Lecture Notes in Computer Science   9737

Commenced Publication in 1973
Founding and Former Series Editors:
Gerhard Goos, Juris Hartmanis, and Jan van Leeuwen

More information about this series at http://www.springer.com/series/7409

Margherita Antona · Constantine Stephanidis (Eds.)

Universal Access in Human-Computer Interaction

Methods, Techniques, and Best Practices

10th International Conference, UAHCI 2016
Held as Part of HCI International 2016
Toronto, ON, Canada, July 17–22, 2016
Proceedings, Part I

 Springer

Editors
Margherita Antona
Foundation for Research & Technology –
  Hellas (FORTH)
Heraklion, Crete
Greece

Constantine Stephanidis
University of Crete / Foundation for
  Research & Technology – Hellas
  (FORTH)
Heraklion, Crete
Greece

ISSN 0302-9743   ISSN 1611-3349 (electronic)
Lecture Notes in Computer Science
ISBN 978-3-319-40249-9   ISBN 978-3-319-40250-5   (eBook)
DOI 10.1007/978-3-319-40250-5

Library of Congress Control Number: 2016940353

LNCS Sublibrary: SL3 – Information Systems and Applications, incl. Internet/Web, and HCI

Printed on acid-free paper

This Springer imprint is published by Springer Nature
The registered company is Springer International Publishing AG Switzerland

Foreword

The 18th International Conference on Human-Computer Interaction, HCI International 2016, was held in Toronto, Canada, during July 17–22, 2016. The event incorporated the 15 conferences/thematic areas listed on the following page.

A total of 4,354 individuals from academia, research institutes, industry, and governmental agencies from 74 countries submitted contributions, and 1,287 papers and 186 posters have been included in the proceedings. These papers address the latest research and development efforts and highlight the human aspects of the design and use of computing systems. The papers thoroughly cover the entire field of human-computer interaction, addressing major advances in knowledge and effective use of computers in a variety of application areas. The volumes constituting the full 27-volume set of the conference proceedings are listed on pages IX and X.

I would like to thank the program board chairs and the members of the program boards of all thematic areas and affiliated conferences for their contribution to the highest scientific quality and the overall success of the HCI International 2016 conference.

This conference would not have been possible without the continuous and unwavering support and advice of the founder, Conference General Chair Emeritus and Conference Scientific Advisor Prof. Gavriel Salvendy. For his outstanding efforts, I would like to express my appreciation to the communications chair and editor of *HCI International News*, Dr. Abbas Moallem.

April 2016   Constantine Stephanidis

HCI International 2016 Thematic Areas and Affiliated Conferences

Thematic areas:

- Human-Computer Interaction (HCI 2016)
- Human Interface and the Management of Information (HIMI 2016)

Affiliated conferences:

- 13th International Conference on Engineering Psychology and Cognitive Ergonomics (EPCE 2016)
- 10th International Conference on Universal Access in Human-Computer Interaction (UAHCI 2016)
- 8th International Conference on Virtual, Augmented and Mixed Reality (VAMR 2016)
- 8th International Conference on Cross-Cultural Design (CCD 2016)
- 8th International Conference on Social Computing and Social Media (SCSM 2016)
- 10th International Conference on Augmented Cognition (AC 2016)
- 7th International Conference on Digital Human Modeling and Applications in Health, Safety, Ergonomics and Risk Management (DHM 2016)
- 5th International Conference on Design, User Experience and Usability (DUXU 2016)
- 4th International Conference on Distributed, Ambient and Pervasive Interactions (DAPI 2016)
- 4th International Conference on Human Aspects of Information Security, Privacy and Trust (HAS 2016)
- Third International Conference on HCI in Business, Government, and Organizations (HCIBGO 2016)
- Third International Conference on Learning and Collaboration Technologies (LCT 2016)
- Second International Conference on Human Aspects of IT for the Aged Population (ITAP 2016)

Conference Proceedings Volumes Full List

Universal Access in Human–Computer Interaction

Program Board Chairs: **Margherita Antona, Greece, and Constantine Stephanidis, Greece**

- Gisela Susanne Bahr, USA
- João Barroso, Portugal
- Jennifer Romano Bergstrom, USA
- Rodrigo Bonacin, Brazil
- Ingo K. Bosse, Germany
- Anthony Lewis Brooks, Denmark
- Christian Bühler, Germany
- Stefan Carmien, Spain
- Carlos Duarte, Portugal
- Pier Luigi Emiliani, Italy
- Qin Gao, P.R. China
- Andrina Granić, Croatia
- Josette F. Jones, USA
- Simeon Keates, UK
- Georgios Kouroupetroglou, Greece
- Patrick Langdon, UK
- Barbara Leporini, Italy
- Tania Lima, Brazil
- Alessandro Marcengo, Italy
- Troy McDaniel, USA
- Ana Isabel Paraguay, Brazil
- Michael Pieper, Germany
- Enrico Pontelli, USA
- Jon A. Sanford, USA
- Vagner Santana, Brazil
- Jaime Sánchez, Chile
- Anthony Savidis, Greece
- Kevin Tseng, Taiwan
- Gerhard Weber, Germany
- Fong-Gong Wu, Taiwan

The full list with the program board chairs and the members of the program boards of all thematic areas and affiliated conferences is available online at:

http://www.hci.international/2016/

HCI International 2017

The 19th International Conference on Human-Computer Interaction, HCI International 2017, will be held jointly with the affiliated conferences in Vancouver, Canada, at the Vancouver Convention Centre, July 9–14, 2017. It will cover a broad spectrum of themes related to human-computer interaction, including theoretical issues, methods, tools, processes, and case studies in HCI design, as well as novel interaction techniques, interfaces, and applications. The proceedings will be published by Springer. More information will be available on the conference website: http://2017.hci.international/.

General Chair
Prof. Constantine Stephanidis
University of Crete and ICS-FORTH
Heraklion, Crete, Greece
E-mail: general_chair@hcii2017.org

http://2017.hci.international/

Contents – Part I

Design for All and eInclusion Best Practices

Universal Access in Architecture and Product Design

Personal and Collective Informatics in Universal Access

Eye Tracking in Universal Access

Contents – Part II

Universal Access to Mobile Interaction

Virtual Reality, 3D and Universal Access

Intelligent and Assistive Environments

Contents – Part III

Technologies for ASD and Cognitive Disabilities

Design for Healthy Aging and Rehabilitation

Universal Access to Media and Games

Universal Access to Mobility and Automotive

Novel Approaches to Accessibility

A Framework for the Development
of Localised Web Accessibility Guidelines
for University Websites in Saudi Arabia

Asmaa Alayed$^{(\boxtimes)}$, Mike Wald, and E.A. Draffan

School of Electronics and Computer Science,
University of Southampton, Southampton, UK
{asialg14,mw,ead}@ecs.soton.ac.uk

Abstract. The number of universities in Saudi Arabia has increased dramatically in the last two decades. As a result the number of their websites has also
increased without any clear guidelines regarding accessibility, which may hinder
some of their disabled users from benefiting from their content. Internationally, a
number of initiatives have been implemented to develop guidelines for web
accessibility such as WCAG to overcome this problem. However, these
guidelines are developed in Western countries and applying them to Arabic
websites can raise more accessibility issues, for example related to culture and
language. In order to enhance the accessibility of Saudi university websites, a
new framework for the development of localised web accessibility guidelines is
presented in this paper. In addition, an evaluation process to validate the
framework is described.

Keywords: Web accessibility · Disability · Localised guidelines · University
websites · Saudi Arabia

1 Introduction

In recent years, the number of people using the Internet in Saudi Arabia has been
increasing dramatically from 200,000 in 2000 to 18,300,000 in 2014 [1] which indicates
that 65.9 % of the population of Saudi Arabia uses the Internet. However, the subject of
web accessibility has remained a problematic issue for Arabic language websites in
terms of accurately assessing whether those with disabilities are able to enjoy their use
on equal terms with their peers [2–4]. This is despite the fact that by 2015[1], there were
over 700 thousand disabled individuals in Saudi Arabia representing almost 8 % of the
total population.

Without suitable web accessibility guidelines and standards the number of people
excluded from obtaining the benefits of accessing the web would definitely increase. This
is an important issue that needs to be taken into account when developing sites, services
and content. A number of initiatives have been implemented to develop guidelines for
web accessibility including the Web Accessibility Initiative Web Content Accessibility
Guidelines (WCAG 1.0) which were published in 1999 [5]. These guidelines were

---

[1] http://rs.ksu.edu.sa/82739.html.

© Springer International Publishing Switzerland 2016
M. Antona and C. Stephanidis (Eds.): UAHCI 2016, Part I, LNCS 9737, pp. 3–13, 2016.
DOI: 10.1007/978-3-319-40250-5_1

revised and became WCAG 2.0 in 2008. At that time, WCAG was internationally known and respected as a 'de facto' standard for Web accessibility [6]. In 2012, WCAG 2.0 finally became an international standard called (ISO/IEC 40500:2012) [7].

Web accessibility guidelines that are developed in Western countries (North America and Western Europe) are followed by some Arabic developers when designing and developing Arabic websites [2–4]. However, some of the success criteria, as part of the guidelines, do not fit all cultures and all languages; a simple example of this is the font size and type. The acceptable font size and type in Latin-based languages would not be accepted in other languages like Arabic, where larger fonts are required for ease of reading. Some symbols are strongly culture-defined because what they represent is not available in another country. Using inappropriate symbols that the user cannot recognise or with which they do not identify reduces the accessibility of the web product. Moreover, the use of certain symbols, icons, or images may be offensive or even against the law in some countries. According to [8], Saudi users prefer to have more images and less text compared to Western countries where there tends to be a preference for more text and fewer images, which can raise a further problem when surfing the web as the Internet speed in the country can be slow and unsatisfactory.

Due to the fact that some people in Saudi Arabia do not listen to music and believe it is forbidden from a religious point of view depending on how conservative they are, if a Saudi user navigates a website that presents a video with music in the background, for example, he might not continue watching it and consequently quit the website. Although, this is not the case for all Arab users, as they differ in their beliefs and traditions, an appropriate way to deal with such a situation is needed, and this is not found in the existing guidelines. So, besides providing text alternatives for the video, the developers would provide a hint for people that there is music in the video, and/or providing another version of the video without music if they prefer no music.

Cloning the WCAG 2.0 guidelines and applying them to Arabic websites would raise more accessibility issues and require different success criteria and possibly even techniques to maintain accessibility levels. This problem has been recognised by a number of researchers, as they recommend adapting the guidelines to the Arabic context [3].

In this paper, related work is discussed in Sect. 2. A new framework for the development of localised web accessibility guidelines for university websites in Saudi Arabia is presented in Sect. 3. Section 4 explains the validation process for the proposed framework. Section 5 discusses the results from the validation process. Section 6 presents the confirmed framework. Finally, Sect. 7 concludes with a summary of the paper.

2 Related Work

Studies on web accessibility in the Arab world started a decade ago when [9] conducted their study on e-government websites in Saudi Arabia and Oman. Since then, there has been limited research to examine web accessibility of Arabic websites, such as [4, 10, 11]. There has been an agreement on the low level of web accessibility in Arab countries and a lack of awareness of its importance. In addition, the localisation to the Arab world and its impact on accessibility have not been investigated by these studies.

Nevertheless, there have been efforts made by different bodies to improve the status of web accessibility in this region. For example, the translation of web accessibility guidelines (WCAG 2.0) into Arabic[2] with the aim of providing better understanding of the them by Arabic native speaker developers. It should be noted that this initiative has a number of weaknesses such as incomplete and inconsistent translation and the use of unfamiliar and inaccurate Arabic words. There appears to have been little effort to understand the Arab people as a target audience, with a lack of localisation of examples within the guidelines. More work is needed in this field to serve the Arab world and this research aims to address the gap.

3 Constructing a New Framework for the Development of Localised Web Accessibility Guidelines for University Websites in Saudi Arabia

In order to construct the framework for the development of localised web accessibility guidelines for university websites in Saudi Arabia, several research areas have been investigated. Each area has an influence on how the framework is constructed. These areas include: web accessibility as the main context, with different guidelines that contribute to accessibility, and also cultural, technical and financial aspects and their impact on accessibility guidelines.

The framework has been constructed in three main phases. The purpose for the first phase was mainly to determine, from literature, the components and aspects that needed to be considered when localising web accessibility guidelines. This resulted in the identification of seven components. These are web accessibility, cultural markers, genre markers, costs, user diversity, Internet infrastructure and technology variety.

In the second phase, the components and all of their subcomponents and elements identified in Phase One were synthesised to form the framework for localised web accessibility guidelines. As this research investigates the localisation to the Saudi context, some of the identified components in Phase Two needed more specification. Two components were specified in detail in this phase: cultural markers and genre markers. Figure 1 shows the proposed framework with all of its components and subcomponents.

A brief description of the components of the framework is as follows:

3.1 Web Accessibility

Web accessibility is concerned with making websites perceivable, operable, understandable and robust [12]. This means that people with disabilities can perceive, understand, navigate, and interact with the web, and that they can contribute to the web [5].

3.2 Genre Specific Cultural Markers

Genre or knowledge domains refer to information types that are presented on the web and describe large categories of websites [13], for instance, news websites or university

---

[2] Available on: http://www.alecso.org/wcag2.0.

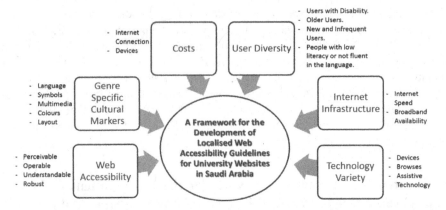

Fig. 1. Proposed framework for the development of localised web accessibility guidelines for university websites in Saudi Arabia.

websites. Cultural markers are interface elements and features that are acceptable and preferred within a particular cultural group [13]. Genre specific cultural markers are elements and features of a specific website genre for a particular cultural group [13].

In the framework, this component contains 5 subcomponents: language, symbols, multimedia, colours and layout. Language comprises 13 elements and multimedia contains 3 elements.

3.3   Costs

Costs of devices and Internet connection could prevent users from accessing the Internet and surfing the Web [14, 15].

3.4   User Diversity

This concerns different users with different abilities, for example: users with disabilities, older users, new and infrequent users and people with low literacy or those not fluent in the language [5, 12].

3.5   Internet Infrastructure

This component comprises two subcomponents that could impact on the ability to connect to the web in a satisfactory manner which may also affect accessibility and personalisation of content: Internet speed and broadband availability in the country [16].

3.6   Technology Variety

Technology variety [17] requires that a broad range of hardware and software are supported. In particular the use of assistive technologies, that are mainly used by people with disabilities, to support functional limitations need to be taken into account.

4 Validating the Framework

Interviews were used to conduct an exploratory study. The interview research method was chosen because it enables in-depth discussion and exploration. Experts were chosen for interview at this exploratory stage to ensure the findings would have more credibility than those from a sample of non-experts [18]. Therefore, the initial framework proposed via a desk-based study was reviewed by interviewing experts developing university websites in Saudi Arabia, or Saudi university researchers working in this area. The process of expert review and validation of the framework is comprised of a number of steps, as shown in Fig. 2:

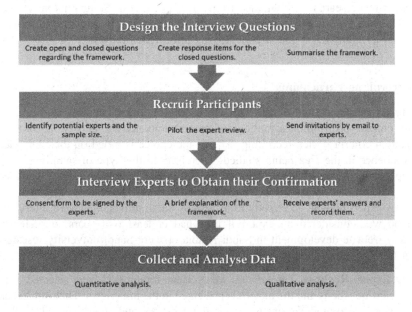

Fig. 2. The process of expert review

4.1 Interview Question Design

The expert review was based on conducting semi-structured interviews with experts. These included both closed and open questions. The closed questions concerned obtaining their opinions on the components and elements of the proposed framework. In addition, the experts were allowed to comment on the proposed components. The open questions aimed to find further components or elements that they recognised but were not identified by the desk-based study.

The Likert scale is a commonly used approach to measure participants' opinions and attitudes regarding a certain statement. Therefore, the closed questions were constructed using a Likert-type scale [19] with the following ratings: strongly disagree = 1; disagree = 2; neutral = 3; agree = 4; and strongly agree = 5. These different ratings are known as Likert items. Table 1 shows the adopted Likert items, their weight and their meaning in the expert review.

Table 1. Likert items with their weight and meaning

Likert item	Weight	Meaning
Strongly disagree	1	This item needs to be excluded from the framework
Disagree	2	This item may need revision or be excluded from the framework
Neutral	3	Exclusion of this item does not affect the framework
Agree	4	This item may need revision to be included in the framework
Strongly agree	5	This item needs to be included in the framework

Since the selected research methods required people as participants, ethical approval to conduct this research was obtained from the University of Southampton (Research Ethics Number 17056). No personal data was collected at this stage; the information collected was anonymised and any identifying information removed.

4.2   Recruiting Participants

Identify Experts and the Sample Size. According to [18], qualitative studies usually depend on non-probability sampling, where participants are chosen according to non-random criteria. When recruiting experts, the choice is based on their knowledge and experience in the area being studied. Therefore, in this type of sampling, sample size depends on saturation [20]. Saturation point is reached when no new knowledge can be gathered, and is usually achieved by 12 interviews [20].

In this expert review, 15 experts from various Saudi universities were interviewed. A person was considered an expert if they had at least two years' experience of university website development in Saudi Arabia or were Saudi university researchers with at least two published papers in this area of research.

Piloting Expert Reviews. Three Saudi web science researchers were selected to pilot the interview questions and the materials presented in the interviews. This was to gather comments and recommendations regarding the questions and other material. Each was met individually, and comments were made. Some questions were recommended to be deleted, and the phrasing of some questions was found to be unclear. After recording their feedback and making the necessary changes, a set of interview questions was created. By the end of the pilot study, the interview questions and other material were ready to be presented to the experts.

An E-mail Invitation to Experts to Participate. After conducting the pilot study, an invitation was sent by email that requested experts' participation. The invitation was in Arabic and included: participant information sheet, approximate duration of the interview and summary description of the framework.

4.3   Interview Experts to Obtain Confirmation

After sending the invitation emails to the experts, 15 of them responded by agreeing to participate and informed us of their preferred way of communication. Appointments with the experts were made for the three month period of September 2015 to November 2015. The time allocated per expert was between 45 and 60 min. The interviews were conducted face-to-face, over the phone and online, according to the availability and location of each expert.

Most of the experts (12) were developers or designers, and the remaining three were researchers in the area of web accessibility. In each interview, the expert was presented with a consent form to sign and then given a brief explanation of the framework and how to respond to the closed questions. After that, the questions were asked and the responses audio recorded by the researcher, after obtaining permission.

4.4   Collecting and Analysing Data

All the interviews were conducted in Arabic and audio recorded, then transcribed. Afterwards, the transcripts were translated from Arabic to English. Arabic native-speaking researchers at the University of Southampton were able to confirm the accuracy of the translated transcripts.

Quantitative Analysis. To analyse quantitative data statistically, the experts' responses to closed-ended questions were collected and entered into SPSS software. The one sample t-test was used to analyse the results. This helps by comparing the mean of a population (μ) with a hypothesised value ($\mu 0$). The hypothesised mean here: $\mu 0 = 3$ which indicates Neutral on the five point Likert-type scale. In addition, the one sample t-test involves testing the null hypothesis against the alternative hypothesis. By convention, the statistical significance level α was set to 0.05 for a 95 % confidence level. The hypotheses for testing each item in the framework are as follows:

- The null hypothesis (H0): If the mean rating is higher than 3 ($\mu > \mu 0$) in all questions, then the item affects localised web accessibility guidelines and needs to be included in the framework. In this case, H0 is accepted and H1 is rejected.
- The alternative hypothesis (H1): If the mean rating is less than or equal to 3 ($\mu \leq \mu 0$), then the item does not affect localised web accessibility guidelines. In this case, H1 is accepted and H0 is rejected.

Qualitative Analysis. To analyse experts' responses to open questions and their comments on the framework components, the interviews were transcribed and saved into NVivo. NVivo is a software tool used to manage and understand textual data, and make the most of it. Experts' responses were tagged using NVivo according to analysis themes and components, collected together into groups, then synthesised.

5   Results and Findings from the Quantitative and Qualitative Analysis

This section discusses the confirmation of the proposed framework. The results of quantitative analysis of responses to the closed questions are discussed first followed by those of the qualitative analysis to the open questions.

Table 2. Statistical results for closed ended interview questions

Component			No	Question	Sig.	Mean	Accepted Hypothesis
Web Accessibility			1	The content of the website must be: Perceivable, Operable, Understandable and Robust	< 0.001	5.00	Null Hypothesis (H0)
Genre Specific Cultural Markers	Language		2	Direction of reading and writing	0.008	3.93	
			3	Uni-case language	< 0.001	3.73	
			4	Formation of the letters	< 0.001	3.80	
			5	Cursive form and paces within and between words	< 0.001	4.27	
			6	Diacritical Marks	< 0.001	5.00	
			7	Homographic language	< 0.001	4.33	
			8	Gender-specific language	< 0.001	3.93	
			9	Font size	< 0.001	5.00	
			10	Font type	< 0.001	5.00	
			11	Type of text emphasis	< 0.001	5.00	
			12	Alignment of text	< 0.001	4.60	
			13	Long sentences	< 0.001	4.33	
			14	Diglossic language	0.001	4.07	
	Symbols		15	Understood and acceptable symbols within the culture for university websites	< 0.001	4.93	
	Multimedia		16	Multimedia appropriateness to the culture in university websites	< 0.001	4.87	
			17	Incorporating music with multimedia provided on university websites	< 0.001	4.67	
			18	Amount of multimedia preferred in the culture for university websites	< 0.001	4.20	
	Colours		19	Acceptable and preferred colours in the culture for university websites.	< 0.001	4.40	
	Layout		20	Acceptable and preferred layout in the culture for university websites	< 0.001	4.47	
Costs			21	High costs of Internet connection and devices	< 0.001	1.87	Alternative Hypothesis (H1)
User Diversity			22	Various Users: disabled, older, inexperienced users and low literacy or not fluent in the language	< 0.001	4.80	Null Hypothesis (H0)
Internet Infrastructure			23	Internet speed in the country.	< 0.001	4.93	
			24	Broadband availability.	< 0.001	4.87	
Technology Variety			25	Various devices, browsers and assistive technology	< 0.001	4.73	

5.1 Results from Quantitative Analysis

The results of the quantitative analysis of experts' responses are summarised in Table 2. They show that the experts had positive attitudes toward inclusion of almost all the components in the framework, with the exception of Costs (Q21). The means of expert opinion are greater than $\mu0 = 3$ and the significance value (Sig.) is less than 0.05. Consequently, the null hypothesis is accepted and the alternative hypothesis is rejected for all questions. This indicates that all these components, subcomponents and elements affect localised web accessibility guidelines for Saudi university websites. In contrast, the mean of experts' responses to questions about inclusion or otherwise of Costs in the framework is less than $\mu0$ ($1.87 < 3$), indicating disagreement. Therefore, the null hypothesis is rejected and the alternative hypothesis is accepted, meaning that this component does not affect localised web accessibility guidelines for Saudi university websites.

5.2 Results from Qualitative Analysis

Experts were asked to identify any other aspects that had not been covered by the proposed framework. Their responses were used to enrich the framework. The following elements were suggested to be added to the subcomponent 'Language':

- Numbers in Arabic websites, as they need to be in one consistent form through the website, whether Arabic or Hindi. (**Expert B**)
- Abbreviations and acronyms in Arabic. Although they are rare, instances occur in Arabic and they do not always use a full stop to discriminate between the abbreviated form of the words and the completed form, which confuses users. (**Expert B**)
- The spacing between lines and paragraphs needs to be more than in English. (**Experts C, D and F**).

Experts N and O suggested web usability as a new component in the framework. They justified this by saying that usable accessibility is important, as the users are involved in the evaluation process. While technical accessibility is evaluated by tools, it does not check for usability for target users.

6 The Framework After Refinement

Based on the experts' responses discussed above, the framework has been refined, as illustrated in Fig. 3. The component of cost has been removed, and web usability has been added to the framework. In addition, subcomponent 'Language' was extended by the following elements: numbers in Arabic websites, abbreviations and acronyms in Arabic and spacing between lines and paragraphs.

This confirmed framework provides the basis for the development of localised guidelines for university websites in Saudi Arabia.

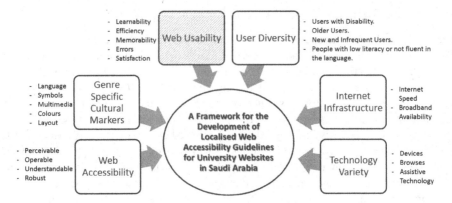

Fig. 3. A framework for the development of localised web accessibility guidelines for university websites in Saudi Arabia - after refinement.

7 Summary and Conclusion

A new confirmed framework for the development of localised web accessibility guidelines for university websites in Saudi Arabia is presented. This paper has described the approach, methods, analysis and results of the experts' evaluation of the components, subcomponents and elements of the proposed framework for localised web accessibility guidelines for Saudi university websites. It has explained the process of expert review as comprising four steps: design interview questions; recruit participants; interview experts; and collect and analyse the data. Open and closed questions have been designed to cover all aspects of the framework. There followed, an expert evaluation study carried out with 15 experts, comprising both web developers and researchers in the area of web accessibility from Saudi universities.

The importance of all components in the proposed framework, apart from one (costs), has been confirmed by the results and findings of the interviews, including their statistically significant results. Furthermore, the framework has been refined by incorporating a new component (web usability). Three new elements emerged from the findings and were added to the 'Language' subcomponent.

The next task will be to develop the localised guidelines. Based on the confirmed framework, the existing WCAG 2.0 guidelines and their success criteria will be divided into two categories: applicable or not applicable to accessibility guidelines for Saudi university websites. Afterwards, additional guidelines that are not identified by WCAG 2.0, but needed for the Saudi websites, will be gathered from the confirmed components. Having completed these tasks, the guidelines will need confirmation from the experts (a group of developers of university websites in Saudi Arabia) in order to ensure they can be applied as techniques that will support WCAG 2.0 success criteria for Arabic websites.

References

1. Internet Usage in the Middle East. http://www.internetworldstats.com/middle.htm
2. Al-Badi, A.: A Framework for Designing Usable Localised Websites. Ph.D. thesis. School of Computing Science, University of East Anglia (2005)
3. Al-Khalifa, H.S.: Exploring the accessibility of Saudi Arabia e-government websites: preliminary results. In: ICEGOV, Proceedings of the 4th International Conference on Theory and Practice of Electronic Governance, Beijing, China, pp. 274–278 (2010)
4. Al-Faries, A., Al-Khalifa, H.S., Al-Razgan, M.S., Al-Duwais, M.: Evaluating the accessibility and usability of top Saudi e-government services. In: Proceedings of the 7th International Conference on Theory and Practice of Electronic Governance, ICEGOV 2013, pp. 60–63. ACM, New York (2013)
5. Henry, S.L.: Understanding web accessibility. In: Web Accessibility, pp. 1–51. Apress (2006)
6. Lewthwaite, S.: Web accessibility standards and disability: developing critical perspectives on accessibility. Disabil. Rehabil. 36(16), 1375–1383 (2014)
7. ISO/IEC 40500:2012. Information Technology: W3C Web Content Accessibility Guidelines (WCAG) 2.0. http://www.iso.org/iso/iso_catalogue/catalogue_tc/catalogue_detail.htm?csnumber=58625
8. Almakky, H., Sahandi, R., Taylor, J.: The effect of culture on user interface design of social media. a case study on preferences of saudi arabian on the arabic user interface of facebook. Int. J. Soc. Educ. Econ. Manag. Eng. 9(1), 107–111 (2015)
9. Abanumy, A., Al-Badi, A., Mayhew, P.: E-government website accessibility: in-depth evaluation of Saudi Arabia and Oman. Electron. J. e-Government 3(3), 99–106 (2005)
10. Khan, M.A., Buragga, K.A.: Effectiveness of accessibility and usability of government websites in Saudi Arabia. Can. J. Pure Appl. Sci. 4(2), 1227–1231 (2010)
11. Mourad, M.B.A., Kamoun, F.: Accessibility evaluation of Dubai e-government websites: findings and implications. J. E-Government Stud. Best Pract. 2013, 1–15 (2013)
12. Web Content Accessibility Guidelines (WCAG 2.0). https://www.w3.org/TR/WCAG20/
13. Barber, W., Badre, A.: Culturability: the merging of culture and usability. In: Proceedings of the 4th Conference on Human Factors and the Web, vol. 7, no. 4, pp. 1–10 (1998)
14. Alrawabdeh, W.: Internet and the Arab world: understanding the key issues and overcoming the barriers. Int. Arab J. Inf. Technol. 6(1), 27–32 (2009)
15. Sait, S.M., Al-Tawil, K.M., Sanaullah, S., Faheemuddin, M.: Impact of internet usage in Saudi Arabia: a social perspective. IJITWE 2(2), 81–115 (2007)
16. Aleid, F., Rogerson, S., Fairweather, B.: Factors affecting consumers adoption of ecommerce in Saudi Arabia from a consumers perspective. In: IADIS International Conference e-Commerce, pp. 11–18 (2009)
17. Shneiderman, B.: Universal usability. Commun. ACM 43(5), 84–91 (2000)
18. Bhattacherjee, A.: Social science research: principles, methods, and practices (2012)
19. Likert, R.: A technique for the measurement of attitudes. Arch. Psychol. 22, 55 (1932)
20. Guest, G., Bunce, A., Johnson, L.: How many interviews are enough? An experiment with data saturation and variability. Field methods 18(1), 59–82 (2006)

Accessibility in Virtual Communities of Practice Under the Optics of Inclusion of Visually Impaired

Luís Felipe Cândido Marques[(⊠)], Daniela Freitas Guilhermino,
Maria Eduarda de Araújo Cardoso, Rafaella Aline Lopes da Silva
Neitzel, Larissa Albano Lopes, José Reinaldo Merlin,
and Giovanne dos Santos Striquer

Center of Technological Sciences,
State University of Paraná, PR Bandeirantes, Brazil
lfelipecm_@hotmail.com, {danielaf,mariaeduarda,
rafaella,larissa,merlin,giovanne}@uenp.edu.br

Abstract. Accessibility aims to ensure better quality of life to people, specially people with disabilities. Thus, it is possible to break down barriers and allow everyone, independently its specificities, have access to the same contents, materials and places equally. Many barriers are still encountered in terms of the accessibility of computing environments for the visually impaired. However, the accessibility should assume a requisite role in the quality of software to enable the inclusion of people with different types of visual impairment in these environments. The Virtual Communities of Practice (VCoPs) are important computing environments that promote interaction and collaboration between people, however, these areas also have many limitations to the inclusion of people with disabilities, including the visually impaired. Thus, this research investigates the visually impaired needs to access the VCoPs, analyzing the main existing guidelines with the aid of some accessibility evaluation tools. With the analysis of the results in accessibility evaluations it is intended to support the design process of inclusive VCoPs for the visually impaired.

Keywords: Accessibility · Visually impaired · Virtual communities of practice

1 Introduction

The [32], defines the web accessibility as people with different sensory conditions can use the web in a process of understanding, interaction, navigation, perception and contribution to the web.

Visual impairment is the disability of higher incidence worldwide. About 285 million of people worldwide have some kind of visual impairment, considering that 39 million are blind and 246 million have low vision [31].

During the construction of an accessible interface to visually impaired are necessary some adaptations that can attend the different types of disabilities, such as: low vision, colour-blind and blind. However, some web accessibility standards are available to assist designers in building their interfaces.

© Springer International Publishing Switzerland 2016
M. Antona and C. Stephanidis (Eds.): UAHCI 2016, Part I, LNCS 9737, pp. 14–26, 2016.
DOI: 10.1007/978-3-319-40250-5_2

The W3C makes clear through researches that many barriers related to accessibility for the visually impaired are still found in computing environments. However, some recommendations are presented in order to make the web an equal access environment for everyone. Some of these recommendations are: to make a great html mark up, non-text content should have a text alternative, the colour may not be used as a visual resource to convey information and make all features available through the keyboard.

Amidst the great technological advancement and the indispensable search for the information and knowledge, the way in which is treated the access and inclusion of the visually impaired to web systems is not often a concern. Among the web systems, virtual communities of practice (VCoPs) have been shown important spaces, mediated by computer, which promote interaction and collaboration between people. Nonetheless, these spaces still present many limitations to the inclusion of people with disabilities, including the visually impaired.

Communities of practice (CoPs), basically, are groups of people who gather to share a common interest. According to [30], the community of practice is made up of people who engage in a process of collective learning, they share concerns and or passion for something they do and they learn how to improve. In CoPs, the experiences are shared over the time and there is a commitment to share knowledge [8].

In this context, this paper aims to investigate the difficulties encountered by visually impaired when accessing VCoPs. In this work, the main accessibility problems will be identified; moreover, improvements and adjustments will be proposed in order to turn communities more accessible for the visually impaired.

2 Community of Practice

Community of Practice is defined by [29] as a group of people who share an interest or passion for a subject and they interact regularly to improve their knowledge on this topic. [17], states that the CoPs have always existed, scattered in various types and with different names. Therefore, it is apparent the importance of these communities in recent times. CoPs are becoming environments that support the exchange of information and cooperation process.

Three characteristics are crucial in any type of CoP [30]: (i) The Domain- the area of knowledge where each member is inside. In this area, the identity of each member and the keys issues that will be addressed in the CoP are defined; (ii) The Community- place where the interaction is proposed. This interaction can be related to interests, learners, or even directed toward a goal; and (iii) The Practice: a process in which people learn with the group how to put in practice the things that they are interested with the aid of tools, stories and experiences. The Table 1 provides a comparison of a CoP to other types of groups, communities and organizations.

In collaborative environments such as CoP, it is of fundamental importance an interaction between the members in order to reach some attributes, whether tools or past experiences that may assist in the construction of learning or problem solving.

In order to seek improvements in individual and collaborative learning, a research work was performed by [23]. The Table 2 presents a summary made by [24] about the research of [23], and demonstrates the main elements of the CoPs and their

Table 1. Comparison between CoPs and other organizations

	What is the objective?	Who participates?	What they have in common?	How long does it last?
Community of practice	To develop members capabilities to build and exchange knowledge	Member who select themselves	Passion, commitment, and identification with the group's expertise	As long as there is interest in to be part of the group
Formal work group	To develop a product or service	Everyone who reports to the group's managers	Work requirements and common goals	Until the next reorganization
Team	To accomplish a specified job	The members are assigned by senior manager	The goals and project's milestones	Until the project has been completed
Informal network	To collect and transmit business information	Friends and business acquaintances	Mutual needs	As long as people have a reason to keep in contact

Source: Adaptation of [30]

interrelations (objectives, characteristics, possible roles and skills that actors can present) that can be used in the learning process of the CoP.

A Virtual Community of Practice (VCoP) is a Community of Practice (CoP) mediated by a computer. [30] states that new technologies, such as internet, have allowed

Table 2. Main concepts and their relationships inherent in CoPs

CP – Main concepts		Authors
COMMUNITY	Motivation; domain; practice	[30]
	Field; goal; structure; composition; cultural diversity	[23]
		[12]
MEMBERS	Personal characteristics; type of involvement; tole; peripheral role	[15], [23]
COMPETENCE	Type of competence	[23]
COLLABORATION	Collaboration goals; collaborative activities; roles involved; geographic dimension; temporal dimension; collaboration resources; communication means; types of interaction	[25]
	Engagement; coordination	[6], [28]
DECISION-MAKING	Decision-making resources; results; actors; strategies	[23]
CP RESOURCES	Record of interaction; CP tools	

Source: Adapted from [23]

the interactions go beyond the geographical limitations of the traditional communities. The facility, speed and low cost of communication through the internet contribute to the creation of VCoPs [7].

The members of VCoPs can benefit themselves with experiences from others members of the community, obtaining information, answers and solutions to problems not solved yet inside their local community or work environment [3].

The VCoPs may present some different functions when compared to CoPs, according to [3]: the sent messages are automatically saved, allowing a person to interact at any time; moreover, it is possible to consult past information; the interactions can be instant, however, most cases do not happen in real time; most often there is no knowledge about the people whom are interacting, and, in this case, it is not necessary to know the people as individual, the goal is to know the knowledge that this person is able to share. It is important to highlight that the ontology proposed by [23], presents the elements and the semantic annotations (objectives, characteristics, possible roles and responsibilities) that may also be related to VCoPs.

3   Accessibility: Under the Perspective of Visual Impairment

The visual impairment can be briefly defined as the partial or complete loss of vision, and, this loss can be acquired throughout life or it can also be acquired from birth. The causes of these deficiencies can be the most varied, from infectious and traumatic causes, to genetics and degenerative causes. According to [11], considering all the disabled people in Brazil, 48,1 % have visual impairment, and considering the whole Brazilian population, 18.8 % have some type of visual disability. In terms of global data, about 285 million people have some kind of visual disability, wherein 39 million are blind and 246 million have low vision [31].

According to [31] the visual function can be classified in 4 levels: (i) Normal vision; (ii) Moderate visual impairment (iii) Severe visual impairment; (iv) blindness. Moderate visual impairment and severe visual impairment are defined by the term low vision. Therefore, the low vision (visual acuity between 0.3 and 0.05 in the best eye, with the best optical correction) and the blindness (the visual acuity is equal or less than 0.05 in the best eye, with the best optical correction) represent the visual impairments which can be caused by different diseases, including the most common ones: near-sightedness, farsightedness, astigmatism, cataracts, glaucoma, colour blindness.

Accessibility aims to ensure better quality of life to people, especially to people with disabilities. Thus, it is possible to break barriers and allow everybody, regardless their difficulties, have access to the content, materials and places equally. The web accessibility means that people with some kind of disability can understand, navigate, perceive and interact with the Web [4]. Also, when the accessibility becomes a requisite in the quality of software, it enables and encourages the inclusion of people in the digital world through related principles, thereby facilitating navigation, the layout and presentation of information [16].

The World Wide Web Consortium (W3C), the main standard organization World Wide Web, has a group targeted to accessibility, the Web Accessibility Initiative (WAI). The WAI has developed the Web Content Accessibility Guidelines (WCAG), which are guidelines that should be followed to turn a website more accessible. With these guidelines, it is possible to turn the content more accessible to all types of people with disabilities, such as visual, auditory, motor, speech or any kind of difficult, and, thus, developing a more useful content for everyone.

The accessibility for the visually impaired is gaining more importance every day. The information, in general terms, must be transmitted and understood by any type of people, and in this way, appears the concern if the means of transmission of messages are able to reach everyone. According to [19], it is important that each person put itself in place and imagine the life of a visually impaired, in order to act in an appropriate and inclusive way with the disabled.

Accessibility for visually impaired is not a simple issue, and, to build a successful interface, it is necessary to follow some logical and functional rules and different ergonomics that can be adapted to the different types of visual impairments such as: blind, low vision, colour blindness [18]. For the visually impaired, some tools that can facilitate their access to information were already developed such as [19]: keyboards in braille, speech synthesis system, and computer screen magnification software.

These tools are only aid mechanisms for access to information. Remembering that for the visually impaired only these tools are not enough for an ideal navigation. The developers must be aware of the standards required in the development and design of interfaces in order to allow the inclusion of people with disabilities.

Regarding the access the information, according to [13], the main difficulties faced by visually impaired who have low vision are: reading texts with small or a colour in particular; distinguish different types of letter; distinguish chromatic colours of contrast or depth and locate and/or follow the cursor and manipulate graphic objects. These can be considered just some of the difficulties faced by people with low vision problems. The W3C, through its major groups related to accessibility, demonstrates that many other difficulties may be encountered; however, these difficulties can be minimized or even solved once its recommendations are followed.

4   Accessibility Recommendations

The WCAG arise in May 1999, with the WCAG 1.0, presenting the simple goal of making the web contents accessible to people with disabilities [27]. In December 2008, it was implemented the WCAG 2.0, with the same goals, but with a more solid basis and updated recommendations, which have been implemented nowadays. Within the WCAG 2.0 it is possible to find guidelines, which are divided into the principles shown in Table 3. These guidelines have no separation by type of disability, however, in a process of analysing them, it is possible to infer which are applicable to visually impaired, whether for blind or low vision people.

The principles are used for better organization and understanding of the guidelines and each one is related to a specific area. The non compliance with these principles turns difficult or impossible the web access for people with disabilities. Therefore, it is of major importance that all websites get adapted to these guidelines during the development and maintenance steps of its websites.

Table 3. Adaptation of principles and guidelines WGAG 2.0

Principles	Guidelines
Perceivable	Provide alternative text for all non-text content so that it can be changed into other forms, according to the users needs, such as large print, braille, speech, symbols or simpler language.
	Provide alternatives for time-based media.
	Create contents that can be presented in different ways (e.g., A simpler page layout) without losing information or structure.
	Make it easier for users to see and hear content including separating foreground from background.
Operable	Make all the functionality available from the keyboard.
	Provide users enough time to read and use content.
	Do not design content in a way that is known to cause seizures.
	Provide ways to help users navigate, find content, and determine where they are.
Understandable	Make text content readable and understandable.
	Make Web pages appear and operate in predictable ways.
	Help users avoid and correct mistakes.
Robust	Maximize compatibility with current and future user agents, including assistive technologies.

Source: Adaptation of [27]

The WCAG guidelines are very important and considered throughout the world, however there are other kinds of models, guidelines and laws, they can be created in a determined region or country. These guidelines do not flee from WCAG standards, however they may have some different standards, or they can also be complementary to WCAG guidelines, helping further the accessibility process for everyone. Some of the most popular models are: E-MAG (Electronic Government Accessibility Model, model created by the Brazilian government) [9]; Sect. 508 (Standard created by United States applicable to types of software, hardware, mobile applications and other information systems) [20]; BITV (Barrierefreie Informationstechnik-Verordnung, accessibility model created in Germany) [2]; Stanca Act (Law passed by the Italian parliament in order to provide information to make the systems more accessible) [21].

5 Accessibility Evaluation in VCoPs for Visually Impaired

When conducting the evaluation, the following methodological steps were considered necessary: (i) selection of accessibility evaluation tools; (ii) selection of VCoPs to be evaluated; (iii) assessment of VCoPs in terms of accessibility requirements, with the support of the selected evaluation tools; (iv) compilation of accessibility requirements for visually impaired; (v) combination of the results obtained from the analysis of recommendations identified in the literature review and also from the evaluations performed.

5.1 Evaluation Tools

From several tests performed it was possible to identify and select the most appropriate accessibility evaluation tools to the objectives of this research, they are: TAW[1], EXAMINATOR[2], ACHECKER[3] e WAVE[4]. These tools are based on the accessibility guidelines recommended by W3C, making an evaluation of web pages and demonstrating possible oversights inadvertencies of the pages related to accessibility.

The Taw, Achecker and Wave tools are included among the most complete tools for accessibility in a survey conducted by [14]. In [14], the work of the different areas of expertise of the evaluation tools are detailed through a comparison; it is possible to understand the particularities of each tool. The Examinator tool was chosen because it was used in [5] work and presented satisfactory results.

The Examinator is an automatic evaluation tool created by UMIC – Agency for Society and Knowledge, IP that is a public institution with legal personality in Portugal. It follows the Web Content Accessibility Guidelines Web (WCAG 1.0) that have as objective, overcome several limitations of the other validators and it can be used to evaluate accessibility of all pages of a site. This tool provides detailed and organized results of evaluations analyses according to 3 levels of priority. The total number of tests that are performed in a web page by this tool are 61 [10].

The Taw tool was created by Fundación CTIC (Technological Centre of Information and Communication) based in Spain and its aim is to encourage, to stimulate and to disseminate web accessibility. It is an online validator based on the Web Content Accessibility Guidelines Web, and, therefore, the validation of a URL generates a HTML report with information about the outcome of the review. The Taw is part of a tools groups, all of these tools follow the same line, in addition these tools are always updating themselves to collaborate as much as they can to web accessibility [22].

The Achecker is an open source accessibility evaluation tool, developed in 2009 by the Adaptive Technology Resource Centre at the University of Toronto in Canada. This tool performs completes evaluations by separating the problems into 3 types: known problems, possible problems and potential problems. During the make an evaluation, the user can chose the desired guidelines and also the final report format [1].

The Wave is an evaluation tool developed by WebAIM (Web Accessibility In Mind) that has its base in United States. This tool was launched in 2001 and has already made millions of web pages evaluations. It has a different way of reporting error when compared to the other tools by showing a copy of the page with errors and warnings found instead of generating a long report with the data. The recommendations are also made in the page copy, which greatly facilitates the visual point and also for analysts, developers and novice researchers in the web accessibility field [26].

---

[1] http://www.tawdis.net.

[2] http://www.acessibilidade.gov.pt/webax/examinator.php.

[3] http://achecker.ca/checker/index.php.

[4] http://wave.webaim.org.

5.2   VCoPs Evaluation

In order to assist in the identification of satisfactory and critical points of the communities of practice accessibility, the accessibility recommendations were organized on aspects of accessibility. As a result, for each aspect was assigned a relevance parameter regarding to accessibility. Thus, for each aspect was assigned a relevance parameter regarding to accessibility (Table 4). The parameters were defined based on the W3C recommendations and also from a data collection related to the needs of the visually impaired.

For the blind, it is necessary the a screen readers support (the screen readers are responsible for going through all the content, providing to the blind user a spoken version of everything that is on the website), thus, the alternative texts in images and elements are essential, and the readers can identify on a page these elements and comprehend its contents. It is also important to have all the features and shortcuts available in the keyboard to make it easier for screen readers.

There were selected 4 communities of practice of large spread and different contexts. These 4 VCoPs were analysed by 4 accessibility evaluation tools, with focus on aspects related to the visually impaired. In the Table 5, the negatives points that were identified in the VCoPs are described. The columns 1, 2, 3 and 4 represent, respectively, the negative points found in the VCoP 1, VCoP 2, VCoP 3 and VCoP 4.

The lack of use of alternative text in images was the main problem found and one of the most worrying ones, this aspect is of extreme necessity for an accessible navigation to visually impaired users.

Within the aspects of texts for images and elements, worth highlighting the following issues: images that do not have an alternative text, images with invalid alternative text, and forms without label or alternative text. These problems are very common within the VCoPs and may even preclude the visually impaired understanding of the content. The visually impaired that is blind needs alternative texts to make possible the reading of contents by a screen reader. The screen reader is a software used to read the screen and make sounds about the contents. Lack of use of alternative texts for elements of a page or the misapplication of these texts is the same as omitting information for visually impaired users.

Another problem frequently encountered was the poor structuring of headers. The headers have a high priority within the contents language; therefore, their poor structuring can greatly complicate the interpretation of the content. To have a great structure is strongly recommended the content to be organized, simplified and comprehensible, thereby facilitating the understanding and do not requiring much effort from the user.

A point to highlight is that the tool that pointed more accessibility problems considering the evaluated aspects was the Taw tool, (19 problems) while the tool that less detected problems was the Examinator (10 problems). The Taw tool is part of an accessibility tools group, and was created as a way to encourage web accessibility; this tool makes its evaluation taking as base the new accessibility guidelines WCAG 2.0, dividing the problems neatly according to 4 principles: perceivable, operable, understandable, robust. The Examinator evaluates according to 3 levels of priority bringing the results in an organized manner. Furthermore, it is noteworthy that the Examinator has a differential; beyond pointing out the negative points, it also brings the positive

Table 4. Relevance of each accessibility aspect for visually impaired in VCoPs

Evaluated aspects	Environmental implication	Relevance
Content language	A simpler and clear language helps the visually impaired interpret the content in an easier way. The structuring and segmentation of the texts using titles, headers, paragraphs and lists are important, because information blocks in excess turns the reading of the visually impaired more difficult.	High
Alternative texts	The visually impaired with blindness needs subtitle to identify the images; these subtitles are of paramount importance for the blind to know where they are accessing. The lack of alternative texts and elements can preclude the comprehension of the content by the blind.	High
Keyboard utilization	It is important to have all the features and shortcuts available in the keyboard. In this way, the user can imagine the contents of the page and can navigate easily. The pages that cannot have their features totally accessed by the keyboard are not accessible for blind.	High
Destination addresses of links	The links should clearly and succinctly indicate where they point. The users can not differentiate the links if they are glued to another without any mark or printable character not "linked" to separate them. It should be available in navigation bars, constituted of lists of links to cluster, thereby facilitating its location.	Medium
Visual representation	It is important to provide way to help the visually impaired user to navigate on the website and find contents easily. The visually impaired with low vision has difficulties in interpreting plans, so the page layout table must be easily visible to the user become familiar with the structure quickly. Also, it is important to differentiate colours between contents and links already accessed and slipt the words into blocks of information.	Medium
Technologies adopted in videos	The criteria to use videos is to ensure that their quality meet the maximum rate of understanding to a deficient with low vision, and, thus, containing a great visual motion detection if they can pass some kind of information, but only it does not solve the problem because for blind people understanding it is necessary pass all possible information of the video through its audio.	Medium
Media duration	Must provide control over the executions of the media such as: stop, resume, cancel, start, rewind, forward and others. The visually impaired needs enough time to read/listen, interpret and use the contend so they can have control over the execution.	Medium
Language	When the site does not indicate the language to the user, they are not able to recognize the site language.	Low

Table 5. Negative points in the VCoPs

Aspects	Sub aspects	Taw				Examinator				Achecker				Wave			
VCoPs		1	2	3	4	1	2	3	4	1	2	3	4	1	2	3	4
Content language	Page title																
	Not descriptive headings and labels																
	Labels misused	x			x												
	Declaration of the type of document																
	Incorrectly structured headers	x		x	x			x	x							x	x
	Unordered lists														x		x
Alternative texts	Images that do not have an alternative text	x		x	x			x	x	x	x		x	x			x
	Images with a too long description	x		x											x		
	Images with invalid alternative texts		x	x						x		x		x	x	x	
	Forms without label or alternative text		x	x								x	x	x	x	x	
	Links without alternative texts			x													
	Element type 'script' without alternative text					x	x	x							x		
Keyboard utilization	Access to buttons, forms and scrips via the keyboard																
Destination addresses of links	Empty links	x			x												x
	Links with the same text and different destinations	x		x					x								
	Links enabled only through scripts							x									
Visual representation	Contrast between the text colour and background										x		x				
	Separation of the first plan from the background									x	x	x	x				
Technologies adopted in videos																	
Media duration																	
Language	Main language of the page					x	x								x		

points of the page. The fact whereby the Examinator detected fewer errors are linked to the type of evaluation that is made, because this tool still evaluates using the old guidelines of WCAG 1.0. Currently, the guidelines WCAG 2.0 are already used, and they contain some changes and inclusions compared to the old guidelines.

Regarding to the VCoPs the evaluated aspects generated an average of approximately 14 accessibility problems per VCoP page. It is noteworthy that the chosen tools have not evaluated the technological aspects utilized in its videos and media duration, even though these aspects are of great importance in terms of accessibility for visually impaired. As the used tools only evaluate the code of web pages, these aspects are not evaluated, however, they can be manually detected by the annalist or programmer without difficult.

6   Conclusion

This paper presented an investigation about the main accessibility problems in VCoPs. After conducting an evaluation of 4 VCoPs using the tools Taw, Examinator, Achecker and Wave, it was possible to identify the main problems faced by the visually impaired when accessing a VCoP.

With the results obtained, becomes evident the aspects that should be improved to have an environment more accessible to the visually impaired. Some of the main weak aspects identified in the analysed VCoPs were problems with alternative text in images and elements, and the poor structuring of headers, which can preclude the user to see, to hear and consequently to understand contents.

Regarding the evaluation tools, we can observe that they present distinct characteristics, each tool has different evaluation mechanisms, and, so they can detect different problems. The interesting fact in use more than one evaluation tool is that, sometimes, a flawed aspect with regards to accessibility that was not detected with a tool can be detected by another, thereby, maximizing the probability of finding accessibility problems.

The tools used showed up significant instruments to support the evaluation of the accessibility and they have identified some accessibility requirements for the visually impaired that can support the design of inclusive VCoPs to these communities. A limitation found in the used tools was the fact that they do not evaluate the technologies adopted in video and media duration. As a future work, we intend to conduct further analysis to improve results and also extend this analysis to other types of online communities.

Acknowledgments. The authors would like to thank Araucaria Foundation for the support in this research.

References

1. Achecker: http://achecker.ca/checker/index.php. Accessed 17 October 2015
2. Bitv: http://www.bitvtest.eu/footer/accessibility.html. Accessed 19 December 2015

3. Correa, M.P.L.: Aprendizagem e compartilhamento de conhecimento em comunidades virtuais de prática: estudo de caso na comunidade virtual de desenvolvimento de software livre debian-br-cdd (2007)
4. Da Silva, F.R., Zschornack, F.: Análise de Acessibilidade em Redes Sociais (2009)
5. De Araújo, C.M.E., Trindade, C.M.E., Da Silva, D.F.G., Garcia, R.A.L., Elero Junior, L.S.: Accessibility in E-Commerce Tools: An Analysis of the Optical Inclusion of the Deaf. In: Antona, M., Stephanidis, C. (eds.) UAHCI 2015. LNCS, vol. 9175, pp. 162–173. Springer, Heidelberg (2006)
6. Deaudelin, C., Nault, T.: Collaborer pour apprendre et faire apprendre – La place des outils technologiques. Presses de l'Université du Québec (2003)
7. De Gouvêa, M.T.A., Paranhos, C., Da Motta, C.L.R.: Comunidades de Prática (2008)
8. Eckert, P.: Communities of practice. Encycl. Lang. Linguist. 2(2006), 683–685 (2006)
9. e-MAG: Modelo de acessibilidade em governo eletrônico (2011). http://www. governoeletronico.gov.br/acoes-e-projetos/e-MAG
10. Examinator: eXaminator Validador de Acessibilidade Web. http://www.acessibilidade.gov. pt/webax/examinator.php. Accessed 16 October 2014
11. IBGE: Instituto Brasileiro de Geografia e Estatística Pessoas com deficiência visual (2010). http://www.ibge.gov.br/estadosat/temas.php?sigla=rj&tema=censodemog2010_defic
12. Langelier, L., Wenger, E. (eds.): Work, Learning and Networked. Cefrio, Québec (2005)
13. De Macedo, M.K.B. et al.: Recomendações de acessibilidade e usabilidade para ambientes virtuais de aprendizagem voltados para o usuário idoso (2009)
14. Mifsud, J.: 10 Free Web-Based Web Site Accessibility Evaluation Tools (2011). http:// usabilitygeek.com/10-free-web-based-web-site-accessibility-evaluation-tools/
15. Miller, G.A.: WordNet: a lexical database for English. Commun. ACM 38(11), 39–41 (1995)
16. Moreira, J.R.: Usabilidade, Acessibilidade e Educação a Distância (2011)
17. Nichols, F.: Communities of Practice. A Startup Kit (2003)
18. Reinaldi, L.R., De Camargo Júnior, C.R., Calazans, A.T.S.: Acessibilidade para pessoas com deficiência visual como fator de inclusão digital-doi:10.5102/un.gti.v1i2.1331. Universitas: Gestão e TI, vol. 1, no 2 (2011)
19. Santos, A.P.A., Carli, B., Cano, P.F.: A Acessibilidade da Informação para Deficientes Visuais e Auditivos. Anagrama: Revista Científica Interdisciplinar da Graduação, vol. 4, no 4 (2011)
20. Section 508: http://www.section508.gov. Accessed 18 December 2015
21. Stanca Act: http://www.agid.gov.it/agenda-digitale/pubblica-amministrazione/accessibilita. Accessed 20 December 2015
22. TAW: http://www.tawdis.net. Accessed 15 October 2015
23. Tifous, A., Ghali, A.E., Dieng-Kuntz, R., Giboin, A., Evangelou, C., Vidou, G.: An ontology for supporting communities of practice. In: K-CAP, pp. 39–46 (2007)
24. Trindade, D.F.G., Garcia, L.S.: Framework Conceitual de apoio ao Design de Ambientes Colaborativos inclusivos aos Surdos. In: Anais do Simpósio Brasileiro de Informática na Educação (2013)
25. Vidou, G., Dieng-Kuntz, R., Ghali, A.E., Evangelou, C.E., Giboin, A., Tifous, A., Jacquemart, S.: Towards an ontology for knowledge management in communities of practice. In: Reimer, U., Karagiannis, D. (eds.) PAKM 2006. LNCS (LNAI), vol. 4333, pp. 303–314. Springer, Heidelberg (2006)
26. Wave: http://wave.webaim.org. Accessed 18 October 2015
27. WCAG 2.0: Web content accessibility guidelines. Web Accessibility Initiative (WAI) (2013). http://www.w3.org/TR/WCAG20/

28. Weiseth, P.E., Munkvold, B.E., Tvedte, B., Larsen, S.: The Wheel of Collaboration Tools: A Typology for Analysis within a Holistic Framework. In: CSCW 2006, Banff, Canada, pp. 239–248 (2006)
29. Wenger, E.: Communities of practice: a brief introduction (2011)
30. Wenger, E.: Communities of Practice. Cambridge University Press, New York (2000)
31. WHO: World Health Organization (2014). http://www.who.int/mediacentre/factsheets/fs282/en/
32. W3C/WAI: Web Accessibility Initiative (WAI). WAI guidelines and techniques. http://www.w3.org/WAI/guid-tech.html

Ontology-Based Adaptive Interfaces for Colorblind Users

Ricardo José de Araújo[1,2], Julio Cesar Dos Reis[3], and Rodrigo Bonacin[1,4(✉)]

[1] FACCAMP, Rua Guatemala, 167, Campo Limpo Paulista, SP 13231-230, Brazil
ricardo.araujo@ifsuldeminas.edu.br, rodrigo.bonacin@cti.gov.br
[2] Instituto Federal de Educação, Ciência e Tecnologià do Sul de Minas Gerais
(IFSULDEMINAS), Pouso Alegre, MG 37550-000, Brazil
[3] Institute of Computing, University of Campinas, Campinas, SP, Brazil
julio.dosreis@ic.unicamp.br
[4] Center for Information Technology Renato Archer, Rodovia Dom Pedro I, km 143, 6,
Campinas, SP 13069-901, Brazil

Abstract. Nowadays, the utilization of colors is essential in the design of rich interactive interfaces. However, the widespread use of colors on the web affects the accessibility of colorblind users. Existing proposals in literature fail in not considering the various types of pathologies and individuals' needs and preferences. This article defines techniques for the development of adaptive interfaces that might facilitate the interaction of colorblind people with web systems. Our research explores the use of ontologies, as suitable artifacts for representing knowledge about types of colorblindness, recoloring algorithms, accessibility guidelines and users' preferences. We define a framework and software architecture that employs such ontology. Prototypes and scenarios illustrate the application of the framework. Obtained results allow determining and automatically applying the best recoloring techniques suited to adapting interfaces for colorblind users.

Keywords: Accessibility · Colorblind · Ontology · Adaptive interfaces

1 Introduction

The recognition of colors plays a central role in users' experience when accessing and interacting with web systems. Colorblindness refers to the inability to perceive certain colors in their natural representations or to make confusions between colors [1]. This pathology affects the functioning of the retina, and consequently, how human eyes interpret colors. This requires improving accessibility of web interfaces for colorblind users. Many typical solutions are exclusively based on increasing the contrast of colors. Nevertheless, these solutions fail in considering individuals' needs and preferences, including aesthetics, devices, culture, hedonic, among other aspects.

Colorblindness hampers users' accessibility in computer systems, which mostly rely on colorful interface elements as design alternatives to represent different aspects of information. When designers and interactive solutions do not take into account their barriers, colorblind users might experience limitations and face difficulties, even in simple tasks. For instance, these users cannot distinguish the colors of visited links in

© Springer International Publishing Switzerland 2016
M. Antona and C. Stephanidis (Eds.): UAHCI 2016, Part I, LNCS 9737, pp. 27–37, 2016.
DOI: 10.1007/978-3-319-40250-5_3

websites and textual information can easily turn out unreadable [2]. While literature has investigated techniques to make systems more accessible to colorblind people (e.g., [3–5]), existing approaches are still insufficient for adequately dealing with various interaction limitations.

This research investigates adaptive users' interfaces to improve the quality of the interaction of colorblind people with web systems. We propose an original framework to enable the adaptation of user interfaces based on ontologies and recoloring algorithms. The framework relies on ontologies referring to syntactic structures that formally express the semantics of domain knowledge. Ontology represents knowledge about design options, users' preferences and algorithms capabilities exploring Web ontology language description and rule languages.

Relying on static and dynamic users' information like their informed preferences, type of pathology, as well as information captured from the interaction context (e.g., the webpage controls activated), the framework performs queries and inferences in the ontology to select instances of adaptation options. Reasoning strategies are employed to leverage the quality and completeness of query results. They express the selected interface elements, algorithms and applicable parameters in order to modify the interface in a specific context.

Our technique explores these facts to automatically perform modifications (e.g., recoloring) on interface elements like imagens, texts and background according to the modeled algorithms and retrieved parameters. This study presents the software architecture that implements the framework and a prototype that illustrates the application and benefits of the proposal for colorblind users. The obtained results highlight the possibility of a more efficient and satisfactory interaction with web systems.

The remainder of this article is organized as follows: Sect. 2 presents the related work on colorblind accessibility; Sect. 3 thoroughly describes the framework and the proposed software architecture; Sect. 4 presents interface prototypes as well as a scenario of use to illustrate the applicability of the proposal; Sect. 5 wraps up with concluding remarks and outlines future research.

2   Research on Colorblind Accessibility

Human Computer-Interaction (HCI) research on colorblind accessibility ranges from the study of theoretical aspects of interaction to new recoloring algorithms. In this section, we focus on related work distributed in four overlapping categories according to their focus: (1) proposal of design accessibility solutions for colorblind users; (2) proposal of software frameworks for adaptive interfaces; (3) studies on recoloring algorithms and strategies; and (4) studies on ontology-based interface adaptation.

The first category includes works that emphasize design methods and techniques to improve the development of accessible interactive solutions. Neris [6], for instance, proposed design principles and method for inclusive adaptive solutions. Their work deals with issues on the inclusive design, such as: how to design adaptive interfaces with users' participation, and how to promote accessibility using adaptive interfaces. Although their investigation contributes providing high-level design principles in the design of interfaces for colorblind users, it does not emphasize specific aspects of recoloring and adaptations for colorblind.

Studies in this category also focus on the definition of tools and technologies for the design of adaptive interfaces for colorblind user's needs (e.g., [7, 8]). These adaptations take place at design time by developers with technical skills, differing from our study that proposes the runtime adaptation according to the several types of color blindness and dynamic aspects regarding users' preferences.

The second category includes research of frameworks for the development of systems with the capability of recoloring according to the users' needs in a (semi)automatic way. Many studies in this category propose alternatives to change the interface colors. For example, the use of constraint-based annotations for express the intended color effects [9], service-based users' preferences adaptation [10, 11], and individualized models based on color calibration [12]. Other investigation uses context information, rules or norms to define adaptation parameters (e.g., [13]).

The majority of the studies in the second category conceives a solution for a specific type of colorblindness (deuteranomaly), and usually changes (or calibration) to support unforeseen situations are complex. Furthermore, the "generic" frameworks remain abstract (or theoretical) and fail in deeply dealing into details with specific situations, which requires recoloring changes. Our proposal constructs a conceptual domain model from the generic concepts to specific and technical aspects of adaptation.

The third category involves recoloring algorithms to improve the perception of web pages, images and other resources by colorblind users. Several studies rely on WC3 standards to propose algorithms that calculate the color distance for representative color, and use interpolation for the remaining colors [14]. Alternatively, other proposals preserve the original colors when the users perceive them well [4].

Performance refers to a recurrent issue investigated by researches of recoloring algorithms, particularly when real-time recoloring is required [15]. One of the open challenges stands for the way of conciliating time performance [16] with perceptiveness [17] and subjective quality of the recoloring results. Other studies explore novel technologies to improve the colorblind using wearable solutions [18].

One key limitation of the studies in the third category is the validation by simulators or experiences limited users' studies in controlled environments (e.g., considering illumination and/or video quality) to evaluate the qualitative aspects of the solutions. We propose to organize (using ontologies) and represent features to reuse the existing algorithms according to the users' needs and preferences; however, it is out of the scope of this article to investigate new algorithms.

The last category includes interface adaptation techniques using ontologies focusing on web accessibility. Semantic Web techniques have been used to provide adaptive interfaces and personalized information [19]. Ontologies are used to represent various aspects of user interface adaptation, including web page structure, users' profile information and context information. For instance, existing studies propose a unified web document model based on specialized ontologies [20]. Their models aim at improving blind users' experience on the web. Further studies propose an ontology to formally represents users' contexts interaction processes, including users' physical, environmental and computational contexts [21].

Other studies emphasize the users' characteristics and needs to provide adaptable interfaces for users with disabilities [22]. This approach employs ontologies to represent the user's profiles and needs, as well as for reasoning proposals. These models are combined with contextual service information to provide automatically adapted interfaces for users with disabilities. Although the research in this category presents several advances regarding adaptive interfaces, which proves to be a promising approach, the analyzed literature still lacks specific aspects on ontology modelling for adapting interfaces for colorblind users.

We argue that a solution considering aspects from the fourth categories (in a proper design) may produce better results for colorblind users. Our research faces issues in smoothly respecting the particularities of each type of colorblindness and preferences of each individual in a seamless way. Adaptive interfaces can be a key component for accessibility [5]; however, studies exploring ontologies for this purpose still deserve further research. Our approach differs from literature by modeling (using ontologies) strategies of design, adaptation and algorithms for colorblind accessibility, which are matched with users' needs and preferences aiming to determine the most suitable recoloring options of adaptation.

3 Framework for Interface Adaptation Based on Ontologies

Firstly, this section presents the proposed framework (Sect. 3.1), including its elements for interface adaptation. Afterwards, Sect. 3.2 describes a software architecture that implements it using web technologies.

3.1 Proposed Framework

We first define an ontology that represents: (i) characteristics and preferences of colorblind users (e.g., types and attributes of color blindness and aesthetics preferences); (ii) aspects of techniques for color adaptation (e.g., rich web interfaces structures, properties of coloring algorithms and contrast modifications); as well as (iii) accessibility guidelines and design issues concerning color requirements. The latter represents W3C success criteria regarding the combination and perception of colors.

The core concepts of the ontology refer to key elements of the proposed framework (cf. Fig. 1). In the first step, colorblind users access a web interface to obtain some content. The INPUT element (top of Fig. 1) involves both static and dynamic relevant parameter data regarding to the user. As the static data, users assign their type of pathology and color preferences. The dynamic part includes parameter related to changeable items according to the context of use, e.g., the current visualized interface components. The context might include, for instance, images, bottoms, background, etc.

The item #5 of the framework (Fig. 1) considers the input data to implement search and inferences in the ontology, which represents colorblindness knowledge. The outcome came from the interpretation of axioms and rules that indicate the procedure and interface setting for adaptation, for example, to change the color of a bottom or to apply a recoloring algorithms to an image.

The element RUNTIME ADAPTATION (bottom of Fig. 1) aims at executing (applying) the interface adaptation techniques according to the results from the ontology and the interaction context. This involves the *application of recoloring algorithms* (6.1) – e.g., change of images' colors; *modification of page elements* (6.2) – e.g., alter color of background, bottoms and menus; and *change of contrast* (6.3) – e.g., highlighting details of an image.

The final output (step 7 of Fig. 1) renders the web page with the adapted interface elements based on the ontological knowledge regarding types of colorblindness as well as users' preferences.

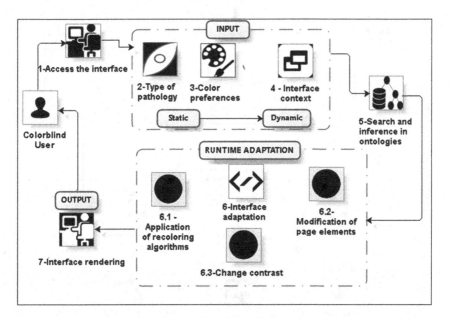

Fig. 1. Framework definition

3.2 Software Architecture

Figure 2 presents the proposed architecture defined with the aim of structuring the development of a software prototype. The architecture involves three main components including: (I) user interface component; (II) algorithms and techniques of adaptation component and (III) data access component.

The data access component stands for storing information of the type of colorblindness and users' preferences about color changes, accessibility standards and ontology data. The component for adaptation makes modifications in web pages via specific algorithms and techniques; it mostly explores PHP functions, Javascript (jQuery) and DOM. For example, we can change the color of all links in a page with a simple jQuery code: *$("a").css("color", "red");* or invoke complex algorithms for recoloring a map. The component II modifies the content to be presented in the user interface (component I) according to the formal statements and rules that analyses the information stored in the data access component. As shows Fig. 2, the interface component allows the rendering of adapted web pages (implemented in HTML and CSS).

. In an overview of the interaction workflow, a user accesses the interface and performs his/her authentication (#1 in Fig. 2). Algorithms and adaptation techniques, which perform propositions of adaptation (#2 in Fig. 2), receive data on the user's type of pathology and his/her personal preferences. In addition, the solution relies on the content and rules for adaptation and accessibility, declared in the ontology. Using the outcome with facts about the adaptation, the component I renders the modified interface (#3 in Fig. 2).

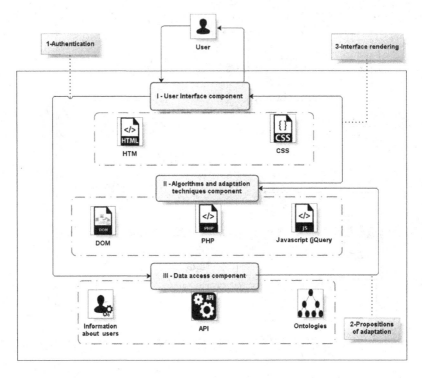

Fig. 2. Software architecture

4   Interface Prototype and Scenario of Application

This section describes the prototypes of interface mechanisms that explore the proposed framework and architecture (Sect. 4.1). In addition, we present an example of execution illustrating the proposed solution and ontology (Sect. 4.2).

4.1   Interface Mechanisms of Adaptation

Figure 3 presents the designed interface prototype, which explores interface adaptation in the context of meteorological images systems. As the basic feature, the prototype allows users to introduce the static data via a registration form typing information related to name, date of birth, username, password and type of his/her pathology, i.e., the type of colorblindness (item 2 in Fig. 3). Based on the available information and content from the underlying ontology, the system then provides alternative colors to be selected by the users according to his/her preferences. This list of alternative colors is determined by the type of pathology and accessibility standards modeled in the ontology (item 3 in Fig. 3). The item 4 (Fig. 3) shows a page with a meteorology image adapted using the most suitable technique to such context of interaction (i.e., meteorological images) and individuals' preferences.

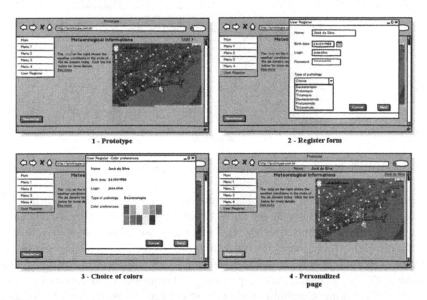

Fig. 3. Software prototype (Color figure online)

4.2 Scenario of Illustration

Figure 4 shows an example of practical scenario to illustrate the execution of our solution. In this scenario, the user needs to access a web page with meteorological information. The system presents a climate map exploring several colors regarding weather events and subtitles to identify them. A user with a normal vision is able to recognize the different colors and the associated events, which is not the case for a colorblind user. For example, such user might observe the map as presented in item 2 of Fig. 4. We may notice that colors of yellow and red tones are confused and the meteorological phenomena represented by the color green remains hardly recognizable in the map. It also makes difficult the identification of subtitles.

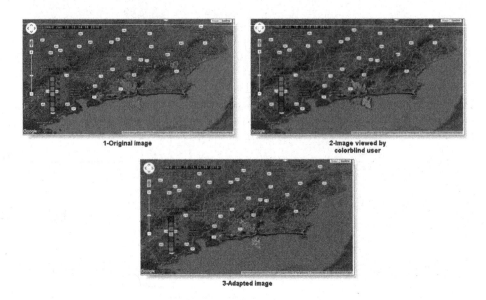

Fig. 4. Example of application (Color figure online)

Figure 5 presents part of a preliminary ontology defined according to our interface adaptation proposal and illustrate the current scenario. In this ontology, an adaptation technique is related to supported standards, useful users' preferences to setup parameters (e.g., of a recoloring tool), pathology types supported by the adaptation techniques, and the access contexts in which the adaptation techniques are applied. Figure 5 also illustrates the hierarchy of classes, including examples subclasses of adaptation techniques: color filters, recoloring algorithms and contrast changes. Note the set of subclasses modeled for the types of colorblindness.

In the present scenario, the system determines the adaptation solution according to the given parameters and ontology, which includes: pathology type (*Defteranopia*); interface context (weather map image); usage context with colors not noticeable in the interface (green and red); and, preference of alternative colors chosen by the user (blue). The system searches for the adaptation techniques described as instances in the ontology of Fig. 5. A simple query (e.g., using Sparql language) in the ontology eliminates algorithms that is not suitable for these parameters. In our scenario, the recoloring algorithm presented in [4] was considered suitable to all the parameters. After applying the execution of adaptation actions (the reprocessing of the image with the algorithm chosen), the new modified image appears to the user in runtime (item 3 in Fig. 4). Colorblind users can more easily distinguish such modified image.

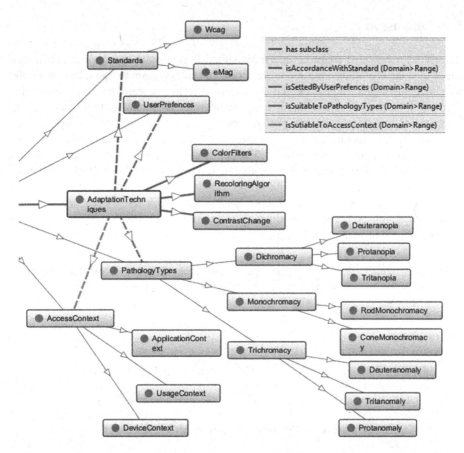

Fig. 5. Excerpt of colorblind ontology for user interface adaptation (Color figure online)

4.3 Discussion

This research obtained a conceptual proposal for interface adaptation and a software prototype elaborated with the aim of providing adaptation mechanisms according to interaction contexts to meet the colorblind users' accessibility needs. The main advantage of the solution is to consider multiple factors that influence on accessibility. This includes several types and subtypes of colorblindness, as well as the users' preferences in the adaptation results.

The proposed framework allows exploring and selecting more suitable adaptation techniques for each situation, such as the adequate recoloring algorithm, according to the domain knowledge formally expressed with ontologies. This meets users' color discrimination needs, while respecting their personal satisfaction. On the other hand, the proposal requires the heavy representation of knowledge and adequate query and reasoning techniques to obtain the adaptation actions. Further studies are needed to investigate additional adaptation mechanisms and scenarios of application.

5   Conclusion

Colorblind users need adaptive interfaces suited to modify colorful elements in web pages to make digital information more accessible and pleasant to them. In this article, we conceptualized a framework that makes use of formal representation of knowledge with ontologies to select and obtain adequate interface adaptation actions according to the interaction context and users' preferences. Our investigation defined a layered software architecture to implement the framework and achieved a functional prototype implementing adaptation mechanisms. The application scenario reveled that ontologies can be useful to achieve complex and complete scenarios of user's interface adaptation. Future work involves the refinement of the adaptation techniques and the research of further ontological properties for supporting the adaptation process. We also plan to conduct thorough experimental evaluations to examine the adaptation results according to the judgment of real colorblind users.

Acknowledgment.   We thank São Paulo Research Foundation (FAPESP) (Grant #2014/14890-0) (The opinions expressed in this work do not necessarily reflect those of the funding agencies.).

References

1. Bailey, J.D.: Color Vision Deficiency: A Concise Tutorial for Optometry and Ophthalmology, p. 16. Richmond Products Inc, Albuquerque (2010)
2. Flatla, D.R., Gutwin, C.: 'So that's what you see!' building understanding with personalized simulations of colour vision deficiency. In: The Proceedings of the 14th International ACM SIGACCESS Conference on Computers and Accessibility, Boulder, Colorado, USA, pp. 167–174 (2012)
3. Troiano, L., Birtolo, C., Miranda, M.: Adapting palettes to color vision deficiencies by genetic algorithm. In: Proceedings of the 10th Annual Conference on Genetic and Evolutionary Computation. New York, USA, pp. 1065–1072 (2008)
4. Kuhn, G.R., Oliveira, M.M., Fernandes, L.A.F.: An efficient naturalness-preserving image-recoloring method for dichromats. In: IEEE Transactions on Visualization and Computer Graphics. Los Alamitos, CA, USA, vol. 14, pp. 1747–1754 (2008)
5. Neris, V.P.A., Fortuna, F.J., Bonacin, R., Baranauskas, M.C.C.: Addressing diversity in web systems with norms and a tailoring-based approach. In: Proceedings of the ADIS International Conference WWW/INTERNET 2011, vol. 1, pp. 19–28 (2011)
6. Neris, V.P.A., Baranauskas, M.C.C.: Designing tailorable software systems with the users participation. J. Braz. Comput. Soc. **18**, 70 (2012)
7. Mereuta, A., Aupetit, S., Monmarché, N., Slimane, M.: Web page textual color contrast compensation for CVD users using optimization methods. J. Math. Model. Algorithms Oper. Res. **13**, 447–470 (2013)
8. Ribeiro, M., Gomes, A.: Recoloração de web conteúdos para daltonicos. In: Conferência Internacional em Design e Artes Gráficas. Lisboa, Portugal, pp. 470–472 (2012)
9. Wakita, K., Shimamura, K.: SmartColor: disambiguation framework for the colorblind. In: SIG ACCESS Conference on Assistive Technologies, New York, NY, USA, pp. 158–165 (2005)

10. Iaccarino, G., Malandrino, D., Percio, M., Scarano, V.: Efficient edge-services for colorblind users. In: Proceedings of the 15th International Conference on World Wide Web - WWW 2006. New York, USA, pp. 919–920 (2006)
11. Malandrino, D., Mazzoni, F., Riboni, D., Bettini, C., Colajanni, M., Scarano, V.: MIMOSA: context-aware adaptation for ubiquitous web access. Pers. Ubiquit. Comput. **14**(4), 301–320 (2009)
12. Flatla, D.R., Gutwin, C.: Improving calibration time and accuracy for situation-specific models of color differentiation. In: Proceedings of the 13th International ACM SIGACCESS Conference on Computers and Accessibility – ASSETS. Dundee, Scotland, UK., pp. 195–202 (2011)
13. Fortuna, F.J., Bonacin, R., Baranauskas, M. Cecília C.: A Framework for Flexibility at the Interface: joining Ajax technology and Semiotics. In: proceedings of 12th International Conference on Enterprise Information Systems (ICEIS 2010), pp. 30–37 (2010)
14. Jefferson, L., Harvey, R.: Accommodating color blind computer users. In: Proceedings of the 8th International ACM SIGACCESS Conference on Computers and Accessibility - Assets 2006. New York, USA, pp. 40–47 (2006)
15. Machado, G.M., Oliveira, M.M.: Real-time temporal-coherent color contrast enhancement for dichromats. Comput. Graph. Forum **29**, 933–942 (2010)
16. Huang, J., Wu, S., Chen, C.: Enhancing color representation for the color vision impaired. In: ECCV Workshop on Computer Vision Applications for the Visually Impaired. Villeurbanne, France., p. 12 (2008)
17. Huang, J.B., Chen, C.S., Jen, T.C., Wang, S.J.: Image recolorization for the colorblind. In: IEEE International Conference on Acoustics, Speech and Signal Processing. Taipei, Taiwan., pp. 1161–1164 (2009)
18. Tanuwidjaja, E., Huynh, D., Koa, K., Nguyen, C., Shao, C., Torbett, P., Emmenegger, C., Weibel, N.: Chroma: a wearable augmented-reality solution for color blindness. In: UBICOMP 2014. New York, USA, pp. 799–810 (2014)
19. Hervás, R., Bravo, J.: Towards the ubiquitous visualization: adaptive user-interfaces based on the Semantic Web. Interacting with Computers. New York, NY, USA, pp. 40–56 (2011)
20. Fayzrakhmanov, R. R., Göbel, M. C., Holzinger, W., Krüpl, B., Baumgartner, R.: A unified ontology-based web page model for improving accessibility. In: Proceedings of the 19th International Conference on World Wide Web - WWW 2010. New York, NY, USA, pp. 1087–1088 (2010)
21. Zakraoui, J., Zagler, W.: An ontology for representing context in user interaction for enhancing web accessibility for all. In: The First International Conference on e-Learning For All. Hammamet, Tunisia, pp. 3–5 (2010)
22. Abascal, J., Aizpurua, A., Cearreta, I., Gamecho, B.: A modular approach to user interface adaptation for people with disabilities. In: 13th International ACM SIGACCESS Conference on Computers and Accessibility, pp. 1–11 (2011)

Usability, Accessibility and Gameplay Heuristics to Evaluate Audiogames for Users Who are Blind

Márcia de Borba Campos[✉] and Juliana Damasio Oliveira

Faculty of Informatics (FACIN), Pontifical Catholic University
of Rio Grande do Sul (PUCRS), Porto Alegre, Brazil
marcia.campos@pucrs.br, juliana.damasio@acad.pucrs.br

Abstract. This paper presents a set of usability, accessibility and gameplay heuristics for audiogames, which have blind persons as intended audience. From the proposed and discussed heuristics, it is possible to determine the main usability, accessibility and gameplay issues in games, serving as a tool to identify the requirements for the game, to develop it and to evaluate it. The process of creating the heuristics was based on 6 steps: exploration, description, correlation, explanation, experimental validation and refinement.

Keywords: Users who are blind · Audiogames · Usability heuristics · Accessibility heuristics · Gameplay heuristics · Evaluation

1 Introduction

This paper presents a proposal for audiogame evaluation based on usability, accessibility and gameplay heuristics. For the scope of this work, audiogames are defined as audio-based games that have blind persons as final users. As a result, we expect the proposed evaluation method to be used during the development cycle of audiogames. This way, we seek to reduce the negative aspects of user experience and, at the same time, to identify and maintain the positive ones that may go beyond usable audiogame design.

Game usability is defined as the degree to which a player is capable of learning, controlling and understanding a game [1]. A system's usability is often defined in terms of effectiveness, efficiency and user satisfaction in a given usage context, along with the ease of using and learning to use the system [2]. Regarding games, these premises are questionable, since they must be more pleasant and entertaining when presenting users with challenges. Thus, the traditional definition of usability is insufficient to characterize the quality of interaction in digital games [3], not to mention that efficiency and effectiveness are secondary criteria for user satisfaction [4] when talking about games. Therefore, applying the general usability heuristics [5, 6] for game evaluation is not enough.

Many game evaluation methods originated in [1, 4, 7, 8]. Federoff [4] created 42 heuristics categorized into game interface, game mechanics and gameplay. Based on the study in [4], Desurvire et al. [7, 8] proposed heuristics organized into gameplay, game story, game mechanics and usability. Pinelle et al. [1] proposed 10 heuristics aiming at usability problems.

© Springer International Publishing Switzerland 2016
M. Antona and C. Stephanidis (Eds.): UAHCI 2016, Part I, LNCS 9737, pp. 38–48, 2016.
DOI: 10.1007/978-3-319-40250-5_4

For audiogame evaluation, accessibility issues must be included [9]. Miao et al. [10] discussed the application of different usability tests with blind, partially blind and sighted users. In their study, they presented the differences in conducting tests and in users' preferences. Petrie and Bevan [11] introduced a range of methods to evaluate accessibility, usability and user experience with information about their appropriate use, strengths and weaknesses. Sánchez et al. [12–14] evaluated different audiogames with blind persons based on usability and user satisfaction criteria. Park and Kim [15] suggested serious game guidelines based on game accessibility, which includes web accessibility, game contents accessibility and gameplay interface accessibility. Campos and Silveira [16] and Yuan et al. [17] described obstacles to digital accessibility that should be avoided in interactive systems and presented alternative input and output devices and interface styles, which attempt to provide a better experience for users with disabilities.

Based on these studies, we chose to adopt evaluation by inspection, in which evaluators explore the game interface using a set of heuristics. The process for developing the usability, accessibility and gameplay heuristics was based on the methodology presented by [18–20], which contains 6 steps. These topics, as well as the detailed heuristics for the evaluation of audiogames for blind persons, are presented and discussed in this paper.

This paper is organized in the following way: Sect. 2 presents works related to game evaluation; Sect. 3 presents the research process employed in formulating heuristics; Sect. 4 presents a proposal for usability, accessibility and gameplay heuristics for audiogames; finally, Sect. 5 presents some conclusions and future work.

2 Related Work

The ISO 9241-11 standard defines usability based on efficiency, effectiveness and user satisfaction criteria. The accessibility issues taken into account by [6] are learnability, memorability, efficiency, safety and satisfaction. However, for games, another analysis is required: one that focuses on user satisfaction over efficiency and effectiveness. [21] defined gameplay as an evaluation tool with 4 components: functional, structural, audio-visual and social playability. Gameplay is related to intuition, fun, challenge and social interaction, when the game is multiplayer [22]. This way, a game has good gameplay when its interface is intuitive and discreet, so that the player can focus on playing, which should be adequately difficult and engaging.

Many game evaluation methods originated in [1, 4, 7, 8]. Federoff [4] discusses usability criteria applied to games and emphasizes that a product's usability cannot be evaluated without considering its context. Thus, she concludes that effectiveness, efficiency and satisfaction are not equally important or applicable when talking about games. Federoff [4] initially conceived 30 heuristics, which were revised after the pilot test with game design professionals. The compiled list of game heuristics was organized into 3 categories and 40 heuristics: game interface (13), game mechanics (2) and gameplay (23). To them are also added those which fit into more than one category, which are game interface and play and game mechanics and play.

Based on the study in [4], Desurvire et al. [7, 8] proposed heuristics organized into Gameplay, Game Story, Game Mechanics and Usability. Desurvire et al. [7] adapted a set of heuristics for productivity software to games. The result was Heuristic Evaluation for Playability (HEP). The HEP heuristics were grouped into four categories: Gameplay (16), Game Story (8), Mechanics (7) and Usability (12). According to [7], HEP is helpful in early game design because it facilitates thinking about the design from the user's point of view. [8] have refined HEP, producing a new list called Game Usability Heuristics (PLAY), intended to help game developers during the entire design process, particularly at the beginning of the concept phase when changes to the design are less costly. The general principles were grouped into categories of heuristics evaluated by question: Gameplay (6 heuristics, 22 questions total), Coolness/Entertainment/Humor/Emotional Immersion (4 heuristics, 4 questions total), Usability and Game Mechanics (9 heuristics, 24 questions total). Some examples of heuristics in the Gameplay category include: enduring play; challenge, strategy and pace; consistency in game world; goals; variety of players and game styles; players' perception of control. One of the advantages described by authors [8] is that the PLAY proposal is modular. This way, a story-less game may be evaluated without the questions related to this heuristic.

Pinelle et al. [1] proposed 10 heuristics aiming at usability problems. The process used to develop the heuristics included identifying usability problems in game design, developing a set of categories by grouping similar usability problems together and creating heuristics for avoiding common usability problems in games.

There are other guidelines for game evaluation. Korhonen et al. [22] propose 29 heuristics organized into three modules: Gameplay, Game Usability and Mobility. Soomro et al. [23] propose 4 categories (Gameplay, Usability, Mobility and Multi-player), which add up to 10 heuristics for mobile games, which can also be used as guidelines by game developers. Korhonen and Koivisto [24] present and describe play-ability heuristics for mobile multiplayer games. Game accessibility is presented and discussed by [9, 15, 17, 25].

3   Usability, Accessibility and Gameplay Heuristics to Evaluate Audiogames

For this study, we created a set of heuristics that can be used as guidelines during the stages of modeling, developing and evaluating an audiogame.

3.1   Research Process

We used the methodology proposed by [18–20] to create the usability, accessibility and gameplay heuristics for the evaluation of audiogames for blind persons. This methodology comprises 6 steps:

1. Exploration: to collect bibliography related to the main topics of the research. We selected bibliography concerning audiogames [14] and game evaluation [1, 4, 7, 8], as well as 18 audiogames and 33 games, which were said to conform to accessibility

recommendations. Three evaluators with experience in usability and games in general took part in this step.

2. Description: to highlight the most important characteristics of the previously collected information, in order to formalize the main concepts associated with the research. Evaluators faced usability issues that were listed in order to be categorized according to game heuristics and Nielsen's heuristics [5, 6], without revising or modifying them.

3. Correlation: to identify the characteristics that the usability heuristics for specific applications should have, based on traditional heuristics and case studies analysis. One evaluator from the previous step took part in this stage, along with 23 undergraduate students who were enrolled in the Human-Computer Interaction course. 102 questions were written to be used as a guide in an evaluation by inspection.

4. Explanation: to formally specify the set of proposed heuristics. This stage allowed the evaluation instrument to be reorganized, eliminating questions that were still present in more than one category. The instrument was reduced to 72 questions.

5. Experimental validation: to check new heuristics against traditional heuristics by experiments, through heuristic evaluations performed on selected case studies. Using the instrument modified by step 4, 6 audiogames were re-evaluated.

6. Refinement, based on the feedback from the validation stage. We carried out successive evaluations to consolidate the set of heuristics proposed for audiogames evaluation. This step provided for a better description of the categories of the proposed heuristics and the commonly identified problems. The instrument was reduced to 44 questions. As a result, we produced a document with identification, definition, explanation, examples and advantages for each heuristic, along with a description of every possible problem that can arise when the heuristic is not taken into account.

4 A Set of Usability, Accessibility and Gameplay Heuristics for Audiogames

Based on the method used, we constructed a list of heuristics for audiogame evaluation, containing usability, accessibility and gameplay heuristics. For each heuristic, there is a definition, an explanation on how to conform to it, example questions, what to avoid when developing audiogames and the related benefits and problems. This method evaluates audiogames that do not have a graphical interface, due to the scope of the research. Should the evaluation be carried out on audiogames with a graphical interface, then questions concerning layout, size and shape of the elements must be included.

Heuristic 1: Visibility of System Status

Definition. The audiogame should keep the user informed through audio about actions that are relevant to the game.

Explanation. This heuristic should prioritize the means through which users will check their score and level and how objects and other characters move. One option is to allow the score and the level to be checked via keyboard shortcuts. For the location of objects and characters, a good option is to use 3D audio.

Avoid. Keys with too many functions. Each key should have a specific function. If many functions are accessed with a single key, the user should be notified about this change.
Example questions. Can the user know their score and level during the game? If approaching or moving objects, is it possible to perceive their location during the game? In mobile audiogames, are vibration effects recognizable?
Benefits. Better use experience, because the user may react to each situation accordingly while playing the audiogame. The user can be aware of the general context of the game.
Problems. When this heuristic is not observed, the user may not know about their progress during the game, possibly feeling frustrated.

Heuristic 2: Similarity Between System and Real World

Definition. The audiogame should use the most natural language possible.
Explanation. The audiogame should avoid the use of technical jargon during the game. Information should be presented in a natural and logical order. The language is advised to be that of the targeted audience or of the game's genre.
Avoid. Words in another language or phrases that belong to other gaming genres.
Example question. Are the concepts used in the audiogame comprehensible?
Benefits. Errors are minimized because the player is used to audiogame concepts. Better understanding of the concepts related to audiogames.
Problems. The user may feel confused when playing the audiogame.

Heuristic 3: User Control and Freedom

Definition. The user should feel in control of the audiogame.
Explanation. The audiogame should allow the user to leave, save different states, return, pause and cancel actions at any time. The application should allow the audio to be adjusted. Keyboard shortcuts are advised for such actions. The state saving functionality can be automatic and, when the game starts, it can load the status and scenery according to the user's level.
Avoid. The mouse should be avoided as a tool to select elements from the interface, as well as to move objects that follow the cursor's position, due to blind persons' lack of precision when using a mouse for this purpose.
Example questions. Does the user feel in control of the application? Can they save the game? Can they return to a previous point? Can they fast-forward the audio queue? Can they rewind the audio queue? Can they adjust audio playback speed? Is it possible to adjust the volume? Can the user select objects on the screen? Can they move the objects?
Benefits. Better use experience. The user feels free to explore the application.
Problems. Without the necessary commands, the user will be unable to control the game.

Heuristic 4: Consistency and Standardization

Definition. Audiogames should be executed via consistent and standardized actions.
Explanation. For games that have a graphical interface, this heuristic may relate to element layout on screen. In the case of audiogames, which do not have graphical interfaces, consistency and standardization relate to the actions that the user must carry out

in order to interact with the game. In this context, it is associated with clicking and interacting with menus such as "play", "return", etc. Controls for taking actions should, when applicable, follow the game industry standards, always produce the same results and be available throughout the entire game. The choice of interaction mechanism should remain the same during the game, including key bindings and menu option layout, for example.

Avoid. Varying the control interface and audio features during the game and choosing unusual key combinations to perform actions.

Example questions. Is there coherence between game controls and their actions? Do keyboard shortcuts follow the game industry standard, when one exists? Do controls remain the same throughout the game? Is menu option navigation standardized? Are the key bindings consistent? Is there a standard for audio volume? Does an element's type of audio remain the same throughout the game?

Benefits. User's confidence may be increased, since actions can become more intuitive.

Problems. User may not understand what must be done in the game and what level they are in.

Heuristic 5: Error Prevention

Definition. The audiogame should prevent the user from making mistakes.

Explanation. In games that have a graphical interface, error prevention can be achieved by disabling unnecessary menu options without removing them from the interface. For audiogames, it is advised that disabled menu options be read with a different kind of voice or in another tone. Keys that perform no action during the game should be disabled. This prevents involuntary user actions from causing errors.

Avoid. Keeping options enabled when they should be disabled. Avoid irreversible actions.

Example questions. Can the user identify when a menu option is disabled? Does the audiogame disable keys that are not used during the game? When the user chooses to leave the game, is confirmation required? Is it necessary to save the game manually?

Benefits. Prevent errors from happening.

Problems. The amount of errors during gameplay may be increased.

Heuristic 6: Recognition Rather than Recall

Definition. The user should recognize what to do when playing the audiogame rather than memorizing it.

Explanation. To allow the user to enhance their skills, the game should be simple to play and memory should not be required for every interaction. For games with a graphical interface, options' icons should be a reminder of their functions. In audiogames that have a menu, options should convey their function through audio. Keyboard shortcuts should be in accordance with what they represent. Future skills should be acquired before they are needed. Sounds for game elements should remind the player of what they mean, especially icon sounds.

Avoid. Menus with too many options or long explanations.

Example questions. Is the menu easy to understand? Are keyboard shortcuts easy to remember? Do objects' sounds remind the player of what they mean?

Benefits. Reducing the player's memory requirement also reduces their mental effort to understand the game.

Problems. The user may feel tired during the game, for they will have to rely on their memory in order to access information on how to play better.

Heuristic 7: Flexibility and Efficiency of Use

Definition. The audiogame should be flexible and efficient, so it can be used by various user profiles.

Explanation. Games usually have different levels of difficulty that require different sets of skills. The game should be flexible so that skills can be developed during the game. It is important for it to have customization mechanisms such as setting key bindings, volume control and sound playback speed. The user should be capable of skipping to the desired piece of information without listening to the entire audio.

Avoid. Large number of keys used simultaneously.

Example questions. Are the controls customizable? Are keystroke sequences easy to perform? Are all controls necessary? Is the choice of simultaneous keystrokes adequate? Does it provide for efficient use by different user profiles?

Benefits. Greater efficiency, helping advanced players and beginners alike.

Problems. May cause the player to lose interest in the game.

Heuristic 8: Aesthetic and Minimalistic Design

Definition. The audiogame should have an aesthetic and minimalistic design.

Explanation. An aesthetic and minimalistic design refers to presenting strictly necessary information to the user, including audio content, visual elements and control actions. In audiogames, this heuristic applies directly to the diversity of sound types and quality, as well as to the use of a haptic interface, when available. The user should be able to tell distinct sounds apart and identify the different situations in which the haptic interface is enabled.

Avoid. Excessive use of different types of audio. Avoid long messages.

Example question. Is the sound quality appropriate? Is the amount of sounds appropriate? Is the usage of the haptic interface appropriate? Is its vibration intensity appropriate?

Benefits. User exhaustion is minimized: too many sounds and vibrations in unnecessary moments cause the user to be upset or distracted.

Problems. Users may have problems telling the various sounds or vibrations apart.

Heuristic 9: Help Users Recognize, Diagnose, and Recover from Errors

Definition. The user should understand when an error occurs and be able to recover from it.

Explanation. In games that have a graphical interface, when the user makes a mistake, a window may be displayed containing further information and an option to close it. In audiogames, information is always conveyed in the form of audio. Thus, messages should be clear and the user should have the choice to pause, repeat or fast-forward them. Furthermore, the message should tell the user clearly what to do to return to a safe situation in the game, for example.

Avoid. Interference or excessive use of error message audio alongside gameplay audio. Screen change for help items.

Example questions. Can the user recover from an error? Does the audiogame provide information on how to leave an undesired state?

Benefits. May minimize frustration, since knowing how to recover from an error reduces the annoyance of it ever happening.

Problems. User may not know how to leave an undesired situation, which may cause frustration.

Heuristic 10: Help and Documentation

Definition. The audiogame should provide help and documentation for the user.

Explanation. Audiogames, as well as games in general, should supply relevant information so the user can learn how to play. Information in an audiogame should be conveyed via audio, especially things such as which keys to use during the game and how to interpret each sound. Help should be available at all times during the game and it should be supplied according to context. Also, a tutorial may be available.

Avoid. Exceedingly long explanation audio.

Example questions. At the start of the game, is the user given enough information to understand it? Is the user given help information according to the context they are in?

Benefits. Better understanding of the game and how to play it. Beginners may become more experienced by going through the documentation.

Problems. Increased error rate, since the user may not know how to use the application.

Heuristic 11: Gameplay

Definition. The audiogame should have gameplay.

Explanation. This refers to having an inviting story, with given goals and rules, levels of difficulty and rewards for the player. Additionally, the game may offer several ways to achieve the same goal.

Avoid. Having the user discover required skills by themselves.

Example questions. Does the audiogame have a clear goal? Does it present different levels of difficulty? Does it present challenges? Does it reward experience, i.e. does the character become stronger as levels are surpassed and secondary goals are achieved? Does the audiogame allow the user to practice a skill, be it physical, mental or social? Does the audiogame offer different ways to achieve its goals?

Benefits. The game becomes more entertaining.

Problems. User will not have motivation to carry on playing.

Heuristic 12: Accessibility

Definition. The audiogame should be accessible to the user.

Explanation. The audiogame should have the capability of being used equally, securely and autonomously by users with disabilities. The chosen kind of platform must be regarded, since the way to interact with devices may vary. On desktops, the keyboard is prioritized, whereas on mobile devices the only interface is the touchscreen. Moreover, mobile devices can be used in different screen orientations (portrait/landscape), so the content must adjust to them and be easily reachable in graphical interfaces. More important pieces of information should be presented first.

Avoid. Conflicting information in graphical interface. On mobile devices, avoid the use of navigation actions that differ from the smartphone's native screen reader standards.

Example questions. Are the more important options presented first? Can the user access options quickly? Can the user start the game from the sound interface without having to activate the screen reader? Should a screen reader be used, is the information accessible?

Benefits. More equal and autonomous use. Obstacles that prevent access to information and gameplay are eliminated.

Problems. Gameplay may be made difficult or unfeasible.

5 Conclusions

Many sets of heuristics for game evaluation have been proposed [1, 4, 7, 8, 22, 24, 26]. However, there are no heuristics currently formalized for audiogame evaluation. In this work, we adapted existing heuristics and created others to cover usability, accessibility and gameplay for audiogame evaluation. They were presented and discussed.

The methodology used to develop the heuristics allowed us to perform an iterative process [18–20], resulting in the refinement of the heuristics and the reduction of the number of questions from 103 to 44. The presented heuristics are reliable for use in software development cycles, but it is still important to perfect them and re-validate them in future work.

As for future work, we intend to analyze as developers and evaluators from the field of game design use these heuristics.

Acknowledgments. This work was supported by the Program STIC-AmSud-CAPES/CONICYT/MAEE, Project KIGB-Knowing and Interacting while Gaming for the Blind, 2014. The authors also thank the human-computer interaction students that participated in this research.

References

1. Pinelle, D., Wong, N., Stach, T.: Heuristic evaluation for games: usability principles for video game design. In: Proceeding of the Twenty-Sixth Annual SIGCHI Conference on Human Factors in Computing System, pp. 1453–1462. ACM, New York (2008)
2. Roger, Y., Sharp, H., Preece, J.: Interaction Design: Beyond Human-Computer Interaction, 3rd edn. Wiley, New Jersey (2011)

3. Barcelos, T.S., Carvalho, T., Schimiguel, J., Silveira, I.F.: Análise comparativa de heurísticas para avaliação de jogos digitais. In: Proceedings of the 10th Brazilian Symposium on on Human Factors in Computing Systems and the 5th Latin American Conference on Human-Computer Interaction, pp. 187–196. Brazilian Computer Society. ACM, New York (2011)

4. Federoff, M.A.: Heuristics and Usability Guidelines for the Creation and Evaluation of Fun in Video Games. MS thesis, Department of Telecommunications, Indiana University, Bloomington, Indiana, USA (2002)

5. Nielsen, J.: Usability Engineering. Morgan Kaufmann, San Francisco (1993)

6. Nielsen, J.: Heuristic evaluation. In: Nielsen, J., Mark, R.L. (eds.) Usability Inspection Methods, vol. 17(1), pp. 25–62. Wiley, New York (1994)

7. Desurvire, H., Caplan, M., Toth, J.A.: Using heuristics to evaluate the playability of games. In: Extended Abstracts on Human Factors in Computing Systems, CHI 2004, pp. 1509–1512. ACM, New York (2004)

8. Desurvire, H., Wiberg, C.: Game usability heuristics (PLAY) for evaluating and designing better games: the next iteration. In: Ozok, A., Zaphiris, P. (eds.) OCSC 2009. LNCS, vol. 5621, pp. 557–566. Springer, Heidelberg (2009)

9. Leporini, B., Paternò, F.: Applying web usability criteria for vision-impaired users: does it really improve task performance? Int. J. Hum. Comput. Interact. **24**, 17–47 (2008)

10. Miao, M., Pham, H.A., Friebe, J., Weber, G.: Contrasting usability evaluation methods with blind users. Univ. Access Inf. Soc. **15**, 1–14 (2014). LNCS. Springer, Heidelberg

11. Petrie, H., Bevan, N.: The evaluation of accessibility, usability and user experience. In: Stepanidis, C. (ed.) The Universal Access Handbook, pp. 10–20. CRC Press, New York (2009)

12. Sánchez, J., Espinoza, M.: Audio haptic videogaming for navigation skills in learners who are blind. In: The Proceedings of the 13th International ACM SIGACCESS Conference on Computers and Accessibility, pp. 227–228. ACM, New York (2011)

13. Sánchez, J.: Development of navigation skills through audio haptic videogaming in learners who are blind. In: Proceedings of the 4th International Conference on Software Development for Enhancing Accessibility and Fighting Info-Exclusion. LNCS, vol. 14, pp. 102–110. Elsevier (2012)

14. Sánchez, J., Mascaró, J.: Audiopolis, navigation through a virtual city using audio and haptic interfaces for people who are blind. In: Stephanidis, C. (ed.) Universal Access in HCI, Part II, HCII 2011. LNCS, vol. 6766, pp. 362–371. Springer, Heidelberg (2011)

15. Park, H.J., Kim, S.B.: Guideline of serious game accessibility for the disabled. In: 2013 International Conference on Information Science and Applications (ICISA), pp. 1–3. IEEE, New York (2013)

16. Campos, M.B., Siveira, M.S., Santarosa, L.M.C.: Tecnologias para Educação Especial. In: IV Congreso Iberoamericano de Informática Educativa. Informática na educação: teoria & prática, vol. 1, Brazil (1998)

17. Yuan, B., Folmer, E., Harris Jr., F.C.: Game accessibility: a survey. Univ. Access Inf. Soc. **10**(1), 81–100 (2011). LNCS. Springer, Heidelberg

18. Inostroza, R., Rusu, C., Roncagliolo, S., Rusu, V., Collazos, C.A.: Developing SMASH: a set os SMArtphones uSability heuristics. In: Computer Standards & Interfaces. LTCS, vol. 43, pp. 40–52. Elsevier, Amsterdam (2016)

19. Jiménez, C., Rusu, C., Roncagliolo, S., Inostroza, R., Rusu, V.: Evaluating a methodology to establish usability heuristics. In 31st International Conference of the Chilean Computer Science Society (SCCC), pp. 51–59. IEEE, New York (2012)

20. Rusu, C., Roncagliolo, S., Rusu, V., Collazos, C.A.: A methodology to establish usability heuristics. In: Proceedings of the 4th International Conferences on Advances in Computer-Human Interactions (ACHI 2011), pp. 59–62 (2011)

21. Järvinen, A., Heliö, S., Mäyrä, F.: Communication and Community in Digital Entertainment Services. Prestudy Research Report. University of Tampere, Finland (2002)

22. Korhonen, H., Paavilainen, J., Saarenpää, H.: Expert review method in game evaluations: comparison of two playability heuristic sets. In: Lugmayr, A., Franssila, H., Sotamaa, O., Näränen, P., Vanhala, J. (eds.) In: Proceedings of the 13th International MindTrek Conference: Everyday Life in the Ubiquitous Era (MindTrek 2009), pp. 74–81. ACM, New York (2009)

23. Soomro, S., Ahmad, W.F.W., Sulaiman, S.: A preliminary study on heuristics for mobile games. In: 2012 International Conference on Computer & Information Science (ICCIS), vol. 2, pp. 1030–1035. IEEE, New York (2012)

24. Korhonen, H., Koivisto, E.M.I.: Playability heuristics for mobile multi-player games. In: Proceedings of the 2nd International Conference on Digital Interac-Tive Media In Entertainment And Arts (DIMEA 2007), pp. 28–35. ACM, New York (2007)

25. Cheiran, J.F.P.: Diretrizes de acessibilidade para jogos (DAJ). http://www.inf.ufrgs.br/~jfpcheiran/diretrizes/

26. Korhonen, H., Koivisto, E.M.I.: Playability heuristics for mobile games. In: Proceedings of the 8th Conference on Human-Computer Interaction with Mobile Devices and Services (MobileHCI 2006), pp. 9–16. ACM, New York (2006)

Authoring WCAG2.0-Compliant Texts for the Web Through Text Readability Visualization

Evelyn Eika[1(✉)] and Frode Eika Sandnes[1,2]

[1] Oslo and Akershus University College of Applied Sciences, Oslo, Norway
{Evelyn.Eika,frodes}@hioa.no
[2] Westerdals Oslo School of Art, Communication and Technology, Oslo, Norway

Abstract. Texts on the web need to be readable in order to be accessible to a wide audience. WCAG2.0 states that tests should not exceed the reading level of upper secondary education. Several readability measures have been proposed over the last century. However, these measures give an accumulated measure of the text and do not help pinpoint specific problems in the text. This paper proposes a text visualization approach that emphasizes readability issues in texts. The texts are visualized in the textual domain. The intention of the visualization approach is to draw the attention of the author towards the aspects of the text that potentially are hard to read, allowing the author to revise the text and consequently making the text more readable.

Keywords: WCAG2.0 · Readability · Visualization · Universal design · Cognitive disability · Dyslexia

1 Introduction

The Web Content Accessibility Guidelines (WCAG2.0) provide a set of minimum requirements that are intended to help make the web accessible to as many people as possible. One of the issues addressed by WCAG is the quality of the text. Criterion 3.1.5 [1] states that: *"When text requires reading ability more advanced than the lower secondary education level ... supplemental content ... is available. (Level AAA)"*. How is one to realize this relatively abstract criterion in practice? As with many of the criteria in WCAG2.0, they are formulated as issues to be checked after the process of designing web content is finished, such as minimum contrast on web pages [2, 3]. The viewpoint taken in this paper is that the most efficient and cost effective way of designing high quality and accessible web content is to incorporate WCAG-requirements formatively during the design process instead of after the design process.

There have been few major advances in the computer-assisted composition of text in recent decades. Perhaps the only exception is tools that support distributed and collaborative writing activities [4]. Most authors use word processors to compose their text. The WYSIWYG (what-you-see-is-what-you-get) editors [5] have become a convention since the graphical user interface became commonplace in the mid 90's. Some individuals still believe that the final presentation should be separate from the task of composition and will therefore use simple text editors to compose their text and later

© Springer International Publishing Switzerland 2016
M. Antona and C. Stephanidis (Eds.): UAHCI 2016, Part I, LNCS 9737, pp. 49–58, 2016.
DOI: 10.1007/978-3-319-40250-5_5

employ typesetting software such as Latex [6]. This is because a focus on the final presentation during the authoring process draws valuable attention from the composition. However, the text editing tools used in the Latex community are probably even less useful for text composition, and often focus on syntax highlighting for Latex commands, rudimentary spelling and grammar checks.

On the other hand, the main objective of the WYSIWYG editor is to represent the text as close as possible to the way it will appear in published form, being it in print, or in electronic form. WYSIWYG editors are becoming increasingly powerful by integrating tools that enhance the authoring process such as on the fly spell-checking, synonyms, antonyms, grammar checks and simple style issues. For example, Microsoft Word typically underlines erroneously spelled words with a red line, while passages with grammatical issues are marked in blue. One drawback of using the blue underlines is that it employs one visualization feature to represent a vast array of grammatical issues, while the red line only indicates one thing – a misspelled word. The blue line does not give a clue to what the particular issue is. The author therefore has to investigate the blue line further by, for instance, mouse-over to get a tool-tip.

The interest in measures of readability has been vast, and a number of readability measures have been proposed and debated over the last century [7]. The WCAG2.0 supplementary documentation also refers to one of these, namely, the Flesch-Kincaid metric. Although many of these methods demonstrate high correlations with actual readability, they are all aggregated measures and do not indicate what the problems are and where these problems are.

This paper proposes a different way of editing documents. The text is not represented in the ad-hoc manner as in a text-editor, or presentation centric as in the WYSIWYG editors. Instead, the text is presented according to commonly cited readability features.

2   Background

The literature on readability is plentiful, and much of the attention has been focused on readability indices, especially readability index validity [7] and readability index accuracy [8]. Researchers have experimented with various ways of optimizing the formulas for quantifying readability [9]. The most commonly cited measurements include Flesch-Kincaid, Gunning Fog and SMOG. A common feature of most of these formulas is the use of sentence length and word difficulty. More recently, readability is also seen in the context of disability, such as dyslexia [10] and multimodal access via screen readers.

Readability formulas are objective and can be computed automatically. They were originally developed for matching the appropriate texts to students with a given reading level. The reading indices should therefore also be suitable for determining readability on the web. However, the readability formulas have been criticized for not capturing real readability. Also, these numbers are not necessarily useful to authors. Qualitative methods have also been proposed such as levelling [11].

There are at least two ways of making text on the web more accessible to a broad audience: during composition or after composition. Several attempts have been made at automatically summarizing and simplifying existing texts. For example, Jing [12] used syntactic knowledge, context information and statistics to remove extraneous phrases from sentences. Chandrasekar et al. [13] experimented with finite state grammars and the Supertagging model for text simplification. More recent approaches are corpus based [14]. Simplification techniques have also been applied to other languages such as Spanish [15]. Common to all automatic approaches is their current inefficiency compared to humans.

It is our belief that the text becomes more readable if the quality of a text is ensured during composition, as it is harder for others to improve a text they have not written themselves, let alone depending on automatic summarizers and text simplifiers. One approach is to give authors tools that allow them to visualize flaws in their writing.

The visualization of text has been proposed to help navigate digital libraries, including galaxies visualization [16], mapping text to surfaces [17], principal components analysis [18], multiple views [19], and self-organizing maps [20]. The purpose is to visualize the relationship between different documents and not express aspects of the document contents per se. Such methods are thus seemingly not helpful to authors.

Other text visualization techniques aim at helping users understand the content of documents. Tag clouds [21] have become widely used where non-stop words in the text are displayed in a cloud-like shape where the size of each word is related to its frequency. Variations on the tag cloud include spark clouds that allow the frequency of terms to be observed over time [22]. Ham et al.'s [23] phrase nets visually show how terms are linked via a user-selected relation, such as finding the family lines in the Bible. Other interesting text visualizations include Wattenberg and Viégas' [24] word tree, which is used to show various forms of a query phrase in a document. Different instances of a query prefix are shown at different levels, and text size is used to communicate importance. This can help a user quickly find a particular instance instead of browsing all instances of the prefix sequentially.

Chung et al. [25] used visualization to help deaf people understand news texts in Korean. They claim that deaf people have difficulty comprehending complex texts as they are more used to visual representations through sign language. Their solution involved identifying the various clauses of text and representing them visually. The clauses are split up and the relationships between the clauses are visualized using arrows.

Kim et al. [26, 27] used shaded dots to visualize the readability of text. At the beginning of a sentence, the dots were white and gradually become darker as the sentence becomes longer. Very long sentences end up with nearly black dots. Punctuation marks such as commas generally add to the readability and these symbols slow the further darkening of the pixels. Kim et al.'s approach makes it easy to get an overview of the difficulty of a text, and in particular, where the challenges approximately occur in the text. The approach therefore provides more useful information than the traditional readability formulas. However, since the visualisations do not show text, it is still not obvious how authors can easily make use of the visualisations to improve their writing.

Oelke et al. [28] developed the VisRA tool for visualizing readability with the intention to help authors compose more readable texts. This tool provides a mixture of both text centric visualisations and other visualisation mechanisms such as correlation maps. Typically, each paragraph is marked with a colour that indicates its readability. In addition, a column on the right indicates which factors affect readability. The factors employed in

VisRa are vocabulary difficulty (percentage of words not found in a list of 1000 most frequent words), word length (average characters per word), nominal forms (a combined measure comprising the noun/verb ratio and the number of gerunds and nominalized words ending with -ity, -ness, etc.), sentence length (words per sentence) and complexity of the sentence structures (the branching factor in the phrase structure tree of a sentence). VisRa illustrates problems at paragraph level but problems at sentence and word level go undetected. Another drawback is that the VisRa tool is not made available to the general research community.

In a similar attempt, Kamakar and Zhu [29] visualized text at paragraph level to assist authors using several indices including Flesch-Kincaid, Gunning Fog, SMOG, Coleman Liau and ARI. Also, three visualization techniques are used, colour-coded circles, colour-coded abbreviations and Chernoff faces. The colour-coded rings show the average readability indices for the paragraphs where red is the lowest readability, going through orange yellow and green being the highest readability. The colour-coded abbreviation view shows each of the indices with the same colour-coding. The Chernoff face visualization shows the five parameters as oval vs. round face, size of the eyes, orientation of the eyes, size of the mouth and orientation of the mouth. One potential problem with Kamakar and Zhu's approach is that it visualizes relatively abstract and aggregated entities – readability indices. It may be hard for the authors to transform this information into concrete text editing improvements. One study by Liu et al. [30] made use of faces. They created an emotion-detecting engine to detect the emotion in writing and then colours and emoticons to convey one of six emotions for a passage of text.

A different visualization approach proposed by Kamakar and Zhu [31] uses bar graphs to represent sentences in terms of word length, levels of grey to represent six levels of word difficulty and white blocks to indicate sentence clauses. Kamakar and Zhu's approach is among the closest to the one presented herein. The major difference between Kamakar and Zhu's method and our method is that they use a different representation of coloured square bars while we only use text. Another difference is that our visualization is simple with less noise, while theirs provides rich details that may divert the users' attention from the important issues.

3   Method

This section outlines the proposed text visualization technique. First, the textual attributes of interest are discussed, followed by the visual mechanisms employed.

3.1   Readability Attributes

This study adopted three key features from the readability research literature: sentence length, word complexity and prepositional phrases. Sentence length is commonly connected to readability, as long sentences are generally considered harder to read than shorter sentences. Word complexity is also highly cited as a factor that affects readability, in particular, syllable count where words with more than two syllables are considered hard words. Prepositional phrases, that is, phrases introduced by prepositions such as on, in, over, etc., are believed to add to the complexity of a sentence if many prepositional phrases are used within the same sentence.

In addition, we propose simply to use paragraph length as a feature of readability measured in number of characters. Long paragraphs are less tempting to read for the impatient reader, may seem overwhelming for less trained readers, and are more time-consuming to navigate for individuals that rely on screen readers.

3.2 Visual Attributes

Visualizations are achieved by employing visual features that are noticeable to the reader. These typically include position, size, shape, orientation, colour and texture. Unlike other text visualization approaches that represent readability in other domains through various transformations [31], our approach operates in the textual domain.

The textual domain imposes certain typographical constraints such as how sequences of letters form words along horizontal lines going from left to right (in languages based on the Latin alphabet). Moreover, word orders are constrained by their respective sentences, and sentence orders are constrained by their respective passages. Therefore, the visual degrees of freedom include the following: (a) positional features, such as horizontal spacing, line breaks, vertical spacing, size, colour comprising text and background colour; and (b) textural features, such as typeface family, bold, italics, superscript, subscript, underline, strikethrough, etc.

3.3 Visualization Framework

Sentence length is central to a majority of readability studies [7]. Sentence length is thus chosen as an attribute. Often length is measured in the number of words per sentence. In this study, the number of characters is used as the unit of measure. In ordinary typeset passages of flowing prose, it is not immediately obvious how long sentences are. To determine the length, the passage must be scanned or read. In our framework, a sentence is represented on a single line up to 100 characters. If a sentence is longer than 100 characters, it is clipped at the end and ellipses (...) are used to signal that the sentence is clipped. Each sentence thus becomes a bar as in a bar graph, where the length of the line directly relates to the sentence length. A non-proportional font where each character has the same width is used to ensure that the representation of length is in the same scale throughout, as illustrated in the examples below.

```
A somewhat longer sentence.
A short phrase.
```

Sentences with several parts separated by commas are divided using a ling break and continued on the next line. That is, the first part to the first comma is placed on the first line, the next part after the comma to the subsequent comma is placed on the next line after indentation, and so forth. This is illustrated in the following example:

```
This is the first sentence,
    it has more parts,
    and even a final part.
```

Another attribute frequently employed in readability studies is word length, usually represented in terms of number of syllables. Several studies consider words with more than two syllables as difficult. We therefore emphasize words with more than two syllables in the text using upper case. In the previous example, the word *sentence* has two syllables (sen-tence), but is incorrectly detected as having three syllables and is therefore marked as a difficult word. The syllable count is approximated using a simple algorithm based around vowel counting. Although the syllable counting procedure is not perfect, it gives a sufficient indication for this application. The visualization is thus:

```
This is the first SENTENCE,
    it has more parts,
    and even a final part.
```

Prepositional phrases are also known to affect readability. The propositional phrases in all sentences with more than one propositional phrase are highlighted. This allows the author to easily spot sentences that may come across as hard to read.

Finally, we expect paragraph length to be a predictor of readability on the web. In typeset text, it is usually quite easy to spot the length of a paragraph, except when a paragraph spans several pages. However, the advantage of perceiving paragraph length from the typeset text is lost with the proposed approach since lines are broken. We therefore introduce different backgrounds to indicate length. That is, the lines of the text for the first 100 words have an ordinary background, the lines for the subsequent 100 words is marked as long. The marking strength is increased for every 100 words; the limit of 100-word paragraph was based on [32].

Note that the word counts are used irrespective of lines since the layout proposed herein breaks up text utilizing more lines than the typeset text. Length marking paragraphs may help authors to know where to rephrase passages, cut text or reorganize the text into different paragraphs.

3.4 Alternative Views

To help authors focus on the most important issues in a text, the text visualizer allows other views besides the view showing the text in its correct chronological order. The sentence viewer lists the sentences in decreasing length, allowing authors to focus on assessing the readability of the longest sentences in the text. The word view lists all words with more than two syllables in decreasing order of syllable length and character lengths. Finally, the passage length view shows the paragraphs in decreasing order according to length.

4   Results

The first example illustrates the technique on a text for children at the level one (Flesch-Kincaid Reading Ease 87.6, Flesch-Kincaid Grade Level 3.2):

```
A young man goes to a SUPERMARKET.
It is his first day at work.
The SUPERMARKET MANAGER says hello with a smile.
Then he gives him a brush.
The young man must clean the floor.
The young man doesn't UNDERSTAND and he says,
        "But I studied at UNIVERSITY."

THE MANAGER then says,
        "Oh,
        I'm sorry.
I didn't know that you studied at UNIVERSITY.
Give me the brush and I will show you how to do it."
```

The layout suggests that this is an easy-to-read text. There are no long sentences and no complex prepositional phrases, but there are a couple of long words. However, these words are well known. The next example shows the same content at a higher reading level (Flesch-Kincaid Reading Ease 82.7, Flesch-Kincaid Grade Level 4.9):

```
A young man goes [TO] a SUPERMARKET [FOR] his first day [AT] work.
The SUPERMARKET MANAGER says hello [TO] him with a smile and then gives him a brush [TO] clean th...
The young man doesn't UNDERSTAND and says,
        "But I studied at UNIVERSITY."

THE MANAGER then says,
        "Oh,
        I'm sorry.
I didn't know that you studied at UNIVERSITY.
Give me the brush and I'll show you how to do it."
```

This passage is more difficult to read as it has fewer and longer sentences with a couple of more complex prepositional phrases. The following example shows the same content with an even higher reading level (Flesch-Kincaid Reading Ease 81.1, Flesch-Kincaid Grade Level 5):

```
A young man goes [TO] a SUPERMARKET [FOR] his first day [AT] work.
The SUPERMARKET MANAGER WELCOMES him with a smile and then gives him a brush to sweep the floor.
The young man looks very SURPRISED and says,
        "But I studied at UNIVERSITY."

THE MANAGER then says,
        "Oh,
        I'm sorry.
I didn't REALIZE that you studied at UNIVERSITY.
Give me the brush and I'll show you how to do it."
```

There is not much visible difference between the two and the readability scores are marginally different. The final example shows an extract from a hard-to-read disclaimer (Flesch-Kincaid Reading Ease -3.4, Flesch-Kincaid Grade Level 25.2):

```
LICENSOR agrees with *** that [FOR] this effort [TO] be SUCCESSFUL,
        LICENSOR and *** need [TO] work TOGETHER [IN] COLLABORATION and COOPERATION [IN] their ...
In PARTICULAR,
        LICENSOR shall assist and consult with *** upon request [ON] any topic REASONABLY RELAT...
        INCLUDING FORMULATION COMPONENTS,
        FORMULATING methods,
        MANUFACTURING methods,
        plant IDENTIFICATION,
        plant MEDICINAL PROPERTIES,
        sourcing of plant MATERIALS,
        INFORMATION [FROM] patients REGARDING SAFETY,
        EFFICACY,
        and side effects,
        INCLUDING ANECDOTAL INFORMATION,
        and any INFORMATION USEFUL [IN] ESTABLISHING a CLINICAL study.
If the ASSISTANCE and CONSULTATION FURNISHED [BY] LICENSOR [AT] the request of *** exceeds TWENTY...
.........LICENSOR.may.charge.a.REASONABLE.CONSULTING.fee.[FOR].such.ASSISTANCE.and.CONSULTATION....
LICENSOR REPRESENTS [TO] *** that [TO] the best of LICENSOR'S KNOWLEDGE and belief,................
.........the.FORMULATION.and.Other.FORMULATIONS,.......................................
.........the.EXCLUSIVE.LICENSE.rights.[FOR].which.LICENSOR.grants.[UNDER].this.Agreement.[TO].***,.
.........are.safe.and.EFFECTIVE.[FOR].the.treatment.of.human.patients.[FOR].the.CONDITIONS.and.D...
*** UNDERSTANDS that such REPRESENTATIONS do not CONSTITUTE GUARANTEES,...........................
.........but.an.ASSURANCE.based.upon.the.TECHNICAL.KNOWLEDGE.and.EXPERTISE.that.the.LICENSOR.has...
```

Clearly, the readability indices are off the scales. A visual inspection reveals that the paragraph itself is too long, and that the sentences are all too long with many prepositional phrases. Moreover, there are many difficult-to-read words. Note also that not all prepositional phrases are detected.

5 Discussion

The focus of the visualization approach is on sentence length and word difficulty. This is based on the assumption that long words and long sentences are difficult to read. Although this is often the case, it is not always true. It is very possible to write incomprehensible short sentences using short words. Some sentences can become easier to read if more words are used, inclusive of appropriate long words. Certain long words are frequently used and are thus well known. One may also argue that rhythm and variation in language make texts easier to read. Fortunately, the proposed approach makes such variations and rhythms visible.

In conclusion, the visualization is not intended to be used to eradicate all long words and long sentences, but rather to make the authors aware of their presence and allow them to deliberate their appropriateness. A potential drawback of the proposed strategy is that the limits are based on fixed pre-determined values. These values may not necessarily be correct for different writing styles and different genres.

6 Conclusions

A text-oriented visualisation approach was presented where the objective is to draw attention to aspects of writing which may reduce the readability of text. The approach is simple and thus easy to implement. However, although the features visualized are useful, the present approach does not capture other important aspects of text that affect readability. It is therefore unlikely that such a tool can be a complete solution. It could be one of many tools in the authors' toolbox. Future work should focus on evaluating the effectiveness of the visualisation and exploring how to automatically detect and visualize deeper attributes of readability, such as the use of transitional words and text coherence. For such purpose, it may be necessary to draw from natural language processing techniques. The approach presented herein may also be applicable to language learning [33] and teaching academic writing [34].

References

1. World Wide Web Consortium, Web content accessibility guidelines (WCAG) 2.0 (2008)
2. Sandnes, F.E., Zhao, A.Q.: An interactive color picker that ensures WCAG2.0 compliant color contrast levels. Procedia Comput. Sci. **67**, 87–94 (2015)
3. Sandnes, F.E., Zhao, A.Q.: A contrast colour selection scheme for WCAG2. 0-compliant web designs based on HSV-half-planes. In: Proceedings of System, Man and Cybernetics Conference SMC2015, pp. 1233–1237. IEEE (2015)

4. Hart-Davidson, W., Spinuzzi, C., Zachry, M.: Visualizing writing activity as knowledge work: challenges & opportunities. In: Proceedings of the 24th annual ACM international conference on Design of communication, pp. 70–77. ACM (2006)
5. DeRose, S.J., Durand, D.G., Mylonas, E., Renear, A.H.: What is text, really? ACM SIGDOC Asterisk J. Comput. Documentation **21**, 1–24 (1997)
6. Lamport, L.: Latex. Addison-wesley, Reading (1994)
7. Janan, D., Wray, D.: Reassessing the accuracy and use of readability formulae. Malays. J. Learn. Instruction **11**, 127–145 (2014)
8. Pitler, E., Nenkova, A.: Revisiting readability: a unified framework for predicting text quality. In: Proceedings of the Conference on Empirical Methods in Natural Language Processing, pp. 186–195. ACL (2008)
9. McLaughlin, G.H.: SMOG grading: a new readability formula. J. Read. **12**, 639–646 (1969)
10. Berget, G., Sandnes, F.E.: Do autocomplete functions reduce the impact of dyslexia on information-searching behavior? The case of Google. J. Assoc. Inf. Sci. Technol. (2015). http://onlinelibrary.wiley.com/doi/10.1002/asi.23572/abstract
11. Fry, E.B.: Text readability versus leveling. Read. Teacher **56**, 286–292 (2002)
12. Jing, H.Y.: Sentence reduction for automatic text summarization. In: Proceedings of the Sixth Conference on Applied Natural Language Processing, pp. 310–315. ACL (2000)
13. Chandrasekar, R., Srinivas, B.: Automatic induction of rules for text simplification. Knowl.-Based Syst. **10**, 183–190 (1997)
14. Chandrasekar, R., Doran, C., Srinivas, B.: Motivations and methods for text simplification. In: Proceedings of the 16th Conference on Computational Linguistics, pp. 1041–1044. ACL (1996)
15. Şaggion, H., Martínez, E.G., Etayo, E., Anula, A., Bourg, L.: Text simplification in simplext. making text more accessible. Procesamiento del Lenguaje Natural **47**, 341–342 (2011)
16. Wise, J., Thomas, J.J., Pennock, K., Lantrip, D., Pottier, M., Schur, A., Crow, V.: Visualizing the non-visual: spatial analysis and interaction with information from text documents. In: Proceedings of Information Visualization, pp. 51–58. IEEE (1995)
17. Rohrer, R.M., Ebert, D.S., Sibert, J.L.: The shape of Shakespeare: visualizing text using implicit surfaces. In: Proceedings of IEEE Symposium on Information Visualization, pp. 121–129. IEEE (1998)
18. Booker, A., Condliff, M., Greaves, M., Holt, F.B., Kao, A., Pierce, D.J., Poteet, S., Wu, Y.J.J.: Visualizing text data sets. Comput. Sci. Eng. **1**, 26–35 (1999)
19. Eler, D.M., Paulovich, F.V., Oliveira, M., Minghim, R.: Coordinated and multiple views for visualizing text collections. In: 12th International Conference on Information Visualisation, pp. 246–251. IEEE (2008)
20. Henderson, J., Merlo, P., Petroff, I., Schneider, G.: Using syntactic analysis to increase efficiency in visualizing text collections. In: Proceedings of the 19th International Conference on Computational Linguistics, pp. 1–7. ACL (2002)
21. Bateman, S., Gutwin, C., Nacenta, M.: Seeing things in the clouds. In: Proceedings of the Nineteenth ACM Conference on Hypertext and Hypermedia, p. 193. ACM (2008)
22. Lee, B., Riche, N.H., Karlson, A.K., Carpendale, S.: Sparkclouds: visualizing trends in tag clouds. IEEE Trans. Visual Comput. Graphics **16**, 1182–1189 (2010)
23. Van Ham, F., Wattenberg, M., Viégas, F.B.: Mapping text with phrase nets. IEEE Trans. Visual Comput. Graphics **15**, 1169–1176 (2009)
24. Wattenberg, M., Viégas, F.B.: The word tree, an interactive visual concordance. IEEE Trans. Visual Comput. Graphics **14**, 1221–1228 (2008)

25. Chung, J.W., Min, H.J. Kim, J., Park, J.C.: Enhancing readability of web documents by text augmentation for deaf people. In: Proceedings of the 3rd International Conference on Web Intelligence, Mining and Semantics, p. 30. ACM (2013)
26. Kim, H., Lee, D., Park J.W.: Textual visualization based on readability. In: SIGGRAPH Asia 2011, p. 9. ACM (2011)
27. Kim, H., Park, J.W., Seo, D.: Readability visualization for massive text data. Int. J. Multimedia Ubiquit. Eng. **9**, 707–719 (2014)
28. Oelke, D., Spretke, D., Stoffel, A., Keim, D.: Visual readability analysis: how to make your writings easier to read. IEEE Trans. Visual Comput. Graphics **18**, 662–674 (2012)
29. Karmakar, S., Zhu, Y.: Visualizing multiple text readability indexes. In: 2010 International Conference on Education and Management Technology, pp. 133–137. IEEE (2010)
30. Liu, H., Selker, T., Lieberman, H.: Visualizing the affective structure of a text document. In: CHI 2003 extended abstracts on Human factors in computing systems, pp. 740–741. ACM (2003)
31. Karmakar, S., Zhu, Y.: Visualizing text readability. In: 2010 6th International Conference on Advanced Information Management and Service, pp. 291–296. IEEE (2010)
32. Markel, M., Vaccaro, M., Hewett, T.: Effects of paragraph length on attitudes toward technical writing. Tech. Commun. **39**, 454–456 (1992)
33. Jian, H.-L., Sandnes, F.E., Law, K.M.Y., Huang, Y.-P., Huang, Y.-M.: The role of electronic pocket dictionaries as an English learning tool among Chinese students. J. Comput. Assist. Learn. **25**, 503–514 (2009)
34. Jian, H.-L., Sandnes, F.E., Huang, Y.-P., Cai, L., Law, K.M.Y.: On students' strategy-preferences for managing difficult course work. IEEE Trans. Educ. **51**, 157–165 (2008)

Inclusive Process and Tool for Evaluation of Accessible User Experience (AUX)

Geordie Graham[1] and Sambhavi Chandrashekar[2](✉)

[1] Career Cruising, Toronto, ON, Canada
geordie@geordiegraham.com
[2] OCAD University, Toronto, ON, Canada
schandrashekar@faculty.ocadu.ca

Abstract. Evaluating user experience (UX) during usability testing is an estab-lished practice leading to the design of more enjoyable information systems and products. Currently no published process or tool exists for UX evaluation for users with disabilities. Accessible User Experience (AUX) focuses on integrating accessibility into UX design to create enjoyable digital experiences for everyone, regardless of age or ability. With a view to developing an AUX evaluation tool and process, the emotional experiences of six blind individuals were explored through interviews along with hands-on sessions with websites/apps using laptops/phones. Comfort, Likability, Autonomy, Agency and Pleasure (consti-tuting the CLAAP framework) were identified as dimensions for developing an AUX evaluation tool, which was tested with the interviewees. 'Pleasure points' were discovered as an alternative concept to 'pain points.' An inclusive process for conducting AUX studies with screen reader users was documented to support UX designers.

Keywords: Blind · Vision impaired · Accessibility · Screen reader · Usability testing · User Experience (UX) · Accessible User Experience (AUX) · Inclusive design

1 Introduction

Users of digital systems and products such as websites and applications (apps) frequently experience a variety of emotions, both negative and positive, while interacting with apps and websites. The affective aspects of such interactions may not be effectively captured during studies of usability, which is defined as "the extent to which a product, service or environment can be used by specified users to achieve specified goals with effective-ness, efficiency and satisfaction in a specified context of use." [1] User experience (UX) is a concept that goes beyond this largely system-oriented paradigm of "effectiveness, efficiency, satisfaction," to take into account a number of user-oriented factors such as likability, pleasure, comfort and trust [2]. User experience differs from 'experience' in a general sense, in that it explicitly refers to the experience(s) derived from users encountering products, services or artefacts through a user interface [3]. The notion of user experience has different meanings for different professionals, with a variety of definitions across different domains [4].

© Springer International Publishing Switzerland 2016
M. Antona and C. Stephanidis (Eds.): UAHCI 2016, Part I, LNCS 9737, pp. 59–69, 2016.
DOI: 10.1007/978-3-319-40250-5_6

UX design, as a field, is concerned with the design of enjoyable websites and apps for users [5]. There are tools used for evaluating UX during usability studies involving users but these do not consider users with disabilities. Although accessibility studies involving users with disabilities do mostly evaluate usability, they have not progressed to the stage of evaluating the emotional experiences of users with disabilities for the purpose designing websites and apps that deliver more enjoyable UX for them. The few studies that took into consideration the emotional experiences of users who are blind, or visually impaired, have primarily revealed these users' frustration regarding the inaccessibility of the websites and apps [6, 7]. An examination of multiple studies describing UX evaluation revealed that these studies were not conducted with users with disabilities.

There are circa 50 tools available to help designers and developers measure and evaluate UX [8]. There is no published process or tool, which specifically describes, or caters to, UX evaluation for users with disabilities. In particular, for users who are blind or visually impaired, who have a distinct disadvantage because much of the content and interaction on websites and apps is visual. Designing for improving the user experience for all users, including blind and low vision users, is essential to make websites and applications more inclusive. A community of UX researchers is aiming to push for greater inclusion in design by developing a Manifesto for Accessible User Experience (AUX) where they urge for a focus of accessibility efforts on delivering quality user experiences [9]. AUX concerns the integration of accessibility into UX design and practice to create "genuinely inclusive high-quality digital experiences for everyone, regardless of disability or age." [10] At the moment, there is insufficient research or dialogue on this topic.

To help mitigate the lack of focus, both academic and professional, on this subject, this study attempts to systematically understand the experiences of users who are blind or visually impaired and the ways in which technology mediates their digital user experience. These users rely on a screen reader[1] to interact with their digital devices. The primary research question examined by this study is: How can a tool be designed for measuring the accessible user experience (AUX) of users who are blind when interacting with websites and applications? An exploratory approach was employed since there is paucity of published information concerning this area. Borrowing methods from the usability and UX domains, interviews were conducted with six screen reader users employing a think-aloud protocol and hands-on activities using their laptop and phone. The data gathered were analyzed to identify the components of an AUX framework that could form the basis for building an accessible evaluation tool.

---

[1] A screen reader is the generic name for a software tool that assists individuals who are blind or visually impaired in interacting with their computing devices. It converts the text, data, and elements displayed on the screen into synthesized speech. It can also send this information to an output device, used by some, called a refreshable Braille display that provides the output in Braille notation.

The objective of this study is to initiate the inclusive design[2] of a tool and document the process for evaluating the AUX of screen reader users[3]. The tool is intended for UX designers to use during usability sessions with screen reader users. To further support UX designers, the process of conducting an AUX session with screen reader users has been documented in detail [11].

2 Theoretical Framework

2.1 User Experience

UX is a multidisciplinary concept. Hassendahl, Sheldon, Mehrabian, Russell, Porat, Tractinsky, Forlizzi, Battarbee and Dewey have made key theoretical contributions to UX design. Of these, the ideas of Hassenzahl [12] and Bevan [2] have been selected because of their simplicity and precision to construct a lens for analysis. Their contributions are listed below:

Hassenzahl (2010)

- Autonomy: Feeling that you are the cause of your own actions rather than feeling that external forces or pressure are the cause of your action.
- Competence: Feeling that you are very capable and effective in your actions rather than feeling incompetent or ineffective.
- Relatedness: Feeling that you have regular intimate contact with people who care about you rather than feeling lonely and uncared for.
- Popularity: Feeling that you are liked, respected, and have influence over others rather than feeling like a person whose advice or opinion nobody is interested in.
- Stimulation: Feeling that you get plenty of enjoyment and pleasure rather than feeling bored and under stimulated by life.
- Security: Feeling safe and in control of your life rather than feeling uncertain and threatened by your circumstances.

Bevan (2008) [2]

- Likability: the extent to which the user is satisfied with their perceived achievement of pragmatic goals, including acceptable perceived results of use and consequences of use.
- Pleasure: the extent to which the user is satisfied with their perceived achievement of hedonic goals of stimulation, identification and evocation and associated emotional responses.
- Comfort: the extent to which the user is satisfied with physical comfort.

---

[2] Inclusive Design is design that considers the full range of human diversity with respect to ability, language, culture, gender, age and other forms of human difference (http://idrc.ocadu.ca/).

[3] This paper will use the term 'screen reader users' when referring to the user group of blind, or visually impaired people, who use screen readers.

• Trust: the extent to which the user is satisfied that the product will behave as intended.

2.2 Non-visual Access

The term screen reader is generic for a system that reads out the contents of the display on a computer or mobile device. There are several screen reader programs available, both commercially and in the form of free, open source software. Some popular commercial screen readers used for accessing the computer/Internet are JAWS, Window-Eyes, HAL, and VoiceOver. Free, open-source screen readers such as NVDA and Orca, as well as low cost products such as System Access, are also available. However, JAWS is reportedly the most popular screen reader in use in North America [13].

There are many studies about barriers to information access when using a screen reader and factors of interface design that facilitate accessibility [14–16]. But there is very little empirical research about what emotions these factors produce in screen reader users. In particular as regards investigating features that produce positive emotions and enhancing the design for a more positive experience. This is a potential area for research.

2.3 Positive Psychology

Positive psychology involves the study of the human pursuit of individual happiness as something central to human life. Until two decades ago, psychology was confined, primarily, to the study of mending an injured or unhappy mind. But, around the turn of the century, Seligman and Csikszentmihalyi [17] started a new paradigm of study termed positive psychology or the "knowledge of what makes life worth living." Since then, happiness has been a subject of many empirical studies [18–21].

Lyubomirsky stated that the pursuit of happiness requires the acquisition of positive experiences on a day-to-day basis with a more general assessment of life as positive and meaningful and that a good part of happiness depends on activities and is, thus, variable. This idea gave rise to the concept of "designing for happiness" in the design domains to provide a positive experience. A natural complement to this idea was the concept of evaluation of users to determine what makes them happy and how happy they become. The theory of positive UX for users with disabilities is a focus this study has drawn from positive psychology.

3 Methodology

Data for the research was primarily derived from interviews with six blind adults living in Toronto (four men and two women aged between 35 and 60 years). The technologies they used to access websites and apps were comparable. All of them primarily used a laptop with Windows Operating System, Firefox browser and JAWS screen reader to interact with websites and web-based apps. All of them used an iPhone to interact with websites and apps. Yet, their profiles showed diversity along occupation, information-seeking interests, nature of use of websites/apps and proficiency in the use of computer/phone, screen reader and websites/apps.

The interviews included semi-structured questions pertaining to the three main areas based on the critical incident technique [22] with abundant hands-on demonstration by participants to substantiate their responses. The three areas were:

Incident(s) where user felt a negative emotion such as frustration or anger while using a website or app.

Incident(s) where user experienced a positive emotion such as happiness or enjoyment while using a website or app.

User's experiences of interacting with a website or app using the phone (with touchscreen and Voiceover) vs. the laptop (with keyboard and JAWS).

The interviews lasted around 90 min, affording adequate discussion about each of the areas noted. Each participant used their own laptop and iPhone to demonstrate their answers and, additionally, to share other related experiences. Data triangulation was achieved through audio recording of the sessions (including think-aloud protocols), video recording of the laptop/phone screen, and observational notes. An initial framework for AUX was derived through a literature survey and environmental scan. This framework comprised likability, pleasure and comfort. An inductive-deductive content analysis of the transcribed data was done using the above framework to arrive at the final AUX framework for the study (described in the next section), which will be strengthened through further inclusive design iterations. Personas were created based on the data of each of the six interviewees to illustrate their diversity as an indicator of the validity of the findings and to enhance communication during discussion of the research outcomes.

4   Findings

4.1   The Framework

Data from the user sessions were analyzed using the lens derived from secondary research based on the concept proposed by Hassenzhal and Bevan. This study resulted in a five-point framework (see Fig. 1) for Accessible User Experience consisting of the following components:

Comfort, Likability, Autonomy, Agency and Pleasure. The framework, acronymized as **CLAAP**, signifies the positive feeling associated with clapping of hands. Proponents of the science of positive psychology state that positive emotions serve as markers of flourishing, or optimal wellbeing [6]. Adopting this premise, the five components above are identified with, and derived through, the study of points of positive experience for the users. The first author proposes the term 'pleasure points' for these points, in contrast to the search for 'pain points' in conventional usability studies.

Based on the five components of the **CLAAP** framework, an AUX evaluation tool was developed in the form of a questionnaire as given below:

CLAAP Framework

Comfort

When the interface is intuitive to use

Likability

When expectations are met or exceeded

Autonomy

When users can perform independently

Agency

When users feel empowered and competent

Pleasure

When users experience engagement

Fig. 1. Diagram of the CLAAP framework

*Imagine that you have just used the {**name of website or app**}. With that experience in mind, please answer the following questions:*

Q1: Does the website or app exceed your expectations? If so, how? Please describe in detail.
  A1:

Q2: What parts of the website or app engaged you the most?
A2:

Q3: Did you find the website or app intuitive to use? If so, describe how?
A3:

Q4: Do you feel that you are able to accomplish all the tasks on the website or app independently?
A4:

Q5: Could you describe your navigation experience on the website or app?
A5:

The tool was sent to all the participants and refined based on the responses and feedback obtained from them. Responses to the tool were sought from all the participants with a reference to "Twitter" because all of them had mentioned that website/app on their favourites list. A detailed protocol for conducting UX studies with participants who are blind was drafted based on the experiences during the interviews. The outcome of this study is thus a process and tool for AUX evaluation with users who are blind.

5   Discussion

This paper presents an exploration of the emotional experiences of persons who are blind when they use websites and apps on their computers and smart phones and develops both an empirically sound process and tool for evaluating the accessible user experience (AUX) aspects of such interactions. Some significant outcomes from the study are an AUX evaluation tool and an analysis of impact of technology on interaction and pleasure points. They are discussed in the following subsections.

5.1   AUX Evaluation Tool

The evaluation tool developed through this study is in the form of an electronic question-naire that is accessible via screen readers. It contains five questions along the dimensions of Comfort, Likeability, Autonomy, Agency and Pleasure (CLAAP.) The dimensions were arrived at qualitatively through analysis of data gathered from six screen reader users. The tool is merely a first attempt at developing a useful AUX resource for UX designers to consider pleasurable user experiences when they work with users who have disabilities.

The evaluation tool that was created with the CLAAP framework is merely a first attempt at developing a useful AUX resource for user experience designers hoping to work with users who have disabilities. The disruptive effect that was hoped to come from this tool is in attempting to influence individuals within both the UX and AUX field to consider the pleasurable user experience for people who are disabled. Those within the accessibility movement have considered user experience for disabled users but have only done so through focusing on the negative feelings associated with pain points and user frustration. The AUX movement is still nascent, and as it has been established in the literature, thus far, very little work has been done within the conventional user experience field to consider disabled users in terms of actually developing evaluation methods to determine pleasurable user experience. The goal of the AUX evaluation tool is to contribute to the AUX field by drawing attention to this disparity and striving to provide a solution that could either inspire some designers and AUX practitioners to consider pleasurable user experience for disabled users within the field and to give other AUX practitioners a tool to assist in usability testing.

The tool was effective in capturing key insights. However, based on responses and feedback obtained from the interviewees, the following points were noted for future refinement:

- Justification for selecting the website or app used for usability testing with the participants should be made known to them.
- If comparison across participants is desired, then specifications must be made about the product to be used (website or app) for the service (such as Twitter) whose usability is being tested. This is because responses about experiences were found to vary across products (website or app)
- Question about agency should be clarified further by adding components relating to adaptation and personalization of sites and apps as they are both concrete examples of user-control to change their computing environment to match their personal preferences.
- Ways of separating pleasurable feedback from positive feedback should be documented.
- The current long answer question format makes it difficult for cross measurement across participants. The inclusion of Likert scale questions that are accessible to screen readers could be helpful to better track measurements across participants as well to help with quantitative data analysis.

5.2 Pleasure Points

Drawing from positive psychology, this study introduced a term 'pleasure points' in contrast to the traditional conversation about 'pain points' that prevail in user testing. Components of a design that evoke positive emotional reactions from users are termed as pleasure points. Two original contributions of this research are: (1) a process to evaluate pleasure points while testing websites and apps with screen reader users and (2) a tool to facilitate the evaluation of pleasure points.

It must be emphasized that the AUX tool was not designed to solely look at pleasure points. Rather, the tool is designed to counterbalance the overemphasis on pain points in UX research. Since this tool evaluates UX and not positive UX, the responses that are resultant from the tool will vary based on the mindset of the user both during and after using the website or app.

5.3 Impact of Technology on Interaction

One of the major insight that came from observations made during the user sessions was that the technological configurations used by participants played a big role in the interaction of screen reader users with websites and apps. Furthermore, it was also seen that the mode of interaction between the technology and the user also contributed to their UX. This provided a useful insight that UX is not just about how a website or app is designed but also how it is caused by the interaction itself. The user's electronic devices such as computer, browser, screen reader and input-output devices/mechanisms, all contribute to their user experience.

Participants were comfortable using both Windows laptop with Jaws and iPhone with Voiceover. Those with greater proficiency seemed to enjoy the experience more. Some participants' enjoyed the experience on their phone more than on the laptop. With audio from the screen reader being common, it appeared that the touchscreen interaction on the phone (versus keyboard on laptop) made it more enjoyable. For the same product, some participants had very different experiences vising website or app on laptop or phone.

An important technology-related emotional experience that was observed in the study was the variance of feelings elicited between engaging in an identical activity on a laptop relative to a phone. This divide is evidenced by through response of the participants the user experience evaluation tool. The tool itself asked the participants for feedback on 5 key metrics of user experience. The site chosen to evaluate upon was twitter and participants had the option of preforming their evaluations on the website or app or in combination.

When the same individuals assessed the site for the same metric (expectations) the results were different. Karan noted that: "the iPhone app is very accessible and easy to use. Although I was pleasantly surprised to find it accessible and I enjoy using it." In contrast, the same user when assessing the website mentioned: "The website is OK to use, but I rather use the iPhone app because I find it easier to use in general." In both instances Karan was preforming the same activities, navigating the site to view content. Yet these observations were not unique. Fatima when asked if they could navigate the website independently described the user experience as "…cumbersome as it takes too much time and effort to perform simple tasks." In contrast, Jose had overwhelming positive experience with the app noting that it had exceeded his expectations as it was: "very accessible, tweets can be sent and navigation happens easily. It should be noted that the comments about the improved user experience for mobile devices revolved less around the screen reader and more focused on the interaction model as evidenced by Jose's describing why he prefers the iPhone to his computer: "…because you can get information with shorter journeys and less keystrokes."

6 Conclusion

With respect to accessing and enjoying digital content, screen reader users today still face many challenges. The web accessibility community is actively working on reducing barriers faced by individuals with disabilities in accessing websites and apps. A core tenet of UX is that all users on the spectrum of human diversity deserve to have a pleasurable experience when using digital products. However, this is not followed in practice. In this context, the contributions of the study, as well as the limitations and plans for future research, are outlined below

6.1 Contributions

This study is intended to reinforce the concepts promulgated in the manifesto of AUX, namely to examine accessibility through the lens of user experience. The study also contributes to the three dimensions of Inclusive Design as identified by the Inclusive Design Research Centre [23].

First, it seeks to **recognize diversity and uniqueness** in individuals by examining the needs of extreme users on the spectrum of individual abilities—in this case screen reader users who are blind—who are commonly ignored as an insignificant set of outliers when considering UX in designing products or solutions for individuals.

Secondly, the study offers an **inclusive process and tool** for evaluating AUX, thus making these easily usable by UX designers for providing a positive experience to all users with varied abilities. Ultimately, the goal of every UX designer is to provide a pleasurable user experience, and people with disabilities should not be left behind.

Thirdly, the study promises a **broader beneficial impact** because the AUX evaluation tool designed to meet the needs of extreme users also has the ability to benefit users with other disabilities, as well as the general population. Even though the tool was designed though interviews with screen reader users, its components could help many other user groups who require accessibility support, such as those with hearing loss, those with low vision and seniors. Moreover, because the tool can be an effective barometer of people's emotional states when using websites or apps, the tool can be used with the general population as well. Thus, a curb cut effect exists. This study thereby contributes to Inclusive Design.

6.2 Limitations and Future Work

This paper is based on a master's research project that was completed within a limited time frame. Hence, this study on AUX evaluation was conducted with a small number of users. By replicating the process with screen reader users with a variety of profiles, interests and proficiency levels, the set of evaluation criteria could be expanded; and the process could be refined.

The AUX evaluation tool developed through this study was based only on interaction with users having vision impairment. To expand the tool and to develop comparable processes for AUX evaluation for users with dexterity/cognition/hearing constraints, similar studies ought to be conducted with these users.

Acknowledgments. Our special thanks are due to Dr. Katherine Sellen for her academic support as the Principal Advisor for this Master's Research Project and to David Lawson for his editorial assistance.

References

1. ISO 9241. Standard on Ergonomics of Human System Interaction (Part 11 1998)
2. Bevan, N.: Classifying and selecting UX and usability measures. In: International Workshop on Meaningful Measures: Valid Useful User Experience Measurement, pp. 13–18 (2008)

3. UX-Whitepaper. http://www.allaboutux.org/files/UX-WhitePaper.pdf
4. All about UX. www.allaboutux.org/ux-definitions
5. Hassenzahl, M., Tractinsky, N.: User experience-a research agenda. Behav. Inf. Technol. **25**(2), 91–97 (2006)
6. Lazar, J., Feng, J., Allen, A.: Determining the impact of computer frustration on the mood of blind users browsing the web. In: Proceedings of the 8th International ACM SIGACCESS Conference on Computers and Accessibility, pp. 149–156. ACM (2006)
7. Lazar, J., Feng, J., Allen, A., Kleinman, J., Malarkey, C.: What frustrates screen reader users on the web. Int. J. Hum. Comput. Interact. **22**(3), 247–269 (2007)
8. UX evaluation methods. http://www.allaboutux.org/all-methods
9. A (Rough) manifesto for accessible user experience (2015). https://medium.com/@accessibleux
10. Sloan, D. (2014). https://www.paciellogroup.com/blog/2014/08/developing-a-manifesto-for-accessible-ux
11. Graham, G.: A process and tool for evaluation of accessible user experience with websites and apps for screen reader users who are blind: Masters degree in inclusive design (research report), OCAD University, Canada (2015). http://openresearch.ocadu.ca/377
12. Hassenzahl, M.: Experience design: technology for all the right reasons. Synth. Lect. Hum.-Centered Inf. **3**(1), 1–95 (2010)
13. WebAIM (2015). http://webaim.org/projects/screenreadersurvey6/
14. Petrie, H., Hamilton, F., King, N.: Tension, what tension?: website accessibility and visual design. In: Proceedings of the International Cross-Disciplinary Workshop on Web Accessibility, New York City (2004)
15. Petrie, H., Kheir, O.: The relationship between accessibility and usability of websites: In: Proceedings of ACM CHI 2007, Human Factors in Computing Systems. ACM Press, New York (2007)
16. Strain, P., Shaikh, A.D., Boardman, R.: Thinking but not seeing: think-aloud for non-sighted users. Paper presented at the CHI 2007, S18, San Jose, CA, 28 April–3 May 2007 (2007)
17. Seligman, M.E., Csikszentmihalyi, M.: Positive Psychology: An Introduction, vol. 55, no. 1, p. 5. American Psychological Association (2000)
18. Kahneman, D.: Thinking Fast and Slow: Farrar, Straus and Giroux, New York (2011)
19. Lopez, S.J., Snyder, C.R. (eds.): Oxford Handbook of Positive Psychology. Oxford University Press, New York (2009)
20. Lyubomirsky, S.: The How of Happiness: A Scientific Approach to Getting the Life You Want. Penguin Press, New York (2007)
21. Seligman, M.E.P.: Flourish: A Visionary New Understanding of Happiness and Well-being. Free Press, New York (2011)
22. Aveyard, H., Neale, J.: Critical incident technique. Res. Methods Health Soc. Care, **253**, 253–264 (2008)
23. IDRC: Inclusive Design Research Centre. http://idrc.ocadu.ca/index.php/resources/idrc-online/library-of-papers/443-whatisinclusivedesign

Personalizing Interaction Focused on a User's Interactive Experience and Potential

Yi Ji[✉]

Guangdong University of Technology, Guangzhou, China
jiyi001@hotmail.com

Abstract. The existing computer system is very powerful and multi-function. Conventional Human Computer Interaction (HCI) mainly focusing on creating interactions to solve common problems rather than extending each user's individual characteristics (McCarthy and Wright 2004) and lead to positive experience (Rogers et al. 2011, Heibeck et al. 2014). A challenge for HCI is how to create Human Computer Interaction in a personal way that leads to the users' desirable experience and extend their potentials. A main goal is to give the opportunity to users to handle complex systems, to present an interface the user wants to see, and to deliver desirable user experiences. We need therefore, a method to "present" typical functionalities to user in an effective and personal way while users are using the computer. This research aims to construct a personalized interaction between the users and computer as a way to integrate the user's experiences and mechanisms of the existing application in a specific interaction context. This research provides an additional perspective on interaction design based on both designers' and users' point of view by adapting computer interactive system based on users' personal needs. At the end of paper, we will create new interactive drawing system that can integrate human cognition and behavior to improve the users' experience by allowing the user to personalize the system.

Keywords: Personalized interaction · Interaction design · User's interactive experience

1 Introduction

Modern computer systems are very powerful and multi-functional. A main goal is to give the opportunity to users to handle complex systems, to present an interface the user wants to see, and to deliver desirable user experiences. Conventional Human Computer Interaction (HCI) mainly focusing on creating interactions to solve common problems rather than extending each user's individual characteristics (McCarthy and Wright 2004) and lead to positive experience (Rogers et al. 2011, Heibeck et al. 2014). One good example is Photoshop, which is designed to allow the users to complete a particular task, which can have up to hundreds of functionalities (Haynes and Crumpler 2001) trough standard interaction model like dropdown menu, tool bar, shrotcut and so on (Evening 2005). Unfortunately, we lack an interaction design system that truly supports user specific interaction. Langdon et al. write that there has been no effective way to

© Springer International Publishing Switzerland 2016
M. Antona and C. Stephanidis (Eds.): UAHCI 2016, Part I, LNCS 9737, pp. 70–80, 2016.
DOI: 10.1007/978-3-319-40250-5_7

build human product interaction that can adapt to end users' individual mental models (Langdon et al. 2012). The way that has been used is of is through "ontologies", yet these ontologies can be hard to build, especially for the very people that are expert in the fields whose knowledge is being captured but who are not experienced in the specialised "modelling" field. In other words, the meanings of interactions are different to convey to divers of end users comprehensively. For that reason, the users have to spend lots of time and efforts to get familiar with an interactive system in order to operate it effective such as finding an appropriate functionality to complete a particular task.

As a result, the majority of its functionalities are rarely being used (Constantine and Lockwood 1999, Følstad et al. 2012) and only a small group of users found the system useful (Marshall et al. 2013). A significant question is that why are computers hard to use? And how to reduce gaps emerged between human and computer during the interaction (Norman 2002, Norman 2007, Nakken 2014). A challenge for HCI is how to create Human Computer Interaction in a personal way that leads to the users' desirable experience and extend their potentials.

2   Personalized Interaction Design

We need therefore, a scheme of methods to "present" typical functionalities to user in an effective and helpful way while users are using the computer. This requires getting the computer to cooperate with what the user think of the system and getting it to present reactions in a meaningful way. To do a good job, the system will have to understand something about what the person is trying to do and what sorts of results will be most interesting to them. For this, we need to adapt user personal model to organize a domain and interact with tools; be able to model the dialogues between a human and the provided system.

This research project aims to construct a personalized interaction between the users and computer as a way to integrate the user's experiences and mechanisms of the existing application in a specific interaction context (Costabile et al. 2006). Bellotti et al. (2002) points out the most important questions that must be overcome by every designer and researcher developing user-centered systems.

1. How does the user address the system?
2. How does the system show the user that it is attending?
3. How does the system understand commands?
4. How does the user get feedback on command execution?
5. How can the user fix errors?

This research provides an additional perspective on interaction design based on both designers' and users' point of view by adapting computer interactive system based on users' personal needs. One particular purpose for this research is going to investigate how to integrate the user's personal experience and behaviour. In this research, by looking beyond common notions of interactions (formalized action), we can increase the possibilities to open a personalizing interaction design system based on a novel co-development, co-creation, and co-ownership interaction composition. These significant features of the novel interaction are represented in the following:

- Co-ownership: the Interaction reflects and responds to the users' thinking, problem and experience dynamically.
- Co-development: the interaction allows users to redefine a special meaning for the interaction by mapping, complementing and integrating existing elements of interaction.
- Co-design: the interaction can be changed by the users based on their interaction experience by customizing a particular interactive system.

3   Design Method

The goal of research is to construct a user-oriented interaction which is called personalized interaction to make computer system easy, efficient and pleasure to the users. At the end of project, we will create new interactive drawing system that can integrate human cognition and behaviour to improve the users' experience by allowing the user to personalize the system. Experiments showed positive user experience plays a key component to produce successful interaction between human and computer (Thüring and Mahlke 2007). In addition, it requires the HCI not only solve a particular task taking

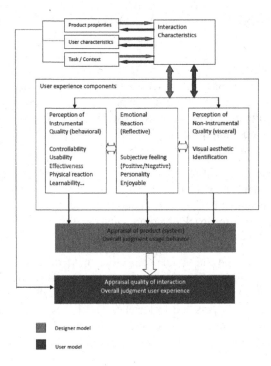

Fig. 1. Structure of constructing personalized Human Computer Interaction (Color figure online)

place in a certain context, but also fulfil the users' individual needs like emotional expression (see Fig. 1).

The project will be carried out in two steps. The first step is to allow computers be able to "see and hear what the user does before they can prove truly helpful" (Pentland 1996). It relays on knowing the type of user; the user's interaction pattern and the user's experience level with the software. The second step is to provide accordingly patterns with corresponding function according to the user's interaction behaviour in shaping software to meet the broad, varied, rapidly changing needs of the users (Rogers et al. 2011).

We use a set of state-of-the-art machine learning techniques to intelligently "learn" from a user's behaviour, making predictions of user's experience level, its typical pattern of usage, and most importantly, to generate a collaborative and personalized interaction to assist the user to have desirable experience. The data of learning the users' dynamic interaction behaviour will be employed to define interaction behaviour algorithm and form in a way that he/she want to cope with.

User interactions with the system does not possess a linear path, it can comprised many "loops" and "branches" between user and system. The Fig. 2 shows a an example of this phenomenon: As one can see that, although these interactions are occurring in a time sequence, however, such behaviour can be drastically different to traditional time-series modelling, such as First order Auto Regressive Model or Hidden Markov Model (Ruber 1989) which assumes a linear progression of observations across time. For this reason, the modelling of complex time-sequence based interactions is of a challenging problem in machine learning research and needed to be studied closely in this project.

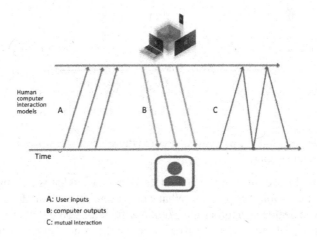

Fig. 2. The sequence of interactions between user and a system

The traditional time series modelling typically assumes the presentence of a series of latent nodes, for example, the syllables in speech recognition, which them can not be directly observed, but only can be inferred from the observation sequence themselves. In the setting of this project, such latent nodes may refer to the "user Intentions", which may take on both discrete and/or continuous state space. Here we illustrate the graphical model for a traditional Hidden Markov Model: (Fig. 3)

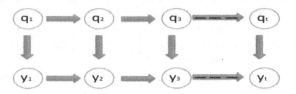

Fig. 3. The graphical model for a traditional Hidden Markov Model

Part of the goal of this project from a machine learning perspective is to find ways to adept the traditional HMM to that of the complex user interaction sequences. If we were try to naively apply them directly, we end up of having the following probabilistic graphical model: (Fig. 4)

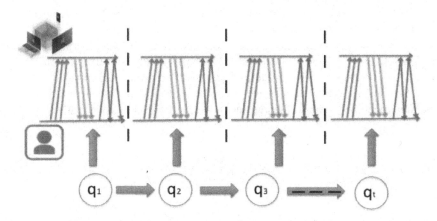

Fig. 4. The graphical model for our proposed model

Having stated this model, we must overcome the several scientific challenges in the realm of machine learning:

1. If we choose the user intention as a discrete value, then, what is the number K, i.e., how many states should be present? What would be an optimal number in this setting
2. How may one decide an appropriate likelihood function given that the observations is in a sequence of interactions between user and the system given a time window? The additional intricacy has been that the number of interactions at each time window may differ therefore, violating the traditional Hidden Markov Model in which the observations are generally of the same dimensionality (hence same family of distributions can be chosen).

In order to resolve these issues, we plan to employ a non-parametric approach, which is the state-of-the-art statistical method in which the number of states as well the parameters associated with each state can be inferred from the data itself. In particular, we will utilise the methods similar to those described in (Fox 2010), where state transitions matrix can potentially go infinite. In order to solve this intractable model, we will use the latest inference work, such as Variational Bayes (Jordan 2010) to provide a faster and accurate computation.

This process is iterative, in such a way that the learning and reinforcements from the users' feedback are updated in an iterative manner. As a result, a personalized Human Computer Interaction can be established as the users know their own context and needs better than anybody else, and they often have real-time awareness of shifts in their respective domains.

To evaluate usability of personalized HCI and the user's experience we are going to use a well-known evaluation analysis method - usability testing to test two types of drawing system by completing some drawing tasks. One is commercial drawing system-Photoshop CS5, the other one is a prototype of new drawing system created by our team.

To construct a suitable environment for usability testing we need to solve practical issues including designing typical tasks, selecting target users, prepare the testing conditions, setting up a variety of tests and dealing with the ethical issues.

The tasks for the usability testing are designed to compare users' experiences when they creating a drawing using the above two drawing systems. There are three drawing tasks:

- Draw a picture by using different drawing tools (pencil, pen, oil pen and crayon).
- Draw multiple pictures with different styles.
- Customize the drawing system (circle, rectangle and square) to product a personal drawing pattern.

Next, we need to select suitable users to evaluate the systems - people that somehow represent those that the product is designed for. For example, some products are targeted at specific types of users like seniors, children, novices, or experienced people. In our case, the product is a digital drawing system, so the specific user audiences are computer users who use drawing systems.

In addition, users' prior experience with a particular classes of product are different so selecting a range of users with different backgrounds is important. For example, a group of people who are using the web for the first time are likely to express different opinions to another group with five years of web experience.

To gather a range of views from different perspectives, we chose two different groups of people: novice users and experienced users with different backgrounds. These two groups of users participated in both prototype studies.

To achieve a gender balance, in the evaluation study we employed an equal number of males and females aged is between 21 and 38, including three males and three females from different disciplines and living areas. In the Hi-Fi prototype study, we recruited 30 representative users from, including 16 males and 14 females. All of them have different study backgrounds and nationalities.

Finally, it is necessary to prepare the test conditions and set up user tests for two studies in a lab situation. For both of the prototype studies, it requires the testing environment to be controlled to prevent unwanted disturbances and noise that may distort the result. As the product we are going to test will mainly be used in an office situation and environment we establish a simulated working environment by setting up a usability testing laboratory to carry out the above user tests. The facilities that have been used in laboratory are different for each of the two user tests. For the first test, after the user experimented with the prototype, we asked them questions to capture their opinions through a semi-structured interview. For the prototype evaluation, we set up a video camera in the laboratory to record all the data that the user generated during operating the provided prototype of the interaction language and the Photoshop CS5. After the user testing, the users were asked to complete the questionnaire.

4   Criteria of Usability Testing

Harker defines usability as the extent to which a product can be used by specified users to achieve specified goals with effectiveness, efficiency and satisfaction in a specified context of use (Harker 1995). In industry area, a well-known deification of the usability is ISO 9241 which is composed of three parts: effectiveness, efficiency and satisfaction (Abran et al. 2003).

According to Nilsson's definition of usability, usability is composed of five quality components (Nielsen 1994):

Learnability: How easy is it for users to accomplish basic tasks the first time they encounter the design?

Efficiency: Once users have learned the design, how quickly can they perform tasks?

Memorability: When users return to the design after a period of not using it, how easily can they re-establish proficiency?

Errors: How many errors do users make, how severe are these errors, and how easily can they recover from the errors?

Satisfaction: How pleasant is it to use the design?

From the above definitions we can see that there are several criteria for usability, but that they mainly relate to two key aspects:

- Usability of product including efficiency, learnability effectiveness; and
- User experience of using the product in a particular situation.

The results of user studies should provide measures of comprehensive base criteria of useability including completion effectiveness, efficiency related to the artefact usability and user experiences. Usability testing is typically carried out in laboratory settings. We designed multiple questions built upon the criteria of usability to evaluate the usability of the new drawing system.

For user experience study, the participants are required to complete a set of drawing tasks by using two digital drawing systems (Photoshop CS5 and a prototype that is built upon ILDP). User satisfaction is assessed based on the users' feedback on their experience with the systems such as satisfaction, fun and/or frustration by using a well-designed questionnaire.

5 Data Analysis

The purpose of data analysis is to develop an understanding or interpretation that answers the basic question being asked. B. Kaplan and J.A. Maxwell give five purposes for using qualitative methods in evaluating computer information systems (Kaplan and Maxwell 2005):

1. Understanding how a system's users perceive and evaluate that system and what meanings the system has for them.
2. Understanding the influence of social and organizational context on systems use.
3. Investigating causal processes.
4. Providing formative evaluation that is aimed at improving a program under development, rather than assessing an existing one.
5. Increasing the utilization of evaluation results.

As we have described, the data gathering method employed in this research is to set up appropriate user tests to assess whether the product we develop is usable and fitting for the intended user population to achieve their objectives. We set up two different prototype studies of a drawing system to clarify our design method. One is usability study and the other one is user experience study.

Accordingly, we employ different data analysis techniques to evaluate the data from each of the two prototype studies. Normally, there are four basic techniques of qualitative data analysis: coding, analytical memos, and contextual and narrative analysis (Kaplan and Maxwell 2005). These methods help us to identify themes, develop categories and explore similarities and differences in the data, and relationships among them.

6 Coding

The coding is created by the users when they doing the usability study focuses on evaluating usability of the domain specific interaction language, which has been developed from the ISO (ISO 9241 Usability Standard) base criteria of task effectiveness and efficiency. For example, we code the participants' performance when they were required to complete few specific tasks by using the new drawing system refer to its usability, effectiveness and efficiency in a specified context of use.

6.1 Analytical Memos

The other analysis method is analytical memos. We asked the participants different questions about their responses to carry out the user experience study. Through these questions we are able to have a deeper understanding of what the participants think about of using the interactive artefact come through the specific interaction. The close questions focus on getting feedback about a particular design feature, such as the way of interaction that the interactive artefact provided. The open question related to exploring the users' individual experiences how well a product supports them to complete a particular task and what other supports are needed. At a result, the general questions (open) and specific questions (close) that contribute to bring comprehensive feedback for the evaluation goal are asked.

6.2 Contextual and Narrative Analysis

For the Hi-Fi prototype study, we use contextual and narrative analysis method to analysis the data that is generated from the observation and user satisfaction questionnaire. Through the Hi-Fi prototype study, we category and analysis the results of user testing to evaluate whether the participants enjoyed using the new drawing system to improve their interaction experience by constructing personalized interaction.

In the Hi-Fi prototype study, we observe user using the Hi-Fi prototype to exam whether the developing product meets users' needs. We use video to capture everything that the users did during the usability testing including keystrokes, mouse clicks, and other interactions. Through the observation data, we can clarify that and analyse what users do and how long they spend on completing different tasks. It also provides insights into users' affective reactions that related to the users' experiences as satisfaction and frustration. Moreover, the user satisfaction questionnaire is used to clarify and deepen understanding of the users' experiences.

7 Conclusion

We designed a specific questionnaire to evaluate users' satisfaction with some specific features of the Hi-Fi prototype. As we mentioned before, the questionnaire that we are created in different levels: visceral, behaviour and affective (Norman 2002). And then, we compare outcomes of users testing performance on manipulating two digital drawing systems and asking the users about their opinions based on their interaction experience through a user satisfaction questionnaire. The first drawing system is a well-known drawing system-Photoshop CS5; the second one is the Hi-Fi prototype of drawing system. The produces qualitative data demonstrates how the different participants make sense of the interactive artefact.

Aims

- This project addresses the user's individual problem of interacting with a particular software.
- Provide a suitable interaction pattern to the user in a right at right place based on a continuing machines learning process to Integrate multi-channel interactive computer interaction like pen/touch type interaction, gesture interaction under a human natural way.

Research outcomes: The expected outcomes include the following:

- Producing an interactive drawing system human computer interaction. This composes of two aspects: one is to build a personalized user interface which can continuously adapt to user's behaviour, create individual user experience. The other one is construct natural interaction that be able to suggest uncommon, but needed function to users through multi-model interaction and automatically customize interfaces through multi-modal integration of functions.

- Providing theoretical and technical preparation and application to explore in-depth study of natural human-computer interaction techniques.
- Research demonstrations will be showcased at international national interactive arts exhibitions.

Part of research outcomes can be used into improving existing commercial system like Photoshop. That means we can cooperate with industry partners to explore variety of more suitable application systems with personalized interaction in many different areas.

References

Abran, A., Khelifi, A., Suryn, W., Seffah, A.: Usability meanings and interpretations in ISO standards. Softw. Qual. J. **11**, 325–338 (2003)

Bellotti, V., Back, M., Edwards, W.K., Grinter, R.E., Henderson, A., Lopes, C.: Making sense of sensing systems: five questions for designers and researchers. In: Proceedings of the SIGCHI Conference on Human Factors in Computing Systems, 2002, pp. 415–422. ACM (2002)

Constantine, L.L., Lockwood, L.A.: Software for use: a practical guide to the models and methods of usage-centered design. Pearson Education, Upper Saddle River (1999)

Costabile, M.F., Fogli, D., Mussio, P., Piccinno, A.: End-user development: the software shaping workshop approach. In: Lieberman, H., Paternò, F., Wulf, V. (eds.) End User Development, vol. 9, pp. 183–205. Springer, Netherlands (2006)

Evening, M.: Adobe Photoshop CS2 for Photographers: A professional Image Editor's Guide to the Creative Use of Photoshop for the Macintosh and PC. Taylor & Francis, New York (2005)

Følstad, A., Law, E., Hornbæk, K.: Analysis in practical usability evaluation: a survey study. In: Proceedings of the SIGCHI Conference on Human Factors in Computing Systems, pp. 2127–2136. ACM (2012)

Harker, S.: The development of ergonomics standards for software. Appl. Ergon. **26**, 275–279 (1995)

Haynes, B., Crumpler, W.: Photoshop 6 Artistry: Mastering the Digital Image. New Riders Publishing, Thousand Oaks (2001)

Heibeck, F., Hope, A., Legault, J.: Sensory fiction: a design fiction of emotional computation. In: Proceedings of the 2nd ACM International Workshop on Immersive Media Experiences, pp. 35–40. ACM (2014)

Kaplan, B., Maxwell, J.A.: Qualitative research methods for evaluating computer information systems. In: Anderson, J.G., Aydin, C.E. (eds.) Evaluating the Organizational Impact of Healthcare Information Systems, pp. 30–55. Springer, New York (2005)

Langdon, P., Clarkson, J., Robinson, P., Lazar, J., Heylighen, A.: Designing Inclusive Systems. Springer, London (2012)

Marshall, R., Cook, S., Mitchell, V., Summerskill, S., Haines, V., Maguire, M., Sims, R., Gyi, D., Case, K.: Design and evaluation: end users, user datasets and personas. Appl. Ergon. **46**, 311–317 (2013)

McCarthy, J., Wright, P.: Technology as experience. Interactions **11**, 42–43 (2004)

Nakken, O.K.: Closing the gap between human-computer interaction and human-human interaction with mobile and sensing systems (2014)

Nielsen, J.: Usability inspection methods. In: Conference Companion on Human Factors in Computing Systems, pp. 413–414. ACM (1994)

Norman, D.A.: The Design of Everyday Things. Basic Books (AZ), New York (2002)

Norman, D.A.: Emotional Design: Why We Love (or Hate) Everyday Things. Basic Books, New York (2007)

Pentland, A.P.: Smart rooms. Sci. Am. **274**, 54–62 (1996)

Rogers, Y., Sharp, H., Preece, J.: Interaction Design: Beyond Human-Computer Interaction. Wiley, New York (2011)

Thüring, M., Mahlke, S.: Usability, aesthetics and emotions in human–technology interaction. Int. J. Psychol. **42**, 253–264 (2007)

How Blind and Sighted Individuals Perceive the Typographic Text-Signals of a Document

Georgios Kouroupetroglou[1(✉)] and Philippos Katsoulis[2]

[1] Department of Informatics and Telecommunications,
National and Kapodistrian University of Athens, Athens, Greece
koupe@di.uoa.gr
[2] Graduate Program in Basic and Applied Cognitive Science,
National and Kapodistrian University of Athens, Athens, Greece
phikats@phs.uoa.gr

Abstract. Typographic, layout and logical elements constitute visual text-signals of a document that carry semantic information over and above its content. Although they are important to the reader, most of the current Text-to-Speech (TtS) systems do not support them. As there is a lack of studies on how blind perceive them and aiming to incorporate them efficiently in advanced TtS systems, we investigate in a systematic way the perception of the main typographic text-signals by 73 blind and sighted students. The results show that both groups of the participants perceive that font-styles are used largely to better locate, recognize or distinguish the topics or specific information in a document. Almost half of the sighted argue that they are useful for the comprehension of the content, but only 4 % of the blind students perceive the same. Most of the sighted participants (68 %) consider that bold is used to indicate an important word or phrase in the text that needs more attention by the reader, but only 23 % of them perceive the same for the italics. 27 % of the blind participants and 23 % of the sighted perceive that the role of font-size is to provide emphasis. Moreover, only 9 % of the sighted students grasp that bold is used for emphasis and 13 % of them that italics is used for light emphasis. Half of the blind participants consider that font-size plays an important role in separating the basic elements of a text (e.g. titles, footnotes), but only 13 % of the sighted believe the same. Finally, the sighted and blind students recognize the titles of a text mainly using non-identical criteria.

Keywords: Document accessibility · Text-signals · Typography · Font-size · Font-type

1 Introduction

Printed or electronic documents (i.e. books, newspapers, magazines, etc.) incorporate, additionally to their content, an amount of visual presentation details, such as typographic elements and arrangement of the content on the page. The title of a section, for example, can be pinpointed by having it one or two lines above the content and with larger font size, compared with the size of the main text. Moreover, bold or color can be used to provide emphasis in a specific word, phrase or paragraph. Rich-text

© Springer International Publishing Switzerland 2016
M. Antona and C. Stephanidis (Eds.): UAHCI 2016, Part I, LNCS 9737, pp. 81–90, 2016.
DOI: 10.1007/978-3-319-40250-5_8

documents preserve all their presentation elements. Besides, plain-text documents ignore them. The textual content of a document is referred as text-document.

The visual elements of a text document can be classified into three layers [1]:

- Logical layer: the content is related to elements of the structure, i.e. titles or headings, paragraphs, sections, chapters, lists, footnotes, simple or complex tables.
- Layout layer: the content is associated with the architectural elements for its arrangement on a page (e.g. text alignment, page margins, columns).
- Typography layer: it includes the elements of font-type, font-size, font-color, background color, etc. as well the elements of font-style (e.g. bold, italics, bold-italics, underline).

The three layers above are not independent, but complementary. Typographic elements can be applied to the textual content itself, as well as on the layout or the logical layer. For example, a word in bold can be used either in a title or to indicate a new term. Further, a title can have bigger font size and be arranged in the center of a line.

The term text-signal has been introduced [2] as the writing device that indicates characteristic elements of a text-document or structure that carries semantic information over and above its content. Text-signals attempt to pre-announce or emphasize content or reveal content relationship [2–7]. Titles, subtitles or headings constitute text-signals [3]. Furthermore, the input-enhancement operation augments the saliency of linguistic attributes through textual enhancement in visual input (e.g. italics, bold) or through phonological manipulations in aural input (i.e. oral repetition) [8].

The three text layers of a document or the text-signals play important roles during the reading of a document: (a) direct the reader's attention, (b) enable specific cognitive processes, (c) facilitate the comprehension of text information, (d) in some cases, influence the memory on text, and (e) direct selective access between and within texts [2].

The use of the typographic elements denotes a number of associated semantics. W3C has introduced unique labels for each of the font-styles bold and italics [9]. But, it has been found that readers use at least eight semantics to characterize bold and italics in a text document [10].

Accessibility of documents for persons with disabilities can be achieved by Text-to-Speech systems [11]. Screen-readers and braille displays constitute common technology for the visually impaired to access the content of a document or the Web [12–14]. Although text-signals are important to the reader, most of the current Text-to-Speech (TtS) systems essentially use documents in plain text [12]. Recently, there is an effort toward the acoustic mapping of visual text-signals through advanced Text-to-Speech systems called Document-to-Audio (DtA) [15]. For the typography layer, two approaches for rendering document signals to auditory modality have been incorporated in DtA: (a) direct mapping and (b) emotional-based mapping [16, 17].

As there is a lack of studies on how blind perceive text-signals and, on the other hand, targeting to incorporate much more efficiently the text-signals in DtA, in this work we explore in a systematic way the perception of the main typographic text-signals of a document by blind and sighted students.

2   Methodology

Of the 73 students who took part in the study, 47 were sighted and the other 26 were congenitally blind, users of braille, who became blind during the first years of their life and did not have a visual memory of the alphabet. The students who were sighted ranged in age from 11 to 16, and the students who were blind ranged in age from 10 to 17.

A research protocol was used in the study consisting of a questionnaire. Questions were presented individually for each participant in a closed-ended or open-ended format on printed paper for the sighted students and in braille for the blind. Participants responded orally with one or more answers for each one of the questions and the researcher was recording them.

3   Results

Question 1: Textbooks include words or phrases in different font sizes from the main text. Why do you think it is useful to have several font-sizes? (Fig. 1).

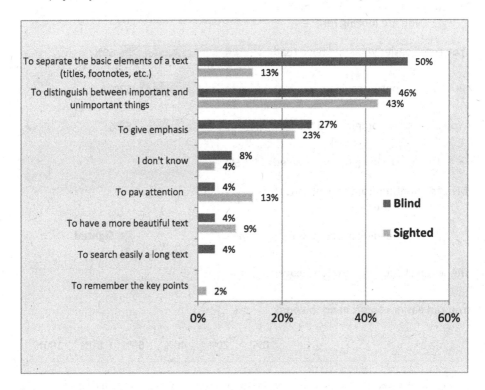

Fig. 1. Answers to Question 1 on the perception of font-size by the blind and sighted students (Color figure online)

Figure 1 shows that half of the blind participants consider that font-size plays an important role in separating the basic elements of a text (e.g. titles, footnotes), but only 13 % of the sighted believe the same. Moreover, 46 % of the blind and 43 % of the sighted participants answered that font-size is used to distinguish between important and unimportant things in a text. Both the groups of the students show almost equally that the third significant role of font-size is to give emphasis to the specific word or phrase.

Question 2 *(for the sighted participants)*: Textbooks include words or phrases in bold, italics or bold-italics. Why do you think it is useful to have these various font-styles?

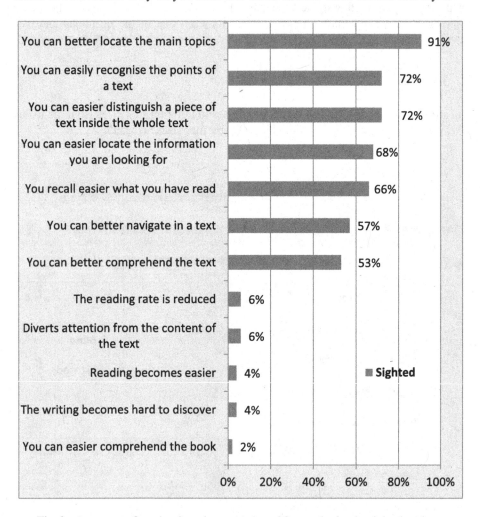

Fig. 2. Answers to Question 2 on the perception of font-styles by the sighted students

The results in Fig. 2 indicate that a significant number (91 %) of the sighted participants consider that font-style plays an important role to better locate the main topics in a text. 72 % of them believe that it helps to easily recognise the points of a text or to distinguish a piece of text inside the whole text. Other significant roles of font-style include the easy location of the information you are looking for (68 %), the easy recall of what you have read (66 %), better navigation in a text (57 %) and better text comprehension (53 %).

Question 3 *(for the blind participants)*: You have heard that text for the sighted people include different styles of characters, such as bold, italics and bold-italics. Why do you think it is useful to have these various font-styles?

35 % of the blind participants (Fig. 3) consider that font-style is used to distinguish some elements of the text or to grab the eye and 27 % to give emphasis at a specific point.

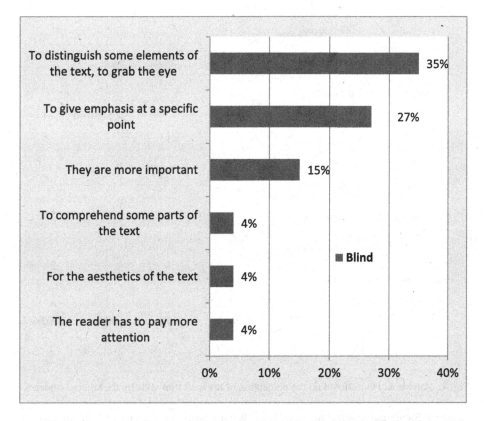

Fig. 3. Answers to Question 3 on the perception of font-style by the blind students

Question 4 *(for the sighted participants)*: What means for you a word or a phrase in bold within a text?

From the results presented in Fig. 4 we see that most of the sighted participants (68 %) consider that the bold font-style is used to indicate an important word or phrase in the text that needs more attention by the reader. Some of them (17 %) believe that the role of the bold is to indicate keywords or new meanings and some (13 %) for the key points of the text.

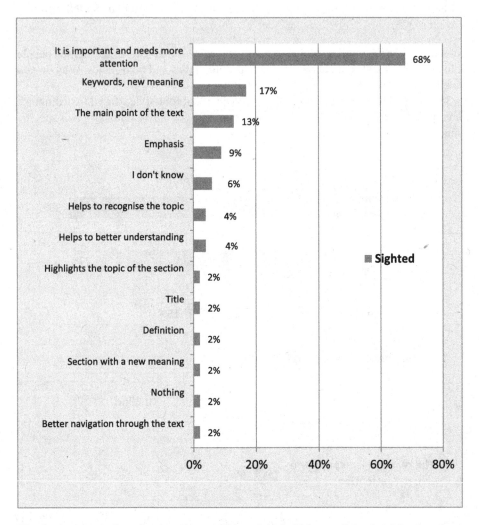

Fig. 4. Answers to Question 4 on the perception of the bold font-style by the sighted students

Question 5 *(for the sighted participants)*: What means for you a word or a phrase in italics within a text?

For the sighted participants (Fig. 5), there is not a dominant view on the perception of the italics font-style in a text. They answered a word or a phrase in italics means that: is important and needs more attention (23 %), is a definition or it is not so important (15 %), it shows a light emphasis (13 %) or it provides additional information (11 %).

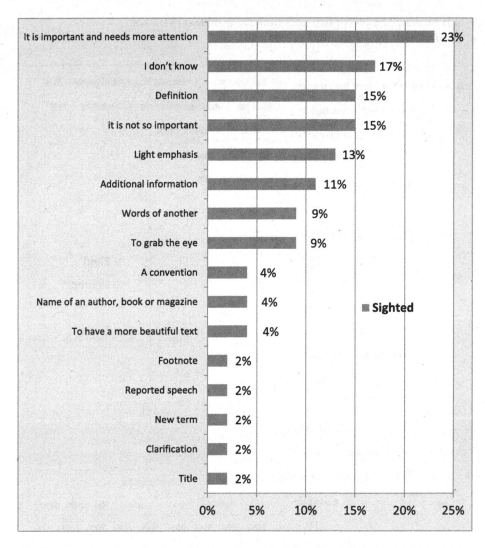

Fig. 5. Answers to Question 5 on the perception of the italics font-style by the sighted students

Question 6: How you recognize the title of a text?

The results (Fig. 6) show that the sighted and blind students recognize the titles of a text mainly using non-identical criteria, but also there are some common ones.

The sighted participants recognize a title mainly from the font features of its characters:

- the bold font-style is the dominant characteristic (83 %) and
- more than half of the students (53 %) from the large font-size.

In contrast, the blind participants recognize a title mainly because:

- it is separated by one or two lines from the main text (81 %) or
- it is followed by a dotted line (77 %).

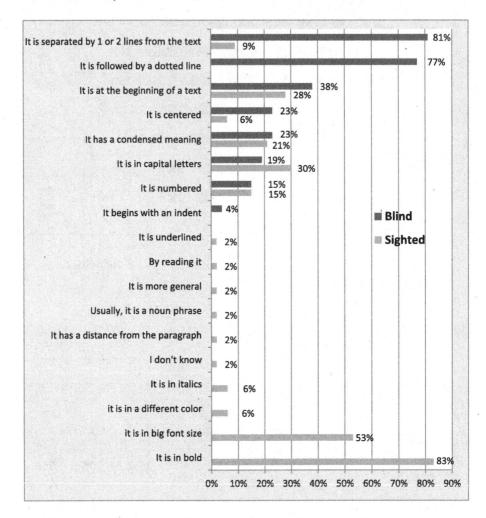

Fig. 6. Answers to Question 6: "How you recognize the title of a text?" (Color figure online)

4   Conclusion

In this study, we explored the ways blind and sighted students perceive the main typographic text-signals and how they recognize headings in a document.

Both groups of the participants perceive that the font-styles are used largely to better locate, recognize or distinguish the topics or specific information in a document, but only a few of the blind (4 %) to ask the reader to pay more attention. Almost half of the sighted argue that they are useful for the comprehension of the content, but only 4 % of the blind students perceive the same. Most of the sighted participants (68 %) consider that bold is used to indicate an important word or phrase in the text that needs more attention by the reader, but only 23 % of them perceive the same for the italics.

27 % of the blind participants and 23 % of the sighted perceive that the role of font-size is to provide emphasis. Moreover, only 9 % of the sighted students grasp that bold is used for emphasis and 13 % of them that italics is used for light emphasis.

Half of the blind participants consider that font-size plays an important role in separating the basic elements of a text (e.g. titles, footnotes), but only 13 % of the sighted believe the same.

The results show that the sighted and blind students recognize the titles of a text mainly using non-identical criteria. The sighted use mainly bold and font-size, but the blind use line separation or a dotted line that follows.

In our future work, we plan to extend the current study by including more text-signals.

Acknowledgements. This research was partially funded by the National and Kapodistrian University of Athens, Special Account for Research Grants.

References

1. Kouroupetroglou, G., Tsonos, D.: Multimodal accessibility of documents. In: Pinder, S. (ed.) Advances in Human-Computer Interaction, pp. 451–470. I-Tech Education and Publishing, Vienna (2008)
2. Lorch, R.F.: Text-signaling devices and their effects on reading and memory processes. Educ. Psychol. Rev. **1**, 209–234 (1989)
3. Lemarié, J., Eyrolle, H., Cellier, J.M.: Visual signals in text comprehension: how to restore them when oralizing a text via a speech synthesis? Comput. Hum. Behav. **22**, 1096–1115 (2006)
4. Lorch, R.F., Chen, H.T., Lemarié, J.: Communicating headings and preview sentences in text and speech. J. Exp. Psychol. Appl. **18**, 265–276 (2012)
5. Spyridakis, J.H.: Signaling effects: a review of the research—Part I. J. Tech. Writ. Commun. **19**, 227–240 (1989)
6. Lemarié, J., Lorch, R.F., Eyrolle, H., Virbel, J.: SARA: a text-based and reader-based theory of text signaling. Educ. Psychol. **43**, 27–48 (2008)
7. Lorch, R.F., Lemarié, J., Grant, R.A.: Signaling hierarchical and sequential organization in expository text. Sci. Stud. Read. **15**, 267–284 (2011)
8. Han, Z.H., Park, E.S., Combs, C.: Textual enhancement of input: issues and possibilities. Appl. Linguist. **29**, 597–618 (2008)
9. W3C: The World Wide Web Consortium. http://www.w3.org
10. Fourli-Kartsouni, F., Slavakis, K., Kouroupetroglou, G., Theodoridis, S.: A Bayesian Network Approach to Semantic Labelling of Text Formatting in XML Corpora of Documents. In: Stephanidis, C. (ed.) Universal Access in HCI, Part III, HCII 2007. LNCS, vol. 4556, pp. 299–308. Springer, Heidelberg (2007)
11. Fellbaum, K., Kouroupetroglou, G.: Principles of electronic speech processing with applications for people with disabilities. Technol. Disabil. **20**, 55–85 (2008)
12. Freitas, D., Kouroupetroglou, G.: Speech technologies for blind and low vision persons. Technol. Disabil. **20**, 135–156 (2008)

13. Isaila, N., Smeureannu, I.: The access of persons with visual disabilities at the scientific content. WSEAS Trans. Comput. **9**, 788–797 (2010)
14. Pavel, O.: Automatic system for making web content accessible for visually impaired users. WSEAS Trans. Comput. Res. **1**, 325–328 (2006)
15. Kouroupetroglou, G.: Acoustic mapping of visual text signals through advanced text-to-speech: the case of font size. WSEAS Trans. Comput. **14**, 559–569 (2015)
16. Tsonos, D., Kouroupetroglou, G.: Modeling readers' emotional state response on documents' typographic elements. Adv. Hum. Comput. Interact. **2011**, 1–18 (2011). doi: 10.1155/2011/206983
17. Tsonos, D., Kouroupetroglou, G., Deligiorgi, D.: Regression modeling of reader's emotions induced by font based text signals. In: Stephanidis, C., Antona, M. (eds.) UAHCI/HCII 2013, Part II. LNCS, vol. 8010, pp. 434–443. Springer, Heidelberg (2013)

Methodology for Heuristic Evaluation of Web Accessibility Oriented to Types of Disabilities

Anyela Orozco[✉], Valentina Tabares, and Néstor Duque

Universidad Nacional de Colombia Sede Manizales, Manizales, Colombia
{alorozcom,ndduqueme,vtabaresm}@unal.edu.co

Abstract. In order to ensure that a Website available is easily accessible to as many people as possible, evaluation processes are carried out on Web accessibility, allowing the identification of issues in the construction of such sites and barriers that may limit access to information. However, making these evaluations can become a time consuming task and produce incomplete results; besides, they are based on general guidelines that do not take into account the particularities of each type of disability. This paper proposes a methodology for heuristic evaluation of web accessibility oriented to types of disabilities, consisting of five stages that allow establishing the level of accessibility and specific problems of a website.

Keywords: Web accessibility · Web accessibility evaluation · Disabilities

1 Introduction

The accessibility of websites is aimed at providing equitable access to information, breaking barriers in some sites in order to provide every human being with this fundamental right. Web Content Accessibility Guidelines (WCAG) 2.0 - W3C/WAI set the accessibility requirements for people with disabilities and are the basis of many automated tools and accessibility evaluation manuals [1].

The evaluation of Web accessibility is a fundamental stage in the process of evolution of accessibility, as it identifies the issues in the processes of construction of websites and the barriers that limit access to information to people with disabilities [2].

Currently, there are different tools for evaluating accessibility, some automatic and others manual, but generally this evaluation process becomes time consuming and produces incomplete results [3]. In some cases, it seeks to establish -from the review of compliance with criteria such as the WCAG - the level of accessibility of a site; however, this process is based on general guidelines that do not take into account the particularities of each type of disability [1].

Since web applications are also dynamic, some initiatives aimed at this situation have developed frameworks for the analysis of the characteristics of these types of sites [4].

Based on the above, this paper proposes a methodology for heuristic evaluation of web accessibility oriented to types of disabilities which consists of five stages that allow

© Springer International Publishing Switzerland 2016
M. Antona and C. Stephanidis (Eds.): UAHCI 2016, Part I, LNCS 9737, pp. 91–97, 2016.
DOI: 10.1007/978-3-319-40250-5_9

establishing the level of accessibility and specific problems of a given website in order to implement improvement strategies.

Section 2 presents some basic concepts related to evaluation of accessibility and Sect. 3 presents related work. The proposed methodology is detailed in Sect. 4, and in the next section is presented an experimental work implementing the proposal. Finally, Şect. 6 presents conclusions and future work.

2 Theoretical Framework

The Web is critical for the society of today, as it has become an essential part in education, work and daily life. For this reason, one should think of a Web that guarantees all members of society access to the services offered [5].

Web accessibility is defined as the possibility that a product, environment or service available through the Internet can be used in equality, safety and comfort by all people, and especially for those with disabilities [6]. Several initiatives have been aimed at achieving a Universal Web that the user can access regardless of the type of hardware, software, network infrastructure, language, culture, geographical location and capabilities [7, 8].

The goal with the Web Accessibility Evaluation is to determine whether the evaluated sites comply with the guidelines and minimum standards that allow access to people with disabilities, identifying possible barriers that may be faced and alternative solutions [9].

Some principles have been defined internationally to guide Web accessibility and that are critical to the evaluation process. The Web Content Accessibility Guidelines (WCAG), proposed by the W3C, are to be highlighted; their main objective is to guide the design of Web pages, reducing information barriers and increasing accessibility [8].

In total, 14 guidelines grouped into 4 principles are presented [10]:

Perceptible: The components of user interface and information must be arranged so that users can perceive them.

Operable: Forms, controls, navigation and other interface elements must allow interaction.

Comprehensible: Content and interface must be easily understood and be semantically rich.

Robust: The content must be consistent and reliable enough to allow use, with a wide variety of user agents, technical aids and prepared for future technologies.

The checkpoints upon which the WCAG are based are assigned to a level of priority that, when evaluating web accessibility, allow the identification of which site is in better conditions. In total, there are three different levels of priority, where Priority 1 corresponds to the points that a web developer must meet because, otherwise, certain groups of users could not access the information on the website. In the case of Priority level 2, points that should be met for certain user groups to easily access the Web are taken into account; and finally, Priority 3 makes reference to the characteristics that enable some users to experience easy access to an inclusive web and with more possibilities [10, 11].

3 Related Work

Here are some works related to the topic of evaluation of web accessibility:

In [1], models are proposed to facilitate automated evaluation of web accessibility for large sites with sophisticated features, where Semantic Web technologies are used structuring results in a standardized way in order to achieve better performance and reuse.

The works presented in [2] describe a measuring process of the level of web accessibility for educational sites, where unfavorable results are obtained for the institutions that own the sites, limiting access to information and services offered to certain people with some specific needs.

The authors of [12] propose a conceptual framework for automatic evaluation of accessibility of Rich Internet Applications (RIAs), including web robot, RIA events controller, WAI-ARIA accessibility specifications, evaluator, and results handler.

In [13], it is proposed a guideline to Evaluate Web page accessibility based on several structural-based accessibility models where an innovative Accessibility-Popularity (A-P) analysis is deployed to measure and, thereby, to modify a Web structure.

An heuristic checklist for an accessible smartphone interface design is proposed in [14]. User requirements are reorganized in statements in six general categories: mechanical controls, display, speech and general operation controls, audio feedback controls, touch-operated controls, and others.

4 Proposed Methodology

From the literature reviewed, it was possible to identify that in most cases the results of accessibility evaluation using tools to perform the process automatically are incomplete, and manual evaluation presents a high degree of subjectivity.

It was also identified that a fully automated evaluation of WCAG is infeasible, since it requires human validation in cases where diffuse, ambiguous and subjective terms are presented. Additionally, automated accessibility evaluation tools are unable to identify problems for a specific type of user [3].

This leads to the need of proposals to integrate the two approaches for better results, but it is also required an approach to accessibility evaluation where special needs are taken into account, since barriers on a website depend to a large extent on the specific conditions of each user.

Below is proposed a methodology for heuristic evaluation for web accessibility, which aimed at guiding the process of accessibility evaluation with a focus on specific disabilities and barriers that could be faced by this group of people. It is sought to respond to the particular conditions of users with respective disabilities and provide a comprehensive evaluation based on a set of heuristics.

This work is based on the methodology proposed in [15] and used in [16], where a series of steps are defined to establish heuristics that support the usability evaluation process. The authors argue that the heuristic evaluation is an inspection method widely used, as it is easy to apply and does not require high costs; however, to avoid overlooking some errors, it requires appropriate heuristics to specific situations.

The defined methodology consists of five stages described below:

Stage 1 - Analysis and Characterization of the Population. This stage reintegrates steps 1 and 2 of the methodology presented in [15], which consist of performing exploration on what is to be assessed and describing the most important features.

For the particular case of the accessibility evaluation process, it is necessary to perform an analysis of the characteristics of the disabled population to which the evaluation will be oriented. Groupings are established according to the needs and barriers that could be faced by these people in order to have an initial idea of how the accessibility evaluation process would be carried out and which elements would be taken into account. This analysis is done considering the literature reviewed where such characteristics are described; it is also recommended an initial approach to the population subject of the definition of the heuristics and subsequent evaluation.

Stage 2 - Definition of Indicators for Evaluation. This step corresponds to step 3, proposed in [15], where the characteristics to be taken into account for the definition of the heuristics are identified.

Once identified and selected the group on which the evaluation will be focused, an analysis of the barriers that these people could face when trying to access the contents of a website is done.

For the definition of indicators to assess whether or not the accessibility criteria are met, WCAG 2.0 and other proposals for manual evaluation of accessibility are used, identifying which elements can be taken into account for the particular case of the group subject of the evaluation.

Stage 3 - Definition of Heuristics. Subsequently, at the third stage, following step 4 of the methodology proposed in [15], a series of heuristics were defined based on the provisions established in the usability evaluation processes, but that fit the criteria to be taken into account specifically in evaluating accessibility.

The indicators proposed at stage 2 are used for the definition of the heuristics, but elements that allow the evaluator a greater understanding of what to evaluate and how to do it are added.

The template presented in [16] is used as a guideline, which consists of an identifier and a name for the heuristic, the detailed explanation of the indicators to be taken into account, examples of cases where the criteria are met or not, and the specific problems arising, which will be used for analysis of results.

Stage 4 - Implementation of Accessibility Evaluation. Once the heuristics to be taken into account for accessibility evaluation are defined, it is necessary to identify the websites to be evaluated, together with the people responsible for conducting the evaluation.

At this stage it is advisable to have a group of evaluators who have different levels of knowledge on the subject of web accessibility and the specific barriers that may be faced by the group of people to whom the evaluation is addressed.

One advantage of this approach is presented when making the evaluation, as the defined heuristics must be carried out in a simple language, with clear examples that facilitate the evaluation process.

Step 5 - Analysis of Results. At this stage the results obtained with the application of stage 4 are taken and analyzed. This is very important because it defines the usefulness of the evaluation process.

Unlike other accessibility evaluation strategies, the application of heuristics makes it easier to guide the process and it is possible to present the results in a clear and understandable way as it works with specific indicators.

A proper analysis of the results is fundamental for the improvement processes to be followed in the institutions whenever weaknesses on the websites evaluated may be found.

5   Experimental Work

In order to make an initial assessment of the proposed methodology, two websites of higher education institutions were selected (http://www.unal.edu.co, http://www.ucaldas.edu.co). The accessibility evaluation was performed only on the home page.

People with visual impairment were selected for the implementation of the first stage of the proposed methodology as target population. After this definition, we proceeded to perform a detailed assessment of their specific characteristics in addition to the barriers commonly faced when trying to access web content.

Taking into account the specific characteristics of the disability, images without alternative text, complex images without detailed description, multimedia elements without textual or sound description and links without significant text are identified as some of the barriers.

Having identified the barriers, the next step was the definition of the indicators that will allow performing the evaluation through the heuristics defined. These indicators were grouped into those that affect the perception of content and those that affect the operation by the user.

After defining the criteria and following the template presented at Stage 3, the heuristics to be applied were established to evaluate the selected websites according to the specific conditions of the visually impaired population. As an example, one of the heuristics designed is presented in Table 1.

The heuristics defined were applied by a group with three evaluators who identified problems in the sites from the heuristics given. Table 2 presents the total amount of problems found, both for heuristic HA01, presented in Table 1, and for heuristic HA02, which evaluates elements related with how the user can interact with the site.

The results show a number of problems taking into account heuristics used. For the first site, a greater number of issues regarding images and other multimedia resources

Table 1. Heuristic, Example

ID	HA01
Name	Multimedia Objects Perception
Explanation	Commonly, visually impaired people use tools that allow them to interact with websites, as is the case of screen readers. These tools require adequate text descriptions to allow the user to access content.
Examples	A video is presented and it has only animations and background sound. It requires a textual or sound description of what happens in the video.
Problems	- One or more images without alternative text are presented. - If the image is complex, a detailed description is presented. - Videos are presented without alternative text. - Videos are presented without alternative sound.

were found, while the second site had a higher number of difficulties with the way the site operates, taking into account elements such as links and buttons.

This evaluation is preliminary and allowed feedback to improve the heuristics defined and also the analysis of other elements that may be considered to carry out this evaluation process.

Table 2. Results of evaluation application

Heuristics	Problems found	
	http://www.unal.edu.co	http://www.ucaldas.edu.co
HA01 - Multimedia Objects Perception	10	7
HA02 - Site Operability	6	9

6   Conclusions and Future Work

A methodology is proposed to evaluate the level of accessibility of a website, following a series of heuristics that support this process and make its implementation easier.

Performing an accessibility evaluation process focused on features and specific barriers for one type of disability, it is possible to get results that meet their needs, identifying the problems with the site, allowing for further adaptation and improvement.

As future work it is proposed the carrying of more tests, involving other types of disabilities, other websites and a greater number of evaluators. It is expected to refine the indicators and heuristics defined, besides the adjustment of the methodology according to more detailed results of validations.

Acknowledgments. The research presented in this paper was partially funded by the COLCIENCIAS project entitled: "RAIM: Implementación de un framework apoyado en tecnologías móviles y de realidad aumentada para entornos educativos ubicuos, adaptativos, accesibles e interactivos para todos (Implementation of a framework supported by mobile technologies and augmented reality for ubiquitous, adaptive, accessible and interactive learning environments for all)" of the Universidad Nacional de Colombia, with code 1119-569-34172.

References

1. Abou-Zahra, S.: A data model to facilitate the automation of web accessibility evaluations. Electron. Notes Theor. Comput. Sci. **157**, 3–9 (2006)
2. Riaño, A., Ballesteros, A.: Análisis de accesibilidad web orientado a la estrategia de gobierno en línea del estado Colombiano (2014)
3. Centeno, L., Delgado, C., Arias, F., Álvarez, L.: Web accessibility evaluation tools: a survey and some improvements. Electron. Notes Theor. Comput. Sci. **157**, 87–100 (2006)
4. Abu, D., Alkhateeb, F., Maghayreh, E.A., Mohammed, A.: The design of RIA accessibility evaluation tool. Adv. Eng. Softw. **57**, 1–7 (2013)
5. Takagi, H., Asakawa, C.: New challenges in web accessibility. Univers. Access Inf. Soc. **13**, 205–226 (2015)
6. Zubillaga del Rio, A., Alba Pastor, C.: Hacia un nuevo modelo de accesibilidad en las instituciones de educación superior. Rev. Española Pedagog. **71**(255), 245–262 (2008)
7. Martínez Usero, J.Á., Lara Navarra, P.: La Accesibilidad de los Contenidos Web, vol. 72. UOC, Barcelona (2006)
8. W3C: Web Accessibility Initiative (WAI). http://www.w3.org/WAI/
9. Pereira, L.S., Ferreira, S.B.L., Archambault, D.: Preliminary web accessibility evaluation method through the identification of critical items with the participation of visually impaired users. Procedia Comput. Sci. **67**, 77–86 (2015)
10. Cooper, M., Reid, L.G.: Web Content Accessibility Guidelines (WCAG) 2.0, pp. 1–24 (2013)
11. Sánchez-Gordón, M.L., Moreno, L.: Toward an integration of web accessibility into testing processes. Procedia Comput. Sci. **27**, 281–291 (2013)
12. Abu Doush, I., Alkhateeb, F., Maghayreh, E.A., Al-Betar, M.A.: The design of RIA accessibility evaluation tool. Adv. Eng. Softw. **57**, 1–7 (2013)
13. Yen, B.P.C.: The design and evaluation of accessibility on web navigation. Decis. Support Syst. **42**, 2219–2235 (2007)
14. Cavuoto, L.A., Benson, K., Tonya Smith-Jackson, M.A.N.: A heuristic checklist for an accessible smartphone interface design. Univers. Access Inf. Soc. **13**, 351–365 (2014)
15. Rusu, C., Roncagliolo, S., Ruso, V., Collazos, C.: A methodology to establish usability heuristics. In: ACHI 2011 Fourth International Conference on Advances in Computer-Human Interactions, pp. 59–62 (2011)
16. Inostroza, R., Rusu, C., Roncagliolo, S., Rusu, V., Collazos, C.A.: Developing SMASH: a set of SMArtphone's uSability heuristics. Comput. Stand. Interfaces **43**, 40–52 (2016)

Development of Universal Design Mobile Interface Guidelines (UDMIG) for Aging Population

Ljilja Ruzic[(⊠)], Seunghyun Tina Lee, Yilin Elaine Liu,
and Jon A. Sanford

The Center for Assistive Technology and Environmental Access, CATEA,
Georgia Institute of Technology, Atlanta, GA, USA
{ljilja, tinalee, y. elaineliu}@gatech. edu,
jon. sanford@coa. gatech. edu

Abstract. The number of older adults using technology is steadily increasing. However, this group of users has faced a variety of user interface (UI) usability issues due to various and multiple age-related limitations they have. Four different strategies designed to solve the usability issues older adults have while interacting with user interfaces were analyzed. When placed in a context of mobile interfaces for older adults, Universal Design (UD), Design for Aging, Universal Usability (UU), and Guidelines for handheld mobile device interface design were not found sufficiently complete and inclusive to meet the usability needs of older adults. There is a need to address these usability needs and reconcile inconsistencies between the four strategies. The purpose of this research study was to develop a robust, integrative set of design guidelines based on the four design strategies to ensure usability of mobile devices by older adults. An example of the application of the guidelines to the mobile interface is presented in the paper.

Keywords: Accessibility guidelines · Design for aging · Human factors · Older adults · Universal design · User interface design

1 Introduction

As the population ages, more older adults are becoming technology users [1]. However, many older adults experience declines in one or more abilities, including reduction in ranges and levels of abilities, such as vision, cognition and dexterity, that can limit their ability to use and interact with technology user interfaces (UIs). Common problems include an inability to understand common icons, taking a long time to complete a task or having poor task performance, making an inordinate number of errors, having difficulty in seeing text, and having problems understanding the relationship between the touchscreen and button manipulation with the response of the interface [2–4]. Despite these issues, product and user interface design can help older adults by incorporating their particular sensory-perception, motor, communication, and mental needs into the design of the interfaces [5].

© Springer International Publishing Switzerland 2016
M. Antona and C. Stephanidis (Eds.): UAHCI 2016, Part I, LNCS 9737, pp. 98–108, 2016.
DOI: 10.1007/978-3-319-40250-5_10

To address issues of usability of UIs by older adults and others with functional limitations, a number of different design strategies have been proposed. Four of the most widely accepted strategies were analyzed as part of this project: Universal Design, Design for Aging, Universal Usability, and Guidelines for handheld mobile device interface design. Universal Design (UD) [6] is a strategy that supports the diverse ranges and combinations of abilities and limitations that characterize this population of users. The purpose of UD is to design for everyone and by doing so, to overcome the barriers to usability that come with aging [7]. In contrast to UD, Design for Aging [8] focuses on older adults' specific and singular limitations. Design for Aging is a strategy that explores the factors that constrain the use of products and user interfaces by older adults, as well as aspects of human-computer interface design that accommodate older users with age-associated disabilities and limitations [9]. Based on UD, which was initially intended to cover design of physical environments (e.g. buildings, spaces, products, graphics), Universal Usability (UU) was developed to support usability, inclusivity, and utility of information and communication technology [10]. It consists of the eight guidelines, called the Eight Golden Rules of Interface Design. Guidelines for handheld mobile device interface design [11] were based on UU, modifying its Eight Golden Rules of Interface Design and adding the guidelines applicable to mobile and touchscreen platforms (See Table 1).

Table 1. Four strategies' specific domains and types of users

Strategies	Specific Domains	Types of Users
Universal Design	Physical environments (e.g. buildings, spaces, products, graphics)	All users
Design for Aging	Technology systems and products (e.g. computer input and output devices, desktop interfaces, helathcare technologies), environments (e.g. lighting, navigational signage), work tasks, and training and instructional programs	Older adults
Universal Usability	Information and communication technology (desktops)	All users
Guidelines for handheld mobile device interface design	Mobile and touchscreen devices	All users

When placed in a context of mobile interfaces for older adults none of these four strategies alone were sufficiently complete and inclusive to meet the range and diversity of usability needs of older adults. To address these usability needs and reconcile inconsistencies among the four strategies, a robust, integrative set of guidelines to ensure usability of mobile devices by older adults was developed. This paper reviews the development and content of the Universal Design Mobile Interface Guidelines (UDMIG), which is based on the four strategies, the extension of the original guidelines into a more comprehensive, inclusive set of design guidelines and details the results of a project to design a mobile interface based on these guidelines [12].

2 Development Process of Universal Design Mobile Interface Guidelines (UDMIG)

The first version of the guidelines, UDMIG v.1.0, which has been previously reported [13], was created by applying Design for Aging, Universal Usability, and Guidelines for handheld mobile device interface design to Universal Design guidelines and its seven principles. UDMIG v.1.0 was developed by expanding the UD principles and guidelines to include components of the other three sets of guidelines. Universal Design was kept as an organizing strategy because of its broad application, inclusiveness, and consideration of all users' ranges and combinations of abilities from the beginning of the design process [14, 15].

However, UDMIG v.1.0 were too simplistic and were based too much on the UD Principles. As a result, they needed further refinement. We further developed and grouped all four design guidelines anew based on the two organizing principles: Person-Environment (P-E) Fit Model [16] and the Guideline Objective as being Prescriptive- vs. Performance-based (See Table 2).

P-E Fit Model. P-E Fit defines the degree to which individual and environmental characteristics match in order to promote healthy aging. Both UDMIG and P-E Fit Theory explore the interaction between aging individuals and their environments [17]. The P-E Fit model examines the match or fit between the competence (or functional ability) of a person and demand of the environment component. When there is a match between person and environment usability is achieved [18]. However, barriers in the environment can create different types and levels of usability problems depending on a person's functional capacity [19].

Here, the person component is a part of all the guidelines, which all describe how to accommodate people with different abilities. The environment component includes the guidelines that describe the design of the touchscreen mobile interface as well as the space requirements and context of use. It is divided into two parts: Micro Environment guidelines (e), which represent those that pertain to the design of the interactive mobile interface, and Macro Environment guidelines (E), which describe guidelines that direct the design of space and context in which the mobile interface is used. The fit (F) component includes the guidelines that guide the design of the interaction between the older adult and the touchscreen mobile interface (See Table 2).

Prescription vs. Performance. The four strategies were also grouped into the prescription vs. performance guidelines. Performance-based guidelines suggest how design can meet the usability goals and objectives without prescribing what to do. In contrast, prescriptive guidelines specify what should be designed to achieve usability. Only several Design for Aging guidelines are prescriptive, while the other three strategies, including the resulting UDMIG v.2.0, are performance guidelines in whole. In addition, a number of Design for Aging guidelines are both performance and prescriptive (See Table 2).

Table 2. The guidelines from the four strategies with the resulting UDMIG v.2.0

Data						Results
Prescriptive D.Guidelines	Prescriptive/ Performance	Performance Design Guidelines				
Design for Aging			Guidelines for handheld mobile device interface design	Universal Usability	Universal Design	Universal Design Mobile Interface Guidelines
DFA1.2.4 50:1 contrast DFA1.3.1 3D and VR displays DFA2.2.2 Speech rates DFA2.2.4 Longer duration sounds	DFA1.2.2 Style sheets DFA2.1.1. Sound volumes; instructions DFA4.2.6 Resolution DFA4.2.7 Built-in controls DFA5.2.3 Search history DFA5.2.5 Navigation assistance DFA5.4.1 Standardized format DFA5.4.3 Current system status DFA5.4.4 Feedback	DFA1.2.5 Color discriminations DFA4.1.1 Default values DFA4.2.8 Adjustable output sound intensity DFA5.1.1 Clutter DFA5.1.2 Adaptability DFA5.1.4 Characters and targets DFA5.2.4 Where the user is DFA5.3.1 Information organization DFA5.3.2 Menu structure DFA5.3.3 Frequent important actions DFA5.4.2 Compatibility DFA5.4.5 Error correction, recovery DFA5.4.6 System tools DFA5.4.7 User levels	MD1. Shortcuts MD3. Dialogs to yield closure MD4. Locus of control MD5. Consistency (platforms) MD7. Error prevention, handling MD8. Short-term memory load MD9. Multiple dynamic contexts MD10. Small devices MD11. Limited and split attention MD12. Speed and recovery MD14. Personalization	UU1. Consistency UU4. Dialogs to yield closure UU5. Error handling UU7. Locus of control UU8. Short-term memory load	UD1a. Same means of use UD1b. Segregating/stigmatizing users UD1c. Privacy, security, and safety available to all UD2a. Choice in methods of use UD2b. Right- or left-handed access/use UD2c. Accuracy and precision UD2d. Adaptable pace UD3b. Consistency UD3c. Range of literacy/language skills UD5a. Hazards and errors UD5d. Unconscious action UD6a. Neutral body position	F1. Same means of use F2. Range of literacy and language skills F3. Choice in methods of use F4. Support of the internal locus of control F5. Right-, left- or no-handed use F6. Accuracy and precision F7. Adaptable pace F8. Consistency with expectations and intuition F9. Dialogs that yield closure F10. Clear and understandable navigation structure F11. Multiple and dynamic contexts F12. Minimized hazards and unintended actions F13. Natural body position _(Fit (Person-Environment Interaction) - F)_
DFA1.2.1 Font size DFA1.2.3 Font type DFA1.2.4 50:1 contrast DFA2.1.2 Frequency > 4000Hz DFA2.1.3 Warning signals DFA3.1.1 Haptic processing DFA4.2.2 Size of the text DFA Auditory warnings	DFA2.2.3 Voice characteristics-situation DFA3.1.2 Upper to lower body sites-vibration DFA4.1.2 Avoid double-clicking DFA4.1.5 Speech recognition control DFA4.1.8 Tactile and auditory feedback DFA4.2.5 Instructions on resolution DFA4.2.9 Warning message DFA4.2.10 Tactile output devices DFA5.2.2 Site map DFA5.4.4 Feedback	DFA1.2.5 Color discriminations DFA1.2.6, DFA5.2.1 Scrolling DFA2.1.4 Redundant information DFA2.1.5 Background noise and reverberation DFA2.2.1 Pauses in speech DFA4.1.7 Large keypad keys DFA4.2.1 Contrast DFA5.1.1 Clutter DFA5.1.3 Temporal constraints DFA5.1.4 Characters and targets DFA5.3.1 Information organization DFA5.3.2 Menu structure DFA5.3.3 Frequent important actions DFA5.4.5 Error correction, recovery	MD2. Feedback MD4. Locus of control MD5. Consistency (platforms) MD6. Reversal of actions MD7. Error prevention, handling MD8. Short-term memory load MD10. Small devices MD11. Limited and split attention MD13. "Top-down" interaction MD15. Enjoyment	UU1. Consistency UU3. Informative feedback UU5. Error handling UU6. Reversal of actions UU7. Locus of control UU8. Short-term memory load	UD1d. Appealing design UD3a. Eliminate complexity UD3d. Information consistent with importance UD3e. Prompting and feedback UD4a. Different modes UD4b. Contrast UD4c. "Legibility" of information UD4d. Differentiate elements UD4e. Compatibility with techniques/devices UD5b. Warnings of hazards/errors UD5c. Fail-safe features UD7c. Variations in hand/grip size UD6b. Operating forces UD6c. Repetitive actions UD6d. Sustained physical effort	e1. Design appealing to all e2. Simple and natural use e3. Informative feedback e4. Use of different modes e5. Maximized "legibility" e6. Simple error handling e7. Easy reversal of actions e8. Low physical effort e9. Variations in hand and grip size _(Micro Environment - e)_
	DFA1.1.2 Non-reflectant materials DFA1.1.2 Adj. light sources DFA4.2.3 Glare DFA4.2.4 Adj. display	DFA1.1.1 Illumination DFA2.1.5 Background noise/reverberation DFA4.1.10 "Homing"			UD7a. Clear line of sight UD7b. Reach to components UD7d. Space for assistive devices	E1. Appropriate lighting and glare E2. Adjustable positioning E3. Minimized background noise and reverberation E4. Space for use of assistive devices _(Macro Environment-E)_

3 Results

3.1 Cross-Walking the Guidelines

To develop a second version of the UDMIG, the four design strategies were cross-walked and categorized by the P-E Fit and Performance/Prescriptive dimensions. Equivalent guidelines from each of the four strategies were mapped onto each other, while unique guidelines were added to the final set to create UDMIG v.2.0 (See Table 3.).

Table 3. UDMIG v.2.0 performance – prescriptive guidelines crosswalk

Prescriptive D.Guidelines	Prescriptive/ Performance	Performance Design Guidelines				
Design for Aging			Guidelines for handheld mobile device interface design	Universal Usability	Universal Design	Universal Design Mobile Interface Guidelines
DFA1.2.4 (F6) DFA1.3.1 (F6) DFA2.2.2 (F7) DFA2.2.4 (F11)	DFA1.2.2 (F6) DFA2.1.1 (F6); (F3) DFA4.2.6 (F6) DFA4.2.7 (F11) DFA5.2.3 (F9,F10) DFA5.2.5 (F10) DFA5.4.1 (F8) DFA5.4.3 (F9) DFA5.4.4 (F9)	DFA1.2.5 (F6) DFA4.1.1 (F11) DFA4.2.8 (F11) DFA5.1.1 (F6) DFA5.1.2 (F11) DFA5.1.4 (F6,F7) DFA5.2.4 (F9) DFA5.3.1 (F9) DFA5.3.2 (F6,F9) DFA5.3.3 (F12) DFA5.4.2 (F8,2) DFA5.4.5 (F12) DFA5.4.6 (F4,F6,F7,F8) DFA5.4.7 (F6)	MD1. (F7) MD3. (F9) MD4. (F4) MD5. (F8) MD7. (F12) MD8. (F6) MD9. (F11) MD10. (F3) MD11. (F3,F5) MD12. (F7) MD14.(F2,F3,F6, F7,F11)	UU1. (F8) UU4. (F9) UU5. (F12) UU7. (F3, F4) UU8. (F6)	UD1a. (F1) UD1b. (F1) UD1c. (F1) UD2a. (F3) UD2b. (F5) UD2c. (F6) UD2d. (F7) UD3b. (F8) UD3c. (F2) UD5a. (F12) UD5d. (F12) UD6a. (F13)	F1 F2 F3 F4 F5 F6 F7 F8 F9 F10 F11 F12 F13 *Fit - F*
DFA1.2.1 (e5) DFA1.2.3 (e5) DFA1.2.4 (e5) DFA2.1.2 (e3) DFA2.1.3 (e6) DFA3.1.1 (e4) DFA4.2.2 (e5) DFA4.2.11 (e6)	DFA2.2.3 (e5) DFA3.1.2 (e4) DFA4.1.2 (e8) DFA4.1.5 (e4,e5) DFA4.1.8 (e4) DFA4.2.5 (e5) DFA4.2.9 (e3,e6) DFA4.2.10 (e4) DFA5.2.2 (e5) DFA5.4.4 (e3)	DFA1.2.5 (e2,e5) DFA1.2.6, DFA5.2.1 (e2,e8) DFA2.1.4 (e4) DFA2.1.5 (e5) DFA2.2.1 (e5) DFA4.1.7 (e9) DFA4.2.1 (e5) DFA5.1.1 (e2,e3) DFA5.1.3 (e6,e7) DFA5.1.4 (e5) DFA5.3.1 (e2) DFA5.3.2 (e2,e5) DFA5.3.3 (e2,e5) DFA5.4.5 (e6,e7)	MD2. (e3) MD4. (e1) MD5. (e2) MD6. (e7) MD7. (e6,e7) MD8. (e2) MD10. (e4,e5) MD11. (e4) MD13. (e2) MD15. (e1)	UU1. (e2) UU3. (e3) UU5. (e6,e7) UU6. (e7) UU7. (e1) UU8. (e2)	UD1d. (e1) UD3a. (e2) UD3d. (e2) UD3e. (e3) UD4a. (e4) UD4b. (e5) UD4c. (e5) UD4d. (e5) UD4e. (e5) UD5b. (e6) UD5c. (e7) UD6b. (e8) UD6c. (e8) UD6d. (e8) UD7c. (e9)	e1 e2 e3 e4 e5 e6 e7 e8 e9 *Micro Environment – e*
	DFA1.1.2 (E1) DFA4.2.3 (E1,E3) DFA4.2.4 (E1,E2)	DFA1.1.1 (E1) DFA2.1.5 (E3) DFA4.1.10 (E4)			UD7a. (E1) UD7b. (E2) UD7d. (E4)	E1 E2 E3 E4 *Macro Environment-E*

The final version of UDMIG 2.0 included all of the guidelines, either in whole or modified, from Universal Usability, Guidelines for handheld mobile device interface design, and Universal Design, whereas 4 of the 52 number of the guidelines in Design for Aging were excluded because of their application to desktops (See Table 4). As an example, half of the 8 UU guidelines (i.e., enable frequent users to use shortcuts, offer informative feedback, design dialogs to yield closure, and support internal locus of control) were included in whole as they apply to mobile devices. In contrast, the other

Table 4. Proportion of design guidance retained from each of the contributing sources

Design Guidelines Analyzed	Number of Guidelines	Number (%) of Guidelines Included in UDMIG 2.0	Number (%) of Guidelines Modified in UDMIG 2.0
Universal Design	30	30 (100%)	8 (26.7%)slightly modified
Design for Aging	52	48 (92.3%)	4 (7.7%) excluded
Universal Usability	8	8 (100%)	4 (50%) modified
Guidelines for handheld mobile device interface design	15	15 (100%)	0 (0%) modified

half of the guidelines (consistency, reversal of actions, error prevention and simple error handling, and reducing short-term memory load) was modified to fit the touchscreen mobile environment. In addition, 8 UD guidelines that cover low physical effort (Principle 6) and size and space for approach and use (Principle 7) were slightly modified to fit the mobile touchscreen environment.

3.2 UDMIG V.2.0

Resulting UDMIG v.2.0 grouped into Fit (F), Micro Environment (e), and Macro Environment (E) guidelines are presented bellow (See Table 5).

Table 5. UDMIG v.2.0

Fit Guidelines (F)	Micro Environment Guidelines (e)	Macro Environment Guidelines (E)
F1. Same means of use	**e1.** Design appealing to all	**E1.** Appropriate lighting and glare
F2. Range of literacy and language skills	**e2.** Simple and natural use	**E2.** Adjustable positioning
F3. Choice in methods of use	**e3.** Informative feedback	**E3.** Minimized background noise and reverberation
F4. Support of the internal locus of control	**e4.** Use of different modes	**E4.** Space for use of assistive devices
F5. Right-, left- or no-handed use	**e5.** Maximized "legibility" of essential information	
F6. Accuracy and precision	**e6.** Simple error handling	
F7. Adaptable pace	**e7.** Easy reversal of actions	
F8. Consistency with expectations and intuition	**e8.** Low physical effort	
F9. Dialogs that yield closure	**e9.** Variations in hand and grip size	
F10. Clear and understandable navigation structure		
F11. Multiple and dynamic contexts		
F12. Minimized hazards and unintended actions		
F13. Natural body position		

3.3 Application of UDMIG V.2.0

A voting ballot was designed using UDMIG 2.0 to integrate visual and audio output without any special adaptations [20]. EZ Ballot interface was designed to meet the guidelines for Fit (F), Micro Environment (e) and Macro Environment (E) as follows:

Fit Guidelines (F).

F1. **Same means of use**. Ballot interface comprises one voting system to all voters regardless of their abilities.

F2. **The range of literacy and language skills**. Universal and recognizable icons were used for text size, audio speed, and contrast; simple Y for Yes, N for No, and I for instructions, and video the instructions on how to use the ballot.

F3. **Choice in methods of use**. Multiple means of input (e.g., touch, stylus) and navigation methods (e.g., Yes/No touch buttons, scroll, and swipe gestures), and output characteristics, including visual (text size, contrast) and audio (speed, volume) were provided.

F4. **Support of the internal locus of control**. Choices of input and navigation methods, multiple visual (text size, contrast) and audio (speed, volume) characteristics, consistency in system navigation, and easy access to all the content (main control pane) were added to enable older adults feel that they are in control.

F5. **Right-, left- or no-handed use**. Inputs were made usable for right- or left-handed older adults by putting the navigation and touch buttons in places that were in natural locations that were easy to reach with either left of right fingers.

F6. **Accuracy and precision**. Large touch-buttons with enough space between the buttons minimize the need for accuracy and precision.

F7. **Adaptation to users' pace**. Ballot interface was designed to support any voter's pace with multiple audio speed options, linear and random access interfaces, and providing a choice for skipping instructions, any races or propositions.

F8. **Consistency with expectations**. The answer to the question on each page was Yes or No. Touchscreen buttons were designed to look touchable.

F9. **Dialogs that yield closure**. Ballot interface provided older adults with the satisfaction of accomplishment and completion, a sense of relief, and an indicator to prepare for the next group of actions.

F10. **Clear and understandable navigation structure**. The instruction was provided to guide on the use of and navigation through the interface, and Review was designed to take the voter to any particular point in the voting system so that older adults could have Clear and understandable navigation structure.

F11. **Multiple and dynamic contexts**. The default setting of the audio output was turned on.

F12. **Minimized hazards and unintended actions**. Yes and No touch buttons were located at the farther left and right sides of the touchscreen, and other touch buttons were placed on the main control panel. The UI began with instructions.

F13. **Natural body position**. Main input buttons were designed at the locations where older adults' hands are in neutral body position (Figs. 1, 2 and 3).

Micro Environment (e).

e1. **Design appealing to all**. Familiar design features were used, institutional appearance was avoided, and human voice was used as an audio sound.

e2. **Simple and natural use**. Guided linear or random access structure that matches the audio interface were provided, the piece-by-piece process broke down a complex task into several easy-to-complete subtasks to reduce complexity, visual clusters were removed, and multiple contest pages on one screen were avoided.

e3. **Informative feedback**. Two ways for verification, a prompt and a sub-review message were provided.

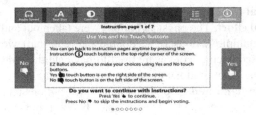

Fig. 1. Instruction page 1

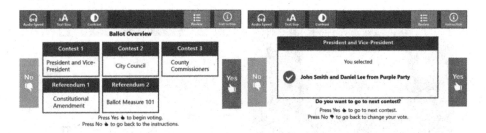

Fig. 2. Contrast (left) and audio speed adjustment (right) pages

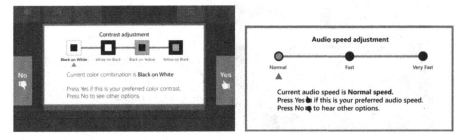

Fig. 3. Ballot overview (left) and President and Vice-President selection (right) pages

e4. **Different modes of use**. Simultaneous visual and audio ballot interface and tactile indicators for locating the touch buttons were provided. Universal icons along with redundant cues (e.g., color, text, and symbols) were used.

e5. **Maximized "legibility" of essential information**. Information was displayed in sans serif and in at least two font sizes: 3.0–4.0 mm (the height of an upper case letter in the smaller text size) and 6.3–9.0 mm (the height of an upper case letter in the larger text size); based on the VVSG (Sect. 3.2.2.1.b.) recommendation. The page title was made bold.

e6. **Simple error handling**. The warnings (under voting, over voting) were designed to prevent mistakes during a voting process, with two ways for verification, a prompt and a sub-review message. Review and Instruction touch buttons were located on the main control panel to be easy to find while isolated from the most used Yes/No touch buttons.

e7. **Easy reversal of actions.** Review page provided easy reversal of actions.

e8. **Low physical effort.** The physical buttons were taken out and instead used large touch buttons, multiple actions (e.g., double tap, split-tap) were avoided, and a single tap was used, tactile icons were used to navigate the older adults' fingers to the location of the touch buttons to ensure Low physical effort.

e9. **Variations in hand and grip size.** Large touch buttons and large tactile icons on the cover of the screen, and sufficient space between buttons were designed for different size of fingers and grip (Fig. 4).

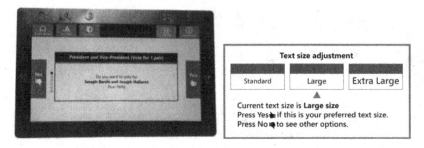

Fig. 4. Tactile cover (left) and text size adjustment page (right)

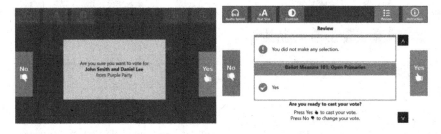

Fig. 5. A prompt message (left) and review page (right)

Macro Environment (E).

E1. **Appropriate lighting and glare.** Adjustable display and adequate lighting need to be provided at the voting poll.

E2. **Adjustable positioning.** Ensure adjustable height, depth, width, and angle from a seating position at the voting poll.

E3. **Minimized background noise and reverberation.** Wireless headphones should be provided to voters.

E4. **Space for the use of assistive devices** needs to be arranged at the voting poll (Fig. 5).

4   Discussion

Older adults as mobile technology users are in a need of user interfaces that fit their needs and abilities. While Universal Design, Universal Usability, and Guidelines for handheld mobile device interface design all guide design of interfaces, when placed in a context of designing interactive mobile user interfaces for older adults these were not found complete. Moreover, UU and UD guidelines were not originally developed for mobile interfaces. UD recently included this platform to a certain extent. In addition, Design for Aging focuses on older adults with their particular limitations usually associated with this end-user group, failing to acknowledge ranges and combinations of limitations older adults have. Adaptation and addition of some of the guidelines were necessary to accommodate design for the interactive mobile interfaces for older adults.

UDMIG v.2.0 are an inclusive and complete set of the guidelines developed to guide design process of interactive mobile interfaces for older adults. They are divided into three sets of guidelines: Fit (F), Micro (e) and Macro Environment (E). Fit Guidelines relate to the interaction between older adults and their environment, Micro Environment guidelines guide design of the touchscreen mobile interface, and Macro Environment guidelines help with the design of the space and context of use. Person component is present in all the guidelines, which all describe how to accommodate people with different abilities, and it was not used as a way of grouping the UDMIG.

The guidelines were based on the established strategies for desktop and mobile user interfaces for older adults and published research on interactive mobile interfaces and designing for aging population. Their significance is in their completeness, and integration of the four common strategies for designing interactive mobile interfaces for older adults. This unique set of the guidelines is useful to Human-Computer Interaction (HCI) researchers working in a field of usability and mobile user interface design as well as to industry leaders who develop mobile devices and applications for our aging population.

References

1. Fisk, A.D., et al.: Designing for older adults: principles and creative human factors approaches. CRC Press, Boca Raton (2012)
2. Becker, S.A.: A study of web usability for older adults seeking online health resources. ACM Trans. Comput.-Hum. Interact. (TOCHI) 11(4), 387–406 (2004)
3. Bederson, B.B., et al.: Electronic voting system usability issues. In: Proceedings of the SIGCHI Conference on Human Factors in Computing Systems. ACM (2003)
4. Chadwick-Dias, A., McNulty, M., Tullis, T.: Web usability and age: how design changes can improve performance. In: ACM SIGCAPH Computers and the Physically Handicapped. ACM (2003)
5. Morrell, R.W.: Older Adults, Health Information, and the World Wide Web. Psychology Press, Hillsdale (2001)
6. Mace, R.: Universal Design: Housing for the Lifespan of all People. US Department of Housing and Urban Affairs, Washington DC (1988)

7. Law, C.M., et al.: A systematic examination of universal design resources: part 1, heuristic evaluation. Univ. Access Inf. Soc. **7**(1–2), 31–54 (2008)
8. Nichols, T.A., Rogers, W.A., Fisk, A.D.: Design for aging. In: Salvendy, G. (ed.) Handbook of Human Factors and Ergonomics, 3rd edn, pp. 1418–1445. Wiley, Hoboken (2006)
9. Zajicek, M. Interface design for older adults. In: Proceedings of the 2001 EC/NSF Workshop on Universal Accessibility of Ubiquitous Computing: Providing for the Elderly. ACM (2001)
10. Schneiderman, B.: Eight golden rules of interface design. Disponible en (1986)
11. Gong, J., Tarasewich, P.: Guidelines for handheld mobile device interface design. In: Proceedings of DSI 2004 Annual Meeting. Citeseer (2004)
12. Kascak, L., Rébola, C.B., Sanford, J.: Integrating Universal Design (UD) principles and mobile design guidelines to improve design of mobile health applications for older adults. In: 2014 IEEE International Conference on Healthcare Informatics (ICHI). IEEE (2014)
13. Kascak, L.R., Lee, S., Liu, E.Y., Sanford, J.A.: Universal Design (UD) guidelines for interactive mobile voting interfaces for older adults. In: Antona, M., Stephanidis, C. (eds.) UAHCI 2015. LNCS, vol. 9178, pp. 215–225. Springer, Heidelberg (2015)
14. Ruptash, S.: Universal Design through Passion, Knowledge and Regulations? Trends in Universal Design, p. 24 (2013)
15. Sanford, J.A.: Universal Design as a Rehabilitation Strategy: Design for the Ages. Springer, New York (2012)
16. Lawton, M.P., Nahemow, L.: Ecology and the Aging Process. Lawton, Spokane (1973)
17. Nahemow, L.: The ecological theory of aging: Powell Lawton's legacy. The many dimensions of aging, pp. 22–40 (2000)
18. Iwarsson, S.: A long-term perspective on person–environment fit and ADL dependence among older Swedish adults. Gerontologist **45**(3), 327–336 (2005)
19. Iwarsson, S., Ståhl, A.: Accessibility, usability and universal design-positioning and definition of concepts describing person-environment relationships. Disabil. Rehabil. **25**(2), 57–66 (2003)
20. Lee, S., et al.: EZ ballot with multimodal inputs and outputs. In: Proceedings of the 14th International ACM SIGACCESS Conference on Computers and Accessibility. ACM (2012)

Developing Accessibility Design Guidelines for Wearables: Accessibility Standards for Multimodal Wearable Devices

Jobke Wentzel[1]([⊠]), Eric Velleman[2], and Thea van der Geest[1]

[1] Department of Media, Communication and Organisation, University of Twente, Enschede, The Netherlands
{m.j.wentzel,t.m.vandergeest}@utwente.nl
[2] The Accessibility Foundation, Utrecht, The Netherlands
e.velleman@accessibility.nl

Abstract. Smart wearable devices are integrated our everyday lives. Such wearable technology is worn on or near the body, while leaving both hands free. This enables users to receive and send information in a non-obtrusive way. Because of the ability to continuously assist and support activities, wearables could be of great value to persons with a disability. Persons with a disability can only benefit from the potential of wearables if they are accessible. Like other devices, platforms, and applications, developers of wearables need to take accessibility into account during early development, for example by including multimodal interfaces in the design. Even though some accessibility guidelines and standards exist for websites and mobile phones, more support for the development of accessible wearables is needed. The aim of our project is to develop a set of guidelines for accessible wearables. Three approaches are combined to develop the guidelines. A scan of the literature was done to identify publications addressing the accessibility of wearables and/or development guidelines. Semi-structured interviews were held with developers of accessible wearable technology. Based on these first activities, a draft set of guidelines is created. This draft is evaluated with developers and researchers in the field of universal design, accessibility, and wearables. Further, the draft is evaluated with visually impaired people (VIP) in interviews. Based on these results, a final set of guidelines will be created. This set is evaluated against an actual project in which apps are developed for VIP. This study is in progress; first results are presented (literature study, semi-structured interviews, first draft of guidelines) and a call for participation in the Delphi study is issued.

Keywords: Accessibility · Wearables · Guidelines · Universal design · Multimodal interfaces · Visually impaired people

1 Accessibility of Wearable Devices

Information, services, and communication are increasingly offered via high-tech ICT application and devices. This development potentially gives visual impaired people (VIP) and persons with other disabilities better and easier access to the information and services. Wearable devices enable users to collect, process, and transfer data without intensive

M. Antona and C. Stephanidis (Eds.): UAHCI 2016, Part I, LNCS 9737, pp. 109–119, 2016.
DOI: 10.1007/978-3-319-40250-5_11

interactions with the device. Wearable devices are worn on, near, or in the body, leaving the hands free. These devices can in some cases be operated by touch, but often performing a certain gesture or giving voice commands are also available as interaction mechanisms. Because many wearables have a multimodal interface, hands-free operating system, and mobile character, wearable devices can be especially useful for persons with a disability. In fact, various assistive devices and applications exist, aimed at VIP [1]. The existing applications support tasks such as navigation, wayfinding, text to speech conversion, and object recognition. To use such devices or applications, users need to hold their assistive device or smartphone, which usually makes them quite obtrusive in daily life activities. In addition, the number of separate devices needed to tackle the different tasks one faces throughout the day can be too much to carry around (e.g. a screen reader, a smart cane, a GPS navigation device, and a magnifier). Wearables are in principle able to take on many of the assisting roles these devices and apps have. The advantage of wearables are that they can offer such support unobtrusively and hands-free.

The potential benefits of wearables can only be realized when the devices, applications, and content are designed to be accessible. A visual display that offers no audio or tactile alternatives, cannot be used by blind persons. Input and output modalities should be multimodal to ensure that users do not have to rely on an interaction modality that is inaccessible to them. To be able to fully participate in society, professionally or personally, persons with a disability should have access to information and communication technology. Not having access to ICT may lead to exclusion and a higher dependence on others or public support [2, 3]. As wearables are increasingly integrated into people's daily life, the digital divide can increase when these wearable technologies are not accessible to everyone. Conversely, accessible wearables open up information support and assistance to persons with a disability and can stimulate empowerment and participation [4]. Given the rise of wearable availability and use by the general public, this is the time to think about design for all and accessibility of wearables.

2   Design Standards for Accessible Wearables

Accessibility should be warranted on different levels: the device or delivery platform (e.g., smartphone, wearable device, desktop computer), the operating system (e.g., windows, Android, iOS), and the content and function (e.g., a navigation support app). Many wearables rely on and synchronize with smartphones. Therefore, the actual accessibility of wearables stretches beyond the wearable device and its application; any necessary supporting devices and applications need to be accessible as well. The accessibility of wearable devices depends on issues resolved in all of these areas. There are guidelines, documents, and support tools for web accessibility, or multimodal interfaces [5]. Legislation that aims to protect persons with a disability from exclusion or discrimination, both online and in the physical world [2, 6] powers the discussion on digital accessibility and the creation of guidelines. Best known are initiatives of the World Wide Web consortium (W3C), which focus on establishing and communicating standards for web accessibility [7]. According to W3C, accessible design has content that is: "(1) Perceivable: Information and user interface components must be presentable to users in ways they can perceive, (2) Operable: User interface components and navigation must be operable, (3) Understandable: Information and the operation of user interface must be understandable, (4) Robust: Content must be robust enough that it can be interpreted reliably by a wide variety of user agents, including assistive technologies" [8]. These generic principles are applicable to new technologies and devices as well. With mobile devices, such as smartphones and wearables, information is at the tip of our fingers wherever we go. To ensure persons with a disability can benefit from these mobile and wearable technologies, they should be accessible. Most smartphones offer disability modes or features and developers can access tools and guidelines to support them to include accessibility features in their products. Certain accessibility features are supported in some wearables, like Google Talkback and VoiceOver in MyGlass app for Google Glass, or Voice Over and Font adjustment in Apple Watch [9–11]. A bridge between web accessibility and accessibility of other devices and applications is acknowledged and supported in WCAG2ICT [12]. This initiative provides guidance to develop non-web documents and software, based on web accessibility guidelines. Specific guidance for the area of wearables is not covered in this initiative however.

Accessibility is best paid attention to throughout the development process, starting in early development phases. Hard numbers on cost effectiveness lack, but various publications indicate that adjusting an already existing design to make it accessible (retrofitting) is more costly than creating accessible sites from the start [13–15]. Furthermore, accessible websites are usable bu larger audience, and can be easier to maintain. Therefore, it is advisable to pay attention to accessibility throughout the development process, starting in early development phases, to create a robust, good technology, without costly redesigns later on [15]. Applying universal design to web design, as well as wearable design can provide an approach to take into account accessibility during early development phases. It can be difficult, stigmatizing, or costly to adapt existing designs to make them accessible. Universal design aims to support individuals by requiring a minimal amount of adaptation, while supporting inclusion of the broadest range of people in daily activities [16]. Seven universal design principles are formulated which provide a starting point or guidance to develop accessible designs. The seven principles are summed up below:

1. Equitable Use: The design is useful and marketable to people with diverse abilities
2. Flexibility in Use: The design accommodates a wide range of individual preferences and abilities
3. Simple and Intuitive Use: Use of the design is easy to understand, regardless of the user's experience, knowledge, language skills, or current concentration level
4. Perceptible Information: The design communicates necessary information effectively to the user, regardless of ambient conditions or the user's sensory abilities.
5. Tolerance for Error: The design minimizes hazards and the adverse consequences of accidental or unintended actions.
6. Low Physical Effort: The design can be used efficiently and comfortably and with a minimum of fatigue.
7. Size and Space for Approach and Use: Appropriate size and space is provided for approach, reach, manipulation, and use regardless of user's body size, posture, or mobility [17].

To provide guidance in creating accessible wearable technology, Tomberg and colleagues discuss universal design principles in the context of wearables [4]. They offer concrete examples of universal design principles applied to wearables, such as multimodal interfaces (vibration or even smell) to communicate perceptible information. In addition, they stress that universal design is a process as well as an outcome that should be applied already in early design phases [4].

Our current project aims to develop and validate accessibility standards for a new generation of smart, wearable ICT devices. We involve developers, designers and technology users with a disability (VIP), to ensure the views and needs of these stakeholders are reflected in the guidelines.

3   User-Validated Accessibility Standards for Wearables

Our project aims to develop and validate a set of guidelines containing accessibility standards for wearables. With the standards we aim out to guide developers beyond web or mobile accessibility. The accessibility standards will focus on wearable technology, with special attention to the multimodal interfaces needed to accomplish accessibility. Multiple stakeholders will be consulted throughout the project, to foster applicability and relevance on various levels. We take a three-track approach to create a set of draft guidelines; a *literature* scan, semi-structured interviews with *developers* regarding their experiences in developing/researching wearables or accessible technology in practice, and *VIP* involvement via interviews. This draft is evaluated and refined in a Delphi study with developers, and in interviews with VIP. In addition, to ensure real-world validity and applicability of the guidelines, a concurrent development cycle is followed and evaluated. In this parallel project, apps for smart glasses are developed for VIP. The results of this development process is evaluated against the newly created guidelines, to assess real-world validity. The research methods are described more precisely below. This study is currently in progress. The first two phases of this study are being finalized; the literature review and expert consultations. Preliminary findings, as well as a preview on future research activities, are described below.

4   Development Process

4.1   Literature Review

Guidelines and publications addressing wearable technology, accessibility and/or multimodal interfaces are collected and analyzed. Documents containing standards, guidelines, or some form of 'lessons learned' concerning accessibility of wearable technology and/or multimodal interfaces are identified by searching Google Scholar, and databases of ISO, BSI, and NEN. Furthermore, key publications' reference lists are scanned for relevant publications. Publications that do not specifically mention wearable technology, but are relevant because of overlap are included. For example, some web accessibility guidelines apply (partially) to wearables too, as do lessons learned from a participatory development process with VIP. Such publications are considered for review.

For every publication, the type of publication is identified (empirical study or standard/guideline). Further, the domain (wearables; website; specific device; multimodal interfaces in general; and focus on participatory or human centered design, no specific domain) and level of instructions/advice (process or technical instructions). The key message and/or lessons are noted down.

4.2 Semi-structured Interviews with Developers

Exploratory semi-structured interviews with developers of wearable/mobile technology are held to further refine the body of readily available guidelines and standards. In addition, reasons for (non) use of such guidelines are explored. Interview questions include:

1. Describe your experience in inclusive design/designing for persons with a disability/ accessibility and/or multimodal interfaces?
   (a) More specifically, describe the project goal and output, timeframe, followed approach.
2. Were end-users involved in the project(s) you described? How?
3. Do you have experience designing for wearable technology?
   (a) How do you think this differs from mobile or non-wearable technology?
4. Which supporting documents/standards/guidelines did you use?
5. What guidelines/standards for accessibility are you aware of?
   (a) Have you used them?
   (b) What are the reasons you use these documents?
6. Do you use any of these [show list] standards or guidelines? If so, which and why?
7. What do you think is missing in the guidelines/standards that are currently available?
   (a) What do you need?
8. How do you keep up to date regarding accessibility developments?
   (a) And regarding wearables?
9. Do you have other comments or suggestions?

Experts who have previously worked on projects developing or designing wearable or mobile technology for persons with a disability or practice universal design were invited to take part in the interviews. In addition, developers or researchers who have experience with multimodal interfaces are invited to participate as well, even if they have no direct experience with wearables or universal design. Respondents are recruited via the authors' networks and via snowball sampling.

4.3 Delphi Study

Based on the literature review and semi-structured interviews, a medium-fidelity draft for the accessibility guidelines will be created. This draft will then be refined via a Delphi study [18]. In this study, developers will be invited to comment on and refine the draft, based on their own views or experiences. Participants who participated in the semi-structured interviews are invited for the Delphi, as well as newly recruited developers and researchers. In three rounds, participants are asked via email to communicate their suggestions about the draft and propose amendments. The Delphi study is will take place between April and September 2016.

4.4   VIP (User) Interviews

Interviews with VIP will be held to establish what they feel should be reflected in the guidelines. Based on the review of available standards and the expert consultations, rough drafts will be created and discussed with VIP. VIP participants are selected for their self-reported type of impairment (congenially or later acquired) blindness, peripheral view, reduced visual field, reduced acuity. The respondents will be recruited mainly via the researchers' network. The interviews will be conducted face to face or via telephone or skype.

4.5   Check Against VIP Smart Glass App Development Project

The final set of guidelines will be checked against a concurrent app development project. In this project, two applications that assist VIP with certain daily life activities will be developed for smart glasses. One of the applications targets emotion recognition, the other application supports navigation/wayfinding. These applications will be evaluated regarding accessibility. Also, the apps and their development process will be checked against the then finished set of guidelines for accessible wearable technology. This way, we will evaluate the guidelines against a real-world project.

5   Results

5.1   Existing Guidelines

Various guidelines and publications holding advice on development of wearables or multimodal interfaces for VIP were identified. A selection of the findings is discussed below.

Several publications that address the development of multimodal interfaces are identified [19–25].

Guidance for developing mobile apps is provided in one publication [26]. It specifically focuses on inclusion in public life by developing applications that assist persons with a disability. Advice on wearable development is provided in several publications [4, 27–32]. Some of these describe the development of applications for persons with an impairment. In one publication, the potential of wearable technology to offer monitoring and an easy means of communication is explored. In this case, research shows that wearables could be used to support persons with a mild cognitive impairment's to participate and become professionally active [30]. A study focusing on VIP shows how co-creation can be applied to develop and test prototypes, for example for to support landmark identification in navigation tasks [31]. It is important to involve end-users (in this case VIP), to ensure that the technology fits their specific needs and situation. In addition, special attention should be paid to the avoidance of 'masking'; blocking the senses (for example with earplugs) [30].

Guidelines that provide very detailed technical advice and instructions regarding (web) accessibility include WCAG 2.0, as well as guidelines focusing on interface design [8, 33, 34]. The gap between web accessibility and the Internet of Things is bridged by initiatives such as WCAG2ICT [12]. It provides guidance for developers non-web documents and software, based on WCAG. Furthermore, the ATAG tool offers developers a means to check and test their designs for accessibility [35]. Ergonomics of human-system interaction are addressed in publications as well, for example [36, 37].

As the identified publications are very heterogeneous, we will evaluate them against quality criteria for guidelines or heuristics [38]. Based on this evaluation (work in progress), relevant heuristics will be included in the draft set of guidelines that will be evaluated in the Delphi study.

5.2 Guideline Use in Practice

So far, various experts (researchers and developers) were consulted regarding their experience with (guidelines for) accessible multimodal interfaces and wearable technology. We interviewed four males and three females, who have the following professions: researcher in the field of haptic wearables, researcher in the field of haptic and tactile feedback, developer, accessibility consultant, researcher and lecturer in the field of human-computer interaction and technological innovation. The respondents had experience with accessibility, designing for persons with a disability, multimodal interfaces, and/or wearable technology. Some main findings are summed up below.

The projects that the respondents mention include consultancy/giving training about web accessibility. Further, the respondents mentioned projects in which wearables for autistic persons, elderly persons with mild dementia, and deaf-blind persons were created. One of te mentioned projects focused on tactile displays for specific tasks/ settings. End-users were not involved in all the projects mentioned by the respondents. Especially in web accessibility consultancy, testing accessibility with end users seemed not to be standard. Most respondents do stress the importance of involving the end-user group and continuously learning from them, however difficult communication sometimes may be (e.g., deaf-blind persons, autistic persons).

Respondents point out that, for as far as they have any experience with wearables, the ergonomics or human factors associated with developing wearables are what make them different from other (e.g., website or mobile) development projects. Issues with comfort need to be resolved. In addition, when there is no display or only limited visual output, the search for alternative ways to convey complex information can be challenging.

The respondents mention having used some guidelines, mostly originating from internal or self-created handbooks. Most respondents are familiar with web accessibility guidelines. Reasons for not using guidelines are the level of specificity; they are either too specific and not relevant for a particular project, or too generic to be of real use. Also, having sufficient expertise is mentioned as a reason not to use guidelines. However, sometimes, guidelines or publications are helpful. For example, when working with very specific target groups (e.g., persons with autism), guidance and examples of how to setup and perform user studies is insightful. Often mentioned strategies of staying informed are colleagues, social and professional media, and conferences.

5.3   Work in Progress

Currently, the literature review is being finalized. In addition, additional semi-structured developer interviews are held. The preliminary results have been analyzed and translated into a draft set of guidelines. Below we describe this draft, and future research activities.

Draft Set of Guidelines. Based on the literature review and interviews, preliminary principles for the development of accessible wearable technology were synthesized and a draft set of guidelines is formulated.

A key necessity for accessibility to a broad audience is the multimodality of the system. Different modalities of interaction with the system should be available and equivalent to each other. Therefore, two principles from the ETSI guideline [20] are mentioned first:

1. Use multimodal presentation of information to allow users with different preferences and abilities to use information in their preferred way.
2. Use multimodal interaction to allow users to interact with a system following their individual preferences and suited to their personal needs.

In addition, the system should provide adequate feedback to its users. What is adequate depends on the need for reassurance, confirmation, or feedback on the one hand, and sensory or cognitive overload on the other hand. A third principle has been formulated:

3. The system or application should provide relevant feedback on the user behavior and the system actions. This can consist of positive confirmation and reinforcement of actions, and/or status or process updates, or notification and instructions on unexpected or incorrect behavior or actions.

Users can have different preferences across different settings. Therefore, the system's settings should be adaptive and/or adaptable. The following principle is formulated:

4. Adaptation of preferred settings (e.g., for input/output modalities, feedback intensity) should be contextual; based on localization, task, and/or user preferences. The system should be self-learning to enable optimal automated adaptive settings.

Wearable technology which is worn on the body, asks for some special attention with regards to ergonomics or human factors engineering. In fact, developers need to ensure that the device can be worn without discomfort and optimally blends into and supports the work or life-processes of the person using it. To voice this concern, the following principles were formulated:

5. The design of the wearable device should take human factors into account, to ensure the device can be used with ease and without discomfort, and without blocking the

users' senses. Special attention should be paid to the range of mobility/movements the person has, and the senses available to the person with a disability.

6. The decision on platform and device should be based on a careful analysis of the user needs and platform/device options regarding accessibility and multimodality.

In the Delphi study, these principles will be further refined and complemented. Developers and researchers in the field of wearables and universal design are invited to share their experiences and thoughts on the draft. In addition, interviews with VIP will be done to learn their take on accessible wearables and values that should be included in the guidelines. The final set of principles (guidelines), is evaluated against actual accessibility development projects.

6   Discussion

The preliminary results of the interviews with developers and reviewers show that there is a need for some form of guidance for developing accessible wearables. The aim of the discussed projects' scopes and aims differ, but even generic guidelines are not used often. This finding is in line with other studies, indicating that even when guidelines for accessibility are known, they may not always be used [39]. As argued, universal design forms a good starting point for formulating guidelines for accessible wearables [4]. The literature and interviews further stress the importance of a human centered - and participatory development approach [31, 40].

The draft guidelines will be refined based on the ongoing analyses of literature and expert interviews. We invite researchers and developers who wish to participate in this project's next research stage, a Delphi study to further finalize the guidelines, to contact us.

Acknowledgements. We thank the researchers and developers who were interviewed thus far for participating in this study. This study is executed within a project (Google Glass For VIP), funded as a Tech4People 2015 grant by the faculty BMS of the University of Twente.

References

1. AppAdvice: Apps For Blind And Visually Impaired. http://appadvice.com/applists/show/apps-for-the-visually-impaired
2. Peters, C., Bradbard, D.A.: Web accessibility: an introduction and ethical implications. J. Inf. Commun. Ethics Soc. **8**, 206–232 (2010)
3. Watling, S.: Digital exclusion: coming out from behind closed doors. Disabil. Soc. **26**, 491–495 (2011)
4. Tomberg, V., Schulz, T., Kelle, S.: Applying universal design principles to themes for wearables. In: Antona, M., Stephanidis, C. (eds.) UAHCI 2015. LNCS, vol. 9176, pp. 550–560. Springer, Heidelberg (2015)
5. Brunet, P., Feigenbaum, B.A., Harris, K., Laws, C., Schwerdtfeger, R., Weiss, L.: Accessibility requirements for systems design to accommodate users with vision impairments (2005). doi:10.1147/sj.443.0445

6. Bickenbach, J.E.: Monitoring the United Nation's convention on the rights of persons with disabilities: data and the international classification of functioning, disability and health. BMC Public Health **11**(Suppl 4), S8 (2011)
7. Berners-Lee, T.: Web Accessibility Initiative (WAI) (2014). https://www.w3.org/WAI/. W3C
8. Caldwell, B., Cooper, M., Reid, L.G., Vanderheiden, G.: Web Content Accessibility Guidelines (WCAG) 2.0 (2008). https://www.w3.org/TR/WCAG20/. W3C
9. Apple: Apple watch accessibility. http://www.apple.com/accessibility/watch/
10. Android: Android Accessibility. http://developer.android.com/training/accessibility/accessible-app.html
11. Google: My Glass Accessibility. https://support.google.com/glass/answer/6057431?hl=en
12. Korn, P., Martínez Normand, L., Pluke, M., Snow-Weaver, A., Vanderheiden, G.: Guidance on Applying WCAG 2.0 to Non-Web Information and Communications Technologies (WCAG2ICT) (2013). https://www.w3.org/TR/wcag2ict/. W3C
13. Sherman, P.: Cost-Justifying Accessibility (2001). https://www.ischool.utexas.edu/~l385t21/AU_WP_Cost_Justifying_Accessibility.pdf. Austin Usability
14. Velleman, E., Van der Geest, T.: Business Case Study Costs and Benefits of Implementation of Dutch Webrichtlijnen. University of Twente, Enschede (2011)
15. Van Der Geest, T., Velleman, E., Houtepen, M.: Cost-Benefit Analysis of Implementing Web Standards in Private Organizations. University of Twente, Enschede (2011)
16. Story, M.F.: Maximizing usability: the principles of universal design. Assist. Technol. **10**, 4–12 (1998)
17. The Center for Universal Design: The Principles of Universal Design, Version 2.0. NC: North Carolina State University (1997)
18. Okoli, C., Pawlowski, S.D.: The delphi method as a research tool: an example, design considerations and applications. Inf. Manag. **42**, 15–29 (2004)
19. Furner, S., Schneider-Hufschmidt, M., Groh, L., Perrin, P., Hine, N.: Human factors guidelines for multimodal interaction, communication and navigation. In: Proceedings of the 19th International Symposium on Human Factors in Telecommunication, Berlin, Germany, 1–4 December 2003 (2003)
20. ETSI EG. 202 191: "Human Factors (HF)." Multimodal interaction, communication and navigation guidelines. ETSI (2003)
21. Baggia, P., Burnett, D.C., Carter, J., Dahl, A.D., McCobb, G., Raggett, D.: EMMA: Extensible MultiModal Annotation markup language (2009). http://www.w3.org/TR/emma/. W3C
22. Bodell, M., Dahl, D., Kliche, I., Larson, J., Porter, B., Raggett, D., Raman, T., Rodriguez, B., Selvaraj, M., Tumuluri, R., Wahbe, A.: Multimodal architecture and interfaces. W3C proposed recommendation (2012). http://www.w3.org/TR/2011/PR-mmi-arch-20120814. W3C
23. Jaimes, A., Sebe, N.: Multimodal human-computer interaction: a survey. Comput. Vis. Image Underst. **108**, 116–134 (2007)
24. Van Hees, K., Engelen, J.: Equivalent representations of multimodal user interfaces: runtime reification of abstract user interface descriptions. Univers. Access Inf. Soc. **12**, 339–368 (2013)
25. Sarter, N.B.: Multimodal information presentation: design guidance and research challenges. Int. J. Ind. Ergon. **36**, 439–445 (2006)
26. Jellinek, D., Abrahams, P.: Moving together: Mobile apps for inclusion and assistance. OneVoice for Accessible ICT (2012)

27. Weller, M.: 10 Top Wearable Technology Design Principles (2014). http://www.designprinciplesftw.com/collections/10-top-wearable-technology-design-principles

28. Motti, V.G., Caine, K.: Human factors considerations in the design of wearable devices. In: Proceedings of the Human Factors and Ergonomics Society Annual Meeting, vol. 58(1), pp. 1820–1824. SAGE Publications (2014)

29. Lyons, K., Profita, H.: The multiple dispositions of on-body and wearable devices. IEEE Pervasive Comput. **13**, 24–31 (2014)

30. Dibia, V., Trewin, S., Ashoori, M., Erickson, T.: Exploring the potential of wearables to support employment for people with mild cognitive impairment. In: Proceedings of the 17th International ACM SIGACCESS Conference on Computers & Accessibility, pp. 401–402 (2015)

31. Ugulino, W.C., Fuks, H.: Prototyping wearables for supporting cognitive mapping by the blind. In: Proceedings of 2015 Workshop on Wearable Systems and Applications - WearSys 2015, pp. 39–44 (2015)

32. Gandy, M., Ross, D., Starner, T.E.: Universal design: lessons for wearable computing. IEEE Pervasive Comput. **2**, 19–23 (2003)

33. Ergonomics of human-system interaction — Part 171: Guidance on software accessibility. ISO (2008)

34. Miñón, R., Moreno, L., Martínez, P., Abascal, J.: An approach to the integration of accessibility requirements into a user interface development method. Sci. Comput. Program. **86**, 58–73 (2014)

35. Richards, J., Spellman, J., Treviranus, J.: Authoring Tool Accessibility Guidelines 2.0 (ATAG) (2015). https://www.w3.org/TR/ATAG20/. W3C

36. Maguire, M.: Methods to support human-centred design. Int. J. Hum Comput Stud. **55**, 587–634 (2001)

37. Ergonomics of human-system interaction - Part 210: Human-centred design for interactive systems. ISO (2010)

38. de Jong, M., van der Geest, T.: Characterizing web heuristics. Tech. Commun. **47**, 311–326 (2000)

39. Lopes, R., Van Isacker, K., Carriço, L.: Redefining assumptions: accessibility and its stakeholders. In: Miesenberger, K., Klaus, J., Zagler, W., Karshmer, A. (eds.) ICCHP 2010, Part 1. LNCS, vol. 6179, pp. 561–568. Springer, Heidelberg (2010)

40. Williams, M.A., Buehler, E., Hurst, A., Kane, S.K.: What not to wearable: using participatory workshops to explore wearable device form factors for blind users. In: Proceedings of 12th Web All Conference - W4A 2015, pp. 1–4 (2015)

A Test Procedure for Checking the WCAG 2.0 Guidelines

Kathrin Wille[1], Cornelius Wille[2(✉)], and Reiner Dumke[3]

[1] Hessian Ministry for Social Affairs and Integration, Wiesbaden, Germany
kathrin.wille@wcag2.de
[2] University of Applied Sciences Bingen, Bingen, Germany
wille@fh-bingen.de
[3] Otto-von-Guericke-University of Magdeburg, Magdeburg, Germany
dumke@ivs.cs.uni-magdeburg.de

Abstract. The Internet is an indispensable part of our everyday life today. Worldwide the number of Internet users from 1997–2014 has increased from 121 million to 2.9 billion - that represents an increase from 2 percent to 40 percent of the world's population [1]. Despite this growth there are barriers to Internet use. This is especially true for people with disabilities. To minimize this, the Web Content Accessibility Guidelines (WCAG) 2.0 specifies guidelines on how a web page can be created to optimize accessibility. In this paper a web-based test procedure as prototype is going to be presented. The accompanying prototype supports the test of all success criteria. The paper is based on an empirical study and evaluation of existing automatic test tools, which are used for the test procedure. As a result, the tester obtains a numerical value about the degree of accessibility. That's a statement of how well the web page meets the success criteria.

Keywords: Accessibility · Test procedure · Test tool · Web page · Web content · Web Content Accessibility Guidelines 2.0 · WCAG 2.0 · Disabilities · Web-based test tool

1 Introduction

The Internet has become commonplace for a significant proportion of the world's population (40 %) [1], for communication, information searches or the purchase of goods, among many other uses. This mobile period ensures that more and more people have access to the Internet on mobile devices. According to Global Web Index [2] 80 % of adult Internet users in the world have a smartphone and almost 50 % a tablet. The increasing development of wearables supports this trend.

Also more and more senior people have discovered the World Wide Web (WWW) as an information and communication medium with many new possibilities. Unfortunately, not everyone has been able to benefit. People with physical or mental disabilities often come up against barriers that make it more difficult or impossible to use the WWW. One example being insufficient contrast between font color and background color or too small font sizes. There is, therefore, a necessity to make web

M. Antona and C. Stephanidis (Eds.): UAHCI 2016, Part I, LNCS 9737, pp. 120–131, 2016.
DOI: 10.1007/978-3-319-40250-5_12

pages more accessible. Also people without physical or mental disabilities benefit from better web page accessibility.

In the international standard Web Content Accessibility Guidelines (WCAG) 2.0 the guidelines for the implementation of accessible web pages are defined and regulated [3]. Single automated test tools partly exist to test these guidelines, such as for checking color contrast, alternative texts or similar. However, for some automated testing is not technically possible, such as to check whether the header structure has been set up correctly and logically or meaningful alternative texts were used for graphics (success criterion 1.3).

The aim of this study is to develop a web-based test-procedure as a prototype, which the WCAG 2.0 guidelines supports. As a result, the tester obtains a statement whether, and to what degree, the guidelines of accessibility are fulfilled on the web page. In the first step, the test procedure is limited only on web pages that are accessible on a desktop PC. In the future, it should be possible to check the accessibility for invoke web pages on mobile devices (smartphones and tablets).

2   Legal Agreements and Standards

"The World Wide Web Consortium (W3C) is an international community where Member organizations, a full-time staff, and the public work together to develop Web standards" [19]. The W3C has published more than 80 standards [6] respectively recommendations, such as HTML, CSS, XML and also the WCAG. This recommendations explain in detail how web pages can accessibly be developed, so that people with disabilities can use the web pages without barriers. It was implemented at the national level in many countries around the world. The Web Accessibility Initiative (WAI) is a working group of the W3C, which deals with the accessibility of web pages, and was significantly involved in the development of WCAG.

Before the structure of the WCAG is described in detail, it is first necessary to define accessibility. The WAI define accessibility as follows: "Web accessibility means that people with disabilities can use the Web. More specifically, Web accessibility means that people with disabilities can perceive, understand, navigate, and interact with the Web, and that they can contribute to the Web. Web accessibility also benefits others, including older people with changing abilities due to aging" [12].

The authors of this article provide a more comprehensive definition of accessibility. The definition of the WAI includes only a certain group of people. The goal of accessibility it is not to offer web pages accessible only for people with disabilities, but also to allow any person to use a web page without barriers. There should be, therefore, an expanded definition of accessibility based on our paper:

"A web page is accessible if the following applies:

1. There is one access for all people to the content and functionality of this web page.
2. This access is equally well available to all people" [9].

This definition brings out the aim of accessibility clearly, because accessibility does not require special solutions for disabled people.

The latest version of WCAG was published in 2008 in the version 2.0 [3]. It was comprehensively revised compared to WCAG 1.0. The differences can be found under [7]. However, the guidelines and success criteria were written in a technology-neutral form and do not contain instructions or programming examples. These are found only in the non-normative documents "Techniques for WCAG 2.0" [5] and "Understanding WCAG 2.0" [4]. So the WCAG is open to new future technologies [8].

The WCAG consists of four principles (perceivable, operable, understandable, robust). These are further subdivided into 12 guidelines that describe the goal accurately. Each guideline contains testable success criteria, which are each associated with a levels of conformance: A (lowest), AA, and AAA (highest). Altogether there are 61 success criteria. In Fig. 1 an overview of the structure of the WCAG 2.0 is shown.

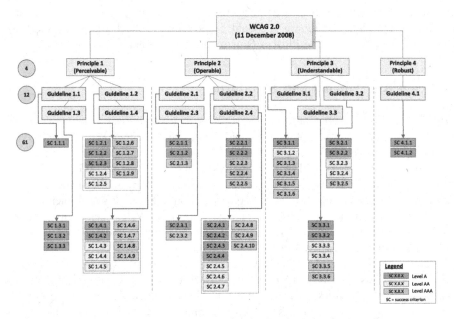

Fig. 1. Overview of the structure of WCAG 2.0 (Color figure online)

3 Test Procedure vs. Test Tools and Automatically vs. Manually Testing

3.1 Test Procedure vs. Test Tools

First we are going to explain, in general, the difference between the terms test procedure and test tools.

Test Procedure. In a test procedure to verify the accessibility of web pages in individual test steps about all success criteria of WCAG 2.0. The test of individual success criteria is carried out either automatically or manually. As a result, it is possible to make a statement about how well accessibility by WCAG 2.0 has been met (degree of accessibility or a statement of levels of conformance). An example of such a test procedure is the "BITV-Test" [14]. Although this procedure is testing the German accessibility guidelines (BITV), these are based on the international WCAG 2.0.

Test Tool. In a test tool, one or more success criteria will test automatically or semi-automatically. Here there are different classifications in terms of platform [15]:

1. **Online Service:** "They work by having the site visitor input the URL of their web page, selecting from any evaluation options, and then selecting a "Go" button or some other method of initializing the program" [15].
2. **Within a browser:** Browser extensions, they provide extra menu options within the browser itself (e.g. as a toolbar).
3. **Within an authoring tool:** These tools have been created to function as part of a web authoring tool, such as Macromedia Dreamweaver or in content management systems. The user can examine their content in the same environment they are using to create this content.
4. **Install on hard drive:** The tools required can be installed on your hard drive. They are able to examine web pages locally.

Examples are extensive tools such as the European project "EIII- European Internet Inclusion Initiative" [13] or WAVE [16], as well as smaller tools such as ContrastFinder [22].

3.2 Automatically vs. Manually Test

For checking the accessibility according to WCAG 2.0, there are already many automated test tools. However, for the web-based test procedure presented here it is not intended that the test of the success criteria is exclusively automated. The reason for this is; when testing accessibility the human inspection plays a major role because not all success criteria are automatically tested. The following example demonstrates this.

```
<img  src = "image/university_logo.jpg"alt = "Logo  of  the
university of Magdeburg"/>
```

The alt attribute (alternate text) is described the pasted image. This is especially important for people who use a screen reader usually blind people. The screen reader reads the content of the alt attribute, so the user knows what is to be seen in the picture. Although an automatic test tool can verify the existence of an alt attribute within an img element, it cannot verify whether the description in the alt attribute fits to the displayed image (success criterion 1.1.1). This can currently only be checked manually [11].

For this reason, the checking of a web page for accessibility must be made in two stages. Firstly, automatic or semi-automatic test tools are used, further an (extra) manual check is carried out on other success criteria by the tester.

4   Empirical Study of Existing Test Tools

4.1   Classification of Automatic Test Tools

For the developed web-based test procedure existing automated test tools for checking individual success criteria of WCAG 2.0 shall be used. An empirical study has been used to evaluate which tools are appropriate. First, a classification of test tools was carried out. Figure 2 shows a subdivision of automatic test tools in three classes [12].

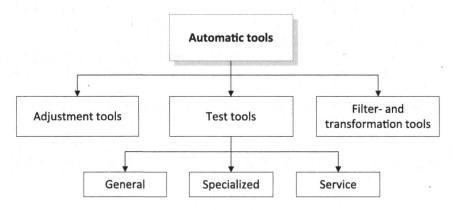

Fig. 2. Overview of various types of automated tools

- **Adjustment tools:** With the help of adjustment tools automatic corrections can be carried out. If an automatic correction is not possible, these tools help the user step by step to carry out any necessary corrections. An example of such an adjustment tool is Tidy. Tidy validated firstly the (X)HTML source code and then shows necessary corrections.
- **Filter- and transformation tools**: With these tools, the page viewed is changed or added directly in the browser. For example, color simulations can be carried out which make it possible to look at a page as they would appear to a person with a certain color vision anomaly. Often these tools are integrated as a browser plug-in .
- **Test tools**:
  - **General test-tools**: The aim of these programs is to find many different barriers. However, the barriers found are often the same, since only a part of the guidelines are automatically tested. One example of this would be the EIII project [13]. With the help of a tabular overview the success criteria that were not met have been explained.
  - **Specialized test-tools**: For these programs only one or a small number of barriers is checked. Frequently, these test tools are better implemented, as is the case with the general test tools, because they are usually very complex. For example, the test tool "Colorblind Web Page Filter" allows to see how an existing web pages appear to colorblind users [26].

– **Service tools**: So far there are very few services. An example of such a service would be the AccMonitor (no longer available) of a given website. This tool constantly monitors and alerts the user with updates regarding barriers, for example via email.

4.2   Evaluation Criteria for the Evaluation of Test Tools

In order to evaluate which of the automated tools is suitable for testing of the success criteria according to WCAG 2.0, the following evaluation criteria were established.

- **For WCAG 2.0 relevant?:** The test tool must check at least one success criterion in WCAG 2.0. There are many old tools that examine, for example, only the guidelines according to WCAG 1.0 and would therefore not be suitable.
- **Freely available?:** Checking accessibility with a tool should be possible for each user. Financial barriers for automatic test tools should be avoided for this reason. Therefore, all commercial tools are ruled out. Only freely available and open source tools should be used.
- **Suitable for web pages?:** Only web pages on personal computers will be monitored and evaluated (see Introduction). Only tools for this purpose come into consideration. Tools that only check other techniques cannot be considered, such as accessible PDF documents.
- **Which platform (online/plugin/Web Editor/HDD):** Sect. 3.1 (Test procedure vs. test tools) explains the different classifications regarding the platform. Additionally it was determined that under the classification "disk" only tools which can be installed on Windows 7 or higher shall be used. In the classification "plugin" only tools which are run in the browsers Mozilla Firefox, Google Chrome or Microsoft Internet Explorer come into consideration.
- **Easy installation:** Here the criteria is whether the installation and also the
- general handling of the tool is possible without problems. Possibly, individual decisions must be made.
- **Language:** The tool must support, at least, the English or German language. This is because the test procedure will initially be used in German-speaking countries.

   If all quoted evaluation criteria are met, the evaluated test tools are approved for the developed test procedure.

4.3   List of Evaluated Test Tools

In the course of an empirical study the test tools were specified and checked according to the evaluation criteria in Sect. 4.2 (Evaluation criteria for the evaluation of test tools). A basis of the examined test tools is provided in the list of the W3C [10] with a total of 38 tools. The licensing of the tools extends to "Commercial", "Enterprise", "Free Software", "Open Source" and "Trail or demo". Because of the determined evaluation criteria only "free software" or "open source" tools are considered for this investigation. Generally, these tools can automatically test one or multiple success criteria of WCAG 2.0. Also, additional tools that were eligible for evaluation were researched through

Table 1. List of evaluated test tools

Name	For WCAG 2.0 relevant?	Freely available?	Suitable for web pages?	Platform	Easy installation?	Language	Is used?
A-Checker [20]	y	y[a]	y	On	y	ger, en, it	y
AccessColor [21]	n	y	y	On	y	en	n
Contrast-Finder [22]	y	y[b]	y	On	y	en, fr	y
Web Accessibility Toolbar [23]	y	y	y	BP	y	en, ger,	y
EIII – Page Checker [24]	y	y	y	On	y	en	y
Tanaguru [25]	y	y	y	On	y	en, fr, es	n[c]

[a]FS,
[b]OS
[c]Important explanations only in french.
Legend: y, yes; n, no; FS, Free Software; OS, Open Source; On, Online; WE, web editor; HD, hard drive; ger, german; en, english; it, italian; fr, french.

internet search engines. A total of approximately 100 test tools were evaluated. The presentation of the complete list of all examined testing tools cannot be shown here for reasons of space. Therefore in Table 1, only an excerpt of the results is presented.

5   Specification and Functionality of the Test Procedure

5.1   Specification and Validation Model

Specification. First, the functional, qualitative, platform-related and process-related requirements were specified in the test procedure. The test procedure differentiates between the two user groups "authenticated" and "non-authenticated user". An authenticated user had significantly more functionalities as compared to a non-authenticated. It can create and select new projects, evaluate and store success criteria, view an evaluation and change and store their personal information. The term "project" refers to the examined web page being checked using the test procedure in compliance with the success criteria. Figure 3 gives a summary overview of the functionalities for an authenticated user. Initially a non-authenticated user must register to use the test procedure.

Validation Model. The fulfillment of success criteria can either be measured by a test tool or (if no tool is available /possible) assessment by the tester. Finally the tester indicates for each of the 61 success criterion if it is "fulfilled", "not fulfilled" or "not applicable". The quality and reliability of the obtained results depends to a large extent

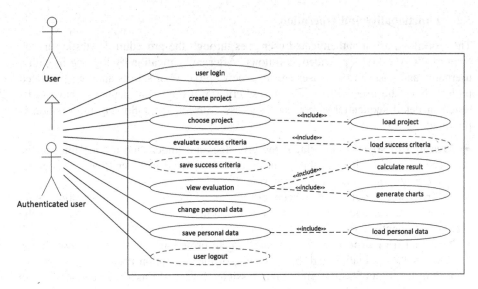

Fig. 3. Use case diagram for an authenticated user

on the test tool and the assessment by the tester. Now, this validation provides the basis for the establishment of a numerical value, the degree of accessibility. Of course, the calculation of such a value will certainly lead to discussion, because the validity of such a value does not tell much about how accessible a web page really is. However, this value should only be used as an additional indicator to assess whether the efforts to implement an accessible web page are on the right track.

A weighting of the success criteria (Level A is more important than Level AAA) will not be considered for the model, because all success criteria are equally important. Therefore, the degree of accessibility is calculated as follows:

$$\text{Degree of accessibility} = \frac{(\text{count fsc} + \text{count nasc}) * 100}{61 \text{ sc}} \quad (1)$$

sc = success criteria
fsc = fulfilled success criteria
nasc = not applicable success criteria

The result calculated will be a value between 1 and 100. A 100 percent accessibility is not possible, therefore, the following classification (Fig. 4) shows the tester how accessible the tested web page is. This classification is based on the BITV test procedure [17].

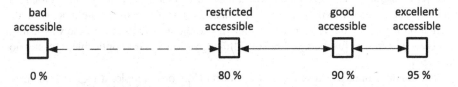

Fig. 4. Classification of the evaluation of the valuation model

5.2   Functionality and Operation

The workflow, as an authenticated user goes through the procedure for testing a web page to WCAG 2.0, is provided as follows. After authentication by logging in with a username and password, the user creates a new "project" or selects an already created project. Now the user will see all success criteria in the main menu that have to be tested in detail sequentially. For each success criterion the following information is provided:

- **Meaning of success criteria:** If the user does not understand the meaning of the success criterion, it is, at this point described in detail in order to avoid incorrect implementation of the success criterion.
- **Information about more references/sources**: If the user wants information about more references and sources, it will be offered here. The web pages of W3C are the most frequently used sources.
- **Test tool and procedure for evaluation**: Information about the test tool that is used for the evaluation and the procedure of the evaluation itself.
- **Examples**: Examples describing the possible situations a user may encounter help in the technical implementation.
- **Evaluate**: If all previously collected information for the tester is clear, he/she can start to evaluate the success criteria using the specified test tools. For this, depending on the success criterion, a number of different questions are available. These questions detect and evaluate all aspects of this criterion. The answers to each question are selected with a drop-down menu (fulfilled, not fulfilled or not applicable) and stored using the "Save" button in the database.

6   Implementation of the Test Procedure

The developed test procedure was implemented as a web-based prototype. A part of the success criteria was selected, to illustrate the test procedure by way of example. The structure of the web page is presented as an overview in Fig. 5.

The three areas header, navigation and content were further specified (1). The navigation is divided into three navigation areas. The first navigation area (2) includes topics on which any user has access, independent of his user group. For example, to get information about the workflow of the test procedure. On the second navigation area (3) there are web forms to authenticate a user. The user can login or register for example. If the authentication is not possible due to incorrect data entry, you will get an error message at this point. If the authentication is successful, then the third navigation area (4) is displayed and for unauthorized users this area is hidden. In this area all the success criteria are listed. Next to each success criterion a traffic light icon in the navigation is visible that is intended to illustrate to the user the status of the verification at a glance (green = fulfilled, red = not fulfilled, yellow = Not applicable, cross = not checked).

The content area can reveal different forms (5), for example, a registration form, contact form or a form to edit the user data. The main function of the test procedure is

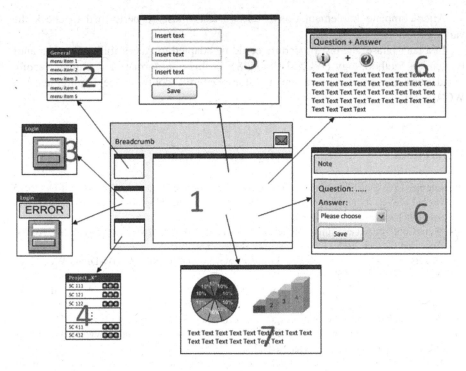

Fig. 5. Design of web-based user interface of the test procedure (Color figure online)

the provision of the questions (6). Each question is answered by means of a drop-down menu. Included are the above mentioned possible answers. Additionally, information is provided for evaluation (see Sect. 5.2 "Functionality and operation"). After pressing the save button, a notice appears about the successful save in the database or an error message. Furthermore, an evaluation of the results (7) is calculated and generated dynamically. This provides information on the achieved level of accessibility.

7   Summary and Outlook

It was developed as a prototype web-based test procedure, which initially checked parts of the success criteria of WCAG 2.0. The human tester is supported by the use of automatic or semi-automatic testing tools. As a result, the degree of accessibility is determined, which gives information about how well the success criteria on the tested website has been respected.

To prepare the prototype for production, further work is needed. First, a full implementation of all the success criteria must be carried out in the test procedure. Moreover, it is desirable that national legislation (for example, the American Secion508 [13] or the German BITV 2.0 [14]) be checked with regard to this test procedure. The national guidelines are similar to the international WCAG to a very large degree.

After complete implementation extensive tests must be performed to check the validity.

In a later phase, the test procedure could be adapted to Accessibility Conformance Evaluation Methodology (WCAG-EM) [18]. In this non-normative document recommendations are given to evaluate a test procedure's conformance requirements of WCAG 2.0.

References

1. Internet Live Stats. http://www.internetlivestats.com/internet-users/. Accessed 08 Oct 2015
2. Global Web Index. http://www.globalwebindex.net/blog/80-of-internet-users-own-a-smartphone. Accessed 08 Oct 2015
3. Web Content Accessibility Guidelines (WCAG) 2.0. http://www.w3.org/TR/WCAG20/. Accessed 09 Oct 2015
4. Understanding WCAG 2.0. http://www.w3.org/TR/UNDERSTANDING-WCAG20/. Accessed 09 Oct 2015
5. Techniques for WCAG 2.0. http://www.w3.org/TR/WCAG20-TECHS/. Accessed 09 Oct 2015
6. W3C Standards. http://www.w3.org/TR/tr-technology-stds. Accessed 09 Oct 2015
7. W3C Standards - How WCAG 2.0 Differs from WCAG 1.0. http://www.w3.org/WAI/WCAG20/from10/diff.php. Accessed 11 Oct 2015
8. Einfach für Alle – Vorsprung durch Techniques: die Umsetzung der WCAG 2.0, https://www.einfach-fuer-alle.de/wcag2.0/. Accessed 11 Oct 2015
9. Meurer, A.: Barrierefreiheit im WWW – Ein Mehrwert für alle?- Design und Implementierung einer barrierefreien Website für das Recherchesystem Infoconnex, Universität Koblenz Landau, Fachbereich Informatik, Institut für Computervisualistik, Diplomarbeit (2003). https://userpages.uni-koblenz.de/~litdb/dasa/thesis/getthesis/93. Accessed 5 Apr 2007
10. W3C – Web Accessibility Evaluation Tools List. http://www.w3.org/WAI/ER/tools/. Accessed 11 Oct 2015
11. Malack, K.: Diplomarbeit Konzeption und prototypische Implementation eines webbasierten Tools zur Selbstevaluierung barrierefreier Webseiten nach WCAG 2.0 (2007)
12. W3C Introduction to Web Accessibility. https://www.w3.org/WAI/intro/accessibility.php. Accessed 23 Jan 2015
13. EIII. http://eiii.eu/. Accessed 24 Jan 2015
14. BITV-Test. http://www.bitvtest.eu/bitv_test.html. Accessed 30 Jan 2016
15. Classifications of Accessibility Evaluation Tools. http://webaim.org/articles/tools/. Accessed 30 Jan 2016
16. Web accessibility evaluation tool (WAVE). http://wave.webaim.org/. Accessed 31 Jan 2016
17. BIK BITV-Test – Beschreibung des Prüfverfahrens. http://www.bitvtest.de/bitvtest/das_testverfahren_im_detail/verfahren.html#c88. Accessed 31 Jan 2016
18. Website Accessibility Conformance Evaluation Methodology (WCAG-EM) 1.0. https://www.w3.org/TR/2014/NOTE-WCAG-EM-20140710/. Accessed 24 Jan 2015
19. About W3C. https://www.w3.org/Consortium/. Accessed 30 Jan 2016
20. Web Accessibility Checker. http://achecker.ca/checker/index.php. Accessed 28 Jan 2016
21. AccessKeys Tools. http://www.accesskeys.org/tools/color-contrast.html. Accessed 28 Jan 2016

22. Tanaguru Contrast-Finder. http://contrast-finder.tanaguru.com/. Accessed 31 Jan 2016
23. Web Accessibility Toolbar. https://www.paciellogroup.com/resources/wat/. Accessed 15 Jan 2016
24. European Internet Inclusion Initiative. http://checkers.eiii.eu/en/pagecheck/
25. Tanaguru. http://www.tanaguru.com/. Accessed 27 Jan 2016
26. Colorblind Web Page Filter. http://colorfilter.wickline.org/. Accessed 31 Jan 2016

Design for All and eInclusion
Best Practices

Is Universal Accessibility on Track?

Julio Abascal[1]([✉]), Luis Azevedo[2], and Albert Cook[3]

[1] Egokituz Laboratory of HCI for Special Needs, University of the Basque Country/Euskal Herriko Unibertsitatea, Donostia, Spain
julio.abascal@ehu.eus
[2] Anditec, Lisbon, Portugal
luis.azevedo@anditec.pt
[3] Faculty of Rehabilitation Medicine, University of Alberta, Edmonton, Canada
ac4@ualberta.ca

Abstract. Even if the evolution of accessibility engineering is generally considered as impressive, one can question whether it is producing the expected result or not. A deeper analysis can discover that theoretical improvements and practical demonstrators coming from research are not producing proportionate enhancements in the lives of users with disabilities. Starting from an analysis of the role of the research, development, and manufacturing, this paper develops a critical review of the current situation regarding the application of science and engineering to the accessibility field, in order to find the cause of possible weak points, failures and misapplications.

Keywords: Universal accessibility management · Social impact

1 Introduction

Universal Accessibility has experienced significant advancement in the last decades due to diverse efforts. A major factor in this advancement has been the application of science and engineering methods and techniques to enhance accessibility. These include pre-market accessibility features included with virtually all mobile and fixed Information and Communications Technologies (ICTs). These features aid those with motor difficulties (e.g., finger dexterity), sensory loss (e.g., low vision or blindness) and cognitive disabilities (e.g., difficulty understanding the operation of features) to access these technologies more easily.

It is evident that in the last decades, Universal Accessibility has very much advanced and the quantity and quality of Assistive Technology products available to people with disabilities has enormously risen. Nevertheless, analyzing the current situation of the Universal Accessibility and the Assistive Technologies available in (some) markets worldwide one can question if there is a balance between the technological, economic effort and the results available. In addition, if this is true, what are the causes and how can it be corrected.

© Springer International Publishing Switzerland 2016
M. Antona and C. Stephanidis (Eds.): UAHCI 2016, Part I, LNCS 9737, pp. 135–143, 2016.
DOI: 10.1007/978-3-319-40250-5_13

2   Manufacturing Accessibility

Assistive technologies and universal design differ in their focus [1]. Assistive technologies are developed and applied to maximize societal participation by individuals with disabilities in carrying out the functional tasks of daily living. Universal design has a focus on the functionality of design for as wide a segment of the population as possible without concern for individual needs [2]. However, many of the accessibility features built into mainstream ICT devices had their origin in assistive technologies. These include: SMS transmission (texting), Closed Captioning, Voice Recognition, On-screen Keyboards, Speech Synthesis, Word Prediction and Digitized Speech. Thus, the assistive technology design parameters, which are more directly related to the needs of individuals who have disabilities should be incorporated into the design of accessible mainstream products as much as possible.

For electronic assistive technologies (e.g., augmentative communication, computer access, appliance control, sensory aids and cognitive assistive technologies) inclusion of the principles of universal design together with the incorporation of accessibility features in mainstream products has made opened new opportunities for people with disabilities [1]. However, universal design does not completely eliminate the need for assistive technologies because the variety and complexity of individual needs are too great for inclusion in a single product [3]. For these assistive technology application areas, two complimentary approaches-universal design and specialized assistive technologies (AT) will be required [3]. Both approaches will require the use of mainstream technologies since low cost AT will depend on the use of mainstream products that have useful AT application features. Mainstream products are likely to be more accessible to people with disabilities even if they are not specifically designed with those individuals in mind, i.e. using universal design principles [3].

ICT devices like smart phones and tablets have the capability of running AT applications previously requiring laptop or desktop computers [4]. Among the thousands of apps developed for these devices, many are directly related to addressing needs of people with disabilities. Many more can be of benefit to people with disabilities even though they were developed for the general population. There is also recognition that ICTs can be a critical enabler to developing countries that are moving toward the information-based society. They can also provide access to society (work, communication, leisure) for persons with disabilities.

A major approach for creating access to mainstream technologies by people with disabilities is the development of specialized application program (apps). These are designed to make a mainstream device (e.g. tablet) operate like a special designed assistive device. A common example is their use for augmentative communication. Many applications function like a full-featured speech-generating device (SGD). The cost of the mainstream technology and app is less that 10 % of a purpose-built SGD. The availability of these mainstream technologies and apps result in increasingly inexpensive hardware and software, availability of alternative access methods and the opportunity to use standard software applications in the same device (e.g., email, internet browsing, word processing) [5, 6]. To use these devices, however, the individual with a disability must be able to access the smart phone or tablet both physically and visually. This is where universal design comes in. The most effective app is useless unless the individual has access to the technology on which it runs.

Mobile technologies utilize an array of highly coordinated fine-motor movements for access (e.g., pinching, swiping left to right, touching) that require significant motor, cognitive, and sensory-perceptual skills, [6]. There is a set of individuals for whom an app and mainstream technology is well suited, but there are many who will not be able to access these options. The number of AT applications is growing rapidly, and there are many for people with disabilities.

Dolic et al. [7] compared the technical characteristics and capabilities of purpose-built SGDs to mainstream tablet devices. A major difference between most SGDs and mainstream technologies is providing access to multiple communication functions and electronic tools (e.g., accelerometers, GPS tracking, cameras) that could enhance access and functionality. Mainstream mobile technologies are frequently smaller and lighter than purpose-built SGDs. Mainstream tablet devices can be as much as 15 times less expensive than purpose-built SGDs, making them more accessible to users in countries where they are not subsidized by medical or social funding agencies. They also include a wide variety range of mainstream smartphone applications such as texting, browsing the internet and GPS navigation [6].

Another aspect is the social impact of special purpose assistive technology. For a child or adolescent using a purpose-built SGD carries a stigma that sends a message about being different and calling attention to his disability. An iPad with and SGD app sends a message that says "I'm cool" and I have the latest technology [6, 8].

Because purpose-built SGDs are often based on custom computer systems and software, the capability of the device cannot be expanded by installing additional applications made by the broader community making them less generally useful than a more universal device. These apps are available with mainstream mobile technologies. Part of the cost difference between purpose-built AT and mainstream technologies with AT apps is the support that AT manufacturers supply [9]. They repair devices that fail to operate properly, often providing service loaners while a device is being repaired. They also assist clients during the assessment process by demonstrating equipment and assisting with obtaining funding for the SGD or other AT. The cost for the additional services that provide obvious benefits to clients is included in the price of the product, making traditional SGD and other AT devices significantly more expensive than comparable mainstream devices. However, the lack of support can be a major detriment, however, for those individuals who purchase a mainstream device and Augmentative and an Alternative Communication (AAC) app and then realize that there is little or no support for their use [10]. "Some service providers for people with disabilities have also been reluctant in exploiting the full potential of "mobile technology aps", as their role and incentives is based on having clients come to them for evaluation and fitting of special assistive technologies." [3, p. 108].

Mainstream smartphone and tablet devices use operating systems developed and optimized for mobile devices where as many purpose-built devices use customized PC operating systems. Mobile operating systems like iOS and Android are optimized for touch screen interfaces and for consuming low power. In contrast to purpose-built SGDs mainstream mobile devices lack alternative input capabilities using switches, head control or eye pointing. Bluetooth-enabled switch interfaces can compensate for this in part [1].

3 Novelty of the Research and Development of Technology Applied to the Universal Accessibility

A large research activity in accessibility can currently be observed. The number of scientific conferences and journals that directly or indirectly cover topics such as design for all, universal design, accessibility and assistive technology has substantiality increased. Our starting point is whether the advancements in practical terms are proportional to the effort devoted to research. Novelty of the results is a key parameter to analyze the evolution of the research in universal accessibility.

The question is: is innovation scarce in accessibility research and development? Speaking about the current situation of HCI research, Kostakos [11] wrote "We simply roll from topic to topic, year after year, without developing any of them substantially", synthesizing the impression shared by several researchers that HCI current paradigms have reached a blockade. The application of HCI techniques to the development of accessible human-machine interfaces is a factor in this blockage. Several researchers have the feeling that the tendency is to "play variations on a theme". Technological advancements frequently allow a number of enhancements in terms of efficiency and reliability, associated with better development, but not the real novelty that can be expected from research. In fact, a superficial analysis of the abstracts of papers published in scientific journals and conferences show some recurrence in a number of topics that already have a consolidated theoretical support. In many cases, small technological contributions to previous findings are found in these papers.

It is remarkable that a large number of technological advancements have occurred without considering accessibility issues. Subsequently, they have required extensive efforts to make them more accessible (when it was possible). For instance, two relatively recent technological advancements have greatly affected the way of life of people with disabilities: the internet/Web and mobile telecommunications. Both of these were initially barely accessible for several people with special needs. Even if currently they represent an open window to social participation for people with disabilities, they have required, and still require, large efforts to enhance their accessibility.

4 Economic Aspects

One of the main reasons for the gap between technological developments and market products can be found in the difficulty of the path from science results and marketable products.

In fact, the economics of universal design have multiple factors. On the one hand modifying a product after production to meet the needs of a person with a disability is expensive and this cost can be avoided by designing in the necessary accessibility features. These universal design features may cost more than a design without them.

Thus, there is a level of skepticism in industry due to the increased emphasis on economic sustainability and profit worldwide [3]. Because of limited profits and very competitive markets companies tend to adopt the concept that "people with limitations should be a duty of the welfare system in the different countries and should not be an obstacle to the main aim of industry, i.e., to the generation of profit" [3]. There are some technologies, such as telecommunications equipment where companies may have a governmental mandate to make the products accessible to a wide range of users "without much diffi-culty or expense." The last part of that quotation gives companies great latitude. To accomplish this goal companies look at the costs and the resources available to address accessibility [12]. Large companies with more resources will be expected to do more than small companies with limited budgets, for large mainstream companies "being forced (e.g., by legislation) to take into account all users is considered by them an undue interference in their goal (serving the mainstream customer and maximizing profits.)" [3].

Time and cost to develop a product can be affected by inclusion of universal design. Bjork [13] evaluated the design of two supportive seating products. One using universal design and the other a modular system that could be adjusted to fit a variety of users. The development of the universally designed system took four times as long as the design and development of the modular system.

4.1 Marketability of the Research Results

Back to the difficulty of converting the results of research into a marketable product, some experts consider that basic science does not need to produce practical results. However, there is some consensus that applied research's results are nearer to the product. We must not forget that research on universal accessibility and assistive tech-nology is clearly located in the area of applied research.

Researchers often complain that their achievements are not welcome by the industry. Research proposals frequently claim that they would end "with a significant contribution to the welfare of people with disabilities…" and similar statements. However, projects too frequently finish with an interesting prototype that is hardly marketable. The reason may be that many projects developed in academia often ignore the requirements that convert a good prototype into a commercial product (that include redesign, manufac-turing, testing, standards compliance certification, drafting manuals, marketing, distri-bution, maintenance, recycling program, etc.).

In general, scientists do not question, "Is there a market for this product?" Therefore, failure to be marketable can be related to the requirements stated by Clarkson [14]: Products must be Functional, Usable, Desirable and Viable (the last in the business/market sense).

Therefore, one of the causes for low marketability can be found in the roots of the research. Several research projects are triggered by the availability of a new techno-logical advancement, that "supposedly can support" the user needs. The problem is that their validity has not been checked by means of rigorous users' needs studies. As a result, these projects frequently produce fancy technology that can hardly be adopted by the users. In addition, good research practices do not mean good product design.

According to Clarkson [14], to manage development risk, the key questions are: "Are you building the right products (or services)" and "Are you building the product right?".

On the other hand, projects developed by academic research institutions have access to recent, expensive and complex technology that facilitates the proliferation of technology availability-driven projects. In addition to produce expensive prototype devices (that are frequently difficult to be understood, learned and used), the use of sophisticated technology makes more complex the process to convert scientific results into marketable products.

5   Political and Social Aspects

Accessibility is far from being "universal", principally due to economical differences [15–17]. Universal accessibility (and Design for all) refers to the quality of being accessible by any individual. Nevertheless, statistical studies show that "universally accessible technology" is out of the reach of the most part of the human population in the world. The most important reason is economical: people with disabilities cannot afford buying accessible equipment, because it is expensive.

The resolution 58th "Disability, including prevention, management and rehabilitation" adopted by the World Health Assembly in 2005 states that 80 % of people with disabilities live in low-income countries and that poverty limits access to basic health services, including rehabilitation services [18]. Citing an study by Frye (1993), Arne et al. [19] state that "rehabilitative services in the developing world reach only 1–2 % of the disabled population", in addition, "Much of the AT in use in these countries are either technically outdated and not adapted to local circumstances or imported sophisticated technology beyond common people's reach".

In the developed world, Assistive Technologies are available to meet the needs of people with disabilities. However, because these devices are very expensive, much of the world cannot acquire AT. Because it is less expensive utilization of mainstream technologies with apps that function like AT devices, as we have described above, is needed to meet the needs of people with disabilities in lower income countries.

Mainstream technology is globally pervasive and its capability is constantly increasing. However, much of this technology is not accessible to individuals with disabilities. Advances in technologies that are not accessible to those with disabilities can increase the gap in available resources for work, school and community living between people who have disabilities and those who do not. As advances occur more quickly, the gap widens faster and the people who are poor and/or disabled lose out even more completely and quickly. This is a characteristic of cultural and societal "progress" over centuries–technology drives change, and creates both positive and negative outcomes in the process [20].

Due primarily to cost and availability of suppliers, much of the world has not had access to assistive technologies. There are many types of assistive technologies, primarily those based on computer technology, that have not been available to much of the world's population. Computer-based AT includes computer access, environmental control, cognitive assistive technologies, and augmentative communication.

Achieving widespread global availability of assistive technology applications at an affordable local price will have to be based on mainstream devices [3]. The largest area of growth internationally is mobile broadband internet access [21]. "Wireless-broadband access, including prepaid mobile broadband, is mushrooming in developing countries and internet users are shifting more and more from fixed to wireless connections and devices" (p. 1). This is good news for the global application of assistive technologies based on smart phones and tablets. However, the cost of these technologies is still too high in many developing countries, and there is a need to develop more affordable devices [4].

The International Telecommunication Union (ITU) the United Nations specialized agency for information and communication technologies provides an annual overview of the world's use of ICTs [21]. The ITU has developed the ICT Development Index (IDI) that compiles 11 indicators of development in communication and technology within a country, divided into access (40 %), use (40 %, percentage of use of internet, broadband and fixed or wired ICT) and skills (20 %, based on literacy and enrollment in secondary and post-secondary education). The IDI allows a more detailed look at ICT development than measures based strictly on number of cellphones or computers.

All of the sub-indices for developing countries increased between 2008 and 2011. The ITU (2013) report presents the IDI score and rank for 152 countries broken into four levels based on IDI levels. The two top levels of ICT use, penetration and skills based on the IDI have 26 % of the world's population and the lower two levels have 74 %. There is still a long way to go before the "digital divide" is narrowed substantially.

6 Weak Points and Misapplications

Regarding the difficulty that techno-science has to produce practical results in the area of accessibility, a number of issues that should be avoided and aspects that should be enhanced can be pointed out:

- Lack of knowledge on user needs. Design flaws or weaknesses relative to accessibility can occur when telecommunication product manufacturers do not focus on needs and preferences of users who have disabilities.
- Use of sophisticated technology makes the products and services more expensive, complex and frequently more difficult to use.
- Ethnocentrically designed devices and services are not able to solve specific accessibility problems in different economic and cultural contexts.
- Policies oriented to support technological research have difficulties to promote the arrival of resulting prototypes to the market.
- Low awareness by scientist of key issues at product conception time, such as the need for efficient provision and delivery systems (prescription, adaptation, tutoring, maintaining, etc.).

In order to enhance the situation, global policies are required that consider the whole population needing accessibility support and the complete lifecycle of the product, in order to produce durable enhancements in the accessibility field.

7 Conclusion

This paper starts from the idea that the technical, economic and personal effort devoted to the development of technical aids and universal accessibility does not seem to have produced proportional results in the availability of advanced support systems for people with disabilities. However, it is currently difficult to find accurate data to support this assertion. Therefore, a detailed taxonomy of the technological applications for accessibility would help to understand the current situation. In addition, we consider necessary to conduct diachronic studies on the evolution of the application of science and engineering to improve accessibility deem. Their results, along with existing synchronic studies of the current state of technology support in the various regions of the world, would allow rigorous re-planning of the techno-scientific efforts.

References

1. Cook, A.M., Polgar, J.M.: Assistive Technologies: Principles and Practice, 4th edn. Elsevier/Mosby, St. Louis (2015)
2. Sanford, J.A.: Universal Design as a Rehabilitation Strategy. Springer, New York (2012)
3. Emiliani, P., Stephanidis, C., Vanderheiden, G.: Technology and inclusion - past, present and foreseeable future. Technol. Disabil. 23(3), 101–114 (2011)
4. International Telecommunication Union. Percentage of Individuals using the Internet report. Per country report and comparative data over the past 10 years. In: Measuring the Information Society. International Telecommunication Union. Geneva (2011). www.itu.int/net/pressoffice/backgrounders/general/pdf/5.pdf
5. Higginbotham, J., Jacobs, S.: The future of the Android Operating System for augmentative and alternative communication. Perspect. Augmentative Altern. Commun. 20(2), 52–56 (2011)
6. McNaughton, D., Light, J.: The iPad and mobile technology revolution: benefits and challenges for individuals who require augmentative and alternative communication. Augmentative Altern. Commun. 29(2), 107–116 (2013)
7. Dolic, J., Pibernik, J., Bota, J.: Evaluation of mainstream tablet devices for symbol based AAC communication. In: Jezic, G., Kusek, M., Nguyen, N.-T., Howlett, R.J., Jain, L.C. (eds.) KES-AMSTA 2012. LNCS, vol. 7327, pp. 251–260. Springer, Heidelberg (2012)
8. Alliano, A., Herriger, K., Koutsoftas, A.D., Bartolotta, T.E.: A review of 21 iPad applications for augmentative and alternative communication purposes. Perspect. Augmentative Altern. Commun. 21(2), 60–71 (2012)
9. Hershberger, D.: Mobile technology and AAC Apps from an AAC developer's perspective. Perspect. Augmentative Altern. Commun. 20(1), 28–33 (2011)
10. Niemeijer, D., Donnellan, A., Robledo, J.: Taking the pulse of augmentative and alternative communication on iOS. Assistiveware, Amsterdam (2012). http://download.assistiveware.com/assistiveware/files/Taking the Pulse of AAC on iOS White Paper.pdf
11. Kostakos, V.: The big hole in HCI research. Interactions 22(2), 48–51 (2015)
12. Schaefer, R., Eikerling, H.J.: Increasing the acceptance of ambient intelligence. In: International Conference on Information & Communication Technologies (ICTTA 2004), Damascus (2006)
13. Björk, E.: Why did it take four times longer to create the Universal Design solution? Technol. Disabil. 21(4), 159–170 (2009)

14. Clarkson, J.: Designing a more inclusive world. In: 2007 Inaugural Conference: Universal Design for the 21st Century: Irish & International Perspectives. Centre for Excellence in Universal Design. http://universaldesign.ie/What-is-Universal-Design/Conference-Proceedings/Universal-Design-for-the-21st-Century-Irish-International-Perspectives/Designing-a-more-Inclusive-World

15. Abascal, J., Barbosa, S.D.J., Nicolle, C., Zaphiris, P.: Rethinking universal accessibility: a broader approach considering the digital gap. Univ. Access Inf. Soc., 1–4 (2015). http://link.springer.com/article/10.1007/s10209-015-0416-1/fulltext.html

16. Warschauer, M., Ahumada Newhart, V.: Broadening our concepts of universal access. Univ. Access Inf. Soc., 1–6 (2015). http://link.springer.com/content/pdf/10.1007%2Fs10209-015-0417-0.pdf

17. Barlott, T., Adams, K., Cook, A.: Increasing participation in the information society by people with disabilities and their families in lower-income countries using mainstream technologies. Univ. Access Inf. Soc., 1–10 (2015). http://link.springer.com/content/pdf/10.1007%2Fs10209-015-0418-z.pdf

18. WHO: Disability, Including Prevention, Management and Rehabilitation. In: 58th World Health Assembly, 97–100. World Health Organization, Geneva (2005). apps.who.int/gb/ebwha/pdf_files/WHA58-REC1/english/A58_2005_REC1-en.pdf

19. Arne, H., Eide, A.H., Øderud, T.: Assistive technology in low-income countries. In: MacLachlan, M., Swartz, L. (eds.) Disability & International Development. Towards Inclusive Global Health, pp. 149–160. Springer, Berlin (2009)

20. Wright, R.: A Short History of Progress. Anansi Press, Toronto (2004)

21. International Telecommunication Union: Measuring the information Society, Geneva, Switzerland. International Telecommunication Union (2013). http://www.itu.int/en/ITU-D/Statistics/Documents/publications/mis2013/MIS2013_without_Annex_4.pdf

Technology for Inclusion and Participation – Technology Based Accessibility (TBA)

Christian Bühler[✉]

TU-Dortmund University/FTB, Dortmund, Germany
`Christian.Buehler@tu-dortmund.de`

Abstract. The UN Convention on the rights of persons with disabilities (UNCRPD) [1] puts a focus on accessibility and technology. Both are considered as a precondition and means to support full participation of people. Today, new technologies provide new options for the support of all people including people with disabilities. The concepts assistive technology and accessibility begin to merge into "Technology Based Accessibility (TBA)". TBA has the potential to make a significant change in the lives of people with disabilities.

Keywords: Technology · Accessibility · Ambient intelligence · Universal design

1 Introduction

The UN Convention on the rights of persons with disabilities (UNCRPD) [1] requests the use of technology as a basic precondition for the full and equal participation and inclusion of people with disabilities. Accessibility is one of the general principles of the convention [1, Art. 3f] and is outlined in article 9. Universal Design is defined in article 2 and is referred to in the general obligations [1, Art. 4f]. Different technologies are mentioned in several articles and the provision of technology at affordable cost is requested. All the available options need to be made available complementing each other [1, Art. 4g, h].

New combinations and implementations of technology based support for all people including people with disabilities open up through new technologies, mobile devices, and the options of a connected environment with ambient intelligence. There is no longer a clear distinction between individual assistive technology and accessible infrastructures: accessibility becomes a result of general installations in the environment, mainstream mobile devices, and cloud based services – "Technology Based Accessibility (TBA)". This TBA approach has the potential to make a significant change in the lives of people with disabilities and for many of us. This paper describes the technology baseline and gives examples for options of TBA.

2 Traditional Approach

People with disabilities are supported by individual assistive technology to provide them with restauration, enhancement, or compensation of functions [2]. This support enables

© Springer International Publishing Switzerland 2016
M. Antona and C. Stephanidis (Eds.): UAHCI 2016, Part I, LNCS 9737, pp. 144–149, 2016.
DOI: 10.1007/978-3-319-40250-5_14

to carry out activities and reach participation levels [3]. For example, for moving around walking is replaced by driving (in wheelchairs and scooters), for interpersonal communication natural speech is replaced by electronic talkers or gestures (sign language), for using books visual reading by audiobooks, and for orientation visual orientation by tactile white canes, etc. In all those approaches a complementation in the infrastructure is more or less needed to make it work: a wheelchair needs an environment without steps and arrangements for vertical access like ramps and elevators; users of white canes need tactile guidance systems on the floor and acoustic traffic lights; users of audio need content in appropriate audio books; users who talk in sign language need partners able to communicate by signing. If both parts, assistive technology and complementing accessibility, are present the activities can be carried out and participation is possible. In the past many recommendations on how to provide accessibility have been formulated and many standards have been developed [4]. However, what happens in an environment which does not provide the accessibility features? Or if the content of interest is not available in appropriate format, or communication partners do not understand signing? Unfortunately, under such circumstances many people face significant barriers towards their activities, participation, and inclusion. Therefore, traditionally the aim was to create more accessible environments and to cover as much of the infrastructure as possible. In practice this decent approach fails frequently due to various reasons. The persons responsible are often simply not aware of the need and the available options for accessibility. Unfortunately, even new infrastructures are set up inaccessible. Redesign and reconstruction of already existing inaccessible infrastructures is often considered as too expensive or conflicting with other requirements. In many countries legislation on accessibility of the built environment, accessible transportation, and accessible information and communication has given strength to the process. The UNCRPD [1] has led to increased awareness and further activities by the ratifying countries. Nevertheless, accessibility is not always and not everywhere implemented.

3   Technology Basis for the New TBA Approach

The technological basis for the new TBA approach builds mainly upon ubiquitous powerful cloud services, ambient intelligence, and mobile devices as individual user interfaces. Today we can already observe that mobile devices like smart phones, smart watches, and navigation systems etc. are in widespread use and are considered as helpful gadgets by many people (for example, many people still read maps but use car navigation on a daily basis). These kinds of systems provide local computing power, versatile operating options, inbuilt sensors, and connections to external sensors, communication between people, local and global data communication, and connection to powerful external services.

Many mobile devices can be considered as personal and individual interfaces to local functions of the device and functionality in the cloud. Small mobile devices need new paradigms of human machine interfacing. For example speech input, signalling, and sound output may be used with a very small device compared to text input and output which requires a display. Modern smart phones provide many interface options which can be set individually: operation without vision (Voice Over ®, Talkback ®), use of gestures, voice input, vibration, options for colour schemes, font size, placement of functions, use of hardkeys and softkeys, visual or audio signalling, etc. With these interfacing options, the devices have the potential to provide individually adapted interfaces for a great variety of user needs including people with different disabilities.

Most important is, however, the range of functionality which can be used via the adapted personal interface. First, access to information and knowledge in the cloud and also humans is provided (via GSM, LTE, WLAN, and Internet). In case of requests encyclopaedias, data bases, search engines, and special services can be addressed to find the information. Second, interactive services allow for reservations, bookings, purchases, bank transfers, updates, maintenance, etc. The use of local sensors and local communications (WLAN, Bluetooth, RFID, etc.) enable e.g. measurements of body functions, activity levels, and exchange and interaction with local appliances like ATMs, ticketing, buses, and smart environments. Third, global sensors like GPS or similar services permit localisation. The combination of these options and the use of local and global computing power open up the potential of the new approach for technology based accessibility. Preconditions are, however, the availability and affordability of devices and network services. This is very much connected with an economy of scale, which means in turn availability and use of mainstream features.

4   Exemplary Solutions of the New TBA Approach

Accessibility needs can be divided in four main areas with some overlapping user requirements: hearing, vision, movement and understanding. This division follows the abilities of people and the connected required support functions. In comparison the four principles of WCAG 2.0 [5] support the structure of a guideline which tells developers what to do. The WCAG principle "Perceivable" corresponds to Hearing and Vision and the principle "Understandable" to understanding, whereas the principle "Operable" and "Robust" and Movement have no direct correspondence, but relations. As the application domain of accessibility is much broader than e.g. web access [6] or access to digital technology [7], the meaning of the terms is much broader. The movement abilities to operate a device correspond to the principle "Operable" but the movement abilities to move around in a physical setting belong to a different category. It needs to be said that for direct movement restauration assistive technologies like crutches, walkers, wheelchairs, etc. will still be needed.

The mobile device is considered as the individual interface. It can be adapted to the individual user needs, maybe by creation of a user profile, using presents from a selection but also by learning systems and dynamic adaptation. This is closely connected to access to digital technology, the domain of the initiative "Raising the floor" [7] and GPII [8].

For many people understanding how an environment is organised and how it can be used is a significant access problem. Physical and also digital environments but also the communication and interaction with people can be very complicated and an accessibility barrier for many people. Cognitive challenges can arise from a health condition, but are often connected also to the level of education and (digital) literacy or simply situation related e.g. concentration under stress or fatigue.

Mobile devices provide a very good basis for supporting memory function, cognition, and understanding. Calendar, daytime schedules, and timed, situation based, or sensory based reminders help to structure daily routines or guide through unknown situations. Again, mainstream software tends to provide many options and a complexity that is not understood by many people. Therefore, the level of complexity needs to be decreased. The functionality needs to be restricted for simplicity and the presentation to and interaction with the user simplified. Here Easy2Read is an important concept, which needs to be further developed by means for content moderation [9–11].

Another support need arises if people move outside their homes, in public spaces, and public transportation. Unfortunately, not all locations are fitted with traditional accessibility features at all or only certain parts of an environment are accessible. Therefore, the first step is to provide information about the situation in buildings [12], public spaces [13], and public transportation [14]. Further, private companies and crowd sourcing initiatives have proven that it is possible to collect data about environments and provide it via the Internet to the general public. Using this information it is possible to carry out an analysis of an environment prior or during the visit of a certain location. It enables e.g. to plan door to door visits with public transportation using the best accessible travel chain and path depending on individual needs [15]. Other options allow finding e.g. accessible restaurants, restrooms, taxis etc. This kind of service can be helpful to support needs of *understanding, hearing, vision, and mobility*. Further, direct interaction with smart buildings is possible, e.g. operation mode of doors (opening time/closing speed), automatic selection of level according to target, internal routing, etc. In the context of mobility car adaptations and driving support systems make car driving accessible for many people. Navigation, lane assistance, automatic parking, collision avoidance, and fully automated driving are options, which are already available or about to leave the labs [16].

Similar navigation technology can be used for pedestrians, including blind people. Instead of tactile elements in the floor the correct moving direction can be taken from the navigation system and the user be informed via acoustic or tactile means [17]. For people with reduced sight details can be enlarged, textually described, or analysed and outspoken. It can be used to recognise landmarks, identify persons, analyse traffic situations, transfer visual information from screens into text, etc.

This is close to concepts of enhanced reality, where scenes are enriched by elements of information and explanation about the immediate surroundings or other aspects of concern in the vicinity or even far away. Mostly, people think of heads up displays and electronic glasses, but the information can also be transferred e.g. as audio. With respect to complexity the services again need to be adaptable to different user needs.

Today pictures and movies are made accessible people with restricted sight via alternative texts which are provided by the producers or providers of the information. In the new TBA approach audio information about pictures and videos will be automatically provided on demand. As a step towards fully automated systems assistance on demand or peer support via internet and social networks will partly fill the gap. The automatic production of subtitles is already available e.g. with YouTube but needs a lot of quality improvement. The apps Greta & Starks [18] can also be seen as a step towards the new TBA approach; the information for subtitles and audio description are still produced in the traditional way but not provided by the movie theatre but through a smartphone. A further step for information and communication access for people who cannot hear is the automatic conversion from speech and written information into sign language provided by avatars. An intermediate step is the provision of sign language interpretation via relay services. For people who cannot see and hear technologies like the LORM-hand [19] can increase access. It is important to realise that only the fully automated conversion of information formats and modes will be able to reach out to all information, without the need for the information provider to follow any accessibility rules. The underlying vision is that by using computing power in the cloud all information and communication can be adapted to the respective individual user needs of each single user in real time.

It needs to be stated that the new approach does not completely supersede the traditional approach. The different concepts will coexist and probably the new approach will gradually take over particular domains whereas assistive technology and traditional accessibility will be needed in others.

5   Conclusions

Accessibility in combination with assistive technology and universal design builds an important precondition for participation and inclusion. New technology, especially ICT, provides innovative solutions for technology based accessibility (TBA), where the borders between accessibility, universal design, and assistive technology become blurred and floating. Powerful services are at hand to provide individual solutions based on user profiles, automatic adaptations, conversions, and translations. As these kinds of services are of general interest for the customers it is very close to Universal Design: optimal solutions to all users based on the respective individual needs. Big threads in this context are design thinking for heterogeneous needs and the usability of the solutions in terms of complexity. Finally, it will not completely supersede the need for traditional accessibility solutions and assistive technology.

References

1. UN: Convention on the Rights of Persons with Disabilities (2006). http://www.un.org/disabilities/convention/conventionfull.shtml. Accessed 30 Dec 2015
2. DIN: DIN EN ISO 9999:2011–10: Title: Assistive products for persons with disability – Classification and terminology (ISO 9999:2011); Deutsche Fassung EN ISO 9999:2011, Deutsches Institut für Normung, Beuth Verlag (2011). http://din.de. Accessed 30 Dec 2015
3. WHO: ICF – Internationale Klassifikation der Funktionsfähigkeit, Behinderung und Gesundheit. Hrsg. v. Deutschen Institut für Medizinische Dokumentation und Information. DIMDI WHO-Kooperationszentrum für die Familie internationaler Klassifikationen. Köln 2004 (2001)

4. Bühler, C.: Universal design - computer. In: Stone, J., Blouin, M. (Eds.), Center for International Rehabilitation Research Information and Exchange (CIRRIE): International Encyclopedia of Rehabilitation (2010). http://cirrie.buffalo.edu/encyclopedia/en/article/146/. Accessed 30 Dec 2015
5. W3C: Web Content Accessibility Guidelines (2008). http://www.w3.org/TR/WCAG20/. Accessed 30 Dec 2015
6. W3C: Web accessibility Initiative. http://www.w3.org/WAI/. Accessed 30 Dec 2015
7. Raising the floor: RtF – Mission statement. http://raisingthefloor.org/who-we-are/mission-beliefs/. Accessed 30 Dec 2015
8. GPII: Global Public Inclusive Infrastructure. http://gpii.net/index.html. Accessed 30 Dec 2015
9. Nietzio, A., Naber, D., Bühler, C.: Towards techniques for Easy-to-Read web content. In: 5th International Conference on Software Development and Technologies for Enhancing Accessibility and Fighting Info-exclusion, DSAI 2013, Procedia Computer Science, vol. 27, pp. 343–349 (2014)
10. Schaten, M.: Barrierefreiheit 2.0 – Ein neuer Ansatz zur verbesserten Zugänglichkeit zu Web-Inhalten für Menschen mit Lernschwierigkeiten. In: TU Dortmund, Eldorado. https://eldorado.tu-dortmund.de/. Accessed 30 Dec 2015
11. Bühler, C., Pelka, B.: Empowerment by Digital Media of People with Disabilities. In: Miesenberger, K., Fels, D., Archambault, D., Peňáz, P., Zagler, W. (eds.) ICCHP 2014, Part I. LNCS, vol. 8547, pp. 17–24. Springer, Heidelberg (2014)
12. Agentur Barrierefrei NRW: NRW Informierbar. http://informierbar.de/. Accessed 30 Dec 2015
13. Sozialhelden, E.V.: Wheelmap. http://community.wheelmap.org/en/about/. Accessed 30 Dec 2015
14. Bühler, C., Heck, H., Becker, J.: How to inform people with reduced mobility about public transport. In: Miesenberger, K., Klaus, J., Zagler, W.L., Karshmer, A.I. (eds.) ICCHP 2008. LNCS, vol. 5105, pp. 973–980. Springer, Heidelberg (2008)
15. Bühler, C., Heck, H., Nietzio, A., Reins, F.: The mobile travel assistance system NAMO with Way-finding support in public transport environments. In: Miesenberger, K., Fels, D., Archambault, D., Peňáz, P., Zagler, W. (eds.) ICCHP 2014, Part II. LNCS, vol. 8548, pp. 54–57. Springer, Heidelberg (2014)
16. Google: Self Driving Car Project. https://www.google.com/selfdrivingcar/. Accessed 30 Dec 2015
17. Mensch, A.: Inklusion 2025 - Zukunftskongress der Aktion Mensch. https://www.aktion-mensch.de/zukunftskongress/dokumentation/panels/technologische-entwicklungen/inklusion-durch-technik.php. Accessed 30 Dec 2015
18. Starks, G.: Kino einfach erleben. http://www.gretaundstarks.de/. Accessed 30 Dec 2015
19. Universität der Künste Berlin: LORM Hand. In: Design Research Lab, Research and Projects. Accessed 30 Dec 2015

Place Brand-Building. *Urban Empathy* as an Evaluation Method

Agata Bonenberg[✉]

Faculty of Architecture, Poznan University of Technology, Nieszawska 13C,
61-021 Poznan, Poland
agata.bonenberg@put.poznan.pl

Abstract. The image of urban areas created by an appropriate urban branding attracts population, when cities compete for inhabitants and businesses. Experience shows that not only the positive visual and spatial features attract people, but also hard to define "atmosphere", mood, city narrative, related to activities, events and history. Author proposes a new method of urban assessment to define features that are important, but difficult to capture - the method of *urban empathy*. The empathetic perception of urban space is a broad-spectrum experience: it can be lived through learning the city's history, narrative, events in a relation to physical urban space. Emotions mapped on urban plan create the emphatic image of the city.

Keywords: Place brand-building · Urban empathy

1 Introduction

The diagnosis of contemporary spatial phenomena in architecture and urban planning taking under consideration changes in cultural, social and economic impact caused by the development of the information society should form the basis for creating new strategies in urban branding. De-industrialization of cities in developed countries, significant mobility of workers, development of information and communication technologies and creative industries cause changes in settlement preferences. New, image of urban areas created by an appropriate urban branding can attract additional population, when places compete for inhabitants and businesses. In order to do that effectively, it is necessary to understand the potentials of place to be presented to the target groups. Experience shows that not only the positive visual and spatial features attract people, but also hard to define "atmosphere", mood, city narrative, related to activities, events and history. The choice of a place/neighbourhood to live in, is often based on emotions and impressions. Author proposes a new method of urban assessment to define these features that are important, but difficult to capture. The method proposed is urban empathy. The empathetic perception of urban space is a broad-spectrum experience. It can be lived through learning the city's history, myths, legends, social relations in a relation to urban space. Furthermore, the approach takes under consideration the view of specific groups of inhabitants.

In a *place brand-building*, urban empathy can be used to evaluate:

© Springer International Publishing Switzerland 2016
M. Antona and C. Stephanidis (Eds.): UAHCI 2016, Part I, LNCS 9737, pp. 150–160, 2016.
DOI: 10.1007/978-3-319-40250-5_15

- predominating emotions connected to the place: curiosity, awe, boredom, distaste and irritation for place marketing and place promotion
- city narrative: history, legend, combined with particular elements of city structure for urban branding
- events contributing to brand-building
- mapping emotions and presenting them on urban plan
- assessment how to create a powerful city brands.

2   Quality of Urban Structures - Assessment

The beauty of urban structures, which through the centuries was derived from the spatial order and quality of life within it, has been moved into the back row of interests of the town planners and spatial planners. Its place was taken by the values based on predomination of rational functionalism strongly related to technology and economy. Urban tradition of the first Athen's Charter introducing division into functional zones continues to be the basis for shaping modern city structures. City space was assigned with functional and economic values, with no regard to emotional values directly related to a sense of beauty or ugliness of the surrounding area. Contemporary idea of a balanced development refers mainly to the issues of nature, economy and sociology; the problematic issues of beauty are pushed to the back of the hierarchy of strategic objectives.

The reason for this are difficulties in defining and assessing beauty, both at the stage of recognition of determinants of spatial development, as well as in the phase of creating scripts for the development of the city structures. However, diagnoses, which do not encompass all significant needs of the residents (including the inbred need for beauty and harmony), imprint themselves negatively on the quality of urban planning.

It is believed that harmony of urban structures has an impact on social order and lack of appreciation for beauty is one of the reasons of urban disintegration and fading identity of cities. In the Beijing Charter of the XIX Congress of the International Union of Architects - UIA, held in June 1999, among the tasks facing the architects of the XXI century there is a postulate of bringing back the soul of cities and towns which characterized them and invoked awe of its inhabitants and visitors during the past centuries.

In modern urbanization, the development of planning procedures based on functional and technological, social and economic analysis significantly outdistanced methods of diagnosis of compositional quality, order and harmony, which may become an object of admiration. The author believes that the ability to find beauty in an urban space is just as important as knowledge of the state of the environment, its physiographics, methods of land use, access to public transportation etc. Our feelings have an objective quality in forming our relationship with our surroundings. The beauty of a city evokes specific feelings providing a sense of order. The ability to recognize beauty is an art in itself. In this case the author suggests to use the method of empathy based on Husserl's cognitive theory (Husserl 1929). Husserl's idea of "feeling empathy", "looking within"; (introspection) was an object of inspiration for many specializations, which treated empathy as a cognitive action method (empathic awareness).

Irena Wojnar (1976) calls upon Arnheim's opinion, "as perception is based on the interaction between the properties of an object and the nature of the entity of the observer, each act of perception is simultaneously an intellectual action".

Steiner Kvale in his work on the effectiveness of research interviews states that empathy is a very sensitive interpretive method of acquiring information. The author emphasizes that "the use of….interviews for research shows the possibilities of applying empathy and emotional interaction to obtain significant knowledge…" (Kvale 1996).

These methods are effective tools in acquiring research material; however, "the outcome of an interview depends on the knowledge, sensitivity, and empathy of the interviewer." (Kvale 1996).

The objective of this work is to present the possibilities of expanding existing urban diagnostic methods by adding urban empathy as a new research tool. In urban planning, empathic perception is a new approach to diagnostic research. It seems that it corresponds well with modern urban planning challenges but also with the necessity of creating the brand of the city.

3   Urban Empathy as a Study Method, Case Study City of Catania, Italy

In direct ties between a man and a city, urban interiors have basic significance. It is they that decide about perception of beauty of the streets, city squares, and housing blocks – designating contact with space. It is not hard to notice, that these components of municipal fabric play a double role. First of all, they have a specific functional designation: to meet the requirements. Secondly, their appearance evokes defined aesthetic experiences related to the form, composition, colour, etc. We can experience certain emotions while contemplating only a view of a part of the city and independently experience different feelings using its functional attributes. Thus, if we like some element of municipal space because it looks pretty, it is still not known as to whether we will be satisfied with its practical usefulness to meet defined needs.

An example of this study is Catania – a city located in the central part of the east coast of Sicily, at the foot of the Etna volcano. This choice is not incidental. A city of ancient origin in a region marked with social and economic problems yet with innovation and ideas for further development. Catania is full of contrasts and contradictions, and the line between beauty and ugliness, free composition and spatial disorder are particularly fragile. Finding an answer to a question what sort of city Catania is will provide a challenge to test the chosen research method. Contrasts resulting from periods of its development and fall marked by the eruption of the volcano Etna can be read in its urban composition. In the disposition of its inhabitants, one can see the love for temporary and substitutive solutions being in opposition to their unfailing faith in the survival after future attacks of nature's element. Their perception of the city encompass a feeling of admiration for the magnificent historical architecture, wonderful climate, but also aversion and fear ensuing from the high crime rate, lack of social and political order and organization. Currently, Catania is undergoing intensive urbanization. Modern building constructions, however, are quite often technologically and stylistically behind the times. At the same time the city is a buoyant centre of science and industry. Innovative technologies are being implemented in a dynamically developing technology park called "Etna Valley". Thus, the multi-layered, contrasting with one another qualities constitute and ideal base for a study allowing to define and systematize groups of qualities, that make an empathic portrait of the city.

Whilst perception of a city takes place only by means of sights, it has a contemplative characteristic; functional perception is dynamic, imposes action. It places a person under pressure of direct contact with specific people, situations, institutions, events - they provide specific experiences (e.g. looking for a parking space, taking care of a matter in a public office, finding a room at a hotel). Activity of an individual is then directed to a specific need related to part of the city's fabric. Positive or negative experiences are related to this activity, combining into a general experience of beauty of the city. The said activity evoking specific feelings can be called "experiencing" the city. Lipps (1987) says that experience is the basis for knowing, it stimulates the human psyche.

How, through this understanding, can one describe the relation between the view of a place and its designated function? It seems that the best cognitive tool here is the concept of empathy. Empathy, for the purpose of further analysis can be defined as the ability to sympathize, imagining the feelings of other people functioning in the observed by us environment. It means placing oneself in the situation of another individual and becoming aware of not only one's own emotional states relating to, for example, admiring an interesting façade but imagining how the people behind the façade live and what they feel. Urban empathy pertains to both: the current moment and to historical retrospect. It therefore means seeing a romantic, picturesque narrow street through the eyes of its impoverished residents, for whom the said picturesqueness is associated with the lack of resources for the repair of plaster falling off, patching up roofs, or replacing old windows and doors. In such case, one is beginning to perceive the picture of the city through the eyes of "another" human being. The concept of empathy was founded on the basis of Edmund Husserl's philosophy. In his speculations, empathy is subjective; it is a multilayered and complex act. For empathy, it is vital to go beyond the boundaries of one's own feelings. Urban empathy is a mutual dependency between my own perceptions and an experience and the ones of the other people living within the landscape admired by me. It is a very specific type of synthesis of aesthetic experiences and functional/utilitarian qualities of the place.

Urban empathy requires careful observation, perception and knowledge. Eyesight carries information about the external state of the observed surroundings; knowledge enables to identify with the mentality and habits of the inhabitants, their culture, and history.

Urban empathy is a specific type of "listening in" to the city. Into what it communicates to us with its appearance, history, tradition, culture, diversity of functions. It is a mental entrance into the world of the residents with their joys, sadness, aspirations, and problems. It also allows to understand places marked with unusual events. In order to see a city, all you need is eyes. In order to understand a city, empathy is vital.

3.1 Mapping of Dominating Emotions

An important factor of our emotional experiences pertaining to Catania is the feelings of relationship with the city and sensations accompanying it. They ensue not only from social relations but also from our bonds with the city space – houses, sidewalks, walls. Gradually interpersonal elements come into play, a specific form of sympathy and antipathy. Such anthropomorphism of emotional experience, assigning human traits to houses and streets is well known to psychologists. Thus, we have cheerful and joyful streets, serious and laughing facades, sad and gloomy courtyards, and tenement houses evoking pity, pathetic, funny, and anguished houses. Specific emotions ensuing from associating with a city, harmony and disharmony, city myths, fashionable and cult places, style of living related to various parts of the city – those are examples of relationships, in which Catania shapes our emotional approach to its space. In a wider sense, this emotional structure of the city tissue builds a bond between a man and the space. Stanisław Ossowski (2004) points to social reaction determinants towards works of art, evoking their communication function. Through analogy, one can risk a statement that in the urban environment emotional relation towards the space also has a social function. It is based on the emotional "interlacing" of social relations, which impact the valorisation of municipal space. Thus, in Catania it is possible to distinguish places evoking different emotional states: curiosity, awe, boredom, distaste, and irritation.

Curiosity. In the narrow streets of the Consolazione district, one finds a romantic ambiance, a fairytale quality of the remarkable former Catania. Consolazione was built in 1669 by the earthquake survivors, inhabitants of the Catania's city centre - hence its

Fig. 1. Catania, Consolazione road. Traditional tenement houses. Drawn A. Bonenberg

name[1]. Single and two storey tenement houses in colours of golden brown and grey, oleander and bougainvillea flowers decorating the balconies, laundry hung up between the buildings create the special atmosphere enhanced by mystery of dark courtyards. A frequent sights here are street stalls with fresh products such as tomatoes, lemons and figs placed in wooden boxes laid out on the street, men involved in discussions standing in front of house entrances. The black volcanic tuff with which the streets were paved reminds of the many eruptions of Etna. The picturesqueness of cosy urban interiors, neglected buildings, awakens our interest, draws us deep into the shadowed courtyards, mysterious alleys and winding streets (Fig. 1).

Awe. Curiosity gives up to awe as we approach the centre of Catania. Going in the direction of the heart of the city we become engulfed in the world of Sicilian baroque. Piazza San Francesco: volcanic blackness of the sidewalk, light yellow façade of the church, pulsating cornices, decorative balconies, pilaster strips, friezes, and plinths. Grid divisions are enlivened by relieves and bas-relieves. Contrast is the main determinant of composition: the still, massive black plinth of San Francesco d'Assisi church, which is contrasted with the light sandstone shade façade with imaginatively formed partly architectural, partly borrowed from theatrical stage design details. Everything vibrates, creating an illusion of movement. Cornices repeat the façade's hollows. Decorative pillars emphasize the corners. The capitals of pilasters peculiarly bend under the solid cornices. Restless surfaces are torn by weaving lines intertwining with each other. Urban interiors are filled with an atmosphere of loftiness and Baroque temperament. The façades of houses, in certain fragments overly expressive, dazzle the viewer and at the same time surprise with the richness of form, the lack of moderation. Overly excessive ornaments in some places border on kitsch. The unique combination of disharmony, dynamics, and contrast evokes the feeling of awe.

Boredom. Completely different emotions are evoked by the development of the Nesima and Monte Po districts. This development started at the beginning of the 70s of the 20th century according to the design made by Federico Gorio and Marcello Vittorini and is a typical example of great suburban apartment complexes constructed according to the ideals of modernism. It is dominated by boredom and monotony: simple concrete forms of high-rise apartment blocks, horizontal windows, flat roofs, and the balconies in repeatable rhythms. The space between buildings is filled with parked cars. Bored groups of adolescents sit on scratched up benches.

Distaste and Irritation. Moving away from the city centre, we come to the Catanian *urban sprawl*. Boundaries of the city are hard to grasp, housing development spills destroying the beautiful landscape. The feeling of boredom is replaced by distaste brought out by chaos in composition of dynamically developing building sites. New developer-made housing estates are located next to warehouse bases, small factories and shopping centres. It is difficult to notice any pedestrians. Roads leading in the direction

---

[1] Consolazione (it.) - consolation, alleviation of misery or distress; comfort.

of the city are overflowing with thousands of cars. Exhaust fumes and noise fill the picturesque valleys of the Catania's suburbs.

Catania provides us with a wide scope of diversified feelings. It evokes curiosity, awe, boredom, distaste, and irritation. Those feelings are transposed unto the spatial structure of the city creating its unique map of emotions (Fig. 2).

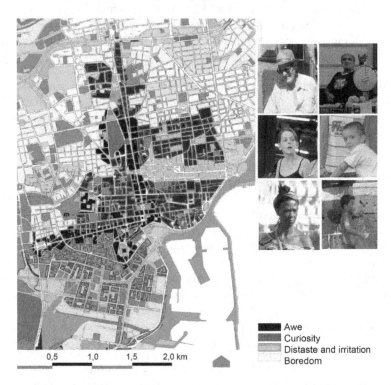

Fig. 2. City of Catania. Mapping emotions in relation to the city structure to support city branding concepts.

3.2 Empathetic Analysis of Beauty

The presented analysis confirmed that urban empathy is an effective study tool of urban structures. It allows to effectively combine aesthetic evaluation relating to the picture of the city and its functional-utility assessment being a decisive factor of comfort and functioning of an urban structure. It enables better understanding of how historical preconditions, tradition and nature shape the face of the city. It makes it possible to prove that beauty of the city structure lies in harmonious integration of views of the city, impressions, values, emotions and symbols, the synthesis of which creates emotional and pragmatic image of the city (Fig. 3).

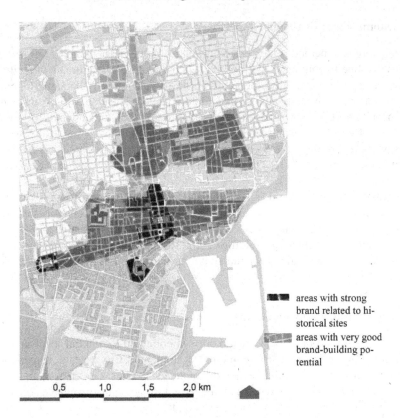

areas with strong
brand related to hi-
storical sites

areas with very good
brand-building po-
tential

0,5   1,0   1,5   2,0 km

Fig. 3. Brand building: City of Catania. Mapping areas with strong brands (based on search-engine popularity rating) with relation to emotional map (Fig. 2.) Areas with strong brand, related to historical sites shown together with areas with good brand building potential (according to author).

Based on this type of comprehension of beauty, its picture becomes more realistic. Captured in such way the city is described in a language of perceptions which with the aid of a set of unique symbols that allow to shape the impression of beauty. The relationship of urban empathy and beauty of the city is based on the fact that thanks to empathy one can read and assess its beauty better. Of course this is not the sole method of perceiving beauty. Urban empathy enriches the existing cognitive methods of the city space, including factors difficult to measure, which have significant impact on urban developments within the space of a city.

3.3   Intersubjectivity of Urban Empathy

Urban empathy enables to recognize subtle dependencies between different interpretations of space. Due to similarities in reactions of different recipients to the defined spatial, social and functional situations, it has interpersonal aspect. Therefore it can constitute a basis for believable urban diagnosis.

3.4   Phenomenology of Urban Empathy

Urban empathy is a method of perception primarily in the phenomenological sense. It stipulates that due to command of emotional states, evoked by the image of a city, its structure and genesis of its development can be recognized. By the same token, its uniqueness can become easily noticed and comprehended. The idea behind this method is a moment of transporting "oneself" into situations of local inhabitants (former and present) and observing their immediate surrounding through their eyes as if travelling together with them through the events which happen to them on a street, a square, in a house. It is the sight of the city "through the eyes" of their feelings, experiences and motivations.

This urban analysis method is conditioned by understanding of emotions of the people who have direct relation with a definite part of a city space. Feelings being a basis of the behaviour, the decisions concerning investments, systems of value and aesthetic sensitivity– all that contributes to building this, and not any other, type of social structure. Such knowledge, when obtained, should constitute significant message for undertaking urban decisions.

3.5   Sense of Municipal Community

Urban empathy on the emotional, historical, symbolic and existential level is a vital element in building a sense of municipal community. City events, experiences, emotions, social stances, cumulative memory of the inhabitants – are an inseparable part of urban science. Perceiving and recognizing them through empathy enables obtaining urban solutions which strengthen group ties and identity.

3.6   Empathy and Urban Context

Urban empathy is especially useful in comprehensive grasp of a context. The key issue here is the history of a place, its identity, ambiguity. In a city space we find various, overlapping levels of experience, which influence emotions and human behaviour. The effect of empathic analysis is, on one hand, discovery of unrecognized contexts, and on the other hand, provision of a critical record of interdependencies which are decisive in the uniqueness of a place.

3.7   Urban Empathy in Spatial Management Plans of Cities

Empathetic analysis is a reliable foundation for making decisions defining the scope of interference in the existing tissue of the city. Prior to undertaking project decisions a planner should ask himself the question: how the project task is going to be understood, and after formulating an answer, seek approval and confirmation within the local community.

4   Scope of Method Application

Empathetic analysis may be carried out for any part of each city. Urban empathy allows to draw out those values, which elude standard urban diagnosis. Analysis conducted in this manner shows that places at first glance unattractive may take on a sparkle, unique character, its own one of a kind individuality. This is the identification of emotional urban structure topography. From this point of view, both intriguing deformity and breathtaking beauty enrich experiences constitute a place's charm and uniqueness.

Empathetic analysis should be skilfully adapted to specific conditions of a location. Its various aspects may be deepened by adapting to the required accuracy of the studies. Using empathetic method in the field of urban studies introduces not only town-planner's imagination in the design process but also interpretive diversity of emotions in urban creativity.

5   Limitations on Method Application

There are some traps in the urban empathy method. For a researcher providing emotional diagnosis, empathy may become a dominant state and be used as an excuse for someone's even the most mistaken urban decision. Such decision, once the motives behind it are understood, may become (wrongly) emotionally justified, because it can be explained by some "discovered" reasons. Empathetic diagnosis without reflection may be a reason for wrong decisions, thus bringing damage to a city. When urban planner attempts to destroy a valuable landscape with an ill-considered decision, one can succumb to a temptation of justifying steps taken. This is the type of extreme subjective empathy that uses excuses such as: 'it was because of pressure', 'effects were needed urgently', 'the investor was impatient', 'people have to live somewhere', or 'the city has to grow'. One can list many such reasons used by architects and town planners to justify their reproachful actions and expecting "empathic" understanding of their conduct.

6   Conclusion

It is the author's belief that implementing urban empathy category into urban assessment would break away from a certain defined scheme of urban studies and the method can be used in creating urban branding strategies. Empathic analysis causes urban studies to become a process emerging from the life schedules of inhabitants, requiring constant effort to discover the city and to perfect its space.

Empathy helps to understand better the genesis of the city. In standard urban research, one makes use of contemporary set of concepts which hamper or make impossible to understand motives and circumstances that occurred long time ago. Due to emphatic analysis it is possible to reach the genesis of the city and to understand specific historical, political, social and economic conditions, which today may appear to be incidental and incongruous.

References

Howard, E.: Garden Cities of To-morrow. S. Sonnenschein & Co., Ltd., London (1902). s.48. The MIT Press Edition (1967)

Husserl, E.: Formal and Transcendental Logic, Trans. D. Cairns. The Hague, Nijhoff (1929)

Hornblower, S.: A Commentary on Thucydides, vol. III: Books 5. s.25-8.109. Oxford University Press, New York (2008)

Krier, L.: Architecture: Choice or Fate. Andreas Papadakis Publisher, Windsor (1998). Wyd. polskie: Krier, L.: Architektura: wybór czy przeznaczenie. Wydawnictwo Arkady, Warsaw (2001)

Kvale, S.: Interviews: An Introduction to Qualitative Research Interviewing. Sage Publications, London (1996)

Lipps, T.: Psychologische studien. Weiss, Heidelberg, desc.w: James, W.: Essays, comments, and reviews, Tom 15. P&F Harvard College (1987). s. 391–394

Misiągiewicz, M.: Architektoniczna geometria. Wydawnictwo DjaF, Kraków (2005)

Camillo, S.: The Art of Building Cities: City Building According to its Artistic Fundamentals. Hyperion Press, Westport (1979)

Tatarkiewicz, W.: Dzieje sześciu pojęć. PWN, Warszawa (1988)

Wojnar, I.: Teoria wychowania estetycznego. Państwowe Wydawnictwo Naukowe, Warszawa (1976)

Research and Intervention to Improve Institutional Structures for Adult AAC Users

Ingo K. Bosse[✉] and Leevke Wilkens

Faculty of Rehabilitation Research, University of Dortmund, Dortmund, Germany
ingo.bosse@tu-dortmund.de

Abstract. In order to promote the establishment and implementation of AAC in facilities for adults with complex communication needs, this study examined: which binding institutional and network structures contribute to the establishment and implementation of AAC, and how AAC can lead to more self-determination and participation in assisted living and sheltered workshop facilities. Additionally, the research examined how a service center, where AAC users give peer advice, can support this process. In order to achieve triangulation, expert interviews, participatory observations and a group discussion were conducted. The definition of the categories is based on the participation model by Beukelman and Mirenda and the International Classification of Functioning, Disability and Health (WHO). The main factors for the successful implementation of AAC are awareness, knowledge, and institutional structures and structural parameters. The results led to recommendations for the implementation of AAC in living and working facilities for adult AAC users.

Keywords: AAC · Adults · Living and working facilities · ICF · Participation model · AAC checklist

1 Introduction

Work is of high importance in our society. To work often means to be included in society and to participate in the achievement of collective goals. We find recognition through work. Work also implies economic independence, identity, and quality of life [16]. Effective communication is essential for employment [5]. For those who are not able to reach their daily communication needs through natural speech, augmentative and alternative communication (AAC) can be seen as a way to reach these goals and to meet the expectations of society. AAC enables working people to communicate their desires and needs and to show their abilities. Forms of work can be the first labor market, self-employment, or university studies, vocational training or an internship. Additionally, for persons with disabilities, the supported employment system exists. In Germany, the most common way of employment for persons with disabilities is in sheltered workshops.

In Germany, the European country with one of the best labor markets, there were 288,000 workplaces in sheltered workshops in 2014 [7]. Renner assumes that the majority of AAC users are working in these sheltered workshops [16]. Terfloth and Lamers have proven that a factor of highest importance for wellbeing at these workplaces, as well as in day activity centers, is the use of appropriate communication [22]. Their SITAS study is one

© Springer International Publishing Switzerland 2016
M. Antona and C. Stephanidis (Eds.): UAHCI 2016, Part I, LNCS 9737, pp. 161–171, 2016.
DOI: 10.1007/978-3-319-40250-5_16

of the few in Germany that has originated evidence-based data about the implementation of augmentative and alternative communication in sheltered workshops and day activity centers. The data are not much better in other countries. Even in Norway, which has a long tradition of inclusive education and a political consensus about the principles of "full employment" and "work for all", an overwhelming number of people with intellectual disabilities and a high number of AAC users still spend their day in segregated work environments or at day activity centers [8]. Since Mirenda claimed that sheltered employment and augmentative communication was an oxymoron [15], the question of if and how AAC can be implemented in sheltered employment, and how this can lead to more self-determination and participation, still remains.

The aim of this study is to examine the self-determination and participation of employees who use AAC. Following the internationally recognized definition of the American Speech-Language-Hearing Association (ASHA), we define AAC as follows:

Augmentative and Alternative Communication (AAC) refers to an area of research, clinical, and educational practice. AAC involves attempts to study and when necessary compensate for temporary or permanent impairments, activity limitations, and participation restrictions of individuals with severe disorders of speech-language production and/or comprehension, including spoken and written modes of communication [1].

Following Beukelman and Mirenda, one can say that there is no typical person who relies on AAC. "Their only unifying characteristic is the fact that they require adaptive assistance for speaking and/or writing because their gestural, spoken, and/or written communication is temporarily or permanently inadequate to meet all of their communication needs. (…) "Without access to speech, these people face severe restrictions in all aspects of life - education, medical care, employment, family, and community involvement, unless they are provided with other communication supports" [5].

To identify beneficial factors and barriers affecting the use of AAC, the International Classification of Functioning (ICF) of the WHO was used. This measure deals with the impact of environmental and contextual factors on the participation of individuals. Another theoretical basis was the participation model by Beukelman and Mirenda. The participation model is a comprehensive and systematic action model for AAC [11]. "It provides a systematic process for conducting AAC assessments and designing interventions based on the functional participation" [4]. Two types of participation barriers are focused: opportunity and access barriers [4]. Access barriers, which are located in the individuals themselves, were not taken into account, because this study focuses on institutional structures. Instead, opportunity barriers were emphasized. These arise from the environment in which the individual lives. Five forms of opportunity barrier are identified [4]. Policy barriers result from laws and rules within a facility, for example the funding of staff and AAC- materials. These are often set out in writing in the concepts and/or model of institutions and facilities [4]. Practice barriers grow out of everyday activities. Everyday activities were no longer questioned [4]. Knowledge barriers emerge if the equipment required is available but nobody has the requisite knowledge to use it [4]. Attitude barriers differ from the others because they arise from negative or restrictive attitudes towards the AAC- user. The AAC-user faces low expectations; simultaneously, the participation opportunities will be limited. This happens because expectations influence the volume of support given to the AAC user [4]. Skill barriers result from a lack of technical, communicative and interpersonal skills [4].

2 State of the Art

The German SITAS study has shown that adjustment of the form of communication to suit the competencies of employees with disabilities is a central criterion for the wellbeing of those who work in sheltered workshops and in day-activity facilities [22]. Nevertheless, there is still a lack of studies on AAC in areas such as working and living. The first studies that investigated the employment situation of AAC-users were conducted in the middle of the 1990s in the USA. The aims of these studies were to conduct the form of employment of those who were using AAC. An overview by Renner concerning the following Anglo-American studies has shown that most of the existing studies have been case studies [17]. There is also a particular research interest concerning the institutional implementation of AAC and existing institutional structures. AAC is not used in working life [16]. As in almost all countries, in Germany AAC first became popular at school and early intervention facilities [3]. The USA had shown a similar progression, but since the 1990s there has been an intensive discourse regarding the employment situation of AAC users [17]. At the same time, more and more children, adolescents and adults are using AAC worldwide. Today, the fields of participation of adults are becoming more focused [2]. A range of noteworthy information regarding the usage of AAC in sheltered employment and other programs for persons with disabilities was gathered from practical experience. Additionally, there is a range of findings on the conceptual level [19, 20]. Authors like Schäffer and Struck state the high demand for development, research and specialized literature on AAC in working life [18]. "Completed studies according the job situation of AAC users in Germany do not yet exist" [17]. But at least, Research-based information about the work situation of persons with complex communication needs does exist. A quantitative investigation conducted by the University of Oldenburg in special schools, educational institutions and institutions of the disabled welfare in north-western Germany shows that only 24.1 % of potential AAC users are actually using an AAC device. At the same time, the high need for training and counseling was assessed [23]. A study by Erdélyi and Thümmel revealed the importance of institutions of the disabled welfare in initiation and facilitation of AAC usage, and how they can approach their work in this regard [9]. Findings from SITAS study show how differently this work is carried out in the different levels of an organization. 81.4 % of managers in educational institutions for persons with disabilities said that AAC was used in varied activities, but only 66.3 % of the employees state the same. On the other hand, teams state that AAC is used, while the management assumes that AAC is not in use [21].

Lage and Knobel Furrer showed that AAC is employed in the context of the disabled welfare on four levels: (1) On the individual level; (2) In the social environment, including training of potential interaction partners (AAC-culture); (3) Within the structural conditions of the living environment, mostly in disabled welfare organizations; and (4) Within society [12]. In the context of this study the levels two "AAC-culture" and three "structural conditions" are particularly relevant. A promising approach for the implementation of AAC is given by systemic organizational development [10]. The aim, as described by Giel and Liehs, is to involve as many elements of the system as possible, and to encourage sustainable development. During this process it is necessary to appreciate the work of the system and its members. In both publications the importance of knowledge management is pointed out.

3 Research Design

In order to conduct the barriers and beneficial factors for the establishment, implementation and networking of AAC, and to track the influence of AAC on the working life of persons with complex communication needs, the following questions were posed:

- Which factors are beneficial to AAC use?
- Which barriers prevent efficient implementation of AAC?
- Which binding institutional structures contribute to the establishment and implementation of AAC?
- Which network structures are beneficial to the establishment and implementation of AAC?
- How does AAC enforce the participation of adults with complex communication needs?

Research partners were (1) A sheltered workshop with around 900 employees with disabilities, with different work areas. In this study, there were three working areas with different tasks. Workers were mainly persons with complex disabilities. (2) A day

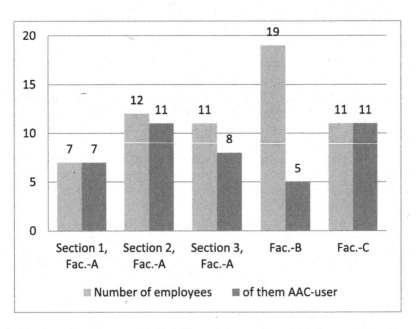

Fig. 1. Number of employees with disability and the number of AAC-users within this group (Color figure online)

activity center for persons with disabilities, where a range of tasks for the meaningful structuring of daily life was provided. (3) A service center for AAC where AAC users gave peer advice and created self-made AAC tools. All three research partners were already using AAC in some way.

At the beginning an analysis of requirements of the extent and need of AAC in these facilities was conducted. A modified questionnaire for adults, based on the questionnaire by Boenisch was used [6]. In order to determine whether and to what extent AAC was already established in these facilities, their format was examined (Fig. 1).

No difference between the usage of AAC as a dialogical or as a structuring tool was considered within this analysis of requirements.

For the following qualitative data collection, method- and a perspective triangulation were used. Expert interviews, a group discussion and participatory observations were

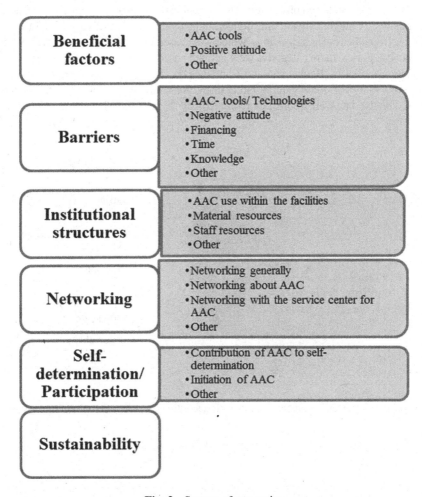

Fig. 2. System of categories

conducted. All three methods were used to answer the research questions, while every method focused on different aspects.

Overall, thirteen expert interviews with employees, management and AAC users were conducted. In the expert interviews with employees and management the barriers, the beneficial factors and the established structures of the institution were determined. In the interviews with AAC users, the frequency of AAC usage and the impact of AAC on their self-determination were deduced. The group discussion focused on the networking structures between and within the different facilities. Five participatory observations supplemented the triangulation, with the aim of gaining knowledge about the implementation of AAC in daily working life. Using this method, beneficial factors and barriers to the implementation and establishment of AAC, as well as the contribution of AAC to self-determination and participation, were to be documented.

In order to analyze the data collected, qualitative content analysis by Mayring was chosen. This method allowed the categorization of data and it's reduce it. Direct comparison between statements and observations was possible because of the prior classification in categories [14]. Categories were thus defined inductively and deductively. First root categories, based on the research questions, which were based on the ICF, were defined. Within these root categories, more categories were defined based on the opportunity barriers of the participation model by Beukelman and Mirenda [4]. The opportunity barriers were used because this study was mainly interested in institutional structures. Following this, categories based on the data were defined more inductively (Figs. 2 and 3).

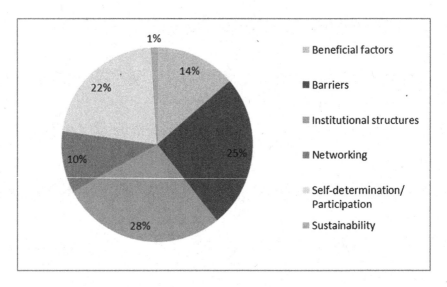

Fig. 3. Expert interviews: number of statements according the categories (Color figure online)

4 Results

Within these categories all statements were conducted by different methods, and were then compared and interpreted. A range of aspects important for establishment, implementation and networking could be identified and brought together for results.

Beneficial Factors. An essential beneficial factor is positive attitude among staff, users and management in the facilities. Positive attitudes strengthen motivation and commitment and therefore bring the establishment and implementation of AAC forward. Knowledge about AAC is also crucial to successful implementation of AAC in the facilities. Nevertheless, the statements about AAC were diverse. General knowledge about AAC is still described as beneficial and necessary for the implementation of AAC. Some of the people interviewed stated that training should be provided and is necessary.

Barriers. A pessimistic attitude can be seen as a barrier. Eye-catching statements, which show that such a pessimistic attitude is present among some employees in the facilities, reveal that awareness about the relevance of AAC is not always in line with statements made by the management. Some employees with disabilities are not seen as being able to use AAC. Some employees consider AAC not as a relief but rather a burden. Another crucial barrier is the technology and the purchase of AAC devices and materials. The service center for AAC did not identify such barriers. Nevertheless, fast- evolving technology makes it difficult for employees to keep up with the latest technologies. Additionally, lack of time is another important barrier. The lack of time results from a shortfall in personnel resources, and insufficient technical knowledge. Another barrier the phenomenon was described, where just one employee had the skills and knowledge about AAC and if he or she leaves the facility the knowledge is not present any more, as well.

Institutional Structures. In this study, institutional structures were defined as the current use of AAC in the facilities, as well as material and personnel resources (qualifications and training). Self-assessment and the definition of qualifications showed a heterogeneous picture. In all conducted facilities, there was a range of AAC devices and materials available, from non-electronic up to complex electronic AAC devices. Different ideas, background knowledge and different professions were used. These different resources determine different use. In some facilities, AAC was used only to structure the day and work, while in others, it was used to communicate, mostly in one-to-one situations.

Networking. It was stated that networking makes enforcing and ensuring the implementation process possible. A close cooperation between different organizations could also be used to create appropriate offers for customers with disabilities. Additionally, it was stated that a networking- facility would be useful to initiate the exchange of e.g., ideas and information. In Dortmund, such a networking-facility has already been founded, but it takes time until every cooperating facility is aware of it. Communication within the facilities is described as situational. Communication with relatives is also important for implementing AAC in the everyday life of a user, and should therefore also be considered.

Self-determination/Participation. All statements regarding the self-determination of AAC users contain the opinion that AAC is contributing to self-determination. The use of AAC is a possibility to encourage communication and therefore enforces participation, even if the potential AAC is providing is not being used to its full extent.

5 Discussion: Recommendations

Based on the results, a general recommendation for the implementation of AAC in facilities of the disabled welfare was created. With the aid of a checklist, employees are able to examine the current state of implementation of AAC in their facility. To enable the implementation, establishment and networking, the general recommendation provides specific recommendation for specific points in the included checklist.

In the following, some recommendations will be presented. Awareness of the importance of AAC for the individuals using it can provide assistance if AAC is embedded in the guidelines of the facility and in quality management. At the same time, it is crucial that the management be demanding in initiating this step. With these actions the establishment of AAC becomes obligatory for every employee. Additionally, awareness of AAC increases. AAC will no longer be an additional service, but will become a compulsory task. The management should also provide enough training in order to ensure that employees gain the knowledge required. This knowledge also needs to be archived, so every employee can have access to information about AAC (e.g., an intranet). In the intranet, information about specialist literature and practical advice for the implementation of AAC in general or with single users should be provided. An essential component of the dissemination of knowledge is networking within and between different facilities. If a range of facilities is linked with each other, it is easier to disseminate knowledge and options for implementation. This can work either through a regular meeting between AAC representatives, or a networking facility. Both possibilities can provide the chance to exchange information or provide support if needed. A university-based networking facility should be taken into consideration, because it would also provide more research opportunities.

Rituals can be used to gain regularity and continuity in AAC use. For example, a gesture of the month can be introduced, in order to expand vocabulary in sign language. Everyday situations should be supported by AAC e.g., a visualized weekly- and daily schedule and menu. In the process, consistent symbols and sign language should be used in order to lay the foundation for the use of just one system in a user's entire lifespan [10].

If different employees are responsible for different tasks, the situation where just one employee has the knowledge and the responsibility can be avoided. A sense of responsibility can be established with binding distribution of tasks for everyone. Nevertheless, the AAC representative should be responsible mainly for the implementation of AAC and for the assessment of individual needs. Additionally, he or she should also be responsible for managing the AAC working group and knowledge management, and should help with the purchase of new AAC devices and materials. Workshops regarding the handling of different AAC devices also seem to be useful. Those might help to keep up with fast-evolving technologies.

6   Conclusion

AAC has come a long way over the past 30 years. At school and in early intervention the field is becoming more and more established. For adults with complex communication needs there is still an urgent need to extend AAC research and intervention [13]. The aim of this project was to design a general recommendation for sheltered employment and day activity centers. Instead of providing rigid facts, this project aimed to present ideas to facilitate the underpinnings already in place. While creating this recommendation, it was attempted to bear in mind that the recommendations provided needed to be economically viable. Nevertheless, it is questionable whether the recommendations are really affordable for the facilities. The costs required should be considered as part of personnel and time management budgets. Certain amounts of time are needed and necessary if AAC is to be implemented. The establishment and implementation of AAC requires a long period, time and patience. The absence of success in AAC initiations can lead to frustration and finally in the termination of an AAC intervention. In order to avoid this, a contact point that provides professional support should be available. This contact point should provide information about progress and motivation if the success is below par and employees must seek professional advice. Communication should be seen as a human right by the management as well as by the employees. It should be supported by the implementation of new control mechanisms. This is the only way to enforce the implementation and establishment of AAC in the whole facility. The management of knowledge is crucial for professionalization including modules "to identify, to gain, to develop, to distribute, to use, to maintain, to assess knowledge and to identify new knowledge objectives" [12]. For further research, the establishment of these recommendations and associated challenges will be of interest. Furthermore, the individual level and the societal level must now be considered [12]. Article 27 of the Convention on the Rights of Persons with Disabilities [24], along with working in sheltered workshops, will enable a focus on the general labor market. Renner shows in his latest analysis of case studies that in Germany, no AAC user working in the general labor market could be found [17]. Occupational participation of persons with complex communication needs is possible, but in Germany there are still many participation barriers that prevent this [17]. There remains a great need for research into the conditions of vocational training, accessible workplaces, the structure of the labor market and the instruments of employment services.

Acknowledgements. The special feature of this study is that the research was conducted by eleven students of the bachelor degree course "Rehabilitation Sciences" at the Technical University of Dortmund in their fifth and sixth semester, with professional support by Prof. Ingo Bosse. I would like to acknowledge the participants of this AAC project group: Leevke Wilkens, Stefanie Fleischer, Annette Stegemann, Johannes Emmerling, Franziska Friedrich, Julia Heimann, Markus Leifeld, Friederike Simon-Kutscher, Judith Wendt, Victoria Wieczorek, Ronja Zimmermann.

References

1. American Speech-Language-Hearing Association. Roles and Responsibilities of speech-language pathologists with respect of augmentative and alternative communication: Position statement (2005). doi:10.1044/policy.PS2005-00113
2. Antener, G., Blechschmidt, A., Ling, K.: Vorwort der Herausgeberinnen. "UK wird erwachsen" und dies in vielerlei Hinsicht. In: UK wird erwachsen. Initiativen in der Unterstützten Kommunikation, pp. 11–18. von Loeper, Karlsruhe (2015)
3. Baunach, M.: Unterstützte Kommunikation und Beruf?! Machen wir uns nichts vor. In: Isaac, Gesellschaft für Unterstützte Kommunikation e. V. (ed.) Handbuch der Unterstützten Kommunikation (pp. 09.003.001–09.005.001), von Loeper Literaturverlag, Karlsruhe (2008)
4. Beukelman, D.R., Mirenda, P.: Augmentative and Alternative Communication. Management of Severe Communication Disorders in Children and Adults. Paul. H. Brookes Publishing Co, Baltimore (1998)
5. Beukelman, D.R., Mirenda, P.: Augmentative & Alternative Communication: Supporting Children and Adults with Complex Communication Needs, 4th edn. Brookes Publishers, Baltimore (2013)
6. Boenisch, J.: Forschungsergebnisse zur Unterstützten Kommunikation bei Kindern ohne Lautsprache- Bundesländer im Vergleich. Ergänzungsband zum Hauptwerk "Kinder ohne Lautsprache – Grundlagen, Entwicklungen und Forschungsergebnisse zur Unterstützten Kommunikation". Von Loeper, Karlsruhe (2009)
7. Bundesarbeitsgemeinschaft Werkstätten für behinderte Menschen: Anzahl der Mitgliedswerkstätten und belegten Plätze nach Bundesländern zum 1. Januar 2014, http://www.bagwfbm.de/category/34. Accessed 16 Oct 2015
8. Engeset, A., Söderström, S., Vik., K.: Day activity centres – work for people with intellectual disabilities: a Norwegian perspective. In: Work (Reading, Mass), vol. 50, no. 2, pp. 193–203 (2015)
9. Erdélyi, A., Thümmel, I.: They know it, but they don´t do it. Forschungsergebnisse zu Barrieren und Förderfaktoren in Bildungssystemen für Schüler mit komplexen Kommunikationsbeeinträchtigungen. In: uk & forschung_4, pp. 4–10 (2014)
10. Giel, A., Liehs, A.: Systemische Organisationsentwicklung in Wohn- und Werkstätten. Ein Träger implementiert UK. In: Antener, G., Blechschmidt, A., Ling, K (eds.): UK wird erwachsen. Initiativen in der Unterstützten Kommunikation. pp. 83–92. von Loeper, Karlsruhe (2015)
11. Lage, D.: Unterstützte Kommunikation und Lebenswelt. Eine kommunikationstheoretische Grundlegung für eine behindertenpädagogische Konzeption. Klinkhardt, Bad Heilbrunn (2006)
12. Lage, D., Furrer, K., Christina: Rahmenbedingungen für die Unterstützte Kommunikation – die neuen Herausforderungen. In: Schweizerische Zeitschrift für Heilpädagogik, vol. 20, no. 11–12, pp. 20–26 (2014)
13. Light, J., McNaughton, D.: Designing AAC research and intervention to improve outcomes for individuals with complex communication needs. In: AAC – Augmentative and Alternative Communication, vol. 31, no. 2, pp. 85–97 (2015)
14. Mayring, P.: Qualitative Inhaltsanalyse. Grundlagen und Techniken. 10th ed. Beltz Verlag, Weinheim (2008)
15. Mirenda, P.: Sheltered employment and augmentative communication: an oxymoron? AAC Augmentative Altern. Commun. **12**, 193–197 (1996)

16. Renner, G.: Berufsvorbereitung für unterstützt kommunizierende Erwachsene. Praxisprojekt des Zentrums für Unterstützte Kommunikation Freiburg. In: Antener, G., Blechschmidt, A., Ling, K (eds.) UK wird erwachsen. Initiativen in der Unterstützten Kommunikation, pp. 43–59. von Loeper, Karlsruhe (2015)

17. Renner, G.: Berufliche Teilhabe (Partizipation) von Menschen mit schwerer motorischer Bewegungseinschränkung und schwerer Kommunikationsbeeinträchtigung. Analyse qualitativer Fallstudien und –beschreibungen. In: Zeitschrift für Heilpädagogik 6, pp. 289–301 (2015a)

18. Schäffer, K., Struck, H.: Unterstützte Kommunikation in den Werkstätten für Menschen mit Behinderung. In: Hallbauer, A. et al. (eds.): UK kreativ! Wege in der Unterstützten Kommunikation, pp. 313–319. von Loeper, Karlsruhe (2013)

19. Schäffer, K., Rosenmeier, A.: UK in den Werkstätten für Menschen mit Behinderung. In: Antener, G., Blechschmidt, A., Ling, K (eds.) UK wird erwachsen. Initiativen in der Unterstützten Kommunikation, pp. 114–121. von Loeper, Karlsruhe (2015)

20. Spindler, C.: (Mit-)Sprache. Unterstützte Kommunikation bei erwachsenen Menschen mit kognitiver Beeinträchtigung als Grundlage für Selbstbestimmung, Empowerment und Partizipation. In: Bollmeyer, Engel et al. (eds.): UK inklusive.Teilhabe durch Unterstützte Kommunikation, pp. 155–169. von Loeper, Karlsruhe (2011)

21. Terfloth,K., Sabo,K.: Lebensqualität durch tätigkeits- und arbeitsbezogene Angebote. In: Fröhlich, A., Heinen, N. et al. (eds.): Schwere und mehrfache Behinderung – interdisziplinär, pp. 345–366. Athena, Oberhausen (2011)

22. Terfloth, K., Lamers, W.: Inklusion einfach machen oder einfach machen? Ar-beitsweltbezogene Angebote für Menschen mit schwerer und geistiger Behinderung im Spannungsfeld von Inklusion/ Exklusion. Rechtsgrundlage – Institution FuB – Professionalität. In: Ackermann, K-E., Musernberg, O., Riegert, J. (eds.): Geistigbehindertenpädagogik!? Disziplin – Profession – Inklusion, pp. 379–407. Athena, Oberhausen (2013)

23. UK- Netzwerk Weser-Ems: Empfehlungen zur Verankerung von Unterstützter Kommunikation in Einrichtungen (2010). http://www.unioldenburg.de/fileadmin/user_upload/sonderpaedagogik/download/Ambulatorium_fuer_Rehabilitation/UK/Netzwerk_Weser_Ems/Empfehlungen_UK.pdf. Accessed 08 July 2015

24. UN – United Nations Convention on the Rights of Persons with Disabilities and Optional Protocol, New York (2006)

25. World Health Organization (WHO) (ed.): International Classification of Functioning, Disability and Health. World Health Organization, Geneve (2001)

About Us, with Us: The Fluid Project's Inclusive Design Tools

Colin Clark[1]($\boxtimes$), Dana Ayotte[1], Antranig Basman[2], and Jutta Treviranus[1]

[1] OCAD University, Toronto, Canada
cclark@ocadu.ca
[2] Raising the Floor - International, Geneva, Switzerland

Abstract. Since 2007, the Fluid Project has been developing an integrated set of inclusive design methods and software tools to support personalization, authoring, and software creation by users within the context of a participatory, open source community. In this paper, we position the Fluid Project's inclusive design practice within the context of interaction, participatory, and universal design methods. We examine and contrast these approaches from the perspective of supporting user creativity throughout the process of designing and using software. The Fluid Project is an open source community of designers, developers, testers, users, and other diverse contributors who might not otherwise fit into the highly technical and exclusive culture of conventional open source software communities.

Keywords: Accessibility · Inclusive design · Co-design · Fluid project · Development tools · Assistive technology · Design methods · User creativity

1 Introduction

We begin by briefly surveying several established design methods, exploring their strengths, weaknesses, and relations to inclusive design. In particular, we examine the degree to which these methods can support diverse participation by users during the design process and beyond. Next, we describe the community-grown design methods employed by Fluid, which blend established techniques with new inclusive methods. The challenges and opportunities of designing within an open source community are discussed; we provide an overview of common open source governance and decision-making processes, examining some of the social and technological mismatches between today's developer-oriented open source practices and our goal of an inclusive, participatory community. We end by discussing how inclusive design and collaboration can be supported by technologies such as Fluid's Infusion framework, which provides the foundation for what we call "user-continued design," where software artifacts can be changed and redesigned even after the initial design process has been completed.

© Springer International Publishing Switzerland 2016
M. Antona and C. Stephanidis (Eds.): UAHCI 2016, Part I, LNCS 9737, pp. 172–182, 2016.
DOI: 10.1007/978-3-319-40250-5_17

2 Design Methods

2.1 Interaction Design

Industry-driven interaction design methods such as those described by Cooper [4], Beyer et al. [2], and IDEO [11] primarily look inward; they are created by professionals and intended for an audience of like-minded designers and managers. These methods aim to provide prescriptive, generalized, and reproducible techniques for managing teams who design commercial software products or offer design consulting services. The predominant emphasis is on "modelling" users, their goals, and their work or organizational processes.

Despite an increased focus on user-centered design, which often invites users into the fold of research in a more active way (as with the human-centric design methods of [11]), such industrial modelling methods maintain the user in a passive role as "consumer" or "customer," often advocating for a rigid design focus on typical or mainstream requirements while explicitly de-prioritizing the "edge cases" of outlying, marginal needs [4].

While this approach may simplify product requirements and focus designers on the most popular features, it also risks excluding the crucial features and customizations that enable people with disabilities to use a software product and which ultimately contribute to greater innovation and to the overall usability of a system [21].

Moreover, interaction design advocates often argue that their subjects (i.e. the individuals who use their software on a daily basis) are unable to be articulate or self-aware about their own technology needs, and that only the software industry can provide design innovation, not users themselves [20]. User input gathered through human-centered design methods tends to be seen only as a means for users to inspire the creative process of "real" designers. The result is that there are few opportunities for individuals to actively contribute to the design process and work alongside professional designers, except as consumers or research subjects.

2.2 Universal Design

Universal design, with an explicit focus on meeting the needs of all individuals, including those with disabilities, substantially expands a designer's creative remit and responsibilities. However, the challenge of universal design is in its emphasis on a single product or design that aims to fit the needs of all users without adaptation or personalization. Ron Mace describes universal design as "the design of products and environments to be usable by all people, to the greatest extent possible, *without the need for adaptation or specialized design*" [our italics] [15]. As the complexity and diversity of today's software grows, it is no longer practical for designers to plan for every user and every feature within a single piece of software, nor to be able to fully understand and obtain expertise in the infinite variety of creative, serendipitous, and unexpected uses that software can be subjected to. Instead, the design process needs to be supported by technologies that provide users with a means to materially change, personalize, specialize, and extend their software environments.

2.3   Participatory Design

Participatory design, in contrast to many interaction design methods, offers the potential for users to more actively engage in the design process. This often takes the form of workshops and scenario-building exercises where users are invited to explore design strategies alongside professional designers [23]. While participatory techniques play a foundational role in the Fluid Project's inclusive design methods, particularly the concept of experienced designers working in harmony with users and other non-designers, we argue that workshops and other "before-the-fact" design methods alone are insufficient for three primary reasons:

1. Participatory design methods do not explicitly provide a means for ongoing community "stewardship" or "curation" of the software product after the initial participatory methods have been completed
2. Additional technological tools are needed in order support ongoing or user-continued design, including the ability for individuals to customize, adapt, and modify a "finished" software product
3. Most user-centered or participatory methods do not fully support the participation of "extreme users" — those at the margins or who have particular needs that cannot be easily accommodated by traditional user research or workshops [18].

3   Fluid's Inclusive Design Tools

Taking up the co-design position that "all people have something to offer to the design process and that they can be both articulate and creative when given appropriate tools with which to express themselves" [19], the Fluid Project has been developing design and technological tools to support user creativity. We aim to extend the design process into the designed artifact itself — to give users the ability to continue the design process themselves, after the specialized design effort has been finished and the product has shipped. This approach to "adaptation as design" extends from creating tools that allow users to configure their own interfaces, to technologies that support remixing, repurposing, and sharing.

Designing inclusively, we have learned, requires more than just design processes, but also new technologies. This is the motivation for tools such as Fluid Infusion [13], a software development framework that enables applications to be reconfigured in context- and preference-sensitive ways, and the GPII Nexus [10], which can integrate diverse software components together in a way that will eventually be supported by graphical authoring and programming tools accessible to non-developers.

3.1   Catalogue of Design Tools

Fluid's software and design tools are rooted in open community practices that emphasize the role of users, especially users with disabilities, as co-designers, "gardeners", and ongoing maintainers of the project's outcomes. Fluid's approach emphasizes the importance of non-prescriptive design methods and self-organizing collaborative teams who freely draw from a toolbox of design approaches (such as those documented in Fluid's Design Handbook [14] and the Inclusive Learning Design Handbook [12]) based on the design context and the needs of participants and project stakeholders. We outline some of Fluid's community-driven design methods below.

UX Walkthroughs are a hybrid technique based on heuristic evaluation and cognitive walkthroughs. They emphasize paired or collaborative evaluation of user interfaces by designers and non-designers alike, and serve to bring a diversity of perspectives to bear on the design process.

The UX Walkthrough technique is a procedure for critically examining a user interface by following one or more predetermined scenarios and making assessments based on common user experience heuristics such as those by Jakob Neilsen [17]. It is an amalgam of several proven conventional inspection procedures, supporting reviewers in making assessments both from the user's point of view and that of a design expert. Pairing actual users up with designers to define scenarios and participate in walkthroughs can further enrich the results.

The multifaceted nature of the UX Walkthrough enables reviewers to make assessments across several dimensions, including: general design quality, task-oriented usability, assistive technology usability, accessibility standards compliance, and code quality. A UX Walkthrough can be performed by novices as well as experienced evaluators. The result is a comprehensive and multidimensional report of usability and accessibility issues in a website or application.

Personas and Use Cases provide models of potential stakeholders who may use a product or service and the scenarios they may encounter when using it. Personas often play an ambivalent role in an inclusive design process; as tools, they offer teams a useful way to identify with and design for certain users, yet they also simultaneously risk stereotyping or reducing users to static, product-oriented identities.

Although personas represent fictional people, their characteristics, needs, goals and motivations are rooted in the insights and feedback collected from various sources including formal or informal research techniques (such as interviews and surveys), or through familiarity with the needs and interests of self, co-workers, friends or family members. They begin as early, provisional sketches and often evolve iteratively as more information is gathered. Personas are behavioural models; they do not represent the full demographics of any given population of complex and unique people. They enable designers, developers and evaluators across a project to keep a broad and diverse collection of stakeholders

in mind. Considering non-obvious or unconventional users helps a design team
to think broadly and stay open to unexpected uses of the systems they are creating. Personas are most useful for inclusive design when they are understood
as full and idiosyncratic individuals, rather than as representatives of a broader
category of disability, age group, or market demographic [18].

Use cases describe particular scenarios in which a persona may encounter and
use a product or service, providing more detail about specific tasks and goals
as well as helping to map out the potential steps in a workflow. User personas
and accompanying use cases are not meant to exhaustively describe all potential
stakeholders or situations; rather they help to illustrate key goals and behaviour
patterns related to the design in question.

When paired with the other tools, particularly User States and Contexts and
UX Walkthroughs, personas and use cases can help to paint a clearer picture
of a broad and diverse range of user needs and preferences. They must be used
with caution, since by their nature they create a distinction between user and
designer, and they must be tempered with the awareness that no single persona
or group of personas can independently determine the full range of potential
uses of a product or service. Most importantly, like the real world, they need
to be understood as always in flux; user needs and goals change significantly in
different contexts and at different times.

User States and Contexts serve to "de-centre" and "multiply" personas,
reducing the risk of stereotyping with personas by emphasizing the dynamic
nature of a user and their needs across different contexts of use. This tool offers
a way to represent and "query" or visualize different user needs and perspectives
individually or in aggregate.

These diagrams can be considered a use-modelling tool for evaluating the
ability of a design to be perceived and operated by users in a wide range of
states and contexts. A user states and context map can be used to demonstrate
the range of needs of users that are represented by a particular persona, or
those of a collection of personas. The map can also be used to consider and
demonstrate how a user's state and context can change in the short term (e.g.
on a daily basis) or the long term (e.g. over a lifetime). Each "constellation" in
a User States and Contexts diagram shows the needs of a particular user in a
specific context, environment, or situation. These diagrams can be layered on
top of each other to plot how needs change across different contexts. Similarly,
diagrams of different users can be clustered in order to analyze relationships
amongst users. This helps to reveal patterns and commonalities that might not
otherwise be obvious when using personas alone, as well as serving to highlight
unique needs, interesting outliers, and edge cases that may suggest new design
opportunities and features (Fig. 1).

Community Design Crits bring together designers, developers, and users to
discuss and critique design artifacts, including ideas, scenarios, mockups, and
in-development software.

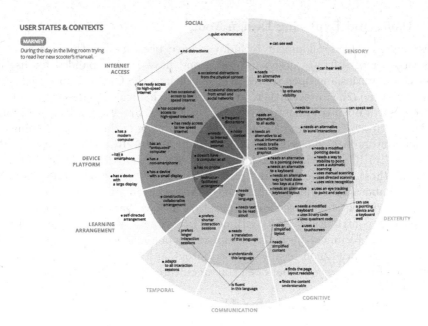

Fig. 1. A user states and contexts diagram.

Design crits provide a space, both locally and remotely via the use of video conferencing tools, for informal feedback and input to be gathered on a regular basis from a group of people with differing perspectives and differing stakes in the design. Gathering feedback in this way allows everyone a chance to participate in the design process from the start and in so doing reduces the typical design/develop/test cycle time.

Open, Transparent Sharing of design artifacts and discussion on mailing lists and other community forums based on "lazy consensus" governance principles [3]. Lazy consensus is a form of community-based decision-making that allows participants to make design and technical decisions freely based on their own personal judgement, trusting that, by virtue of the fact they are working openly and visibly, others will be able to speak up, contribute, or ask questions if issues arise.

When working transparently, diverse participation in the design process is more likely, because those who wish to get involved and who have access to the content and tools can contribute. Accessible and open communication tools can provide both a means of alerting the community to a group discussion or other activity, as well as a means of distributing collaborative artifacts including meeting minutes, design mockups, and other relevant information.

3.2   Using and Exploring Design Tools

These design and development techniques have been used with some success on a number of software design projects, and have been expanded for use in other communities and open source projects such as the Global Public Inclusive Infrastructure [22]. However, there are significant challenges to designing within the context of open communities, many of which we are still exploring. In particular, meritocratic governance runs the risk of being exclusive and dominated by contributors in privileged positions (socially, culturally, technologically, and economically) if a system is not in place to ensure that diverse contributions, especially those by non-coders, are recognized and promoted [7]. Access to open source collaborative forums, which are often synchronous, require high bandwidth, or privilege text-based communication over verbal or visual means, can limit diverse contributions. We continue to experiment with, evaluate, and test new social and technical methods for supporting ongoing engagement by individuals with disabilities, non-technical contributors, and those who might otherwise be excluded from conventional open source culture.

4   Technological Tools for Design

Technological tools to support such open and interactive design processes are, in our experience, relatively scarce. This is not only a result of the rarity of the processes they would support, but also because the underpinning for them is missing at the technological level. In this section, we survey the parallel story of technologies designed to support software developers in order to highlight what is missing for inclusive design, and to imagine the types of support which could be created for a community-oriented design process.

4.1   Distributed Version Control for Software Developers

Distributed version control systems gradually took over from traditional centralized version control systems during the 2000s. Distributed versioning offers a more democratic, "peer to peer" model for managing community assets, rather than the previous authority-based model whereby the definitive version of a community asset was stored in a nominated central repository. The most widely-used system of this kind currently is git [8], designed by Linux architect Linus Torvalds in response to problems he faced managing a very large source code base of millions of lines of code shared amongst thousands of contributors. Especially as hosted by the hugely popular infrastructure site GitHub [9], git offers important new affordances for software developers, beyond those directly implied by adopting an open source contribution model.

Amongst the most interesting for our purposes is GitHub's *review model*. This allows a suggested contribution to a project to enter a rich interactive lifecycle centred around a git artifact known as a *pull request* — a request by the contributor that their work be accepted (pulled) into the community's shared project. GitHub's pull request review interface provides the following facilities to contributors:

1. **Difference focused**: the interface highlights the differences between the project's state before and after the contribution is accepted. It is possible to navigate to complete views of project artifacts before and after the contribution.
2. **A Content-focused discussion**: comments can be attached to particular parts of the contribution. These can start off a dialogue between the contributor and other project members which remains attached to the particular content it is relevant to.
3. **An archived record**: even after the contribution is accepted into the project (or perhaps rejected) the pull request interface remains permanently available in the archive, making it easy to revisit and understand previous discussions.

It is worth noting that this pull request workflow is particularly a facility of GitHub rather than simply git itself, although it is enabled by the core technology of git. Unlike git itself, GitHub is not an open source project and its free-tier facilities are provided to the open source community as part of a wider commercial offering. However, alternatives to Git and free alternatives to GitHub exist, such as Gitorius on git, or the darcs hub [5] on darcs (although this currently has no pull request UI).

4.2   Nothing for Designers

Nothing similar to GitHub's pull request user interface and workflow currently exists to facilitate contributions to open source culture from non-developers. Because of this, open design teams are often left to devise ad hoc processes, such as exchanging designs as "rendered" image files (e.g. bitmaps and PDFs) using Dropbox [6] or other cloud file sharing systems, attachments to wiki pages, email, and so on. As a result, comments and discussion are separated from the design artifacts and occur in parallel channels such as emails, IRC chats and Skype messages. There is no easy way to interleave comments, suggestions, and critiques with a design "source" file, and it can be difficult to publicly archive and preserve such discussions for future reference. This complicates lazy consensus and collaborative governance for design, and makes it difficult to establish stable, shared archives of design knowledge within a community to help bring newcomers on board.

Additionally, none of the design tools most commonly in use today have accessibility features to facilitate contributions from individuals with disabilities, such as the ability to attach descriptive text narratives to wireframes and mockup images. This huge discrepancy between the quality of tools provided to technical as opposed to design contributors further erodes the ideology of a "meritocracy" in open source communities.

4.3   Fluid's Dream of an Inclusive Tool Chain

We dream that the same community affordances can be extended to all kinds of contributors. The technical, economic, and social barriers to this are, however, significant. Providing, for example, an accessible equivalent to Adobe's Illustrator or similar visual design tools is a prohibitive task. Even where open source alternatives to popular commercial visual design tools exist, they are unlikely to provide useful accessibility and collaborative features that can be integrated with robust, decentralized version management in a manner suitable for nontechnical users. Such tools will likely never be developed without a fundamental change to both the economics and practices of software design and development. Indeed, such a collaborative, accessible design tool could likely never stand alone as a single product; it could only be viable within the context of a broad collection of mutually-supportive technologies that take the needs of inclusion and collaboration into account at each infrastructural level.

5   Building an Inclusive Tool Chain

The primary aim of Fluid's Infusion framework is to provide the foundation for such an inclusive tool chain, including supporting "user-continued" design. The needs of inclusion and collaboration both induce similar kinds of requirements on software and content creation processes.

5.1   Working with Design Landmarks

At the technical level, one of the strategies we have found to be effective in Infusion for supporting both adaptability and collaboration is to provide **landmarks** in a design — named architectural points that can be used to focus discussion as well as used to target further design or customization after the fact by users. We take our inspiration from the kinds of landmarks visible in HTML documents, which can be successfully referenced by means of a vocabulary of *CSS selectors* [16]. Landmarks can, for example, take the form of *tag names*, *CSS class names*, or other attributes of a document node. By referencing these landmarks using CSS selectors, designers can meet both the needs of styling (using CSS rules) and further authoring (by using document-oriented manipulation tools such as the jQuery library). Landmarks are also valuable for supporting collaborative design tools, since they provide a means to attach comments and document-directed discussion to the design. Such CSS rules have been an early success for inclusive design, allowing designers and developers to share access to a design space in a harmonious way.

Infusion aims to bring the affordance of these selectors and rules not just to markup and styling, but to the rest of the software development process. This is accomplished by organizing Infusion applications into *cellular units* named *components* that can be referenced by means of a CSS-like system of **IoCSS rules**, allowing components to be easily altered, replaced, or removed at any time. This casts the world of software development more in terms of document authoring than source code editing, with its final artifacts taking the form of structured trees with landmarks rather than binary opaque blobs [1]. The key difference between such document-based software and traditional code is that it is intended to be modifiable at any point in the software's creation and use lifecycle. By providing an infrastructure which is suitable for authoring such trees, and for casting designs both visual and architectural in terms of them, we aim to support the creation of inclusive, collaborative workflows for designers of all kinds, including users.

5.2 Requirements Beyond Frameworks

Despite our technical efforts, we recognize that collaborative, open, and participatory design communities cannot be supported solely by means of a development framework. Other requirements need to be met through:

– Building up hosting infrastructure for applications and data, and the tools and infrastructure needed to manage it
– Building up community structures and workflows for welcoming, supporting and reviewing contributions
– Building up and curating shared understanding of productive ways of casting and solving design and implementation problems, organized, for example, in "handbooks" of design guidelines, "bestiaries" of real-world problems and their solutions or other approaches like those listed in Sect. 3.1.

6   Conclusion

The design processes and technologies we describe here aim to support new forms of participation in open source software and to ultimately provide users with the ability to materially redesign and adapt software themselves. These goals are, needless to say, highly complex, ambitious, and challenging. We believe that such processes and tools need to be prototyped, evaluated, and refined within the context of open, collaborative communities that recognize the many and diverse contributions necessary to make highly usable software. Our approach continues to evolve and grow based on real-world experience designing and implementing software for a variety of projects, and we invite others to join our community and help creatively explore these issues with us.

The authors would like to thank James Yoon and Sepideh Shahi for their contributions to the design methods described in this paper.

References

1. Basman, A., Clark, C., Lewis, C.: Harmonious Authorship from Different Representations. Psychology of Programming Interest Group Annual Conference 2015. http://www.ppig.org/sites/default/files/2015-PPIG-26th-Basman.pdf
2. Beyer, H., Holtzblatt, K.: Contextual Design: Defining Customer-Centered Systems. Morgan Kaufmann Publishers, San Francisco (1998)
3. Capra, E., Wasserman, A.I.: A framework for evaluating managerial styles in open source projects. OpenSource Dev. Communities Qual. **27**, 1–14 (2008). Special Issue of IFIP International Federation for Information Processing

4. Cooper, A., Robert, R., Cronin, D.: About Face 3: The Essentials of Interaction Design, p. 80. Wiley, Indianapolis (2007)
5. Darcs Hub. http://hub.darcs.net/
6. Dropbox (service). Wikipedia. https://en.wikipedia.org/wiki/Dropbox_(service)
7. Emke, C.A.: The Dehumanizing Myth of the Meritocracy. Model View Culture 21 (2015). https://modelviewculture.com/pieces/the-dehumanizing-myth-of-the-meritocracy
8. Git. https://git-scm.com/
9. Github. Wikipedia. https://en.wikipedia.org/wiki/GitHub
10. Clark, C., Basman, A., Bates, S.: The Nexus. GPII Wiki, 10 March 2016. https://wiki.gpii.net/w/The_Nexus
11. IDEO. Methods. Design Kit. http://www.designkit.org/methods
12. The Inclusive Learning Design Handbook. The FLOE Project. http://handbook.floeproject.org/
13. Infusion. Fluid. http://fluidproject.org/products/infusion/
14. The Fluid Design Handbook. Fluid Project Wiki. https://wiki.fluidproject.org/display/fluid/Design+Handbook
15. Mace, R., et al.: The Principles Of Universal Design. https://www.ncsu.edu/ncsu/design/cud/about_ud/udprinciplestext.htm
16. Getting Started with CSS Selectors. Mozilla Developer Network. https://developer.mozilla.org/en/docs/Web/Guide/CSS/Getting_started/Selectors
17. Neilsen, J.: 10 Usability Heuristics for User Interface Design. Neilsen Norman Group. https://www.nngroup.com/articles/ten-usability-heuristics/
18. Pullin, G., Newell, A.F.: Focussing on extra-ordinary users. In: Stephanidis, C. (ed.) HCI 2007. LNCS, vol. 4554, pp. 253–262. Springer, Heidelberg (2007)
19. Sanders, E.B.N.: From user-centered to participatory design approaches. In: Frascara, J. (ed.) Design and the Social Sciences. Taylor and Francis, London (2002)
20. Skibsted, J.M., Hansen, R.B.: User-led innovation can't create breakthroughs; just ask apple and Ikea. Fast Company, 3 March 2007. http://www.fastcodesign.com/1663220/user-led-innovation-cant-create-breakthroughs-just-ask-apple-and-ikea
21. Treviranus, J.: Leveraging the web as a platform for economic inclusion. Behav. Sci. Law **32**, 94–103 (2014)
22. Vanderheiden, G., Treviranus, J.: Creating a global public inclusive infrastructure. In: Stephanidis, C. (ed.) Universal Access in HCI, Part I, HCII 2011. LNCS, vol. 6765, pp. 517–526. Springer, Heidelberg (2011)
23. Wakkary, R.: A participatory design understanding of interaction design. Science of Design Workshop. CHI (2007)

New Initiatives for the Empowerment of People with Activity Limitations – An Analysis of 1,005 Cases of (Digital) Social Innovation Worldwide

Jennifer Eckhardt, Christoph Kaletka[✉], and Bastian Pelka

TU Dortmund University, Dortmund, Germany
{eckhardt,kaletka,pelka}@sfs-dortmund.de

Abstract. The paper exploits an extensive quantitative case mapping to blend three strands of research: First, social innovation will be considered as an approach to improve and/or guarantee social inclusion for people with activity limitations. Secondly, ICT will be understood as a means to empower people with activity limitations; and thirdly, the needs of vulnerable people will be regarded as a lens for scrutinizing those two approaches: How can ICT based social innovation/digital social innovation (DSI) empower people? The analysed cases shed light on the phenomenon of "digital social innovations" and allow first insights into their practice. The paper illustrates a quantitative overview of the actors behind these initiatives, their funding structures and drivers and barriers. In a conclusion, the new phenomenon of "digital social innovation" is described in contours.

Keywords: Social innovation · ICT · Digital inclusion · Digital social innovation

1 Introduction

Social welfare systems and public services are under pressure in many countries as a result of the financial crisis and global challenges. In 2013 the European Commission has launched a policy instrument to address these challenges by suggesting a "European" approach to modernizing welfare systems; the "Social Investment Package" (SIP)[1]. This collection of suggestions

- "guides EU countries in using their social budgets more efficiently and effectively to ensure adequate and sustainable social protection;
- seeks to strengthen people's current and future capacities, and improve their opportunities to participate in society and the labour market;
- focuses on integrated packages of benefits and services that help people throughout their lives and achieve lasting positive social outcomes; (…)"[2]

---

[1] Communication from the Commission to the European Parliament, the Council, the European and Social Committee and the Committee of the Regions: Towards Social Investment for Growth and Cohesion – including implementing the European Social Fund 2014-2020. COM(2013) 83 final. See: http://ec.europa.eu/social/main.jsp?catId=1044.

[2] http://ec.europa.eu/social/main.jsp?catId=1044.

© Springer International Publishing Switzerland 2016
M. Antona and C. Stephanidis (Eds.): UAHCI 2016, Part I, LNCS 9737, pp. 183–193, 2016.
DOI: 10.1007/978-3-319-40250-5_18

The SIP identifies eight target groups that would profit most from this modernization of welfare services; "older people" and "disabled people" being two of them. In its core the SIP urges Member States to prioritise social investment and the modernisation of their welfare systems in order to reach the inclusion and welfare goals of the EU 2020 strategy. Social innovation (SI) is an essential element of the SIP, highlighting SI as a policy instrument for addressing vulnerable people's needs.

International innovation research is providing numerous indications of a fundamental shift in the innovation paradigm towards social innovation [1]. This new paradigm is characterized by the innovation process opening up to society, its orientation towards the major societal challenges, and a stronger recognition of social innovations complementary to technological innovations [2]. Social innovation is understood as a new combination or figuration of practices in areas of social action, prompted by certain actors or constellations of actors, with the goal of better coping with needs and problems than is possible by use of existing practices. An innovation is therefore social to the extent that it varies social action, and is socially accepted and diffused in society. This definition exceeds a normative understanding of social innovations as 'good' or socially desirable. It also enlarges traditional technologically oriented innovation concepts. Such a comprehensive understanding of innovation may also serve as an answer to a situation where the limits of strictly policy-driven programmes on the one hand and social entrepreneurship and civil society initiatives on the other hand become obvious. Therefore, it is important to better understand the potential and mechanisms of intersectoral approaches for solving the grand societal challenges such as a better inclusion of people with activity limitations.

While "in recent years, social innovation has become increasingly influential in both scholarship and policy" [3], there is still no sustained and systematic analysis of social innovation, its theories, characteristics and impacts. But, Misuraca et al. [4] conclude that "(…) social innovation - and more concretely ICT-enabled social innovation - can provide an important contribution to social policy reform, providing new/better/different ways of integrating the provision of social services."

This political backdrop is used to investigate findings from an extensive analysis of social innovation cases, for the first time empirically describing this new concept of addressing needs; produced by the EU funded research project "Social Innovation – Driving Force of Social Change" (SI-DRIVE, 2014–2017). In a first step the characteristics of SI initiatives will be described in order to understand the objectives, processes and outcomes of this emerging phenomenon.

2   The Dataset

2.1   Methodological Approach

SI-DRIVE has mapped social innovation projects and initiatives all over the world via desk research and interviews. 1.005 cases – exploiting existing descriptions of social innovation initiatives - have been collected; with 25 project partner institutions contributing to the sample. For the first time, socially innovative projects and initiatives around the world have been analyzed and compared in such quantities, allowing for analyses with a special thematic focus.

The 1.005 cases are the result of an expert based selection. Social innovation experts from all world regions, all of them either SI-DRIVE project partners or advisory board members, were asked to identify cases which meet the criteria of the working definition of social innovation.[3] These cases could be in different stages of the innovation process, from ideation, implementation, imitation/diffusion up to the stage where the solution has already been institutionalized.

A survey template consisting of open and structured questions was developed for the data collection of all cases. A case is defined as follows:

1. A case is what the experts define as a relevant social innovation project/initiative.
2. A case has to show novelty of the social practice and first diffusion in society.

From these 1,005 cases, 240 cases (23,9 %) showed an inclusive character, 172 initiatives targeted people with activity limitations (17,1 %) and strive to facilitate their integration into society. 328 initiatives are either inclusive or integrative (32,6 %). The overlap between those groups is 42 initiatives which are targeted towards people with activity limitations and inclusive at the same time.

325 initiatives of the whole sample built their service on digital technologies, making them "digital social innovations". 134 initiatives are "digital social innovations" that are either inclusive or targeted at people with activity limitations or both (Table 1).

Table 1. Count of initiatives in the different subgroups and in total

	Total	Non-ICT-based	ICT-based
All cases	1005	680	325
Inclusive and integrative initiatives	370	236	134
Inclusive initiatives	240	150	90
Integrative initiatives	172	116	56

2.2   Definitions: People with Activity Limitations and Inclusive Initiatives

The various terms and unclear definitions which dominated the discourse on disability, impairment and activity limitation for a long time shared foremost a traditional individual-centric view on people with activity limitations that located the disability in the bodily, sensual or mental functions of the affected persons themselves. Since the implementation of the *International Classification of Functioning, Disability and Health* (ICF), a stronger focus on participation in various dimensions of society as a crucial part of the concept of disability and therefore a more differentiated framework for the description of individual physical and mental statuses is regarded as widely accepted. A person's level of functioning therefore derives from the dynamic interactions between environmental and personal factors as well as the individual health conditions.

---

[3] The composition of world regions follows the United Nation's macro geographical (continental) regions and geographical sub-regions classification.

Following the ICF, it can be said that people are disabled by environmental (i.e. inaccessible environments) and structural factors (i.e. insufficient provision of assistance) which are not compatible to their own functioning.

The *United Nations Convention of the Rights of persons with Disabilities* (CRPD), a human rights charter that clarifies the common human rights for people with disabilities, renounces a specific definition of disability and herein implies the understanding of disability as a part of the human condition that highly depends on the particular cultural and temporal context. The CRPD has set new goals for policy and decision making as it emphasizes every person's right to fully participate in society and its various domains of everyday life. Using the ICF as a bridge between scientific values and the political and social values expressed in the rights in the CRPD, is a conception oriented towards the "rights approach to disability" that finds its expression within the paradigm shift mentioned above [5]. Seeing ICT as a vehicle to ensure empowerment and participation, it becomes necessary to develop indicators which allow research on these issues. By analysing cases which are inclusive in their basic orientation, meaning the needs of persons with disabilities are mainstreamed from an early stage of the initiative, and by differentiating them from cases which are especially directed towards people with activity limitations and those cases which fulfil neither of those characteristics, this evaluation strives to generate comparative statements concerning these groups. To exemplify this differentiation, one example from every sub-group (with a focus on ICT) is illustrated below:

Inclusive Initiative:

- *Wehelpen* is a participatory online platform based in the Netherlands, which facilitates and simplifies (informal) care in society, in terms of searching for, offering and organising it without any costs involved.[4] The project targets all Dutch residents, irrespective of personal preconditions. The platform enables people offering their help as well as indicating need for help. The initiators want to de-anonymize cities and neighbourhoods and provide an easy way for inhabitants to get in touch to each other and raise the level of empathy and care. The platform itself works with icons, aside from descriptions, making it easier to understand for people with mental handicaps. The webpage is constructed in a way that people with sight limitations owning special internet browsers have easy access. People with activity limitations are not in the focus at all, whereas all infrastructure is designed in order to meet as many needs as possible for potential users.

Integrative Initiative Directed Towards People with Activity Limitations:

- *LIFEtool* is a non-profit organisation and is located in Linz/Austria.[5] They offer counselling and training as well as soft- and hardware products for augmentative and alternative communication (AAC). Accessible software programs and apps as well as computer input devices for children, adolescents, adults and elderly with

---

[4] https://www.wehelpen.nl/.
[5] http://www.lifetool.at.

disabilities, their relatives, educators and therapists are developed and put to use in order to reduce external assistance needs for people with activity limitations by providing technical and digital devices to the people which are matching exactly to what they really need. Because the leverage point and goal of this initiative is the integration into social and working life, it is classified as an integrative initiative rather than an inclusive one.

Inclusive Initiative Directed Towards People with Activity Limitations.

• *Sydney's pioneering system of accessible pedestrian signs* (Australia)[6] aims to increase consistency, accessibility, sustainability and city legibility. It's a coordinated and easy to understand system which should encourage people to walk more in the city by improving the city's wayfinding strategy. I.e. new pylons, flag signs, finger signs as well as tactile and audible indicators allow people with activity limitations to perceive the wayfinding system. Pylons and tactile signs will also feature QR tags that can be used for digital links to city websites, transport for information and timetables as well as destination tourism information. In this way people with activity limitations become main addressees of this new system but the system itself follows a *design for all* approach targeting environmental and structural factors and seeking improvement for everyone.

3   Findings

The findings presented here are supposed to provide a first quantitative insight into the emerging topic of (digital) social innovation for people with activity limitations. Therefore, different perspectives into the subsets of cases of digital social innovation for people with activity limitations within the 1,005 cases will be developed. The focus lies on two sets of key questions to build an understanding of this new and forasmuch unrecognized phenomenon in the field of welfare services. First: Who are the actors involved, what is their sectoral origin and in how far is cross-sectoral collaboration a trademark of the cases identified? And second: How can the innovation process be characterized, including questions regarding drivers and barriers, the role of ICT, or the topic or policy field in which they are operating.

3.1   Who? Actors and Collaboration

People with activity limitations are a primary target group of social innovation initiatives. While 23,9 % of the 1,005 social innovation cases identified worldwide show an inclusive character, meaning they are accessible, available and affordable for everyone interested, 17,1 % (172 social innovation initiatives) specifically focus on or actively involve people with activity limitations. This is remarkable since activity limitation was not a specific criterion in the expert-based selection process in the SI-DRIVE project which analyses social innovation in all its diversity (from education, employment and poverty reduction,

---

[6] http://www.sydneymedia.com.au/accessible-signs-open-up-city-streets/.

health and social care to transport and mobility as well as environment and energy supply). But people with activity limitations are differently addressed within different world regions: Western and Northern Europe seem to play an "early adopter" role – with 57,5 % (77 cases) of all digital social innovation cases for people with activity limitation can be found in one of these two regions. Surprisingly, North America scores low in the number of ICT enabled social innovation for people with activity limitations – only three cases could be found in this region. This result may also lead back to a small number of cases in North America in general and especially within those policy fields foremost actively in the field of inclusive policy (Table 2).

Table 2. Distribution of ICT-based inclusive initiatives to the world regions

World region	Total	% of all inclusive ICT-based initiatives	% of all inclusive ICT-based initiatives in the resp. World region
Northern EU	28	20,9	24,6
Western EU	49	36,6	14,8
Eastern EU	9	6,7	10,7
Southern EU	15	11,2	13,9
North America	3	2,2	8,8
Latin America	4	3,0	7,7
Africa	5	3,7	6,6
Middle East	5	3,7	25,0
Asia	5	3,7	5,4
Russia	3	2,2	8,1

Social innovation initiatives are led by men: 54,8 % of the main representatives of the initiatives mapped are male, 45,2 % female. In inclusive initiatives and those focusing on people with activity limitations, 51,4 % of the main representatives are male and 48,6 % are female. Inclusive initiatives based on DSI are represented by male contact persons in 53,2 % of the cases. While it is evident that the field of social innovation is a very recent field in general (86,2 % of the initiatives were funded after 2001), the DSI-sector can be described as even younger in its character. 93,7 % started their work after the year 2001 from which 46,5 % of the inclusive initiatives focusing ICT were funded within the last five years.

Social innovation is characterized by an innovation process opening up to society. Our sample therefore investigated the sectoral origin of actors involved in the initiatives. The theoretical claim is substantiated by empirical results which show that multiple actors are involved in most of the 1,005 initiatives: 68,7 % of the initiatives comprise at least one actor from the private sector; 70,8 % from the public sector and 74,7 % from the civil society sector. At an average, one initiative involves partners from 2,14 of the mentioned three sectors. This result is remarkable. It shows that while the civil society and its social economy initiatives play a significant role, and social economy entities are certainly "important agents in the battles against social exclusion, poverty and environmental degradation, and key actors in the creation of social capital and the delivery of public services" [6], the third sector is not the source of social innovation. Actors from

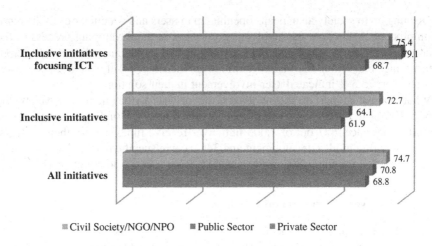

Fig. 1. Sectors actively involved in the initiatives in % of the specific samples

the public and private sector are almost equally involved. These figures are very similar for initiatives using ICT means or addressing people with activity limitations; the overall finding of well connected initiatives is true for all subsets of social innovation initiatives (see Fig. 1). Especially concerning inclusive initiatives operating with ICT, the public sector seems to be from great importance. While this sector is involved in 70,8 % of all mapped cases the inclusive initiatives focusing ICT indicated participation of the public sector in 79,1 % of the cases. In general, initiatives with a focus on ICT seem to be more oriented towards cooperation and transfer, as they state slightly more involvement of partners from the various sectors (except of the private sector).

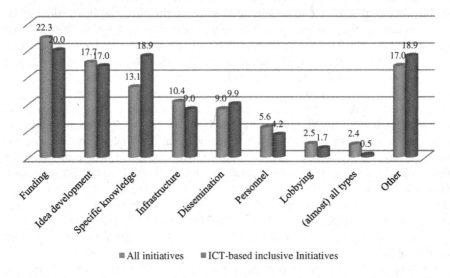

Fig. 2. Types of support provided to the initiatives through partner organizations in %

Opening up to society also means opening up to users and beneficiaries in the innovation process. Asking for the involvement of users in the developing process of the initiatives, 61,5 % stated that beneficiaries participated in the innovation process from an early stage on. Within the inclusive initiatives focusing ICT this number is considerably higher: 75,5 % indicated user-involvement in their solution.

What types of support do the involved actors provide to the initiatives? Among the support that those initiatives get from their involved actors, "funding" seems to be of outmost importance. 627 out of 1,005 initiatives receive funding from their partners, 482 are supported in idea development and 349 receive specific knowledge. This links to the insight that funding is the most crucial issue for social innovation [7] (Fig. 2).

3.2   How? Drivers, Barriers and ICT Use

The use of ICT in supporting social innovation is widely discussed [8–11]. ICT seems to be a strong catalyst in promoting, fostering and sustaining social innovation initiatives as modern digital technology seems to support the co-operation and networking attitude of social innovation initiatives – especially for vulnerable target groups [12, 13]. Therefore, the SI-DRIVE dataset asked for the importance of using ICT in the initiative. 325 out of 1,005 cases of SI are building on digital technologies; and 32.7 % of the social innovation cases aiming at people with activity limitations are making use of ICT.

Our sample of 1,005 initiatives of social innovation worldwide differentiated seven practice fields of social innovation: Education, employment, environment, energy, transport and mobility, health and social care, and poverty reduction. Initiatives are relatively evenly spread over these practice fields (between 8,0 and 18,4 %). But a focus on use of ICT within these initiatives reveals an interesting cohesion: Among digital social innovation cases, the topic "health and social care" is addressed by 34,3 %, making "health and social care" the most addressed topic by digital social innovation, while initiatives dealing with environmental or energy issues rarely build on digital social innovation (1,5 and 0,7 % of the cases). Initiatives with an inclusive character and those addressing people with activity limitations can be found predominantly in the fields of health and social care (31,6 %), education (18,6 %) and poverty reduction (16,2 %). For every initiative in the sample, experts were asked to name the three strongest drivers and barriers and rank them from 1 to 3. In 448 of 1,005 cases, the most important drivers are the individuals involved along with their competences, motivation and networks pushing the initiative forward. With 44.6 %, this is by far the strongest rank 1 driver for the whole sample, followed by the innovative environment as a whole in which the initiative has been created (99/9.9 %), solidarity (87/8.7 %), ICT (81/8.1 %) and governance/politics (80/8.0 %). Looking at rank 2, there are three drivers of considerable importance: The innovative environment (193/19.2 %), followed by individuals, networks and groups (185/18.4 %) and solidarity (135/13.4 %). Looking at the 370 cases with an inclusive character and/or addressing people with activity limitations, the picture is comparable.

Looking at the three most important barriers the initiatives have encountered, funding challenges are clearly the biggest issue (for 29.7 % of the initiatives this barrier is the most important one). This is followed by a lack of personnel (10.5 %), knowledge gaps (10.0 %), legal restrictions (9.5 %) and missing political support (8.1 %). In contrast to traditional innovations, competitors are seldom considered a barrier (3.6 %).

For inclusive initiatives and those focusing people with activity limitations the problem of funding seems to be even bigger: 34,1 % of them see it as the highest barrier, followed by lack of personnel (13.8 %), knowledge gaps and legal restrictions (both 9.7 %).

For even 35.1 % of the ICT-based initiatives in this group (inclusive/activity limitations) funding challenges dominate. Knowledge gaps also pose a considerable barrier (16.4 %).

4   Discussion

People with activity limitations are an important actor and target group for social innovation initiatives worldwide. At the same time, a considerable share of social innovation initiatives are inclusive, meaning they are accessible, available and affordable to everyone interested and are treating the needs of people with activity limitations as cross-cutting themes in their everyday-work. Having in mind that social innovation has gained importance for societal development as a whole, and solving the grand challenges society is facing today, the concept has to be systematically explored in order to reap its full potential in the field of inclusion and for the actor group of people with activity limitations. This group is not limited to being receivers and the object of social innovation approaches, but they play an active role in the SI process, especially in the field of DSI.

As the analysis of the SI-DRIVE dataset has shown, this process is characterized to a large extent by intersectoral cooperation of public, private and civil society actors. Social innovation initiatives acknowledge the importance of involving actors from all fields of a "quadruple helix for social innovation", bringing together civil society (marginalized persons' stakeholders), policy making, economy and research in any kind of solution. Results have shown a high prevalence for inclusive initiatives focused on ICT to involve the public sector while they generally seem to put greater emphasis on cooperation and knowledge transfer. This raises questions such as how professionalized this cooperation is, how it can be supported and how intermediary actors, such as social innovation labs and centres, can help to better facilitate cooperation throughout the whole social innovation process.

ICT use also plays an important role for many SI initiatives and is an important driver, leading to 'digital social innovation' (DSI) as a specific sub-set of social innovation and an emerging object of research. This suggests a strong role of digital/social media for today's social innovation empowerment activities: A lot of today's social innovation activities are driven by social entrepreneurs cooperating via social media or are addressing digital inclusion. Though, a large share of DSI initiatives for people with activity limitations seems to be confronted with funding challenges as one of the main barriers.

What we were able to provide, on the basis of the quantitative mapping, is a general overview of ICT-driven social innovation initiatives which are inclusive or which focus on people with activity limitations, highlighting the actors involved, the importance of intersectoral collaboration, and drivers and barriers encountered. Given the policy background and the expectations towards social innovation as a new way of addressing vulnerable people's needs, our empirical results are showing that (digital) social innovation indeed can be an instrument for addressing the needs of people with activity limitations – but our comparative study also indicates huge differences between world regions: While western and norther European countries seem to exploit the added value of digital technology combined with social innovation for the needs of people with activity limitations, other world regions are showing a different picture. The most interesting facet of analysed cases is their approach to stakeholder involvement; most cases of social innovation are actively involving actors from several societal sector and therefore follow the approach to build their services on "multiple shoulders". Moreover, the active involvement of people with activity limitations seems to be a common approach within social innovation initiatives.

References

1. Howaldt, J., Butzin, A., Domanski, D., Kaletka, C. (eds.): Theoretical Approaches to Social Innovation - A Critical Literature Review. A Deliverable of the Project: 'Social Innovation: Driving Force of Social Change' (SI-DRIVE). Sozialforschungsstelle, Dortmund (2014)
2. Howaldt, J., Schwarz, M.: Social innovation: concepts, research fields and international trends. In: Henning, K., Hees, K. (eds.) Studies for Innovation in a Modern Working Environment - International Monitoring, vol. 5 (2010). http://www.sfs-dort-mund.de/odb/Repository/Publication/Doc%5C1289%5CIMO_Trendstudie_Howaldt_Schwarz_englische_Version.pdf
3. Moulaert, F., MacCallum, D., Hamdouch, A., Mehmood, A. (eds.): KATARSIS. Social Innovation: Collective Action, Social Learning and Transdisciplinary Research (2010b). http://cordis.europa.eu/documents/documentlibrary/124376771EN6.pdf
4. Misuraca, G., Kucsera, C., Lipparini, F., Voigt, C., Radescu, R.: ICT-enabled social innovation in the support to the implementation of the social investment package – IESI report D1.2. JRC Technical reports (2016)
5. Bickenbach, J.: Monitoring the United Nation's convention on the rights of persons with disabilities: data and the international classification of functioning, disability and health. In: What is Disability? UN Convention on the Rights of Persons with Disability, Eligibility Criteria and the International Classification of Functioning, Disability and Health, Rome, Italy, 19–20 April 2010
6. Scoppetta, A., Butzin, A., Rehfeld, D.: Social innovation in the social economy and civil society. In: Howaldt, J., Butzin, A., Domanski, D., Kaletka, C. (eds.) Theoretical Approaches to Social Innovation - A Critical Literature Review. A Deliverable of the Project: 'Social Innovation: Driving Force of Social Change' (SI-DRIVE), pp. 79–96. Sozialforschungsstelle, Dortmund (2014)
7. Terstriep, J., Kleverbeck, M., Deserti, A., Rizzo, F.: Comparative report on social innovation across Europe. Deliverable D3.2 of the Project «Boosting the Impact of SI in Europe Through Economic Underpinnings» (SIMPACT), European Commission – 7th Framework Programme: European Commission, DG Research & Innovation, Brussels (2015). http://www.simpactproject.eu/publications/reports/SIMPACT_D32.pdf
8. Bria, F.: Growing a digital social innovation ecosystem for Europe. DSI final report (2015). https://www.nesta.org.uk/sites/default/files/dsireport.pdf

9. Millard, J., Carpenter, G.: Digital technology in social innovation: a synopsis. In: A Deliverable of the Project: "The Theoretical, Empirical and Policy Foundations for Building Social Innovation in Europe" (TEPSIE), European Commission – 7th Framework Programme. European Commission. DG Research, Brussels (2014a). http://www.tepsie.eu

10. Millard, J., Carpenter, G.: Case study analysis report of online collaboration and networking tools for social innovation. In: A Deliverable of the Project: "The Theoretical, Empirical and Policy Foundations for Building Social Innovation in Europe" (TEPSIE), European Commission – 7th Framework Programme. European Commission. DG Research, Brussels (2014b). http://www.tepsie.eu

11. Misuraca, G., Colombo, C., Radescu, R., Bacigalupo, M.: Mapping and analysis of ICT-enabled social innovation initiatives promoting social investment. In: Integrated Approaches to the Provision of Social Services, European Commission's Joint Research Centre, Institute for Prospective Technological Studies, JRC Technical reports Series (2015)

12. Bühler, C., Pelka, B.: Empowerment by digital media of people with disabilities. In: Miesenberger, K., Fels, D., Archambault, D., Peňáz, P., Zagler, W. (eds.) ICCHP 2014, Part I. LNCS, vol. 8547, pp. 17–24. Springer, Heidelberg (2014)

13. Kaletka, C., Pelka, B.: (Digital) Social innovation through public internet access points. In: Antona, M., Stephanidis, C. (eds.) Universal Access in Human-Computer Interaction. Access to Today's Technologies. LNCS, vol. 8547, pp. 201–212. Springer, Switzerland (2015). doi: 10.1007/978-3-319-20678-3_20

Investigating Motivational Aspects of Brazilian Elderly to Interact with Digital Games

Gleice Souza, Luciana Salgado, Esteban Clua,
and Daniela Gorski Trevisan$^{(\boxtimes)}$

Department of Computer Science,
Fluminense Federal University (UFF), Niterói, Brazil
{gramos,luciana,esteban,daniela}@ic.uff.br

Abstract. The increase in the number of world's elderly people has encouraged the research about human-computer interaction relating to the elderly. Recent studies indicate that digital games could bring benefits to the elderly, such as cognitive stimulation and relaxation. These benefits can help prevent some types of diseases related to old age. However, very few elderly take advantage of these benefits because they do not aware of it and do not have reasons or abilities to play digital games. This work focuses on investigating what are the elements that may encourage (or not) elderly people to interact with digital games and may offer relevant insights to games developers to motivate this target audience. For this, we organized a workshop to conduct a qualitative study with elderlies. Our findings showed up some elderly preferences, which may be converted into new design characteristics, although some positive and negative motivations of elderly Brazilians related to digital games are similar to the ones of the elderly in developed countries, according to the related work.

Keywords: Senior gamers · Elderly · Motivational aspects · Game design

1 Introduction

Biological and psychosocial changes are natural in the aging process and can affect different aspects in the elderly lives and even limit the realization of certain activities [1]. Recent research indicates that digital games are able to bring benefits to the elderly. These range from relaxation [2, 3], which provide cognitive stimulation to prevent some types of diseases related to old age [3, 4], to physiotherapy and rehabilitation benefits by using games to perform exercises [5]. However, the Information and Communication Technologies (ICT), especially games, are still little used by the elderly. Selwyn and co-authors [6], for example, claim that many of them do not use the computer games because they do not identify the need to use this feature.

To helping older people to overcome their limitations through digital games is, therefore, necessary to overcome a motivational barrier [7]. According to Elliot [8] motivation may be defined as the energization (i.e., instigation) and direction of behavior. Approach and avoidance motivation differ as a function of valence: in approach motivation, behavior is instigated or directed by a positive/desirable event or

M. Antona and C. Stephanidis (Eds.): UAHCI 2016, Part I, LNCS 9737, pp. 194–203, 2016.
DOI: 10.1007/978-3-319-40250-5_19

possibility; in avoidance motivation, behavior is instigated or directed by a negative/ undesirable event or possibility. However, motivation does not depend on individual factors only, it is also linked to social and cultural factors that can facilitate or hinder people's behavior. The way people act is also delimited by their cultural practices [9, 10]. Studies conducted in the Netherlands, Belgium and Portugal, for instance, have identified some necessary features in digital games to attract the elderly as well as some emotional aspects existing in this relationship [1, 2, 11, 12]. However, these studies were conducted in countries with different social and cultural context of Brazilian reality.

According to the World Health Organization[1], the elderly population in developing countries consists of individuals aged from 60 years. In this segment of the population are included people with different socio-economic, demographic and epidemiological characteristics. In order to find out the motivations of Brazilians elderly related to digital games, we conducted a qualitative study that investigated the preferences, motivations and opinions of older people, mainly guided by the following research question: What are the reasons for the older people to play (or not) digital games?

The paper is structured in four sections. After the introduction, we present the study methodology. Next, our findings from the study and triangulation. Finally, our conclusion and possibilities for future work.

2   Methodology

2.1   Half-Day Workshop

We conducted a qualitative study to investigate the preferences, motivations and opinions of older people, mainly guided by the question: What are the reasons for the older people to play (or not) digital games?

In order to answer our research question, we used a non predictive paradigm with interpretative and qualitative methods [15]. We performed a half-day workshop with 5 (five) elderly participants, divided into 4 steps: pre-session (S1), game session (S2), focus group (S3), participatory design (S4).

Participants' Profile. We recruited five women aged between 60 and 77 years. They have family income ranging from one to twelve times the basic salary in Brazil, three of them have the equivalent to a high school education and two of them have a graduation degree. Most participants have vision, some motor and memory limitation as well as hearing problems. All participants have a computer (desktop) at home and some basic experience with this device. The participant with the highest family income have also a tablet device. Despite their computer experience, participants affirmed to have a reasonable difficulty with digital technologies, in general. Finally, all participants play digital games (e.g. patience, crossword puzzles and minefield).

Pilot Study. To ensure that the workshop would be feasible and would allow the collection of the desired data, we conducted a previous pilot study with an elderly participant of 81 years old. The pilot study allowed us to identify the needs for

---

[1] http://www.who.int/en/ (last accessed in November, 2015).

improvement in devices, data collection and the needs for adjustments in the questionnaires questions to estimate their previous knowledge about games. During the pilot, we also learn that it was necessary to help them while develop ideas for creating new games.

Workshop Steps. The workshop was held in a half day, divided into four stages: pre-session (S1), game session (S2), focus group (S3), participatory design (S4). In the first stage of the workshop (pre-session) the participants filled the agreement term and a questionnaire with questions about socioeconomic data, leisure activities and level of experience with digital games. Instigated by the questionnaire questions participants commented freely about digital games, so we also could collect data from the participants' speech. In the second workshop stage (game session) we aim at observing the participants at interaction time with digital games. They were invited to interact with three different devices: notebook, tablet and smartphone. Because the number of devices were smaller than the number of participants, we asked them to form two pairs and one participant played alone (Fig. 1).

Fig. 1. Participants interacting with different devices in the gaming session stage

At this stage the participants were presented to six casual games, the device that they would play each game and its features. We choose the games based in the following criteria: be casual; with various interaction styles; have two games for each interactive device. All participants played six games alternating the devices between them. Participants received no prior instruction of how to play, so we can see how the elderly get to explore a new game and so identify potential interaction problems caused by the lack of prior experience with the game. The observers (researchers) were available to answer questions if a participant ask for help to avoid bothering them. The empirical data collected at this stage are from audio and video records while participants interacted with the games.

In the third stage (focus group) we collected participants' perceptions in the previous gaming session experience. Empirical data were collected from the audio records of participants' speeches in response to questions raised by observers about the games and devices used before.

In the last stage we conducted a participatory design session. The purpose of this step was to determine what characteristics are necessary and important when designing a new game for this public. To keep the focus on the elderly users we a *personna* based on the results of previous studies [13], see Fig. 2. Then we invited participants to think about a game to be played by the *personna*. We, then, asked them questions about the game's features. When needed we presented some examples to clarify possibilities and ideas mentioned for them. After defining the features, we designed the game with the participants' help and the aid of colorful markers and a whiteboard shared by everyone.

Rita is 69 years old and she likes to watch TV, do crossword puzzles and read to distract. She has a desktop computer at home that she uses to read email, access the internet and access the social networks. Rita is curious to play digital games, but she thinks does not have time for this and believes that she is not able to play this type of game. Rita does not see well without glasses and sometimes has trouble remembering details like where she left the pen she was using.

Fig. 2. Personna used to guide the participatory design session

The participants identified themselves with the *personna* and felt free to express their needs, opinion related to the game. The use of *personna* was a good tool for researchers to talk about the focus, game preferences and game appeal with the participants.

2.2 Data Analysis

The empirical data from the participants' speeches produced in each workshop step was analyzed, separately, using the discourse analysis technique [14]. We carried out a systematic exploration of discourse material to find out meaning. First, we applied an intra-participant analysis to identify meaning of categories from each participant. Afterwards we applied inter-participant analysis to identify the meaning categories recurring across multiple participants' discourse. Finally, we drew up our conclusions (positive and negative motivations issues) based on the set of categorized meanings that help us to answer our research question.

To validate the results obtained through the discourse analysis and confirm which motivations diverge or converge with those involving elderly people of other nationalities, we performed an exogenous triangulation [15, 16]. For that, we considered the related literature involving elderly and games [1, 2, 11, 12, 17–19]. Those studies were conducted in developed countries, which have a different socioeconomic and cultural reality of the developing countries reality such as Brazil. The main findings are shortly described in the next section. Due the lack of space, they are followed by our findings in triangulation phase.

3 Findings

With the application of discourse analysis technique, we identified two meaning categories, which emerged from the participants discourse in the workshop. The reasons for seniors do not play digital games were grouped in the category named as negative motivations. Based on the evidences we arrived at two sub-categories of meanings that synthesize these reasons: (i) believe that he/she will not be able to play successfully; and (ii) to have difficulties related to accessibility and usability problems. In the category of positive motivations, participants evidences that lead older people to take an interest in digital games were identified and synthesized into six subcategories of meanings: (i) be encouraged by others to play; (ii) it is possible, but not obliged, to interact with others; (iii) obtain benefits with the game; (iv) play autonomously; (v) have a nice experience with the game; (vi) create the game itself.

3.1   Negative Motivations

Believe that He/She Will Not Be Able to Play Successfully. Sometimes elderly people do not experience a new game because they believe that they do not have the capabilities to play. Several factors lead them to have this belief, but the main reasons are: their physical impairments or limitations related to their age; some bad previous experience; the fact that digital games are not of/for their generation.

The reasons identified in our workshop that converged with related works are: believe they do not have enough skills to play; memory problems; and lack of experience with digital devices. The fear that the elderly have in doubt about their capacity to play is not only related to digital games. In the study reported by Vasconcelos et al. [1], several participants indicated that they could not solve the game in a book without help because they do not have enough skills to perform those activities. The authors argued that engage in gaming experience, it is sometimes a challenge for the elderly and for this reason the game should be easy enough to allow a wide range of users. According to Smeddinck et al. [18] during recruiting participants for the study, some seniors mentioned reserves in order to play digital games based on motion. Thus, the elderly have shown to be afraid of using an unknown device whose interaction happens through movements, as well as participants of our workshop expressed concern in interacting with a device to which they were unaccustomed. In the study performed by Gerling et al. [17], the authors reported that most seniors who participated in the study were not able to recall the movements necessary to interact with the game and needed help to perform the correct movements. This difficulty meets the concern pointed by our workshop participants that reported to believe that they could not play due a memory problem.

Have Difficulties Related to Accessibility and Usability Problems. The main difficulties encountered by participants in our workshop were generated by accessibility and usability problems and such difficulties have leaded them to a poor user experience. We found the following recurrences by triangulating these results with related literature about accessibility problems: reduced size of the interface elements; lack of local language support; and quick responses required from players. Usability problems that were also observed in other studies were: ineffectiveness or absence of instructions and input data not intuitive. For example, in the work of Vasconcelos et al. [1], the authors cited a problem of usability involving non-intuitive data input mappings. The authors reported that seniors who participated in the study had to enter information via a virtual keyboard on the tablet, but they invariably ended up down the keyboard for longer than necessary, so that the letters were switched automatically to other symbols.

Another problem of usability is discussed by Nap et al. [2], in which one of the study participants said could not understand the rules of a specific game, demonstrating that the instructions of this game were not efficient. We also found in this study the recurrence of all accessibility issues that arose during our workshop. The main observed and recurrent problems were: difficulties with the high interaction speed required by some games or the speed of the game in the final levels; problems with the size of some elements of the game interface; and most participants had difficulty in understanding the content of the games that is presented in English. Finally, the games interfaces should incorporate usability and accessibility guidelines for the elderly public overcomes the barriers they face.

3.2   Positive Motivations

Be Encouraged by Others to Play. Receive an indication of a game or be taught to play, can be an incentive for seniors to play. The importance of being encouraged by others is also reported by De Schutter and Vanden Abeele [11], which mentioned the fact that one of the participants of their study begun to play encouraged by his son.

It Could be Possible, But Not Obliged, to Interact with Others. The ability to interact with others is a good thing for the elderly, since the player can also play alone. Through the workshop results, we found out that one of the envisioned reasons for this is that not everyone have someone available to play with. We also find evidence of this in the study of Nap et al. [2], where one of the participants said to be not practical to play with other people, because his grandchildren live in another country. In addition, the authors report that although most of the old players have rejected the idea of playing games with other people, some of the old players like the idea of playing digital games with family or friends in the same room. On the other hand, De Schutter [12] claims that social interaction was the least popular motivation among the reasons cited by the old players, but the social interaction was shown to be the most important feature for players to invest more time in games. Given this contrast posted by the De Schutter [12], perhaps the seniors players are just looking for older playing partners. In contrast to that, the results of our workshop explain that older people can enjoy playing with people from any age. This result can be a specific characteristic from the Brazilian public that deserves to be deeply investigated in future works.

Obtain Benefits Through the Game. One of the factors that make sense for the elderly playing digital games is the possibility of obtaining benefits through the game. Thus, the elderly need to identify benefits *a priori* that they will get if playing digital games. Exercise their memories and learning about something through the digital game were the benefits identified in our workshop, which have also appeared in previous works. For instance, De Schutter [12] argues in his work that AVGUG instrument (Video Analysis Game Uses and Gratuities) [20] seems to lack of motivations that are targeted specifically for the elderly public, such as memory or skill training, keeping up to date and learning about technology. In the work of Abeele [19], most of games suggested by the elderly in brainstorming sessions offer the possibility of enriching the user's knowledge. Some examples of that are cultural or touristic quizzes.

Play Autonomously. To be able to interact with a digital game without help was extremely rewarding for the participants who managed this. But for the elderly feel able to play autonomously they need a game that is easy to understand, offer an efficient interaction with them and have efficient instructions. Playing a game that is familiar for them in the physical environment is one of the alternatives that the elderly found to play digital games more autonomously once they are aware about the game rules. These findings are converging with the results pointed by Vasconcelos et al. [1], De Schutter [12], Nap et al. [2] and De Schutter and Vanden Abeele [11]. De Schutter and Vanden Abeele, for instance, reported that some participants said that digital games have given to them a sense of freedom contributing to a sense of autonomy. In the list of guidelines suggested by Gerling et al. [17] for full body interaction they argued that the menus, startup and shutdown routines of the game should be sufficiently easy for the elderly users encouraging them to play independently.

Have a Nice Experience with the Game. Relaxation, distraction, fun, and feel challenged were the experiences provided by games, which participants of our workshop demonstrated to appreciate. In the study by De Schutter [12], be challenged received the highest score among the reasons provided by AVGUG instrument (challenge, social interaction, distraction, fantasy and excitement). In addition to this, distraction and excitement were among the top three reasons that lead the participants to play digital games. Distraction, fun and excitement were aspects also reported by study participants of Smeddinck et al. [18]. The fun also appears as a positive factor in the elderly experience in De Schutter and Vanden Abeele [11], Nap et al. [2] and Gerling et al. [17] studies. In the work of Nap et al. [2], in addition to the fun, the authors found out that the elderly also judge relaxation as one of the main motivations for playing digital games. For participants of the De Schutter and Vanden Abeele study [11], besides fun and challenge, digital games were also used to fill the time. At this point, it is relevant to note that spending time was not a valid experience or motivation observed in our study. On the other hand be challenged was a recurrent motivation because it is related to the fact the game should meet a specific goal bringing a benefit to the player, usually by learning something new.

Create Their Own Game. To participate in the creation process of a game can motivate seniors to play this game. Among the studies addressed only the work of Abeele et al. [19] investigated the possibility of including older people in the game development process and they also noted a good motivation of seniors participants in creating their own game. However, it is not clear in that work whether seniors who participated in the study had suggested game design features. Apparently, the participation of the elderly was limited to the conceptual step what can result in a game with limited attractive design features for older players.

In the participatory design phase of our workshop was possible to observe a set of design characteristics focused on elderly players. The following characteristics are also present in the literature: to have support to the player language, to have good artistic quality; to be configurable, to have missions, to be able to play for a short period of time, to have mobility, to allow collaboration, to have a wide variety of games, to provide help on context of use. Additional design characteristics were pointed in our workshop. They are: to have possibility to play in full screen, to have good soundtrack, to have characters with good empathy with the player, to provide game with third-person perspective, to have an exploratory environment, and at last, to have a good storytelling.

However, because participatory design was not the main focus of this study and thus we are not able to affirm if these design features are specific to the elderly Brazilian public or not. In this direction, a more detailed survey of the existing literature may point to new directions in the possibility of inclusion of elderlies in the game development process and clarifying such cultural aspects.

4 Final Considerations and Future Directions

This work aimed at investigating what motivates (or not) elderly people to play digital games. A half-day workshop (with 5 female participants) was organized as a means to collect data about their experience while interacting with this kind of applications. The four steps of the workshop gave us the opportunity to capture different and complementary visions about some motivational aspects of Brazilian elderly to interact with digital games.

We highlight three contributions that, in our view, can be of interest and value for other researchers and practitioners involved in HCI, game design and design for elderly. One is that our findings suggest that the creation of games in participatory design activities with elderlies is a very promising approach. It was surprising the engagement of the participants to create a new game. They became excited and motivated about the task and to find a good story to involve the *persona in the game*. So, the workshop procedures (questionnaire, game session, participatory design) showed itself as a good environment to investigate specific issues to elderlies.

The second contribution we would like to highlight come from our findings related to negative motivational aspects. The ease of use is the most crucial quality factor to elderly people. The absence of this factor determines the general attractiveness of a game or device. In our study, all the participants elect as *the worst game*, the one which they have more difficulties to interact.

Finally, the positive motivational aspects pointed that the elderly have interest in new and different games. The participants showed a high level of interest for games that they never have played before. We suspect that digital versions of already known games are just a start point to attract them. However, as time goes, they need to be motivated by innovations or challenges, although the results of our study show they are afraid of making mistakes.

In conclusion to this paper, we underline that our contributions open avenues for future work. Besides the new features to design, unlike research in other countries, our findings also showed that Brazilian older people can enjoy playing with people from any age. The study of motivational aspects of elderly to interact with digital games followed by the creation of a game in a collaborative way are just the first steps to the development of attractive games and maybe be viewed as an attempt to propose a list of *"do's and don'ts"*. Future work could create, implement and evaluate the game (proposed by elderlies) to advance the scientific knowledge about this theme and also validate the design characteristics pointed in the design participative session. We also plan to organize others empirical studies to investigate the interaction of elderly people without experience with digital games.

Acknowledgment. The authors would like to thank all participants who participated in empirical studies and contributed to the research reported in this paper. Additionally, the authors thank CNPq and FAPERJ for financial support received for this research.

References

1. Vasconcelos, A., Silva, P.A., Caseiro, J., Nunes, F., Teixeira, L.F.: Designing tablet-based games for seniors: the example of CogniPlay, a cognitive gaming platform. In: Proceedings of the 4th International Conference on Fun and Games, pp. 1–10. ACM (2012)
2. Nap, H., De Kort, Y., IJsselsteijn, W.: Senior gamers: preferences, motivations and needs. Gerontechnology **8**, 247–262 (2009)
3. Ijsselsteijn, W., Nap, H.H., de Kort, Y., Poels, K.: Digital game design for elderly users. In: Proceedings of the 2007 Conference on Future Play, pp. 17–22. ACM (2007)
4. Clark, J.E., Lanphear, A.K., Riddick, C.C.: The effects of videogame playing on the response selection processing of elderly adults. J. Gerontol. **42**, 82–85 (1987)
5. Smith, S.T., Schoene, D.: The use of exercise-based videogames for training and rehabilitation of physical function in older adults: current practice and guidelines for future research. Aging Health **8**, 243–252 (2012)
6. Selwyn, N., Gorard, S., Furlong, J., Madden, L.: Older adults' use of information and communications technology in everyday life. Ageing Soc. **23**, 561–582 (2003)
7. Carvalho, R.N.S., Ishitani, L.: Motivational factors for mobile serious games for elderly users. In: Proceedings of XI SB Games, pp. 19–28 (2012)
8. Elliot, A.J.: Approach and avoidance motivation and achievement goals. Educ. Psychol. **34**, 169–189 (1999)
9. Reeve, J.: Understanding Motivation and Emotion. Wiley, Hoboken (2009)
10. Deci, E.L., Ryan, R.M.: Intrinsic Motivation and Self-determination in Human Behavior. Springer Science & Business Media, New York (1985)
11. De Schutter, B., Vanden Abeele, V.: Designing meaningful play within the psycho-social context of older adults. In: Proceedings of the 3rd International Conference on Fun and Games, pp. 84–93. ACM (2010)
12. De Schutter, B.: Never too old to play: the appeal of digital games to an older audience. Games Cult. **6**, 155–170 (2010)
13. Souza, G.R., Trevisan, D.G.: Estudo investigativo sobre idosos, jogos e suas motivações. Cadernos de Informática **8**, 35–40 (2014). Available only in Portuguese
14. Nicolaci-da-Costa, A.M., Leitão, C.F., Romão-Dias, D.: Gerando conhecimento sobre homens, mulheres e crianças que usam computadores: algumas contribuições da psicologia clínica. In: IV Workshop sobre Fatores Humanos em Sistemas Computacionais, Florianópolis (2001)
15. Creswell, J.W., Miller, D.L.: Determining validity in qualitative inquiry. Theory Pract. **39**, 124–130 (2000)

16. De Souza, C.S., Leitão, C.F.: Semiotic engineering methods for scientific research in HCI. Synth. Lect. Hum.-Centered Inform. **2**, 1–122 (2009)
17. Gerling, K., Livingston, I., Nacke, L., Mandryk, R.: Full-body motion-based game interaction for older adults. In: Proceedings of the SIGCHI Conference on Human Factors in Computing Systems, pp. 1873–1882. ACM (2012)
18. Smeddinck, J., Gerling, K.M., Tiemkeo, S.: Visual complexity, player experience, performance and physical exertion in motion-based games for older adults. In: Proceedings of the 15th International ACM SIGACCESS Conference on Computers and Accessibility, p. 25. ACM (2013)
19. Abeele, V.V., Husson, J., Vandeurzen, L., Desmet, S.: A soft approach to computer science: designing & developing computer games for and with senior citizens. J. Game Dev. **2**, 41–62 (2007)
20. Sherry, J.L., Lucas, K., Greenberg, B.S., Lachlan, K.: Video game uses and gratifications as predictors of use and game preference. Playing Video Games: Motives Responses Conseq. **24**, 213–224 (2006)

Identifying and Addressing Critical Usability Issues to Strengthen Nurses' Interactions with Health IT

Nancy Staggers[1,2(✉)], Beth Elias[3], Ellen Makar[4], Jane Hunt[4], and
Gregory L. Alexander[5]

[1] Summit Health Informatics, New Orleans, USA
nancystaggers@sisna.com
[2] University of Utah, Salt Lake City, UT, USA
[3] Virginia Commonwealth University, Richmond, VA, USA
belias@vcu.edu
[4] Department of Health and Human Services, Washington, D.C., USA
makarelv@gmail.com, janehunt@comcast.net
[5] University of Missouri, Kansas City, USA
AlexanderG@missouri.edu

Abstract. Technology usability, especially electronic health record (EHR) usability, is a global concern for clinicians. Despite critical user experience (UX) issues, nurses are not vocal about interactions with health IT. The purpose of this project was to identify nurses' health IT UX issues and propose solutions for them. Using a snowball sampling technique, 25 experts were interviewed using a semi-structured format. Three themes emerged from content analysis (1) The Burdens of Health IT, (2) The Voice of Nursing, and (3) We Need a New Vision. Lack of cognitive support underscores the burden theme. The voice of nursing is missing throughout the systems life cycle, and a need exists for new visions of EHRs and training delivery. Solutions include the need for national leadership, modular redesign of EHRs to support the way nurses think and do work, and a concerted effort to incorporate UX methods into health IT design in the future.

Keywords: User experience · Usability · Nurses · Health information technology · Electronic health records

1 Introduction

Technology usability, especially electronic health record (EHR) usability, is a global concern for clinicians. In the U.S., physicians are exceptionally vocal about poor EHR usability and impacts on their productivity as well as their reimbursement. The American Medical Association and 30 other medical organizations wrote to the Office of the National Coordinator for health Information Technology (IT) deploring EHR usability and provided six recommendations for essential EHR usability [1]. In late March 2015, EHR issues became an epicenter of health IT user experience (UX) difficulties when The Joint Commission (TJC), a U.S. accrediting body for health organizations, created a new alert concerning health IT-related sentinel events. TJC completed an analysis of 3,375 adverse event reports from January 2010 to June 2013. These included 120 health

© Springer International Publishing Switzerland 2016
M. Antona and C. Stephanidis (Eds.): UAHCI 2016, Part I, LNCS 9737, pp. 204–213, 2016.
DOI: 10.1007/978-3-319-40250-5_20

IT-related sentinel events [2]. A full one-third of these events emanated from computer-user interface issues and another 24 % were related to workflow and communication issues. TJC issued the alert because these kinds of issues can affect patient safety, clinician productivity and organizational quality measures.

At 3.1 million professionals, nursing is the largest group interacting with health IT nationally in the U.S. [3] and globally. As seen in Fig. 1, nurses represent the largest number of EHR users in the U.S. and they experience critical user experience issues with EHRs as well as other health IT. These issues are different than those for more vocal professionals such as physicians. Yet, nurses are less outspoken about their UX issues.

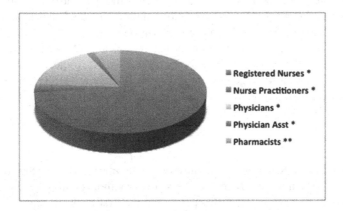

Fig. 1. Proportion of RNs to Other Professions in the U.S.* http://kff.org/state-category/providers-service-use/, 2016 ** http://www.bls.gov/oes/current/oes291051.htm, 2014. (Color figure online)

Individual research studies are available on the topic of nurses and UX issues, though a national view does not yet exist. For example, Drew and colleagues observed nurses responding to 2,558,760 unique alarms generated by physiological monitors over a month's time in five intensive care units. A full 88 % were false positives for arrhythmias, impacting productivity and creating issues with alarm fatigue [4]. A usability evaluation by Staggers et al. examined barcode medication administration design and found 99 usability problems, 15 of which were classified as catastrophic due to the potential for patient harm [5]. The sum total of the issues impacted patient safety, nurses' productivity and being able to obtain the "big picture" of the patient in 150 Veterans Administration facilities using this application in the U.S.

In addition to EHRs, the work of nursing increasingly includes point-of-care devices such as smart intravenous medication infusion pumps, which incorporate information technology that is like a desktop computer [6]. These system and device interfaces are therefore becoming more complex. Many of these devices and systems are products purchased from different vendors resulting in multiple complex interfaces, using different interaction designs that must be mastered before they can be used efficiently and effectively.

The healthcare model is also evolving in the U.S., with increased involvement of information and communication technologies to care for patients in their homes, provide telehealth services and make use of health apps that are used on smart devices to track and manage chronic conditions [7]. As patients with chronic conditions and lower acuity health problems are being pushed back into their homes, patients who are admitted to hospitals are more seriously ill than in the past [8]. One could argue that caring for these complex patients increases information needs, requiring nurses to interact with health IT even more frequently. In fact, nursing will be increasingly called on to work with patients and existing/emerging technologies to improve patient outcomes. Equally important is that nurses will need to act in their traditional role as patient advocates in this technology-rich environment.

These recent studies and care complexity issues likely identify only the tip of the iceberg of nurses' current UX concerns. No systematic methods exists to collate and analyze UX issues for any health professional group. Therefore, the purpose of this project was to describe nurses' usability issues with health IT and to develop recommendations for improving health IT usability for nurses. The project was sponsored by the Health Information Management and Systems Society (HIMSS) User Experience and Nursing Communities as well as the American Nurses Association.

2   Methods

This project was conducted under the guise of a 5-member team from the HIMSS User Experience (UX) Committee. Team members are the authors of this paper. This descriptive, exploratory project included two phases. In the first phase of the study, requests for usability case studies were distributed via informatics and the American Nurses Association list serves. Second, snowball sampling was used to select national nursing, nursing informatics and UX leaders and experts for interviews. After obtaining participants' consent, the team used a semi-structured interviewing technique with probes to interact with experts. The interviewers used a structured script to ask participants to describe critical usability issues for nurses in their interactions with health IT. Follow-up questions asked participants to describe the significance of the issues, why they thought they occurred, the prevalence of issues in other sites and last, experts were asked to identify solutions for UX issues. Interviews were audio-recorded; extensive notes were taken and independently verified by two team members. Content analysis was used to analyze the data [9, 10] and to identify appropriate, preliminary thematic content.

3   Results

For the first phase, the listserve requests went to thousands of nurses, but the request for case studies resulted in only 12 uneven submissions, making this method ineffective and the data not representative. The second phase included interviews with 25 experts who were UX professionals (4), nursing informatics/nursing UX leaders (9), UX nurse researchers (6) and site leaders such as chief nursing or medical informatics officers (6). The representation was across federal/non-federal institutions, acute care and long-term care, various health IT vendors, and academic/non-academic organizations. Twenty of the participants were professional nurses who had expertise in UX and health IT.

Interviews lasted an average of 25 min with a range of 18–55 min. The results in this paper represent preliminary analyses of the interview data.

3.1 Themes on UX Issues and Solutions

Three themes emerged through preliminary content analyses (1) *The Burdens of Health IT* (2) *The Voice of Nursing* and (3) *We Need a New Vision*. Discussion of each follows.

The Burdens of Health IT. This theme includes myriad design and technical issues. Experts indicated health IT developers do not yet understand nurses' work or cognitive processes so these are not reflected in current technology design. For example, the work of nursing includes non-linear where tasks, such as medication administration, often clustered across multiple patients. In contrast, EHRs are designed to allow a view of one patient's information at a time, making information retrieval difficult to support clustered activities. Moreover, as one UX expert noted, EHRs miss the main points about nurses' activities. An example concerns barcode medication administration which focuses on assuring the medication in hand is being given to the correct patient, but it does not support higher level cognitive activities such as, "Is this even the right medication for this patient given her condition?" or "Do the patients' symptoms indicate another medication might be superior?" Another example is deploying an adult EHR in a pediatric setting creating a mismatch of care requirements, e.g., for weight-based dosing and age-based care, resulting in increased patient safety issues and inefficiencies.

As a snapshot of the health IT burdens, a nurse-author who was interviewed for this project published her accounting of interactions with her site's EHR:

I do understand why thoroughness in documentation matters legally, but sometimes wonder if sadists designed our software. It should not be easier to order a sweater from Lands End than to chart on my patients, but it is. Click, scroll, type, enter. Here's the menu with twenty choices, none of them the one I need. Here's the point where I need information from two different screens, but there's no way to toggle between them. Here's the screen with thirty discrete options to check, but the window it opens up only shows me five at a time. New lab results, X-rays, CT scans, MRIs: none of those generate an alert and the screen is full of minute icons, some of which represent functions I don't use or even understand [11].

These kinds of cognitive-task mismatches result in not only a lack of health IT support for the cognitive processes that are at the core of nursing practice, but a frustration that comes from increased cognitive burdens. Similarly a UX expert indicated that not all nursing activities are "orderables," meaning not all are driven by physician-related orders, a dependent activity central to EHR interactions. In addition to and dependent and inter-dependent activities, nurses perform independent activities. For instance, nurses' independent discharge teaching may uncover the fact that an older patient has no one to care for him at home, a fact that could contribute to a readmission within 30 days and greater morbidity.

More important, nurses are knowledge workers who must think critically about patients and their care. The current design of EHRs can impede this thinking. A prime example is the EHR design and federal requirements that have resulted in extensive documentation requirements for nurses, especially around entering data for others' needs such as for quality improvement departments and to meet new federal guidelines, e.g., Meaningful Use. One expert counted the number of clicks to enter a nursing admission assessment: 532. Assessments alone can take 30–60 min of a shift to chart, according to experts. Moreover, finding pertinent data in the sea of text is difficult.

Designs are particularly problematic for information synthesis around handoffs, medication management, and communication activities. Care handoffs, as noted by many experts in this project, are a particular source of UX "pain points" [12, 13] because nurses must conduct "information foraging" in the EHR to construct the full picture of patients' episodes of care.

The impacts of these health IT pain points occur across all healthcare delivery sites and vendors. Patient safety is at risk when the goals around patient care get lost as nurses struggle to use health IT. Inefficiencies are a particular impact and can result in delays in decision making and care rendered, e.g., a 1.5 h delay in the administration of pain meds during a system downtime experienced by one expert.

Organizations typically purchase disparate systems and smart point-of-care testing devices resulting in poor interoperability and data isolation. Information is siloed between fragmented systems and in devices such as vital sign machines that are not integrated with EHRs. Despite these issues, nurses are expected to adopt and use these systems, a real technology dilemma. Hybrid systems using both technology and paper are also common which further increases data isolation. The lack of interoperability and hybrid systems hinder both the nurse's ability to locate information quickly and obtain the holistic patient view required to provide safe and appropriate patient care.

The *Burdens of Health IT* theme also includes perceived time away from patients due to increased interaction time with technology. This decreases the nurses' awareness of their patient's status. All these IT burdens result in inefficiencies. Work-arounds, lack of fit to workflow, loss of productivity and threats to patient safety are outcomes of the health IT burden for nurses.

The Voice of Nursing. The *Voice of Nursing* is absent in all the phases of the health IT systems lifecycle from the selecting, purchasing, developing/tailoring and implementing processes. If nurses are present in the selection/purchasing process they are often an executive who does not represent the voice of the point-of-care nurse who will be using the purchased system. While nurses may be consulted during the tailoring or development process, this consulting is typically more casual and informal. UX methods are seldom employed (although they are being increasingly used by health IT vendors). Implementation processes do include nurses, although the extent of involvement is under-representative of the numbers of nurses in both acute and longterm care facilities.

Because of this, health IT systems and tools are seen as a "no-win" for many nurses, who must simply use without complaint whatever technology appears in their facilities. Unlike physicians, nurses are employed by the institution, giving them little recourse if EHRs are purchased without an end-user viewpoint or if technology is not integrated.

Experts thought nurses often received inadequate and inconsistent training. Typically go-live or new personnel training was provided, but no training was done after that. Training models are often "train the trainer," meaning that training and education quality and effectiveness eroded over time once the initial expert trainer left the site.

A New Vision for EHRs. Despite the progress for EHRs globally, new visions for this technology are necessary. A main re-envisioning would be designing acute and longterm care EHRs with a patient-centered focus. For inpatient care, the current focus is primarily internal processes for departments – laboratory, radiology, pharmacy, etc. Orders management modules are typically "glued" over these functions. Data are aggregated by patient identification numbers for results and orders, but EHRs do not yet support full processes of care such as seeing the "picture of the patient" or even having relevant data integrated across intra-facility or external sites around the reason for admission. A simple example is following patients as they traverse across the surgical process from admission to the operating room (OR) to the post-anesthesia care unit (PACU) to intensive care (ICU) to a surgical floor and then to home and follow-up with their surgeon and primary care provider. Current EHRs do not show integrated data for these patients such as estimated blood loss from the OR or even medications given intraoperatively once patients leave the OR/PACU setting.

Supporting care for complex patients is even more difficult. For instance, oncology patients are seen by myriad health professionals in myriad departments both in and outside a facility supported by a particular EHR. Some data, such as chemotherapy or TPN (total parental nutrition) may still be on paper versus in electronic media. Issues are compounded in long-term care when even basic connectivity and integration challenges are amplified. For example, skilled nursing facilities rely on outside labs and radiology, so lack of this basic integration results in a paucity of patient-centered information. Creating a full accounting of care is difficult at best in any setting. Having a patient-centered focus would mean re-designing EHRs to support these transitions, data syntheses and "telling the story" of the patient across settings and units.

Another expert suggested re-envisioning EHRs as a communication (versus billing or physician-centric) system. Communication is central to patient care, especially in the acute care setting. Current EHRs were not designed with this requirement in mind. Current communication is done by phone, email and verbal methods as well as, to a lesser extent, by clinical notes. Complex patients generate hundreds of separate notes filed in EHRs, making it difficult to track relevant and timely information. Instead, communication is often informal and frequently verbal.

Last, several experts suggested the need for new education and training models that include training beyond mere go-live. In particular, training models should be discipline-specific and based upon workflow. Although none of the experts recommended de-installing technology, critical improvements are needed in the near future.

4 Discussion and Conclusions

This preliminary analysis shows that nurses experience significant health IT usability issues, some that can result in increased risk to patient outcomes. Significant health IT design issues exist across settings, particularly for handoffs, medication management and communication activities. Experts thought the voice of nursing was missing in all phases of the systems lifecycle and they suggested new visions for the redesign of technology to support acute and longterm care. Nurses are experiencing increased cognitive burden from the very technology whose purported benefit is that it is supposed to reduce the burden of care as well as the risk of patient harm.

The reasons bedside nurses did not respond to our initial request to share their health IT experiences are not clear, but several reasons are possible. First, point-of-care and bedside nurses are focused on patient care needs at the moment. Most nurses are under severe time constraints as they care for patients, and they also may think they just have to adapt to whatever technology an organization deploys. Nurses often work in survival mode to assure adequate care is rendered during a shift. Managing or improving technology can be well beyond their primary goal of completing patient care. Another expert mentioned that once a work-around is created to a UX issue, nurses may see the issue as resolved and not requiring attention. Nurses can feel that they have no voice in technology decisions or as experts in this study indicated, they may not even know to whom to take their issues and complaints about health IT. Last, fear of retribution was mentioned during informal discussions and interviews. Nurses who speak out may find they are labeled as trouble-makers or their performance evaluations may identify them as not being team players.

4.1   Health IT Transformation

Solutions identified by the participants require that we look beyond the installed base and think of health IT as a process of continual, incremental transformation. Most organizations have installed technology, and, as noted earlier, de-installation will not help them attain their institutional and patient experience goals.

Partnering is required among health IT vendors, healthcare organizations, UX professionals and nurses to guide the evolution of health IT and support patient and organizational needs. The voice of the largest group of health IT users can give vendors the real-world feedback they need to support the process of care transformation. The voice of nursing

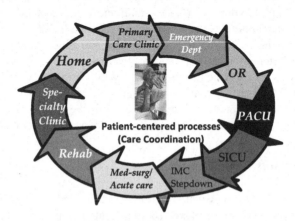

Fig. 2. A Model of Patient-Centered, Communication Health IT Copyright Nancy Staggers, 2015. Reprinted with permission.

can also guide organizations in the purchase and effective use of tools and systems that represent significant costs in budgets. The impact of incorporating UX professionals into the partnership will serve as a bridge between the nurses and the efforts of vendors to transform health IT ensuring a continuous feedback loop.

In addition to partnering, a new vision of health IT is needed: as a patient-centered communication system (see Fig. 2). Technology is seen as a triad of care support: technology, patient and nurse. The new vision must also consider health IT as part of an ecosystem that can bring risk and gains. Leaders may think EHR redesign is overwhelming, but one UX expert suggested using a modular approach to redesign versus a whole-scale overhaul. This approach is successfully used by Goggle. For example, medications management or handoffs could serve as a starting point.

4.2 Standardization

Standardization was also identified as an essential solution across a number of entities and issues. Standardization is needed in areas from health IT design guidelines from developers/vendors to documentation standards at a national level. For instance, each site currently tailors a vendor's system de novo and also develops its own set of nursing assessment forms. However, an admission assessment to a neonatal intensive care unit in San Francisco is unlikely to be very different from one in New York City. Thus, an opportunity for standardization is available nationally and to some extent, globally.

Standardization for technology project implementations and training also exists. Again, each organization designs its education and training de novo. While some peculiarities within sites exists, most training can be standardized according to the product being implemented. Known project management principles can be employed. Continual and refresher training could reduce variability in health IT interaction quality. Training would also be designed using workflow pertinent to user groups.

4.3 The Voice of Nursing

Nurses are knowledge workers and act as an information and communication hub for the healthcare team; thus, nurses' voices must be reflected in technology design, purchasing, deployment and evaluation.

The voice of nursing around health IT is also needed at all levels in a healthcare organization. Nurses' role as patient advocate extends to health IT so nursing input into purchasing, design and tailoring decisions is essential. Successful organizations will recognize nurses as knowledge workers engaged in complex activities which are currently poorly understood by others.

This means that increased nursing leadership is needed on UX issues in health IT. Nursing needs a digital strategy, a strategic direction that focuses on why nurses use particular technology, what health IT does and what it can do to support the evolution of nursing practice. In the plan, a home needs to be assigned for nursing UX issues, both locally and a home for UX issues is needed nationally. Clinicians need the ability to collect UX issues and find solutions for them.

4.4 Uptake of UX Tools

Tools exist for integrating UX professionals, their practices and methods. These include the HIMSS Usability Maturity Model, National Institutes for Standards and Technology (NIST) usability documents and SAFER guidelines. The HIMSS Usability Maturity Model was developed by the HIMSS UX committee and is tailored to the health IT domain. It describes 5 stages of organizational maturity for UX and provides steps to attain each stages [14]. NIST has created a series of documents for the design and testing of EHRs, e.g., NIST 7804 on evaluating EHR designs [15]. Last, the U.S. Office of the National Coordinator for Health IT created SAFER guides. These are guides for organizational self-assessment in safe use of health IT such as: High priority practices, contingency planning, system configuration, system interfaces and computerized provider order entry [16].

Experts in this project agreed that current technology designs do not support nurses' work or provide needed cognitive support. Impacts span patients, nurses, local organizations and the national healthcare system. Clearly, EHRs must be re-conceptualized to be patient-centered, to support communication, to be interoperable and to support team-based processes. The voice of nursing must be included in all phases of the systems lifecycle.

4.5 Significance and Comparison with the Literature

The results of this project demonstrate widespread UX issues for nurses in both acute and longterm care. The impacts are non-trivial: risks to patient safety, increased cognitive burdens, loss of productivity and other inefficiencies. This project provides a national snapshot of the state of UX affairs with health IT in the U.S. Thus, it expands what is known for individual UX studies.

This project bolsters available literature cited earlier. It is also consistent with a recently released report from the National Quality Foundation [17]. The report outlines the potential for health IT to create new hazards and recommends a framework for health IT safety measurement. Of importance here, one of the key areas is including user-centered design methods and testing to promote health IT safety.

5 Future Research and Project Limitations

Future research might include systematic assessments of novel designs to solve complex health IT issues identified here particularly for care transitions (handoffs), medication management and care communication. Researchers might develop and evaluate future visions for health IT and/or EHRs to promote safety and efficiency. Limitations to this project include the lack of sampling for clinical areas outside acute and long-term care such as telehealth, public health and home health. Future researchers may wish to conduct a similar project for those areas. The project lacked the view of point-of-care nurses, despite our efforts at requesting their input. However, site experts interviewed in this project should have been able to represent their views. Future researchers may want to interview nurses in person versus listserve requests.

References

1. AMA.: AMA board chair: HHS should address EHR usability issues immediately. American Medical Association (2014). http://www.ama-assn.org/ams/pub/amawire/2013-may-15/2013-may-15-general_news1.shtml. Accessed 29 Jan 2016
2. TJC: Safe use of health information technology. Safe use of health technology. The Joint Commission, vol. 54, 31 March 2015. www.jointcommission.org. Accessed 27 Jan 2016
3. AACN: Nursing Fact Sheet. American Association of Colleges of Nursing (2011). http://www.aacn.nche.edu/media-relations/fact-sheets/nursing-fact-sheet. Accessed 29 Jan 2016
4. Drew, B.J., Harris, P., Zegre-Hemsey, J.K., Mammone, T., Schindler, D., Salas-Boni, R., et al.: Insights into the problem of alarm fatigue with physiologic monitor devices: a comprehensive observational study of consecutive intensive care unit patients. PLoS ONE 9, e110274 (2014)
5. Staggers, N., Iribarren, S., Guo, J.W., Weir, C.: Evaluation of a BCMA's electronic medication administration record. West J. Nurs. Res. (2015)
6. Elias, B.L., Moss, J.A., Dillavou, M., Shih, A., Azuero, A.: Evaluation of nursing student perspectivesof a simulated smart pump. Clin. Simul. Nurs. 9, e3599–e3606 (2013)
7. Demiris, G., Kneale, L.: Informatics systems and tools to facilitate patient-centered care coordination. Yearb. Med. Inform. 10, 15–21 (2015)
8. Jacob, E.R., McKenna, L., D'Amore, A.: The changing skill mix in nursing: considerations for and against different levels of nurse. J. Nurs. Manag. 23, 421–426 (2015)
9. Hsieh, H.F., Shannon, S.E.: Three approaches to qualitative content analysis. Qual. Health Res. 15, 1277–1288 (2005)
10. Patton, M.: Qualitative Research and Evaluation Methods. Sage, Thousand Oaks (2002)
11. Brown, T.: The Shift: One Nurse, Twelve Hours and Four Patients' Lives, p. 117. Algonquin Books, Chapel Hill (2015)
12. Collins, S.A., Mamykina, L., Jordan, D., Stein, D.M., Shine, A., Reyfman, P., et al.: In search of common ground in handoff documentation in an intensive care unit. J. Biomed. Inform. 45, 307–315 (2012)
13. Staggers, N., Clark, L., Blaz, J.W., Kapsandoy, S.: Why patient summaries in electronic health records do not provide the cognitive support necessary for nurses' handoffs on medical and surgical units: insights from interviews and observations. Health Inform. J. 17, 209–223 (2011)
14. HIMSS. HIMSS Usability Maturity Model (2015). http://www.himss.org/ResourceLibrary/ContentTabsDetail.aspx?ItemNumber=39016. Accessed 26 Jan 2016
15. NIST: Technical Evaluation, Testing and Validation of Electronic Health Records. NISTIR 7804. National Institutes of Standards and Technology, Gaitherburg, MD (2011). http://www.nist.gov/healthcare/usability/. Accessed 29 Jan 2016
16. ONC: SAFER: Safey Assurance Factors for EHR Resilience. Office of the National Coordinator for Health IT; Washington D.C. (2014). https://www.healthit.gov/sites/safer/files/guides/safer_highprioritypractices_sg001_form_0.pdf. Accessed 29 Jan 2016
17. NQF: Identification and Prioritization of Health IT Patient Safety Measures. National Quality Forum. HHSM-500-2012-000091-Task Order HHSM-500-TO016-Task Order 16. Department of Health and Human Services, Was 17 November 2015. http://www.qualityforum.org/ProjectEventsList.aspx?projectID=77689. Accessed 27 Jan 2016

Design with Me: I Have Special Needs! The Case for Cerebral Palsy

Josiane Tochetto[✉], Cayley Guimarães, Ana Luiza Maranho, and Ana Luísa Tartari

Federal University of Technology – Paraná (UTFPR), Curitiba, Brazil
jotochetto@gmail.com, cayleyg@utfpr.edu.br,
maranhochyla@gmail.com, analuisa.tartari@live.com

Abstract. The HCI community has an important task of bringing the requirements of people with special needs to the forefront. Thus, all involved can help inform the design of systems that promote quality of life, inclusion and citizenship for a large portion of individuals and groups. This article presents a process that draws from universal and participatory design, as well as intellectual tools, such as mental and empathy maps, to help designers to inform design of artifacts. As per the proposed framework, it also presents a set of suggestions of artifacts and systems to be built that are centered on persons with Cerebral Palsy.

Keywords: Cerebral palsy · Special needs · Universal and participatory design · Empathy map

1 Introduction

People with special needs have been excluded from society: they suffer daily through life-threatening situations that go unattended, mostly due to lack of awareness, proper practices and policies, tools and education, among others. People with special needs do not fulfill their human potential. This article follows the HCI community lead of designing for people with special needs to aid them in their social inclusion and citizenship. It presents an HCI process that relies on various theories, frameworks and tools with which to inform the design of artifacts. It also presents an initial set of artifacts needed that are centered on persons with Cerebral Palsy (CP).

CP can be described as a group of non-progressive motor syndromes, caused by injuries or abnormalities in the brain, which occur during birth or the first years of development. CP is not a disease to be removed: rather, one can think of people with CP as presented with a different way to experience human life. As such, families, healthcare personnel and those with the syndrome are in need of artifacts and educational tools - usually in the form of Assistive Technology (AT). AT are devices that enable people to perform tasks by providing enhancements and new interaction methods to accomplish such tasks. CP syndrome has a gamut of symptoms that range from low to high degree of motor and cognitive impairment. Thus, Universal Design (i.e. design of inclusive, accessible artifacts) should be used basically to generate initial ideas - and then the design should be tailored almost on an individual basis.

© Springer International Publishing Switzerland 2016
M. Antona and C. Stephanidis (Eds.): UAHCI 2016, Part I, LNCS 9737, pp. 214–222, 2016.
DOI: 10.1007/978-3-319-40250-5_21

2   Related Works

Livox [1] is an App that enhances communication by using tablets. The proposed app can be seen as an improvement of the board of communications that up until now have been the most traditional way used by the CP community for their communication needs. But it still presents a series of challenges for the ones with severe motor impairments.

CP Family Network [2] Special Website aims to support and inform families about CP in general. However, there is little allowance for peer-to-peer information exchange.

Data about CP should be made visual – but to our knowledge there is little to no compilation of the existing graphics into information vectors. The CerebralPalsy site [3] makes extensive use of info graphs to explain CP causes, types, some treatments and data on daily life routines.

3   Design for CP

This article describes the requirement acquisition phase of a design process used by the research group in order to inform design of AT for several groups with specific needs. It has been used by Guimarães et al. [8] to design educational artifacts to teach Portuguese and Sign Language for Deaf children, among other uses. It vastly relies on the participation of members of the community as designers throughout the entire process, thus allowing for a more efficient process that yields better-designed systems (i.e. systems that correspond to the needs and expectations of the end user).

Figure 1 shows the proposed process to aid the design of Intellectual Interaction artifacts. Intellectual Artifacts can be defined as social interactions, mediated by

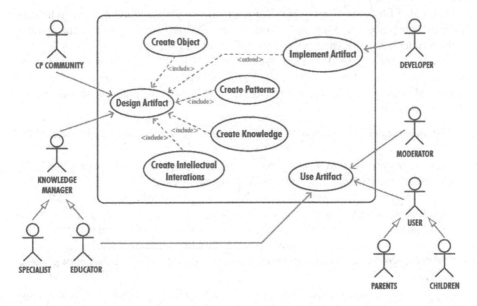

Fig. 1. Process to inform design for people with disability. Source [8]

computational artifacts that stimulate the use of intellectual processing for knowledge creation and overall development; the ensuing systems are based on cognitive theories for mind and physical development [8]:

As per the proposed process, in order to Design an artifact, the designer will use a series of cognitive and design tools (i.e. Empathy Map; Observation; Mental Map; Design of Service; Design Thinking, among others) to interact with the stakeholders (the user herself, educators, family members, specialists etc.) to better understand the person, her daily activities and her environment. These tools will help create knowledge, patterns and the design of the artifact.

In tandem with Human-Centered Design (HCD), designers must look at the individual person, and focus on her needs, identifying what she can or cannot do in her daily life. The process helps the designer to achieve such goal with the use of some cognitive and design tools.

Initially, the designer should follow the guidelines of the World Health Organization (WHO) [4], which provides the International Classification of Functioning, Disabilities and Health (ICF) that focus on the limitations for social participation in the environment where the person lives. The ICF broadens the designer's view beyond deficiency to inform design that promotes functional activities in all aspects of the individual's life in regards to her inclusion in her social context.

The use of simulations and ethnographic observation methods helped the researchers to understand the environment and its various aspects, such as human interactions, activities, and limitations, among others. The insight gained from the observation of the user in her environment proved valuable in understanding the actual features needed on the artifact [6]. The simulations and in situ observations carried out by the researchers provided a richer insight into the person's needs in her environment; researchers became more aware of the real, every day issues.

The use of Empathy Maps (EM) allows for better understanding of the stakeholders (their thoughts, needs and feelings). Additionally, EM provide insight into the features of the artifact being designed, according to Gray et al. [5].

The Empathy Map (EM) is a tool used to get to know the stakeholders, the way they think and feel. According to Gray et al. [5], EM aid in developing an agile profile of the users. EM centers on people (in our case, people with CO). Figure 2 shows the six different aspects:

- "Think and Feel" corresponds to dreams, ambitions, frustrations, motivations of the audience;
- "See" corresponds to how they contact to others, where do they work, how they experience things, how they see the others reactions, etc.;
- "Hear" corresponds to what do their friends say, what influences them, how they socialize, what they hear about yourselves, etc.;
- "Say and Do" corresponds to what kind of attitude do they have, what they talk about, what does their day look like, how does they react to some stimulus, etc.;
- "Gains" corresponds to what they want to reach: desires, needs, measure of success, etc.; and,
- "Pains" corresponds to what they face: fears, frustrations, obstacles, challenges, etc.

Figure 2 shows an Empathy Map complete, with actual needs, feelings and desired changes that were gathered by the research team with the community. The process of generating the EM was very helpful for the designers: real empathy was created for the everyday plight of people with CP that would otherwise be clouded by misinformation, lack of adequate communication and overall prejudice: a lot was learned about the syndrome and how it affects each individual differently that could not have been learned by literature review, or even by talking to family and professionals.

The use of EM allowed the designers to approach the requirements truly from the perspective of the person with CP – especially considering that most of them difficulties to communicate their thoughts and feelings. It became clear the need for AT, but also for technologies that would play into their sense of self, dignity, humanity and social inclusion.

Although it is very had to determine the extent to which the cognitive functions of persons with CP are preserved, the EM revealed that, in most cases, those individuals were very aware of their condition, and were deeply affected by the misconceptions

Fig. 2. Empathy map (based on what people with CP feel)

about them and the way they are treated by people who didn't understand them: there is no need for sympathy or patronizing.

This acknowledgement emphasized the general feeling that the first and foremost way designers can help people with specific needs is by providing educational tools about their conditions to the public in general, and to family and health care providers in particular.

Still on the requirements phase, and extending on the ideas of simulations and observations, designers should create Mental Maps (MP) with the aid of all involved. The use of MM allows for the generation, organization e mapping of ideas through synthesis and association of thoughts and experiences [7]. MM provide an approach and expansion of scope through various angles and interpretations that allow an easy visualization of the initial idea and its scenario in context.

Figure 3 shows part of the MM centered on the person with CP and its links with the CP environment. The resulting MM contains 8 main categories in which the aspects derived from the research were listed. This kind of organization allowed for deeper understanding of the types of systems that are needed.

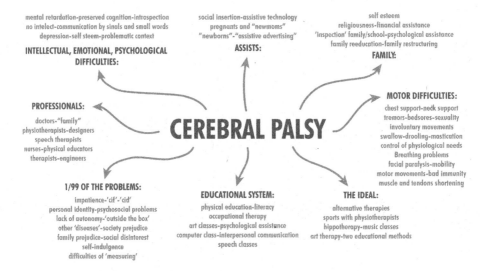

Fig. 3. Partial mental map

The use of MM and EM allowed for insights about the needs, scope and relations among the issues (i.e. how some of the issues were linked to one another, and how one issue would cause dire consequences on other issues). Thus informed, the designers were able to come up with high level suggestions of systems that would greatly improve the quality of life of all involved.

4   System's Suggestions for CP

Here are some examples of the needs for artifacts, processes and systems that came up in our research: a 3D process to get measurements to build protheses and orthesis; virtual reality boards to enhance communications (the system would project objects within a category and the person would select her choice - e.g. food - apple, to convey that she wants to eat an apple); An information system to support the family - documentaries, educational videos, access to health care, support group etc.).

Information Systems:

- Information System Vector/Portal for families and health care providers;
- Information System Vector/Portal with guidelines to educate society in general on how to interact with people with CP;
- Universal Design of communication devices;
- Forum and/or specific channel for open, peer-to-peer discussions about experiences, tips, feelings etc.;
- Virtual material to demystify CP and to prevent exclusion, with the participation of people with CP;
- App for connecting people with CP, your family's, institutions and promote integration, interaction, information exchange, etc.;

Educational Systems:

- Repository of information and communication (storage, retrieving and sharing); Economic and operational model for such repository;
- Repository of educational videos – along with its operational model (criteria for who can post; what can be posted; etc.) and generation and distribution of such videos;
- Alternative and extended communication via computer mediated Assistive Technology;
- Alternative and extended communication via other media (banners, posters etc.);
- Peer-to-peer online/virtual (computer mediated) discussion groups to promote support, experience exchange etc.;
- Development of Learning Objects to be made universally available;
- Development of awareness and simulation workshops.

Ideas for professionals:

- Universal Design of rehabilitation artifacts;
- Universal Design of artifacts for social integration;
- Universal Design of educational tools.

Ideas for families:

- Posters with support information;
- Digital information material;
- Call Center (and its business models) to provide information, support, assistance (psychological or social);

- Raise awareness and pride: events, social projects, socialization tools;
- National monitoring system to support families, educators and healthcare providers for newly born children with CP;
- Access to low-cost Assistive Technologies via new productions methods, research initiatives, operational material etc.;
- Webinars (online conferences) with specialized professionals;
- Artifacts that promote child's autonomy.

Ideas for help providers:

- Health care integration system to lower costs;
- Research into new born stimulation;
- Awareness and training for professional.

Ideas for general problems:

- General purpose artifacts to improve skills and promote physical and emotional independence;
- Enhance communication board;

Ideas for Intellectual, emotional, psychological difficulties:

- Artifacts to increase awareness within the family;
- Virtual reality tracking devices to activate digital systems for Internet access and other activities;
- Virtual reality for emotional education and life-enriching experiences;
- Virtual reality system to help access the cognitive level of the child;
- Assistive technology to stimulate intellectual development.

Ideas for motor deficiencies:

- Artifacts to help develop muscular strength;
- Health, balance, position sensors;
- Haptica devices for health monitoring and stimulation;
- Sensors for measuring and adjusting physical pressure in devices for facilitate movement;
- Exo-scheleton.

Considering that the support of the family is paramount for the child's development, priority was to develop an information system. Figure 4 is shown here as an example of one of the many research fronts that have to be addressed.

Figure 4 shows the prototype of a system that is being developed as per the process to provide families with information about CP, educational videos and to serve as a platform for support group, exchange of experiences, etc.

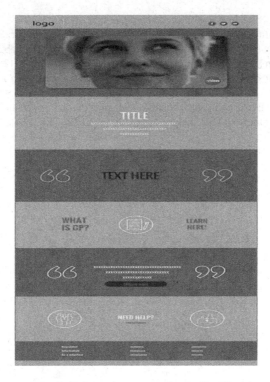

Fig. 4. Information system for the families

5   Conclusion (Discussions)

The proposed framework aims to help the HCI community to gather requirements to inform the design of systems with limited capacities (namely, in this article, people with Cerebral Palsy). It provides a sensible use of intellectual tools that help bridge the communication gap with members of the CP community. It has been extended to help design of artifacts for Deaf people also. In that regard, the proposed framework proved to be most valuable, as shown by the real insights that the researchers were able to get into the CP community. Those insights are here presented in the form of suggestions for system development.

One limitation is that this article does not provide enough solutions to the problems: rather, it presents the community with a series of suggestions of needed systems that were identified during the research. The important task of implementing, testing and validating of the suggestions is left to the community.

References

1. Lixon App. https://youtu.be/f-ejWyPSves
2. CP Family Network. http://cpfamilynetwork.org/

3. The CerebralPalsy Site. http://www.thecerebralpalsysite.co.uk/
4. WHO. http://lndufmg.blogspot.com.br/2005/10/o-impacto-da-cif-na-paralisia-cerebral.html
5. Gray, D., Brown, S., Macanufo, J.: Game Storming. O'Reilly Media, Sebastopol (2010)
6. Fraser, H.: Design Works. Rotman-UTP Publishing, Rio de Janeiro (2012)
7. Lupton, E., Phillips, J.C.: Graphic Design: The New Basics. Princeton Architectural Press, New York (2008)
8. Guimarães, C., et al: Internet artifacts for bilingualism of the deaf (Sign Language/Portuguese). In: Proceedings of the 46th HICSS, vol. 46, pp. 40–49. IEEE CPS, Wailea (2013)

Running on the Gatherun Cloud Platform: Using Self-determination Theory to Increase Motivation to Participate in Sporting Events

Tsai-Hsuan Tsai[1(✉)], Hsien-Tsung Chang[2], Yu-Wen Lin[1],
Yi-Hao Hu[2], Chih-Wei Chen[3], Yi-Cheng Chen[3], and Wei-Hung Wu[3]

[1] Department of Industrial Design,
Chang Gung University, Taoyuan, Taiwan
ttsai.cgu@gmail.com
[2] Department of Computer Science and Information Engineering,
Chang Gung University, Taoyuan, Taiwan
[3] Metal Industries Research & Development Centre, Kaohsiung, Taiwan

Abstract. For the purpose of stimulating the interest in and motivation of exercise participation by the exercise group (e.g., roadrace runner) and the potential exercise group (e.g., spectators) through the use of social technologies, the social exercise platform developed in this study uses the currently popular road race as the central core, utilizing the characteristics of social media and the self-determination theory as the design rationale to design suitable social exercise features. Finally, the system usability is verified with mobile-specific heuristic guidelines; the results show that the newly developed system is in line with usability standards.

Keywords: Road running · Mobile application · Cloud competition · Self-determination theory · Virtual game · Avatar creation · Exercise participation · Spectator participation · Heuristic evaluation

1 Introduction

Sports motivation has always been one of the topics on which sports psychologists and researchers have focused. As people grow from children to adolescents to adults, their exercise activity rate starts to decrease, as does their competitive motivation for sports participation [1]. Studies have noted that exercise habits in early adulthood lay the foundation for individuals' future exercise behavior; thus, studying the exercise participation motivation of adults is particularly important [2, 3]. Deci and Ryan [4] propose self-determination theory (SDT) to understand motivation in human behavior. The basic assumption of SDT is that human behavior is related to three variables of psychological needs, namely, autonomy, competence, and relatedness. When these three needs are satisfied, people's execution motivation in any field will be performed in a more dynamic and sustained manner. Currently, SDT is widely used in physical exercise behavioral research. Frederick and Ryan [5] demonstrate that interest, entertainment, and a sense of competence can positively predict people's weekly exercise hours.

© Springer International Publishing Switzerland 2016
M. Antona and C. Stephanidis (Eds.): UAHCI 2016, Part I, LNCS 9737, pp. 223–230, 2016.
DOI: 10.1007/978-3-319-40250-5_22

Mullan and Markland [6] indicate that it is easier for people with exercise autonomy to participate in and draw positive experiences from exercise activities. Edmunds et al. [7] establish an intervention method based on SDT and find that people who need more exercise facilitation and support tend to be more autonomous and have more motivation to participate in exercise. Patrick and Canevello [8] develop computer software containing demand support as the exercise coach of users, and they note that people who need more support tend to have more autonomy and competence in exercise behavior, which indirectly induces higher levels of exercise frequency, persistence and entertainment. Additionally, some research uses SDT to investigate the motivation of people who share physiological information on social websites after walking or exercising [9, 10]. In terms of practical applications, there already exist health and fitness apps that contain autonomous motivation, competence motivation, and relatedness motivation. For example, Nike+ Running contains a fitness trainer function that can be used by users in independent training; additionally, Endomondo provides a challenge mode that stimulates the competence motivation of users. The goal of relatedness motivation design is to allow exercisers to post and share their exercise information within the software or on an external website. The abovementioned studies show that applications of modern mobile technology can indeed raise people's physical health awareness and facilitate the establishment of exercise habits. Moreover, the introduction of social platforms changes exercise from "one person" endurance-concentrated training into a social activity consisting of "a group of people"; these platforms influence not only the behavior of the exerciser but also the exercise participation motivation of spectators on the social platform. Unfortunately, the developed exercise-related fitness applications mostly concentrate on the exercisers themselves, ignoring the spectators on social platforms. For the purpose of stimulating the interest in and motivation of exercise participation by the exercise group (e.g., road-race runner) and the potential exercise group (e.g., spectators) through the use of social technologies, the social exercise platform developed in this study uses the currently popular road race as the central core, utilizing the characteristics of social media and SDT as the design rationale to design suitable social exercise features. Finally, the usability of the system is evaluated through a mobile-specific heuristic evaluation checklist.

2   Gatherun Design and Development

Compared to other types of exercise, running has low requirements for professional competence and technical proficiency and is not constrained by hardware facilities and equipment limitations such as site or the urban-rural gap. Running, which has become a popular sport, has the lowest participation requirements, and various types of marathon and road running activities have become fashionable. Accordingly, the Gatherun system uses the road race as the implementation case and designs a social feature that allows the participation of both exercisers and spectators, based on SDT and the need for autonomy, relatedness, and competence noted above. The Gatherun mobile application was jointly developed by the Digital Media Lab and WIDE Lab of Chang Gung University in Taiwan and the Metal Industries Research and Development Center in Taiwan to help Taiwan's Global Solution International Co., Ltd., which is a professional manufacturer of fitness appliances and systems, and will support the official version of iOS 8.0 or higher of all iPhone operating systems; Gatherun be published in March 2016 on the App Store for consumer download. The main features of Gatherun are described below.

2.1 Establishing User Need for Autonomy Through a User-Friendly Interface Design and Virtual Game Environments

Autonomy in SDT means that the individual is the action initiator and has freedom of choice, including personal self-determination, self-regulation, and self-selection. In terms of using fitness applications, autonomy means providing users the choice of favorite and satisfactory self-enjoyment decisions. In addition, a friendly user interface (UI) design also has the ability to raise user autonomy needs. In terms of raising user autonomy needs, first, the developed Gatherun system provides a simple and friendly user interface that can be easily operated by a novice. Second, the setting function enables personalized settings, such as the UI layout mode and privacy settings. Furthermore, concepts of cloud competition, avatar creation, and game enjoyment are incorporated so that users can have efficient game-based player performance and an effective enjoyable experience through participating in running on the Gatherun cloud platform (see Figs. 1 and 3).

2.2 Establishing User Need for Relatedness Through Cloud Competition and Spectator Participation

The need for relatedness stated in SDT refers to the degree of affective connection with other people produced during an individual's behavior process. When the environment provides sufficient acceptance, caring and warmth, and emotional power, the individual can be encouraged to accept various obstacles and challenges, thus achieving the purpose of psychological growth. For example, in road running, under normal circumstances, the runner typically runs individually, without company. Although a road race can achieve the goal of popular participation, the limitations of time and location often prevent people from actually joining the race. Therefore, the developed Gatherun platform provides users with the cloud race feature. Figure 1 shows that compared to a real road race event, holding a cloud road race has far fewer practical constraints and can enable users at various times and locations to simultaneously conduct a road race in a virtual environment. A real map function can allow users to observe the actual location of other racers (Fig. 2). The Gatherun system also emphasizes the participation of spectators; through the support of community friends, the relatedness motivation of individuals can be raised. The real-time spectator function allows spectators to participate in the ongoing virtual road race. In addition to displaying the instantaneous information of runners, spectators can interact with avatars (runners) through, for example, voice messaging to instantaneously encourage runners (as in Fig. 3). In addition, the common photo gallery function, as shown in Fig. 4, can gather images taken by road race participants (including runners and spectators) during the race into an event-concept shared album, allowing Gatherun users to browse and share on the community platform at any time.

Fig. 1. Cloud virtual road race feature, enabling individual runners to participate in a virtual race with other runners.

Fig. 2. Real map feature, showing the locations of other runners

Fig. 3. Real-time spectating feature, enabling spectators to watch an ongoing road race and encourage race runners through instant voice messaging.

Fig. 4. Common photo gallery, using the road race as a group to compose a commonly shared album.

2.3   Establishing User Need for Competence Through Avatar Creation

The competence stated in SDT refers to the degree of the sense of control and mastery of the external environment by an individual, that is, the individual's sense of whether the external demand can effectively be met by the individual's own ability. To obtain a sufficient sense of competence, an individual may select jobs or tasks that are perceived as challenging. In terms of using fitness applications, the competition mode typically stimulates the motivation of exercisers more than independent road running; thus, many fitness applications provide community friends with an achievement leaderboard to induce competence motivation. To raise the competence needs of the users participating in the road race, road racers are created as avatars and used as self-symbolic imagery in the game-based virtual environment established by Gatherun. The avatar level-up standard is judged by the road running performance and race participation status of users. From novice to professional, the avatar levels, in order, are bulldog, cat, fox, deer, and leopard. Different avatars show different participant rivalries and the real-time performance in the race, as shown in Fig. 5.

Fig. 5. Use avatar creation, forming a virtual and immersive gameplay environment

3 System Validation

This study uses the mobile-specific heuristic guideline proposed by Yáñez Gómez et al. [11] as the Gatherun system validation method. According to the 13 usability heuristics of Yáñez Gómez et al. the Gatherun system does not contain one of the items: the help and documentation sub-heuristic. Therefore, this item is eliminated, and the system usability evaluation is performed according to a 12-item mobile-specific heuristic guideline. It is important to note that we invited five interactive interface design and mobile application development experts to conduct the usability test; two of them have an information engineering background and are well experienced in mobile application development, whereas the other three experts have a digital media background and numerous system interface design experiences and had previously performed system usability assessment tests. The experts tested the system usability by using a mobile-specific heuristic checklist. In addition, the experts identified design weaknesses and defined the usability issues through the exchange of opinions and discussion. The 12-item usability heuristic-based assessment results are as follows:

- Visibility of the system status: The Gatherun interface design can easily recognize the current feature location, and the information display is clear and easy to understand. Adding visual cues in the interface swap feature is recommended.
- Match between the system and the real world: There is true correspondence with the user operation. When operating various functions, users can instantly sense changes in the interface.
- User control and freedom: Gatherun system operation is simple and easy to learn; functional operation has obvious distinguishability. Providing default values to more conveniently initiate the virtual race function is recommended.
- Consistency and standards: The color, font, and icons displayed by the system are highly uniform and in line with the design principles. Permanently adding a logout function in the main feature manual is recommended.
- Error prevention: No error handling mechanism is provided; however, the system is easy and has simple operations that can reduce the error occurrence rate. Imposing an input length limit to avoid use input errors is recommended.
- Recognition rather than recall: The Gatherun system provides an icon supplemented with text options, which can increase the degree of system recognition and reduce cognitive load without excessive user memorization.
- Flexibility and efficiency of use: The system feature display is clear, not requiring any special memory or search. Locating the friend search function on the homepage to increase usability is recommended.
- Aesthetic and minimalist design: The graphical interface design is exquisite, beautiful, clean, and simple.
- Helping users recognize, diagnose, and recover from errors: No issue assistance feature is provided. Adding a feature introduction to help novices quickly understand system features is recommended.
- Skills: Technical operation is in line with the normal range of user operational abilities.

- Pleasurable and respectful interaction: A graphical interface is provided, and the game-based interaction can raise usage enjoyability.
- Privacy: The level of privacy is very low, suited for use on a personal mobile device. When it is used on a public device, adding a foreign device login warning is recommended.

4   Conclusion

To raise the performance of exercisers and the interest in and willingness to participate of spectators, based on the three basic psychological needs defined by SDT, this study develops a mobile road running community group application – Gatherun. The Gatherun system provides a cloud competition to enable individual runners in different locations and time to participate in a virtual race scenario. Avatar creation and a game-based virtual environment provide users a fun and diverse experience model. Furthermore, to enhance the social interaction between users (exercisers and spectators), in addition to the runners participating in a race, spectators can also participate in a race and encourage follow runners instantly through the instant spectating feature. The common photo gallery feature can record the race status, and photos can be shared with all race participants and users. Finally, the system usability is verified with mobile-specific heuristic guidelines; the results show that the Gatherun system is in line with usability standards. The system will be improved in the future based on expert recommendations.

Acknowledgements. We thank all of the individuals who participated in the study. This research was funded by Taiwan Metal Industries Research & Development Centre, Chang Gung University, and Taiwan Ministry of Science and Technology (MOST103-2221-E-182-051-MY2).

References

1. Leslie, E., Fotheringham, M.J., Owen, N., Bauman, A.: Age-related differences in physical activity levels of young adults. Med. Sci. Sports Exerc. **33**, 255–258 (2001)
2. Laakso, L., Telama, R.: Sport participation of Finnish youth as a function of age and schooling. Sportwissenschaft **1**, 28–45 (1981)
3. Telama, R., Silvennoinen, M.: Structure and development of 11-to 19-year-olds' motivation for physical activity. Scand. J. Sports Sci. **1**, 23–31 (1979)
4. Deci, E.L., Ryan, R.M.: Intrinsic Motivation and Self-determination in Human Behavior. Springer, New York (1985)
5. Frederick, C.M., Ryan, R.M.: Differences in motivation for sport and exercise and their relations with participation and mental health. J. Sport Behav. **16**, 124–146 (1993)
6. Mullan, E., Markland, D.: Variations in self-determination across the stages of change for exercise in adults. Motiv. Emot. **21**, 349–362 (1997)
7. Edmunds, J., Ntoumanis, N., Duda, J.L.: Testing a self-determination theory-based teaching style intervention in the exercise domain. Eur. J. Soc. Psychol. **38**, 375–388 (2008)

8. Patrick, H., Canevello, A.: Methodological overview of a self-determination theory-based computerized intervention to promote leisure-time physical activity. Psychol. Sport Exerc. **12**, 13–19 (2011)
9. Gard, D.E., Sanchez, A.H., Starr, J., Cooper, S., Fisher, M., Rowlands, A., Vinogradov, S.: Using self-determination theory to understand motivation deficits in schizophrenia: the 'why' of motivated behavior. Schizophr. Res. **156**, 217–222 (2014)
10. Stragier, J., Evens, T., Mechant, P.: Broadcast yourself: an exploratory study of sharing physical activity on social networking sites. Media Int. Aust. **155**, 120–129 (2015)
11. Yáñez Gómez, R., Cascado Caballero, D., Sevillano, J.-L.: Heuristic evaluation on mobile interfaces: a new checklist. Sci. World J. **2014** (2014)

Universal Access in Architecture
and Product Design

Internal Diversification – Developing a Research Method of Urban Planning

Wojciech Bonenberg[✉]

Faculty of Architecture, Poznan University of Technology, Poznan, Poland
wojciech.bonenberg@put.poznan.pl

Abstract. The paper presents a method of urban diagnosis based on internal diversification analysis. The method has been created to obtain a tool for construction of a strategy resulting in improving quality of space. It takes into account specific determinants that are associated with internal relations within urban areas. This method has been developed at the Faculty of Architecture of Poznan University of Technology and implemented in the research on the Poznan Metropolitan Area. The concept of micro-divisions and internal diversification within metropolitan areas still remains a subject of discussion among professionals, as it is treated in a number of ways. The idea that the relations between structural units in urban space are not limited to the impact they have on one another and that intensity of such interrelations varies, constituted a significant element of the previous models. In recent models, the type (quality) of interaction between the units is perceived as a substantial element. From this point of view, the impact of one unit on another can be advantageous or damaging. By labelling the negative impact with a minus, positive one with a plus, and the lack of impact with a 0, all possible types of influence can be classified in six different ways: mutual negative impact between two units $(-,-)$, mutual positive interactions $(+,+)$, the $(+,-)$ relation, the $(+,0)$ relation, the $(-,0)$ relation, the $(0,0)$ relation. The above-mentioned types of relations became the basis for diagnosis of spatial conflicts and possibilities of sustainable development of the Poznan Metropolitan Area.

Keywords: Urban planning · Diversification · Interactions

1   The Description of the Problem

This paper is a synthesis of research on urban planning within the Poznan Metropolitan Area carried out by a team of scientists of the Faculty of Architecture, Poznan University of Technology. The spatial structure of the Poznan Metropolitan Area is currently undergoing deep structural transformations. Therefore the method implemented focuses on preventing a progressive depreciation of architectural and urban environment, on a degradation of urban landscape and social structures due to uncontrolled investment encroachment on city centres, as well as on the ineffectiveness of the existing spatial planning system. The method is based on analysis of an internal diversification of urban areas. Research related to spatial divisions and diversification of settlement network has been quite significant, especially on the national and regional level.

© Springer International Publishing Switzerland 2016
M. Antona and C. Stephanidis (Eds.): UAHCI 2016, Part I, LNCS 9737, pp. 233–241, 2016.
DOI: 10.1007/978-3-319-40250-5_23

This paper synthesises research on urban planning within the Poznan Metropolitan Area carried out by the team of scientists of the Faculty of Architecture of Poznan University of Technology. The spatial structure of the Poznan Metropolitan Area is currently undergoing deep structural transformations. Therefore the method implemented focuses on preventing a progressive depreciation of architectural and urban environment, on a degradation of urban landscape and social structures due to uncontrolled investment encroachment on city centres, as well as on the ineffectiveness of the existing spatial planning system. The method is based on analysis of an internal diversification of urban areas. Research related to spatial divisions and diversification of settlement network has been quite significant, especially on the national and regional level.

The phenomenon of internal diversification is perceived and evaluated in many different ways. There are egalitarian attitudes regarding planning and local policy as a tool of eliminating differences between particular units inside the city structure. This is result of a specific vision of development related to spontaneous, bottom-up tendency to get assimilated and copy up-to-date models. The unification of urban environment is a visible effect of this phenomenon, related to contemporary global mass culture.

The other point of view refers to an internal diversification of urban areas as an important factor of development. It is believed that internal diversity is a value that gives a competitive advantage, saves expenses on overcoming existing differences and diverts them to the benefit of local communities. In this situation it is important which elements are diversified. Too large differences in income per capita among the residents are a negative phenomenon, as an economic stratification and a high level of poverty causes social pressure inside urban areas.

This problem relates specifically to the city centres and is observed in many European metropolitan areas and is also present in the Poznan Metropolitan Area-[1]. This is the area that plays an important role in economic growth, employment and competitiveness. But it also faces serious problems: unbalanced urban development, areas of economic and social marginalisation, environmental degradation, insecurity and decay of social relationships. Appropriate internal relationships between urban units mean rational redevelopment of spatial, cultural and economic structures in the city. The research is not only about renewal of neglected areas, but also about finding efficient management methods. Such upgrading prevents a future stagnation, a decline in urban activity, and also an improper development of urban areas.

2   Internal Diversification of Urban Areas

The problem of internal diversification of urban areas has recently acquired significance due to growing interest on part of investors in old, neglected city centres. It has a record of unsuccessful attempts to tamper with the historic urban tissue, which is reflected in vanishing street identity, standardization of neighbourhoods and a lack of legibility of urban space. Actual planning efforts are often reduced to new investments in the existing urban structure or improving technical conditions of technical infrastructure. It is very rare that the problem is placed in the broader framework of social, cultural and environmental categories. In this context a few positive examples of successful regeneration projects that have led to rational transformation of the urban space can be pointed out. However, in the face of today's needs of the investment market and the scale of modernization demand, these cases form only a small fragment of investment interference in the structure of degraded central areas. Most of the projects are intended to suit commercialized, short-term interests of investors. This leads to evident failures of regeneration projects and to deterioration of the urban quality in general.

One of the reasons that behind this is the lack of methodological guidance that would allow analyzing internal relations between adjacent urban units. Internal diversification analysis emphasizes the principle that a metropolitan area is not neutral in terms of economics. To put things simple, spatial diversification has been explained here as a natural result of economic inequalities. Among them, as a result of income disparities, groups with the highest income occupy the most attractive territories [2]. This is part of a general problem including the relations between spatial behaviour and economy [3]. Many models based on systemic economic approach to spatial planning emerged in the first half of the 20th c. Zofia Dembowska [4] provides a detailed description of these models. Among them the group of *gravity and potential models* is worth mentioning, which concern spatial and economic interrelations between settlement units to their economic potential and distances between them. These models are based on analogies to Newton's theory of gravity. In this approach, relations between units located in the immediate vicinity of each other are the strongest. From a classical point of view, the strength of the relation is directly proportional to these units' potential product and inversely proportional to the squared distance. The first attempts to apply the *gravity* and potential models in spatial and economic issues took place as early as in the 19th c. Johann Heinrich von Thünen in his theory of agricultural production location, published in 1826, pointed out the advantages given by the fact that production was situated in a place which had positive relations compared to other acceptable locations. These advantages depended, in his opinion, on the distance and costs involved in the transport of the produce [5]. Carey [6] noted that the bigger the population is in a given area, the larger force it has of attracting migrants. He described gravity as directly proportional to the area size and inversely proportional to the distance. Ravenstein in the study called "The Laws of Migration" [7] showed the great force of attraction related to industries located in large English and Welsh cities. In his opinion the size of workers migration depended on the distance between the place they lived in and the migration targets. In 1929, Reilly [8] applied a gravity model to study the impact of city size on retail development. He described this impact as directly proportional to the number of city residents and inversely proportional to the square root of the distance from another city.

Contemporary models, where index of the power is identical as the one used in Newton's model of gravity, i.e. <2>, are rare. This index is usually derived experimentally. The index of the power derived empirically is a result of an intuitive assumption that the resistance related to the distance depends on the type of interaction. In other words, the distance between the two units has a different impact on e.g. relations of goods exchange, number of commuting people, housing and leisure conditions etc. Lakshman and Hansen [9], in their model of potential retail market, assumed that the index of the power of distance between these zones equals 2.6 in order to determine interactions between the two areas. O'Sullivan [10] showed that the index of the power of distance variable for British cities varies from 1.3 to 4.8 depending how intensive the urbanization of region is. An interesting attempt at a systemic approach constitutes models based on the analysis of "taken opportunities" in the behaviour of settlement inhabitants [11]. In Poland, research in this area has been carried out since the 1970s by Tadeusz Zipser. It refers to, so called, balancing movements in the development of a territory to ensure balance between travel destinations and noted acceptations [12].

3   Model of Relations Between Space Units

The idea that the relations between structural units are subject to diversified sub-relations, which vary in direction, intensiveness and quality, constitutes further development of these models. Here, the type (quality) of interaction between the units is an important element [13]. From this point of view, the impact of one unit on another can be beneficial or not. By labelling the negative impact with a "minus", positive one with a "plus", and lack of impact with a "0", all possible types of influence can be classified in six different ways.

3.1   Mutual Negative Impact

Mutual negative impact, labelled with $(-,-)$, takes place when each of the two spatial units has a negative impact on the other. This situation is present when two units use the same insufficient element of urban infrastructure. For instance, using the same transport system by housing and manufacturing units can lead to high congestion on roads and extend the time needed to get home or to supply manufacturing materials, causing significant losses in each unit. The size of the negative impact can change, and even be completely reduced by establishing different hours in which the transport system is by the two subjects used. In many modern designs, architects and urban planners try to answer the question of the extent to which units co-existing in a given area can tolerate competitive usage of the same, limited resources of urban environment.

3.2   Mutual Positive Impact

Mutual positive interactions between two units, labelled with $(+,+)$, take place when each unit benefits from the relation with the other. Examples of this relation include benefits related to the location of retail, cultural, and educational services near residential developments. This type of interaction is seen as one of the reasons why spatial development is concentrated in such areas, and a cause of increased prices of properties located there.

More and more frequently, the mutual benefits of the compact model of urbanization are pointed out, especially if they bring closer places of work and residence. Koppenhöfer [14] says that majority of workplaces should be located using the following rule: bring work to people, and not the other way round. The vicinity of places of work and residence reduces congestion on roads, takes pressure off the public transport, creates social bonds, enables working women to look after their children and run their households, and makes it easier to work part-time. It is also worth mentioning that locating places of work in deteriorating, central districts is considered as a basic condition of the revitalization. Linking workplaces with residential, retail, and service developments stimulates urban and economic activity positively. This is a come-back to traditional mode of placing living spaces, workplace and shop in one building, an approach common in the past centuries. This model is popular even today in Middle and Far East cities, and has been recently applied in the revitalized urban quarters of many European cities.

3.3 "Plus-Minus" Relation

The $(+,-)$ relation takes place when one of the unit harms the other, but draws benefits for itself. A typical example here is the inconvenience related to heavy industry being located close to residential and service territories. Disturbing elements include dust, gas, and noise emissions. At the same time, such a close location is beneficial for the manufacturing sites, giving them easy access to workforce, convenient links with research and scientific institutions as well as services. Such a conflict occurs between location and development of the Volkswagen aluminium foundry situated within the Wilda residential area in Poznan. This situation has recently been widely covered in the local press.

3.4 "Plus-Zero" Relation

The $(+,0)$ relation takes place when one of the units benefits from the other, and the latter does not incur any losses. Examples include the relations between territories designated for leisure and residence, offices and service areas – provided that leisure areas are adequate for the expected number of users. Such interaction has no negative impact on leisure areas, while supporting neighbouring areas due to their increased attractiveness enhanced by convenient access to places where people can relax and use leisure facilities.

3.5 "Zero-Minus" Relation

The $(0,-)$ relation takes place when one of the units harms the other, and the latter draws no benefits from this relation. Examples include the post-industrial areas located in the city centre. The "unused railway tracks" area in Poznan is an unnecessary burden for PKP (Polish Railways) and produces no benefits to the company. The impact on units located in its vicinity is negative, as the potentially attractive central area remains "frozen".

3.6 "Zero-Zero" Relation

The $(0,0)$ relations take place when two units do not influence each other. This type of interaction is likely to be very rare and it may even not exist in practice.

3.7 Model

The dependencies presented above lay at the heart of the proposed model.

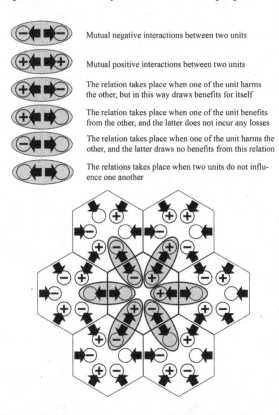

Fig. 1. Model of relations between the identified urban units

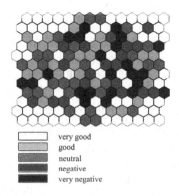

Fig. 2. Assessment of the metropolitan area space. Profit and loss balance ensuing from mutual relationships between the neighbouring spatial entities.

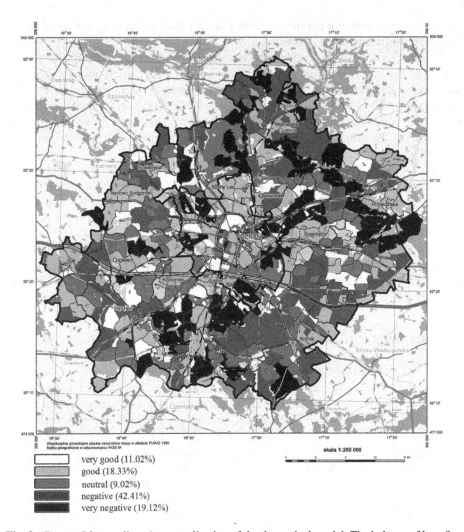

Fig. 3. Poznan Metropolitan Area, application of the theoretical model. The balance of benefits and losses resulting from the neighbourhood of urban units.

After their analysis it is possible to diagnose the settlement system in the context of:

– spatial conflicts that lower the quality of the space,
– sustainable spatial development.

It needs to be pointed out that both the criteria influence the attractiveness of the metropolitan space, property prices and strength of attracting new investors.

Figure 1 shows a theoretical approach to the presented model. Figure 2 shows a profit and loss balance ensuing from mutual relationships between the neighbouring spatial entities. Assessments are presented as a five-grade scale. The very good grade refers to entities that benefit the most from the close proximity to nearby ones. At the opposite end of the scale there are entities evaluated as very bad, which incur the most losses from their dysfunctional neighbourhood.

Figure 3 shows the use of the model in research concerning the sustainable development of the Poznan Metropolitan Area. The studies were carried out by a group of architecture students in July 2015 as part of their summer internship. As part of the research an urban visit was carried out to an area of 2162 km^2 with 878,000 inhabitants. For partial assessment the expert Geo Urban Centric method was used that had been developed by the Institute of Architecture and Spatial Planning, Poznan University of Technology, Poland.

The research territory was divided into 311 spatial units the borders of which match the borders of urban estates and divisions, as well as natural borders determined by watercourses, streets, railway lines and other physiographic objects. The isolated spatial units match the surveying sections found in the national register of territorial division (TETRYT) maintained for the purposes of public statistics.

On the basis of detailed analysis of the internal dependencies it was found that 11.02 % of the Poznan Metropolitan Area is characterised by very good grades coming from the relationships among neighbouring spatial units. 9.02 % of the area has neutral relations, 42.41 % – bad, and 19.12 % – very bad.

4 Summary

The (+,+), (+,0), (0,0) relations between spatial units improve the stability of the entire urban system. These relations cause no losses in any of the spatial units if one of them is located close to the other unit. For instance, functional and spatial arrangements of many villages and towns near Poznan were not changed for many centuries until their stabilized relations (+,+), (+,0), (0,0), changed into (−,−), (0,−) (−,+). This process was triggered by economic and demographical changes. First of all, rapid migration of people due to a high demand for workforce in newly built factories in the 19th c. and the first half of 20th c. The (−,−), (0,−), (−,+) relations resulted in changing functional and spatial characteristics of the area urbanized in compliance with economic reasons. Further changes have occurred with development of individual car transport and unrestricted spread of even small villages at the end of the 20th c.. Entire systems have lost their stability due to rapid changes in the way land was used. The urban sprawl phenomenon has also led to the disintegration of historical settlement tissues. Throughout the Poznan Agglomeration competitive displacement of "weaker" functions (agriculture) by "stronger" functions (housing, wholesale) have distorted the area characteristics.

The changes aim at obtaining better conditions of functioning by each structural entity at the cost of the neighbouring ones. The urban layout is destabilised by conflicting interests of neighbouring land users.

From this point of view, the process of metropolitan area development can be treated as a permanent functional evolution of individual structural units related with an ongoing balancing of economic benefits. In this interpretation, the process of development dispersion can be explained by excessive economic weakness of agricultural units. The gap between prices of agricultural land and building plots, powered by underestimation of the distances, causes people to build their houses in the suburbs and to commute to work by car.

The presented model is a simplification of complex urban processes related to competitive use of land. This allows for effective assessment of urban space quality based on analysis of internal diversification of the metropolitan area.

References

1. Bonenberg, W.: The enigma of metropolis: its spatial diversity and methods of diagnosis. Tech. Trans. Czasopismo Techniczne **8-A**(14), 33–38 (2015)
2. Kilroy, A.: Intra-Urban Spatial Inequality: Cities as Urban Regions. MIT and UNDP, World Development Report, Reshaping Economic Geography (2009)
3. Ponsard, C.: Ekonomiczna analiza przestrzenna, pp. 10–11. Wydawnictwo Akademii Ekonomicznej w Poznaniu, Poznan (1992)
4. Dembowska, Z.: Planowanie przestrzenne w ujęciu systemowym. PWN, Warszawa (1979)
5. Potrykowski, M., Taylor, Z.: Geofrafia transportu, pp. 42–44. PWN, Warszawa (1982)
6. Carey, H.C.: Principles of Social Science. J. B. Lippincott and Co., Philadelphia (1958)
7. Ravenstein, E.G.: The laws of migration. J. Stat. Soc. Lond. **48**(2), 167–235 (1885)
8. Reilly, W.J.: Methods for the Study of Retail Relationships. Bureau of Business Research. University of Teras, Austin (1959)
9. Lakshmanan, T.R., Hansen, W.G.: A retail market potential model. J. Am. Inst. Planners **31**, 134–144 (1965)
10. O'Sullivan, P.M.: Variations in distance friction in Great Britain. Area **2**(70), 36–39 (1970)
11. Stouffer, S.A.: Intervening opportunities: a theory relating mobility and distance. Am. Sociol. Rev. **5**, 845–867 (1940)
12. Zipser, T.: Modele symulacyjne wzrostu miast oparte na modelu wyboru celów. Przegląd Geograficzny XLIV, z 3, pp. 479–494 (1972)
13. Bonenberg, W.: Przemysł w mieście. Ekologiczna metoda modernizacji zakładów przemysłowych zlokalizowanych na obszarach intensywnie zurbanizowanych. Zeszyty Naukowe Politechniki Śląskiej. Gliwice (1985)
14. Koppenhöfer, K.A.: Miejsce pracy w środowisku. w: Architektura w przemyśle, przemysł w architektkurze. Mat. Konf, Seminarium Architektury Przemysłu. Ustroń, Gliwice (1977)

Exploring Downloadable Assistive Technologies Through the Co-fabrication of a 3D Printed Do-It-Yourself (DIY) Dog Wheelchair

Rickee Charbonneau[✉], Kate Sellen, and Angelika Seeschaaf Veres

Ontario College of Art and Design University, Toronto, Canada
rc11wg@student.ocadu.ca,
{ksellen,aseeschaafveres}@faculty.ocadu.ca

Abstract. This paper explores Downloadable Assistive Technologies (DAT) and the possibilities as well as the limitations of publishing and fabricating DAT through online 3D printing communities. A design probe was used for this research within the context of *Thingiverse*, in the form of a 3D printed dog wheelchair design probe – the *FiGO Dog Wheelchair*. *FiGO enabled an exploration of co-customization of tools and processes for DAT, issues of design and communication around modification and personalisation, with several other themes emerging from the research.* It is concluded that implementing communication guidelines for publishing DAT on *Thingiverse* by involving both end users as well as health professionals in the research process is vital to the process of co-fabrication and modification in an open design context.

Keywords: 3D printing · Co design · Digital fabrication · Assistive technology · Open design · *Thingiverse*

1 Introduction

As digital fabrication is rising in popularity and becoming more accessible to consumers, people are participating more frequently in the practice of downloading, fabricating, and publishing 3D models or design blueprints online. There are no limits to the variations of objects that can be found and downloaded from various online 3D printing model repositories. *Thingiverse*, for example, has grown into a massive community since its launch in 2008. *Thingiverse* "reached a landmark one million uploads and 200 million downloads" on October 29 2015 [1]. While the growth of participation is irrefutable, many questions arise from the practice of sharing, creating, downloading, and printing downloadable designs, including the questions of motivation, community, safety, disruption, and the design and availability of technologies that make digital fabrication possible.

Downloadable Assistive Technologies (DAT) is one area of growth in digital fabrication where many of these questions are starting to emerge, and is an area that the *Thingiverse* community is actively engaging in. In fall 2015 *Makerbot* announced the *Assistive Technology Challenge* [2], where community members were encouraged to

M. Antona and C. Stephanidis (Eds.): UAHCI 2016, Part I, LNCS 9737, pp. 242–250, 2016.
DOI: 10.1007/978-3-319-40250-5_24

design assistive technologies to be printed by a *Makerbot*. DAT are an interesting subject of research because issues of motivation, community, safety, and disruption [3] are recognizable in the challenge that DAT represent to the prevailing model of medicalized assistive devices [4].

DAT refer to designs of assistive technologies uploaded online with the intention of being downloaded and fabricated by an end user. This activity is based on the concept of *Open Design* - the material or physical equivalent of *Open Source* software [5]. While users are often required to conform to standardized medical or assistive devices, 3D printing of DAT enables users to customize their devices for both functional and aesthetic reasons that can lead to a better outcome and fit for users needs. Hurst and Tobias explore in their paper this idea of customization and outcome and suggest, "empowering users to make their own Assistive Technology can improve the adoption process (and subsequently adoption rates) [of assistive technologies]" [6]. Users can express themselves through individualized assistive technologies that are customized to be optimally functional for them as well as being aesthetically pleasing. However a number of concerns arise. DAT may not all be rigorously tested and approved by medical professionals – as is the case for traditional assistive devices. The potential for modification and innovation is clear, but there are risks taken on by end users in terms of potential adverse or neutral outcomes, and there may also be a certain resistance from the medical community, as they do not believe makers will perform the necessary thorough risk assessments that a health professional might provide. In a recent study looking at challenges associated with DIY assistive technology in the context of children with disabilities, medical professionals who were participants in the study "questioned whether or not non-professionals would have the required engineering knowledge and experience to be able to take similar precautions [as they do in their practice]" [7]. Designers of DAT play a role in this milieu, potentially managing trade-offs between articulating highly constrained (commercial) design and completely open (downloadable) design in order to produce safe (regulated) design while keeping the design open for innovation.

In this paper, we explore the issues of DAT design through reflection on a DAT design probe [8]. The design probe took the form of a prototype DAT of the *FiGO Dog Wheelchair* designed for a French Bulldog in a collaborative design process with the dog and its owner. The design probe enabled the exploration of themes relating to the open design context of assistive technology and digital fabrication: design modification/remixing over time, the need to address risk and novice maker education, and online offline user engagement. These themes are discussed and relating research questions and implications for design are explored.

2 Design Probe

FiGO, a DIY dog wheelchair [see Fig. 1], was chosen as a case study to explore DAT due to the nature of the current pet product sector. The pet product sector is not widely regulated and as such it is a sector where customized or personalized items are common and are often created without expert or regulatory oversight. There are fewer barriers to designing, fabricating, and testing products for pets, similar in many ways to the situation for the human DAT sector. As noted by the American Pet Product Association, there are very few listed regulatory requirements for pet products other than for pet food or pesticide products [9], and products that are intended to be worn by pets, or to be used for exercise or pet housing, are not regulated.

Fig. 1. The *FiGO Dog Wheelchair* (photo courtesy of Pete Thorne)

The design probe *FiGO* is a 3D printable dog wheelchair kit that aims to disrupt the current market for assistive pet devices. Commercial wheelchairs for domestic animals are very expensive (rear-support-only dog wheelchairs costing up to $525.00) [10] and often inaccessible to many pet owners due to cost and availability of veterinarians and veterinary orthotists with dog wheelchair expertise. Issues of access arise for individuals who need a pet wheelchair for their animals at short notice due to a trauma related injury to the pet, when on a budget, at a remote location, or perhaps for temporary purposes during recovery from surgery. Embedded in the concept of *FiGO* is the empowerment of individuals to build their pet's wheelchair with a combination of relatively available digital fabrication (3D printing) and easily available traditional making or small-scale construction. *FiGO* uses parametrically designed 3D printed joint pieces that fit into acrylic or aluminum tubing, which can be easily customized to the dog for both functional and aesthetic purposes. All materials used in the kit that are not 3D printed can be sourced locally at most hardware stores.

The kit includes 10 3D printed customizable joint pieces in total that can be printed with a variety of consumer grade 3D printers in ABS or PLA plastic. The printer used for this iteration was a *Makerbot* Replicator 2X. Each piece takes roughly an hour to print, so the print time can be averaged to 10 h. Other than the time commitment, the material cost is very low as long as the pet owner or fabricator has access to a 3D printer. Increasingly, public spaces such as libraries and schools are providing publicly accessible 3D printing facilities and equipment, for instance in Toronto, *Makerbots* are available to be booked for use at the Toronto Public Library for public use [11]. Spools of ABS and PLA plastic cost roughly $45 USD at the time of writing [12], and *Makerbot* suggests that 1 kg spool can print up to 392 chess pieces [13]. While this does not give a measure of how much a spool can print in volume, it gives an estimation of how many *FiGO* pieces can be printed with one spool (each *FiGO* piece being no larger than 2–3 chess pieces) – using this data *FiGO* pieces that require printing could be produced for less than $5 USD. The other components of this specific French Bulldog wheelchair were acrylic tubing ($7 USD), straps to support the dog in the wheelchair ($3 USD), wheels ($5 USD) and leg bag ($5 USD), totalling in a material cost of $25 USD.

3 Design Process

3.1 Participatory Approach

The creation of *FiGO* was achieved through a series of rapid prototypes that helped inform further iterations of the overall design. The end user became a participant in this process, through involvement in the ideation process and also in the ideation of the concept and subsequent two iterations of the design. Collaboratively, the aesthetic qualities of the wheelchair were determined based on the owner's dog's personality and how they wanted to express that personality given a range of choices for material and finishes.

Though the design outcome is a kit that enables users to build their own dog wheelchairs, the first author produced the prototypes together with the participant (dog owner) as a co-designer. While the design and initial prototype fabrication did involve parametric design and fabrication knowledge, the design was developed with the consideration that it should be easily produced without extensive knowledge of fabrication.

This co-design process began from a user-initiated interaction on a popular *Facebook* trading group based in Toronto called the *Bunz Trading Zone*. The *Bunz Trading Zone* is an online community that aggregates requests for trades posted by users. It is important to note that it is a completely non-monetary platform. Members of this community often use this group as a space to trade goods and services, with the ultimate goal to re-appropriate used items. However, this group is much more complex than simply a platform for trading. It has grown into a very large community that engages in storytelling, knowledge, and skill sharing. In this group, a user posted a story about their French Bulldog that was in need of a wheelchair to support her back legs that were rapidly losing function. The first author reacted to this posting by offering to help design a wheelchair for the dog. As a trade for the first author's design services, another user of the *Bunz* community stepped in and provided a high quality photo-shoot of the work for documentation purposes. After this introduction, conversation quickly moved from the Bunz community onto other media such as texting and email, as the first author and participant were getting acquainted with one another.

3.2   Design Process and Fitting

The creation of the FiGO Dog Wheelchair involved the following phases that are commonly used by professional designers: market research, expert research, design brief development together with client to establish functional needs and goals of the project, measuring and fitting to the physiognomy of the dog, iteration, and production of final prototype wheelchair.

Prior to meeting the design participant, the first author researched existing dog wheelchair designs. Researching wheelchair designs developed by experts in pet assistive technology was important for collecting information on how to adapt and remake the rear support dog wheelchair into a much more aesthetically pleasing and affordable design, while retaining its original functionality. Assistive technology design expertise is often missing from a platform such as *Thingiverse*, as it is a platform of makers who produce many objects very rapidly and who may not perform extensive background research. The lack of digital presence of research and expertise on dog prosthetics represents a gap in knowledge availability and sharing in the community.

The initial project meeting between the participant and the first author involved taking a series of measurements to properly size the components of the design to the dog's challenged physiognomy due to paralysis of the back legs. Measurements were based on sketches of the design that were inspired by research on existing commercial dog wheelchairs. During the prototyping process, as the design was being realized more substantially, it was clear that some measurements were missing and needed to be taken to move forward. A photo of a French Bulldog with two colored lines visualizing areas that needed to be measured was provided to the participant so that these measurements could be recorded. Once the initial prototype was produced, the dog was secured to the chair and appeared to provide a good fit based on how the dog interacted with the device. However to firm up this assumption a veterinarian will be consulted to confirm that this assistive device does not have any undesired long term effects for the dog. This process revealed the need for clear visual documentation of guidelines for measuring a dog for a wheelchair and for involvement of veterinary expertise.

4   Outcomes and Experience

4.1   Design Choices

The dog wheelchair 3D printed joint pieces were initially designed to imitate rounded plumbing fittings. It was discovered that geometric shapes were much more appropriate for 3D printing as they tend to stick more strongly to the machine bed, minimizing the potential warping of the piece. This also provided an interesting design aesthetic that further differentiated the joint pieces from plumbing fittings. The 3D printed pieces, which could be printed in a wide variety of colors, were printed in a bright purple as suggested by the participant. 3D printed nylon was explored as a possible material for this project due to its flexibility and strength, but its inaccessibility to consumers and incompatibility with most consumer grade 3D printers made ABS and PLA the obvious material choices for the project.

The wheelchair structure was built using clear acrylic tubing. While this was an appropriate solution for the French Bulldog, what was learned from this process is that dogs will require different materials, depending on the dog's weight and breed. A benefit from the acrylic is that it allows the end user to fill the tubes with glitter or other craft materials to further enhance the look of their wheelchair. The French Bulldog's chair was filled with purple glitter. The wheels were purchased from a local hardware store, but future iterations of this wheelchair will likely make use of rollerblade wheels and standard skate bearings to ensure that many communities can access all materials locally.

4.2   Novice-Designer Relationship

In this case, the designer was an expert in the phases of the design process and the development and fabrication of 3d printed components in combination with the other elements such as harness and wheels to create this assistive dog wheelchair, and the novice was an expert in their requirements for the end product. Working with the end user directly provided a rich understanding of their needs and how to meet them. The end user was well researched in their dog's condition and was able to provide knowledge on the subject, based on interactions with their veterinarian, which informed design decisions (notably the incorporation of 3D printed pieces that include additional supportive straps on the chair). They also developed a bag that held up their dog's legs so that could be fastened to the wheelchair. This helped reveal the need for the wheelchair to be very adaptable (and thus, open) so that it can be used to support a varying degree of severity of paralysis in other dogs.

5   Scaling the Project

5.1   The Thingiverse Platform

The *FiGO* project currently exists as a project page on *Thingiverse*, where it can be accessed and downloaded for fabrication. *Thingiverse* is currently the largest virtual 3D printing community, which makes it a great site for dissemination, awareness, and accessibility. The first author chose to publish the project on this online platform, where the project can be openly accessed, to gain a further understanding of risk management, and to learn more about what different users may need in terms of instructions to successfully build the project by themselves. In order to more smoothly transition into this platform, the design would ideally need to be adapted to ensure that it is a feasible project for novice users who do not have a designer or experienced maker close-by.

5.2   Design Customization

Thingiverse [14] enables users to adapt existing projects to suit their specific needs, provided that they have the knowledge required to amend a design. In *Patterns of Physical Design Remixing in Online Maker Communities*, the authors describe that while the ability to more easily customize (or remix) designs though *Thingiverse's Customizer* application has catalyzed a huge influx in design authors, designs produced through this tool are very rarely interacted with by members of the community once they have been published [15]. Other explorations of specific DAT expertise and participation in open design also indicate the need for designing in customization opportunities [17] in a way that is enabling for novice makers.

5.3   Lack of Feedback for Design Iteration

There seems to be very little engagement around improving and iterating on designs from members of the community (novice makers) that may lack technical expertise to produce novel designs.

Thingiverse has the infrastructure in place to allow users to post, share, and fabricate 3D printed projects via a project page which varies from a completely empty page with no added author information or guidelines, to elaborate DIY style step-by-step instructions. One aspect of the *FiGO* experience that *Thingiverse* is lacking is offering opportunities for dynamic interaction that a community such as the *Bunz Trading Zone* so effortlessly invites. *Thingiverse* could benefit from a space that would elicit impromptu connections to bring together end users, designers, engineers, and makers. In fabrication practice taking place exclusively online, potentially complex projects such as DAT may require alternative forms of engagement with the project author such as video chat, or a dedicated collaborative space other than the comments thread paired to a project page. *Thingiverse Groups* [14], *Makerbot's* attempt at community forums, could be a starting point for this style of interaction.

5.4   Co-creation Potential in Online Platforms Vs. Direct Interactions

After engaging in this design probe experience, it seems highly unlikely that an individual could receive the same value out of a completely online co design experience (with reduced or minimal interaction), as opposed to a local co design project. We recognize that there is some need for more than what is currently available on *Thingiverse*. There was much value gained from designer interaction with the end user: aligning goals and expectations for the project, ensuring a plausible, functional design, and also learning from the iterative experience for both designer and pet owner. This process of engaging with the end user could also empower them to appropriate the project and potentially improve upon it [4], or at the very least learn the skills to be able to repair the dog wheelchair if necessary.

It would be interesting to study what tools could teach or encourage novice makers to participate in improving designs in more indirect ways. An example of a community that has structure that allows this level of participation is GitHub, a social open-source programming community, where members can post issues [16] on projects, which are comments or annotations that often inform authors of bugs in their code, or perhaps to address areas that could be improved upon by the authors. Members can resolve issues themselves, but are not required to do so to be productive contributors to a project. The support of active communities and techniques for supporting skill building and the inclusion of novice users is an area not well explored currently in the open designs with a physical outcome as end result.

6   Emerging Themes and Future Directions

A number of larger themes emerged and were explored in this study. This research project has enlightened the need for involving multiple stakeholders in the process of documenting and developing DAT with specialty skills in dog prostheses identified as a gap in current participation in online Open Design [5] initiatives. There remains unresolved risk and safety issues, how these risks may be controlled through a variety of mechanisms including the parametric design files themselves, support tools (fitting tool), and through risk and safety communication possibly through structured communication templates – although this is one of many possible vehicles. The study has also provided insight into the level of clarity needed when giving or providing design instructions that could be enhanced by visual supports such as video or animated instructions. Currently, the use of support materials and the communication of design modification boundaries and safe fabrication and use has not been the subject of liability claims to our knowledge. However, legal liability and the development of safeguards for use of DAT may emerge overtime as use of DAT expands.

References

1. Celebrating a Maker Milestone: 1 Million Uploads on MakerBot's Thingiverse, 29 October 2015. http://www.makerbot.com/blog/2015/10/29/celebrating-a-maker-milestone-1-million-uploads-on-makerbots-thingiverse. Accessed 10 Jan 2016
2. Assistive   Technology   Challenge   (n.d.).   http://www.thingiverse.com/challenges/AssistiveTechChallenge/. Accessed 20 Jan 2016
3. Buehler, E., Branham, S., Ali, A., Chang, J.J., Hofmann, M.K., Hurst, A., Kane, S.K.: Sharing is caring: assistive technology designs on thingiverse. In: Proceedings of the 33rd Annual ACM Conference on Human Factors in Computing Systems, pp. 525–534. ACM, April 2015
4. Hayes, J., Hannold, E.L.M.: The road to empowerment: a historical perspective on the medicalization of disability. J. Health Hum. Serv. Adm. 352–377 (2007)
5. van Abel, B., Evers, L., Troxler, P., Klaassen, R.: Open design now: why design cannot remain exclusive (2014)
6. Hurst, A., Tobias, J.: Empowering individuals with do-it-yourself assistive technology. In: The Proceedings of the 13th International ACM SIGACCESS Conference on Computers and Accessibility, pp. 11–18. ACM, October 2011
7. Hook, J., Verbaan, S., Durrant, A., Olivier, P., Wright, P.: A study of the challenges related to DIY assistive technology in the context of children with disabilities. In: Proceedings of the 2014 Conference on Designing Interactive Systems, pp. 597–606. ACM, June 2014
8. Mattelmäki, T.: Design Probes. Aalto University, Espoo (2006)
9. Law Library Article (n.d.). http://www.americanpetproducts.org/law/lawlibrary_article.asp?topic=62. Accessed 5 Jan 2016
10. Rear Support Dog Wheelchair I K9 Carts The Pet Mobility Experts (n.d.). http://www.k9carts.com/rear-wheelchair. Accessed 5 Jan 2016

11. Digital Innovation Hubs 3D Design & Printing (n.d.). http://www.torontopubliclibrary.ca/using-the-library/computer-services/innovation-spaces/3D-design-print.jsp. Accessed 11 Feb 2016

12. MakerBot Filament (n.d.). http://store.makerbot.com/filament. Accessed 4 Feb 2016

13. A Matter of Scales: How Much Can You Print with a Single 1 kg Spool? 24 February 2012. http://www.makerbot.com/blog/2012/02/24/a-matter-of-scales-how-much-can-you-print-with-a-single-1kg-spool. Accessed 11 Feb 2016

14. Thingiverse Groups (n.d.). https://www.thingiverse.com/groups. Accessed 10 Feb 2016

15. Oehlberg, L., Willett, W., Mackay, W.E.: Patterns of physical design remixing in online maker communities. In: Proceedings of the 33rd Annual ACM Conference on Human Factors in Computing Systems, pp. 639–648. ACM, April 2015

16. Bissyandé, T.F., Lo, D., Jiang, L., Reveillere, L., Klein, J., Le Traon, Y.: Got issues? Who cares about it? A large scale investigation of issue trackers from github. In: 2013 IEEE 24th International Symposium on Software Reliability Engineering (ISSRE), pp. 188–197. IEEE, November 2013

17. Moraiti, A., Vanden Abeele, V., Vanroye, E., Geurts, L.: Empowering occupational therapists with a DIY-toolkit for smart soft objects. In: Proceedings of the Ninth International Conference on Tangible, Embedded, and Embodied Interaction, pp. 387–394. ACM, January 2015

Architecture of Absurd

Klaudiusz Fross[✉], Katarzyna Ujma-Wąsowicz, Ewa Wala,
Dorota Winnicka-Jasłowska, Anna Gumińska, Michał Sitek, and Agata Sempruch

Faculty of Architecture, Silesian University of Technology, ul. Akademicka 7,
44-100 Gliwice, Poland
klaudiusz.fross@wp.pl

Abstract. Ergonomy is not automatically attributed for an architectonic projects. Construction regulations and norms partially guarantee ergonomic solutions. But still, there is a free, great field for creative work (visions, ideas) for designer. Architects can, but do not have to, use ergonomic principles in projects. They can also freely omit them. We know, that high quality ergonomic buildings are functioning, in built environment, as well as unergonomic and ineffective ones, so-called "ill". Why is it like that? Why architects are enabled to design unergonomic, "ill" objects? Why the investor agrees to inefficient building? Is such an object a success or a failure? Authors think that this subject is extremely current, because it makes us notice, a big amount of basic project errors in buildings. The article presents and discusses examples of pleasing from the outside but non-ergonomic, ineffective and non-functional buildings - the masterpieces of architecture. This type of design is called - "the architecture of absurd" (Fross 2015). It also indicates that using a methodology of qualitative research, evaluate the design at the stage of concept and programming. Design with the principles of ergonomics guarantees the future quality of the object [5].

Keywords: Architectural design · Ergonomics in the design · Building quality evaluation · Revitalisation · Ergonomy of space · Supplementary buildings · Energy-efficient architecture

1 Introduction

Daily reality of architect-practitioner is the perfect background for scientific discussion about architecture. The article elaborates on quality factors closely associated with the architects' work. There can be seen two main approaches, the first one: ignorant attitude to designing and making decisions according to subjective views, "because it seems right to me", "because I know better", with main focus on the artistic side of architectural works, using superficial inspirations, implementing self ego in terms of creating design, and the second one: professional preparation of pre-design phase, based on knowledge which comes directly from the source of the built environment assessments and from its users, with full scheme. Of course, the second approach does not preclude the creation of architect's work and designer's self-realization (Fross et al. 2014, 2015).

Certainly, it is a great effort to plan and implement an object, but its maintenance is even more difficult. High operating costs, ineffectual space or lack of customers'

© Springer International Publishing Switzerland 2016
M. Antona and C. Stephanidis (Eds.): UAHCI 2016, Part I, LNCS 9737, pp. 251–261, 2016.
DOI: 10.1007/978-3-319-40250-5_25

satisfaction, as a result, translates into serious trouble for the owner of the facility and its future. The full realization of business aims is threatened. The authors feel that there is wispread belief - to build an object is intrinsically a success- and yet this is just a beginning. The building is not a goal in itself, but it's a factor to achieve one. It is a wrapper for different types of activities, as well as the implementation of business plans. Even social and welfare objects are subjects for market, competitiveness, efficiency or economy. These days, thinking about operating costs (energy efficiency, maintenance, property taxes) and constantly growing and changing needs of users should be the priority. That is why it is so important, on planning and programming stage, to analyze the future operating costs, to create capabilities of buildings' transformations for future needs (currently unknown), universalism of object, flexibility and adaptability. One of the best methods of managing the mentioned problem is a good preparation of the pre-design phase. It is fair to say that one of the most important project stages, affecting the success of the investment, is the programming phase with pre-design qualitative research. Construction design is a creative continuation of the program assumptions, while a lack of programming or superficial, subjective decisions making in this area cause a lot of errors [5, 6, 10, 13].

2   Examples of Authors' Own Research

2.1   Research 1 – The Swimming Pool Building (2015)

Aim of Research. Research concerns the functioning of eight years old public indoor pool. It is an object which annual losses exceed the capabilities of municipality. Its future in the current financial state is threatened.
The main aim of the research was to assess the actual quality of the object and land development in terms of: technical, functional, organizational, behavioral and economic quality. The attractiveness from the position of the client and cognition of people's views was also important. It was crucial to search solutions to: reduce the amount of design errors (operational and organizational), improve the efficiency of the swimming pool and modify use of space, meet business priorities (investor's goals), lessen operating costs, propose ideas for additional sources of income to meet the requirements and needs of users, new investment opportunities [7].

As a result a set of information about an object, land use, its condition, problems, mistakes, the positives, good sides, strengths and opportunities was obtained. Conclusions and guidelines were used to develop a diversified recovery program and the concept of change. Research, recovery program and the concept were made within 3 months.

Research Methods. In order to familiarize oneself with the current state of building, numbers of proven techniques were used. The methods and techniques are: arranging interviews; loose, spontaneous conversations; telephone interviews; surveys; opinions in the region; internet reviews; users' ratings; building rounds; observational studies on usage and users' behavior inside the object and its surrounding; qualitative research (in following categories: technical, functional, organizational, behavioral and economic) by author's method of qualitative assessments of objects in use "in 8-steps" [5, 6]; way-finding; analysis of land development; analysis of information about the municipality area; a comparative testing, simulations, inspirations; graphical analysis on projections; evaluation of website and advertising folder – information about object and its services; analysis of the concept of area development by the pool from 2009; analysis of the progress priorities of the community – strategy up to 2015.

As a result, an expert assessment of the quality aided by residents users, managers and team representatives opinions was made. In order to evaluate qualitatively a number of expert groups were developed, under the guidance of K. Fross (architect, researcher and teacher) and A. Sempruch (student of Faculty of Architecture) were developed. Selected aspects were consulted with the economist (M. Fross) and the appraiser for construction quality (M. Czyszek) [8].

To obtain the opinions of the pool and land use a simple questionnaire was carried. Surveys were addressed to the municipal office workers, students and teachers of primary school and junior high school. The main questions are: Enumerate elements that are missing or malfunctioning in the building pool (highlight one of the most important); Enumarate the advantages of swimming pool building, that make you feel good in it (highlight one of the most important); What can be improved or changed in the pool building to make it function better or appear more attractive?; Your ideas for further development of the entire recreational complex and the surrounding area [7, 8] (Fig. 1).

Fig. 1. The swimming pool building and qualitative research (Fross, Sempruch).

Research Results. Polling gave 234 statements including 55 adults (teachers and officials) and 179 school children and youth. The survey provided an opportunity to express themselves and to draw attention to the problems related to the subject of research. Many expert opinions were covered with assessments of users obtained in the surveys, interviews, loose conversations and phone calls. This demonstrates the validity and confirmation to expert indications which ran independently and at different times. There also appeared a list of beginning proposals for changes.

For the present poor condition of the property, two basic elements are significant: numerous design errors – primary defects of the building; management of facility and investment. Designed and submitted to the use object with initial defects, had a direct impact on annually number of customers, which is constantly decreasing, and as a result rising operating costs. Conclusions from the study were used as guidelines for the recovery program (Fross 2015).

2.2   Research 2 – Panoptic Architecture – Who Needs It? (2015)

Aim of Research.   Architect, in the act of creating, like an artist, is struggling with the same degree of materials and ideas. Like the manager of a large company he must respond quickly and flawlessly to the capabilities, needs and requirements of contemporary times. This is because the human dreams, which were always at the beginning of thinking about the structures creation are changing, as well as changes to the material architecture (Juzwa et al. 2012). Architects often fall into the trap of their own ideas. Sometimes implemented structures do not go hand in hand with human well-being and perception of the environment. One of such examples is disproportionate to the gains, wonder material, which is glass.

The aim of this study was to analyze the changing in the last few years trends in the organization of architectural space and attempt to answer the question whether the new, young generation ignores, in times of the internet and social networks, the issue of privacy in that space. Setting out in contemporary embodiments, trends of "panoptical architecture" were considered. Accepted methods of research included analysis of the literature of evolutionary transformations and surveys.

Research Results.   The definition of "panoptical architecture" is closely linked to the so-called *panopticon space*. This term comes from the name of the prison, which was conceived in the eighteenth century by Jeremy Bentham – in this facility, the supervision and control were hidden so that the prisoners did not know if and when they are being watched. Enthusiasts-designers of panoptical architecture, which is synonymous with glass architecture, are convinced that it gives a sense of security (I can see everything), spaciousness and aesthetic. However, if designed space is serving an inappropriate function, it applies the opposite effect - a person feels spied on and hemmed.

In 40–50 s of XX century, the dream of European modernism about glass houses, where large transparent panes of glass define the physical boundary between the inside and the outside, was moved to the USA. The transparency of these walls makes them almost absent. This kind of architectural manifesto, which are "houses aquariums" (Ransworth Haus nad Fox River – arch. Mies van der Rohe/1951, house in New Canaan – arch. Philip Johnson/1949) did not work, as a space to live, work or even study.

Transparent compartments indoor (research was focused on this particular matter) set limits, which are often invisible (like "Predator" in Cameron's film from 1987). We should, of course, talk about their advantages, which are: the integration of space, an opportunity to observe the changing shapes, opening for viewing, the security against noise and adjustment of the appropriate microclimate. However, irrefutable drawbacks of glass walls (usually performed in the non-profile system) is a disturbance of privacy and often imperceptible drafting of obstacles [11]. Despite many signals coming from users that is undoubtedly impressive fluidity and blurring the boundaries between the inside and the outside world in certain circumstances is not desirable. On the other hand, continuation of this trend is one of the characteristics of contemporary architecture. Of course, today technology offers solutions for transparency limitation of partitions or allows its individual control. Wall are enriched with moving parts or casings are made of glass with controlled transparency (laminated glass). So what if these solutions are much more expensive and often disturbing convention (the idea) of designer?

Recently, two independent teams of researchers at the Faculty of Architecture, Silesian University of Technology carried out studies, in which particular interest included the issue of perception of existing facility and its interaction with the environment, understood as a need for "being" among the people and as one that should allow privacy. Several newly constructed objects of science (universities) were checked. The studies leave no illusions, under which circumstances shaping specific (in this case - panoptical) aesthetics were associated by the user more with an absurd than the architectural work.

Selected comments [7, 8, 10] can be written as follows: the user's problem is often irresistible awareness of being watched – this raised the question from both students and academic staff (refers to lecture halls and the rooms of individual work); glazing leads to distraction at work, moving out silhouettes of people bother to focus on lectures, exercises, individual interviews; the idea of glass walls/panoptical space is aesthetically, but not functionally acceptable; glass walls reflect sound, which can be uncomfortable - it affects the poor audibility of speech; fully glazed halls sometimes cause excessive supply of sunlight, which interferes with visibility [7, 8, 10].

In contemporary buildings many beautiful and functional glass interiors can be found. However, considering the fact that they are only positively received, if the man is staying there occasionally - such experiment can be carried out. Panoptical architecture is not tolerated by users in places where they are learning and working (therefore staying in one area for a few hours).

2.3   Research 3 – Glass Houses - The Dream and Reality

Aim of Research. House and apartment for the average person is the closest part of architecture, which is used every day. It is a place of rest, an oasis that provides a sense of security and privacy. A sensation here is a glass house, often called the home aquarium. Thanks to the transparency of the glass enclosure it allows to enjoy the view of the environment, but it also raises a lot of doubts about the quality of living. The aim of the study is to attempt to answer the questions: Whether in residential buildings such high transparency of the form is justified? Whether the glass house can be a rational and ergonomic? Would average people like to live in such a house? What are the reasons to decide on the implementation of home aquariums?

Research Methods. The research used literature studies, own observations and surveys on a group of 170 respondents.

Research Results. Idea of glass houses was forming at the turn of the 19th and 20th century - from the beginnings of glass architecture and implementation of Crystal Palace (Paxton 1851), glass skeletal structures formed by representatives of the Chicago School, to the ideas of Paul Scheebart in writing Glasarchitektur and futuristic visions of cities of the future by Bruno Taut (Stadtkrone 1914). Paul Scheebart was writing: *"Our culture is at some point a product of our architecture. If we want to raise culture to a higher level, we need to change our architecture. (...) However, we can only introduce glass architecture that lets in the light of the sun, moon, stars, not only by a few windows - but through as many walls that are entirely of glass as possible - with colored* *glasses."* (Scheerbart 1914). In his conceptions he sketched the image of a new world and a better society, which, thanks to new materials and modern technology, and the openness of the structure of glass and steel, had to give hope for a better future [11]. A similar vision was also presented by the Polish writer Stefan Żeromski, in his novels: *Uroda życia* (1912) and *Przedwiośnie* (1921–24) (Żeromski 1972). In theme of glass houses writer presented the utopia of "new and better civilization". It was a criticism against the Polish situation after 1918, and at the same time dream of a free, fair and beautiful Poland. The presented ideas influenced the views and projects of architects gathered around Bauhaus. Effect of their work was glass pavilion *Glashaus* (Taut 1914), the first glass curtain walls (Gropius and Meyer 1919) and pioneering concept of a glass skyscraper (van der Rohe 1921).

The first houses aquariums appeared exclusively in the 30 s in 20th century - in projects of Keck brothers, then in realizations: Farnworth villa in Plano (van der Rohe 1945–50) and Glass Hause in New Canaan (Johnson 1949). These buildings consistently implemented the principle of "less is more". In the aphorism, Mies van der Rohe expressed limited language of architecture to structures ("skin and bones" of building, in other words coating and steel frame) and aesthetic restraint (eliminating the visual chaos). Their simple cubic forms, using lightweight steel frame and glass cover, initiated fascination with vision of houses fully open to the surroundings. Although these buildings were not without drawbacks resulting from the contemporary technological limitations and inconvenience associated with the use of comfort they have become the archetype of modern glass houses. In order to preserve privacy around the property of *Glashaus*, Johnson built a huge stone fence. Such action indicates that the concept of openness form of a glass building does not always go hand in hand with the needs of users. The development of materials technology and modern building techniques in the late 20th century created new possibilities for the use of glass in buildings. Good technical parameters of glass and more excellent technical solutions of glass partitions these days allow us to meet the high expectations of designers and users. These activities make the idea of glass houses still alive. Houses aquariums are implemented in different parts of the world, various climatic and local conditions. Although the main inspiration for their implementation is the landscape, there are existing buildings that at a particular location and the location are quite surprising, such as House NA designed by Sou Fukimoto in the suburbs of Tokyo. The house is encased by panes of clear glass (also part of sanitary). It is extremely open to both inside and outside. It provides plenty of natural light, but it also reveals the privacy of residents. It is a total negation of a traditional house - shelter. Inside, there are installed curtains, which allow visual separation of space and if it is necessary (especially at night) they protect it from the eyes of pedestrians. In the view of the street, the house gives the impression of scaffolding and temporary structure. For owners it is the fulfillment of youthful dreams. However, in the future, it can become for them cumbersome and irrational for them.

Although contemporary glass houses use modern materials and technologies, large glass panes make them energy-intensive and expensive objects. They often do not meet the legal requirements needed to obtain a building permit (relating to the size, arrangement of glazing and its technical parameters). Interiors of glass houses are exposed to the phenomenon of x-rays, large diurnal temperature variation, overheating in the summer, especially during the endless heat or chilling in the winter, when there is frost and snow. Fully transparent walls eliminate visible borders between the interior and the exterior, as in the case of residential houses is not always seen as positive. The average person expects stability in the home, privacy and security. Glass walls are associated with transparency, fragility and cold. Surveys conducted by the author showed that the majority of respondents positively perceive glass buildings (89,4 %). Few is willing to live in a glass house. 38.2 % of respondents would not like to have glass walls, stairs and ceilings in their home. Their reluctance is explained by the lack of trust in the glass solutions, lack of sense of security, privacy, high costs and problems with keeping it clean.

Despite many shortcomings, glass houses are still considered contemporary and intriguing. They are carried out mainly for reasons of prestige. They are often an experiment with the use of new or enhanced technologies. Sometimes they are the embodiment of unusual, extravagant ideas that have little to do with rationality and ergonomic apartment. Arising occasionally, they still arouse great interest [11].

2.4   Research 4 – Supplementary Buildings in Historic City Centers in Terms of Ergonomic Quality - Examples of Polish Cities

Aim of Research. Supplementary buildings within the historic downtown areas are often shaped differently from the ambient environment. Street space is changing its nature and aesthetics, which should come from the cultural heritage of the area. It is obvious that transformation of the space is continuous. However, it should refer to the existing historical space and cultural heritage, enriching it with new quality values. Supplementary buildings, which are implemented without the protection of the existing urban fabric, degrades the functional and the aesthetic quality of the space and affect the right use and acceptance of that structure aesthetics.

The aim of the study was to analyze the development of supplementary buildings due to the preservation of the quality and continuity of the particular area heritage.

Research Methods. The study was conducted using the methodology of qualitative research in Polish cities, particularly in the downtowns with historic buildings from at least the 19th century. The method and location of the complementary architecture with respect to the historical buildings and effects of the non-adapted new buildings to the existing was studied. It was dealt with the following criteria: composition, proportions of the interior, cross-section of urban street, quality and ergonomic of space in those realizations. The study was carried out "in situ" in the field, on the basis of photographic documentation.

Research Results. The analyzed supplementary buildings, revoked in relation to the existing ones into the quarter, comes often from the 60 s, 70 s of the 20th century. In the obtained places there were created small squares of green, or hardened widens of the street, side blind walls of existing buildings stayed unused. The result is a new type of street frontage with impaired composition and function of the street, as well as the quality of the interior space of the street. Examples of such activities are complementary building projects in Prudnik, Gliwice, Zary and other cities.

There can also be seen that the revitalization of downtown areas tend to expand the traditionally accepted line of demarcation in the buildings of 19 and 20 century. One such example is the revitalization of Elblag and other cities where the destroyed historical buildings were reconstructed. The results are buildings with aesthetic referencing to the historic buildings, but street spaces are too large, devoided of greenery, small architecture, they are ergonomically unsuitable (Fig. 2).

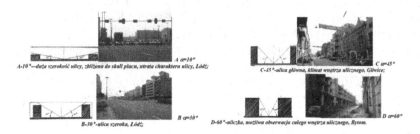

Fig. 2. Central angle street influencing the perception and the perception of the interior street (Gumińska).

Supplementary buildings in the Polish cities in combination with historical downtown buildings often disturbs, shaped by centuries, traditional construction of division of spatial order and urban heritage. Frontage of the street is often deformed, its continuity is disturbed, it is transformed into a smaller quarters. The research, cited above, indicates the importance of the proportion of the streets and the method of forming the frontage of the streets in the historical areas for the quality of the revitalization [2–4].

2.5 Research 5 – Airport Terminal

Aim of Research. Designing facilities accompanying passenger in public transport is associated with the movement analysis of large users groups over time. A special role in these studies is played by tools for simulation at the design stage to find the space in which there are problems with liquidity flow of users. The aim of such simulation experiments is to eliminate bottlenecks in the transfer of passengers between their zones of operation. The experience of the author's concern analyse the flow of passengers through airport terminals. Tests performed on the objects indicate that the airport terminals have the potential retrofit of existing architectural and construction solutions, in order to increase flexibility and ergonomics supporting the four processes of passenger service: check in luggage, security checks, boarding, baggage collection at the arrivals.

Research Methods. Most of the carried out research works were based on the analysis of statistical data and personal observations executed by a group of trained participants. With the ability to work with statistical data describing the changing dynamics of passenger traffic over the five years preceding the period of observation realized in the frames of research, it was possible to determine the periods of peak traffic at terminals in both annual and selected for detailed observation daily events during the four weeks. During the research there was used the access to the monitoring system in selected areas, and there were conducted numerous interviews with airport staff. Thanks to the cooperation of all companies working in the port area it was possible to conduct follow-up of operations performed in areas protected and not accessible to passengers areas. The collected information can be used for studies and comparative analyzes carried out in the future on other objects and off-site testing.

Research Results. Research indicates two groups of factors that determine the appearance of problems at the level of functional and ergonomic use. The first group is related to the evolutionary process of the expansion of the existing terminal facilities. A huge impact on this group have also economic, time and organizational constraints (lack of ability to close the port for the duration of the work under construction). These factors often result in serious accumulation of strange design solutions. We can find a variety of bizarre technical and spatial remedies. During the works on objects, group of researchers has observed: columns located on the main paths of horizontal communication between the zones; stairs being a result of design errors caused frequent accidents and injuries among users, exposes manager of the object to the additional costs associated with the payment of compensation; deficit space necessary to handle passengers in a standard consistent with user expectations and aspirations of the port authorities; the lack of flexibility of space - placing the area of maintenance of luggage prevents the expansion or replacement of devices without serious interference in the structure of the building; incompatibility technological solutions within the volumes; erroneous decisions on zones supporting passenger service - in one of the buildings placing of public functions was offered on the third floor.

Another type of errors associated with designing of airport terminals is a lack of understanding of the processes implemented in the zones and functional changes in these processes in the perspective of modernization and development. A common phenomenon in airport terminals designing is a revaluation of usable space. This is due to the lack of knowledge about how the future object will be working. Dynamics of changes in air services is strongly linked with global markets and fuel economic and political situation.

Easy to obtaining EU funding for the construction or modernization of airports has led to different, sometimes very extreme events. An example of a negative situation can be Ciudad Real airport (spanish.: *Aeropuerto Central Ciudad Real*, code IATA: CQM, kod ICAO: LERL). After three years of operation, the airport was closed. Airport which with the infrastructure costs 1.1 billion euros, was in 17 of July 2015 sold to Chinese company - Tzaneen International for the amount of 10 850 euros.

3   Summary and Conclusions

These days, quality is a standard and duty, not the added value. The high aesthetic quality does not justify the designer errors in other qualities. Quality designing with the use of qualitative research is also a standard and obligation. If, objects were designed according to these priorities, there would be no problems with the buildings, financial loss, user satisfaction, and thus the need for qualitative assessments or remedial programs. The arrogance of a group of architects presenting only artistic approach must end (fashionable design, interesting detail, attractive inspiration, the idea) and they have to start designing on the basis of knowledge, needs and priorities, well-prepared program and the qualitative research before project (which does not exclude high-quality aesthetic). This is in line with the latest global trends in design – design using studies: *Research by Design* and *Design by Research* [5] (Fig. 3).

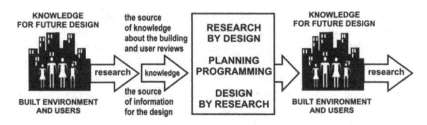

Fig. 3. Flow chart describing additional sources of knowledge and information derived from studies of the built environment and its users (the author's elaboration, 2015).

It is important to study and analyze the needs of today's users (the new information society). The former features of architectural space changed their definitions and images under the new requirements, both: organizational and behavioral. Intuitive design does not work, what can be provided by some Polish projects, for example Academic facilities, which were mentioned in the article (publication). For example, the current prevailing trend of open space areas, multi-purpose, among others, with functions to learn and stay for students, usually in Polish conditions "do not work", because the needs associated with the forms of activity and types of work between classes, performed by students are not understood. In Western Europe, mainly in the UK, there are carried out researches paying special attention to this case and on their basis, effective changes in existing buildings are introduced and new buildings are built based on constructive proposals [13, 14]. In Poland, the architects still rely on their intuition and inspiration, not always correctly interpreted the Polish or local conditions (Winnicka-Jasłowska D.: The space science of the modern university. The role of research of pre-programming new functions of universities. Monography Silesian University of Technology, Gliwice 2016).

References

1. Bell, P., Greene, T., Fisher, J., Baum, A.: Environmental Psychology. Wadsworth Publishing Company, Belmont (2000)
2. Brzezicka (Gumińska), A.: Contemporary interference tissue regeneration in the historical city. In: Balcer-Zgraja, M. (ed.) Modern architecture 8. System - Structure - neighborhood, Rybnik 2014, Proceedings. Silesian University of Technology, Faculty of Architecture. Gliwice, Architectural Design Department (2014)

3. Brzezicka (Gumińska), A.: Modernization of the central areas of historical buildings nineteenth/twentieth - century cities as a way to improve energy facilities. In: Bać, A., Kasperski, J. (eds.) Trends in Development of Energy - Efficient Construction and the Use of Renewable Energy Sources in Lower Silesia. Collective work. [Electronic document]. Publishing Wydaw, Wroclaw University of Technology, Wroclaw, the Optical Disk (CD-ROM), pp. 165–174, bibliogr. 31 pos (2013)

4. Brzezicka (Gumińska), A.: Place identity urban space of all sizes in all technical. In: Juzwa, N., Szulimowska-Ociepka, A. (eds.) ULAR 7, Renewal of the Urban Landscape. Monograph = Urban Landscape Renewal. T. 1, The Future of Medium-Sized Cities, pp. 451–460. Gliwice Silesian University of Technology Faculty of Architecture, bibliogr. 17 pos (2013)

5. Fross, K.: Ergonomics in the practice of project architect on selected examples. In: Kurosu, M. (ed.) HCI 2014, Part I. LNCS, vol. 8510, pp. 77–85. Springer, Heidelberg (2014). ISBN 978-3-319-07232-6 (Print) 978-3-319-07233-3 (Online)

6. Fross, K.: Architect-researcher as a model combination of research and design practice on examples. In: Charytonowicz, J. (ed.) Advances in Human Factors and Sustainable Infrastructure, Proceedings of the 5th International Conference on Applied Human Factors and Ergonomics AHFE 2014, Kraków, Poland, 19–23 July 2014, Las Vegas (2014). ISBN 978-1-4951-2092-3

7. Fross, K., Sempruch, A.: The qualitative research for the architectural design and evaluation of completed buildings – part 1 – basic principles and methodology. ACEE **8**(3), 13–19 (2015). Silesian University of Technology

8. Fross, K., Sempruch, A.: The qualitative research for the architectural design and evaluation of completed buildings – part 2 – examples of accomplished research. ACEE **8**(3), 21–28 (2015). Silesian University of Technology

9. Fross, K., Winnicka-Jasłowska, D., Gumińska, A., Masły, D., Sitek, M.: Use of qualitative research in architectural design and evaluation of the built environment. In: AHFE – HFSI 2015, Session: Ergonomical Evaluation in Architecture, Las Vegas (2015)

10. Juzwa, N, Ujma-Wasowicz, K.: Large scale architecture. Design human factors and ergonomics aspects based on state-of-the-art structures. In: Duffy, V., Gavriel, S. (eds.) 4th International Conference on Applied Human Factors and Ergonomics, AHFE 2012, San Francisco, Boca Raton, USA, 21–25 July 2012

11. Wala, E.: Szkło we współczesnej architekturze (Glass in Contemporary Architecture). Silesian University of Technology, Gliwice, Poland (2012)

12. Weston, R.: 100 Ideas that Changed Architecture. Laurence King Publishing, London (2011)

13. Winnicka-Jasłowska, D.: Quality analysis of polish universities based on POE method - description of research experiences. In: Antona, M., Stephanidis, C. (eds.) UAHCI 2015. LNCS, vol. 9177, pp. 236–242. Springer, Heidelberg (2015)

14. Winnicka-Jasłowska, D.: Ergonomic solutions of facilities and laboratory work-stands at universities. In: Stephanidis, C., Antona, M. (eds.) UAHCI 2014, Part IV. LNCS, vol. 8516, pp. 314–321. Springer, Heidelberg (2014)

Aging Society in Wroclaw's Prefabricated Housing Estates

Barbara E. Gronostajska[1(✉)] and Andrzej M. Wielgus[2]

[1] Faculty of Architecture, Wroclaw University of Technology, Wrocław, Poland
barbara.gronostajska@pwr.edu.pl
[2] Wroclaw Medical University, Wrocław, Poland

Abstract. The paper presents following researches: study the social transformations in selected prefabricated housing estates related to the aging of the society (age structure, family status, physical fitness), conduct social research on the elderly in selected prefabricated housing estates (household structure, family status, physical fitness, assessment of physical activities, leisure activities).

The studies conducted in one large prefabricated housing estates in Wrocław – Szczepin to meet the needs of aging society.

In the 1970s and 1980s the prefabricated housing estates were in the first social cycle. They were inhabited by young people, most often families with small children. Once they became adults, the children moved out, leaving their aging parents in these dwellings. Therefore, today, these estates are mostly inhabited by the elderly, who are often lonely. This is the second social cycle of these estates. As a result new problems emerged related to the needs of this particular group of tenants/inhabitants, which had not been taken into consideration when these housing estates were being designed.

Keywords: Design for aging · Quality of life

1 Introduction

Considerable part of the Polish society lives in prefabricated housing estates, commonly called "bleak housing projects". 1970s and 1980s were the "Golden Period" of large panel construction in Poland. With time, such housing estates were affected by ageing. Along with the age of housing estates, the advancing age of its occupants resulted in change of their social structure. In 70s and 80s the estates were inhabited by young people, mostly families with children. Having grown up, children moved out of these flats and left their ageing parents alone. That is why these housing estates are mostly inhabited by elderly people who often live alone. As a result new problems connected with addressing the needs of this particular group of tenants/occupants emerged. Analyses presented in this study continue my over ten-year research of problems inherent for prefabricated housing estates. Despite constantly growing number of new flats, prefabricated housing estates are still home to a large portion of population in Poland (approximately 12 m, which amounts to about 30 % of the entire population). It should also be mentioned that these buildings are not in such a bad technical condition as the media or press seem to suggest in broadcasts and articles,

M. Antona and C. Stephanidis (Eds.): UAHCI 2016, Part I, LNCS 9737, pp. 262–271, 2016.
DOI: 10.1007/978-3-319-40250-5_26

which has been confirmed by research conducted by the Faculty of Civil Engineering of the Wrocław University of Technology. The fact that occupants of prefabricated housing estates get older and their needs keep changing with time is an important aspect of this study.

The aim of this study is to show social changes resulting from ageing of the society and taking place on prefabricated housing estates. Therefore an important aspect of the project is to conduct social research and evaluate the quality of the environment in which elderly people live, and then to select solutions which can improve their quality of life based on their real needs and their psychophysical abilities. Social psychology shows close relationship between a human being and his/her living environment. Maslow's or Gehl's theories are well known. According to Maslow, human motivation changes as needs are satisfied at each subsequent level of personal development. Human needs are hierarchical in nature and thus need to be fulfilled in a given order: first fundamental needs have to be met in order to effectively meet the higher needs. The most fundamental needs are physical requirements for survival: need of food, shelter and clothing. Safety needs, which come second, take precedence when the first are relatively satisfied. A man in extreme hunger (need for survival) will primarily think of food, and only after satisfying this hunger will he turn to the higher need of safety. Once physiological, financial and emotional safety is present, the need of belongingness and love emerges. Man is a social being and needs to feel loved, liked and accepted by others. The fourth in the hierarchy is the need of self-esteem, related to self-respect, whereas the need of self-actualization is at the top. On the other hand, the Danish psychologist J. Gehl, who also deals with similar issues, identifies three other types of needs that should satisfy the occupants, which are as follows: the feeling of safety (home, protection from pollution and noise, safety of communication), physiological needs (rest, food, drink, sleep, air, light, hygiene), psychological needs (contact, belonging, orientation possibilities, identification).

It can thus be concluded that there is a close link between the quality of residential environment and the quality of life of the elderly. It is evident that satisfaction of people with their place of residence is closely connected to specific requirements related to age. Therefore it is important to learn about all the problems and aspects related to the ageing process.

Analyses show that the Polish society will keep getting older and older. The topic is also more and more popular with the media. Therefore, the needs and abilities of this particular social group should be closely investigated. The issue is very complex as it combines many problems. Dealing with the issue of the elderly in Poland is connected primarily with establishment of Polish standards of conduct, since economic, social, philosophical and religious situation differs from solutions worked out in the West (and for this reason they cannot be adopted directly in Poland). For many years Western European countries have developed a model of retirement homes, which are very popular there. Yet, Polish reality is different than in the West. It must be stressed that not all elderly persons will end up in retirement homes. They are too expensive or offer poor living conditions. Most of today's retirement homes can be commonly labelled as "dying homes", where the elderly end up not of their own volition, but are most often placed there by their families. Such facilities are in poor condition and the housing conditions make the elderly feel lonely, abandoned and often ill.

It must be stressed that majority of elderly persons does not want to move out of their homes. Therefore they should be allowed to live in their previous residential environment as long as possible. It is even more important since research shows that one of the conditions for good physical fitness in old age is being independent. Such independence is possible primarily by owning and taking care of an apartment, which makes us feel "at home". People say that "old age is not designed properly", but it comes to all of us and we should already start thinking about the conditions in which we want to spend the last years of our lives. That is why any voice that promotes dignified ageing and shows how to live and spend leisure time is worthy of attention.

Conducted research shows that initiatives must be directed at three fundamental issues:

- improvement and adjustment of residential environment to changing needs,
- education of the elderly at various levels, taking into account their actual abilities,
- broadly defined encouragement of the elderly.

2 Old Housing Estate – Old Person

The housing estate selected for analysis is Szczepin – the estate erected in 1970's with the use of large panel construction technology. The analysis includes historical context, cultural environment and architectural and urban solutions, including location, basic parameters, land development and its morphology. Social structure, types and possibilities of leisure activities were also subject to analysis. Investigating the structure of housing estate with regard to the elderly, their needs and ability to adjust to the needs of this increasingly numerous group of occupants is also an important element of research (Table 1).

Table 1. Analysis of prices of flats in the resale market, Szczepin north

Localization	Size	Number of rooms	Year of erection	Price
Zachodnia str.	55 m^2	3	1970	5 436 PLN
Zachodnia str.	39 m^2	2	1970	6 138 PLN
Poznańska str.	49 m^2	3	1972	5 680 PLN
Mł. Techników str.	39 m^2	2	1970	6 128 PLN
Mł. Techników str.	48 m^2	2	1970	6 653 PLN

The profile is based on analysis of the real property market performed with real property agencies and shows that 40 % of their current turnover includes flats on prefabricated housing estates. Surprisingly, these flats are not as cheap as one might assume. In Wrocław the average price of a prefabricated flat built before 1990 is lower in comparison to new flats, but the difference is only about PLN 300–400 per m^2. What is more, in some cases the prices are higher than the average price of flats in the resale market. The price analysis was performed for flats located at the prefabricated housing estate subject to research, located in the western area of Wrocław. The buildings were erected in the period from 1970 to 1980.

The above analysis of prices of flats in the resale market suggests that they are very similar to prices of flats in the primary market (development flats). It gives rise to questions about the grounds for such "attachment" of the Poles to "prefabs", since popular opinion about such estates suggests their attitude should be quite contrary. Given these data, one should take a closer look at the location of such housing estates within the city, their communication links, quality and proportion of green areas, availability of services as well as architectural and functional solutions for the buildings and urban planning solutions.

3   Szczepin North

3.1   Location of the Area, Basic Parameters

The area is located within Stare Miasto (Old Town) district. It is quite close to the city centre, 2 km from the Old Market and about 800 m away from the outbound route to Zielona Góra. Boundaries of the estate are outlined by Zachodnia Street in the south, Młodych Techników Street in the east, Ścinawska Street in the north and Poznańska Street in the west. The analysis covers real properties with total area of 8 ha (400 m × 200 m) and occupied by 3000 people.

The area is located in the western part of the Old Town. It is adjacent to residential areas in the south, recreational facilities in the east and west, and educational facilities in the north (Figs. 1 and 2).

Fig. 1. Plan of Szczepin North.

Fig. 2. View on the estate, Szczepin North

3.2   Cultural Environment

Cultural context of the estate involves facilities located in its direct proximity:

A. brick building of the Complex of Schools No. 18. The building was erected in 19th century in accordance with assumptions of neoclassical architecture. The school consists of two 4-storey buildings (A and B). The area between the buildings is filled with greenery. During Spring and Summer the area makes a perfect place of relaxation for students during their breaks. Complex of Schools No. 18 combines Junior Secondary School No. 37 with classes specializing in sports (swimming, handball, athletics, judo) and classes specializing in mathematics and IT with Secondary Technical School of Mechanical Engineering No. 3, providing its students with education in the following specializations: mechanical technician, electrical technician and mechatronics technician. The school has over 60-year history. It has signed contracts for long-term cooperation with such enterprises as Pneumat System Sp. z o.o., Viessmann, Ruukki Polska Sp. z o.o., Volz Gruppe, ABB in Poland, Elektrotim S.A. and Wrocław University of Technology. The cooperation is aimed at better conditions of vocational education. The facility can boast thousands of graduates, including distinguished representatives of technical, academic and political elite of the city. It provides its students with conditions for comprehensive development and thorough education in particular areas of specialization within particular types of schools. It owes its potential to professional teaching staff and modern equipment. Its back-up facilities include multimedia room, computer rooms, Multimedia Centre with 24/7 Internet access, gyms equipped with electronic running track, complex of courts for team games (including 350-m running track, the long jump runway), lecture theatre, Multimedia Information Centre and a rich film library. Security within the facility is ensured with vision monitoring system. Both, the library and the reading room are properly equipped and student-friendly. Numerous student and school events are held at the school "Icarus" Club. Both buildings have their own cafeterias which offer rich selection of hot meals.

B. Christ the King Church – Roman Catholic parish run by the Society of St. Francis de Sales. The building of the church from 1971 has been designed by a famous architect, Witold Molicki. Construction of the church took a long time and it lasted from 1978 to 1991. It is a distinctive and recognizable spot in the neighbourhood as well as the city. Apart from the church itself, the building houses the Dominic Savio Private Salesian Grammar School. It has been designed as two-level structure. The upper level houses the church, the lower level houses the monastic chapel. Form of the building is a reference to regular pyramid made of four parts (each part makes ¼ of the pyramid) with various heights. Projection of the church is an example of central layout and it is based on the square. The ceiling is decorated with a structure resembling a crystal whereas the space above the altar is filled with the sculpture of Christ the King by R. Zamoyski.

3.3 Development Morphology

The estate was created by W. Molicki. Spacial structure of the estate is dominated by multi-family development areas. They consist of middle-rise and high-rise buildings erected mostly with the use of panel slab technology and fitted with external thermal insulation to a large extent. The estate is not fenced off which makes it easily accessible. Moreover, it has a network of paths across the greenery which allows its occupants to move about freely and in pleasant surroundings. The analyzed area has compact, rectangular layout divided by Litomska Street into two, clearly defined parts with transparent urban development.

Analysis of the estate in terms of urban development shows the following:

- The estate is friendly and receives positive opinions from its occupants.
- It has transparent layout with clearly designed, green, enclosed interior spaces and good proportions taking human scale into account.
- Parking space is separated from recreational areas (Fig. 3).

Fig. 3. View on the estate, Szczepin North

3.4 Communication

Analysis of communication within the housing estate shows the following

- The existing roads provide good connection with the city center and other parts of Wrocław.
- Thanks to convenient connections with outbound and bypass roads getting out of the city is quick. Difficulties in communication result from heavy traffic at Legnicka Street during rush hours but occupants can avoid this route by taking one of two neighbouring streets with lower traffic congestion – Zachodnia and Długa.
- The nearest bus and tramway lines (500–800 m away) provide its occupants with direct access to 20 % of the entire area of Wrocław.
- Convenient location of bus and tram stops which can be found no further than 500 m from one's place of living.
- Significant shortage of parking space is visible within the estate despite outlined parking lots and garages, which forces its occupants to park their vehicles with violation of traffic regulations (on pavements, lawns and greens).
- Shortage of bicycle lanes, especially within internal area of the estate.
- Poor quality of pedestrian routes which are unaesthetic and have no amenities for the disabled.

3.5 Recreational Areas and Greenery

Analysis of the estate with regard to recreational areas and greenery shows the following:

- The housing estate has sufficient quantity of recreational areas within public space and its occupants are glad to make use of them.
- Very large recreational areas are available within its semi-public space (quarters of the estate's developments). Yet, the area does not necessarily correspond with the quality. The areas are rather untended.
- Considerable part of the estate is filled with greenery (including high, middle and low vegetation). Sadly, it is usually far from tidied up or well kept - lawns are trampled down, choked with weeds and not mown.
- Elderly occupants are very eager to make use of recreational areas.

3.6 Social Infrastructure

Analysis of social infrastructure of the estate shows the following:

- The estate has good access to a number of facilities, especially educational ones, which can be enjoyed by the elderly, e.g. swimming pool at the school.
- Availability of commercial services is rather limited.
- The estate can boast a social club which is available also to the elderly.
- Catering services are missing and it takes a long walk to other areas of the estate to find them, which is a serious drawback for those elderly who prefer to eat out.
- Not all services are accessible for the elderly and disabled. Some facilities are located on higher storeys which are accessible only by stairway (no wheelchair access ramps, lifts or platforms).

3.7 Technical Condition of Buildings and Infrastructure

Technical condition of buildings can be qualified as average. Residential buildings have been erected with the use of Wrocław Panel Slab technology:

- All buildings are supplied with central heating (municipal network), water and gas.
- Some flats are equipped with air conditioning systems. Yet, such systems are private investments and air conditioners are installed on balconies and exterior walls which affects aesthetics of the building in a negative way.
- 5-storey buildings have no lifts whereas 11-storey buildings have been equipped with such facilities.
- All buildings have undergone thermal performance improvement.
- Majority of flat owners replaced old windows with new ones.
- Most staircase entrances are accessible for the disabled.

3.8 Demography

Large proportion of occupants are persons over 60 (about 40 %). These people have been living on the estate from its beginnings. They moved into their flats as young couples and have been living there until today.

At the beginning of 21st century, after 2006, a considerable number of young people appeared on the housing estate. It resulted from the onset of new financial programme called RnS (A Family in its Own Home). The programme enabled families to take advantage of preference mortgage loans. During that period many young couples purchased flats on this estate as they were relatively inexpensive and rather small whereas proximity of recreational areas and educational services made (and still makes) it a perfect location for young couples with children. They can be seen within recreational areas on a daily basis.

3.9 Accommodation Options

The estate offers accommodation in a variety of dwellings, from studio apartments to four-room flats. The estate has been developed with 4 types of buildings: 11-storey buildings with staircases and corridors and 5-storey buildings with staircases, housing 2 or 3 flats on every storey. Despite the fact that the estate has been designed and erected with the use of industrial technology, structure of flats is diversified. It results, among others, from diversified size of individual units.

4   Swot Analysis for Aging Society in Szczepin Housing Estate

Strengths.

Urban planning aspects	Architectural and technical aspects	Social and economic aspects
Good public transport solutions costs	Technical installations available in flats	Relatively low maintenance costs
Large number of basic services	Functional flat layouts – well-planned	Knowing one's neighbours and strong social bonds within the community
Proximity of recreational areas and sports facilities	Flat sizes – usually adequate for couples or single persons (2- and 3- room flats)	Availability of co-financing from EU funds
Considerable size of areas filled with greenery	–	–
Significant amount of space	–	–
Good local infrastructure	–	–

Weaknesses.

Urban planning aspects	Architectural and technical aspects	Social and economic aspects
The housing estate has not been adjusted to the needs of the elderly – numerous obstacles	No lifts in staircases of 5-storey buildings	No funds for renovations and modernizations
No solutions for bicycles	Staircase entrances have no access ramps or railings – obstacles	Migration of the young from this type of housing estates
Insufficient amount of parking space	No benches or bicycle parking racks near staircase entrances	Being used to living in the same place
No separate parking space for the disabled	Flats do not match the needs of the disabled (wheelchair users)	Housing estates with majority of elderly occupants
Various condition of the Greenery	No common areas inside buildings	Flats rented temporarily to students
–	No private gardens	–

Opportunities.

Urban planning aspects	Architectural and technical aspects	Social and economic aspects
Housing environment advantageous for the elderly	Flats adapted for the elderly – after modernization	Winning EU, municipal or special purpose funds
Construction of additional buildings for the elderly within the estate	–	–

Threats.

Urban planning aspects	Architectural and technical aspects	Social and economic aspects
Introduction of buildings made by property developers (fenced off estates) on the estate can lead to uncontrolled congestion of development	Without renovation and adaptation technical condition of buildings will deteriorate	Loneliness caused by absence of contacts with the surrounding world (obstacles)

5 Summary

A considerable proportion of the Polish society lives on housing estates from 1970s erected with the use of panel slab technology. Despite constant warnings pertaining to poor quality of materials, standardization of solutions and flat sizes, such estates still hold positive opinions of their occupants. Analyses conducted in this study confirm such opinions. Location of such housing estates is one of their major strengths. In many cases such estates are located nearby city centers and benefit from good public transport solutions. Another essential element affecting the quality of living is proximity of broadly defined services, including trade, education and recreation. The estate analyzed in this study can boast services at a level higher than satisfactory. It is distinguished by large areas filled with greenery as well as recreational, relaxation and sports facilities. One might say that it makes a good place to spend one's free time. Yet, the issue of the elderly is an important aspect of further advancement of this type of housing estates, as they keep growing in number and their living environment has not been adapted to their needs. Some financial outlays might improve quality of life by introducing a number of solutions that would make life of the elderly and disabled easier and more comfortable. Such solutions can be divided into the following groups:

a. Adjustment, b. Adaptation, c. Intensification, d. Reduction, e. Cohousing.

References

1. Arthur, P., Passini, R.: Wayfinding-People, Signs, and Architecture. McGraw-Hill, New York (1992)
2. Gehl J.: Życie między budynkami, Wydawnictwo RAM (2009)
3. Gronostajska, B.: Kreacja i modernizacja przestrzeni mieszkalnej. Oficyna Wydawnicza Politechniki Wrocławskiej, Wrocław (2007)
4. Jordan, S.D.: The subtle differences in configuration of small public spacer. Landscape-Archit. **68**, 487 (1978)
5. Zych, A.A.: Moderacja rozwoju – wyzwaniem dla gerontologii edukacyjnej. Gerontologia Polska **12**(3) (2004)

Impact of New Construction Technologies on Sustainable Hotel Design

Joanna Jabłońska, Elżbieta Trocka-Leszczyńska, and Romuald Tarczewski[✉]

Faculty of Architecture, Wroclaw University of Technology, Wrocław, Poland
{joanna.jablonska,elzbieta.trocka-leszczynska,
romuald.tarczewski}@pwr.edu.pl

Abstract. One of the important trends in contemporary design of hotels is to obtain environmental compatibility. This is manifested on the one hand in the search for the special locations of these facilities, and on the other hand – in giving them a very sophisticated, organic form. The specific location means scenically attractive site, surrounded by spectacular natural forms. These can be, for example hardly accessible mountain slopes, old abandoned quarries, desert areas, or even the sea bottom surrounded by coral reef. Until relatively recently, both the construction process and operation of hotels in such locations was extremely difficult or even impossible for technical reasons. Also, nature conservation considerations constituted a serious obstacle, because often these areas are protected by law. Technological development enables to overcome these barriers, and limitation for designers is often only imagination. This is manifested in the second-mentioned aspect of striving for environmental compatibility – organic shaping the architectural forms. During several years of development of so called free-forms in architecture, often called "the Bilbao effect", have been developed appropriate design tools, which in combination with modern technologies open up completely new possibilities for architects. This article is an attempt to summarize the most important issues in this respect, illustrated with most characteristic examples.

Keywords: New construction technologies · Sustainable hotel design

1 Introduction

Travelling for various non-profit purposes is known since ancient times. Just to remind Pausanias and his "Description of Greece" (2nd century AD). But the term "tourist" appeared only in the nineteenth century, in Stendhal's novel "Memoirs of a Tourist" (*Memoires d'un touriste*), in 1838 [2]. Since then, the importance of tourism has increased greatly. Changed its definition and understanding, and significant changes took place within it.

Modern tourism is one of the most profitable businesses in the world, a phenomenon characterized by great dynamics of development, but also associated with adventure. Multifaceted and interdisciplinary nature of tourism means that it is defined in several ways. Tourism is of interest to many sciences, because it is a social phenomenon, psychological, cultural, economic and spatial. A different look at this area has a

© Springer International Publishing Switzerland 2016
M. Antona and C. Stephanidis (Eds.): UAHCI 2016, Part I, LNCS 9737, pp. 272–281, 2016.
DOI: 10.1007/978-3-319-40250-5_27

geographer, sociologist, economist and politician. Tourism is defined differently from various viewpoints, e.g. demand and supply. Modern tourism is also a kind of "escape from reality". The search for what we do not have at home. Tourism is searching for unexplored.

Changes occurring within the tourism were reflected in the architecture of objects generated for this industry. These changes concerned both function and form of buildings. The development of tourism generated an increase in the number of new investments. In recent years the phenomenon appeared in a sense the other way round. There arise architectural buildings – hotels, which are themselves generators of tourism development. They attract by their unusual form, location in hard to reach places, or the scope of the offered attractions. This was made possible through the use of new constructional technologies, as well as redefining the paradigm of tourist attractiveness.

2   Tourism and Its Form of Activities

Tourism refers to the activity of visitors [7]. According to United Nations recommendations IRTS 2008 [3], tourism is defined as a subset of travel, which in turn refers to the activity of travelers. A traveler is someone who moves between different geographic locations for any purpose and any duration, while a visitor is a traveler taking a trip to a main destination outside his/her usual environment, for less than a year, for any main purpose other than to be employed by a resident entity in the country or place visited.

Typology of tourism involves many aspects of this phenomenon and is very extensive. Due to the complex nature of tourism a one common model of its classification has not been developed yet. United Nations recommendations [3] provide its basic outline but in studies of many authors can be found much more extended versions.

The following three basic forms of tourism can be distinguished in relation to the country of reference: domestic tourism, inbound tourism and outbound tourism. These three basic forms can be combined in various ways to derive other forms: internal tourism, national tourism and international tourism.

Classification of tourism is related to the trip, which notion refers to a round trip. It's the travel by a person from the departure from his usual residence until he returns [7]. When taken by visitors they are tourism trips. They are usually associated with different forms of tourism, and may be characterized by [3]:

- main purpose
- types of "tourism product"
- duration of a trip or visit
- origin and destination
- modes of transport
- types of accommodation.

One of the most important of the above characteristics and from the standpoint of this paper – is the main purpose. It is defined as the purpose in the absence of which the trip would not have taken place [3]. According to this criterion, we can distinguish the following main purposes:

- personal
  - holidays, leisure and recreation
  - visiting friends and relatives
  - education and training
  - health and medical care
  - religion/pilgrimages
  - shopping
  - transit
  - other
- business and professional.

The main purpose of the trip is at the same time closely related to the specific types of "tourism products", such as culinary tourism, ecotourism, city tourism, sun-and-sand tourism, agro-tourism, health tourism, winter tourism, etc. One of the important tourism consumption products is accommodation service for visitors.

3   Accommodation Services for Visitors – A Challenge for Architecture

From the short list of "tourism products" presented above arise great diversity of forms of providing of accommodation services for visitors. Each type of tourist activity has slightly different requirements in this regard. This has a direct impact on the architectural form of facilities for accommodation [1].

Such facilities must combine different, often conflicting requirements. Hotels house a number of different functions at the same time. These functions depend on the standard of the hotel and are related to the operation of specific forms of activity. Their spatial interweaving affects the size of the rooms, the span of construction, loadings etc. Another very important aspect is to find the appropriate means of architectural expression and harmonious fitting of building into surrounding terrain. As a result, there are many possible configurations of functional layouts, which are shown schematically in Fig. 1.

Designing of such functionally complex objects must of necessity be a fully integrated process, in which all participating branches collaborate closely since the initial phases. Advantageous aspect of such organization of the design process is the possibility of use and harmonious integration of the latest technological advances in all branches [5, 6].

There are two trends in the application of new technologies. One of them is the so-called "architecture of exaggeration". Emerging objects manifest their largeness and extravagance. Their form is far from traditional, often flashy, exposes the functions located inside. A good example is the Marina Bay Sands Hotel in Singapore.

Second trend is the opposite of the previous one. It includes objects that try as much as possible to integrate with the surrounding environment. Often they use the natural spaces, e.g. caves or rock caverns. It can be divided into two sub-trends. The first is minimalist, preferring modesty and simplicity, and even – to some extent – poverty. The other, avoiding ostentation requires the use of sophisticated techniques due to the specific locations. In both can be seen desire to preserve the principles of environmental compatibility.

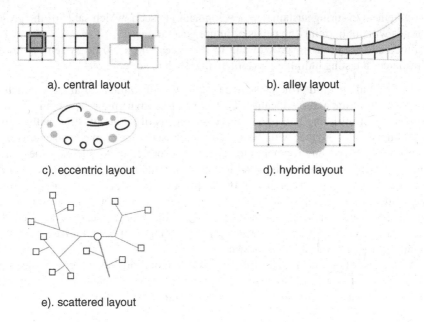

a). central layout   b). alley layout

c). eccentric layout   d). hybrid layout

e). scattered layout

Fig. 1. Various functional arrangements of hotel facilities

4 Principles of the Theory of Environmentally Compatible Structures

The theory of environmentally compatible structures is an applied subject of environmental sciences in the field of civil engineering and architecture. It focuses on restoration of clean environment and minimization of any environmental pollution effect in the phases of design, technology and use of buildings and structures [6].

It is an extension of the classical theory of architectural and structural design. According to it, any design has to ensure [4]:

1. safe resistance of the designed structure against all external loads or effects, to which it may be subjected over the whole life span,
2. responsibility, that the structure will serve the purpose for which it was designed or redesigned, throughout the expected life cycle.

The third, supplementary environmental condition has to ensure, that:

3. during all phases of the life cycle of the structure, its environmental pollution effect is reduced to minimum. The last design condition is meant to protect the local, regional and global clean environment.

These three assumptions lead to the formulation of the three globally valid basic principles:

1. an axiom of global equilibrium: global lasting dynamic equilibrium in nature must be preserved

2. a statement ensuring sustainable development i.e. such, which satisfies the present needs without harming the needs of future generations
3. a theorem of "limits to growth and to resources": in a closed system of limited resources a lasting unlimited quantitative growth is not possible.

The first and the third principles are based on globally valid natural laws, which are independent on time and the locality. They express the dynamic global equilibrium of the diversity of all living and non-living components of nature existing within given natural limits, in accordance with the principle of preservation of mass and energy, such as clean atmospheric environment etc. The second principle is reflecting the general moral and social attitude for the need to maintain sustainable development with due regard to the economic and social activities [4]. For practical design purposes, these three fundamental principles must be transformed into a practically acceptable and applicable version. Such transformed versions of these principles are designated as "design characteristics" [4]. The design characteristics must be optimized in order to maximize protection of the environment.

The process of optimization is different for different problems, different objects and different types of structure. However, it is possible to formulate appropriate strategies in order to introduce formulated above principles into practice [4].

5 Influence of Environmental Compatibility on Architectural Design

Architectural design is a very specific field, located on the border between art and science of engineering. Its social impact is very large, as architectural objects because of their scale and function have a significant impact on both the daily human life and on the environment. They can help to raise its value or increase its degradation. They are an important element of the landscape. Therefore, the implementation of the principles of environmentally compatible constructing is particularly important.

Below are given few areas of the tourist activity, where can be observed such a design approach. They relate to embedding objects as close to the surrounding environment as possible, to ensure, of full contact residents of with Nature. They also include examples of rehabilitation of devastated environment both natural and man-made, and the location of accommodation in places previously inaccessible.

5.1 Embedding of Facilities in the Surrounding Nature

One of the most popular solutions for environmentally compatible structures is locating scattered accommodation units in almost untouched natural environment. This protects existing resources, avoiding e.g. cutting down trees. At the same time close contact with nature is the basis to create a completely different man-environment relationship.

Depending on the technology used and the characteristics of the specific location there are various optional solutions. Popular is locating apartments in a completely different way than traditional buildings. They can e.g. be stretched between the slopes of the ravine using

a)   b)

Fig. 2. Residential units and swimming pools interwoven with natural environment, Resort Spa Treehouse, Bali island, Indonesia [8]

a lightweight, non-invasive visually structure, leaving space to the maximum extent open to the environment, Fig. 2(a).

Fig. 3. Freestanding accommodation units among the trees, Resort Spa Treehouse, Bali island, Indonesia [8]

Fig. 4. Residential units suspended from trees, Resort Spa Treehouse, Bali island, Indonesia [8]

Very common is location of independent accommodation units scattered among the high forest, where their design gives the impression that they are part of the forest, Fig. 3. Alternatively, they may be suspended to trees, further increasing the impression Fig. 4. It is worth noting how diverse architectural forms can be obtained in these objects and how well they integrate with the environment. This method of location is applied not only to rooms but also to the supplementary functions, for example swimming pools, Fig. 2(b).

5.2   The New Facility as a Form of Rehabilitation of the Natural Environment

Locating hotel facilities in places where environment is degraded through intensive human activity, may be one of the roads leading to his rehabilitation. Substantial costs associated with the process of rehabilitation make that locating there standard housing construction is not economically justified. However, in the case of hotels, especially of high standard the bill of expenditures and payback time looks completely different. The rate for one-day stay in such a facility may be higher than the monthly rent for a multi room apartment. An additional source of income are different kinds of dedicated, specific tourism product oriented activities. Thus, despite the large amount of capital expenditures realizations of such objects are not at all uncommon.

An example might be Songjiang Quarry Hotel, located within the one hundred meters deep abandoned and half flooded quarry near the base of Tianmashan Mountain in the Songjiang District of Shanghai, Fig. 5. The facility takes advantage of gorgeous location. The idea of realization of this unique object was presented by the international consulting firm Atkins and undertaken by Shanghai Shimao Property Group [9].

Undertaking such difficult construction works was possible thanks to the latest technology in the field of geotechnical and structural engineering. As a result, devastated environment of the quarry turned into a unique spot in terms of landscape, attracting tourists with its uniqueness. The facility is in the final phase of realization.

5.3   The New Facility as a Form of Rehabilitation of the Man-Made Environment

Old, abandoned objects whose functional usefulness already exhausted, can be for the environment as burdensome as the site of the intensive exploitation of natural resources. If these objects can be relatively easily subjected to demolition, the problem is of a smaller scale. If the demolition of such a facility and rehabilitation of land remaining after demolition is technically difficult and expensive, the problem becomes serious. One way to deal with such situations is practiced in cities transformation onto objects with luxurious apartments – lofts. In the case of objects located outside the cities, and those whose primary function is far from residential function, it is possible to convert them into tourist facilities.

An example of this is the development of an old fortress, Spitbank Fort, located one mile out to sea off the coast from Portsmouth Harbor in Hampshire, U.K. This 134 year old object, in the past part of the defense system of the British coast against enemy ships has been converted into luxury tourism facility, Fig. 6. It contains currently luxury guest rooms, bars, restaurants etc. [10]. The building, rather than pose a threat to the environment has become a valuable part of the tourism infrastructure.

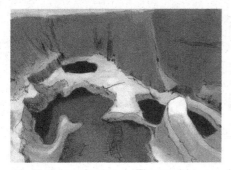 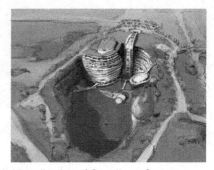

<table>
<tr><td>a). Abandoned quarry in Tianmashan Mountain</td><td>b). Visualization of Songjiang Quarry Hotel</td></tr>
</table>

Fig. 5. Songjiang Quarry Hotel near the base of Tianmashan Mountain in the Songjiang District of Shanghai [9]

Fig. 6. Spitbank Fort – fortress off the coast near Portsmouth Harbor in Hampshire, U.K. [10]

5.4 Development of Facilities on Surface of the Seas

Futuristic plans to create floating islands have been created for a long time. Due to the feeling of insecurity caused by the alleged global warming, they have become recently popular again. There are many projects of floating habitats, units on the scale of a medium-sized city, able to function independently. Suffice it to mention in this context, projects of Vincent Callebaut.

On this wave also they began to emerge projects of smaller floating accommodation objects constituting a new form of hotel facilities. They are basically large boats, adaptable to a variety of outdoor activities, including the opportunity to observe the underwater world. An example of such a project, which is recently loudly presented in the media is the Solar Floating Islands in the Maldives developed by Michele Puzzolante from MPD Designs, Fig. 7.

Fig. 7. Visualization of the Solar Floating Islands in the Maldives, developed by MPD Designs, U.K. [11]

According to this concept, the hotel would be a kind of a mooring station for the team of floating units, each of which is designed for four people. Its users can choose whether they want that their unit moves through the surrounding waters, or prefer to remain in the base, taking advantage of additional services [11].

5.5 Development of Facilities in the Depths of the Seas

The next step, after the of floating islands, in the development of water areas for tourism is locating permanent objects on the seabed. Particularly attractive are the areas of coral reef, due to the possibility of direct observation of outstanding natural beauty. Below is one of the projects of this type, which is in the initial stage of preparation for implementation. This is the Planet Ocean Underwater Hotel, a proposition of the company based on the Florida island of Key West, Fig. 8.

Fig. 8. Visualization of the prefabricated modular facility developed by the Planet Ocean Underwater Hotel, Key West, U.S. [12]

This is a modular structure which can be assembled in various configurations. The hotel will be deployed at a depth of around 8.5 m. In the facility will be located all the necessary functions, including rooms allowing organization of events such as meetings, weddings etc. [12].

6   Conclusions

Presented above basic principles of designing environmentally compatible facilities and examples of their practical implementation show how much they can contribute to the architectural design. On the one hand it is possible to achieve a new level of protection of the environment from the adverse effects of human activities, and on the other hand, they trigger a great potential in the creation of architectural form.

References

1. Błądek, Z. (ed.): Modern hotel industry. From design to equipment (in Polish). Nowoczesne hotelarstwo. Od projektowania do wyposażenia. Oficyna Wydawniczo-Poligraficzna "Adam", Warszawa (2010)
2. Cymańska-Garbowska, B., Steblik-Wlaźlak, B.: Tourism. Vol. I: Fundamentals of Tourism (in Polish). Turystyka. Tom I: Podstawy turystyki. WSiP, Warszawa (2013)
3. United Nations, Department of Economic and Social Affairs, Statistics Division: International Recommendations for Tourism Statistics 2008 (IRTS 2008). http://unstats.un.org/unsd/publication/Seriesm/SeriesM_83rev1e.pdf. Accessed 26 Feb 2016
4. Végh, L., Végh, P.: Environmentally compatible structures (ECS) – introduction into the theory of ECS. In: Domingo, C., Lázaro, C. (eds.) Evolution and trends in Design and Construction of Shell and Spatial Structures. CEDEX, Madrid (2009)
5. Vickers, G.: 21st Century Hotel. Laurence King Publishing, London (2005)
6. Watson, H.: Hotel Revolution. Wiley, Chichester (2005)
7. World Tourism Organization (UNWTO): Glossary of tourism terms. Update 2014. https://s3-eu-west-1.amazonaws.com/staticunwto/Statistics/Glossary+of+terms.pdf. Accessed 26 Feb 2016
8. http://nexttriptourism.com/resort-spa-treehouse-tourism-bali/resort-spa-treehouse/. Accessed 09 Nov 2015
9. http://www.amusingplanet.com/2012/10/construction-of-amazing-underground.html. Accessed 09 Nov 2015
10. http://www.gizmag.com/spitbank-fort-hotel/26303/?li_source=LI&li_medium=default-widget. Accessed 09 Nov 2015
11. http://www.dailymail.co.uk/travel/article-2579216/The-luxury-floating-island-resort-future-tourism-comes-145MILLION-price-tag.html. Accessed 09 Nov 2015
12. http://www.gizmag.com/planet-ocean-underwater-hotel/40753/?li_source=LI&li_medium=default-widget. Accessed 09 Nov 2015

Structure vs. Ergonomics in Contemporary Hotel Design

Joanna Jabłońska[✉], Elżbieta Trocka-Leszczyńska, and Romuald Tarczewski

Faculty of Architecture, Wroclaw University of Technology, Wroclaw, Poland
{joanna.jablonska,elzbieta.trocka-leszczynska,
romuald.tarczewski}@pwr.edu.pl

Abstract. The structural system is not only a carrier of architectural form, but also an important factor in the process of formulating the spatial-functional plan of facilities. Its impact goes far beyond the basic function of ensuring safety of the building. Proper coordination of architectural solutions and structural system allows zone optimization, influences layout arrangement and interiors span and therefore has a strong impact on ergonomics of room solution. Moreover, it allows combining (correct mutual positioning) of the various zones in the building, deployment of special and additional functions (e.g. swimming pools, conference centers, parking lots, etc.). Such interaction is also crucial for matching the hotel facilities to the surrounding environment. Presented article is a summary of research on architecture to structure relation, in pursuit of optimal solutions for maximizing safety and comfort of use in contemporary hotels. The needs of people with impaired physical of psychical conditions were also taken into account.

Keywords: Contemporary hotel design · Structural system · Interdisciplinary co-creation

1 Introduction

In the fully integrated design process architecture and structure are elaborated simultaneously in a close cooperation of branches. Such approach is dictated by direct relation between form and its' support. If these two are properly solved, than whole investment can be optimized as far as: costs, ecology, user and fire safety are taken into account. When incorrectly placed: structure span, load barring and support elements, can ruin functionality and elasticity of large scale spaces (like: swimming pools, SPA areas, conference halls, ball rooms, sport facilities), room dimensions or may become hazard for people suffering from different kinds of chronical or temporary psychophysical disabilities. On the other hand optimal solutions allow strengthening architectural expression, harmonious fitting of building into surrounding and most of all provide long-lasting security of whole investment. In light of these arguments this article was dedicated to present a short description of study process and conclusions on search for optimal and ergonomic relation between architecture and structure in contemporary European hotels.

M. Antona and C. Stephanidis (Eds.): UAHCI 2016, Part I, LNCS 9737, pp. 282–292, 2016.
DOI: 10.1007/978-3-319-40250-5_28

2   Aspect of Time in the Design

Consideration of architecture and structure mutual relation must be always carried out in four dimensions – three spatial dimensions and time. This is the problem of transience of architecture.

The buildings are aging in several aspects: technical, functional and aesthetic. According to [11] average period of "life of the building" is approx. one hundred years, of course, with deviations in either direction. After this period, each object – except perhaps for monumental buildings – exhausts its usefulness, in at least one of the aforementioned aspects. Then, the decision as to its further fate is necessary. There are only two possibilities: modernization or demolition. This dilemma arises in the categorical form at the end of the "life of the building", but in fact the whole period is a process of formation spread out over years (preparation of investment, design and realization), because of constant need to adapt facility to changing conditions of use. However, these transformations may have minor intensity. "End of life" states the moment when possibilities of the continuing modernization exhausted and there must be decision taken on radical changes [10]. The more building is susceptible to continues upgrading, the more moment discussed can be postponed. In this context, it is essential that initially adopted solutions are as flexible as possible, allowing transformation of the building to the maximum extent.

In presented study firstly three dimensions were simplified and expressed in layouts and sections, which is fully sufficient for engineer considerations and interpretations. For aspect of time, structure duration was estimated and given in the discussion part of paper.

Research was carried out on a theoretical background (literature survey) and in a practical aspect (case study on site and in text sources). There have been around 30 examples analyzed, selected in to order obtain most diversified architecture-structure relations. Studies are based on European examples, taking into account, that each culture (European, Asian, American, African, etc.) has different customs in space arrangement [4] and uses diversified construction methods and materials. Due to need for limiting text content only conclusions from this part were discussed in "typology" paragraph. Further on synthesis was used to form concise typology and extract main cases form A-D for buildings' layouts and 1–4 for its' cross-sections. Having main aspects emerge a discussion was executed with use of: critical analysis, cooperative synthesis and synthesis. The same methods were used for conclusions section.

3   Functional Typology of Hotel Buildings

The functional layouts which are applied in the design of hotels appear in great diversity. However, their visual differentiation does not interfere with the finding of common features, allowing building a systematic classification. Based on highly diversified source typologies (created for hotels or buildings of public use) [1, 3, 6–9, 12–14] and taking into account the structural aspects of the building, the following systematics of layouts have been created (Fig. 1):

- central – containing also atrium arrangements – (with structure and service elements in the center of the layout) – case A
- alley – containing multi-alley, bay and angled or organic linear solutions – (with structure and service elements placed along corridors and lateral walls of rooms or external facade) – case B
- eccentric – notion used by [3] – (with unusual layout form, therefore with asymmetrically placed structure and service places) – case C
- hybrid – containing also nested arrangements – (connecting two or more aforementioned systems) – case D
- scattered – a group of independent small buildings (bungalows) (not considered in this study).

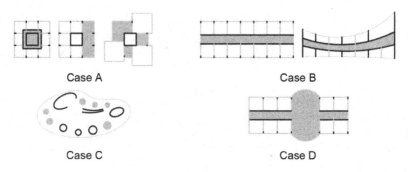

Case A   Case B

Case C   Case D

Fig. 1. Typology of layouts with consideration of hotel building's structure

The presented typology significantly generalizes and idealizes the actual schemes, however, thanks to this enables finding common features of objects. In particular, it allows defining concerns that are closely related with residential floor planning, which serves as a base for all most important investment considerations on economy or ergonomic aspects. Arrangement of the structural system is not the least important of them.

4 Review of Feasible Structural Systems

When analyzing the feasibility of various functional variants and different architectural forms of hotel facilities, one should systematize the means that are available to designers. The carrier of architectural content (functional and visual) is a structural system. Its primary function is to transfer all loads that act on the object on the ground and provide it with sufficient rigidity and reliability. However, these basic tasks can be achieved through the use of very different technical solutions. From their selection depends the implementation of architectural assumptions.

It is assumed that the most important criterion for the classification of structural systems is type of elements responsible for providing spatial rigidity of the building. On this basis, Khan and Moore [5] developed the following classification:

- shear systems: shear wall, shear frame, braced frame (longitudinal, crosswise, mixed)

- core systems: central core, split core, end core, atrium core (single, multiple)
- core-frame and core-outrigger systems: shear wall core, rigid/braced frame core
- partial tubular systems: end channel framed tube with interior shear trusses, end channel and middle framed tube
- tubular systems: framed tube, perforated shell tube, deep spandrel tube, single tube, tube-in-tube
- core-tubular systems.

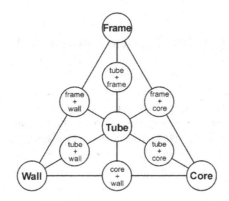

Fig. 2. Classification of structural systems in outline, based on Khan and Moore [5]

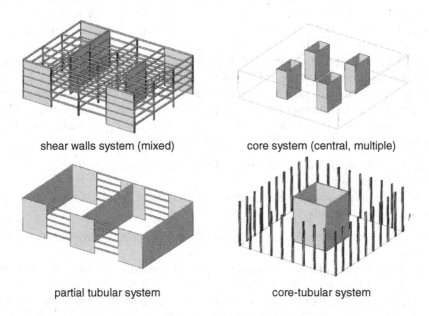

shear walls system (mixed)   core system (central, multiple)

partial tubular system   core-tubular system

Fig. 3. Schematic diagrams of selected structural systems

This classification considers four main types of elements providing rigidity due to their geometry, while showing how they can be meaningfully combined. The outline of this classification is shown in Fig. 2. These general relationships are implemented in practice by a variety of technical solutions. For example, the core can be realized as set of RC walls or as a braced frame. Similarly, is with shear walls system. This makes the vocabulary at the disposal of designers very rich and allows the implementation of different objectives. This is illustrated by examples of selected structural systems in Fig. 3.

5   Challenges to Structural System Due to Functional Layout

An important aspect of the choice of structural system is its accommodation to different functional schemes. Hotels are objects in which this problem is particularly evident. The reason for its occurrence is the spatial interweaving of different functions, which requires from the structural system varied parameters for: a span, height, loadings, a dynamic impact, a size of openings, etc. These parameters in a specific way interfere with each other, and their simultaneous fulfillment is often a challenge. This can be illustrated by a simple example of the hotel, where in underground part parking is located, above – a block of conference and restaurant facilities, then the hotel rooms and – at the top – SPA with pool and block of restaurants again. Each of these functions requires a different design grid, spans and imposes different loads. If we combine this with supplementary office function connected with the hotel – what is very common – the situation becomes even more complicated. This is the first group of concerns closely related to hotels' structural systems, which serves as a base for all most important investment considerations on economy or ergonomic aspects.

As outlined in Sect. 3, selection of the structural system optimal to the functional layout used in the particular hotel, is one of the most important issues, which a designer faces. Systematization of variable decision parameters allows their mutual customization. Introduced classification allows creation of a direct link between structure and function at the level of idealized schemes. To each of the cases presented on Fig. 1 can be assigned an appropriate structural system. Exemplary relations are presented below:

- case A – tubular systems, core-tubular systems, core-frame systems
- case B – shear systems
- case C – multiple cores systems, partial tubular systems, tubular systems
- case D – shear systems.

The apparent obviousness of these relationships does not detract from their practical usefulness.

The second group of concerns related to applied structural systems is related to the above-mentioned interweaving of functions with very different requirements to the structural system. The four specific, most likely appearing basic cases can be specified (Fig. 4).

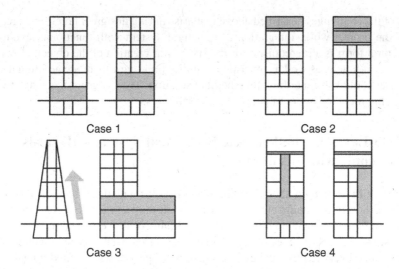

Case 1   Case 2

Case 3   Case 4

Fig. 4. Typology I. Hazards for support structure: case 1 – large scale rooms below rooms, case 2 – heavy load rooms on upper floors, case 3 – diversified layout on reach floor, case 4 – atrium.

Case 1 occurs when large scale rooms (span reaching up to 20 m and more) are located in the lower part of the building: on an underground floor, a ground floor or a first floor. This causes the separation of the upper storeys' structure from the foundations. This is a very common situation. In absolute majority of cases it is impossible and unreasonable to continue on the upper floors structure retaining the large span, divided functionally by non-structural walls. Thus, the structure of the upper storeys' (which require reduced spans) is somehow suspended over the lower portion and must be supported bypassing it.

As the case 2 is recalled a situation where heavy load rooms are located on the top of the building, i.e. public use spaces: swimming pools, SPA areas, Wellness and gyms (sport machines and equipment, water), as well as maintenance rooms: archives (paper) or storage (spare room furnishing, equipment).

Case 3 is connected to floor layout design, thus building with nonstandard, "fancy" forms, like: containing parts which are quite different in height (e.g. divided into plaza and tower), with varied layout on each floor, with narrowing or widening cross-section towards top, etc.

Case 4 includes buildings with atrium, which are quite popular in overall hotel design, especially in tall buildings. The latter pose additional challenges for the structure, however their structural systems are included in the above presented classification and will not be discussed separately here.

Additionally, one can distinguish case 5, which is not represented in Fig. 4. This is a situation in which in the building is located underground parking, which structural grid design is different (not necessarily of a greater span) than the structural grid of the storeys' located above. This very common situation may also occur in all four of the aforementioned cases, imposing additional limitations as to the range of solutions available.

All of the challenges described above that arise during design of hotels are a regular part of the project work. Integration of structural system with functional layout and architectural form is a prerequisite for the successful creation of the object. However, in the case of hotels, as well as other public utility buildings, there are additional challenges that could substantially affect the final solution. They concern the adaptation of the object to meet the needs of people with disabilities.

6   Meta-Level of Challenges to Structural System – Hazards for People with Disabilities

All public utility buildings should be tailored to persons with disabilities. These people require creation of a specific environment in which they can feel safe and function in spite of limitations. When creating such an environment it is essential to eliminate all obstacles, barriers and sources of interference that – irrelevant to people without disabilities – can be very tedious and even dangerous for people with limited fitness.

Incompatibility of structural system and functional-aesthetic solutions can be a major source of problems in the use of the building. The following hazard areas can be distinguished:

- limitations on the freedom of forming the functional layout
- limitations within communication zones
- adverse properties of elements of the structural system regarding serviceability limit state
- imposition of disturbances in the perception of space.

The first group of hazards can be easily identified. Limitations on shaping the functional layout may arise from the fact that the modular grid of structural system has a different size than the grid resulting from functional layout. Such incompatibility is often the result of the above-mentioned interweaving of the functional zones in the building. In certain arrangements of the structural system may appear also constraints associated with the emergence of large structural elements which separate zones on their both sides (e.g. shear walls). Also, in a situation when a zone is not physically divided into two separate parts, it is possible occurrence of individual structural components (e.g. columns) limiting functional development of the space or enforcing its division. Additionally, such structural components can be positioned improperly relative to the curtain walls, thereby restricting access to them. It happens that in the building occur structural components of floors which are of significant physical height, reducing the usable height of the interior and possibly limiting lighting the space with natural light.

The above-mentioned hazards are even more serious if appear within the communication zones. Incorrectly placed and designed: pillars or load bearing walls – inclined, blocking main communication routes, untypically or unexpectedly located, as well as narrowings between structural elements, lowered beams or lintels may create serious threats for people with impeded: sight, hearing, walking and psychological abilities. Among them should be mentioned a risk of: collision, impact, stumbling, confusion and complete blockage of a passage, should be mentioned [2]. What is even more improper, structure may cause insufficient space for maneuvering i.e. on a wheelchair or with use of canes, balconies or electric charts, disable access to furniture or equipment and at times limit necessary "kinesthetic space".

However the main task of the structural system is carrying the loads and providing rigidity of the building, its usefulness also depends on other features, commonly referred to as the "serviceability limit state". Insufficient load capacity components, which results in excessive deflection may restrict placement in certain areas of function that cause the occurrence of significant loads. This may in further consequence lead to excessive vibration of the structure. Both of these phenomena are very unfavorable from the point of view of people with disabilities, because they can hinder their movement and cause confusion.

Issue is related to another area of hazards concerning disturbances in the perception of space. This involves not only a decrease in comfort but also even harmful phenomena like material born sounds and vibration transition to the residential areas. Further on elaborated phenomena can cause disorientation through misleading echolocation. Of course, it should be emphasized that the insufficient rigidity of the structure is not the only possible source of undesirable vibrations in the building. Another important source of it may be installation and fittings: elevators, HVAC and similar which can induce and distribute waves. These causes can be quite effectively eliminated by proper insulation and localization of expansion joints. Vibration may also come from outside of the building, i.e. from infrastructural sources (roads, railways, metro, traffic) and propagate through the foundations in the entire object. By careful design of foundations, a lot of vibrations may be avoided. This case, however, is complex and calls for actions, which description is beyond the scope of this paper.

To give an example (Fig. 5a, c) of hotels in Greece and Spain show how distinctly pillars and support walls can limit both vertical and horizontal communication space. This makes it insufficient for people moving on wheelchairs and especially electrical chars and scooters. The later are wider (about 70 cm of width) than typical charts (width around 63 cm), thus require more space that usually recommended in norms. Also people using canes or just having troubles with walking, require additional side area. In other of studied hotels (in Spain) an inclined wall (Fig. 5b), covered by very reflective materials, was used, just by the main entrance. Designers deciding on such solution must be

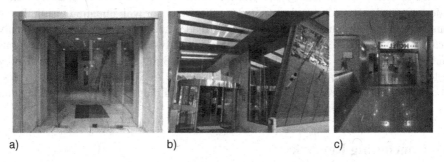

a)   b)   c)

Fig. 5. Examples of hazards arising from the structural system: (a) pillars and structural walls distinctly limit the vertical communication area (hotel in Greece), (b) inclined wall with reflective materials by main entrance (hotel in Spain), (c) pillars and structural walls distinctly limit the horizontal communication space (hotel in Spain).

aware that uneven angles change echolocation sensation. This method of space orientation is consciously used by people with impaired eye-sight but also is unknowingly used by many human beings to strengthen the information they gather from other senses during movement. Moreover highly reflective, shining and bright material used for building this compartment may be hazardous for all users by creating unexpected reflections, glares and effect of blinding lights during night time (passing car reflectors).

7   The Added Value Which Can Bring Properly Designed Structural System

Common is awareness that well-designed structure can significantly enhance the architectural form, which is the carrier. During case studies it was also confirmed that properly designed structure can optimize space for movement, orientation and visibility. Very good example of such solutions was pillars (Fig. 6a) in one of the hotels in Greece.

a)   b)   c)

Fig. 6. Examples of structure as a support for the ergonomic architecture: (a) chamfered and well-marked pillars (safety feature) allow orientation in a vast space of a hall (hotel in Greece), (b) even and parallel walls allow fluent movement along them (hotel in Greece) (c) extruded plinth supporting an atrium widow allows safe movement and visibility (hotel in Czech Republic).

In a vast hall space arranged with large, wide columns, chamfered at both sides. Not only their placement help to move and orient in space, but their dark colors at the background of lightly colored materials, clearly stated their presence. Moreover softly arched sides provided safety for people moving on wheelchairs or with impaired vision. In the same hotel (Fig. 6b) another observation was made. Long, parallel walls, additionally marked with elongated carpet boundary patterns, clearly determined walking directions and served as an extra movement support if needed. Similar function was fulfilled by boldly extruded plinth, which was a base for hotel in Czech Republic (Fig. 6c). Additionally this element protected people with sight disabilities form random walking into the glass.

8   Concluding Remarks

In the conducted study there were identified the main areas of the hazards that in the hotel facilities are associated with the applied structural solutions. Methods of solving these problems in turn can qualify for the two groups. The first of these is to obey the technical correctness of applied solutions, the use of appropriate materials and taking into account issues of serviceability. This eliminates problems described in Sect. 6.

Another approach is required to solve problems related to interweaved functional layouts and related changes in a structural system. Rational procedure for solving these problems is to find "common parts" and adapt to them requirements of specific solutions for individual functional zones. It is an approach in which we replace the local optimization by global optimization. The final resulted solution is not ideal in terms of the needs of each zone but allows "optimal" design of the building as a whole.

Despite of method selected it is crucial to integrate work of an architect and structural engineer in order to provide best possible solutions for people with disabilities. Presented number of cases and structure solutions allows designers to adjust particular situations to all diversified variants of functional plan. In this way, they are able to provide users not only with proper safety in a hotel, but even can increase comfort in movement of people with impaired hearing, vision, walking or psychical abilities. Thus, theoretical examples given can be used for practice, as well as carrying out future studies on ergonomic of mutual architecture and structure relations.

References

1. Błądek, Z. (ed.): Modern hotel industry. From design to equipment (in Polish). Nowoczesne hotelarstwo. Od projektowania do wyposażenia. Oficyna Wydawniczo-Poligraficzna "Adam", Warszawa (2010)
2. Brawley, E.C.: Design Innovations for Aging and Alzheimer's. Creating Caring Environments. Wiley, Hoboken (2006)
3. Gregory, R.: Key Contemporary Buildings. Plans, Sections and Elevations. Laurence King Publishing, London (2008)
4. Hall, E.T.: The Hidden Dimension. Polish translation: Ukryty wymiar. trans. Hołówka, E., Warszawskie Wydawnictwo Literackie "MUZA" SA, Warsaw (2003)
5. Khan, F.R., Moore, W.P.: Tall Building Systems and Concepts. American Society of Civil Engineers, New York (1980)
6. Kosar, L.: Lifestyle hotels – new paradigm of modern hotel industry. Broj **14**:39–50 (2014). www.visokaturisticka.edu.rs/docs/tupos/tupos14/rad3.pdf. Accessed 4 Nov 2015
7. Niezabitowska, E.: Designing of Office Buildings, Part 1 (in Polish). Projektowanie obiektów biurowych.Cz. 1. Historia. Rodzaje obiektów biurowych. Politechnika Śląska, Gliwice (1997)
8. Popławski, B.: Designing of Higher Education Buildings (in Polish). Projektowanie szkół wyższych. Arkady, Warszawa (1982)
9. Rutes, A.W., Penner, H.R., Lawrence, A.: Hotel Design Planning and Development. W.W. Norton and Company Inc., New York, London (2001)
10. Tarczewski, R.: Transience of architecture – technical, social and environmental aspects. In: SGEM 2015 International Multidisciplinary Scientific Conference on Social Sciences and Arts. Book 4: Arts, Performing Arts, Architecture and Design. STEF 1992 Technology, Sofia, pp. 757–764 (2015)
11. Technical report 14177: 1994 (E) Classification of Information in the Construction Industry, ISO (1994)
12. Vickers, G.: 21st Century Hotel. Laurence King Publishing, London (2005)

13. Watson, H.: Hotel Revolution. Wiley, Chichester (2005)
14. Wilczyński, J.: Hotel and Its Infrastructure (in Polish). Hotel i jego infrastruktura. Fundacja Rozwoju Uniwersytetu Gdańskiego, Gdańsk (2010)

Mobile Bathroom – Ideas and Solutions

Anna Jaglarz[✉]

Faculty of Architecture, Wroclaw University of Technology, Prusa Street 53/55,
50-317 Wroclaw, Poland
anna.jaglarz@pwr.edu.pl

Abstract. The trends based on modern technologies and joining hygiene, recreation and other additional functions in the bathroom space, indicate that it is not the place that meets only hygienic needs, but it can be an independent multifunctional module equipped with extra features which conventional bathroom does not provide. The basis of this solution is the ability to locate it anywhere - if necessary, the ability to transfer and install it in the new space.

The consequence of thinking about the hygienic-sanitary space in this way is a flexible, modular shaping of bathrooms and the introduction of mobile elements of equipment, that in addition to their output function, receive additional abilities to adapt them to the changing requirements of users, and the possibility of transformation and portability after their installation.

Thanks to the advanced technology used in multifunctional and mobile sanitary devices, modern bathrooms and their equipment can ensure, anywhere and even in a small space, comfort and safety related to personal hygiene and the corresponding aesthetics of the interior, for all users - children, the elderly, the disabled and other people requiring special, extra care.

Keywords: Mobile bathroom · Modular bathroom · Portable bathroom · Multifunctional devices

1 Introduction

Currently, activities related to hygiene and personal care require more and more space and equipment. New other purposes of bathroom also require new elements and additional space for their location and space associated with their use. The freedom of shaping the bathroom is limited not only by its size, but also the need to connect to the plumbing. Not everywhere you can place a bathtub below the floor level, not always you can find a place for the sauna. However, thanks to modern technology, changes in the needs and preferences of people following under the influence of fashion or new lifestyle, can be variously included in the existing and planned interiors, by adapting them to contemporary requirements. With advanced technology, modern equipment can provide, even on a small area and in a small space, widely understood comfort of personal hygiene and the corresponding aesthetics of the interior.

The observations and analyzes the latest trends in shaping the hygienic-sanitary space confirm that the contemporary bathroom can not only meet the diverse needs of its users, but should also have certain characteristics that affect the way their

© Springer International Publishing Switzerland 2016
M. Antona and C. Stephanidis (Eds.): UAHCI 2016, Part I, LNCS 9737, pp. 293–304, 2016.
DOI: 10.1007/978-3-319-40250-5_29

implementation and degree of satisfaction. Desirable features of contemporary bathroom include multi-functionality, mobility, flexibility, modularity, transformability, portability, adaptability, adjustability, space-saving, compactness.

The multifunctional device is a combination of functions and tasks that are traditionally provided for several individual devices. This combination reduces the space occupied by separate mono-functional appliances and allows for extra space. Taking into account the limitations of bathrooms area especially in multi-family residential buildings, both in newly designed and existing (adaptation), retrieval of space in bathroom is very important from the point of view of the demand for physical space for users.

Mobile bathroom is equipped with flexible devices which allow to easy maneuvering after mounting, with the possibility of moving, changing location and functioning in different interiors. The solution in the form of a bathroom with the equipment contained in a container that can be moved is also defined as a mobile bathroom.

2   Mobile Bathroom in the Past

The first attempts to create a mobile bathroom appeared in the thirties of the twentieth century with the development of industrial production. Although many of the concepts of prefabrication appeared at the time - one-piece components and entire bathrooms - it was mostly about the use of the basic advantages of prefabrication, which was the ability to combine all the necessary elements to develop a complete facility for hygiene. Then began the pursuit of a properly designed and fully equipped hygienic and sanitary facilities that would be comprehensive and coherent, both in terms of functionality and design. Application of new materials and experimental prefabrication of certain elements were directed towards reducing the costs of manufacture and use. As a result of numerous analyzes and the consideration of the issue by many designers, small functionally designed cabin began to spread.

In 1938, Richard Buckminster Fuller created a completely sealed unit *The Dymaxion Bathroom* that could be moved and adjusted in the middle of the prefabricated structure of its *The Dymaxion House*. It consisted of two parts: in one of them was a bathtub with shower, in the second part was a sink and toilet. The whole thing was made of nickel-coated copper plate, although Fuller had planned the use of plastic, and its appearance alluded to the submarine. The device was patented in 1938 and could be produced in the factory and installed in homes by simply connecting to the water supply and sewage system. At the same time leading architects working in France, Edouard Jeanneret, better known as Le Corbusier, who thought that the bathroom should be a machine for washing the body, and Charlotte Perriand, at *the World Exhibition* in 1937 showed their famous "sanitary cabin" intended for use in hotels. This cabin produced by Jacob Delafona contained a sink and toilet, which could be converted into a bidet and shower. Later, in 1970, Charlotte Perriand presented a different version of the bathrooms. It was made of PVC and intended for the winter sports resort in Les Arcs. With the help of Breton, a producer of polyester bathroom equipment for the Navy, Charlotte Perriand designed a complete bathroom, which was shaped in one piece and supplied ready to install. The entire cabin consisted of the modeled bathtubs, sinks, shelves and toilet, together with all accessories, even lighting. The idea was also sold successfully in hotels in Japan, a country with a strong tradition of bathing and where space saving solutions are necessary [3] (Figs. 1 and 2).

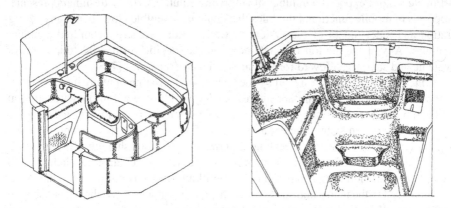

Fig. 1. The concept of integrated bathroom *Dymaxion Bathroom* designed by Fuller in 1938 (Source: own work based on 7, 10).

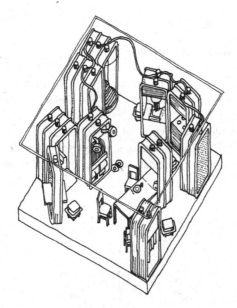

Fig. 2. Example of the use of container furniture designed by Ettore Sottsass in 1972 (Source: own work based on 7).

The perception of living space with an area of hygiene and sanitation was gradually changing. Similarly, the general relationship of man with the surrounding objects, which in addition to new forms gained new functions was increasingly becoming different. Already in the mid-seventies the goal of many leading designers was creating such elements of housing equipment and facilities that could be moved and quickly adapt to other places.

In 1972 the exhibition *Italy: The New Domestic Landscape* at the Museum of Modern Art in New York exposed a number of surprising solutions. Some designers presented proposals of mobile functional modules that could be assembled together in any configuration and independent of the system of walls. Ettore Sottsass submitted container furniture. Any configuration of containers with a specific residential function, also hygienic and sanitary, allowed for various spatial combinations [7, 8].

Total Furnishing Unit designed by Joe Colombo, consisting of many interconnected residential segments, was another interesting proposal at the exhibition. Locating all residential and sanitary functions in the possible smallest space, in the block with an area of over a dozen square meters and their ability to adapt to the current needs and requirements of users, was a milestone in terms of conscious shaping of home space. Rectangular volume of no more than twenty cubic meters, contained a kitchen, bathroom, bedroom and living room and could fulfill all functions inserted into any space and connected to the mains and sewage system. The new approach to the way of shaping residential buildings was the result of a mechanistic consideration of the majority of issues relating to human. People from the days of *the Industrial Revolution* were surrounded by more and more machines and accustomed to their presence, and even began to live in them [7].

3   Multifunctional Bathroom Facilities

Search for a combination of several functions in one facility in order to expand hygienic and sanitary spaces resulted in a devices that resembled modern machines in both appearance and character.

Multifunctional modules inclusive toilet, bidet, sink, shower, joined together by a common outlet and sometimes partially closed water cycle allow for any placing them in the bathroom, while ensuring the necessary water, sewer and often electricity connections.

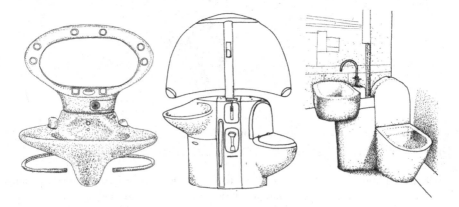

Fig. 3. Multifunctional bathroom configurations - sink integrated with mirror, lighting and accessories, combination of sink and toilet (Source: own work based on 7).

The lighting, radio, electric toothbrush and sensors that control water temperature and flushing the toilet may be an additional elements.

Other examples of multifunctional hygienic and sanitary devices are so-called "bathroom hybrids" or combinations of sinks and toilets or sinks and urinals. These objects have a special system water saving and are equipped with an additional tank for waste water coming from the sink, which can be reused to flushing [5] (Figs. 3 and 4).

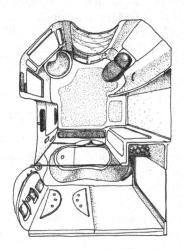 

Fig. 4. Hygienic and relaxation capsule designed by Fabio Lenci in 2000 (Source: own work based on 6).

The object in which a number of technical achievements have been applied and properly adapted to the bathroom area, is hygienic and recreational capsule, designed by Fabio Lenci and presented at the exhibition *Linee d'aqua* during *the Milan Trade Shows Mostra Convegno Expocomfort* in 2000. Bathroom created by Fabio Lenci is based on already known and currently used technologies. And although applying them to such an extent in the hygienic-sanitary space seems still quite unusual, further domestication process when users will be directly confronted with modern technology in the near future is inevitable. Fabio Lenci considering wide problem of hygiene and recreation, gathered all the technological innovations, combined them in a small space and prepared for the role of the bathroom that seems to live their own "electronic" life. Undoubtedly, such understanding of hygiene and healthy lifestyle may in the near future to revolutionize the bathroom. It will no longer be a facility used only for hygiene purposes, but it will become an independent module, that will be equipped with functions which traditional bathroom has not had so far. The basic principle of this solution is the ability to locate it anywhere - if necessary, the possibility of moving, installing and adjusting it to a new apartment.

The consequence of thinking about domestic space in this way is the use of a flexible equipment, which in addition to its essential function, obtains additional abilities to adjust to the changing needs of users. It is not too complex, as regards the "mobile" elements of bathroom equipment, that is, for example, furniture and accessories, but all starts to become complicated when the use of the facility require a permanent connection to the water and sewage systems. In this respect, hygienic and sanitary space and its equipment is a real challenge for designers and builders. Built-in, concealed systems that are simply in terms of assembly and allow for reorganizing the whole bathroom without destruction, without breaking existing walls and building new ones, appear to be one way in response to the need for changeability and adjustability. This solution greatly simplifies the adaptation of the existing interior. Adjustable concealed frames can help you set the bathroom devices at the proper height. Many of the appliances can be easily removed and installed in the new location. These include, among others, multifunctional shower bars and panels that can be easily removed and changed, light shower cabins with the ability to move and function in almost any interior, bathtubs, which can be transferred to any place, portable saunas [6, 8].

4 Mobile Devices

The next step in direction of flexibility, adjustability and easy adaptability are mobile devices that allow you to maneuver them and regulation after their installation. These include shower bars with adjustable height and shower panels and sets additionally equipped with rotating nozzles to provide multiple variants of shower.

Mobile sink placed on special guides, so that it can be moved up and down, thereby adjusting its height, is another convenient and ergonomic solution. The folding portable shower cabins are mobile devices that can also be very useful.

Analysis of various ways of adapting equipment to the needs of users indicates that most of multi-functional and mobile elements of equipment is designed for all users of the bathroom, including children and disabled. Additionally, we can see solutions that specifically meet the needs of users who require special, extra care. Example of actions increasing both comfort and safety of user is the toilet with a slide-out shelf supporting feet. This support makes possible not only comfortable and safe use the toilet by children, but also it allows posture correction of an adult during this action. Special sink applied to the bidet,

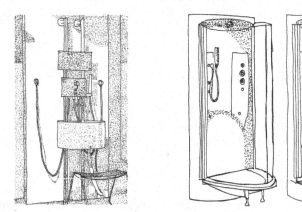

Fig. 5. Mobile devices - sliding sink, portable shower cabin (Source: own work based on 9, 14)

folding and reducing its size to the dimensions of a small suitcase is another convenience for small children getting to know the rules of personal hygiene. Some companies offer a little bigger suitcases, or even trunks, in which bathroom accessories can be packed and transported. Such solutions, however, are quite extraordinary, perhaps intended for those users who are used to "living out of a suitcase" [6, 8, 15] (Figs. 5, 6 and 7).

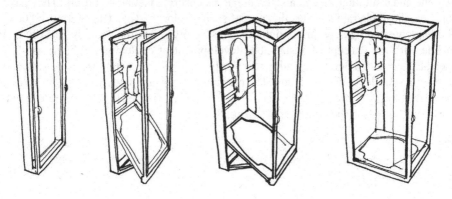

Fig. 6. Mobile devices - folding, portable shower cabin (Source: own work based on 14)

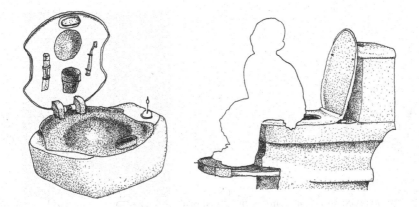

Fig. 7. Interesting mobile bathroom equipment designed not only for children (Source: own work based on 8).

5   Mobile Bathrooms - Modules, Cabins, Boxes

Among the concepts of mobile bathrooms we find many examples of compact, modular, portable, space-saving and at the same time fully equipped and functional objects and structures that contain all the necessary hygienic and sanitary elements. The important thing is the simple principle of the transformation of the individual elements. Their preparation for use and hiding after working should not be too complicated and uncomfortable. Free user access and ease of use are essential for the proper functioning of such facilities.

Mobile, portable bathrooms often taking the forms of multifunctional modules, cabins and boxes are intended to place into small available spaces in apartments and houses. They can be attached with minimal construction, installation and mounting work.

Aquabox designed by Massimo Brugnera is one of the interesting solutions that have come into view recently. In this compact bathroom in addition to the basic functions of hygiene and sanitation we can also find features ensuring wellness of users. They have for use: adjustable rain shower, function of sauna, color therapy. The interior of "box" is complemented by appropriate lighting. The facility is environmentally friendly and in line with the concept of sustainable development of contemporary bathrooms. A special system of water saving allows to purify waste water coming from the sink and shower, and collect it in a 80 l tank. The purifier and tank are parts of the whole system inside the object. The reclaimed water can be recycled and reused to flush the toilet bowl, or for other needs in the household [2] (Fig. 8).

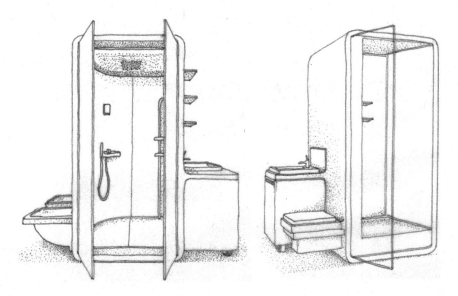

Fig. 8. *Aquabox* - compact bathroom designed by Massimo Brugnera (Source: own work based on 2).

Another example of mobile bathroom is *The Roca Box*, one of the winning projects in the Roca Jumpthegap 2009 Contest. Designers from Valencia created "Box" - modular bathroom system that consists of different types of modules: one containing a toilet and sink, the next including a shower, a small seat and two shelves with towel racks and another module which is a space-adding element containing additional floor space and storage. The last closing segments can be opened or completely locked by a solid wall or wall with the door. Module consisting the basic elements of bathroom equipment, the toilet and sink, is able to work independently of the other parts as a simple bathroom. *The Roca Box* is ecologically oriented saving water and energy. It includes additionally water tanks and heat pump. Water used in the shower and the sink is stored in the water tank which supplies the toilet cistern. The heat pump utilizes the warm, humid air from the inside of the bathroom to heat the space and water. This modular eco-friendly functioning bathroom is low on space, but at the same time high on efficiency [11, 13] (Fig. 9).

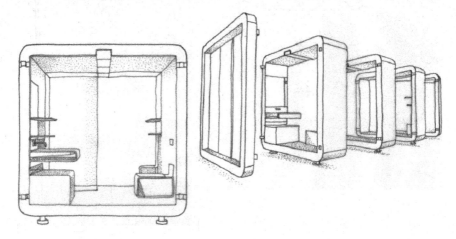

Fig. 9. *The Roca Box* - mobile, modular bathroom designed by *Yonoh Studio* in 2009 (Source: own work based on 11).

The manufacturers of *Design Odyssey* have proposed a mobile, modular and transforming bathroom facility that is not a cabin or a box, but it is all-in-one rotating fixture or rather fixture set which contains several hygienic and sanitary functions. This object consist of a series of "vertebrae" that are stacked on one another. Each level rotates independently and fulfills a different tasks: wc supplemented with compartments for toilet accessories, sink and basin complemented with built-in soap dispenser and standard mixer tap, storage spaces and cistern topped off by a shower elements with pull-out shower heads. This space-saving vertical bathroom facility is the perfect solution that allows to pack everything into an incredibly small space and provides the ability to apply it even in the surface limited places. Its capacity to rotate of individual elements enables different settings and configurations that can be adjusted to need of user and to size and shape of the bathroom [4] (Fig. 10).

Mobile bathroom is a solution that can be very useful in cases where living space is very limited and we have a small surface to organize hygienic and sanitary part of the apartment. As it turns out, sometimes even one room can guarantee the possibility of doing all the tasks and functions necessary for everyday life. Among the many examples of mobile sanitary facilities that save the space we can find such solutions, which provide total access to the devices when necessary, and then can hide them. Proposals of bathrooms with the possibility of such a metamorphosis may be different. An interesting and convenient solution is to organize the whole system on a regular grid composed of repetitive elements - modules, in which are inscribed various parts of bathroom facilities. Sink, toilet, shower disappear in the structure of the entire system and layout. The other modules are used to storage and concealment of plumbing and electrical connections. The individual appliances and all system are integrated with one wall structure creating design idea of modular, transformable, space-saving bathroom. It simple and aesthetic

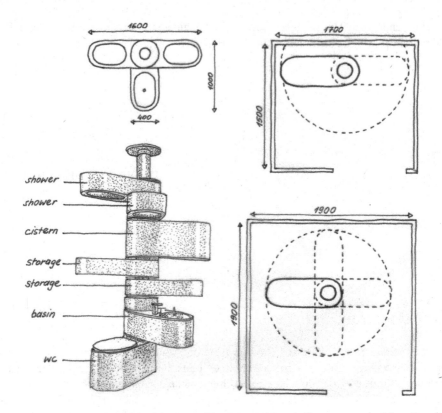

Fig. 10. Mobile bathroom design idea created by *Design Odyssey* (Source: own work based on 4).

solution based on regular divisions provides the simplicity and convenience of using facilities and offers a unified design concept for both the bathroom and the whole room [1, 12] (Figs. 11 and 12).

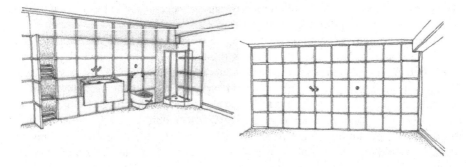

Fig. 11. Example of modular, transforming bathroom design (Source: own work based on 1)

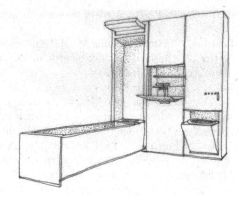

Fig. 12. *Cirrus MVR* - mobile, space saving bathroom designed by Michael Trudgeon (Source: own work based on 12).

6   Conclusion

Research and analysis in the field of mobile bathrooms lead to different ideas and solutions. There are many examples of multifunctional devices that combine the tasks normally provided for several separate appliances. Multifunctional devices allow to save bathroom space which is often very limited.

Other examples, in the form of portable, flexible, transforming devices, or entire compact bathroom cabins with equipment, are shaped in a way that ensures the ability to function in different places, and the ability to easily adapt to changing needs and requirements of users.

The widely understood mobility of the bathroom objects is determined by the following features:

- the ability to fulfill the necessary functions and tasks, not only basic health, hygiene and sanitary functions, but also additional associated with wellness, relax and recreation,
- the ease of access and comfort and safety of using,
- the ability to adapt to changing functional and physical possibilities and needs of users,
- the flexibility in shaping the functional and spatial arrangement in relation to the user needs and the size, shape and type of interior,
- high technical and material quality providing usability, reliability, durability and aesthetics,
- minimizing the cost of installation, maintenance and modernization,
- consideration of environmental criteria and environmental friendliness.

References

1. All-in-One Modular Transforming Bathroom Design. http://dornob.com
2. Aquabox by Massimo Brugnera. http://www.coroflot.com

3. de Bonneville, F.: The Book of the Bath. Rizzoli International Publication Inc., New York (1998)
4. Functions, 1 Fixture: Modular Metal Bathroom Design Idea. http://dornob.com
5. Jaglarz, A.: Sustainable development in the concepts of modern bathrooms. Procedia Manufact. **3**, 1638–1645 (2015)
6. Kubasik, A.: Kapsula Kosmicznej Higieny, Lazienka, Publikator, Bialystok (2001)
7. Kubasik, A.: Lazienka jako Maszyna? Lazienka, pp. 52–55. Publikator, Bialystok (2000)
8. Kubasik, A.: Mobilne Konfiguracje, Lazienka, Publikator, Bialystok (2002)
9. Kubasik, A.: WC Underground, Lazienka, Publikator, Bialystok (2003)
10. Lupton, E., Miller, J.A.: The Bathroom. The Kitchen, and the Aesthetics of Waste. A Process of Elimination, p. 35. A Kiosk Book, New York (1992)
11. Modular Bathroom is Low on Space but High on Efficiency. http://dornob.com
12. Small Bathroom, Big Idea: Space-Saving Fold-Out Fixtures. http://dornob.com
13. Yonoh: 'Box' a Modular Bathroom System. http://www.designboom.com
14. Zukowski, J.: Dwa Pomysly pod Prysznic, Lazienka, Publikator, Bialystok (2003)
15. Zukowski, J.: Kabina Transformujaca, Lazienka, Publikator, Bialystok (2002)

The Role of Architecture and Ergonomics on Shaping the Domestic Kitchen

Przemyslaw Nowakowski[✉] and Jerzy Charytonowicz

Faculty of Architecture, Wroclaw University of Technology, Wroclaw, Poland
{przemyslaw.nowakowski,jerzy.charytonowicz}@pwr.edu.pl

Abstract. Acquiring of knowledge concerning problematic aspects of household chores, in particular complex kitchen chores, as well as dining culture can influence the possibility of shaping more optimal living conditions. It is a completion of ergonomic design of particular zones of home. The household living space can be divided into the leisure area (together with rooms and potential outdoor areas) and service area, with kitchen and bathroom. The needs connected with regaining strength needed for further work activities are fulfilled the leisure space, while the service area is designed to complement the functions of the leisure area. However strict appointing of areas for leisure, work and auxiliary activities is often impossible. It is caused, among others, by a necessity of performing such diverse activities as: cleaning works, taking care of children, preserving optimal microclimate conditions.

Concentration on those issues serves as an evaluation of the role of the kitchen in the housing structure, as well as in the daily lives of the householders. Modern housing and real estate market offer houses with diverse programmes and functional and spatial layouts. Nowadays, a kitchen area is planned in every house and flat. However, there are several variants provided: a separate kitchen, a kitchen area joined onto the living room or a small partial kitchen. Despite the functional programme of houses and kitchens, house chores have and still constitute a significant share of daily life of householders. Moreover they are necessary in order to fulfill basic existential needs as well as higher needs (e.g. social integration by activation of members of household).

Keywords: Ergonomics · History of architecture · Housing · Domestic kitchen · Kitchen design

1 Introduction

The type of kitchen equipment depends on individual ways of preparing meals, in particular in relation to the food industry and food service offer. Formerly it was necessary to work singlehandedly in kitchen, especially in extended families and because of lack of processed food. Processing of food produce obtained directly form fields or slaughter (mainly household-based) prolonged the process of preparation and required involvement of several people. Moreover, the offer of food service was not diverse and it was not available for the majority of society. Nowadays many people abandon the idea of having "a traditional kitchen" with three meals a day, and they rely on dishes

© Springer International Publishing Switzerland 2016
M. Antona and C. Stephanidis (Eds.): UAHCI 2016, Part I, LNCS 9737, pp. 305–314, 2016.
DOI: 10.1007/978-3-319-40250-5_30

prepared outside the household. This phenomenon escalates together with an increase in the number of one- and two-person households. What is more, the extension of time of gainful activity enforces a resignation from performing of some of traditional chores (e.g. preparation of preserves, complex meals, baking, etc.), despite owning a kitchen equipped with numerous technological tools and mechanical devices.

Kitchen equipment is a derivative of current technological progress. What prejudged of its use until the half of 20th was the way of kindling and maintaining fire. It is the hearth which determined the kitchen space of the house. What is more, high temperature did not serve only for heat treating of food produce, but also for heating of houses. Burdensomeness of kitchen chores was related not only to the possibility of obtaining and processing of food, but also to the conditions of clean water access, storing of products and waste disposal. Concentration of work in kitchen caused that it has always been equipped with numerous tools (e.g. cutlery and dishes). Throughout centuries they were very expensive and difficult to purchase. Many of them were used even by several consecutive generations. Only the popularization of industrial production ensured a higher supply and assortment of everyday use equipment. In turn the use of engines (first steam and later electrical) and their miniaturization enabled mechanization of various chores and replacement of the strength of human muscles with machines [8].

Mechanical and engine-driven devices enabled a reduction of physical effort devoted to, i.a. preparation of meals. What is more, permanent access to fully or partly processed food products frees from the necessity of making stock and initial processing of food. The abovementioned mechanization and industrial processing of food however did not result in considerable shortening of time spent on performing kitchen chores [4, 5]. Together with an increase in the standard of living (e.g. hygiene and diversification of menu), the number of possessions etc., a lot of activities accompanying the process of cooking has prolonged. Moreover, new chores and activities have arisen. Running of a modern household requires time-consuming planning. Making savings in household budgets enforces to take on additional activities connected with, e.g. shopping for cheaper goods in further away parts of the city.

The analysis of the role of kitchen in the structure of housing requires i.a. stating of basic human needs, such as: the need of providing of fullness (understood in both literal ad metaphorical sense), as well as the need owning a house. Moreover, the paper elaborates on the role of work in human life, as well as the distinction between the gainful and household activities. It also focuses on the distinction of the specificity and complexity of kitchen, and indication of the role of architecture and ergonomics in shaping of the material environment of people. Architectural designing furthers creation of a sense of comfort and space necessary to fulfill various needs. "Classical ergonomics" used to concentrate on individuals in their work environment. However nowadays the scope of interest of modern ergonomics was broadened also by the household environment, which serves people, among others, to maintain an optimum psychophysical condition and the ability to perform gainful activity. The paper will presents several theses validating the choice of the selected topic, such as:

- kitchen chores are among the most complicated and time-consuming household activities;

- running of a kitchen is as complex economical (managing of the budget), organizational (the order of chores and managing of the resources), culture-forming (maintaining of traditions and relations), as well as preventive (managing of diets and psycho-physical condition of householders) activity;
- household chores are usually performed at the expense of so-called "free time" which theoretically should be devoted to relaxation;
- preparing of meals can mapping a particular lifestyle and culinary tastes.

2   The Role of Fire in Households and Lives of People

Possession of fire or heat of the oven supports running of a household chores and importance of availability of food resources and rules concerning in formulating of work conditions, as well as the kitchen space itself.

Throughout centuries, the central place outlining the living, and especially kitchen, space was the hearth. Fire was necessary for heating of rooms and for heat treating of food products into easily assimilated and warming meals. Together with gasification and electrification the form of the heating medium has changed. Traditional flame was replaced by invisible thermal radiation transferred directly into the dishes. As a result the integrating role of fire ceased to exist. Directed heat is available instantly, without having to perform previous laborious activities, such as: kindling of fire, providing of firewood or cleaning of fireplace.

3   The Role of Organization and Rationalization of Work in Forming of Households and Comfort of Home Life

Technological development was accompanied with gradual rationalization and organization of work. Even in ancient times the issues concerning functioning of households were intuitively and scientifically considered. As the annual cycle of chores (also kitchen-related) enabled people to systematize certain regularities and recurrences of some activities. Specific rules were passed on to following generations by participation in everyday chores. Possible changes and improvements aimed at a reduction of effort or expenditure of supplies. The abovementioned issues also received attention from researchers of various aspects of human life. The most famous authors were inter alia Xenophon, Aristoteles, Leon Battista Alberti, Catherine Beecher, Christine Frederick, Bruno Taut, Margarete Schütte-Lihotzky. Their observations and results were presented in numerous tracts and textbooks. A number of particularly old publications nowadays have only a cognitive value, however, all of them confirm the importance of household chores in everyday life, as well as in shaping of household forms and organizing of households.

4   The Role of Kitchen Chores and Dietary Habits in People's Lives

The work conditions in kitchen are not only a derivative of the development of civilization, but also development of culture, culinary tastes, tradition and dietary possibilities. Obtaining and processing of food produce, preparing and consuming of meals required a proper organization of household, and often engaging of work of even several people. Shared meals might be an opportunity to develop closer relations between the members of family and close friends. Serving varied meals and the culture of their consumption influence the character of chores connected with food preparation and cleaning up, and, as the result, the functional and spatial layouts of kitchens and whole households.

5   The Changes in Kitchen Layouts and Equipment Against the Changes in Housing Development

The analysis of the evolution of the household environment shows the placement and role of kitchen space in the house structure. It influenced the shaping of the living conditions, performing of household chores and ways of meals preparation in the context of constantly changing construction conditions, social relations (mainly in the scope of functioning of single households), and even everyday life. The previous diversity in wealth influenced not only the forms and decor of houses, but also the organization of household chores and ways of preparation of meals.

The "artisanal" character of production throughout centuries resulted in individual character of constructed buildings. Spatial functioning of houses was also influenced by numerous gainful activities. Kitchen with the source of heat (hearth), in particular, concentrated the majority of everyday chores. Multifunctional rooms were also places of fulfillment of other needs, such as: sleeping, studying and hygienic and sanitary activities. Functioning of bigger households and having bigger families in former centuries required hiring service. It was not until the industrialization of production, in 19th century, when the work environment was gradually assigned. The range of household activities was therefore limited to performing cleaning and kitchen chores. The disappearance of gainful activities and share of service in performing of everyday chores considerably influenced the change of forms of houses and shaping of their contemporary models.

The modern types of housing and kitchen obtain from the early 20th century. In 1920's there was the concept of the "laboratory kitchen". It was introduced together with popularization of the Frankfurt model. This probably was the time of the most intensive interest in the issues concerning housework and striving for achievement of a high hygienic and functional standard in houses. It was believed back then that systematizing and shortening of the kitchen work zone closed in a small room was the key to limit everyday laborious effort and "free" the householders from house chores [12]. However, latter savings resulted in discreditation of the laboratory standard, as often the kitchens were too small and dark and were designed for only one person to work in.

Placement of basic equipment and the countertop made it impossible to set apart even small dining areas, which hindered the possibility of integration of household members.

Houses "without servants" with monofunctional rooms (and kitchens) were popularized during the interwar period, thanks to various social trends and "modernism" in architecture. This type of housing became popular after the II World War as a result of, among others, the development of industrial technology in housing and class-less societies. This period distinguishes itself by significant culture and civilization progress, reflected also in new forms of housing. Nowadays is possible to choose the type and size of house and mono- and multi-functional character of the kitchen, which depended not only on individual needs, but even more so on specific situation on the real estate market.

Modern house kitchens are places of merging of contrary behaviours of their users. On one hand householders use there numerous improvements, technological novelties and kitchens are places where "modern" lifestyle is popularized, on the other hand, kitchens are also places where old recipes are reused and former well-known cooking and baking techniques applied. Kitchens are also places of family bonding and maintaining traditions. Therefore kitchens are spaces where old tradition and new trends meet. Moreover using of advanced gastronomic techniques strengthens their specialist character, as modern kitchens are often referred to as "house laboratories" [1].

Nevertheless regarding technical and cultural issues of modern kitchens one may notice certain dissonance. Together with increasingly better equipment of work areas with various devices, often a decrease in the cooking abilities of users can be noticed [6]. Those lower predispositions towards kitchen chores result mainly from lack of time and willingness to continue former culinary traditions, as well as the availability of highly processed food and a growing demand for ready-made dishes and increasing number of households with only one or two householders. As single people often find preparing three courses a day as irrational for economic reasons (e.g. time, usage of energy and water).

The course of the kitchen work can be divided into four, the most important functional zones: thermal heat treating, food storage, water supply and doing the washing-up and waste and sewage disposal. Spatial distinguishing of specialist zones used for performing certain activities results from the complexity of the whole course of action and process of meal preparation. Rationalization and shortening of time spent on performing chores required a selection of proper and modern equipment. Currently used technical conveniences previously often were not known. What is more, the prototypes of nowadays popular devices were often considerably difficult to operate in everyday use.

The most attention deserves the evolution of the heating medium, which throughout the centuries determined kitchen space and the scope of activities related to broadly understood heat treating of food. The evolution of heating device resulted mainly from a need to reduce exhausting heat during work, as well as use of fuel and increase the efficiency of heating of prepared meals. Initially fire was lit on bare ground. With time hearths were placed on elevated podiums. However, preparation of meals with an open fire was time-consuming and not effective, and the work itself was exhausting. A significant convenience was the use of manufactured coal ovens with a closed hearths. Nevertheless they were not popularized until 19th century. Since the turn of 19th and 20th century, gas and electric cookers have gained considerable popularity. Finally they replaced coal ovens and are still widely used. Modern kitchens are places where more devices used for heat treatment of food can be found, among them we can distinguish: microwave ovens, food steamers, coffee presses, barbecues, deep fryers. Currently produced devices are high quality both in case of usability and technology, what is more they are more energy saving [2, 10].

The quality of food depends on the conditions of maintaining and extending of use-by date of various food products, as well as the ways of their preservation and evolution of space and devices used for their storage. Formerly their storage required a big space, even having separate rooms (pantries, cellars). The most effective and popular means of storage was maintaining food in low temperatures. Initially the refrigeration technique was used in food industry and then in single households [2]. In contemporary kitchens refrigerators and freezers are commonly used, and they are often combined in one device.

The running of a household and meals preparation requires the use of water. In industrialized countries its abundance was ensured thanks to a well-developed water-works infrastructure. However, clean water used to be a commodity in short supply and was available only for the minority of population. As a result, the majority of population drank contaminated water. This condition was partly caused by everyday activities of people and penetration of human waste into water intakes. What is more, among people there was a lack of basic knowledge of bacteriological threats, which prevailed until the second half of 19th century [10]. It is only then, when more complex actions concerning the amelioration of bacteriological quality of water were undertaken.

Lack of direct water intakes in former houses impeded fulfillment of nutritional and hygienic needs, as well as cleaning activities performed in houses. The need of brining the water from outside resulted in an increase of time and burdensomeness of everyday chores. Currently water is available even in several places in houses (usually in kitchens and bathrooms). However its effortless and carefree consumption, not to mention its wasting, is no longer possible, as high payments and ecological awareness impose rationalization (saving) actions, aiming at limitation of its excessive use. Special water taps and modern devices using smaller amounts of water gain popularity and are installed in an increasing number of households.

Nowadays, together with meal preparation and other household chores there is a necessity of waste and sewage disposal. While former household managing did not generate big amounts of waste, as a lot of it was reused [11]. The development of hygienic and sanitary standards at the end of 20th century forced food manufacturers to pack even the smallest quantities of food. The most commonly used packaging is made of plastic. Current, broadly understood consumption is therefore related to a growing quantity of various, usually non-biodegradable, waste. Its disposal is usually trouble-some for single households, especially in small flats and in municipal services. Therefore many countries decided to undertake complex actions aiming at limitation of waste in already congested landfills. Various initiatives also focus on households themselves. A proper recycling taking place already in the household kitchen is supposed to further separation of biodegradable organic waste and recycled materials, as well as reduction of the amount of waste.

Other waste created in the course of performing of chores requiring the use of water is sewage. Its disposal used to be particularly inconvenient and non-effective. Pouring them in front of the house only partially solved the problem. Dampness of the environment, bacteriological contamination and irritating foul odor were the causes of a low quality of life, frequent illnesses or even epidemics. An evident improvement of sanitary conditions took place only thanks to installation of sewage systems and draining sewage outside houses into combined sewerage networks or holding tanks [7, 11].

The abovementioned functional zones should be analyzed according to the ergonomics, load and burdensomeness or efficiency of work, as well as threats to both health and safety, hygiene, and even the influence on the environment. The latter issue has a particularly important meaning in current times. Modern societies show a better recognition and understanding of the influence of even the smallest households on the condition of the environment. It is also postulated that the "consumption" of certain raw materials and products, in particular water and energy should be reduced.

6   The Evolution of Kitchen Equipment and Furniture Forms

Since the appropriate furnishing decides on the level of work comfort in kitchens. Formerly the kitchen chores were performed by the members of lower-class. That is why the rooms where the work was done were less representative, particularly in wealthier houses. Therefore kitchen equipment (together with furnishings) was quite poor. The majority of dishes were left out, next to the hearth. Technical equipment was manufactured using craft production, that is why it was expensive and inaccessible [3]. Only thanks to the development of industrial production a bigger supply of furniture and household goods was provided. What is more, various mechanical devices became available at that time. However, the development of mechanization of household chores was possible only after the popularization of miniaturized electrical engines. Which became the basis for the development of new branches of production, manufacturing household goods.

The specificity of production required a certain degree of unification of products, and, in case of maintaining of the kitchen layout, also the size coordination. The introduction of modular typification of furniture and devices in the half of 20th century completely changed the look of kitchens, and the built-in equipment became popular. This also coincided with an increase of hygienic requirements [13]. Maintaining the continuity of furniture enabled keeping kitchen rooms cleaned easily. Those technical solutions come from the pre-war "laboratory" kitchen models. Despite an advanced standardization, it is possible to create all possible spatial, functional and aesthetical layouts in household kitchens. Modern furniture systems come in a rich offer of finishing materials and colours, while household goods are able to satisfy even the most refined culinary tastes and prepare all imaginable dishes. The functional quality of household equipment is comparable with professional gastronomic devices [10].

The supplements to the furniture systems provide a possibility of a more concentrated and ordered storage of tools, dishes and tableware, as well as food products. This is particularly important in case of houses and flats without such storage spaces as: pantries, cellars and utility rooms.

7   The Influence of Technical Progress on Time and Labour Input in House Kitchens

The changes in the housing development, functional layouts of flats, furnishings, tools and use of mechanical devices and machines may positively influence the organization and efficiency of housework, shortening of its time, lowering of burdensomeness and effort, as well as increase the sense of security. However, the aforementioned changes resulted neither in "freeing" of householders from the chores, nor in a considerable reduction of their number. The amount of time spent on meal preparation almost has not changed. However, many of former, laborious activities, which required substantial physical strength have been reduced or eliminated. On the other hand, the intensity of performing of other activities has increased, and new chores have occurred. The evolution of kitchen chores and accessibility of increasingly diverse food products result in disappearance of various devices, which used to be applied in the majority of households [9].

Technical conveniences are used in kitchens mainly in order to improve the work conditions and the quality and diversity of prepared meals. They play an important role in achieving satisfying conditions for running the whole household. Additionally, they influence planning and the course of household chores, social relations between householders, ways of guest entertaining, pro-ecological actions, as well as a subjective sense of comfort at home.

8   Summary

Presented analyses includes a synthetic glance at a short view of problematic aspects concerning shaping of household environment, especially the kitchen space in relation to everyday chores, eating culture, as well as fulfilling human lower and higher needs. However, the scope of the research paper was not limited only to the kitchen itself. The paper also takes into account the technical and social factors shaping houses and conditions of running of households in different times. The obtained results enabled me to examine everyday effort put in household kitchens and appreciate not only the culinary effects of work. Among the most crucial findings there are:

- technological and social changes led to undermining of the traditional order and division of roles in households, as well as to devaluation of the prestige of the role of a "housewife";
- currently there is a trend of dividing household chores based on partnership and including all householders in running a household;

- more freedom and new situations taking place in households, unlike the organized activities in the work place, can incentivise more creative behaviour, further advance in civilization, as well as arising of new threats to health and accidents;
- kitchen chores are still the most complicated among all the household chores;
- in many households, householders prefer using processed foods and food services in order to shorten the time of kitchen chores (part of former food preparation activities was taken over by food industry);
- functional and spatial programme of kitchens is influenced by lifestyle of house-holders: types of prepared meals and ways of their consumption;
- the significance of kitchen in the household structure and lives of families used to be determined by the attitude towards work (household chores used to have a low social status);
- proper layout of technological process and usage of increasingly more technologi-cally advanced equipment enables a reduction of physical effort and the most burden-some and unfulfilling tasks;
- replacing of human effort with machines is limited and does not ensure "freedom from household chores";
- form of kitchen (open and separate kitchens, laboratory or multifunctional kitchens) is a result of the size and layout of houses or life style;
- proper choice of furniture and technical equipment may be assisted expertise from such fields as: architecture, interior design, industrial design, catering technology, household economy, etc.;
- care concerning functional and aesthetic qualities of kitchens furthers more positive attitude towards chores, increases motivation towards household activities and elevates the rank of kitchen both in house structure and everyday life of householders;
- there is a rise in awareness of the influence of households on the environment, which enforces, i.a. saving actions concerning the use of energy, water and reduction of wasted food products;
- running a household requires constant, laborious organization of work, division of responsibilities and performance of additional chores, unknown in the past;
- nature and burdensomeness of household, and especially kitchen, chores currently is a derivative of lifestyle, ergonomics awareness and technological progress.

The issue of shaping of housing environment, mainly the matter concerning work and relaxation, is rarely researched. There is a particular lack of cross-sectional research depicting course of historical change in broadly understood comfort of life in the house-hold environment.

The paper can become a publication enabling acquiring cross-sectional knowledge concerning the conditions of shaping of housing architecture and interior design, with a particular focus on kitchen space, as well as used technical conveniences. It can also be used in practice. Analyses of functional and spatial layouts and technical solutions in kitchens supports the process of interior design and selection of equipment which can answer diverse and changing needs of their users. Acquiring the knowledge of technical progress and characteristic traits of devices provides awareness concerning validity of using of certain conveniences. Such knowledge can contribute to functional programming of kitchens, as well as entire houses, according to traditional and current (modern) requirements and expectations.

Researches concerning culinary habits required looking at kitchen space from a broader perspective. The shaping of kitchens should be seen in relation to social and civilization changes. It may be useful to use various information, not only from the field of architecture and interior design, but also concerning social environment and economic and technological conditions, and such technical fields as: architecture, interior design and history of technology, as well as humanities: history of everyday life, material culture, family, customs and work rationalization. Wider scope of research may be used by specialists from fields other than architecture, such as: economists (especially house economy specialists), specialists of organization and management, health and safety advisors, mechanical engineers, technicians of catering quality and technology. It can be useful when analyzing the changes in running of households, especially in relation to technological determinants of human environment.

References

1. Aicher, O.: Die Küche zum Kochen. Das Ende einer Architekturdoktrin, p. 21. Callwey Verlag, München (1982)
2. Andritzky, M.: Oikos. Von der Feuerstelle zur Mikrowelle. Haushalt und Wohnen im Wandel, pp. 165--239. Anabas Verlag, Giessen (2000)
3. Benker, G.: In alten Küchen. Einrichtung – Gerät – Kochkunst, p. 34. Callwey Verlag, München (1987)
4. Ehling, M.: Wo bleibt die Zeit? Die Zeitverwendung der Bevölkerung in Deutschland 2001/2002, p. 17. Statistisches Bundesamt, Wiesbaden (2003)
5. Ehling, M.: Zeitbudget in Deutschland – Erfahrungsberichte der Wissenschaft, p. 174. Statistisches Bundesamt, Wiesbaden (2011)
6. Flagge, I.: Geschichte des Wohnens. Von 1945 bis heute. Aufbau – Neubau – Umbau, p. 764. Deutsche Verlags-Anstalt, Stuttgart (1999)
7. Fuhrmann, B.: Geschichte des Wohnens. Vom Mittelalter bis heute, p. 36. Primus Verlag, Darmstadt (2008)
8. Giedion, S.: Die Herrschaft der Mechanisierung. Ein Beitrag zur anonymen Geschichte, p. 604. Europäische Verlagsanstalt, Hamburg (1994)
9. Meyer, S.: Technisiertes Familienleben. Blick zurück und nach vorn, p. 194. Edition Sigma, Berlin (1993)
10. Mielke, R.: The Kitchen. History, Culture, Design, pp. 15, 28, 133. Feierabend Verlag, Berlin (2004)
11. Morlok, J.: Keine heisse Asche einfüllen. Über den ehwigen Kampf gegen den Müll, pp. 8, 32. Werbeagentur Keck, Grossostheim (1998)
12. Taut, B.: Die neue Wohnung. Die Frau als Schöpferin, p. 96. Verlag Klinkhardt und Biermann, Leipzig (1928)
13. Wenke, H.: Küchenplanung. Die Haushaltsküche in Theorie und Praxis, p. 45. Verlag Die Planung, Darmstadt (1964)

The Unconventional Tribune Profiles in Architectural Designing of Stadiums

Zdzislaw Pelczarski[✉]

Faculty of Architecture, Bialystok University of Technology, Bialystok, Poland
pelczarski.z@wp.pl

Abstract. One of the key issues in designing of stadiums is to define the profile of the stands. By this term is meant a contour of the vertical cross-section of the tribunes, which is carried out in a plane perpendicular to the edges of the rows of seats. Such a profile reflects the spatial relations between theoretical points of the eye, arranged in individual rows, specifying their horizontal and vertical displacement relative to neighbouring points. It also allows you to determine the extent of visibility of the arena for each of them, using graphs of visibility. But it is also determined by considerations of communication links between the individual rows of seats by using the stairs. These stairs must however be adapted to the human motoric ability. Today, due to economic reasons, the designers completely abandoned the use of curved profile, replacing it with a sloping straight line. Existing standards limit this slope up to 35°. Reminiscent of the curved profiles are currently used broken linear profiles, as the continuous or balcony types. The author takes many years of research on the designing of modern stadiums, especially in shaping large spectator zones. Presented in this article unconventional solutions of modern stadium stands profiles are the result of these studies. These proposals improve much the parameters of visibility, comfort and safety of spectators. They contribute as well in the development on the field of stadiums designing, bringing a new values, such as quite new architectural forms in shaping interiors of these objects.

Keywords: Architectural designing · Tribune profile · Modern stadium

1 Introduction - Definition of the Research Problem

Forms of the interiors of modern stadiums are the result of a compromise between functional, technological and economical determinants. The main task of the designer is to provide every spectator a clear view of the playing field. This does not mean, however, that the image quality for each of them can be the same. The field of view of each viewer is determined by sight lines creating shape of so called the pyramid of view, which base is a rectangle of the pitch, and its top is located in his theoretical point of eye. Two parameters are crucial for the quality of the image of the pitch rectangle. These are: the height of elevation of eye point above the level of the arena, and the distance between this point and side lines of the playing field. The most essential for the perception is the height of the image, reflected on the retina inside the eye of the observer. It depends directly on the so-called vertical viewing angle. The larger the angle is, the higher the

© Springer International Publishing Switzerland 2016
M. Antona and C. Stephanidis (Eds.): UAHCI 2016, Part I, LNCS 9737, pp. 315–326, 2016.
DOI: 10.1007/978-3-319-40250-5_31

height of the image field. In other words, the larger the vertical angle of view, the more we see from the top. On the other hand, small vertical viewing angles correspond to the flat images, with a small depth of the optical perspective [1].

The solutions of profiles of the stadium stands, commonly used in today's architectural practice, can be described as the profiles of the bowl-shaped. They form two or three-tier structures [2, 3]. The lower tiers are characterized by the slightest inclination. This slope is gradually increasing on the upper tiers, reaching the maximum allowable angle of 35° [4, 5]. This arrangement results in that the images of the pitch surface seen from the lower tiers are flat, having a small height, while the images of the players figures are reaching the greatest height. Paradoxically, the images of the playing field are the highest from the upper tiers, characterized by the highest readability of further and closer plans. At the same time, however, the sizes of the images of player figures are the smallest, due to the significant distance from the observer. The above-described circumstances constitute a justification of the undertaken research. Their aim is to determine whether it is possible to use stand profiles with better characteristics than conventional one and to determine the conditions for their application in practice. The second objective is to define the determinants of visibility for spectators located at the lowest tiers. It is necessary to establish a strict criterions regulating the minimum standards for images quality which can be achieved of these places. Another, taken into account, issue is the impact of new profiles on architectural forms of stadium interior (Fig. 1).

Fig. 1. An example of the interior of a modern soccer stadium of medium size. Commerzbank Arena, Frankfurt, 2005 (Photo: author).

2   Lines of Eye Points as a Representation of the Profiles of Stadium Stands

The undertaken research on the stadium stand profiles requires to introduce a few basic concepts, for the analytical reasons. One of them is a "theoretical point of eye". This is the point embodying the geometric center of the lens of the human eye. For simplicity of the optical analysis assumed that each observer is represented by the only one point of the eye, located on the vertical axis of symmetry of the pair of eyes. With these assumptions, the location of each of the many thousands of points of the eye can be defined using the coordinates in the Cartesian system of axes x, y, z.

Figure 2 presents fragment of a classical arrangement of the spectator zone on the stadium. A horizontal shift of the eye points is equal to the predetermined width of the rows. This parameter affects the degree of comfort and safety of spectators, as it affects the size of the space assigned to the individual seats and the space devoted to communication and evacuation [6]. Mutual elevation of the eye points, situated as adjacent to each other, ensures proper raise of the line of sight over the head of the viewer situated below, allowing to see the so-called point of focus.

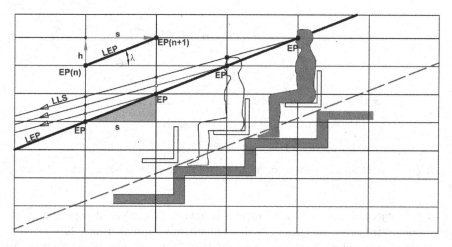

Fig. 2. The definition of the line of eye points (LEP) and the lowest line of sight (LLS) (Source: author)

Drawing through each point of the eye the set of horizontal and vertical lines gives in result a grid of the stand profile. If, however, all the eye points will be connected by continuous line, in the result of this will be obtained the linear image of the profile.

The research instruments described above i.e. *Point of the Eye, Grid of the Stand Profile* and *Lines of Eye Points*, despite its simplicity and without any limitations, enable to carry out assumed studies. They are also very useful in the designing practice because, thanks to their brevity, allow the architect for simultaneous controlling of many issues in design process and taking a quick correcting decisions.

3   The Issue of Vertical Viewing Angle

As mentioned earlier, the quality of vision of the playing field surface is determined mainly by the so-called vertical viewing angle. The essence of the meaning of this angle explains Fig. 3. For the analysis has been chosen theoretical point of the eye EP (n), distant horizontally from the nearer point of focus F1 by the value SEP(n) and raised above the surface of the arena of value HEP(n). The graph is a vertical section of the pyramid of pitch view, running through the center line of the playing field. Vertical viewing angle (α) of the width of the pitch is included between the line of sight SLF2 of further focus point F2 and line of sight SLF1of closer focus point F1. Its value is the difference between the inclination angle (ßf1) of the line of sight SLF1 and inclination angle (ßf2) of the line SLF2.

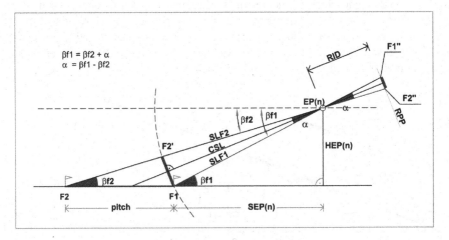

Fig. 3. The vertical angle of view of the pitch field (α) and the relative retinal image of this field (F1"–F2"); (Source: author).

For an objective comparison of images receiving by the visual apparatus of the observers located in various places of the stadium interior, author have developed its own method of so-called *the relative retinal image*. The sight lines of focus points (F1 and F2) extended beyond the point of the eye EP(n), while piercing the back plane of projection (RPP) will appoint the images of these points (F1"and F2"). The image of the pitch width, obtained in this way, can be called *relative retinal image*, provided, however, that the distance between the rear projection plane and the point of the eye will be the same in each case of the analyses. With such an assumption have been obtained an optical system that simulates the interior of the eyeball, the essence of which is a constant distance between the central point of the lens and the surface of the retina.

The dependences, graphically shown on Fig. 4, suggest that the greater is the vertical viewing angle of the pitch, the greater is its relative retinal image. It is also clear that the vertical viewing angle is greater while the position of the point of eye is closer in relation to the observed object and raised higher above it.

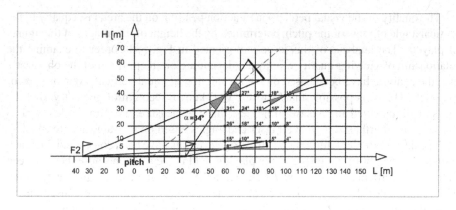

Fig. 4. The impact of the eye point position in the space on the size of the vertical angle of view of the playing field and the size of its relative retinal image (Source: author).

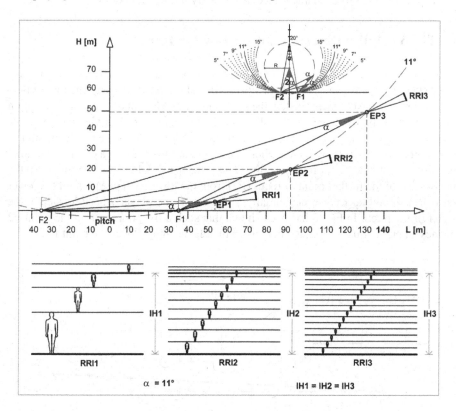

Fig. 5. The characteristics of relative images of the playing field at a constant vertical angle of view (α) and different positions of the eye points (EP) (Source: author).

The quality of the visual perception of action pending on the arena is, equally to the vertical angle of view of the pitch, determined by the height of the images of the figures of players. The analysis of this issue is presented in Fig. 5. In order to examine the relationship of viewing quality of players, depending on the position of the observer's eye, the analysis have been based on the assumption of equal vertical angle of view of the pitch. This was possible thanks to the well-known theorem of geometry, that the measure of inscribed angle is two times less than the measure of central angle based on the same arc. Furthermore, that all inscribed angles based on the same arc are equal.

The three extremely different positions of eye points have been considered. For each of them the height of the image of the playing field is the same, because they are seen in the same vertical angle of view. As shown in the Fig. 5 in the image for the eye point EP1 (coordinates: L = 54 m, H = 5 m) the height of player silhouette housed only 3 times in height of the pitch image. In the case of the eye point EP2 (coordinates: L = 92 m, H = 21 m), this parameter reaches the number 8.5. Eye point EP3 (coordinates: L = 132 m, H = 48 m) is characterized accordingly by the number of 14.

4   The Visibility Determinants of Lowest Tier

As has been earlier mention, commonly used in today's architectural practice profiles of the stadium stands can be named as the profiles of the bowl-shaped. The lowest tiers of these profiles are characterized by the slight slope. The height of eye points elevation for that part of the tribunes is small. This results in a slight vertical viewing angles of the playing field, what gives a flat images of it. Figure 6 presents the results of studies of this problem. According to the author, it is necessary to establish a criterion defining the minimum standards for image quality. This criterion should be to determine that the line of view of the further point of focus (F2) from the lowermost eye point of the lower tier (EP1) should take place tangentially to the top of the player's head located at the center of the pitch. In Fig. 6 has been shown that such a line, drawn from the point F2 reaches a height equal of the two heights of the player figures over the point F1.

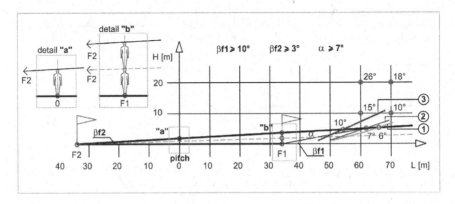

Fig. 6. The postulated rules for determining the minimum vertical angle of view of the pitch and the position of lowest points of the eye at lowest tiers (Source: author).

The slope of this line will be ßf2 = 3°. If the lowest points of the eye will lie on that line and at the same time will ensure at least the vertical angle of view of the pitch α = 7°, it give that the depth of view of the playing field will be 3 heights of the footballer. Figure 6 shows also that the exemplary stand profiles of modern stadia have significantly lower fragments of the spectator zones, which do not meet the described criterion. These are the profile sections which are situated below the proposed regulation line.

5 Propositions of Unconventional Profiles of Stadium Stands

As previously has been shown (Fig. 4) the height of the image of the field is all the higher the larger is the vertical viewing angle. This angle whereas is all the greater the closer and the higher above the pitch is located the point of the eye. These statements indicates the guidelines for searching profiles of grandstands which are characterized by the best parameters of visibility. It results from them that profiles the best visibility should be located in a space that provides the greatest vertical angles of view. Meeting that condition requires that the lines of eye points defining these profiles should have the inclination much greater than accepted by today standards. The farther part of the discourse presents several examples of unconventional solutions. Their common feature are the significant slopes of the profiles achieved by the use of large vertical offsets of the position of the adjacent eye points. Conventional communication and evacuation systems in the interiors of modern stadiums are based on the use of corridors in the form of stairs between sectors. The slope of these stairs is equal to the slope of the terraces of the rows of seats and cannot exceed 35° (Fig. 7). The inclination of the lowest line of view, reached in this type of stands, is the result of its minimal raising (c = 12 cm) above the point of the eye, situated in the next row below or above balustrade. The profiles characterized by the slope greater than 35° require very different solutions of communication and evacuation. Due to the significant height differences between adjacent rows, repeatedly exceeding the height of 50 cm, these solutions require the use of the balustrades or countertops at the edges of the rows. The presence of these elements in the space in front of the eye points determines the course of the lowest line of view, which must run tangentially into the upper edges thereof, or above them. The significant inclination angle of the line of view determines one of the essential values represented by a steep profiles. Thanks to these characteristics, these profiles can be placed in the close proximity of the borders of the observation field. This statement contains a conclusion, that The most important parameter determining the quality of the profile is the slope of the lowest line of sight. When this slope is larger the quality of vision become higher. Studies of the presented examples of non-conventional profiles show that the steepest slope of the lowest line of sight is achieved in these solutions in which the communication passage is located on the back, behind the seats (Figs. 9 and 11). In the proposals when the communication paths ere running in front of rows of seating the inclinations of the lowest lines of vision are smaller, although the slope of the lines of eye are very large (Fig. 8). Particularly noteworthy is in the author's opinion the example shown in Fig. 10. In this case were used the high seats (the barium type), rotating with pneumatically adjustable height. As a result, the eye point of the sitting and standing person are at the same level.

High situated point of the eye in such a sitting position allows to achieve a much greater slope of lowest line of sight over the tip of the railings than in normal sitting position. The advantage of this profile is also the fact that the lowest line of sight of the eye point in a sitting position extends above the head of a person standing close to the balustrade at the level of the row situated below. The proposed solution responds to the demands of the fans, who argue that welding them to the seats reduces the spontaneous cheering.

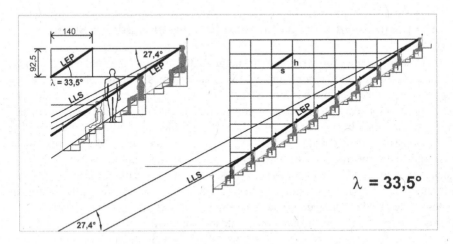

Fig. 7. The proposal of lowered passage in front of a seat (Source: author)

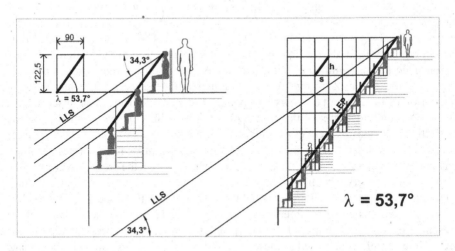

Fig. 8. The proposal of classic width arrangement of the rows and their significant vertical offset (Source: author).

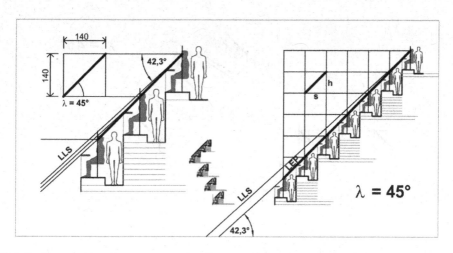

Fig. 9. The proposal of lowered passage at the back of a seat and the countertop at edge of the row (Source: author).

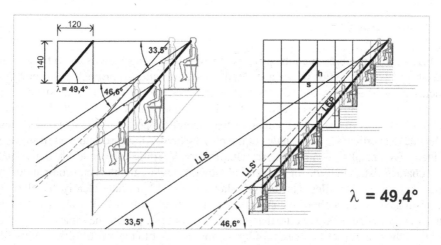

Fig. 10. The proposal of the rotating barium type seats, with pneumatically adjustable height and passage in front of a seats (Source: author).

In the discussed example there is possibility of the participation in a match in both position simultaneously - sitting or standing - while visibility conditions for the latter are even better than the first.

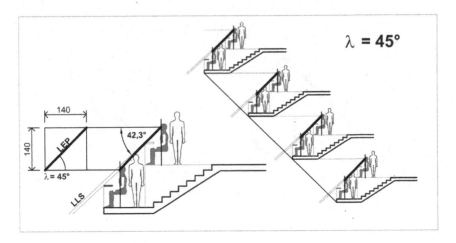

Fig. 11. The arrangement of the spectator zone with a reverse angle of inclination by using stands of the double rows (Source: author).

6 Conclusions[1]

On Fig. 12 has been presented the profiles of several modern stadiums in confrontation with the proposed profiles which are based on unconventional, presented earlier, new functional arrangements of the rows. The analyzed profiles of stadium stands are presented in the form of lines of eye points. At the points of intersection of the horizontal and vertical lines of the grid, simulating the theoretical points of the eyes, has been indicated the vertical viewing angles of the playing field, which are achieved from each of them. As a result, when reading the charts of each profile one can easily determine their characteristics in terms of the vertical viewing angles, and thus can compare each other of considered profiles. The analysis shown in Fig. 12 indicates clearly that all tiers of, postulated by the author, unconventional theoretical profiles PTP-1 and PTP-2 are situated in the zone of large vertical angles of view of the pitch. At the same time all the points of the eye of each of these profiles are much closer to the line of focus points F1 than their counterparts from the stands of the exemplary stadiums. The special emphasis requires fact, that lines of the eye points representing the lowest tiers has a very steep slope reaching up a value exceeding 50°. The effects of the application of postulated by the author a new profiles are fully apparent on Fig. 13. It presents the cross section of the stadium, which allows for an assessment of the shape and scale of this space, defined by the presence of closing it stands. Even more clearly the features of this space are illustrated on Figs. 14A and B as the schematic silhouettes of stadium interiors. These silhouettes, derived from the application of unconventional profiles PTP-1 and PTP-2, have been compared with the one of most representative contours characteristic for contemporary stadium interiors (Fig. 14C).

---

[1] In the years 1994–2007 the author was the chief architect of the reconstruction of the Silesian Stadium in Chorzow, Poland.

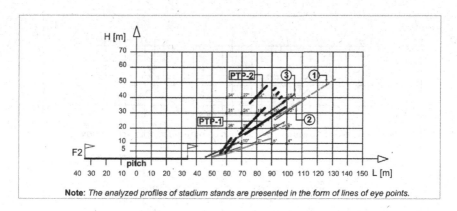

Note: *The analyzed profiles of stadium stands are presented in the form of lines of eye points.*

Fig. 12. The comparative analysis of the postulated theoretical profiles of stands and the selected profiles of modern stadiums (should be considered together with Fig. 13) (Source: author).

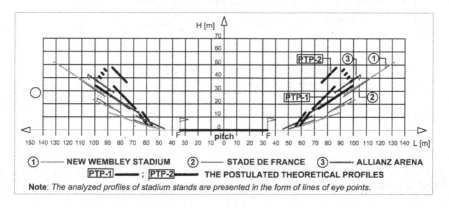

① ------- **NEW WEMBLEY STADIUM**   ② ------- **STADE DE FRANCE**   ③ ------- **ALLIANZ ARENA**
PTP-1 ------- ; **PTP-2** ------- **THE POSTULATED THEORETICAL PROFILES**
Note: *The analyzed profiles of stadium stands are presented in the form of lines of eye points.*

Fig. 13. The juxtaposition of analyzed profiles in the form of a cross section through the interiors of stadiums (Source: author).

In conclusion, we can say that the interior resulting of the PTP-2 profile deserves to be determine as "interior of a flowerpot shape", interiors resulting of the PTP-1 can be called as "interiors of a plate shape", while most of existing today stadiums belong to the "interiors of bowl shape" category. In the author's opinion, the proposals of new, unconventional grandstand profiles improve significantly the parameters of visibility, comfort and safety of spectators. They could contribute as well in the development on the field of stadiums designing, bringing a new values, such as quite new architectural forms in shaping interiors of these objects.

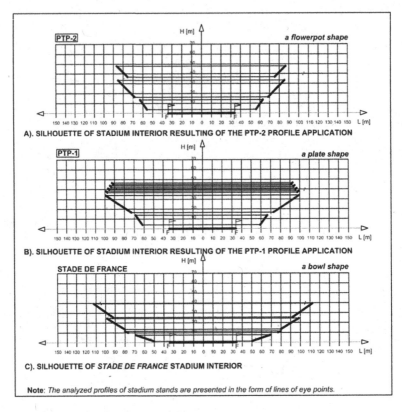

A). SILHOUETTE OF STADIUM INTERIOR RESULTING OF THE PTP-2 PROFILE APPLICATION

B). SILHOUETTE OF STADIUM INTERIOR RESULTING OF THE PTP-1 PROFILE APPLICATION

C). SILHOUETTE OF *STADE DE FRANCE* STADIUM INTERIOR

Note: *The analyzed profiles of stadium stands are presented in the form of lines of eye points.*

Fig. 14. Comparison of the silhouettes of stadium interiors resulting from the use of postulated profiles with the classic profile of contemporary stadium (Source: author).

References

1. Pelczarski, Z.: Widownie współczesnych stadionów. Determinanty i problemy projektowe (Grandstands of the Contemporary Stadiums. Determinants and Design Problems), pp. 69–81, 97–151, 212–219. Oficyna Wydawnicza Politechniki Bialostockiej, Bialystok (2009)
2. John, G., Sheard, R.: Stadia: A Design and Development Guide, pp. 105–120. Routledge, Abingdon (1997)
3. Nixdorf, S.: Stadium ATLAS: Technical Recommendations for Grandstands in Modern Stadiums, pp. 256–345. Ernst & Sohn, Berlin (2008)
4. FIFA/UEFA: Technical Recommendations for the Construction or Modernisation of Football Stadia, FIFA, Zurich (1994–2014)
5. EN 13200-1: Spectator facilities - Part 1: Layout criteria for spectator viewing area–Specification (2003)
6. The Green Guide: Guide to Safety at Sports Grounds. HMSO, London (1990, 1997)

A Study of Product Form Design Using the Theory of Archetypes

Meng-Dar Shieh[1]([⊠]), Fang-Chen Hsu[2], Jia-Shiuan Tian[1], and Chien-Nan Chen[1]

[1] Department of Industrial Design,
National Cheng-Kung University, Tainan, Taiwan, ROC
mdshieh@gmail.com
[2] Department of Multimedia and Entertainment Science,
Southern Taiwan University of Science and Technology, Tainan, Taiwan, ROC
id9lelva@gmail.com

Abstract. The objective of this paper is to design product forms by using the theory of archetypes. The investigation contains three topics and there are three main steps. The first step is to develop the personality adjectives for these twelve archetypes. The second step is to investigate the definition of twelve archetypes by professionals. Simplified descriptions were used to define the twelve archetypes. Riders who were familiar with these bicycles quantized the questionnaire of the Blue Bicycle brand's triathlon bikes. Based on products' images, the Likert scale was used to evaluate the degree of conformity for each archetype so as to determine the primary archetype and the secondary archetype of this bicycle product series. Cluster analysis was then utilized to classify the bicycle models. In the third step, after several primary archetypes of this brand's triathlon series bikes were identified, the personality adjectives obtained in the first step and the archetypes obtained in the second step were used in the Likert scale experiments based on the images of this bicycle series. Factor analysis was used to reduce the dimension of personality adjectives of similar characteristics. Regression analysis was then used to calculate the weight of each factor and determine the relationship between consumers' degree of preference and the willingness to buy.

The final brand archetypes of the Blue Bicycle obtained by the analysis were the explorer, the ruler, and the hero. The adjectives of the three archetypes mentioned above were classified according to similar characteristics by factor analysis and three types of personality traits were formed. These personality traits were "optimistic and independent character", "daring to express character", and "brave explorer character" respectively. The results of the regression analysis of product preferences and the willingness to buy for the Blue Bicycle triathlon series bikes indicated the existence of significance.

Keywords: Archetype theory · Twelve archetypes · Product form design · Cluster analysis · Factor analysis · Regression analysis · Triathlon bike

© Springer International Publishing Switzerland 2016
M. Antona and C. Stephanidis (Eds.): UAHCI 2016, Part I, LNCS 9737, pp. 327–339, 2016.
DOI: 10.1007/978-3-319-40250-5_32

1   Introduction

During concept formation in the product development process, product designers consider the scenarios of using a product and a character image, which belongs to it is then built. Similarly, consumers buy a product depending on whether it complies with their own preference based on the appearance of this product. The "product personality" has become a medium for demonstrating the individual characteristics.

A product with a story makes people reminiscent of something [1]. The "archetype" term contains a range of a population, a type of culture, a type of characteristic, which is shared by people. It is provided with stories and no longer is limited to any specific personality trait. It can generate all-embracing story patterns accordingly. The archetype psychology is also known as the analytical psychology or Jungian psychology, which was proposed by Carl Gustav Jung, a famous Swiss psychologist. The archetype imagery is provided with a common essence and is embodied in different forms or images as the myth elements around the world. After that, based on the "archetype theory" of psychology, the "brand archetype" had been proposed [2].

Therefore, the theory of twelve archetypes was used to analyze the characteristics of the Blue Bicycle and to create an approach for applying the archetype theory so as to build the brand image exclusively for the Blue Bicycle brand. Just like a brand, a product also has a role and a story that belong to it [1]. This theory concluded these story implications and the archetype roles effectively and ingeniously.

2   Background

2.1   Archetype

Jung proposed that the collective unconscious archetype language is expressed in the form of various types of imagery, illusion, and symbols [3]. He also proposed that an "archetype" represents the ideology of people's common viewpoint. Campbell presented the "archetypes" behind a plurality of myths in a book [4]. His research focus was on the adventure stories of the Hero in different cultures. He explained that these stories imply structures of an identical pattern behind the stories except for the Hero character. That is to say, although the contents of myths or legends in various cultures are different, they eventually lead to the identical archetype theme. "Archetype" is a type of tendency and it builds various types of meaning and imagery upon a population. The imagery can be of various patterns in details but the fundamental framework model remains unchanged. An archetype may remain unchanged and it can be used as the foundational framework, while every archetype has its own "symbol" which bears the concrete imagery in different environments [3]. For the imagery or meaning of a symbol archetype, Jung proposed that "We do not have our symbolic life; we need a symbolic life urgently and only have a symbolic life. We have demands for our soul every day and everything of life has already turned old. This is the reason why this type of person gets nervous temperament."

Scholars afterwards kept carrying out studies and analyses on Jung's doctrine. His concept was further classified in a more refined way. According the book authored by

Mark and Pearson, archetypes are classified into twelve types [2], and each one has its own personality trait, imagery, and shadow. The characteristics and personality of every archetype are described as follows.

The Innocent: Motto is "Be yourself by yourself". Happy-go-lucky and smile as much as you like! The consent is to follow your inclinations of being yourself and lives to your best value as long as you follow a few simple principles.

The Explorer: Motto is "Do not get me trapped". Curiosity and adventure are every individual's instinct. A plurality of fairy tale stories talk about the scenarios of looking for treasures, challenging the sea, and pursuing for dreams.

The Sage: Motto is "The truth will get you relieved". The Sage plays the role of a belief among the population and gives you advices for the positive direction when you get lost. It is inward-looking, calm, and sometimes a bit humorous.

The Hero: Motto is "Where there is a will there is a way". The Hero defeated the evil, overcame adverse conditions, crossed tough challenges, and triggered people's feeling of justice. Directors and writers in new approaches have continuously interpreted this kind of stories.

The Outlaw: Motto is "Rules are to be broken". The Outlaw owns the charm of the forbidden fruit. Sometimes the value embodied by the Outlaw is more impressive and real than the main character. This is just like modern young people who put tattoos with violent images or intentionally get hair dye with bright colors to make themselves stand out from the others.

The Magician: Motto is "Dream came true". The characteristic of the Magician is to make things turn magic. The Magician can be dated back to the ancient witch doctors and wizards in the villages. The other embodiments of the Magician include alchemists, Taoist priest, astronomers, and psychologists.

The Regular Guy: Motto is "All men are created equal". The characteristics of the Regular Guy are ordinary and mediocre, inconspicuous, and easily neglected.

The Lover: Motto is "You are the only one in my heart". The Lover often appears in our life. It is not limited to the love between couples but family love, friendship love, and romantic love are all included in this scope.

The Jester: Motto is "If I can't dance, I don't want to be part of your revolution." The Jester includes a clown, and anyone just like a kid who likes to joke or play a trick. They brings joys to the people around, enjoy the simply for enjoyment, enjoy life, or interact with people.

The Caregiver: Motto is "Love your neighbor as yourself". The Caregiver is an altruist, who is driven by generosity and passion, and desires to help others without asking for return.

The Creator: Motto is "Anything you can imagine can be created." The stereotype of the Creator is loving to explore and imagine expressed by the form of matter. The most common examples of the Creator are artists, designers, writers, inventors, and entrepreneurs.

The Ruler: Motto is "The right is not everything but the only". The Ruler has commands and authority to put plans or actions into effect. When thinking about the Ruler, the most common opinion are emperor, queen, chief executive officer, and almighty mom.

2.2   Brand Definitions

This is an era of an international village and entrepreneurs expand their business across the border and create their own commercial territory. Entrepreneurs collaborate and compete with each other. Therefore to stand out from the competitors on the market, the concept of brands gradually formed. Since the market place is constantly changing, merchants not only need to grab the business opportunities, but also to understand customers' mentality. The customer connections became rather important.

Kolter defined six levels for a brand as attributes, benefits, values, culture, personality, and user which are described as follows [5]. The brand value is an enterprise's commitment to its consumers. Sometimes consumers buy a product not for the product itself, but for the meaning behind the product. Therefore, the meaning endowed to a brand is very important since this determined a brand's consumer group [6, 7]. Along with the fierce competition due to internationalization, more complex markets and more picky consumers appeared [8–12]. People often discuss products which correspond to their personality or of similar characteristics [13, 14]. We obtain feedbacks and the sense of recognition from these types of products.

The twelve-archetype theory in mentality was used in this study so as to investigate the archetype personality positioning of the Blue Bicycle brand triathlon series bikes. This is to understand the primary archetype and the secondary archetype of this product series and to provide this brand with a definite character image.

3   Research Process and Methods

The emphasis of this study is on the customers of the Blue Bicycle brand triathlon series bikes so as to understand this brand's archetype image and product form for the consumers. There are three stages as follows. In the first stage, since the twelve archetypes cannot embody their characteristics, the subjects were asked to describe the personalities based on the archetype characteristics and to screen out the adjective vocabularies for the twelve archetypes. To ensure the precision of these adjectives, forty people with design background were asked to carry out adjectives and imagery developments by the brainstorming method. After that, these adjectives were quantized to conduct a preliminary statistics so as to reduce the number of personality adjectives for each archetype between ten and fifteen. Three professionals were interviewed and they are respectively a mental consultant, a psychiatrist, and an industrial designer in the industry. They were asked to screen out the adjectives until only five adjectives were left for each archetype. Each of these adjectives is a symbol of the personality archetype and there is individual personality behind each of them.

In the second stage, the above-mentioned three professionals were asked to include the symbol concepts described by the twelve archetypes into the questionnaire and there are a total of twelve questions. Subjects were asked to compare seven samples of the Blue Bicycle triathlon bikes and evaluate the degree of the twelve archetypes for these seven product samples. The highest score obtained by summing the acquired data up can serve as the primary image or the potential image to be referenced by product designs or marketing for future Blue Bicycle products. The products can be more abundant and highly changeable. At the same time, cluster analysis was also used to classify the seven samples by the archetype attribute groups.

In the third stage, the Blue Bicycle archetype images investigated in the previous stage were used to investigate consumers' assessment for the archetype adjectives of Blue Bicycle. The questionnaire involved the Likert scale experiments [15] for the evaluations. Factor analysis was used to understand which adjective is the primary factor so that personality adjectives of similar properties can be collected into a factor group. After that, regression analysis was used to understand the relationship and influence of factors, degree of preference, and the willingness to buy. This stage helps understand the relationship between Blue Bicycle archetypes, and the influence on consumers' degree of preference and the willingness to buy.

3.1   Questionnaire for Statics the Twelve Archetype Adjectives

Seven bicycle models of the Blue Bicycle triathlon series bikes were analyzed and the product form designs and image positioning were discussed in this study with purposes as follows. The product forms and image styles of the Blue Bicycle brand were provided as a reference. The Blue Bicycle triathlon series bikes are listed in Table 1 as follows.

Table 1. Blue Bicycle brand's triathlon series bikes

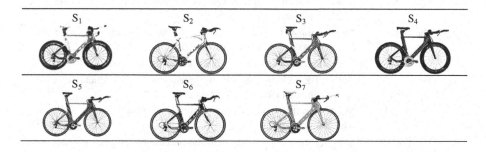

This study aimed at archetype adjectives for carrying out quantization statistics. The number of valid/returned questionnaires is 63/82. There are 38 females and 25 males in the age of 15 to 25 years old. The constraint is that a person can select ten adjectives for each archetype, and the top fifteen adjectives were selected after statistics.

The top ten of The Innocent personality adjectives are naive, pure, optimistic, genuine, kind-hearted, childish, not artificial, carefree, content, and casual. The top ten of The Explorer personality adjectives are brave, dauntless, adventurous, freedom-lover, passionate, curious, forthright, eccentric, steadfast, and eager to do well. The top ten of The Sage personality adjectives are sedate, smart, calm, intelligent, rational, profound, inward-looking, mellow, attentive, and rigorous. The top ten of The Hero personality adjectives are valiant, dauntless, hot-blooded, feeling of justice, heroic, leadership, decisive, self-confident, reliable, broad and level. The top ten of The Outlaw adjectives are traitorous, rebellious, aggressive, fanatic, high-handed, violence, arbitrary, fractious, assertive, stubborn. The top ten of The Magician personality adjectives are mysterious, intelligent, spiritual, smart, sensitive, smart, attentive, quick-witted, calm, and unworldly. The top ten of The Regular Guy personality adjectives are unostentatious, content, compliant, mean, veracious, lukewarm, amiable, honest, casual, and loyal. The top ten of The Lover personality adjectives are romantic, attractive, caring, gentle and soft, sentimental, charming, sweet, elegant, agreeable, and passionate. The top ten of The Jester personality adjectives are not artificial, bold aesthetic, casual, optimistic, pure, droll, humorous, genuine, straightforward, informal. The top ten of The Caregiver personality adjectives are humanitarian, altruistic, agreeable, patient, caring, attentive, kind-hearted, amicable, ardent, gentle and soft. The top ten of The Creator personality adjectives are perceptual, eccentric, self-confident,

Table 2. Investigating the definitions of twelve archetypes with professionals

No.	Archetype	Definition
1.	The Innocent	This world is pure and cute, let us take smile and blissful toward the future
2.	The Explorer	There is no dream that cannot be achieved! Challenge yourself and conquer extremity
3.	The Sage	Gold is tried in the fire. Gospel is not afraid of evil. No longer puzzled, all suffering is readily solved
4.	The Hero	My mission is to rescue the world. Brave and confident, sweep the barriers and march toward the target
5.	The Outlaw	Rules are exactly to be broken, reveals much as you like!
6.	The Magician	With brisk melody, the velocity transformed into magical power, surpass the distance between times
7.	The Regular Guy	Maybe I will lose in the crowd, but I am willing to become a star, which sets off the moon
8.	The Lover	Interpret the most moving emotion; release the elegant and attractive romance
9.	The Jester	Others laugh at I being too insane, I laugh at others for not understanding
10.	The Caregiver	Full of your love, bring the blissful to people!
11.	The Creator	An unfailing supply of inspiration, engrave a brilliant life at every moment
12.	The Ruler	Follow my footsteps; walk on the front end of the scratch line

spiritual, crazy, sensitive, unworldly, casual, quick-witted, and smart. The top ten of The Ruler personality adjectives are leadership, high-handed, decisive, steady, arbitrary, of outstanding talents, proud, heroic, lonely, and serious.

3.2 Definitions of Twelve Archetypes by Professionals

Based on the archetype theory proposed by Mark and Pearson, we carry out the assessment on the personality adjectives of archetypes. It is also required to define the attributes of the twelve archetypes for the quantitative survey in order to conduct the follow-up experiment in the second stage.

3.3 Questionnaire for Statics the Primary Archetypes

By using the above-mentioned methods, this study includes three portions. The first portion deals with the "construction of twelve archetype adjectives". The second portion deals with "Blue Bicycle brand archetype positioning and the construction of classification model for bicycle models". The third portion deals with "the relationship and influence of the brand image of the Blue Bicycle brand's primary archetype on the degree of preference and the willingness to buy".

At the present stage, the bicycle images are provided for consumers, and then requests them to evaluate the characteristic of twelve-archetype in five levels (-2 to 2). After the summation of the scores of the seven bicycles, the series of the primary and secondary archetypes were obtained as shown in Table 4. The number of returned valid/questionnaire was 73/97, and the demography of these subjects is as Table 3.

Table 3. The demography of subjects

No.	Item	Statics
1.	Gender	54 males, 19 females
2.	Age	23 between 15–25, 35 between 25–35, 11 between 35–45, and 4 between 45–55
3.	Place of residence	Northern region 13, central region 13, and southern Taiwan 47
4.	Money possibly to be spent on a bicycle	30000 below is 36, 30000–60000 is 6, 60000–100000 is 14, 100000–150000 is 14, 150000–200000 is 1, and 200000–250000 above is 2
5.	Taking bicycling exercises	Yes 40; no 33
6.	Classes attended	None: 13, Olympics standard: 19, Super ironman: 6, semi ironman: 5

The types and descriptions of the Archetypes are indicated in Table 2 as A1 ~ A12. It was thus known that the archetype ranking of the Blue Bicycle triathlon series bikes is The Explorer (A2), The Ruler (A12), and then The Hero (A4). The archetype personality

Table 4. Total scores obtained by the summation of personality scores for different archetypes

·	Innocent	Explorer	Sage	Hero	Outlaw	Magician	Regular guy	Lover	Jester	Caregiver	Creator	Ruler
	A_1	A_2	A_3	A_4	A_5	A_6	A_7	A_8	A_9	A_{10}	A_{11}	A_{12}
S1	−5	72	16	72	31	17	−22	−37	−23	−13	30	52
S2	35	29	44	−1	−33	13	47	18	−28	19	8	16
S3	−21	76	30	62	67	22	−31	−3	−36	−18	27	49
S4	−36	55	50	44	63	44	−16	−26	−18	−33	10	70
S5	−9	35	26	12	−2	19	18	−33	0	−20	−6	15
S6	−5	26	22	23	24	5	−4	−31	−23	−13	15	38
S7	89	22	−14	−24	−16	37	15	69	3	37	28	−19
Total	48	**315**	174	**188**	134	157	7	−43	−125	−41	112	**221**

Table 5. Personality adjectives of primary archetype adjectives

No.	Primary archetype	Personality adjective
1.	The Explorer (A_2)	Brave, dauntless, adventurous, freedom-lover, passionate
2.	The Ruler (A_{12})	Leadership, high-handed, arbitrary, of outstanding talents, proud
3.	The Hero (A_4)	Valiant, feeling of justice of, hot-blooded, heroic, decisive

adjectives of the three primary archetypes are shown in Table 5. These personality adjectives are used to conduct the factor analysis in the next stage.

3.4 Cluster Analysis of the Twelve Archetypes and the Primary Archetypes

Cluster analysis of product samples S1 ∼ S7 was carried out by using the twelve archetypes A1 ∼ A12 as variables based on the ranking of the archetype images for this product series. The status, after grouping the samples of Blue Bicycle triathlon series bikes, is shown in Fig. 1 and all samples can be classified into 3 groups, wherein S5, S6, and S2 formed the first group and the style of S7 differs very much from the other six bicycles. Therefore, S7 was independent from the others while S1, S3, and S4 are the third group.

Archetypes of Blue Bicycle are The Explorer (A_2), The Ruler (A_{12}) and The Hero (A_4). These three types of archetype served as variables and the seven samples were classified into three groups (Fig. 2). The first group includes S_1, S_3, and S_4. The second group includes S_2, S_5, and S_6 while S_7 was independent from others. It is important to note that the result, which contains three variable groups is similar to the result obtained in the previous section.

3.5 Questionnaire of the Main Personality Adjectives

Via the experiments in the second stage, it is known that the Blue Bicycle triathlon vehicle image archetypes include The Explorer (A_2), The Ruler (A_{12}) and The Hero

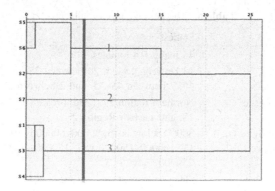

Fig. 1. Cluster analysis of the twelve archetypes for the product samples

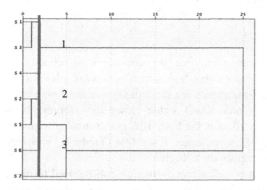

Fig. 2. Cluster analysis of three types of archetypes

(A_4) based on each sample's archetype classification. Nevertheless, the ranking of Blue Bicycle triathlon series bikes images requires the analyses of the character charm for each archetype image. Therefore, a questionnaire survey on the three types of archetype adjectives with a total of fifteen personality adjectives was conducted. By means of factor analysis, we analyzed three types of personality adjectives for the archetypes' universality. A regression analysis of the factor analysis results was carried out so as to understand the degree of each factor's influence on the degree of consumers' preference and their willingness to buy. In the investigation of this stage, the number of questionnaires valid/returned was 59/92. The demography of these 73 people is as follows (Table 6).

3.6 Factor Analysis for the Types of Personality Adjectives

It is required to understand the weighted deviation so as to examine the results' consistency and reliability based on the theory of variance. The inspection criterion of the reliability is Cronbach's α coefficient, which is a nonnegative number. $0.35 < \alpha < 0.7$ is medium reliability, and $\alpha > 0.7$ indicates a high reliability. In typical and actual

Table 6. The demography of subjects

No.	Item	Statics
1	Gender	45 males, 14 females
2	Age	13 between 15–25, 20 between 25–35, 22 between 35–45, 2 between 45–55, and 2 between 55–65
3	Place of residence	Northern region 27, central region 12, Southern region 18, and Eastern Region 2
4	Money possibly to be spent on a bicycle	30000 below is 15, 30000–60000 is 19, 60000–100000 is 11, 100000–150000 is 7, 150000–200000 is 4, 200000–250000 above is 3
5	Bicycling frequency	Once or many times per week is 33, once two weeks 7, once three weeks 1, once a month or above 12, and none 6
6	Classes attended	Never attend: 20, other bicycle racing 11, Olympics standard 12, super ironman 9, semi ironman 7

practices, $\alpha \geq 0.6$ can claim that the questionnaire reliability is acceptable. The Cronbach's α of this analysis is 0.946, which means the reliability is acceptable. Factor analysis at the same time carries out the validity verification, taking eigenvalue as 1 to determine factor standard. KMO Value closer to 1 represents the sample interval common factor of the effect is the best. This questionnaire's cumulative of this case is 73.439 %, KMO > 0.9, significance $P < 0.001$ (Table 7). This indicated that its finding is valid and the credibility is high.

The ingredient matrix after transformation can be used to observe the personality adjectives of the archetypes, which can be concluded as three types of personality traits. While the three types of archetype's personality adjectives are distributed to each component, which are shown in Table 7. The factors of the first group contain the personality adjectives of three archetypes. And the factors of the second group contain the personality adjectives of two types of archetypes. The first factor's (C1) personality adjectives are mostly provided with independence, optimistic upward of right side characteristic, which belong to extraversion personality trait. Thus, this factor was named "optimistic and independent" type. The second factor's (C2) personality adjectives, as compared to C1 and C3, are provided with power, explicit. It was named "dare-to-express" type. The third factor's (C3) personality adjectives are all personality factors of The Explorer. So it was named "brave explorer" type.

A regression analysis was conducted on these three types of factors so as to understand which factor has the influence at the consumer degree of preference and the degree of willingness to buy. The final results of the factor analysis indicated that the Blue Bicycle images cannot be represented by a single archetype. However, these archetypes have common personality traits, which are "optimistic and independent", "dare-to-express", and "brave explorer" types.

Table 7. Matrix after transformation

	Element		
	C_1	C_2	C_3
Proud	**.887 A_{12}**	.070	.143
Outstanding talents	**.858 A_{12}**	.176	.208
Arbitrary	**.732 A_{12}**	.336	.270
Valiant	**.719 A_4**	.357	.202
Hot-blooded	**.701 A_4**	.457	.207
Freedom-lover	**.644 A_2**	.428	.268
Feeling of justice	**.621 A_4**	.499	.161
Adventurous	**.595 A_2**	.428	.373
Heroic	**.564 A_4**	.441	.214
High-handed	.198	**.819 A_{12}**	.107
Leadership	.141	**.795 A_{12}**	.307
Passionate	.384	**.729 A_2**	.180
Decisive	.445	**.679 A_4**	.130
Dauntless	.234	.192	**.903 A_2**
Brave	.310	.248	**.869 A_2**
Eigenvalues	5.097	3.690	2.229
Variance (%)	33.982	24.599	14.858
Cumulative variance (%)	33.982	58.581	73.439
Cronbach's α value	.946		
Kaiser-meyer-olkin value	.916		
Significance	.000		

3.7 Linear Regression Analysis of Triathlon Series Bikes' Personality Trait Factors

After the factor analysis, a linear regression analysis was performed so as to determine the relationship between the three personality traits and the degree of user's preferences about the Triathlon series bikes. This study emphasizes on the product form design with consumer's perception while the price, service attitude, other factors are excluded. The result of this product series' personality styles with the consumer mentality motivation relationship is shown as following regression model, and P < 0.01 (with significance).

Stoichiometric regression model : $Y = 3.370 + 0.593 * C1 + 0.457 * C2 + 0.281 * C3$

This regression equation was used to estimate the degree of preference answered by each subject so as to calculate the standard deviation between the actual value and the predicted value. The average value of the degree of preference is 0.404. Next, another linear regression analysis was performed so as to investigate the relationship between the three personality traits and the consumer's willingness to buy the Triathlon series bikes. The result is shown as following regression model, and P < 0.01(with significance).

Stoichiometric regression model : $Y = 3.245 + 0.693 * C1 + 0.307 * C2 + 0.178 * C3$

By means of this regression equation, users can estimate and calculate the actual/predicted values and the standard deviation of subject's willingness to buy. The average value is 0.419 in this study.

4 Conclusions

A product form design approach, which utilizes the theory of archetypes was investigated in this study. Cluster analysis was applied so as to classify the bicycle models. The final archetypes of the Blue Bicycle obtained by this study were The Explorer (A_2), The Ruler (A_{12}) and The Hero (A_4). Factor analysis was used to reduce the dimension of personality adjectives with similar characteristics. Three personality traits were obtained, which are "optimistic and independent", "daring to express", and "brave explorer" types respectively. Regression analysis was then used to determine the relationship between consumers' degree of preference for these three personality traits and their willingness to buy due to these personality traits. The results of the regression analysis indicated the existence of significance with regard to consumers' product preferences for these three personality traits as well as the willingness to buy the Blue Bicycle triathlon series bikes due to these personality traits. The theory of archetypes can also be applied to analyses related to Kansei engineering for any future research.

References

1. Woodside, A.G., Sood, S., Miller, K.E.: When consumers and brands talk: storytelling theory and research in psychology and marketing. Psychol. Mark. **25**(2), 97–145 (2008)
2. Mark, M., Pearson, C.S.: The Hero and the Outlaw: Building Extraordinary Brands Through the Power of Archetypes, 1st edn. McGraw-Hill Education, New York (2001)
3. Casement, A., Jung, C.G.: Key Figures in Counselling and Psychotherapy Series. SAGE Publications Ltd., London (2001)
4. Campbell, J.: Hero with a Thousand Faces. The Collected Works of Joseph Campbell, 3rd edn. New World Library, Novato (2008)
5. Kotler, P.: Marketing Management: Analysis, Planning, Implementation, and Control. The Prentice-Hall Series in Marketing, 8th edn. Prentice Hall, Upper Saddle River (1994)
6. Harris, F., de Chernatony, L.: Corporate branding and corporate brand performance. Eur. J. Mark. **35**(3/4), 441–456 (2001)
7. Klaus, P.: The case of Amazon.com: towards a conceptual framework of online customer service experience (OCSE) using the emerging consensus technique (ECT). J. Serv. Mark. **27**(6), 443–457 (2013)
8. Balmer, J.M.T.: Corporate branding and connoisseurship. J. Gen. Manag. **21**(1), 24–46 (1995)
9. Balmer, J.M.T.: Corporate identity, corporate branding and corporate marketing - Seeing through the fog. Eur. J. Mark. **35**(3/4), 248–291 (2001)
10. Balmer, J.M.T.: Explicating corporate brands and their management: reflections and directions from 1995. J. Brand. Manag. **18**(3), 180–196 (2010)

11. Balmer, J.M.T.: Corporate brand management imperatives: custodianship, credibility, and calibration. Calif. Manag. Rev. **54**(3), 6–33 (2012)
12. Kapferer, J.-N.: The New Strategic Brand Management: Advanced Insights and Strategic Thinking. New Strategic Brand Management: Creating & Sustaining Brand Equity, 5th edn. Kogan Page Limited, London (2012)
13. Janlert, L.-E., Stolterman, E.: The character of things. Des. Stud. **18**(3), 297–314 (1997)
14. Adiloglu, F., Akinci, S.T.: Interdisciplinary design studio education: place through the activity of play. Cypriot J. Educ. Sci. **3**(6), 140–149 (2011)
15. Likert, R.: A technique for the measurement of attitudes. Arch. Psychol. **22**(140), 1–55 (1932)

Personal and Collective Informatics in Universal Access

Group Level Versus Society Level of Computing

Dipta Mahardhika[✉] and Taro Kanno

Cognitive Systems Engineering Lab., Department of Systems Innovation, Graduate School of Engineering, The University of Tokyo, Tokyo, Japan
dipta@cse.t.u-tokyo.ac.jp, kanno@sys.t.u-tokyo.ac.jp

Abstract. In this paper, a meso-level of computing is added to the four-level model by Whitworth [1]. This meso-level is called group-level computing. It exists between the individual level and society level. The main difference between group-level and society-level of computing is the social tie involved between the members. One function of the social tie is to give a regulation for the interaction between the members. One implication to design and development of systems is that group-level computing will need to consider a group-cognition model, instead of individual cognition model. For the society level, the design should focus on creating a regulation of its member behavior and interaction, since there is no social tie to regulate their interaction.

Keywords: Group-level computing · Society-level computing · Social tie · Group cognition

1 Introduction: Levels of Computing Evolution

Computer technology and its interaction with human have been studied in many aspects, especially in recent years. The focus of studies have ranged from hardware level to social level. Whitworth [1] defined four level of computing evolution which also defines different level of analysis towards sociotechnical system. This leveling is not meant to create a partition of analysis, but instead providing different ways to see technology in human's life. There are four levels in his definition, i.e., mechanical (hardware) level, informational (software) level, personal level, and social level.

Sociotechnology or sociotechnical study is an emerging field studying the interaction between technology and social system. Recently, more attention is put into it due to the high adoption of social media and internet in the society's life. Bunge [2] mentioned that sociotechnology is the process of applying insights from the social sciences to design policies and programs.

It is important to see sociotechnology from the viewpoint of its user. In HCI, the user of the system is the human. Thus, the study focuses on human's cognitive ability and limitation in using computer. On the other hand, the user of technology in a sociotechnical system is an entity called 'society'. Whitworth called this 'community'. The problem is that society or community is loosely defined here. One property that we can clearly draw from those concepts is that there are two or more person in the given system. This definition is very broad since the research can range from about communication

© Springer International Publishing Switzerland 2016
M. Antona and C. Stephanidis (Eds.): UAHCI 2016, Part I, LNCS 9737, pp. 343–350, 2016.
DOI: 10.1007/978-3-319-40250-5_33

between two persons using messaging technology up to the use of social media in the world-scale.

The objective of this paper is to discuss this definition of sociotechnology in the field of computing system, particularly the leveling as proposed by Whitworth. A meso-level computing will be discussed in this context, including its implication in research and development.

2 Types of Social Aggregates and the Use of Technology

In the field of group dynamics, Forsyth [3] classified social aggregates into four types, although he admitted that this classification is not necessarily exhaustive. They are primary group, social group, collectives, and categories. This categorization has also been validated by Lickel et al. [4]. Each of this categorization has some different characteristics, such as their social tie, permeability, and time span.

Primary group refers to an intimate clusters of close associates, such as families, or good friends. This kind of groups tends to have intensive interactions, and those are mostly for maintaining the intimate relationship. The size of primary group is usually small. On the other hand, social group tends to be larger and less intimate than primary group. This kind of groups is often task oriented. Some examples are sports group, fraternities, military squad, companies, and so on.

Collectives are usually large, spontaneous social aggregates. The members have loose or no emotional relationship, and are usually strangers to each other. However, they are tied to each other by spatial proximity, common rule, norm, or purpose. Some examples are audience of a concert, queue, riot, and so on. Social categories are similar to collectives in that the members have no emotional relationship. However, they are tied by their similarity or common feature, such as interest or cultural background. Some examples are American, women, fans of a certain music group, and so on. It is important to note that if a social category does not have a social implication to a 'member', then this is not regarded as social aggregate for this particular 'member'. If the presence of that category influence a member's behavior towards other member or any person outside the category, then it is a social aggregate.

In the context of technology usage, each type of aggregation uses technology in different ways. Family may use phones to communicate with family members. Team may use group application such as Trello[1] or github[2] to coordinate their work progress. One example of collective in the context of technology usage is where some strangers in Facebook comment to a single viral video and may have short a discussion or even an argument. For the social category, one example is where a number of people with similar interest or background create a group to share information about the latest trend about their interest or latest news related to their background. Wikipedia[3] writers and readers can be categorized into this category.

---

[1] Project management tools https://trello.com/.

[2] Software development management tools https://github.com/.

[3] Online encyclopedia https://www.wikipedia.org/.

Some recent trend of sharing-economy, collaborative consumption, or peer-to-peer, is also an example of how a social collective or category utilizes technology. AirBnB[4] and Uber[5], for example, connects a group of room or car owners, to their users. The room or car owners do not know each other, neither they know the user personally. However, they interact through a single system, and an action of a member (such as a review) can influence other member's decision.

3   Differences Between the Two Types of Aggregations

Main significant difference between the first two types and the latter two types mentioned above are the degree of how much the individual members know about other members personally. Other differences are interaction, timespan, and permeability. These differences are used as the basis to distinguish between group-level computing and society-level computing. Hereinafter, primary group and social group will be referred to as a group, while social collective and social category will be referred to as a society.

3.1   Social Ties and Interaction

Social tie between two agents can be observed in the way they communicate with each other. Every communication can be viewed from content dimension or relational dimension. The content is the mere information delivered to the receiver. The relationship dimension is where the communication affects the relationship or perceived closeness between the speakers. A social tie may be indicated by a strong communication in the relationship dimension. It may be in the form of exchanging identities, background, asking conditions, showing affection, and so on.

Social tie can act as a regulation in the interaction between members of a social aggregate. Social regulation in the form of social facilitation or inhibition are affected by the presence of other people, and also the nature and quality of the relationship [5].

In the case of a group, it is reasonable to assume that everybody knows everybody, or at least most of them. Every interaction done between members are recognized as interaction with a particular person(s) that they know. When they exchange some information, the information receiver may care about both the content of the information and who the information provider is. Each of the member is connected in a socially meaningful way.

As mentioned above, social tie is indicated by more (or at least balanced) communication in the relation dimension. This is important to maintain the social tie among the members. It is well recognized in the field of team science that both relation-oriented and task-oriented communication are important for the team performance (see, for example, [6]).

In the case of a society, the members do not know each other. Interactions in society are content oriented or transactional, since there is no social tie to maintain. When there

---

[4] Accommodation sharing platform https://www.airbnb.com/.
[5] Ride sharing platform https://www.uber.com/.

is an information exchange between members, the receiver may only care about the content of the information and not about the information provider. For example, in the case of commenting, arguing, or reposting a video in a social media, the actor do not really care about from whom the viral video came from or who the person one is arguing with. One might want to know what kind of stranger (educated, uneducated, and so on) he is arguing with, but since there is no social tie, one may not care about "who this person is" in a socially meaningful way.

Another example, a user of AirBnB do not need to know who the owner of the rented room is. As long as the room, price, and other non-personal factors satisfy the user's need, transaction can happen.

Sometimes intense interaction can happen between certain members, and they formed a stronger social tie. For example, some Wikipedia writers of a certain topic can create a meet-up event, and have more intense discussion or personal interaction. In this case, they shifts from a society to a group.

3.2   Permeability

Social tie is formed by dyadic ties between the members. When a new person wants to enter a group, he or she needs to create a social tie with each member of the group, or at least most of them. Moreover, social tie between the members can be a strong emotional tie, or regulated by a rule (such as initiation ceremony). This makes entering (or leaving) a group relatively difficult, compared to a society.

When a new person want to enter a society, he or she can join even without knowing the existing member personally. Leaving a society is easy since there is no social tie between the members.

3.3   Timespan

Timespan for a social aggregate can be defined as a relative span for a particular member. Once a person is no longer a member of that aggregate, for this particular person, the timespan has finished, even though the other members are still forming the aggregate. In primary group, timespan can be very long, even up to the members' whole lifetime. Timespan in social group is relatively shorter. It is usually determined by the task or purpose of the group. Once the purpose has achieved, or once the membership has finished (graduated from school, and so on) the life of the group for that particular member is also finished.

For social collectives and categories, if we see it from the perspective of the member, the timespan can be very short compared to the timespan of a group. In the case of sharing economy like Uber, the interaction between the members (driver and user) is limited to the span of the transaction. After the transaction is done, the interaction is finished. When the user or the driver use the system next time, the person that they will interact with will probably be a different person.

On the other hand, if we see it from the aggregate itself (without considering whether the members are the same or not), a society can have a longer timespan than a group. In the context of technology usage, there is not so much example because internet and social media are still a recent trends (around a few decades). However, we can imagine that, for example, as long as Wikipedia still have users, then the timespan of the so-called "Wikipedia users" will not finished even though the writers or the readers may come and go.

3.4   Role of Technology

A research about the difference between online and offline friendship [7] showed an importance of offline relationship over the computing system. When a friendship formed online (the members initially met in the internet) and then they develop their communication offline as well, the quality is higher than a group that merely meet and maintain their relationship online. This shows that the role of computing system is secondary to the social tie itself. In a group, the role of computing system in the whole system is to mediate the interaction between its members. Figure 1 illustrates this interaction. When a person interact with the computing system, the interaction is actually intended for the other member of the group.

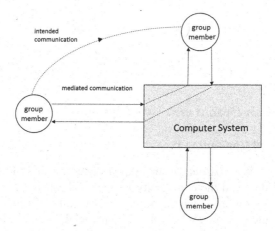

Fig. 1. Computing systems in a group

In a society, traditional relationship between members usually was in the form relationship between a person and an institution. For example, traditional business form of service, good, and information provision usually consisted of providers and consumers, where usually the providers are institutions or companies. However, AirBnB, Rakuten[6], and Wikipedia allows users to interact with each other in the role of a consumer or a provider. The company themselves does not provide any content (service, goods, or information) to the consumer, they only provide the platform of interaction.

However, in the consumer's perspective, those companies including the content may still be perceived as a single entity. The interaction is not perceived as interaction with another member of society, but between the consumer and the company as an entity. As

---

[6] Online shop platform http://www.rakuten.co.jp/.

mentioned above, interaction in the society level is transactional, and users do not care about the person who actually provide the content. The role of the computing system is not mainly to mediate the interaction between members, but to integrate the contents provided by some members, which later are consumed by other members. Figure 2 illustrates the interaction.

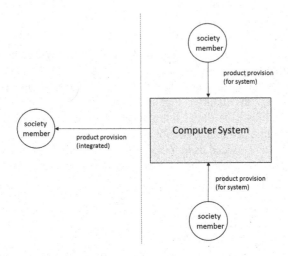

Fig. 2. Computing system in a society

4   Implication on Design and Development

4.1   Group-Level of Computing

As discussed above, it is reasonable to say that there is a meso-level of computing between the individual and the community level. This level is where the user of the technology is a social aggregate where the members are all connected by social ties – a group. One implication is how researcher should model the user of the computer.

HCI field is rooted in cognitive science, specifically, cognition of individual person. When we want to study HCI aspect of a group, a group cognition model should be used as well. Chant and Ernst [8] and Tuomela [9] suggested that group cognition is more than just sum of individual cognitions. Group cognition is the combination of individual cognition and a particular relationship among the cognition. Kanno et al. [10], and Mahardhika et al. [11] suggest that the particular relationship is called mutual belief. There are three belief layers when a person interacts with another person. When a person think or intent (or having any kind of cognition) of something (first layer), he compares that to two other things. Those are: what the other partner thinks (second layer), and what the other partner believes about one thinks (third layer). If all of these three layers are the same, they are said to have a mutual belief. If there is some difference, it will be a trigger for interaction.

One example of this concept is the adaptation of closed-loop communication. When two or more people chat in a group (like LINE or Facebook messenger), the members usually want to know whether his/her message has been delivered or read. This is implemented in a feature called read receipt, where the sender of message gets a notification whether the message has been read by the receiver or not.

This simple "closed-loop" communication is crucial in real-life team [12]. It will decrease the possibility of misunderstanding which can lead to worse performance. In primary group interaction, like communication between family members or romantic couple, such feature will help them in comparing the belief layers and thus reducing misunderstanding and maintaining the social tie.

4.2 Society-Level of Computing

In contrast with the meso-level, the macro level of computing lacks of social ties. In this level, the form of interaction are no longer personal.

Society level computing is powerful in many things. Twitter was used extensively to relay information during Japan great Tohoku earthquake. Facebook was the main communication media to coordinate the Arab spring demonstration. Wikipedia is the biggest online encyclopedia created by thousands of people that are strangers to each other.

In the above examples, the people involved care most about the information being circulated. Identities like names and profile pictures may be visible, but people rarely affected by it. One example was mentioned by Suler [13]. Interaction over the cyberspace can minimize people's status and authority. In the real face-to-face world, someone's status and authority may affect how people interpret information given by this person. In the cyberspace, however, they have less impact.

The lack of social tie can be problematic. As mentioned in the previous section, social tie can act as interaction regulation so that people will behave in a certain way, adjusting with their counterpart. In the absence of social tie, problems like online disinhibition effect [13] and cyberbullying [for example, 14] can be more prevalent.

Therefore, in this level, system developers need to create a system that can utilize the potential of the members in achieving the system's goal, while minimizing the adverse effect of the lack of social ties. Since the regulation from social tie does not exist, other forms of regulation should be integrated into the system. It should be both in the technical aspect (moderation, strict registration requiring personal data, privacy control, etc.) and in the social regulation aspect (law, etc.).

5 Conclusion

In addition to mechanical level, informational (software) level, personal level, and society level, there is group-level of computing. The main difference of group-level and society-level is the presence and absence of social ties among the members in the system.

For the group level, models of group- or team-cognition should be employed more to support the goal of the group. Besides, maintaining social tie between the group members is an important part of the interaction. System designer should also help the users in maintaining the social tie.

For the society level, technical and social regulation should be designed to replace the missing regulation provided by social tie.

References

1. Whitworth, B., Ahmad, A.: The Social Design of Technical Systems: Building Technologies for Communities. The Interaction Design Foundation, Denmark (2014)
2. Bunge, M.: Social Science Under Debate: A Philosophical Perspective. University of Toronto Press, Scholarly Publishing Division, Toronto (1999)
3. Forsyth, D.R.: Group Dynamics. Wadsworth, Cengage Learning, Belmont (2010)
4. Lickel, B., Hamilton, D.L., Wieczorkowska, G., Lewis, A., Sherman, S.J., Uhles, A.N.: Varieties of groups and the perception of group entitativity. J. Pers. Soc. Psychol. **78**, 223–246 (2000)
5. Buck, R., Losow, J.I., Murphy, M.M., Costanzo, P.: Social facilitation and inhibition of emotional expression and communication. J. Pers. Soc. Psychol. **63**, 962–968 (1992)
6. Mohammed, S., Ferzandi, L., Hamilton, K.: Metaphor no more: a 15-year review of the team mental model construct. J. Manag. **36**, 876–910 (2010)
7. Antheunis, M.L., Valkenburg, P.M., Peter, J.: The quality of online, offline, and mixed-mode friendships among users of a social networking site. Cyberpsychology J. Psychosoc. Res. Cybersp. **6**, art. 6 (2012)
8. Chant, S.R., Ernst, Z.: Group intention as equilibria. Philos. Stud. **133**, 95–109 (2007)
9. Tuomela, R.: Shared Belief (2001). http://www.sciencedirect.com/science/article/pii/B0080430767010007
10. Kanno, T., Furuta, K., Kitahara, Y.: A model of team cognition based on mutual beliefs. Theor. Issues Ergon. Sci. **14**, 38–52 (2013)
11. Mahardhika, D., Kanno, T., Furuta, K.: Team cognition model based on mutual beliefs and mental subgrouping. J. Interact. Sci. **4**, 1 (2016)
12. Salas, E., Sims, D.E., Burke, C.S.: Is there a "Big Five" in teamwork? Small Group Res. **36**, 555–599 (2005)
13. Suler, J.: The online disinhibition effect. Int. J. Appl. Psychoanal. Stud. **2**, 184–188 (2005)
14. Udris, R.: Cyberbullying among high school students in Japan: development and validation of the online disinhibition scale. Comput. Hum. Behav. **41**, 253–261 (2014)

The Falsified Self: Complexities in Personal Data Collection

Alessandro Marcengo[1], Amon Rapp[2(✉)], Federica Cena[2], and Marina Geymonat[1]

[1] Telecom Italia - Research and Prototyping, Via Reis Romoli 274, 10148 Turin, Italy
alessandro.marcengo@telecomitalia.it
[2] Computer Science Department, University of Torino, C.so Svizzera 185, 10149 Turin, Italy
amon.rapp@gmail.com, cena@di.unito.it

Abstract. Personal Informatics systems collect personal information in order to trigger self-reflection and improve self-knowledge. Users can now choose among different wearable devices for collecting these data according to their needs and desires. These tools exploit not only different shapes and physical forms, but also diverse technologies and algorithms, which may impact the effectiveness of data gathering. In this paper we explored whether there are significant differences in their reported measures and how these can impact the user experience, along with the perceived accuracy of the gathered data and the perceived reliability of the device. To this aim, we carried out an autoethnography which lasted 4 weeks, monitoring the number of steps and the distance covered during the day and the sleep period through different wearables. The results showed that there are wide differences among diverse tools and these differences greatly influence how data collected and devices used are perceived.

Keywords: Quantified self · Personal informatics · Self-tracking · Wearable devices · Autoethnography

1 Introduction

Technological advances in wearable and ubiquitous technologies have recently opened new opportunities for Personal Informatics (PI). These systems aim to leverage sensors and mobile devices for collecting personal information in order to trigger self-reflection and enhance self-knowledge [1].

While first PI systems were employed mainly in clinical purposes for supporting patients in self-tracking dysfunctional behaviors or problematic medical conditions, they were then adopted by researchers, technical fanatics, and members of the Quantified Self community. Quantified Selfers use them to discover factors that may influence their behaviors, and are engaged in self-experimentation, i.e. the practice of systematically changing aspects of daily lives in order to discover variables that affect physical parameters, psychological states, and, by and large, aspects of daily life [2, 3]. However, thanks to the recent diffusion of wearable devices on the market, we are assisting to the commercialization of a plethora of tools that track a variety of personal information, from steps to sleep, from posture to arousal levels, from heartbeat to blood pressure.

© Springer International Publishing Switzerland 2016
M. Antona and C. Stephanidis (Eds.): UAHCI 2016, Part I, LNCS 9737, pp. 351–358, 2016.
DOI: 10.1007/978-3-319-40250-5_34

These instruments take mainly the form of wearables that users can choose according to their needs: for example, physical activity can be traced by necklaces (Misfit Shine), bracelets (Jawbone Up), watches (Apple Watch), or mobile apps that run on the user's smartphone (Moves). All these technologies measure steps by leveraging not only different forms, that can be differently integrated in people's daily lives and personal styles, but also different technologies and algorithms, which can affect the data accuracy.

Moving from these considerations, we aimed at understanding whether there were significant differences in the reported measures and their possible causes (e.g., characteristics of the device, the position in which they were worn, etc). Moreover, we aim at studying the possible effects of these differences on the perceived accuracy of the gathered data and on the consequent perceived reliability of the device. To this aim, we carried out a four-week autoethnography, monitoring the number of steps, the distance covered during the day and the sleep period with different devices. The results of the study are somehow surprising: (i) the gathered data for the same target parameter were very different depending on the device used, and the difference depended mainly on where the devices were positioned and on the user's habits; (ii) this affected the perceived reliability of the devices fostering the research of alternative strategies for accounting the data collected.

The paper is structured as follow. Section 2 provides the most relevant related work in relation of technologies for self-tracking and their reliability. Section 3 provides a picture of the practice of autoethnography both in anthropology and in Human-Computer Interaction. Section 4 describes the setting of our research while Sect. 5 describes its results. Finally, Sect. 6 concludes the paper providing the future directions of the work.

2   Related Work

Different works have explored how users perceive accuracy and reliability of wearable devices and ubiquitous technologies.

Kay et al. [4], for example, investigated how users perceive accuracy, finding how they react negatively when perceive inaccuracies and which kind of unrealistic expectations they have about their weight. Lazar et al. [7], in their study on why and how users abandon their smart devices, noted how they place a great deal of importance on accuracy, impacting the kind of devices they choose and keep using, and being one of the main cause of the abandonment of these self-tracking tools.

Consolvo et al. [5] found differences in participants' reactions to diverse kinds of errors in detecting data. They found seven types of errors made by the fitness device they were evaluating: (i) errors in the start time; (ii) errors in the duration; (iii) errors about confusing an activity it was trained to infer with another it was trained to infer; (iv) errors about confusing an activity it was not trained to infer with one it was trained to infer; (v) failures to detect an activity it was trained to infer; (vi) failures to detect an activity it was not trained to infer; and (vii) errors in detecting an activity when none occurred. Participants were particularly frustrated when the device failed to detect any activity when they performed an activity that the tool was trained to infer, or when the device detected an activity when none occurred: these two kinds of error questioned the overall credibility of the device. The other type of perceived error that had a great impact on the device's credibility was when the device detected an activity when none occurred.

Mackinlay [8], instead, focused on how users test the accuracy of a device's measurements, reporting barriers in evaluating and bettering the accuracy of their data due to the limited visibility of the system's status that undermined the users' endeavors in calibrating and testing the device.

Yang et al. [6] analyzed 600 Amazon reviews and interviewed 24 participants describing the different methods that users employ to assess accuracy of their self-tracking devices identifying the issues they encountered. They found that differences in users' expectations, physical characteristics, types of activities and lifestyle made them to have different perceptions of the devices' accuracy. The authors conclude how it is essential to focus on how users perceive and assess accuracy of their data in order to determine the reliability of the self-tracking devices. They further suggest (i) to support testability, (ii) to increase transparency of what these instruments can and cannot recognize and (iii) to allow for ways to calibrate the device to personal movement patterns and purposes, enabling users "to record unique movements into a device to let the device know which movements to record and which to ignore" [6].

3   The Autoethnographic Method

We employed an autoethnographic method in order to detect differences among different self-tracking devices and the impact they may have on the user experience. Autoethnography is an ethnographic method in which the fieldworker's experience is investigated together with the experience of the other social actors observed. It is considered valuable on its own and it is reported in the ethnographic recounting [9]. This makes autoethnography close to the autobiographical genres of narration, tying the personal to the social and the cultural in a multi-level form of description of reality [10]. The autoethnographer uses her self-observation and the episodes happened to her as a starting point to make reflections on cultural and social accounts, for returning then to her self and her interpretations of what she observed.

"Autoethnography requires that we observe ourselves observing, that we interrogate what we think and believe, and that we challenge our own assumptions, asking over and over if we have penetrated as many layers of our own defenses, fears, and insecurities as our project requires" [11]. Goodall [13] stresses that good autoethnography "completely dissolves any idea of distance, doesn't produce 'findings,' isn't generalizable, and only has credibility when self-reflexive, and authority when richly vulnerable… When it is done well, we can learn previously unspoken, unknown things about culture and communication from it"

Autoethnography has been employed in HCI for evaluating technologies and gaining empathy with users of various types of devices [16]. It has been used in autobiographical design as a design research method that "drawing on extensive, genuine usage by those creating or building the system" allows designers "to uncover detailed, subtle understandings that they likely wouldn't have found with other user-centered design techniques because they might seem unremarkable" [14].

The recent popularity of this kind of self-study has to be retraced to the need of finding less-demanding techniques than traditional ethnographic methods, which are very expensive in terms of time and costs [15]. "Typically, ethnography will take place over a period of several months with at least the same amount of time spent in analysis and interpretations of the observations" [Bentley]. So they can be inscribed in those approaches called as "rapid ethnography", which aims to understand users and their environments in a shortened timeframe [18].

O'Kane et al. [16], for example, used autoethnography for evaluating a wrist blood pressure monitor used by people with conditions of hypertension. They found that this method enables researchers "to understand and empathize with the experiences mobile device users can face in difficult to access contexts", allowing them "to better understand user experiences with mobile devices, including mobile medical technology, especially during non-routine times that can be difficult to study in-situ with traditional user studies" [16]. By using this method we tried to overcome the difficulties in observing users in private setting, such as during sleep, gathering a variety of data that would have been impossible to collect otherwise.

4   Ethnographic Setting

In the light of the aspects identified above and the chosen autoethnography methodology, we choose for a four week session of self-observation wearing different kinds of wearable devices.

The parameters that we decided to compare were the *steps* and the estimated *distance* covered during the day and the total amount of *sleep* (also segmented into *light/heavy sleep* and *awake time)* for each sleep cycle.

The wearable instruments have been differentiated depending on the model and the position on the body; it was also used an application running background on the phone in order to collect data during the day (*steps* and *distance*).

The purpose of the experiment was to understand, in an explorative way, whether there were significant differences in the resulting measures and whether they could be attributed to the characteristics of the devices or to the position in which they were worn. The objects chosen in particular were the following, each one placed in a different position on the ethnographer's body (the first author):

- Withings Activité on the right wrist: the Withings Activité is primarily a classical watch that also measured *steps* and *sleep,* it does not require to be recharged and it is waterproof, this will let you keep it continuously with no need to ever separate from it.
- Shine Misfits necklace: the Misfits Shine is a waterproof unit that can be worn in various positions, the one that offers the least friction is the use in combination with the necklace accessory. It does not require to be recharged.

- Sony SWR30 on the left wrist: the Sony SWR30 is a hybrid between a smartwatch and a wristband. It has indeed both telephony and logging features. It is waterproof and requires to be briefly recharged every 5/6 days.
- GoogleFit application running background on a Sony Xperia Z3. This application uses the accelerometer of the phone for the *steps* estimation and the GPS signal to calculate the *distance* covered.

The starting hypothesis has been that the recorded data would not suffer the influence of the body positioning, recording approximately the same values regardless of the device used. The app on the phone has been used as a method of comparison between wearable and non-wearable paradigm. Actually the result has been quite surprising. In the four weeks period the recorded data resulted completely different especially as a function of the body positioning of the device and the distortions in the accuracy caused by the peculiarities of the personal lifestyle.

5   Results

Analyzing *sleep* related data, there were several interesting findings, particularly related to the aspects that follow.

Regarding the *sleep* total amount logs the data results reliable with negligible deviations in the order of minutes. However, it has emerged as the *sleep* total amount recorded by the Misfit Shine worn as a necklace is always higher of about thirty minutes. This point, in relation to the personal experience appears due to the fact that the necklace considers the horizontal still position as "sleeping" not taking into account that in fact the user might be lying reading a book before falling asleep. So the *sleep* total amount will always be increased by the reading time in the bed. Furthermore, by comparing the data with the personal observation it is clear that the device with higher accuracy results the one worn on the right wrist (Withings Activité). This is because the right wrist makes possible to discriminate the browsing of pages in a horizontal still position as "non sleep" (obviously in the case of a left-handed user the most discriminating device would be the one on the left wrist).

What emerged in a rather surprising way is the total discrepancy between the different devices about the light sleep and deep sleep data. It was not possible to discriminate any specific reason related to the positioning of the device for the differences in the data collected, so we have to hypothesize that the cause relies in the poor quality of the algorithms that discriminate against the two types of *sleep*. About the *steps* logging the following evidences have emerged. The total *steps* amount is strongly affected by the location on the body on which the device is worn and the wearer's activities dictated by his specific lifestyle. Indeed in relation to the data collected by Withings Activité on the right wrist it has been observed that on days in which the tester has performed much talk in public (meetings, presentations, etc.) *steps* were very biased towards high figures due to the gesticulation of the speech. On the other hand the opposite effect was found in some other lifestyle variables. In particular, the data has been surprisingly distorted toward low figures for the device worn on both wrists for two conditions. The first one is about walking while pushing a stroller. In this case probably the algorithm does not register the dangling of the hands and does not log the activity as *steps*. The second one occurs walking while carrying a moderately heavy bag (e.g. a small suitcase) depending which hand holds the bag. Lastly we recorded a highly distorted *steps* data toward low figures for the phone app due to the fact that the device failed to record in all the occasions when the phone was placed outside of the user's pockets (e.g. weekend, sports, home, etc.).

About the covered distance the data appear completely unreliable: this does not seem due to the position on the body but mainly in relation to the calculation algorithms embedded by the device manufacturer. The conversion from *steps* to *distance* covered appears totally arbitrary, making this the more improbable data among the information collected. The coupling of geo positioning does not seem to improve the accuracy since most of the *steps* are made indoor on the same spot (gps geo positioning seems to work better for outdoor sport situations, like running, hiking, etc.).

In general, on the weekend all the data appear distorted by incomplete or peculiar usage of the devices due to different life activities (i.e. working in the garden, playing with kids, etc.).

Because all the distortions in the measures noted by the ethnographer, however unexpected, he developed a quite disturbing feeling. In particular, the ethnographer had the impression that the devices were drawing, despite the limited nature of data collected, a false self, an image in which the ethnographer could not identify himself. The impression was that the measures were counterfeiting his self-perception.

In the light of these aspects that have become evident at the beginning of the autoethnography the ethnographer developed some strategies targeted to consider only the data streams deserving good accuracy in relation with his personal lifestyle. For example, the total *sleep* duration data stream he considered closer to reality was the one coming from the right wrist (Withings Activitè). Instead, the accuracy related to heavy/light sleep patterns remained completely unknown for the above reasons.

In terms of total *steps* instead the more accurate data stream was considered the one provided by the Misfits Shine necklace as its position on the body was not affected by the oscillation (or not) of the arms. Even in this case, however, the measures of the distance covered and the calories burned appeared totally unreliable and obscure.

It appears that even if all the devices could be able to record several measures (e.g. *Sleep + Steps*) no one resulted enough accurate in all the measures: this led to the necessity of splitting on two different devices, in two different parts of the body the recording of the different data streams.

From these considerations some design insights can be derived such as the manufacturer's need to consider different designs for different usage styles induced by different types of users with different habits (e.g. reading in the bed, pushing a stroller, carrying a folder, gesturing or drawing a lot during work time). These could be condensed into a few personas that can lead to different models of the same device or different tracking algorithms on the same device. This customization may be transferred directly into the experience of the user by collecting certain aspects of her habits that may impact on the accuracy of the device, possibly also advising her on the best body location in which to wear the device in relation to her personal lifestyle.

6   Conclusion and Future Work

The goal of this paper is to study the differences in the measures reported by different PI tools and to investigate possible causes, as well as to discover if such differences have effects on the perceived data accuracy and device reliability. To this aim, we carried out a four-week autoethnography, monitoring the number of steps, the distance covered in a day and the sleep period through different tools. The results of the study showed that (i) there are wide differences due to the device position and the user lifestyle, and (ii) this lack of reliability requires the user to search for personal strategies for making the data accountable.

The next step will be to study different devices with more subjects, in order to confirm our initial findings. Moreover, we want to investigate in a deeper way the subjective users' perceptions with respect to the reliability of the device in relation to the accuracy of the data gathered. We want also to study whether different visualizations may affect the user's perception of the reliability of the data collected. A further interesting experiment would be a comparison with data gathered through a specialized medical device in order to evaluate which commercial device is actually more effective in terms of accuracy.

References

1. Li, I., Dey, A.K., Forlizzi, J.: A stage-based model of personal informatics systems. In: 28th International Conference on Human Factors in Computing Systems, pp. 557–566. ACM Press (2010)
2. Marcengo, A., Rapp, A.: Visualization of human behavior data: the quantified self. In: Huang, L.H., Huang, W. (eds.) Innovative Approaches of Data Visualization and Visual Analytics, pp. 236–265. IGI Global, Hershey (2013)
3. Rapp, A., Cena, F.: Self-monitoring and technology: challenges and open issues in personal informatics. In: Stephanidis, C., Antona, M. (eds.) UAHCI 2014, Part IV. LNCS, vol. 8516, pp. 613–622. Springer, Heidelberg (2014)
4. Kay, M., Morris, D., Schraefel, M.C., Kientz, J.A.: There's no such thing as gaining a pound: reconsidering the bathroom scale user interface. In: ACM International Joint Conference on Pervasive and Ubiquitous Computing (UbiComp 2013), pp. 401–410 (2013)
5. Consolvo, S., McDonald, D.W., Toscos, T., Chen, M.Y., Froehlich, J., Harrison, B., Klasnja, P., LaMarca, A., LeGrand, L., Libby, R., Smith, I., Landay, J.A.: Activity sensing in the wild: a field trial of ubifit garden. In: Proceedings of the SIGCHI Conference on Human Factors in Computing Systems (CHI 2008), pp. 1797–1806 (2008)
6. Yang, R., Shin, E., Newman, M.N., Ackerman, M.S.: When fitness trackers don't 'fit': end-user difficulties in the assessment of personal tracking device accuracy. In: The 2015 ACM International Joint Conference on Pervasive and Ubiquitous Computing (UbiComp 2015), pp. 623–634. ACM, New York (2015)
7. Lazar, A., Koehler, C., Tanenbaum, J., Nguyen, D.H.: Why we use and abandon smart devices. In: the 2015 ACM International Joint Conference on Pervasive and Ubiquitous Computing (UbiComp 2015), pp. 635–646. ACM, New York (2015)
8. Mackinlay, M.: Phases of Accuracy Diagnosis:(In) visibility of System Status in the Fitbit. Intersect: The Stanford Journal of Science, Technology and Society 6, 2 (2013)

9. Tedlock, B.: From participant observation to the observation of participation: the emergence of narrative ethnography. J. Anthropol. Res. **47**(1), 69–94 (1991)

10. Ellis, C., Bochner, A.: Autoethnography, personal narrative, and personal reflexivity. In: Denzinand, N.K., Lincoln, Y.S. (eds.) Handbook of Qualitative Research, 2nd edn, pp. 733–768. Sage, Thousand Oaks (2000)

11. Jones, S.H., Adams, T.E., Ellis, C. (eds.): Handbook of autoethnography. Left Coast Press, Inc, Walnut Creek (2013)

12. Tami, S.: Performing autoethnography: an embodied methodological praxis. Qual. Inq. **7**(6), 706–732 (2001)

13. Goodall, Jr., H.L.: Notes for the autoethnography and autobiography panel NCA. National Communication Association Convention in New York City (1998)

14. Neustaedter, C., Sengers, P.: Autobiographical design: what you can learn from designing for yourself. Interactions **19**(6), 28–33 (2012)

15. Cunningham, S.J., Jones, M.: Autoethnography: a tool for practice and education. In: the 6th ACM SIGCHI New Zealand Chapter's International Conference on Computer-Human Interaction: Making CHI Natural (CHINZ 2005), pp. 1–8. ACM, New York (2005)

16. O'Kane, A.A., Rogers, Y., Blandford, A.E.: Gaining empathy for non-routine mobile device use through autoethnography. In: the 32nd Annual ACM Conference on Human Factors in Computing Systems (CHI 2014), pp. 987–990. ACM, New York (2014)

17. Bentley, R., Hughes, J.A., Randall, D., Rodden, T., Sawyer, P., Shapiro, D., Sommerville, I.: Ethnographically informed systems design for air traffic control. In: Conference on Computer Supported Cooperative Work, pp. 123–129 (1992)

18. Millen, D.R.: Rapid ethnography: time deepening strategies for HCI field research. In: Boyarski, D., Kellogg, W.A. (eds.) the 3rd Conference on Designing Interactive Systems: Processes Practices Methods and Techniques (DIS 2000). ACM, New York (2000)

Work Motivating Factors of the Communications in a Crowd-Powered Microvolunteering Site

Takahiro Miura[1]([✉]), Shoma Arita[2], Atsushi Hiyama[2], Masatomo Kobayashi[3], Toshinari Itoko[3], Junichiro Sawamura[4], and Michitaka Hirose[2]

[1] Institute of Gerontology, The University of Tokyo, 7-3-1, Hongo,
Bunkyo-ku, Tokyo 113-8656, Japan
`miu@iog.u-tokyo.ac.jp`
[2] Graduate School of Information Science and Technology, The University of Tokyo,
7-3-1, Hongo, Bunkyo-ku, Tokyo 113-8656, Japan
[3] IBM Research – Tokyo, 19-21 Hakozaki, Nihonbashi, Chuo, Tokyo 103-8510, Japan
[4] Japan Braille Library, 1-23-4 Takadanobaba, Shinjuku-ku, Tokyo 169-8586, Japan

Abstract. Various systems have been developed to support and motivate volunteer activities for people with disabilities. "Minna de DAISY" is a microvolunteering system, powered by an open-source social networking system and web application, of character corrections. This system demonstrated that digital books could be efficiently produced for the visually impaired through the manual correction of errors using volunteers. According to participant interviews, those who were aware of their social contribution had a higher motivation to do social work. The feeling of community involvement promoted continuous participation. However, these studies do not precisely discuss the contribution of communication between system managers and participants. Some literature reported that interactions in a social network improved participant awareness of the purpose of their work. In this study, we aim to demonstrate the effect of communication on participant motivation and likelihood to continue microvolunteering.

Keywords: Crowdsourcing · Motivation · Communication · Social networking · Microvolunteering · Facilitation

1 Introduction

Along with the increased popularity of crowdsourcing, an increasing number of crowd-powered volunteering websites have emerged. There have been conceptual studies that aim to help people with visual impairments using volunteers. The *social accessibility* program proposed by Takagi et al. aims to improve the accessibility of inaccessible websites [26]. *VizWiz* proposed by Bigham et al. enables visually impaired smartphone users to identify items in the real world [3]. We also proposed and evaluated a crowdsourced digitalization concept for handwritten real-world accessibility information [22]. From the results of these studies, we

© Springer International Publishing Switzerland 2016
M. Antona and C. Stephanidis (Eds.): UAHCI 2016, Part I, LNCS 9737, pp. 359–370, 2016.
DOI: 10.1007/978-3-319-40250-5_35

show that the collective power of crowdsourcing volunteers can improve accessibility more quickly than using only local volunteers.

Recently, Kobayashi et al. developed a microvolunteering system called *Minna de DAISY* (the "DAISY by everyone" in English), [19] powered by the open-sourced social networking system (SNS) OpenPNE, and a character corrections web application [16,23]. This system showed that by using volunteers, it was possible to efficiently manually correct errors in text DAISY (Digital Accessible Information SYstem) that had resulted from the optical character recognition (OCR) of scanned books. They analyzed both motivated and unmotivated system participants and the factors that contributed to their motivation levels [19]. According to interviews, participants who were aware of their social contributions had more motivation towards social work, and their feeling of community identification promoted continuous participation. They also reported that there were encouraging effects associated with game-like feedback and visualization elements.

However, these studies did not precisely discuss or analyze the effect of communication between system managers and participants. Some literature reported that interactions in company's and business' SNSs are one of the most important factors towards work performance [8]. In this study, we aim to demonstrate the effects of communications within the SNS on the participants' motivation to microvolunteer. We mainly analyzed communication logs in our microvolunteering system as mentioned above, and investigated its influences on volunteers' actions, such as their continuous involvement and performance.

Our research questions are as follows:

Q1. What are some characteristics of communication with well-performing workers?

Q2. Can the responses of the microvolunteering site operator of contribute to the members' performances?

Q3. What are elements of the effective facilitation for operators?

2   Related Work and Issue on This Study

Various systems have been developed to support and motivate volunteer activities for people with disabilities. Recently, more assistive tools for facilitating volunteer activities have been developed. This is due in part to the popularization of smartphones for people with and without disabilities, and the increased awareness of the utility of concepts such as collective intelligence, crowdsourcing, and human computation [14,18,25].

2.1   Crowd-Powered Volunteering Systems for Securing Real-World Accessibility

One of the representative tools is *VizWiz*, proposed by Bigham, that can help visually impaired people recognize graphical information in the real world [3].

In the *VizWiz* scheme, when the visually impaired take and upload a picture of something they want to know, volunteers tell them what it is. Lasecki et al. have continued to improve and evaluate *VizWiz* by implementing a function for streaming video and audio [20]. In addition, a variety of similar tools are available using smartphones. Smartphone applications such as *TapTapSee*, *CamFind*, and *Talking Googles* can be downloaded from the *AppStore*, and be evaluated on their usability [13].

In addition to these applications, there are systems that share real-world accessibility conditions. Holone et al. developed a system that hovered entered accessibility conditions on the *OpenStreetMap* [12]. However, based on an evaluation of the system in Norway, it was reported that there were some issues, such as securing and sharing quality accessibility information, privacy, and security problems. Tarkiainen et al. proposed a web-based system for checking accessibility conditions in Finland [28]. In addition to what was done in Finland, Goncalves et al. developed a tool that easily shared accessibility conditions. They reported that by using the tool, users' awareness of environmental accessibility and their willingness to participate in volunteer activities was raised [10]. Hara et al. proposed a crowd-powered accessibility condition checker on bus stops using *Google Street View* [11]. In this system, crowd workers were asked to select the location of accessible or inaccessible bus stops and traffic signs. Based on the results of machine learning using the workers' markings, the system automatically recognized public transit locations. Moreover, Miura et al. proposed the concept of crowd-powered conversion that could convert handwritten accessibility information provided by professionals in disability service offices to electronically accessible information [22]. They compared crowd conversion results with the previous results from a real-world accessibility assessment [21], and then reported that the results from crowd worker input and assessment volunteers were similar. To improve information quality, like other researchers, the authors emphasized the importance of the facilitation of worker collaboration.

2.2 Microvolunteering Systems for the Accessibility of Web Materials and Downloadable Contents

In the last ten years, many studies focused on improving the accessibility of digital media have accumulated.

The *ALT-server*, one of the initial studies on securing web site accessibility, had volunteers enter alternative text for images on web pages [7]. *WebInSight* improved the efficiency of this scheme by combining it with image analysis [4]. Takagi et al. proposed the *social accessibility* concept system that improves the accessibility of inaccessible websites using volunteers [26]. In this concept system, when computer users with blindness, or volunteers, reported problems with an inaccessible web page, volunteers modified the problems according to system guides. Though these projects had some positive results, according to the study, the problem arose on how to ensure and sustain volunteer numbers [27]. They also pointed out the necessity of ensuring an effective motivating structure to maintain the worker community.

Various studies have examined the creation scheme of books for people with visual impairments. *Bookshare* created almost 0.3 million accessible books utilizing a combination of a library support system and a support framework for people with disabilities [1]. Kobayashi et al. proposed and evaluated a microvolunteering system [2] that can streamline the creation of accessible text DAISY books using crowdsourced volunteers [19]. According to their research, 537 participants, 34 % of which were seniors, conducted over 17 million micro-tasks, such as character corrections. In this system over 1100 text DAISY books were created in two years. They found that young and elderly participants contributed to the creation of text DAISY over the short and long-term, respectively. In addition, they were able to maintain participant motivation by helping them visualize their contributions. Since we expect that seniors will gradually become more interested in crowd work [6], additional studies are needed to discuss motivational maintenance methods that appeal to not only young but also senior crowd workers.

2.3   Analysis of Social Network Sites (SNSs)

Social network sites (SNSs) are web-based services that facilitate the creation of relationships among participants. According to Ellison's definition, these sites provide individuals with three functions: (1) constructing a public or semi-public profile within a bounded system, (2) articulating a list of other users with whom they share a connection, and (3) viewing and traversing their list of connections and those made by others within the system [9].

The relationship-building function provided by an SNS enables the provider to not only reinforce mutual connections among many unspecified members, but also to connect business partners and partners-to-be, and to record and analyze communication concerning specific events. For instance, in the case of a disastrous earthquake, a microblogging site provided their users with the ability to exchange their information. Specifically, they were able to exchange information on damages done and their evacuation location, in addition to sharing their feelings and comforting each other [24]. DiMicco et al. demonstrated that interactions in a company's SNS can enhance their awareness of their contribution to the company and thus enhance their work performance [8]. The *TurkOpticon* served as a quasi-union for crowd workers in the *Amazon Mechanical Turk* and helped facilitate a healthy relationship between clients and workers [15].

Most microvolunteering sites exploit SNS functions. A recent study by Kim et al. revealed that SNSs are able to engage younger generations in philanthropy. This is due to the social capital formed by SNSs that is used to promote awareness of volunteer activities [17]. The previously mentioned *VizWiz* incorporated characteristics of SNS and was released as VizWiz Social, which provided a friendsourcing function [5]. The aforementioned *Minna de DAISY* also integrated SNS elements, such as a forum and microblogging functions to facilitate smooth communications among the participants and managers [19]. These features particularly encourage young participants.

Table 1. The number of member IDs in the end of 2013, 2014, and 2015.

Year	2013	2014	2015
The number of new member IDs	299	149	314
The cumulative number of member IDs	299	448	762

However, to date, the type of interchanges contributing to motivating volunteer work remains unclear. In addition, in most other systems, little is known about how SNS communications vitalize users and increase microvolunteering awareness. Therefore, we decided to set research questions as mentioned above and analyze conversation logs from a microvolunteering site.

3   Materials and Method

The material includes the communication logs obtained from the microvolunteering system "Minna de DAISY" [2] in the period from October 2013 to December 2015 (800 days). The records can be divided into two types: members' microblogging comments and comments in the forum-type Q&A system. The former can be characterized as *Twitter*-like short comments displayed in a timeline-like manner. The latter can be categorized as a community-based bulletin board system that non-anonymized members mainly use to discuss how to correct OCRed books. The two logs include 1345 tweets and 3154 comments, respectively. These logs are associated with 537 member accounts (the number of IDs was 762, as shown in Table 1) and can be analyzed based on network analysis. Also, some of these tweets have tags including five category types such as general notices, requests for a text DAISY, notifications of brand new books, Q&A on corrections, and sandbox, as shown in the upper part of Table 2.

In this report, we mainly analyzed brief characteristics of the tweets. First, we added tags to the tweets that had no tag. The additional tags included seven categories such as communications, greetings, general Q&A, progress tweets, irregular notifications by administrators, server problems, and discussions on the system & interfaces, as shown in the lower part of Table 2. Then, we checked the relationship between characteristics of the participants and the corresponding tweets contents. Second, transitions of tweet communications and relationship among participants and the operator group were analyzed based on directed graphs of partial and entire periods. The graphs were generated with the R statistical language and the SNA package. At that time, we calculated some centrality indices and then discuss the participants' connections network of the microvolunteering site. The centrality indices included centralities of information, betweenness, PageRank, and degree, as illustrated in Table 4.

4   Results and Discussion

4.1   Tweets Categorization

Table 2 shows the tweets breakdown classified by brief and specific categories. The tweets in the notifications by the system & administrators category mainly included requests for a text DAISY that probably were posted by visually impaired volunteers. As expanding the scale of the microvolunteering site, this tendency became strong.

Table 2. Tweets breakdown classified by brief and specific categories in entire period (October 2013 – December 2015), 2013, 2014, and 2015. Since some of the tweets classified by the authors had some tags, a total of these tweets were larger than exact number of the tweets.

Category		Frequency			
Brief category	Specific category	Entire	2013	2014	2015
Notifications by the system & administrators	General notices	34	5	20	9
	Requests for a text DAISY	216	3	90	123
	Notifications of brand new books	197	63	129	5
	Q&A on corrections	184	57	31	96
	Sandbox	21	4	4	13
Subtotal:		652	132	274	246
Not notifications	Communications (Whole)	381	135	194	52
(Classified by the authors)	Communications, greeting	37	22	13	2
	Q&A, general	16	5	9	2
	Individual progress	47	18	21	8
	Irregular notices by administrators	107	18	67	22
	Server problems	76	7	39	30
	Discussions on the system & interfaces	133	29	99	5
Subtotal (tags):		797	234	442	121
Subtotal (exact number of tweets):		693	204	379	109
Total (tags):		1449	366	716	367
Total (exact number of tweets):		1345	336	653	355

In the category "not notifications," there were many irrelevant interactions to book corrections. However, the number and rate of these tweets tended to decrease (66 % (2013) → 51 % (2014) → 48 % (2015)). The same tendency can

Table 3. Tweets breakdown classified by tweeted participants category in entire period (October 2013 – December 2015), 2013, 2014, and 2015. These categories were defined by Kobayashi, et al. [19].

	Classified group (ref. Kobayashi, et al. [19])					
	Top performers	Spectators	Occasional workers	Longtailers	Unclassified	Admin. & system
2013	11 (16 %)	5 (7 %)	14 (21 %)	0 (0 %)	0 (0 %)	38 (56 %)
2014	36 (31 %)	4 (3 %)	3 (3 %)	4 (3 %)	0 (0 %)	71 (60 %)
2015	9 (26 %)	1 (3 %)	2 (6 %)	11 (31 %)	0 (0 %)	12 (34 %)
Entire	56 (25 %)	10 (5 %)	19 (9 %)	15 (7 %)	0 (0 %)	121 (55 %)

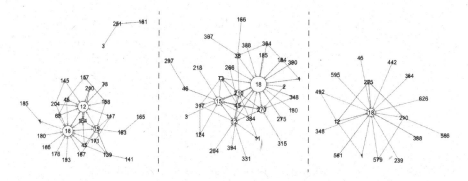

Fig. 1. Directed graphs of the participants' communications in 2013 (left), 2014 (middle), and 2015 (right). The size and the numbers of edges represent degree of connections and participants' IDs, respectively.

be observed in the tweets about individual progress. As the microvolunteering site matured, participants had become to communicate less each other and to concentrate more on their job. The discussions on system and interface in 2013 and 2014 are more than that in 2015. This fact was because the start-up stage of the microvolunteering site had more problems in the system architecture and the interface while in 2015, the interface became improved and sophisticated, and the participants became familiar with the system.

Table 3 shows the number of tweets in the category of "not notification" classified by the user performance. This user classification was employed along with the study by Kobayashi et al. [19]. Excluding the category "admin & system," the top performer group tweeted more than the other groups in all periods. In particular, the contents of top performers' tweets occupied most in all the categories in Table 3.

4.2   Directed Graphs and Centrality Indices

Figure 1 shows directed graphs of participants' tweets communications in 2013, 2014, and 2015. In all the periods, the participant #18 played a most

Table 4. Centrality indices calculated based on the directed graphs shown in Fig. 1. The indices includes information, betweenness, PageRank, and degree centralities.

2013

Order	ID	Information	ID	Betweenness	ID	PageRank	ID	Degree
1	18	1.08E-14	18	35.3	18	0.064	18	0.181
2	12	1.08E-14	15	18.8	12	0.047	12	0.142
3	15	1.08E-14	12	17	15	0.039	15	0.116
4	164	1.08E-14	139	5.6	251	0.023	164	0.065
5	45	1.08E-14	1	5.2	164	0.022	45	0.052
6	46	1.08E-14	163	5.2	139	0.02	46	0.052

2014

Order	ID	Information	ID	Betweenness	ID	PageRank	ID	Degree
1	18	7.435	18	38.2	18	0.061	18	0.154
2	15	5.279	15	19.7	15	0.035	15	0.089
3	210	4.622	12	10.5	12	0.025	12	0.065
4	270	4.379	35	8.2	270	0.025	210	0.065
5	12	4.011	270	6.4	210	0.024	270	0.065
6	45	3.458	210	6.1	45	0.019	45	0.049

2015

Order	ID	Information	ID	Betweenness	ID	PageRank	ID	Degree
1	18	11.465	18	85.8	18	0.053	18	0.435
2	12	2.898	210	12.2	210	0.014	12	0.116
3	210	2.599	12	1.2	12	0.013	210	0.116
4	275	2.564	275	0.8	275	0.01	275	0.087
5	579	1.787	1	0	579	0.007	1	0.058
6	1	1.78	2	0	1	0.007	492	0.058

important role in the interaction network, and the #12 and #15 also contributed much to the network. Since all of them belonged to the administrator group, the communications in the microvolunteering site resulted from the dedicated and frequent communications by the administrator group. Table 4 illustrates the top six centrality indices in the participants' group. The table indicated that #18 performed best in all the period and all the indices. This fact also suggested that the microvolunteering site comprised similar social network to star network. As time passed by, the relative influence of #18 tended to increase because the frequency of tweet communication decreased particularly in 2015. Excluding the administrator group, most of the participants with the high centralities such as #164, #251, #210 belonged to top performer group. This fact can be suggested that this kind of communication can promote the activities of the volunteers.

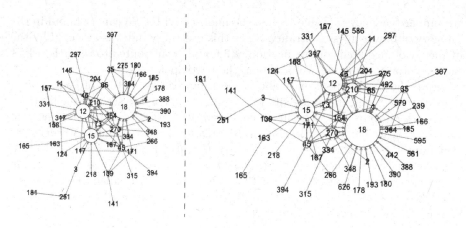

Fig. 2. Directed graphs of the participants' communications in 2013–2014 (left), and the entire period 2013–2015 (right). The size and the numbers of edges represent degree of connections and participants' IDs, respectively.

Table 5. Centrality indices calculated based on the directed graphs shown in Fig. 2. The indices includes information, betweenness, PageRank, and degree centralities.

2013–2014								
Order	ID	Information	ID	Betweenness	ID	PageRank	ID	Degree
1	18	6.983	18	32.2	18	0.066	18	0.134
2	15	6.109	15	22.3	15	0.041	15	0.084
3	12	5.403	12	9.6	12	0.034	12	0.074
4	210	4.385	3	5.1	210	0.02	210	0.045
5	45	3.896	46	4.6	45	0.019	45	0.04
6	164	3.871	45	4.1	270	0.019	270	0.04
2013–2015 (Entire period)								
Order	ID	Information	ID	Betweenness	ID	PageRank	ID	Degree
1	18	9.167	18	36.8	18	0.061	18	0.144
2	15	6.97	15	19.5	15	0.029	12	0.076
3	12	6.836	12	9.8	12	0.029	15	0.072
4	210	5.531	210	5.3	210	0.02	210	0.051
5	164	4.309	3	4.5	270	0.014	45	0.034
6	270	4.261	46	4.1	45	0.014	270	0.034

Figure 2 shows the transitions of the social network in the microvolunteering site. It can be found that there are the increase of the edges and the nodes and the connections concentration to the particular participants including administrators (#18, #12) and top performers (#210). Table 5 describes the top six centrality indices in the participants' group in the periods 2013–2014 and 2013–2015. There are similar tendency to Table 4 while the unobserved ID #3 can be found in the category of betweenness centrality. Since this centrality index is reflected by the frequency of mediated communication, #3 mainly contributed to the network as the mediator of communication among the participants.

From the results mentioned above, work motivating factors of communications in the microvolunteering site can be concluded as the smooth facilitations by operator group. Their frequent communications and diligent responses to volunteer participants can develop and increase the participants' awareness to contribute the site and continue the job on the site. The participants who conducted tweet communications tended to belong or came to belong to the group of top performers, though not even that, the group of longtailers. For motivating these performers, it is important for operators of microvolunteering site to interact them frequently and sincerely.

5   Conclusion and Future Work

For demonstrating the effects of communications within the social network on the participants' motivation to microvolunteer, we analyzed communication logs in the microvolunteering system named *Minna de DAISY*. We also discussed its influences on volunteers' actions, such as their continuous involvement and performance. The achievements of this report are as follows.

- Based on the results of the tweet breakdown, the participants belonging to top performer group tended to not only work more than the others but also communicate frequently in the social network on the microvolunteer site.
- Work motivating factors of communications in the microvolunteering site can be concluded as the smooth facilitations by operator group. In order to motivate these performers, it is important for operators of microvolunteering site to interact them frequently and sincerely.

Our future work includes more detailed analysis of the communication logs. Though we mainly analyzed the relationship of communicated participants, it is also important to check the specific contents of the logs.

Acknowledgments. This research was partially supported by the Japan Science and Technology Agency (JST) under the Strategic Promotion of Innovative Research and Development Program. We thank the staff members of the Japan Braille Library for their support and the programmers of the IBM Research Tokyo. We also thank all of the participants in the *Minna de DAISY*.

References

1. Bookshare. http://www.bookshare.org/
2. Minna de DAISY. https://ebis.cyber.t.u-tokyo.ac.jp/

3. Bigham, J.P., Jayant, C., Ji, H., Little, G., Miller, A., Miller, R.C., Miller, R., Tatarowicz, A., White, B., White, S. et al.: VizWiz: nearly real-time answers to visual questions. In: Proceedings of the 23nd Annual ACM Symposium on User Interface Software and Technology, pp. 333–342. ACM (2010)

4. Bigham, J.P., Kaminsky, R.S., Ladner, R.E., Danielsson, O.M., Hempton, G.L.: WebInSight: making web images accessible. In: Proceedings of the 8th International ACM SIGACCESS Conference on Computers and Accessibility, Assets 2006, NY, USA, pp. 181–188. ACM, New York (2006). http://doi.acm.org/10.1145/1168987.1169018

5. Brady, E.: Using social microvolunteering to answer visual questions from blind users. SIGACCESS Access. Comput. **111**, 26–29 (2015). http://doi.acm.org/10.1145/2809904.2809910

6. Brewer, R., Morris, M.R., Piper, A.M.: "Why would anybody do this?" Older adults' understanding of and experiences with crowd work. In: Proceedings of the SIGCHI Conference on Human Factors in Computing Systems, CHI 2016 (2016)

7. Dardailler, D.: The ALT-server ("An eye for an alt") (1997). https://www.w3.org/WAI/altserv.htm

8. DiMicco, J., Millen, D.R., Geyer, W., Dugan, C., Brownholtz, B., Muller, M.: Motivations for social networking at work. In: Proceedings of the 2008 ACM Conference on Computer Supported Cooperative Work, pp. 711–720. ACM (2008)

9. Ellison, N.B., et al.: Social network sites: definition, history, and scholarship. J. Comput.-Mediated Commun. **13**(1), 210–230 (2007)

10. Goncalves, J., Kostakos, V., Hosio, S., Karapanos, E., Lyra, O.: IncluCity: using contextual cues to raise awareness on environmental accessibility. In: Proceedings of the 15th International ACM SIGACCESS Conference on Computers and Accessibility, p. 17. ACM (2013)

11. Hara, K., Azenkot, S., Campbell, M., Bennett, C.L., Le, V., Pannella, S., Moore, R., Minckler, K., Ng, R.H., Froehlich, J.E.: Improving public transit accessibility for blind riders by crowdsourcing bus stop landmark locations with google street view: an extended analysis. ACM Trans. Accessible Comput. (TACCESS) **6**(2), 5 (2015)

12. Holone, H., Misund, G.: People helping computers helping people: navigation for people with mobility problems by sharing accessibility annotations. In: Miesenberger, K., Klaus, J., Zagler, W.L., Karshmer, A.I. (eds.) ICCHP 2008. LNCS, vol. 5105, pp. 1093–1100. Springer, Heidelberg (2008)

13. Holton, B.: A Review of the TapTapSee, CamFind, and Talking Goggles Object Identification Apps for the iPhone (2013). http://www.afb.org/afbpress/pub.asp?DocID=aw140704

14. Howe, J.: The rise of crowdsourcing. Wired Mag. **14**(6), 1–4 (2006)

15. Irani, L.C., Silberman, M.S.: Turkopticon: interrupting worker invisibility in amazon mechanical turk. In: Proceedings of the SIGCHI Conference on Human Factors in Computing Systems, CHI 2013, NY, USA, pp. 611–620. ACM, New York (2013). http://doi.acm.org/10.1145/2470654.2470742

16. Ishihara, T., Itoko, T., Sato, D., Tzadok, A., Takagi, H.: Transforming Japanese archives into accessible digital books. In: Proceedings of the 12th ACM/IEEE-CS Joint Conference on Digital Libraries, pp. 91–100. ACM (2012)

17. Kim, Y., Lee, W.N.: Networking for philanthropy: increasing volunteer behavior via social networking sites. Cyberpsychology, Behav. Soc. Network. **17**(3), 160–165 (2014)

18. Kittur, A., Chi, E.H., Suh, B.: Crowdsourcing user studies with mechanical turk. In: Proceedings of the SIGCHI Conference on Human Factors in Computing Systems, pp. 453–456. ACM (2008)

19. Kobayashi, M., Arita, S., Itoko, T., Saito, S., Takagi, H.: Motivating multi-generational crowd workers in social-purpose work. In: Proceedings of the 18th ACM Conference on Computer Supported Cooperative Work and Social Computing, pp. 1813–1824. ACM (2015)

20. Lasecki, W.S., Thiha, P., Zhong, Y., Brady, E., Bigham, J.P.: Answering visual questions with conversational crowd assistants. In: Proceedings of the 15th International ACM SIGACCESS Conference on Computers and Accessibility, ASSETS 2013, NY, USA, pp. 18:1–18:8. ACM, New York (2013). http://doi.acm.org/10.1145/2513383.2517033

21. Miura, T., Yabu, K.i., Sakajiri, M., Ueda, M., Suzuki, J., Hiyama, A., Hirose, M., Ifukube, T.: Social platform for sharing accessibility information among people with disabilities: evaluation of a field assessment. In: Proceedings of the 15th International ACM SIGACCESS Conference on Computers and Accessibility, ASSETS 2013, NY, USA, pp. 65:1–65:2. ACM, New York (2013). http://doi.acm.org/10.1145/2513383.2513391

22. Miura, T., Yabu, K., Sakajiri, M., Ueda, M., Hiyama, A., Hirose, M., Ifukube, T.: Evaluation of crowdsourced accessibility information sharing. J. Technol. Persons Disabil. 3, 232–245 (2015)

23. Neudecker, C., Tzadok, A.: User collaboration for improving access to historical texts. Liber Q. 20(1), 119–128 (2010)

24. Qu, Y., Huang, C., Zhang, P., Zhang, J.: Microblogging after a major disaster in China: a case study of the 2010 Yushu earthquake. In: Proceedings of the ACM 2011 Conference on Computer Supported Cooperative Work, CSCW 2011, NY, USA, pp. 25–34. ACM, New York (2011). http://doi.acm.org/10.1145/1958824.1958830

25. Quinn, A.J., Bederson, B.B.: Human computation: a survey and taxonomy of a growing field. In: Proceedings of the SIGCHI Conference on Human Factors in Computing Systems, CHI 2011, NY, USA, pp. 1403–1412. ACM, New York (2011). http://doi.acm.org/10.1145/1978942.1979148

26. Takagi, H., Kawanaka, S., Kobayashi, M., Itoh, T., Asakawa, C.: Social accessibility: achieving accessibility through collaborative metadata authoring. In: Proceedings of the 10th International ACM SIGACCESS Conference on Computers and Accessibility, pp. 193–200. ACM (2008)

27. Takagi, H., Kawanaka, S., Kobayashi, M., Sato, D., Asakawa, C.: Collaborative web accessibility improvement: challenges and possibilities. In: Proceedings of the 11th International ACM SIGACCESS Conference on Computers and Accessibility, pp. 195–202. ACM (2009)

28. Tarkiainen, M., Back, A., Hulkkonen, J., Konkkola, K.: Crowdsourcing accessibility related information from POI-destinations in Finland. In: 18th ITS World Congress (2011)

Creating a Sense of Unity: From Quantified Self to Qualitative Space

Fatemeh Moradi[✉] and Mikael Wiberg

Department of Informatics, Umeå University, Umeå, Sweden
{fatemeh.moradi,mikael.wiberg}@informatik.umu.se

Abstract. The design and usage of Personal Informatics (PI) systems have been subjects of rapidly growing interest in recent years. PI systems are typically designed to monitor individuals' physical activity and encourage them to be more active, thereby 'hacking' the habit of prolonged sitting. Most PI systems focus solely on collecting quantitative data to encourage self-reflection and are therefore sometimes discussed in terms of the Quantified Self movement. However, this perspective is wholly focused on individual bodily movements and neglects the role of architectural spaces. This paper discusses an ongoing project focused on PI systems design at the intersection of bodily movements and the office as an architectural space. Taking this as a point of departure, we introduce a simple prototype interactive lamp known as the NEAT lamp, which was designed, implemented and evaluated in relation to everyday office work. The rationale underpinning the prototype's design is presented, followed by the results of a real-world evaluation of its effects in practice. We also discuss the role of the NEAT lamp as an ambient light that promotes awareness of sedentary behavior in the office as an open architectural space. Finally, we highlight the role of ambient displays as a medium for creating a sense of unity between the self and the architectural space, and propose that this observation suggests that we should move the discussion away from "quantified selves" towards qualitative spaces.

Keywords: Personal informatics · Design · Notification systems · Ambient light · Architectural space

1 Introduction

Interest in the design and development of personal data gathering systems has recently increased substantially because of their usefulness in the context of self-reflection and self-monitoring (Swan 2012). Concepts such as Personal Informatics (PI) and the Quantified Self (QS) have motivated researchers in the field of Human-Computer Interaction (HCI) to explore various aspects and designs of such interactive systems (Li et al. 2010; Ploderer et al. 2014). Many personal informatics systems have been designed, ranging from mobile applications to wearable sensors (Swan 2012; Ploderer et al. 2014). In addition, some researchers have explored novel ways of designing, resulting in the creation of ambient displays and informative art pieces intended to improve efficiency in self-reflective applications (see e.g. (Jafarinaimi et al. 2005; Hazlewood et al. 2011; Burns et al. 2012)).

© Springer International Publishing Switzerland 2016
M. Antona and C. Stephanidis (Eds.): UAHCI 2016, Part I, LNCS 9737, pp. 371–381, 2016.
DOI: 10.1007/978-3-319-40250-5_36

The term "Personal Informatics" first gained currency among the HCI community in 2010 (Li et al. 2010), and the majority of the research interest in such systems is rooted in a utilitarian perspective whereby PI and QS are seen as tools for promoting self-reflection and behavior change (Ploderer et al. 2014). More recently, a number of researchers have expanded their focus beyond traditional PI research by attempting to promote certain experiences as well as the gathering of quantified personal data (Elsden et al. 2015). These investigations have focused on mapping out novel design opportunities and challenges to broaden the field of PI and QS. In particular, they have emphasized revisiting reported experiences with similar systems from a more critical and holistic point of view (Wiberg and Moradi 2013; Ohlin and Olsson 2015). As suggested by Kirk et al. (2015), this expanded focus will open up new horizons for design and research opportunities within our field.

Beyond the traditional first-person/user-centered perspective surrounding the design of PI systems, our work suggests that it is important to recall that bodily movement is affected by (and in some cases, configured by) the surrounding architectural space. An architectural space can fuse our image of ourselves and articulate our experience of the being-in-the world. One important architectural space in which many people spend much of their adulthood is the traditional office environment. According to the United States department of labor, adults aged 25 to 54 with children spend more than 8 h per day on work-related activities in office spaces (Bureau of Labor Statics).

Throughout history, designers and technocrats have planned workspaces in order to increase productivity and efficiency (Moradi and Wiberg 2013). As a result of this development, our bodies have become significantly inactivated and sedentary in the physical architectural spaces where work is performed, i.e. in office spaces. During the 80 s and the 90 s there was a heavy focus on office workspace design from an ergonomics perspective. During this period "efficient" workspaces were designed – but this "efficiency" was defined in terms of reducing or even eliminating physical movement in office spaces (Barnes 1953; Corlett 1983). As a consequence, prolonged sitting emerged as a risk factor associated with increasing all-cause mortality as well as mortality due to cardiovascular disease (CVD), certain types of cancer and non-CVD/non-cancer mortality in adults (Levine 2004; Van der Ploeg et al. 2012). In addition, the reduction in physical activity together with increased food consumption has increased the risk of weight gain and obesity, which is associated with an increased risk of cardiovascular disease (CVD), certain types of cancer, and non-CVD/non-cancer mortality.

The interdisciplinary InPhAct research project aims to address the increasingly important health problems associated with increasingly stationary working patterns in modern office workspaces. In our project we are addressing this problem from a multitude of perspectives and accordingly our project team includes researchers with various backgrounds and competences from disciplines including Informatics, Medicine, and Architecture. This allows us to simultaneously adopt medical, architectural and technological perspectives when attempting to determine how the traditional office environment, as a potentially dangerous setting from a health perspective, could be re-imagined and ultimately re-designed. Our main objective is to identify ways of increasing physical activity in office workspaces and thus to break the habit of prolonged sitting during office hours.

The authors of this work have backgrounds in Informatics and HCI. Here, we seek to contribute to the overall project by answering the following research question: *"How can we design an ambient notification system that stimulates increased bodily movement during office hours and how can we understand what this reconfiguration of the office space means not only in technical terms but also from an architectural point of view?"* With this question as our point of departure, we use this paper to present a suitable notification system (the NEAT lamp), the conceptual work that led to the design of the NEAT lamp, and some preliminary results from an early evaluation of this prototype system.

2 Our Research Approach

In our project we have been influenced by the concept-driven design method (Stolterman and Wiberg 2010), which we have taken as our guiding approach for advancing the design of PI systems in office environments. This method focuses heavily on producing knowledge in the form of theoretical and conceptual developments and then articulating and manifesting this knowledge in the form of a prototype (Stolterman and Wiberg 2010). Broadly, it can be described as an explicitly concept-driven design method that emphasizes theorizing about the nature of the interactions of interest and then manifesting the identified concepts in a concrete design.

To establish an appropriate and well-grounded concept, we conducted an ethnographic study in a contemporary office-based workplace over a period of 80 days in the fall of 2013 in order to understand local movement and mobility in the landscape. The aim of this study was to characterize the bodily movements and mobility patterns of office workers within an office-based landscape. Unlike other ethnographic studies that have investigated mobility in workspaces (Bellotti and Bly 1996; Luff and Heath 1998), we did not focus on the employees' working procedures and the role of mobility in increasing workers' efficiency. Instead, our main interest was in assessing the role of architectural elements in fostering bodily movements among the office workers. Because we were interested in whole–body movement, data were gathered by mapping the walking paths taken by workers. By mapping and drawing office workers' daily walking paths, we gathered visual data, which were supplemented with field notes, informal interviews and photographs (see Fig. 1).

Observation alone was not considered to provide a sufficiently robust foundation for theorizing on the nature of the interactions that occurred in the workspace or for the development of novel prototype concepts. However, we considered it necessary to immerse ourselves in the office space to acquire a deeper understanding of the context, forms, materials and cultural values that were hidden in the work environment. We therefore considered our preliminary ethnographic study to be an essential component in the process of producing theoretical and conceptual knowledge. The nature of design ethnographic studies requires the researcher to seek inspiration everywhere during the field study (Clarke 2010). During our observational study, we quickly became sensitive towards particular objects in the workspace and their contexts as architectural elements. In particular, the apparent relationship between the two provided a valuable inspiration

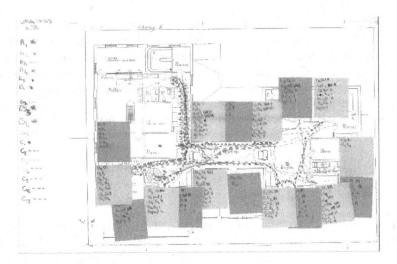

Fig. 1. An example of the visual data collected during our ethnographic study. This data presents the walking paths of the office workers during a typical working day.

for our design by revealing the potential benefits of harmonizing the office workers' bodily movements with the architectural space and thus creating a sense of unity.

NEAT-Lamp. The interdisciplinary perspective adopted in this work gave the advantage of being able to integrate the results of our ethnographic study with previously published research on sedentary behavior in offices from the fields of Medicine and Architecture. The Public Health literature includes several publications describing efforts to increase physical activity in workspaces and break the habit of prolonged sitting (McAlpine et al. 2007; Thorp et al. 2012; Van der Ploeg et al. 2012). One of the concepts that has been explored extensively in this context is the role of "Non-Exercise Activity Thermogenesis" (NEAT) in reducing the risk of chronic disease associated with prolonged sitting (Levine 2004). Put simply, NEAT is any physical activity other than intensive exercise, such as standing while working or taking a short walk.

Returning to the project's initial objectives, we explored ways to develop a concept-based prototype that would foster physical activity in workspaces and also achieve saturation within the context of the office space. Based on our study, we quickly concluded that the new design should be a simple subtle prototype that would not demand extra attention from the office worker. In other words, we were looking for a non-intrusive design that would not disturb the workflow within the office. Keeping simplicity as our driving motto in this process forced us to analyze and evaluate the situation at hand in a very fundamental way, taking our cue from a statement made by John Maeda in his book *The Law of Simplicity*: "simplicity is about subtracting the obvious, and adding the meaningful" (Maeda 2006).

Because the project's primary aim was to break the habit of prolonged sitting and increase physical activity in offices, we were drawn to the simple concept of notifications. Modern digital lives are filled with various notifications, especially in the context of office work. While office workers are familiar with the concept of being notified, these notifications are typically screen-based and serve work-related purposes. Such screen-based notifications are striking and demanding. We conceptualized the NEAT-Lamp prototype by referring back to the idea of increasing NEAT as an effective way of breaking the habit of prolonged sitting and promoting physical activity while keeping the design simple and subtle, and without imposing extra burdens on the office workers. The NEAT-Lamp was conceptualized around the idea of designing a notification system in the form of an ambient display with the form factor of a traditional desk lamp (see Fig. 2). In this way, the NEAT lamp can retain the advantage of being a notification system without becoming a burden or a distraction during the process of work. The design of peripheral display-based notification systems intended to break the habit of prolonged sitting has been explored before (Jafarinaimi et al. 2005). However, these designs have not been evaluated anything like so thoroughly as the NEAT-Lamp.

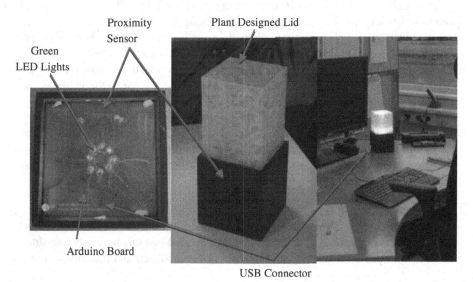

Fig. 2. The NEAT-Lamp and its components. In the right you can see how the NEAT-Lamp notifies an office worker of sedentary behavior.

From a technical perspective, the NEAT-Lamp is a sensor-based notification system connected to a computer via a USB connector and it is placed on the table in front of the office worker (see Fig. 2). If the data from the sensor indicates that the worker has been stationary for 25 min or more, the NEAT-Lamp will turn on. Similarly, the lamp will automatically turn off if the office worker changes his/her position. Whereas most screen-based notification systems have timers, the lamp avoids presenting any information regarding time. This was a deliberate decision intended to prevent the worker from being unduly distracted by the lamp. Moreover, reducing the information supplied in a given message increases the attention that is paid to it and makes us appreciate all that is less, more (Maeda 2006). To promote a sense of affiliation to this simple lamp, we decided to refine the aesthetics of the prototype. As shown in the figures, the lamp emits green light through a translucent plastic lid bearing a plant-like pattern that is intended to remind people in the office of living plants and thus make the lamp more meaningful (see Fig. 2). In addition to being a tangible artifact that gives workers reminders to avoid sitting for prolonged periods, the NEAT lamp was found to have a hidden conceptual feature that was discovered during our second study.

This prototype was tested several times during the design process and then in a three-week pilot study. Based on the results obtained in these tests, we employed it in a second ethnographic study, which lasted for ten weeks and was conducted in the fall of 2014. During this test, six NEAT-Lamps were tested by six office workers the same office-based workspace that was examined in the first study. As in the first study, workers' daily movement patterns were monitored and recorded, both before and after the introduction of the NEAT-Lamps to the setting. To obtain data amenable to statistical analysis, the six participants who volunteered to test the prototype wore step-counters while at work, both before and after the installation of the NEAT-Lamps. Each participant was asked to only carry the step counters during working hours when in the office space. After the observational phase of the study had finished, semi-structured interviews were conducted with each of the six participants. In general, the participants responded well to the design and claimed that the NEAT-Lamp had functioned as a positive reminder to hack their habits of prolonged sitting. Each participant reacted to the lamps in their own way: some of them preferred to switch position when notified by the lamp, for example by going from a seated to a standing working position. Others took the lamp's activation as a cue to take a short walk. The installation of the lamps triggered a significant increase in the number of steps taken by the participants; one participant's step count increased by more than 20 % after the lamps' installation relative to that during the pre-installation phase.

The Hidden Feature. Like most PI systems, the NEAT-lamp was designed to inspire workers to increase their daily step counts and generally be more mobile in the workplace. However, our second ethnographic study revealed that this was only one side of the story. It is well established that prototypes are multi-faced and thus open to many

The NEAT-Lamp

Fig. 3. The light from the NEAT-Lamps shines on the ceiling, creating an intersection between the body and the architectural space.

different meanings (Zumthor et al. 2006). Consequently, combining a prototype's evaluation with an ethnographic study creates an opportunity to identify any silent or hidden features that the prototype may exhibit. Our prototype NEAT-lamp was found to have such a hidden feature, which had been overlooked during the design process. Specifically, during the second ethnographic study we observed that the light emitted by the lamps shines upwards onto the ceiling. Because the study was conducted in an office with an open space environment, the green light shining on the ceiling was visible across the architectural space. The workers in the office quickly picked up on this hidden feature, which represents a novel example of the intersection between the interaction design and the architectural space (Wiberg 2015). This intersection contains hidden meanings associated with the office worker's bodily movement and the workspace that he/she inhabits (see Fig. 3).

In other words, this hidden feature creates a unity between the bodies inhabiting the space as elements of the architectural space and the architecture itself. Such a reflection of the self onto the ceiling can be seen an initial step in the design of PI systems that go beyond the quantification of the self and instead seek to make the space qualitative in a way that encourages reflection on our behaviors. However, it is important to recall that such designs can provoke other challenges, mostly relating to privacy and user confidentiality. The NEAT-lamps do not present major issues of this sort because they do not gather any personal private data and only respond to routine stationary/sedentary behavior in the workspace. Regardless, once we recognized the potential implications of the lights shining on the ceiling, we asked the participants if they were comfortable to continue with the study. All six participants were comfortable with this feature of the lamps and found that it made them more interesting and appealing. In particular, they were fascinated to see how this feature would influence the movement patterns of other workers in the office who were not taking part in the study. Accordingly, this hidden feature created social reflection and informal discussions among the office workers in the office space. In particular, they became interested in discussing how often they moved around during their working hours in office. This experience with the NEAT-lamp made the office workers realize that they have significant ability to shape their architectural space, causing them to recognize themselves as active architectural elements in the office. Being and moving in the workspace was now not only a matter of the self but also a noticeable factor in configuring the quality of workspace.

3   Moving Beyond

The NEAT-Lamp is an example of a concept-driven design situated in the context of office work and architecturally manifested as a physical object that sits on the desk in the office space.

This prototype is similar to other situated designs in that it is embodied, adapted and articulated inside the architectural space (McCullough 2007). Theorizing from the observations presented above, one could say that architectural spaces are shaped by our experiences of being. This is clearly reflected in the results of our second ethnographic study but can also be linked back to the early work of the renowned phenomenologist,

Martin Heidegger. As Heidegger noted, a building is not only related to dwelling but also a sense of being (Heidegger 1971). The term phenomenology means looking at phenomena or viewing their essence. As a school of thought, it basically focuses on how perception, thought, emotion and actions are directed toward things. In the context of this work, taking a phenomenological approach means engaging in a pure "act of looking" that reveals a robust connection between our ethnographic studies, the NEAT-Lamp and its effect on architectural space.

Fascinatingly, many architectural theorists have argued that phenomenology has the ability to bring us closer to our existential being and permits us to understand architecture as part of our life-world (Shirazi 2014). Individual architectural phenomenologists have theorized this field in rather different ways, however; here, we mainly draw on the theories of Norberg-Schulz and Pallasmaa.

The Heideggerian architectural phenomenologist Christian Norberg-Schulz regards phenomenology as a method for penetrating into the world of everyday existence. He thus contends that it is imperative to adopt a phenomenological approach towards humanity and the environment (Norberg-Schulz 2000). His argument for this proposition begins with the different understandings of Descartes' life-world relationships. Descartes divides life into the opposition between subject and object. While engaging with things as objects, we tend to establish a quantitative relationship towards them, which would lead to a mechanical view of world-life. As a result, the world-life is reduced to an abstraction and space is understood as a system lacking quality (Shirazi 2014). This quantitative approach leads to atomization and thus dominates all aspects of modern life. This reduction towards an understanding of life solely in terms of numeric facts has indeed influenced the way we design PI systems to promote bodily movement in architectural space. It could therefore be useful to incorporate phenomenology into our design thinking as a way of moving beyond this numerical abstraction. Natural experiences of the life-world are neither subjective or objective but rather fundamentally qualitative and should be understood as unified phenomena (Norberg-Schulz 2000). For Norberg-Schulz, phenomenology works better than psychology and sociology because it considers the unity of life and place: life is related to place and a true analysis of place will embrace life (Shirazi 2014). In other words, our being-in-the-world combines aspects of "*how*" and "*where*". Space is considered as a dimension of human existence not just our thoughts and perceptions.

From another perspective, this defective view of architectural space is the result of the supremacy of vision over the other senses in western cultures. This dominance of the visual sense in modern life has been greatly enhanced by the proliferation of screens - from TVs and PCs to small mobile displays. As Pallasmaa states, this leads to an architecture that decenters and isolates the body (Shirazi 2014). For Pallasmaa as a Merleau-Pontian, 'a sense of sight' had supremacy over the Cartesian eye because it is an embodied vision that incarnates part of the 'flesh of the world' (Pallasmaa 2012). Pallasmaa thus argues that the fact of experiencing the architectural space is a multisensory act where the qualities of materials' spaces and scales are measured not only by vision but also through the nose, skin, and ear as well as the muscles and bones (Shirazi 2014). We thus experience the architectural spaces we inhabit with all of our senses in a bodily interaction. He then goes further, saying "*Experiencing a space or a house is a dialogue, a kind of exchange: I place myself in the space and the space settles in me*" (Shirazi 2014). In this existential experience, the body and the space unite and fuse, giving rise to a body-space: "*A building is encountered; it is approached, confronted, related to one's body, moved through, utilized as a condition for other things*" (Pallasmaa et al. 2005).

We thus live in 'the flesh of world', which corresponds to an extension of our being. Architectural spaces articulate this experience and give it meaning. Bearing in mind the role of architectural space in configuring our daily bodily experiences, interaction design can enhance this relationship. Our NEAT-Lamp is a concrete example of an interaction design that serves as an architectural element, reinforcing bodily experiences through a phenomenological perspective within the workspace (see Fig. 3). As noted above, the NEAT-Lamp was designed with the objective of moving beyond numeric representations of physical movement. In addition, there was a deliberate attempt to conceptualize the core of the design towards ambient display. Both of these points can be linked to the two basic intentions of Norberg-Schulz and Pallamaa. The reflection of the lamp's light from the ceiling not only links the sky and earth as discussed by Norberg-Schulz (Shirazi 2014) but also creates a sense of sight and glance (Pallasmaa 2012). This reflection of light is a unifying act that links bodies to the architectural space and represents a superior form of embodiment when compared to screen-based notifications. It is argued that experiencing a space means participating in a dialogue between the space and the body; adopting a suitable interaction design-based approach in the development of PI systems could foster such dialogues. This would mean that in addition to being experienced, our bodily movements could be translated by the architectural space into personal or social meanings that are broadcasted to its inhabitants.

4   Conclusion

We hope that the presentation of our prototype in this paper will help to open up a discussion on new ways of designing PI and QS systems. Our prototype NEAT-Lamp (see Fig. 2) is a simple design that has been implemented and tested in a real setting where it functioned as a motivating element, encouraging users to see and use their bodies as interactive elements within this architectural space (Wiberg 2015). We also wish to point out that this ambient notification system creates an intersection between the body and the architectural space (see Fig. 3).

At the same time, there exists a unitary point of view in architectural thinking that considers all the elements within the space and the way they co-create an architectural form (see e.g. (Zumthor et al. 2006; Pallasmaa 2009; Shirazi 2014)). Bodies within the space are among these elements. This relationship between the body and the architectural space can create meaningful insights of self and being. There have been attempts within the field of HCI to use architectural thinking as a way of grounding new interaction designs and to move towards using interactive technologies as architectural elements (Wiberg 2015). Similarly, some architects have adopted a phenomenological perspective on architectural design. As Pallasmaa stated, "*the ultimate meaning of any building is beyond architecture, it directs our consciousness back to the world and towards our own sense of self and being*" (Pallasmaa 2012). By focusing on the intersection of interaction design and architectural space when designing PI systems, we move beyond the traditional first-person/user-centered perspective and create new horizons for examining the lived experience of such systems. As noted above, new voices are calling for novel designs in PI that go beyond the individual, contain dynamic trajectories, and represent data in new ways (Ohlin and Olsson 2015). Fusing our moving bodies through the use of ambient displays in the architectural spaces we inhabit can be seen as one such design. By adopting similar architectural thinking, we can expand the field of PI and interaction design in general as a way of unifying bodily movement with space to create a novel understating of self and being-in-the-world.

References

Barnes, R.M.: Motion and Time Study Applications. Wiley, Hoboken (1953)

Bellotti, V., Bly, S.: Walking away from the desktop computer: distributed collaboration and mobility in a product design team. In: Proceedings of the 1996 ACM Conference on Computer Supported Cooperative Work. ACM (1996)

Bureau of Labor Statics: Bureau of Labor Statics, 26 October 2015. http://www.bls.gov/tus/charts

Burns, P., Lueg, C., Berkovsky, S.: Activmon: encouraging physical activity through ambient social awareness. In: CHI 2012 Extended Abstracts on Human Factors in Computing Systems. ACM (2012)

Clarke, A.: Design Anthropology. Actar, New York (2010)

Corlett, E.: Analysis and evaluation of working posture. In: Ergonomics of Workstation Design, vol. 13. Butterworths, London (1983)

Elsden, C., Kirk, D., Selby, M., Speed, C.: Beyond personal informatics: designing for experiences with data. In: Proceedings of the 33rd Annual ACM Conference Extended Abstracts on Human Factors in Computing Systems. ACM (2015)

Hazlewood, W.R., Stolterman, E., Connelly, K.: Issues in evaluating ambient displays in the wild: two case studies. In: Proceedings of the SIGCHI Conference on Human Factors in Computing Systems. ACM (2011)

Heidegger, M.: Building dwelling thinking. In: Poetry, Language, Thought, vol. 154 (1971)

Jafarinaimi, N., Forlizzi, J., Hurst, A., Zimmerman, J.: Breakaway: an ambient display designed to change human behavior. In: CHI 2005 Extended Abstracts on Human Factors in Computing Systems. ACM (2005)

Levine, J.A.: Nonexercise activity thermogenesis (NEAT): environment and biology. Am. J. Physiol. Endocrinol. Metab. **286**(5), E675–E685 (2004)

Li, I., Dey, A., Forlizzi, J.: A stage-based model of personal informatics systems. In: Proceedings of the SIGCHI Conference on Human Factors in Computing Systems. ACM (2010)

Luff, P., Heath, C.: Mobility in collaboration. In: Proceedings of the 1998 ACM Conference on Computer Supported Cooperative Work. ACM (1998)

Maeda, J.: The Laws of Simplicity. MIT Press, Cambridge (2006)

McAlpine, D.A., Manohar, C.U., McCrady, S.K., Hensrud, D., Levine, J.A.: An office-place stepping device to promote workplace physical activity. Br. J. Sports Med. **41**(12), 903–907 (2007)

McCullough, M.: New media urbanism: grounding ambient information technology. Environ. Plan. B Plan. Des. **34**(3), 383–395 (2007)

Moradi, F., Wiberg, M.: Redesigning work-from sedentariness to activeness. Procedia Technol. **9**, 1005–1015 (2013)

Norberg-Schulz, C.: Architecture Presence, Language and Place (2000)

Ohlin, F., Olsson, C.M.: Beyond a utility view of personal informatics: a postphenomenological framework. In: Proceedings of the 2015 ACM International Joint Conference on Pervasive and Ubiquitous Computing and Proceedings of the 2015 ACM International Symposium on Wearable Computers. ACM (2015)

Pallasmaa, J.: The Thinking Hand. AD Primer, London (2009)

Pallasmaa, J.: The Eyes of the Skin: Architecture and the Senses. Wiley, Hoboken (2012)

Pallasmaa, J., MacKeith, P., Tullberg, D.C., Wynne-Ellis, M.: Encounters: Architectural Essays. Rakennustieto Oy, Helsinki (2005)

Ploderer, B., Reitberger, W., Oinas-Kukkonen, H., van Gemert-Pijnen, J.: Social interaction and reflection for behaviour change. Pers. Ubiquit. Comput. 18(7), 1667–1676 (2014)

Shirazi, M.R.: Towards an Articulated Phenomenological Interpretation of Architecture: Phenomenal Phenomenology. Routledge, Abingdon (2014)

Stolterman, E., Wiberg, M.: Concept-driven interaction design research. Hum. Comput. Interact. 25(2), 95–118 (2010)

Swan, M.: Sensor mania! The internet of things, wearable computing, objective metrics, and the quantified self 2.0. J. Sens. Actuator Netw. 1(3), 217–253 (2012)

Thorp, A.A., Healy, G.N., Winkler, E., Clark, B.K., Gardiner, P.A., Owen, N., Dunstan, D.W.: Prolonged sedentary time and physical activity in workplace and non-work contexts: a cross-sectional study of office, customer service and call centre employees. Int. J. Behav. Nutr. Phys. Act. 9(1), 128 (2012)

Van der Ploeg, H.P., Chey, T., Korda, R.J., Banks, E., Bauman, A.: Sitting time and all-cause mortality risk in 222 497 Australian adults. Arch. Intern. Med. 172(6), 494–500 (2012)

Wiberg, M.: Interaction design meets architectural thinking. Interactions 22(2), 60–63 (2015)

Wiberg, M., Moradi, F.: Information and engagement in personal informatics systems design. In: The Power of Information Conference, Brussels, 20–23 January 2013

Zumthor, P., Oberli-Turner, M., Schelbert, C., Binet, H.: Thinking Architecture. Birkhäuser, Boston (2006)

A Provenance Model for Quantified Self Data

Andreas Schreiber[✉]

Distributed Systems and Component Software, German Aerospace Center (DLR),
Linder Höhe, 51147 Cologne, Germany
Andreas.Schreiber@dlr.de
http://www.dlr.de/sc

Abstract. Quantified Self became popular in recent years. People are tracking themselves with Wearables, smartphone apps, or desktop applications. They collect, process and store huge amounts of personal data for medical and other reasons. Due to the complexity of different data sources, apps, and cloud services, it is hard to follow the data flow and to have trust in data integrity and safety. We present a solution that helps to get insight in Quantified Self data flows and to answer questions related to data security. We provide a provenance model for Quantified Self data based on the W3C standard PROV. Using that model, developers and users can record provenance of Quantified Self apps and services with a standardized notation. We show the feasibility of the presented provenance model with a small workflow using steps data from Fitbit fitness tracker.

Keywords: Provenance · Quantified self · Personal informatics · Trust · Ontology · PROV

1 Introduction

In almost any medical visit nowadays it is common to collect additional data of a patient in form of a medical history or raw data such as weight, height and blood pressure. The data gives doctors additional knowledge about your health status, possible treatments or signs of diseases.

A self-surveillance of personal data is called Quantified Self (QS) [2,5,18]. It is a recently upcoming movement that describes a community of people (users) who record and analyze data about themselves for medical reasons, self-improvement, technological interests, or other reasons. The user collects various types of data related to him, to get a better understanding of himself. The main differences between the data collected in a medical visit and recorded by the user are, that the data recorded by the user can cover a much wider area of interest (e.g., calories consumed or distance walked) and additionally it is recorded in a much shorter period, enabling precisely analytics, that result in more reliable diagnostics than in any medical history collected by the doctor.

The goals of the community are supported by software developers and manufacturers that are providing applications and devices for the user that are easy

© Springer International Publishing Switzerland 2016
M. Antona and C. Stephanidis (Eds.): UAHCI 2016, Part I, LNCS 9737, pp. 382–393, 2016.
DOI: 10.1007/978-3-319-40250-5_37

to use and mostly interoperable with each other, so that the user can create a flexible chain of different devices and programs that are analyzing his data and showing him easy understandable results. But, for example, questions like *"Can I trust the developer with my data?"* or *"How dangerous can it be quantifying and optimizing myself without proper medical support?"* are now hard to answer by users.

To answer those questions and to understand how the data of the user is created, manipulated and processed, the provenance [15] of that data can be recorded and analyzed. Provenance has many synonyms like lineage, genealogy or pedigree that results from different domains in which they were elaborated separately until a few years ago.

By capturing and storing provenance self-trackers could answer questions regarding the creation process of his data, security aspects, and even determining the trustfulness of his diagnostic results (Sect. 3.1). Like any database management system, a provenance system needs an underlying data model (provenance data model) that defines the data that will be captured in QS workflows.

Our main contributions are an ontology (Sect. 3.2) and a provenance model for quantified self workflows (Sect. 3.3). It gives a starting point for the exploration of provenance in QS and related fields, such as telemedicine. We show the feasibility of the provenance model by an example where we record the provenance of simple process. We query steps data via the Fitbit API, clean the data, and visualize the data (Sect. 4).

2   Provenance of Electronic Data

The definition of *provenance* is: *"Provenance is a record that describes the people, institutions, entities, and activities involved in producing, influencing, or delivering a piece of data or a thing. In particular, the provenance of information is crucial in deciding whether information is to be trusted, how it should be integrated with other diverse information sources, and how to give credit to its originators when reusing it. In an open and inclusive environment such as the Web, where users find information that is often contradictory or questionable, provenance can help those users to make trust judgments [16]"*.

With the previous definition, World Wide Web Consortium (W3C) started in 2011 and finalized in 2013 the generic provenance model PROV-DM [16] and an ontology PROV-O [12], inspired by various different approaches [14], that is adaptable to any domain. The general provenance model can be seen as a property graph with three different types of nodes: *Entities*, *Activities*, and *Agents*. Entities represent physical (e.g., a scale), digital (e.g., data), conceptual (e.g., a plan), or any other kinds of objects. An activity is a process that uses or generates entities and that can be associated with an agent, meaning that the agent is responsible for the activity.

Provenance is being recorded during runtime of a process. To make QS workflows provenance-aware requires to gather information that is required by the provenance model. This information is stored in a provenance database or provenance store. For example, ProvStore [8] is publicly available provenance store.

Large provenance graphs of long running real world workflows are stored in scalable databases (e.g., Neo4j [20]). For analyzing provenance data, visualization is a feasible method. Several solutions to visualize provenance exist. For example, publicly web-based tools such as PROV-O-Viz [4], desktop tools such as VisTrails [1], or numerous other graph visualization tools exist.

3   Quantified Self Provenance Model

One of the main tasks of provenance is to answer questions regarding the process that led to a specific piece of data, its corresponding data and agents that were involved in the progress. Since provenance data could be anything related to the origination process, some sort of filter is needed, so that a provenance system can focus its resources into recording specific data, rather than simple audit everything possible.

In data modeling such a focus is usually described with use cases. Because one of the tasks of provenance is answering questions, it is obvious that for this case, to describe the focus through questions which are of interest to be answered. These questions can be modified or extended during the modeling process, because the interest on which they are based could change during a project's lifetime.

3.1   Provenance Questions for Quantified Self

In this section, ten questions will be presented and explained regarding their importance and rationale of them. These questions are just an excerpt of the many possible provenance questions in this domain, but enough to give an overview about its feasibility. With additional questions, the resulting provenance model may need to be extended too.

The following questions were formalized from the position and interest of a regular user [9]. To keep the generalized QS provenance model simple and reduce the complexity of the provenance system, mostly very general questions were considered.

Entity Focused Questions

– *What data about the user were created during the activity X?* Sometimes the user would want to know how much data of him was collected during an activity. This question aims to reveal all data generated during a specific activity.
– *What data about the user were automatically generated?* This question is a specialized form of the previous one. Since all data during an activity can be classified into automatically and manually generated data, this question sets a focus on the first one.
– *What data about the user were derived from manual input?* Although the user might know which data he entered, this question aims to reveal the data, which was derived from his manual input. Sometimes it's not clear to the user, what others could spy out with that data.

Activity Focused Questions

- *Which activities support visualization of the user's data?* In some complex cases, there can exist possibilities to use software or hardware in ways that the user did not know. This question aims to reveal all possibilities on visualizing the user's data.
- *In which activities can the user input data?* Like the previous question, this question aims on possible activities on hardware or software that the user is not aware of. In this case he could want to know which devices, applications and web services support manual data input.
- *What processes are communicating data?* This general question would reveal the complete QS workflow to the user. Depending on the effort a user takes in quantifying himself, he might loose the overview of his QS workflow. By answering this question, the user could easily keep the overview of it.
- *Which activity generated the origin of data X?* The final activity focused question more complex. Some users might want to know how a specific entity came into existence, especially where the origin data came from.

Agent Focused Questions

- *What parties were involved in generating data X?* This question, due to agent-focused view, aims like many questions of this view, a security or trustiness aspect of the QS workflow. Often the user shares data through applications and web services and view the visualized results without knowing who processed his data. This question shall reveal all parties that take responsibility in generating a specific piece of data.
- *What parties received access on data X?* Although the user may know who processed his data, it is more crucial to have particular access on a specific data, reusing it several times. This questions targets to reveal all security issues which the user might be not aware of.
- *Can other parties see user's data X?* In some applications and web services, the user can grant access of his data to other people (e.g., for competitive reasons). To get an overview, which users he had given access to a specific piece of data, is this questions target.

3.2 Quantified Self Ontology

Capturing provenance with a generic data model could be implemented easily, but the missing semantics would constraint the information gain of such a provenance system. Due to this, we developed a QS ontology. Based on Noy's and McGuinness' ontology creation guide [17], it allows inferring semantics onto PROV-DM types and relations.

Our ontology is directly related to PROV-DM with a similar hierarchy and labels (Fig. 1). Since it infers semantics on an already defined data structure, our ontology is structured into three domains: *Agents*, *Activities*, and *UserData*.

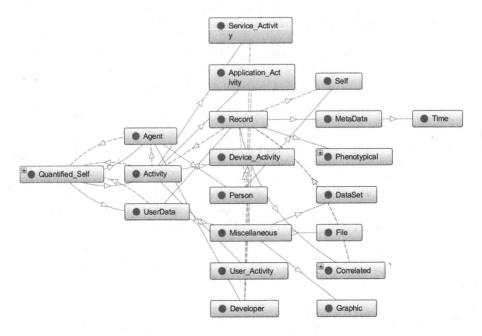

Fig. 1. Quantified self ontology.

Each domain extends PROV-DM: *Agents* ↦ *Agents*, *Activities* ↦ *Activities*, and *Entities* ↦ *UserData*.

The extensions to PROV-DM's *Agent* class are straightforward. We created a *Developer* as a subclass of *Agent*. *Developer* can be both, a *Person* or *Organization*. In the QS domain, a *Developer* produces software or hardware for users. The difference if he is a person or organization is irrelevant. Additionally, in QS the user signifies semantically more than any normal person and thus we added the class *Self* as a subclass of PROV-DM's *Person*.

We added few more subclasses to *Activity*: *User-*, *Device-*, *Application-* and *Service-Activity*. Although these activities could be structured into many fine granulated subclasses, we decided to keep the ontology on an abstract level at first and extend it if needed.

The *Entity* class had the most new semantics added. *UserData* is a subclass of *Entity*, which represents all data generated or related to the user. Since in QS various forms of data exist, we defined two subclasses: *Miscellaneous*, which represents all forms of data that are no original measured or recorded data (e.g., *Graphics*, *DataSets* or abstract *Files*), and *Record*, which represents real original (raw) data set with *Integer*'s, *Float*'s, *Double*'s, or *String*'s.

3.3 Provenance Model

Based on a requirements study of QS workflows and analysis of documentation from breakout sessions at QS Conferences (such as the QSEU14 Breakout

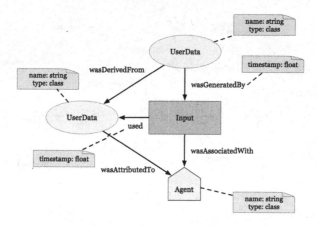

Fig. 2. PROV model for user input.

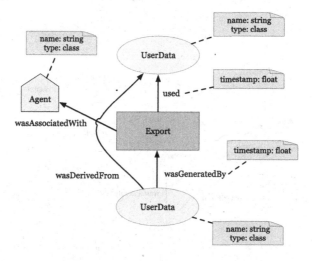

Fig. 3. PROV model for exporting data.

session on Mapping Data Access [19]), we developed a provenance model for QS workflows.

The possible activities in QS workflows are categorized into five abstract functionalities: *Input, Export, Request, Aggregation,* and *Visualization.* We defined a provenance sub model for each of these abstract functionalities.

Input. Specifies the functionality of using raw data from the user (through interaction or devices with sensors) and generating structured data from it (Fig. 2). Usually every QS workflow needs such a functionality to record data from the user.

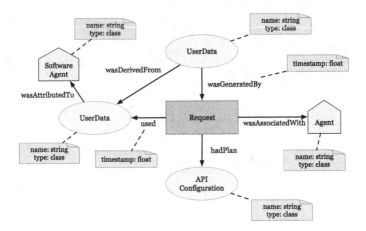

Fig. 4. PROV model for requesting data from a Web Service or Cloud service.

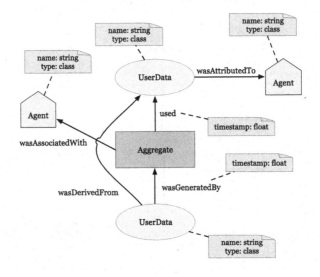

Fig. 5. PROV model for aggregating from two or more data sources.

Export. Specifies the functionality of exporting data from the current system into a format that is readable for other computer systems or humans (Fig. 3). Since a user usually uses more than one device, this functionality is processed multiple times, until the user see the visualized results.

Request. This functionality is in many QS workflows, where the user stores his data via Web Services or at Cloud Services. Often clients of these services requests data regularly from other Web Services or applications to update their data set (Fig. 4). Also, the user can trigger this functionality if the system does not update the data automatically.

Aggregation. A user usually records his data over time to interpret knowledge from it. This data needs to be aggregated with software capable of storing and updating data sets (Fig. 5). Many portals and desktop applications are aggregating heterogeneous data to create a deep knowledge about the user and help him understand his data [10].

Visualization. For many users who track themselves over a longer period, the visualization of their data over time in various graphics is a common approach to reveal knowledge of his data to them (Fig. 6).

4   Example: Visualizing Fitbit Data

To illustrate provenance recording, the following shows a very simple example. In this, steps data is requested from the Fitbit API [3], the data is cleaned and then visualized. We implemented the full example with Python and some supporting libraries, such as *python-fitbit* [11], *pandas* [13], and *matplotlib* [6]. In this example, we use a Python library [7] for storing the provenance and for generating a graph of it. During each step the actual Python command are preceded or followed by command for adding information to the provenance document.

Note: The following example is not complete. Some commands are left out. The full example is available online as Jupyter notebook[1].

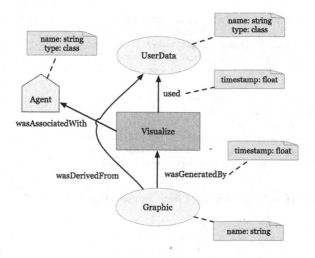

Fig. 6. PROV model for visualizing user data.

---

[1] Available at https://github.com/onyame/quantified_self_prov.

Loading Python Module and Initializing Empty PROV Document

```
from prov.model import ProvDocument
prov = ProvDocument()
```

Defining Namespaces

```
prov.add_namespace('qs', 'http://software.dlr.de/qs/')
prov.add_namespace('user', 'http://software.dlr.de/qs/user/')
prov.add_namespace('userdata', 'http://software.dlr.de/qs/userdata/')
prov.add_namespace('graphic', 'http://software.dlr.de/qs/graphic/')
prov.add_namespace('library', 'https://pypi.python.org/pypi/#')
prov.add_namespace('fitbit', 'https://www.fitbit.com/user/')
```

Adding Python Modules as PROV Entities

```
prov.entity('library:fitbit',
  {'prov:version': fitbit.__version__ })
prov.entity('library:pandas',
  {'prov:version': pd.__version__})
prov.entity('library:matplotlib',
  {'prov:version': matplotlib.__version__})
```

Adding User as PROV Agent

```
agent_user = prov.agent('user:onyame@googlemail.com',
  {'prov:type': 'prov:Person', 'qs:fitbit:id': '%s' % user_id})
```

Getting Values from Fitbit Web Service

```
t1 = strftime("%Y%m%dT%H%M%S%Z", gmtime())
ts = fitbit_client.time_series('activities/steps',
                               user_id=user_id, period='1y')
t2 = strftime("%Y%m%dT%H%M%S%Z", gmtime())
entity_timeseries = prov.entity('userdata:timeseries')
prov.activity('method:time_series', t1, t2,
  {'prov:type' : 'qs:request'})
prov.wasGeneratedBy(entity_timeseries, 'method:time_series', t2)
prov.used('method:time_series', 'library:fitbit')
prov.wasAttributedTo(entity_timeseries, agent_user)
```

Producing a Graph from the Time Series Data

```
steps.plot(label='Steps')
entity_plot_steps = prov.entity('graphic:steps')
activity_plot = prov.activity('method:matplotlib_plot', t1, t2,
  {'prov:type': 'qs:visualize'})
prov.used(activity_plot, entity_steps)
prov.wasGeneratedBy(entity_plot_steps, activity_plot, t2)
prov.wasDerivedFrom(entity_plot_steps, entity_steps)
prov.wasAssociatedWith(entity_plot_steps, agent_user)
```

The result is a provenance document represented as a graph (Fig. 7). This shows how the steps graphic (entity *graphic:steps*) is generated using data gathered from the Fitbit API via a library (entity *library:fitbit*).

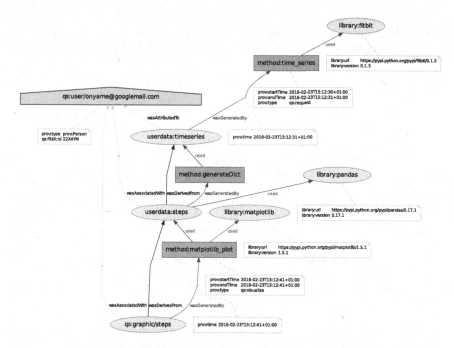

Fig. 7. Provenance of a graph with daily steps. The PROV document is available online in the ProvStore: https://provenance.ecs.soton.ac.uk/store/documents/113488/

5   Conclusions and Future Work

We provided an ontology and a provenance data model for Quantified Self data. Both are based on the open W3C standards PROV-O and PROV-DM. The provenance model reflects all essential data processing steps, which occur in todays QS applications. The provenance model in its current version is relatively abstract. This abstract definition allows modeling a great variety of QS data flows, but it should be improved to be more specific in upcoming versions.

Future work will focus on deployment of provenance recording in real-world QS applications. For example, the provenance of a whole workflow of steps data from a device or sensor, via smartphone apps and cloud services, to aggregation and visualization portals. The challenging task is to add provenance recording to legacy hardware and software in cases where manufacturers and companies are not collaborating.

Another future topic is to elaborate the queries of recorded provenance data. Based on provenance of full QS data flows meaningful insights should be generated. Important will be, to answer questions regarding security and safety of data.

Acknowledgements. We would like to thank Bojan Janisch (Bonn-Rhein-Sieg University of Applied Sciences), for his supportive work he did during his master project.

References

1. Bavoil, L., Callahan, S.P., Crossno, P.J., Freire, J., Vo, H.T.: VisTrails: enabling interactive multiple-view visualizations. In: pp. 135–142. IEEE (2005)
2. Choe, E.K., Lee, N.B., Lee, B., Pratt, W., Kientz, J.A.: Understanding quantified-selfers' practices in collecting and exploring personal data. In: Proceedings of the 32nd Annual ACM Conference on Human Factors in Computing Systems, pp. 1143–1152. ACM (2014)
3. Fitbit: Fitbit developer api (2016). https://dev.fitbit.com
4. Hoekstra, R., Groth, P.: PROV-O-Viz - understanding the role of activities in provenance. In: Ludäescher, B., Plale, B. (eds.) IPAW 2014. LNCS, vol. 8628, pp. 215–220. Springer, Heidelberg (2015)
5. Hoy, M.B.: Personal activity trackers and the quantified self. Med. Ref. Serv. Q. **35**(1), 94–100 (2016)
6. Hunter, J.D.: Matplotlib: a 2d graphics environment. Comput. Sci. Eng. **9**(3), 90–95 (2007)
7. Huynh, T.D.: A python library for W3C provenance data model supporting PROV-JSON import/export (2014). https://github.com/trungdong/prov
8. Huynh, T.D., Moreau, L.: ProvStore: a public provenance repository. In: Ludaescher, B., Plale, B. (eds.) IPAW 2014. LNCS, vol. 8628, pp. 275–277. Springer, Heidelberg (2015)
9. Janisch, B.: Developing an abstract Quantified Self Provenance-model. Master project, University of Applied Sciences Bonn-Rhein-Sieg (2015). http://elib.dlr.de/100752/
10. Jones, S.L.: Exploring correlational information in aggregated quantified self data dashboards. In: Adjunct Proceedings of the 2015 ACM International Joint Conference on Pervasive and Ubiquitous Computing and Proceedings of the 2015 ACM International Symposium on Wearable Computers, pp. 1075–1080. ACM (2015)
11. Kelly, I.: python-fitbit - fitbit api python client implementation (2016). https://github.com/orcasgit/python-fitbit
12. Lebo, T., Sahoo, S., McGuinness, D., Belhajjame, K., Cheney, J., Corsar, D., Garijo, D., Soiland-Reyes, S., Zednik, S., Zhao, J.: PROV-O: The PROV ontology, 30 April 2013. http://www.w3.org/TR/2013/REC-prov-o-20130430/
13. Mckinney, W.: pandas: a foundational python library for data analysis and statistics. In: PyHPC 2011: Workshop on Python for High Performance and Scientific Computing, SC11, Seattle, WA, USA, 18 November 2011
14. Moreau, L., Groth, P., Cheney, J., Lebo, T., Miles, S.: The rationale of PROV. Web Seman. Sci. Serv. Agents World Wide Web **35**, Part 4, 235–257 (2015)
15. Moreau, L., Groth, P., Miles, S., Vazquez-Salceda, J., Ibbotson, J., Jiang, S., Munroe, S., Rana, O., Schreiber, A., Tan, V., Varga, L.: The provenance of electronic data. Commun. ACM **51**(4), 52–58 (2008)

16. Moreau, L., Missier, P., Belhajjame, K., B'Far, R., Cheney, J., Coppens, S., Cresswell, S., Gil, Y., Groth, P., Klyne, G., Lebo, T., McCusker, J., Miles, S., Myers, J., Sahoo, S., Tilmes, C.: PROV-DM: The PROV data model, 30 April 2013. http://www.w3.org/TR/2013/REC-prov-dm-20130430/
17. Noy, N.F., Mcguinness, D.L.: Ontology development 101: A guide to creating your first ontology (2001). http://www.ksl.stanford.edu/people/dlm/papers/ontology101/ontology101-noy-mcguinness.html
18. Picard, R., Wolf, G.: Sensor informatics and quantified self. IEEE J. Biomed. Health Inform. **19**(5), 1531 (2015)
19. QSEU14: Breakout: Mapping data access, 23 August 2014. https://forum.quantifiedself.com/t/breakout-mapping-data-access/995/4
20. Schreiber, A., Ney, M., Wendel, H.: The provenance store prOOst for the open provenance model. In: Groth, P., Frew, J. (eds.) IPAW 2012. LNCS, vol. 7525, pp. 240–242. Springer, Heidelberg (2012)

Understanding the Experience of Situated Mindfulness Through a Mobile App That Prompts Self-reflection and Directs Non-reactivity

Ralph Vacca[✉] and Christopher Hoadley

New York University, New York, USA
{ralph.vacca,tophe}@nyu.edu

Abstract. This paper explores how mobile technology may be able to activate and support mindfulness states while users are situated in everyday life. Interviews with users on the use of a mobile app that was designed to prompt self-reflection and direct non-reactivity, suggest that activating situated mindfulness, may lead to differences in the kind of self-reflection individuals engage in. In addition, a situated approach may alter the way in which we engage in being non-judgmental and non-reactive, bringing the focus to the contents of mental events rather than the process. This paper concludes with implications for the design of mobile technology seeking to prompt and support mindfulness states while situated in everyday life.

Keywords: Mindfulness · Situated cognition · Self-reflection · Self-awareness · Emotional health · Persuasive design · Mobile learning

1 Introduction

In the past decade, mainstream interest in mindfulness has fueled a growth in research in the psychology, mental health, and contemplative studies fields. The growing interest in mindfulness has led to an increase in software applications seeking to support the cultivation of mindfulness. Despite the origins of mindfulness that embed the practice within the context of ethical action and compassion [1], Western psychology commonly defines mindfulness mainly as consisting of the two components of attentional control and non-reactivity [2] with more recent research teasing out these two components more distinctly [3].

Currently there is still very limited empirical research on the potential role technology can play in the cultivation of mindfulness, specifically in prompting attentional shifts that are self-reflective in nature, and supporting non-reactivity [4]. Yet it has been argued that, for a variety of reasons, mobile technology can be particularly effective toward the goal of cultivating mindfulness [4]. From the research that has emerged, the majority focuses on supporting meditation practices with some research also exploring the use of persuasive design techniques to promote tracking. For example, mobile technology has been explored as a way to support self-monitoring [5, 6], and deliver audio-guided meditation and psycho-education [7, 8]. Our initial analysis of the landscape yielded common design approaches

© Springer International Publishing Switzerland 2016
M. Antona and C. Stephanidis (Eds.): UAHCI 2016, Part I, LNCS 9737, pp. 394–405, 2016.
DOI: 10.1007/978-3-319-40250-5_38

currently taken such as directed instruction, interactive instruction, prompted engagement, social engagement, and tracking and aggregation. Remaining unexplored is the how mobile technology may provide an opportunity to situate mindfulness practices in the authentic context of everyday life. The idea that one can be prompted to enter into mindfulness states with the support of a mobile app is riddled with both technical and contemplative issues. While the technical focuses on usability aspects of interrupting everyday life with bothersome notifications, the contemplative issues highlight the issue with operationalizing – and in some cases corrupting – certain phenomenological aspects and traditional conceptualizations of mindfulness.

Using a mobile app, SIMA (Situated Interactive Mindfulness App), this paper explores how prompting self-reflection and supporting non-reactivity is experienced when situated in users' everyday life. Through a qualitative research approach we explore the question of how a mindfulness state is activated and supported in everyday life using a mobile app, and how the self-reflective and non-reactive aspects of mindfulness are experienced. Our findings suggest that activating a mindfulness state in individuals may require designing for the support of reflection-in-action rather than reflection-on-action. In addition, designing for cultivation of mindfulness through a situated approach may alter the way in which non-reactivity can be supported, bringing the focus more to the contents of mental events rather than the process.

2 Situated Mindfulness: Theoretical Framework

Mindfulness is commonly defined as consisting of two overarching components of present-moment awareness and non-judgment [9]. Historically, the origins of mindfulness stem from Buddhist traditions whereby mindfulness was seen as an ethical practice which was thought not just to reduce clinging and attachment (core parts of human suffering), but was also thought to be essential to being a compassionate and an enlightened being [1]. In this section we discuss the theoretical foundations on which SIMA was designed. First we define mindfulness as a state and why self-reflection and non-reactivity are related. We then explore the concept of situated mindfulness, which combines the idea of being in a mindfulness state, and being situated in everyday contexts that influence the thoughts and emotions brought in and out of attention during a mindfulness state (e.g., thoughts while at your office desk at work, interacting with friends, etc.).

2.1 Mindfulness as a State

There are two common approaches taken in operationalizing mindfulness. The most common is a trait-based approach where instruments such as the FFMQ (Five Facet Mindfulness Questionnaire) seek to capture self-reported behaviors that point to a dispositional tendency that can also change with prolonged mindfulness training [10–13]. However, another approach is to view mindfulness as a temporary state that can be induced by an individual with effort [14, 15]. Theoretically these two approaches may be related in that continued mindfulness state induction and maintenance may lead to changes in mindfulness traits. Our focus in this study was on mindfulness as a state, however current measures such as the TMS (Toronto Mindfulness Scale) [16], were developed around meditation practices not non-meditation practices, which was our design focus. We sought to tease out the two factors curiosity and decentering that underlie the TMS measure to inform our own design and qualitative data collection.

Curiosity. The curiosity factor is defined as reflecting an attitude of wanting to learn more about one's own experiences. The authors of the TMS measure argue that empirical derivation of the curiosity factor also encapsulates the attentional self-regulation component suggested in Bishop's definition – present-moment awareness – in that one cannot be curious, open or accepting of experiences one has not brought into their attention [16]. Research has shown that non-secular meditation approaches that allow for taking an investigative interest in mental events (e.g., Mindfulness-Based Stress Reduction) have the tendency to lead to improvements in curiosity as compared to meditation approaches that discourage investigative interests in mental events (e.g., Shambala meditation) [16]. In our design, the key to cultivating curiosity then is the meta-cognitive process of self-reflection where one observes internal events such as thoughts and emotions, and does not inhibit investigative interest in such mental events.

Decentering. Decentering is the second factor in the mindfulness state construct, and is defined as reflecting a shift from identifying personally with thoughts and feelings to relating to one's experience of a wider field of awareness [17]. In other words, decentering is about seeing one's thoughts and feelings as passing mental events in the mind rather than reflections of reality. The notion is that by observing one's mental events, there is the ability to not cling or attach to one event, but focus instead on the process of the ongoing flow of mental events. At the heart of such decentering is an attentional shift between mental events. For example, in meditation practice, such as Vipassana, one focuses on breathing while directing attention back and forth from an ongoing flow of mental events, and breathing. In the shift, there is an "un-clinging" that occurs, decentering one's mental state of self-reflection. Some debate the term decentering in that it suggests a top-down conceptual processing whereby the mind focuses on the content of mental events rather than a bottom-up approach that remains on a phenomenological level of awareness [18]. For instance, in Buddhist Vipassana traditions the idea is to eventually experience mental events within the phenomenological field with no effort required to actively regulate or reappraise what is experienced rather than actively work to regulate mental events [14]. Key to cultivating decentering then is supporting a degree of attentional shifting towards and away from mental events (i.e., thoughts and feelings).

2.2 Situated Mindfulness

So how do the factors of curiosity and decentering that comprise the mindfulness state construct relate to being situated in everyday life? Our study seeks to posit this idea of situated mindfulness – a mindfulness state that makes use of situated contexts external to one's mental events (e.g., being at work before a big presentation, or coming home after a stressful day). Situated mindfulness includes such contexts as part of the attentional shifting process, incorporating such shifts under the curiosity and decentering factors. For example, one would be aware not just of being happy, but being happy because one is about to eat. The positing of situated mindfulness presents challenges, not just in the design of an intervention that can accomplish such experiences, but also in possibly distorting initial conceptions of what it means to be mindful.

The value of incorporating situational context into how we understand mindfulness states stems from the concept of situated cognition, which posits that the situations that comprise our everyday life (i.e. authentic contexts) deeply influences how we make meaning [19]. The idea that that knowledge is contextualized in an experiential framework is relevant to mindfulness states in that the investigative interests at the core of curiosity may or may not change in ways that are beneficial when including the situational contexts that may have influenced such mental events. The incorporation of situational context in self-reflections may change how we experience curiosity within a mindfulness state. Furthermore, including situational contexts in how we shift our attention during decentering may change how we experience the non-reactivity that characterizes a decentered state.

Yet there are challenges in conceptualizing mindfulness as explicitly situated. Primarily there is the technical challenge of managing such attentional shifts between internal mental events, and external situational influences. Also there is the question of how this may distort, either beneficially or negatively, our conceptions of "being mindful." In other words, it is not clear how we may experience mindfulness states, when there are explicit attempts to include in our self-reflection and attentional shifting, the influence of situational contexts on our internal mental events.

3   Systems Design: Situated Interactive Mindfulness App (SIMA)

SIMA (Situated Interactive Mindfulness Application) is a mobile phone application that uses prompted self-reflection and directed non-reactivity as core design approaches to the curiosity and decentering factors of mindfulness states.

The experience begins when the user first enrolls in the ten-day workout that consists of a set number of mindfulness activities for them to engage in daily. Each day, the user is prompted to commit to engaging in the activities for the day (Fig. 1, left). At this point the user can choose to not accept the daily commitment, and instead continue the workout starting the following day. From our usability studies we found that the integration of a daily commitment decreased perceived inflexibility of the system when variations from day-to-day occurred, and increased engagement.

Once a user decides to commit for the day, they are prompted a maximum of three times a day to "check-in" (Fig. 1, right), in the form of a push notification. In our preliminary usability studies, three times a day seemed to be the number of check-ins that did not overwhelm or annoy users, but still allowed us to capture enough variation within the day in terms of situational contexts. When creating an account, the user initially sets the time they start their day, and the system automatically spaces out the check-ins based on 14 h of wake time.

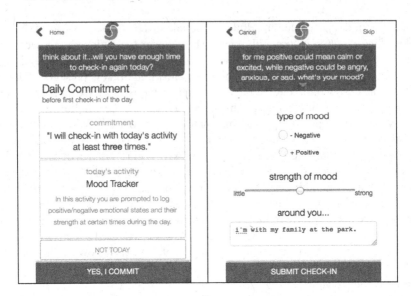

Fig. 1. Screenshots of SIMA making a daily commitment (left), and receiving feedback (right)

The workout for this study prompted self-reflection using two different kinds of activity check-ins, a "general" check-in activity and a "specific" check-in activity. In general check-ins, users are prompted to direct their attention to their current mood or thoughts, and take note of the situational context (e.g., Fig. 1, right). In specific check-ins users are prompted to contrast their current mental events with a specified one (e.g., gratitude). The five different activities used in the workout are listed in Table 1, by day. For example, in days 3 and 4, users received the gratitude check-in where they are prompted to track (type in) a sense of gratitude and make note of the situational context. In all check-ins users engage in a form of tracking and are then taken to a directed non-reactivity screen where users are instructed to not react to the mental event they are attending to (i.e., analyze or seek to change it).

Table 1. List of workout activities by day

Day(s)	Type	Activity name	User input
1–2	General	Thought tracker	Short description of thought and context
3–4	Specific	Gratitude	Sense of gratitude and context
5–6	General	Mood tracker	Magnitude and valance of mood and context
7–8	Specific	Compassion	Sense of compassion and context
9	General	Thought tracker	Short description of thought and context
10	Specific	Negative self-talk	Sense of self-criticism and context

We engaged in several interactions of design and usability studies to reduce confusion with the check-in process and directions. We settled on thought and mood tracking as the general check-ins in that they correspond to the typical mental events in a mindfulness state. Deciding on the specific check-ins was more challenging in that there are a multitude of contexts that could be focused on. We focused on gratitude, compassion, and negative self-talk in that these contexts were the least geo-location and temporal restrictive and are the most common contexts used in mindfulness-based therapeutic approaches.

This design foregrounds situated mindfulness and draws on theory in several ways. First, users are prompted to direct their attention in specific ways throughout their day and to include their situated surroundings as part of the focus of their attention. Second, users are directed to not-react to mental events.

3.1 Methods

This qualitative study relied on semi-structured interviews with a sample of seven young adults ages 18–30 to explore the experiential ramifications of our system design; quantitative assessments of mindfulness outcomes and in-depth analysis of behavior logs are left to future work. Two of the participants were male, and all participants were recruited in New York City via flyers, social media, and snowball sampling. To participate, individuals must have not engaged in more than 5 h of total meditation in the past year, but had engaged in at least one hour of mindfulness meditation in the past year. While we did not use prior meditation experiences as a basis for comparison, we felt those that had previously experienced mindfulness meditation may be more readily able to speak to amorphous concepts of present-moment awareness and mind wandering that overlap with curiosity and decentering.

Participants engaged with SIMA over ten days using their own mobile phone and then completed an interview at the end of the study. The study was designed as 10 days based on our experience in usability studies that showed there was familiarity with the mechanic of responding to prompts after two days, and engagement fatigue after 10 days, given our relatively meager compensation of a $10 Amazon gift card. The focus of the study was on how different forms of prompted self-reflection and directed non-reactivity designs influence how curiosity and decentering are experienced.

The semi-structured interview at the end of the study focused on five aspects of the mindfulness experience: prompted self-reflection, curiosity, non-reactivity, decentering, and the situated nature of the interactions with the mobile app. Specifically, the interview questions adopted many concepts from the Toronto Mindfulness Scale (TMS) quantitative instrument that, while focuses on meditation-based approached, were expanded to meet our needs to understand curiosity and decentering aspects of a non-meditation-based approach, and the situated prompted self-reflection and directed non-reactivity design approaches to those factors. The TMS itself was not integrated in that the TMS is more relevant after each meditation session rather than in aggregate, and has been validated for meditation-based approaches. Perhaps future work can address this limitation. We analyzed interviews from all of the participants using thematic analysis [20]. The audio recordings were transcribed and analyzed for emergent themes. Five of the seven participants engaged in a second interview after our analysis to tease out additional information on their experience. The next section presents the themes that emerged and are relevant to guiding the design of situated mindfulness interventions.

4 Results

This section focuses on how the design approaches of self-reflection and directed non-reactivity impacted users' experiences of using SIMA to activate and support a mindfulness state while situated in their day-to-day life.

4.1 Prompted Self-reflection on Curiosity Factor of Mindfulness State

The first overarching theme that emerged was around self-reflection itself. There was strong evidence that SIMA's prompted engagement approach through the use of check-ins (i.e., notifications) engaged participants in self-reflection. Every single participant recalled moments where the prompts triggered an attentional shift to current mental events. Through phrases such as "I thought to myself", "I noticed I felt", it was clear that the check-ins throughout the day did elicit self-reflection in participants. For instance, one participant Randy shared that, "I got the notification and then tracked my mood. I thought to myself, what am I feeling and then the thoughts that seemed to be associated with that mood." Another user Sharon described how the mood tracker activity, "let me checkin with myself." For Jay labeling his mood required momentary self-reflection where he would, "see if the labels made sense, and if I was really feeling what I thought I was feeling."

The implications here are that push notifications, directing users to explicitly shift attention to their current mental events, is a promising design approach. However, with that said, there were variations in the kinds of self-reflection that were experienced, and aspects of the usability design that influenced the how self-reflection was experienced or engaged with.

Self-reflection as Retrospective and In-Action. Almost all of the participants made a distinction between retrospective and in-action reflection when sharing their experience with the prompted self-reflection approach taken by SIMA. In retrospective self-reflection the focus was not a present-moment mental event, but rather a mental event that had occurred previously and was being brought into focus. In contrast, in-action self-reflection served to bring attention to present-moment thoughts or emotions.

Key to these differences in how self-reflection was experienced was the degree to which the prompted check-in specified a mental event to focus on. As shown in Table 1, SIMA provides both general and specific mental events as part of the check-in activities. For example in prompts that specified a mental event Jay recalled, "I remember one checkin asked me to reflect on being grateful about something that occurred, so I thought back to see if I could remember an occasion." This contrasted with check-ins designed without specifying a mental event (i.e., general), prompting users to record their general current mood or thoughts.

However, the sequence of the check-in itself also played a role in differences between in-action and retrospective self-reflection. There were differences in how the same checkin was experienced later in the day versus earlier in the day. For example, when Sharon discussed her experience with an activity that prompted her to focus on feelings of compassion (i.e., specific mental event), she initially was, "trying to remember what had happened" (i.e., retrospective), while, "the check-ins later in the day were different. I was noticing things in the moment." Other users shared a similar experience whereby an initial check-in that prompted a shift in attention to a specific mental event (e.g., gratitude) initially triggered a retrospective self-reflection, yet as the day progressed they engaged in in-action self-reflection as they anticipated subsequent check-ins would ask them to report on such events.

One question that emerges is whether or not differences in self-reflection matter when it comes to how curiosity is experienced. Given curiosity is largely defined as present-moment awareness, in-action self-reflection is more aligned with curiosity than retrospective self-reflection. Furthermore, the very idea of making use of the situated context is lost during retrospective self-reflection where the present-moment context does not relate in any way to the act of self-reflection.

In terms of the design implications, our findings may suggest that general prompts not specifying mental events to focus on are more likely to trigger in-action self-reflection than prompts that specify a mental event to reflect on. However, specifying a mental event such as gratitude or compassion, may still elicit in-action self-reflection if the user anticipates having to check-in throughout the day and self-monitors for such mental events.

Situated Effort and Engagement. The use of daily check-ins via notifications throughout the day meant the availability of attention and willingness to engage varied. While 83 % of users completed all three daily check-ins for the 10 days, and every participant engaged in at least two check-ins for the 10 days, users shared that had they not been part of a formal research study their engagement would have been lower for certain check-ins. Most by users cited perceived effort as influencing whether they ignored a check-in or engaged with it.

Once again differences between focusing on a general or specific mental event played a role. Across most users the check-ins that prompted a focus on a specific mental event, were perceived to require more effort. For example Claudia shared she "had one checkin on negative self-talking where I couldn't remember a moment, so I didn't know what to checkin with." Since our analysis linked specific mental events to retrospective self-reflection, this may suggest that retrospective self-reflection was perceived to require more effort since one may confront difficulty in recalling an event or taking time to recall.

Another aspect of the perceived effort was timing of the check-ins. Every user noted day-to-day variations as influencing their perceptions of how much effort would be required to engage in a check-in. For instance Nambia felt "it was easier to checkin when I had some downtime or I noticed something." Jay shared that "I don't think you're ever going to be able to get the timing right on the check-ins, I know for me some days it was right in the middle of something, ... like I can't do this right now."

The design implication here is that focusing on in-action self-reflection may in turn also decrease users' perceived effort to engage.

4.2 Directed Non-reactivity on Decentered Factor of Mindfulness

In meditation, decentering occurs through both observing the coming and going of thoughts, and the act of letting go – freeing the individual from clinging to a single thought and shifting focus into the past and the future, rather than the unfolding present. SIMA attempted to engage participants in decentering through the use of directed non-reactivity, where they were explicitly directed not to react or attempt to analyze the focus of their attention, but merely become aware of it. The question is how does SIMA's approach to decentering change the way decentering is experienced.

Snapshot and a Shift. Differences between in-action and retrospective self-reflection influenced how users experienced attentional shifting that is at the heart of decentering. Reflection-in-action occurred most when check-ins served as a reminder to keep self-monitoring top of mind rather than elicit the self-reflection itself. In other words, the self-reflection was occurring in-between check-ins, therefore the attentional focus was different than in retrospective self-reflection experiences where the check-in itself directed the self-reflection and tracking at the same time. This is important because from deeper discussions with users, the in-between check-ins self-reflection took on a more attentional shift dynamic more similar to meditation experiences.

Check-ins that focused on a specific mental event allowed for a shifting between the current situational context and another specified mental event. For example if a user had on their mind the imperative to self-monitor compassionate thoughts, a situation in which they are angry may elicit a shifting towards a new more compassionate form of the mental event. As one user put it, "if I was thinking about the upcoming check-in, it did color my interactions a little." Jay shared that, "I was thinking about being grateful, and then when I was so angry one time, I thought – I'm so grateful I'm not that [expletive]." These experiences suggest that attentional shifting between mental events may better be induced through supporting reflection-in-action rather than retrospective self-reflection.

Non-reactivity as Highly Content-Oriented. Our findings suggest that the overall degree of attention shifting, when it did occur, was fairly limited. As discussed earlier, some check-ins resulted in little if no attentional shifting (i.e., snapshot) while others led to a more of an attentional shift. In the check-ins that did support attentional shifting, did so by prompting the user to hold a mental event to focus on in mind (e.g., being grateful) and contrast it with mental events as they occurred in-situ. The result is not just a limited attentional shift in that the contrast only occurs once, but an overall focus on the content of the mental events themselves. In discussing non-reactivity to mental events, every participant focused on the content of the mental event, rather than a focus on the ongoing process of mental events, as in mindfulness meditation.

For instance, many users sought to explore alternatives to the contents of the mental events they were focused on. Randy put it, "I found myself thinking about all the other times I felt happy, when I felt sad, or some positive things I could say to myself when I thought about the bad things I say to myself." Namibia shared that she, "also thought about all the times I wasn't being compassionate when I was being compassionate, not as a judgment, just as a ... hey wait a minute moment." The result of a content-oriented focus is that users felt a deeper analysis would have been helpful. As put by Randy, "I felt like the activities just tracked stuff and then asked me not to do anything about it." He continued," I mean what was the point? Either help me notice stuff in a specific way or help me do something after I notice it, but to do neither felt like a waste of time."

The design implications here is that while providing a specific mental event may induce reflection-in-action and better support attentional shifting, it also may lead to an increased content-centric experience. While this in turn may break from the traditional mindfulness orientation of not focusing on the contents or analysis of mental events, there may be opportunities for the integration of emotion-regulation strategies, which are commonly integrated in non-meditation therapeutic approaches such as Mindfulness-Based Cognitive Therapy (MBCT). For example, once users have noticed a context in which they could have more compassionate thoughts, rather than just direct users to not-react, they may be asked to reframe existing mental events with the more compassionate bent. This is stretching far beyond the original intent of mindfulness non-reactivity, but would be one direction that responds to users' inquiries into ways the app could help them engage in more self-regulatory behaviors – such as cognitive reappraisal [21].

5 Conclusion and Future Work

The idea of situated mindfulness and approaching it through the design principles of prompted self-reflection and non-reactivity then is not just meant to be yet another tool in the kit for mindfulness technology designers. Rather, it also presents a questioning around how technological mindfulness interventions operationalize mindfulness as a construct and in turn design for the activation and support of mindfulness state in-situ. We found that prompted self-reflection in-situ can be designed to support retrospective and in-action self-reflection, with in-action self-reflection more in line with the factor of curiosity of a mindfulness state. In regards to the use of directed non-reactivity, we found that a difference in the way self-reflection was experienced was pivotal. When self-reflection was more in-action, decentering relied more on attentional shifting, while retrospective self-reflection took on a more snapshot feeling. In turn, in directed non-reactivity during in-action self-reflection there was less of a focus on self-regulation. In summary, it may be that a focus on in-action self-reflection through specific mental events may benefit future designs. However, it is not clear what an increased content-centric focus means for decentered aspects of a mindfulness state. While it may be in line with user feedback and some therapeutic interventions, it may challenge definitions of decentering and non-reactivity, and align more with ideas of cognitive reappraisal and emotion regulation than traditional mindfulness.

Future work should consider a narrower focus on in-action self-reflection through the use of activities that direct the focus of attention on specific mental events, which in turn better explore a content-centric nature of the decentering experience. Exploring self-regulatory directions (e.g., cognitive reappraisal) rather than non-reactivity in the form of directed inhibition may provide deeper insights into how decentering can be experienced. In terms of methodology, future work may benefit from integration of quantitative assessments to at least contextualize any thematic findings. This may include pattern analysis of behavior logs, or require tweaking instruments such as the Toronto Mindfulness Scale (TMS) to adjust the notions of curiosity and decentering to be applicable a situated context versus a set temporal period (i.e., meditation). A key limitation that future work may also address is how data is collected on mindfulness states. A per-session data collection approach through daily journaling might be stronger than an aggregate interview approach at the end alone.

References

1. Bodhi, B.: What does mindfulness really mean? A canonical perspective. Contemp. Buddhism. **12**, 19–39 (2011)
2. Bishop, S.R.: Mindfulness: A Proposed Operational Definition (2004)
3. de Bruin, E.I., Topper, M., Muskens, J.G.A.M., Bögels, S.M., Kamphuis, J.H.: Psychometric properties of the five facets mindfulness questionnaire (FFMQ) in a meditating and a non-meditating sample. Assessment **19**, 187–197 (2012)
4. Plaza, I., Demarzo, M.M.P., Herrera-Mercadal, P., García-Campayo, J.: Mindfulness-based mobile applications: literature review and analysis of current features. JMIR mHealth uHealth **1**, e24 (2013)
5. Kauer, S.D., Reid, S.C., Crooke, A.H.D., Khor, A., Hearps, S.J.C., Jorm, A.F., Sanci, L., Patton, G.: Self-monitoring using mobile phones in the early stages of adolescent depression: randomized controlled trial. J. Med. Internet Res. **14**, e67 (2012)
6. Reid, S.C., Kauer, S.D., Dudgeon, P., Sanci, L.A., Shrier, L.A., Patton, G.C.: A mobile phone program to track young people's experiences of mood, stress and coping. Soc. Psychiatry Psychiatr. Epidemiol. **44**(6), 501–507 (2009). Development and testing of the mobiletype program
7. Glück, T.M., Maercker, A.: A randomized controlled pilot study of a brief web-based mindfulness training (2011)
8. Morledge, T.J., Allexandre, D., Fox, E., Fu, A.Z., Higashi, M.K., Kruzikas, D.T., Pham, S.V., Reese, P.R.: Feasibility of an online mindfulness program for stress management–a randomized, controlled trial. Ann. Behav. Med. **46**, 137–148 (2013)
9. Kabat-zinn, J.: Mindfulness-Based Interventions in Context: Past, Present, and Future, pp. 144–156 (2003)
10. Van Dam, N.T., Earleywine, M., Borders, A.: Measuring mindfulness? An item response theory analysis of the mindful attention awareness scale. Pers. Individ. Differ. **49**, 805–810 (2010)
11. Kohls, N., Sauer, S., Walach, H.: Facets of mindfulness – results of an online study investigating the Freiburg mindfulness inventory. Pers. Individ. Dif. **46**, 224–230 (2009)
12. Baer, R.A., Smith, G.T., Hopkins, J., Krietemeyer, J., Toney, L.: Using self-report assessment methods to explore facets of mindfulness. Assessment **13**, 27–45 (2006)
13. Cardaciotto, L., Herbert, J.D., Forman, E.M., Moitra, E., Farrow, V.: The assessment of present-moment awareness and acceptance: the Philadelphia mindfulness scale. Assessment **15**, 204–223 (2008)
14. Chambers, R., Gullone, E., Allen, N.B.: Mindful emotion regulation: an integrative review. Clin. Psychol. Rev. **29**, 560–572 (2009)
15. Williams, J.M.G.: Mindfulness and psychological process. Emotion **10**, 1–7 (2010)

16. Lau, M., Bishop, S.R., Segal, Z.V., Buis, T., Anderson, N.D., Carlson, L., Shapiro, S., Carmody, J., Abbey, S., Devins, G.: The Toronto mindfulness scale: development and validation. J. Clin. Psychol. **62**, 1445–1467 (2006)
17. Teasdale, J.D., Moore, R.G., Hayhurst, H., Pope, M., Williams, S., Segal, Z.V.: Metacognitive awareness and prevention of relapse in depression: empirical evidence. J. Consult. Clin. Psychol. **70**, 275–287 (2002)
18. Grabovac, A.D., Lau, M.A., Willett, B.R.: Mechanisms of mindfulness: a Buddhist psychological model. Mindfulness (N.Y.) **2**(3), 154–166 (2011)
19. Lave, J., Wenger, E.: Situated Learning: Legitimate Peripheral Participation. Cambridge University Press, Cambridge (1991)
20. Adams, A., Lunt, P., Cairns, P.: A qualitative approach to HCI research. In: Cairns, P., Cox, A. (eds.) Research Methods for Human-Computer Interaction, pp. 138–157. Cambridge University Press, Cambridge, UK (2008)
21. McRae, K., Ciesielski, B., Gross, J.J.: Unpacking cognitive reappraisal: goals, tactics, and outcomes. Emotion **12**, 250–255 (2012)

Eye Tracking in Universal Access

Assessing Levels of Attention Using Low Cost Eye Tracking

Per Bækgaard[✉], Michael Kai Petersen, and Jakob Eg Larsen

Cognitive Systems, Department of Applied Mathematics and Computer Science,
Technical University of Denmark, Building 321, 2800 Kongens Lyngby, Denmark
{pgba,mkai,jaeg}@dtu.dk

Abstract. The emergence of mobile eye trackers embedded in next generation smartphones or VR displays will make it possible to trace not only what objects we look at but also the level of attention in a given situation. Exploring whether we can quantify the engagement of a user interacting with a laptop, we apply mobile eye tracking in an in-depth study over 2 weeks with nearly 10.000 observations to assess pupil size changes, related to attentional aspects of alertness, orientation and conflict resolution. Visually presenting conflicting cues and targets we hypothesize that it's feasible to measure the allocated effort when responding to confusing stimuli. Although such experiments are normally carried out in a lab, we have initial indications that we are able to differentiate between sustained alertness and complex decision making even with low cost eye tracking "in the wild". From a quantified self perspective of individual behavioural adaptation, the correlations between the pupil size and the task dependent reaction time and error rates may longer term provide a foundation for modifying smartphone content and interaction to the users perceived level of attention.

Keywords: Eye tracking · Attention network

1 Introduction

Low cost eye trackers which can be embedded in next generation smartphones will enable design of cognitive interfaces that adapt to the users perceived level of attention. Even when "in the wild", and no longer constrained to fixed lab setups, mobile eye tracking provides novel opportunities for continuous self-tracking of our ability to perform a variety of tasks across a number of different contexts.

Interacting with a smartphone screen requires attention which in turn involves different networks in the brain related to alertness, spatial orientation and conflict resolution [20]. These aspects can be separated by flanker-type of experiments with differently cued, sometimes conflicting, prompts. Dependent on whether the task involves fixating the eyes on an unexpected part of the screen, or resolving the direction of an arrow surrounded by distracting stimuli, different parts of the attention network will be activated, in turn resulting in varying reaction times [7].

© Springer International Publishing Switzerland 2016
M. Antona and C. Stephanidis (Eds.): UAHCI 2016, Part I, LNCS 9737, pp. 409–420, 2016.
DOI: 10.1007/978-3-319-40250-5_39

The dilation and constriction of the pupil is not only triggered by changes in light and fixation but reflect fluctuations in arousal networks in the brain [13], which from a quantified self perspective may enable us to assess whether we are sufficiently concentrated when we interact with the screens of smartphones or laptops, carrying out our daily tasks. Likewise the pupil size increases when we face an unexpected uncertainty [1], physically apply force by flexing muscles, or motivationally have to decide on whether the outcome of a task justifies the required effort [23]. Thus, when we perform specific actions, the cognitive load involved can be estimated using eye tracking. The pupil dilates if the task requires a shift from a sustained tonic alertness and orientation to more complex decision making, in turn triggering a phasic component caused by the release of norepinephrine neurotransmitters in the brain [2,8], which may reflect both the increased energization as well as the unexpected uncertainty related to the task [1].

Whereas these results have typically been obtained under controlled lab conditions, we explore in the present study the feasibility of assessing a users level of attention "in the wild" using mobile eye tracking.

2   Method

2.1   Experimental Procedure

This longitudinal study was performed repeatedly over the course of two weeks in September-October 2015. Two male right-handed subjects, A and B, (of average age 56) each performed a session very similar to the Attention Network Test (ANT) [7] approximately twice every weekday, resulting in 16 resp. 17 complete datasets, totaling 9.504 individual reaction time tests. The experiment ran "in the wild" in typical office environments off a conventional MacBook Pro 13" (2013 model with Retina screen) that had an Eye Tribe Eye Tracker connected to it. The ANT used here is implemented in PsychoPy [18] and is available on github [4]. Simultaneously, eye tracking data is recorded at 60 Hz and timestamped for synchronization through the Eye Tracker API [21] via the PeyeTribe [3] interface.

Before the actual experimental procedure starts, a calibration of the Eye Tracker is performed. The experiment contains an initial trial run that the user may select to abort, after which 3 rounds of $2 \cdot 48$ conditioned reaction time tests follows (Fig. 1); each test is conditioned on one of 3 targets: *Incongruent, Neutral* or *Congruent* and on 4 cues: *No Cue, Center Cue, Double Cue* or *Spatial Cue*. At the start of each test, a fixation cross appears, and after a random delay of 0.4–1.6 s the user is presented to a cue (when present for the particular condition). 0.5 s later the target appears, either with incongruent, neutral or congruent flankers. The user is instructed to hit a button on the left or right side of the keyboard with his left or right hand depending on the direction of the central arrow of the target, which appeared above or below the initial centred fixation cross. Half the targets appear above and half below the fixation cross, and left/right pointing central arrows also appear evenly distributed.

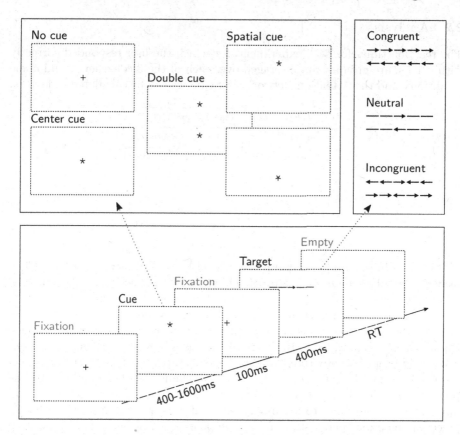

Fig. 1. This Attention Network Test procedure used here: Every 4 s, a cue (either of 4 conditions (TOP, LEFT)) precedes a target (either of 3 congruency conditions (TOP, RIGHT)), to which the participant responds by pressing a key according to the central arrow. The reaction time differences between cue- and congruency conditions form the basis for calculating the latencies of the attention, orientation and conflict resolution networks.

The resulting reaction time "from target presentation to first registered keypress" is logged, together with the conditions of the individual tests, whether the user hit the correct left/right key or not, and a common timestamp. For further details on the ANT please see [7].

Each test takes approximately 4 s to perform. With 2·3 repetitions of all combinations of conditions, left/right arrows and above/below targets, this results in $6 \cdot 12 \cdot 2 \cdot 2 = 288$ single tests. The user has the option of a short break after each 96 performed tests. A typical session with calibration, experimental procedure and short breaks lasts approximately 25–30 min.

2.2   Analysis

The reaction times for each experiment, for which the user responded correctly within 1.7 s, are grouped and averaged over each of the 3 congruency and 4 cue conditions, and the Attention Network Test timings can be calculated as follows:

$$t_{\text{alertness}} = \overline{t_{\text{no cue}}} - \overline{t_{\text{double cue}}}$$
$$t_{\text{orientation}} = \overline{t_{\text{center cue}}} - \overline{t_{\text{spatial cue}}}$$
$$t_{\text{conflict resolution}} = \overline{t_{\text{incongruent}}} - \overline{t_{\text{congruent}}}$$

where

$$\overline{t_{\text{cond}}} = \frac{1}{N} \sum_{i|i=\text{cond}}^{N} t_i$$

Linear pupil size and inter-pupil distance data can be somewhat "noisy" when recording in office conditions. After epoch'ing to corresponding cue times for the individual tests, invalid/missing data from blink-affected periods are removed, and a Hampel [9] filter is therefore applied, using a centered window of ± 83 ms (shorter than a typical blink) and a limit of 3σ, to remove remaining outliers. Data is then downsampled to 100 ms resolution using a windowed averaging filter, and scaled proportionally to the value at epoch start (cue presentation), so that the resulting pupil dilations represent relative change[1] vs the pupil size at cue presentation. This last part was done to compensate for varying environmental luminosity changes and, to some degree, to offset any effect from immediately preceding reaction time test(s) and to compensate for accidental head position drift.

Time-locked averaging is then done by grouping data from similar conditions within each experiment, from which the group-mean relative pupil dilations can be derived.

At the same time, the inter-pupil distance is calculated, to ensure that pupil size changes would not be the accidental result of moving the head slightly during the experiment. Additionally, a "baseline" experiment has been performed, recording eye tracking data in a condition where no action can be taken by the user and when no arrow-heads are visible on the targets but otherwise presented in similar conditions, in order to rule out that the recorded pupil dilations would be the result of (small) luminosity changes caused by the presented cue and targets, or a result of slightly changing accommodation between the focus points of the cue and the target.

The inter-pupil distance variation was found to be significantly smaller (typically much less than 0.2 %) than the recorded pupil dilations, and the "baseline" experiment could not account for the recorded pupil dilations from the real experimental procedure either; it just showed the expected random variations.

---

[1] The data received from the eye tracker is uncalibrated and cannot easily be referenced to a metric measurement.

The data processing has been done with iPython [19] using the numpy [22], matplotlib [11], pandas [15], scipy [16] and scikit-learn [17] toolboxes.

3 Results

3.1 Attention Network Test Timings

Table 1 shows the aggregate Overall Mean Reaction- and Attention Network timings for each subject A and B, with estimates of the variation over the week. The figures are not significantly different from what is found in [7]; the MeanRT reported here is slightly higher than an estimated 512 ms in the reference, whereas the alertness, orientation and conflict resolution are slightly lower or similar to the 47 ms, 51 ms and 84 ms reported.

Table 1. Average Reaction- and Attention Network-Times over all correctly replied experiments for the two week period for either user (the variation over the period is given as estimated ± Sample Standard Deviation of the aggregate values), in milliseconds.

Subject	MeanRT	Alert	Orient	Conflict
A	577 (±54)	27 (±21)	22 (±18)	85 (±16)
B	559 (±55)	35 (±17)	49 (±15)	81 (±17)

There are, however, behavioural variations in reaction time throughout the weeks. Figure 2 shows the variation of the derived ANT timings throughout the experimental period, and the relative error rate for each experiment. The variation appear to be statistically significant, as can be estimated from the standard error of the mean (the shaded area), and may reflect underlying states of varying levels of attention, fatigue and motivation.

To sum up the behavioural results, A shows a somewhat increasing trend in error rate related to the objective task performance, whereas B shows a diminishing difference between the three estimated measures of conflict resolution, spatial orientation and alertness reaction time.

3.2 Pupil Dilations

The group-mean relative linear pupil dilations for each of the 3 congruency conditions are illustrated in Fig. 3.

Pupil dilation responses are all epoch'ed to the cue (at time 0 ms) and target presentation (time 500 ms). A small and slow pupil dilation onset is seen <300 ms after cue presentation, followed by a larger response likely triggered by the target presentation, with an onset of approximately 700 ms and a peak approximately 1300 ms after target, with some variation between conditions, subject and eye.

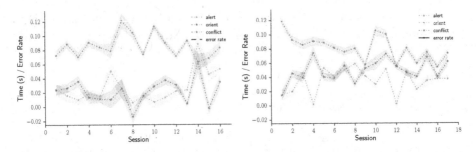

Fig. 2. Attention Network Timing over all sessions in the two week period. Conflict Resolution (RED) is slower than Alertness (GREEN) and Orientation (BLUE). A (LEFT) shows an increasing error rate trend (SOLID); Conflict Resolution for B gradually approaches the other latencies. Both A and B have large variations over time, pointing to varying levels of attention, fatigue and motivation. (Color figure online)

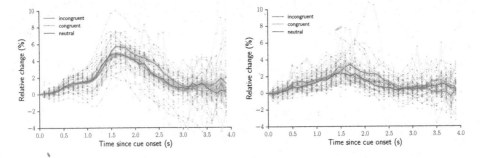

Fig. 3. Averaged left-eye pupil dilations for each session, coloured according to congruency (A (LEFT) and B). All-session average shown in bold, with the shaded area representing the standard error of the mean. The average incongruent (RED) pupil dilation is stronger than the others, indicating a higher cognitive load. (Color figure online)

Even though the experimental conditions are not directly comparable, [14] reported comparable peak latencies at 1400 ms after stimulus for a Stroop effect experiment. Our results are thus in line with these previous findings of pupil dilations, as well as with those reported in earlier processing load experiments [12] at approximately 900–1200 ms. The initial onset of the pupil dilation can occur even faster in some conditions [6,10] although generally onset and peak latencies appear to be within the 150–1400 ms.

The incongruent pupil dilation is larger than the more similar neutral and congruent dilations; there is however no such difference when comparing the 4 cue condition (not shown). The incongruent pupil dilation also has a tendency to appear slightly later (most easily visible for A), consistent with the longer reaction times for the inconsistent condition.

Figure 4 shows the (relative) pupil size BLUE vs the median value over a selected period that covers 48 reaction time tests, in this case for B, for two different experiments. Test-related pupil dilation responses, that occur every 4 s, are not immediately visible in this graph due to random noise and a relatively strong longer-periodic variation over 20–60 s². The GREEN curve shows the relative variation of the inter-pupil distance, with variations an order of magnitude smaller than the pupil size changes.

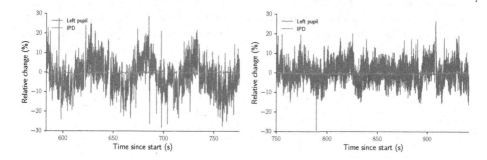

Fig. 4. Filtered pupil size plots; 48-test long sections of two experiments (B, left-eye). Relative inter-pupil distance (GREEN) indicates stable eye-to-screen distances. (Color figure online)

Figure 5 shows the area under the pupil dilation curve between 1.5–2.5 s after cue (1.0–2.0 s after target) for each experiment, serving as a very rough indicator of the relative cognitive load caused by the tests. From these, also a δ(incon) can be calculated by subtracting the congruent value from the incongruent.

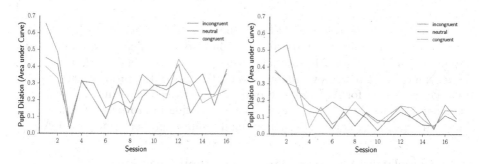

Fig. 5. Area under left-eye pupil dilation curves $[1.5, 2.5]$ s for each session, indicative of cognitive load, grouped after congruency. Both A (LEFT) and B show initial training effects; only A however shows an increasing trend in cognitive load for the remaining sessions. (Color figure online)

---

2 A frequency domain analysis of the signal shows, however, a distinct peak at 0.25 Hz, as expected.

It is seen that both A and B have larger pupil dilation responses for the initial two experiments, after which the level is lower. For B it remains at lower levels, indicating a training effect. For A, the pattern is less clear, with possibly an increased load towards the end of the two week period.

3.3   Predicting Congruency Condition from Pupil Dilations

In order to verify how well previous pupil dilations allow predicting the class of congruency condition, a subset of the 3 within-experiment 96–average pupil dilation responses from each subject were ordered in each of the 6 possible permutations of the 3 congruency conditions. A neural-network type classifier was then trained to identify which of the 3 averaged pupil dilations were the incongruent.

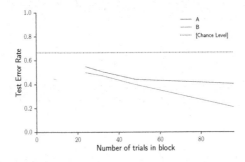

Fig. 6. Test error rates (0.9/0.1 train/test split) predicting averaged 3 s incongruent pupil dilations after cue vs number of averaged experimental tests. At 48 averaged experimental tests, the test error rate at 50 % is clearly below chance (66.6 %, dotted). (Color figure online)

Figure 6 shows the resulting test error rate vs. the number of averaged experimental tests, dividing the 96 equal-condition responses of each experiment into groups of 96, 48, 32 or 24 tests, and using a test/train split of 0.9/0.1. The performance is clearly above chance level (66.6 %), and approaches 80 % accuracy for B vs 60 % for A. Even at groups of 24 averaged experimental tests, the classifier operate above chance level, with continuing improved performance for larger groups for B, however only marginally improving performance for A.

3.4   Correlating Response Times and Pupil Reactions

Table 2 show the Pearson Correlation Coefficients for all combinations of Attention Network- and Reaction-Times, Pupil Dilation metrics and Time-of-Day for each subject, as it varies over the two week period. As the data sets are small (16 and 17 sets), caution is needed when judging the significance levels (p-values).

With some variation between subjects, pupil dilation responses appear correlated.

Table 2. Pearsons correlation coefficients between key metrics for A (Top) and B. A shows negative correlation between mean reaction time and error rate ("speed-accuracy tradeoff"). B (opposed to A) shows correlation between pupil dilations and error rate, possibly indicating a different response to varying levels of fatigue or motivation; additionally alertness (and partly orientation) may inversely correlate to pupil dilations. Both show expected correlations between pupil dilation metrics.

	Att.-Net/Reaction Time			Pupil Dilation					
	Orient	Conflict	μ(RT)	Incon	Neutral	Con	δ(Incon)	ToD	Errors
Att.-Net/Reaction Time									
Alert	0.112	−0.047	−0.189	−0.013	−0.131	−0.011	−0.008	0.061	−0.051
Orient		−0.548[†]	−0.468*	0.274	0.269	−0.020	0.402	0.132	0.270
Conflict			0.474*	−0.081	−0.149	0.035	−0.147	0.330	−0.416
μ(RT)				0.002	0.049	−0.069	0.068	0.237	−0.635[†]
Pupil Dilation									
Incon					0.767[‡]	0.701[‡]	0.737[‡]	0.062	−0.098
Neutral						0.752[‡]	0.362	0.222	0.109
Con							0.034	0.000	−0.018
δ(Incon)								0.087	−0.121
ToD									0.066

Two-tailed significance less than *7.5%, [†]5% and [‡]0.25% marked.

	Att.-Net/Reaction Time			Pupil Dilation					
	Orient	Conflict	μ(RT)	Incon	Neutral	Con	δ(Incon)	ToD	Errors
Att.-Net/Reaction Time									
Alert	0.015	−0.107	0.438	−0.499[†]	−0.534[†]	−0.231	−0.576[†]	0.062	−0.358
Orient		−0.094	0.352	−0.474*	−0.407	−0.559[†]	−0.155	0.056	−0.386
Conflict			0.289	0.431	0.439	0.362	0.309	0.411	0.301
μ(RT)				−0.220	−0.286	−0.173	−0.173	0.481*	−0.400
Pupil Dilation									
Incon					0.894[‡]	0.817[‡]	0.746[‡]	−0.026	0.725[‡]
Neutral						0.831[‡]	0.549[†]	−0.184	0.701[‡]
Con							0.224	−0.020	0.626[†]
δ(Incon)								−0.021	0.501[†]
ToD									−0.215

Two-tailed significance less than *7.5%, [†]5% and [‡]0.25% marked.

Subject A shows correlation between orientation and conflict resolution timings, which is however not seen at all for B. A also may have some correlation between mean reaction time and orientation resp conflict resolution timings, which are however again not quite as present with B.

Subject B shows correlation between alertness timing and both incongruent, neutral and δ(incon) pupil dilations, as well as correlation between orientation timing and congruent pupil dilations. These are not present for A, however. Also, there are indications of a correlation between the time of day and the mean reaction time; the experiments done on B were spread out over larger sections of the day than for A, which might explain why this is not seen for A.

[7] reported correlations between the conflict resolution timing and the mean reaction time over a large group of people. As such, the conditions are not similar to the within-person variation, but it might be worth pointing out that a similar correlation is partly present for A and cannot be ruled out for B.

4 Discussion

Using low cost portable eye tracking to measure the variations in pupil size, we have initial indications that we were able to differentiate and predict whether users were engaged in more complex decision making or merely maintaining a general alertness when interacting with a laptop, over nearly 10.000 tests. A parallel single-experiment study [5] repeating the experimental setup with nearly 10.000 additional tests over 18 more subjects, have confirmed that similar significant pupil response differences characterize the contrasts between incongruent versus neutral or congruent task conditions.

In the present study, we found a significant difference based on the left eye pupil size for the conflict resolution task in contrast to the attentional network components of alertness and re-orientation, but not between these two latter tasks. These results may reflect findings in other studies indicating that the phasic component in attention is predominantly triggered by tasks requiring a decision, whereas the tonic alertness may suffice for solving less demanding tasks like responding to visual cues or re-orienting attention to an unexpected part of the screen [2] as seen in the "baseline" experiment, where no decision needs to be made and no motor cortex activation takes place.

From a quantified self perspective of individual behaviour, using mobile eye tracking to assess levels of engagement, the relations between pupil size (a possible quantification of the cognitive load), and error rate/reaction time (a quantification of the objective task performance), indicate individual differences among the subjects' behavioural adaptation to the attentional tasks. Participant A is apparently coping with the cognitive load by trading off speed and accuracy to optimize performance, as indicated by the lack of correlation between pupil size and either of the performance related measures. However, for Participant B the correlation between pupil size and accuracy may suggest a behavior characterized by applying more effort to the task if the number of errors increase.

As we have in this study only used the pupil size as a measure of attention, even without considering the spatial density of fixations or the speed of saccadic eye movements that could entail further information, we suggest that mobile eye tracking may not only enable us to assess the effort required when undertaking a variety of tasks in an everyday context, but could also longer term provide a foundation for continuously adapting the content and interaction with smartphones and laptops based on our perceived level of attention.

Acknowledgment. This work is supported in part by the Innovation Fund Denmark through the project Eye Tracking for Mobile Devices.

References

1. Ang, Y.S., Manohar, S., Apps, M.A.J.: Commentary: noradrenaline and dopamine neurons in the reward/effort trade-off: a direct electrophysiological comparison in behaving monkeys. Front. Behav. Neurosci. **9**, 310 (2015). http://www.ncbi.nlm.nih.gov/pmc/articles/PMC4644795/pdf/fnbeh-09-00310.pdf, http://journal.frontiersin.org/Article/10.3389/fnbeh.2015.00310/abstract

2. Aston-Jones, G., Cohen, J.D.: An integrative theory of locus coeruleus-norepinephrine function: adaptive gain and optimal performance. Ann. Rev. Neurosci. **28**(1), 403–450 (2005). http://www.annualreviews.org/doi/abs/10.1146/annurev.neuro.28.061604.135709

3. Bækgaard, P.: Simple python interface to the Eye Tribe eye tracker (2015). https://github.com/baekgaard/peyetribe/

4. Bækgaard, P.: Attention Network Test implemented in PsychoPy (2016). https://github.com/baekgaard/ant

5. Baekgaard, P., Petersen, M.K., Larsen, J.E.: Differentiating attentional network components using mobile eye tracking (in preparation)

6. Beatty, J.: Task-evoked pupillary responses, processing load, and the structure of processing resources (1982)

7. Fan, J., McCandliss, B.D., Sommer, T., Raz, A., Posner, M.I.: Testing the efficiency and independence of attentional networks. J. Cogn. Neurosci. **14**(3), 340–347 (2002). http://www.mitpressjournals.org//abs/10.1162/089892902317361886

8. Gabay, S., Pertzov, Y., Henik, A.: Orienting of attention, pupil size, and the norepinephrine system. Attention Percept. Psychophysics **73**(1), 123–129 (2011). http://www.ncbi.nlm.nih.gov/pubmed/21258914

9. Hampel, F.R.: The influence curve and its role in robust estimation. J. Am. Stat. Assoc. **69**(346), 383–393 (1974). http://www.tandfonline.com//abs/10.1080/01621459.1974.10482962

10. Holmqvist, K.: Eye Tracking: A Comprehensive Guide to Methods and Measures. Oxford University Press, Oxford (2011)

11. Hunter, J.D.: Matplotlib: a 2D graphics environment. Comput. Sci. Eng. **9**(3), 99–104 (2007)

12. Hyönä, J., Tommola, J., Alaja, A.M.: Pupil dilation as a measure of processing load in simultaneous interpretation and other language tasks. Q. J. Exp. Psychology Sect. A **48**(3), 598–612 (1995). http://www.tandfonline.com//abs/10.1080/14640749508401407

13. Joshi, S., Li, Y., Kalwani, R.M., Gold, J.I.: Relationships between pupil diameter and neuronal activity in the locus coeruleus, colliculi, and cingulate cortex. Neuron **89**(1), 221–234 (2016)

14. Laeng, B., Ørbo, M., Holmlund, T., Miozzo, M.: Pupillary stroop effects. Cogn. Process. **12**(1), 13–21 (2011)

15. McKinney, W.: Data structures for statistical computing in python. In: Proceedings of the 9th Python in Science Conference 1697900(Scipy), pp. 51-56 (2010). http://conference.scipy.org/proceedings/scipy2010/mckinney.html

16. Oliphant, T.E.: SciPy: open source scientific tools for python. Comput. Sci. Eng. **9**, 10–20 (2007). http://www.scipy.org/

17. Pedregosa, F., Varoquaux, G., Gramfort, A., Michel, V., Thirion, B., Grisel, O., Blondel, M., Prettenhofer, P., Weiss, R., Dubourg, V., Vanderplas, J., Passos, A., Cournapeau, D., Brucher, M., Perrot, M., Duchesnay, É.: Scikit-learn: machine learning in python. J. Mach. Learn. Res. **12**, 2825–2830 (2012). http://dl.acm.org/citation.cfm?id=2078195, http://arxiv.org/abs/1201.0490

420   P. Bækgaard et al.

18. Peirce, J.W.: PsychoPy-psychophysics software in python. J. Neurosci. Methods **162**(1–2), 8–13 (2007). http://dx.org/10.1016/j.jneumeth.2006.11.017
19. Pérez, F., Granger, B.E.: IPython: a system for interactive scientific computing. Comput. Sci. Eng. **9**(3), 21–29 (2007). http://ipython.org
20. Posner, M.I.: Attentional networks and consciousness.. Front. Psychol. **3**, 1–4 (2012). http://www.ncbi.nlm.nih.gov/pmc/articles/PMC3298960/
21. The Eye Tribe: The Eye Tribe API Reference. http://dev.theeyetribe.com/api/
22. Van Der Walt, S., Colbert, S.C., Varoquaux, G.: The NumPy array: a structure for efficient numerical computation. Comput. Sci. Eng. **13**(2), 22–30 (2011)
23. Varazzani, C., San-Galli, A., Gilardeau, S., Bouret, S.: Noradrenaline and dopamine neurons in the reward/effort trade-off: a direct electrophysiological comparison in behaving monkeys. J. Neurosci. **35**(20), 7866–7877 (2015). http://www.ncbi.nlm.nih.gov/pmc/articles/PMC4644795/pdf/fnbeh-09-00310.pdf, http://www.jneurosci.org/cgi//10.1523/JNEUROSCI.0454-15.2015

An Overview of How Eye Tracking Is Used in Communication Research

Nadine Bol[1]([⊠]), Sophie C. Boerman[1],
Jennifer C. Romano Bergstrom[2], and Sanne Kruikemeier[1]

[1] Amsterdam School of Communication Research/ASCoR,
University of Amsterdam, Amsterdam, The Netherlands
{n.bol,s.c.boerman,s.kruikemeier}@uva.nl
[2] Facebook, Menlo Park, USA
jennifer@romanocog.com

Abstract. Eye tracking gives communication scholars the opportunity to move beyond self-reported measures by examining more precisely how much visual attention is paid to information. However, we lack insight into how eye-tracking data is used in communication research. This literature review provides an overview of how eye tracking is used in communication research by examining published articles from the top-25 ranked communication journals between 2005 and 2015. Our results showed that most eye-tracking research was employed in the field of advertising. Furthermore, most studies used eye tracking to measure (visual) attention and used this as the study's dependent variable. A wide variety of eye-tracking measures were reported, including fixation time, fixation count, and visual shifts, and a wide variety of eye-tracking devices were used. Our results highlight opportunities for using eye tracking as well as identify other ways of using eye tracking to maximize its potential in communication research.

Keywords: Eye tracking · Communication research · (Visual) attention · Research methods

1 Introduction

Eye-movement data gives communication scholars the opportunity to examine more precisely how much visual attention has been paid to information [1–3]. Moreover, eye tracking moves beyond self-reported data by offering a rather objective measure that shows how visual and textual information is processed [4]. Tracking individuals' eye movements allows researchers to see what individuals find interesting and, possibly, gain insight into how information is perceived [5].

Although eye-tracking technology has been available for more than a century [4], the use of eye-movement data within the field of communication is remarkably limited. This is incredibly surprising as such data is of crucial importance for communication scholars. Mediated communication always involves some kind of material, both visual and textual. Yet, communication researchers have less knowledge about the actual attention people give to this information, as it is often assumed that self-reported measures are an indication of attention. Using eye-movement data, communication

© Springer International Publishing Switzerland 2016
M. Antona and C. Stephanidis (Eds.): UAHCI 2016, Part I, LNCS 9737, pp. 421–429, 2016.
DOI: 10.1007/978-3-319-40250-5_40

scholars may have a better understanding about which information receives attention. For example, eye-movement data can help gain insight into how online health information is processed (e.g., textual or visual information or both [6]). Moreover, eye tracking can be used to make ads more effective or give insight into how people select and read news about public affairs.

This study aims to contribute to this interesting – but understudied – area of research by exploring how eye tracking is currently used within communication research. This study takes the form of a literature review and examines thoroughly and systematically which measures and eye-tracking systems are deployed, and in which context and country the data were collected. We also describe the materials and samples used. As a result of this close examination of previous work, this study offers directions for future communication research in various fields that wish to use eye-movement data.

2   Method

2.1   Search Procedure

To find eligible studies that used eye tracking in communication research, we focused on articles published in the top-25 ranked communication journals from January 1, 2005 to December 8, 2015 (see Appendix for a list of the top-25 ranked communication journals). This top-25 list was based on the 5-year impact factor as indicated by the ISI Web of Knowledge [7] on November 25, 2015. Our focus on the top journals enabled us to provide an overview of the usage of eye tracking in the most important outlets in the field of communication. We used the Communication & Mass Media Complete database to search for eligible studies in the specific journals. Search terms included "eye track*" (All text field) and the name of the journal (Source field): this procedure was repeated for each of the 25 journals.

2.2   Data Extraction

For each article, the following characteristics were extracted: eye-tracking measures, type of eye-tracking measure (i.e., dependent variable, independent variable, mediator, moderator), intended communication measure, study sample (i.e., sample size, type of participants), material format, eye tracker specifications, field, and country (see Table 1).

3   Results

3.1   Study Selection

The search procedure yielded 90 articles. After screening the full-text content of these articles, 70 references were excluded, because they did not report on eye-tracking data (e.g., only mentioned eye tracking as recommended future methodological research approach, reported on previous eye-tracking studies). The remaining 20 articles were screened for data extraction of which the results are reported below.

Table 1. Main characteristics of included studies

Author (year)	Journal	Eye-tracking measure	Variable type	Communication measure	Field	Material format	Sample	Eye tracker	Country
Bassett-Guntera et al. (2014)	JoHC	Dwell time	DV/IV	Attention	Health	Text on screen	Undergraduate students (N = 77)	The Eyelink II	Canada
Beattie et al. (2010)	JLSP	Fixation time; % fixation; fixation count (40 ms)	DV	Attention	Language	Video	Students (N = 10)	ASL Model 504	UK
Bente et al. (2008)	HCR	Unclear	DV	Visual Attention	CMC	Text, audio, video	Convenience sample (N = 150)	Mediascore, 25 Hz	Germany
Boerman et al. (2015)	JoA	Fixation time (80 ms)	MED	Visual attention	Advertising (TV)	TV program	Undergraduate students (N = 149)	SMI RED, 120 Hz	The Netherlands
Dix et al. (2010)	JAR	% (fixation) time	DV/IV	Banner eye gaze	Advertising (TV)	Video ads	Adult TV viewers (N = 248)	FaceLAB	Australia
Galesic et al. (2008)	POQ	Fixation time; fixation count (100 ms)	DV	Attention	Public opinion	Survey questions	Convenience sample (N = 108)	Tobii 1750, 50 Hz	US
Hartmann et al. (2013)	IJAR	Fixation time; fixation count; visit count	DV	Attention	Advertising (print)	Print ad	Undergraduate students (N = 75)	Tobii T60	Unknown
Heath (2009)	JAR	Number of fixations-per-second	DV	Attention/processing	Advertising (print & TV)	Print & video ads	Convenience sample (N = 17)	Unknown	UK
Heath et al. (2009)	JAR	Number of fixations-persecond	DV	Attention	Advertising (TV)	Video ads	University staff and students (N = 28)	Unknown	UK
Janssens et al. (2012)	IJAR	Number of jumps between page and ad (200 ms)	MC/MOD	Divided attention	Advertising (online)	Online ads (webpages)	Undergraduate students (N = 58; N = 66; N = 71)	SMI RED, 50/60 Hz	Belgium
Mackert et al. (2013)	JoHC	Fixation time; fixation count	DV	Attention	Health	Nutrition label information	University staff and literacy program partici-pants (N = 49)	Tobii T60	US
Neale et al. (2013)	JAR	Eyes-on-screen in seconds	DV	Exposure time	Advertising (TV & online)	Still & video ads	Representative US & Australian sample (N = 35)	Mirametrix system	US & Australia

(Continued)

Table 1. (*Continued*)

Author (year)	Journal	Eye-tracking measure	Variable type	Communication measure	Field	Material format	Sample	Eye tracker	Country
Pan et al. (2007)	JCMC	Fixation time; fixation count; pupil dilation; scanpaths (50 ms)	DV	Trust and implicit awareness	CMC	Webpages	Undergraduate students (N = 16)	ASL Model 504, 60 Hz	US
Perego et al. (2010)	MP	Fixation time; fixation count; path length; visual shifts (100 ms)	DV	Cognitive processing	Language	Video	Under/postgraduate students (N = 16)	Tobii 1750, 50 Hz	Hungary
Sanders-Jackson et al. (2011)	HCR	Fixation time	DV	Visual Attention	Public health	Video ads	Convenience sample of smokers (N = 71)	ASL Model 504, 19"	US
Siefert et al. (2008)	IJAR	Ratio time in/off center screen; ratio time on/off screen; eye movements and fixations inside screen but not in center	DV	Central tendency; screen time; visual processing activity	Advertising (TV)	Video ads	Convenience sample (N = 100)	Unknown	US
Smit et al. (2015)	JAR	% fixations during first 5 s; % fixations on text, brand, visual (100 ms)	DV	Visual attention	Advertising (print)	Magazine ads	Representative samples (N = 105)	Tobii	The Netherlands
Steele et al. (2013)	JAR	Fixation time	DV	Visual attention	Advertising (TV & online)	Video & online ads	Representative samples (N = 129; N = 122)	Tobii, 17"	US
Treutler et al. (2010)	JAR	% fixation time	DV	Visual attention	Advertising (print, radio, TV, online)	Display & video ads	Representative sample (N = 114)	Unknown	Canada
Turner et al. (2014)	JoHC	Gaze duration (100 ms)	DV	Visual attention	Health	Products on screen	Undergraduate students (N = 89)	MyTobii D10, 17"	US

Abbreviations: JoHC = Journal of Health Communication; JLSP = Journal of Language and Social Psychology; HCR = Human Communication Research; JoA = Journal of Advertising; JAR = Journal of Advertising Research; POQ = Public Opinion Quarterly; IJAR = International Journal of Advertising Research; JCMC = Journal of Computer-Mediated Communication; MP = Media Psychology; DV = dependent variable, IV = independent variable, MED = mediator, MC = manipulation check; CMC = Computer-mediated communication.

3.2 Study Characteristics

The included studies mostly reported on eye-tracking data in the field of advertising [8–16], but some eye-tracking studies were also conducted in (public) health [1, 17–19], language studies [20, 21], and computer-mediated communication [22, 23]. Nine studies reported on fixation time [1, 8, 10, 15, 18, 20, 21, 23, 24] or relative fixation time (% fixation time) as eye-tracking measure [9, 14, 16, 20]. Six articles reported on fixation count [10, 18, 20, 21, 23, 24], two on number of fixations-per-second [11, 12], and two on scan paths [23, 24] and visual shifts [24]. Furthermore, one study reported on (re)visit counts [10], one on gaze duration [19], one on dwell time [17], and one on number of jumps between page and ad [13].

The majority of studies used these eye-tracking measures to capture (visual) attention ($n = 15$) and used these measures as the study's dependent variable ($n = 18$). Most material formats included ads, either in the form of print [10, 11, 14], video [1, 9, 11, 12, 15, 16, 20, 24–26], or online [13, 15, 16, 25]. Other non-advertisement material formats included video clips [20], survey questions [21], nutrition labels [18], web-pages [23], and products [19]. Although nine articles employed eye tracking on more than 100 participants [8, 9, 13–16, 21, 22, 26], more articles reported on samples below 100 participants ($n = 11$). The 20 articles showed a wide variety of eye-tracking apparatus used. Seven studies assessed the eye-tracking measures using a Tobii eye tracker [10, 14, 15, 18, 19, 21, 24], three used the ASL Model 504 [1, 20, 23], and two used an SMI [8, 13]. All studies were conducted in Western countries (e.g., the US, Western Europe).

In addition, we noted that different eye trackers measure data with different Hz, which indicates the number of times data is acquired within one second, and different studies use different thresholds with regard to the minimum milliseconds required for a fixation to be registered. Our results showed that some studies use eye trackers with a gaze sample rate of only 25 Hz [22], whereas others collect their data at 120 Hz [8]. Fixations were mostly registered after 100 ms [14, 19, 21, 24], and range from 40 ms [20] to 200 ms [13]. However, most studies did not provide specifications on Hz and ms.

4 Discussion

This literature review explored how eye tracking is used in communication research. The results show that, although a significant number of articles mention the method, only few actually report on eye-tracking data. Eye tracking appears to be mostly used in the field of advertising, and typically quantitatively. In general, it is used to measure (visual) attention to specific content, assessed by a variety of eye-tracking measures, such as fixation time, fixation count, and visual shifts. Furthermore, eye tracking in communication research is employed on various material formats, such as print, video, and webpages.

Our findings suggest that other possible uses of eye tracking, such as usability research or even qualitative usage, seems to be neglected in communication research. Based the low numbers of studies that have employed eye tracking, and because the method could be used for many different goals, we believe that eye tracking has much more potential in communication research. Such potential may include using eye-tracking measures to indicate different communication measures, such as interest [27], applying eye-tracking methodology to other fields of communication research, such as political communication, and extending eye-tracking practices to mobile devices, such as smartphones and tablets [28].

The reported eye-tracking studies often involve rather large samples of more than 100 participants. This is in contrast to non-academic, practical usability research that includes eye tracking, that often uses smaller samples. Although there is no magic number for proper sample size, there is much debate about what sample size is sufficient for eye-tracking research [29]. A meta-analysis may be a potential next step that could reveal interesting insights about effect sizes and power in these studies. Nevertheless, eye tracking can provide various valuable measures, which can give clear insights into the effectiveness of communication materials. However, most of the studies only report one or two measures.

Given the wide variety of eye-tracking devices used in the different studies, it is uncertain whether the eye-tracking data is comparable. Different eye trackers measure data with different Hz, which means that the data acquired from these different devices vary in accuracy. Related to this issue is the difference between studies in the minimum milliseconds required for a fixation to be registered. Whereas some studies use a threshold of 80 ms [8], others register fixations after 100 ms [14] or 200 ms [13]. Moreover, several studies do not specify the minimum milliseconds for a fixation to be registered. It is thus debatable whether we can compare often-used measures such as fixation time and fixation count. We believe that communication research could benefit from more consistency in usage of eye trackers and thresholds and that future studies should make it a priority to include these specifications in their publications.

Another remarkable observation was that all studies were conducted in Western countries (e.g., the US, Australia, The Netherlands, Belgium, and the UK). Future research should be administered in non-Westerns countries, and may even consider comparing attention to communication in Western to non-Western countries. This is especially important because people from different cultures, with different languages and writing systems, may process written messages and even videos differently.

Altogether, this review provides insight into the usage of eye tracking in communication research. Based on our findings, we have formed several directions for further research. Despite these benefits, it is important to note an important limitation – communication research may not be always only published in top-25 ranked communication journals. Thus our review is not a complete overview of *all* eye-tracking studies. However, it provides insights about eye-tracking usage in the most important outlets in the field of communication.

Appendix: Top-25 Ranked Communication Journals (Alphabetical Order)

Communication Monographs
Communication Research
Communication Theory

Health Communication
Human Communication Research
Information Communication & Society
International Journal of Advertising
International Journal of Press-Politics
Journal of Advertising
Journal of Advertising Research
Journal of Communication
Journal of Computer-Mediated Communication
Journal of Health Communication
Journal of Language and Social Psychology
Journal of Social and Personal Relationships
Management Communication Quarterly
Media Psychology
New Media & Society
Personal Relationships
Political Communication
Public Opinion Quarterly
Public Understanding of Science
Research on Language and Social Interaction
Science Communication
Telecommunications Policy

References

1. Sanders-Jackson, A.N., Cappella, J.N., Linebarger, D.L., Piotrowski, J.T., O'Keeffe, M., Strasser, A.A.: Visual attention to antismoking PSAs: smoking cues versus other attention-grabbing features. Hum. Commun. Res. **37**, 275–292 (2011). doi:10.1111/j. 1468-2958.2010.01402.x
2. Romano Bergstrom, J.C., Erdman, C., Lakhe, S.: Navigation buttons in web-based surveys respondents' preferences revisited in the laboratory. Surv. Prac. **9**, 1 (2016)
3. Romano Bergstrom, J.C., Olmsted-Hawala, E.L., Bergstrom, H.C.: Older adults fail to see the periphery during website navigation. Univ. Acc. Inform. Soc. 1–10 (2014). doi:10.1007/s10209-014-0382-z
4. Poole, A., Ball, L.J.: Eye tracking in human-computer interaction and usability research: current status and future prospects. In: Ghaoui, C. (ed.) Encyclopedia of Human Computer Interaction, pp. 211–219. Idea Group Inc., Pennsylvania (2006)
5. Duchowski, A.: Eye Tracking Methodology: Theory and Practice. Springer Science & Business Media, London (2007)
6. Bol, N., Van Weert, J.C.M., Loos, E.F., Romano Bergstrom, J.C., Bolle, S., Smets, E.M.A.: How are online health messages processed? Using eye tracking to predict recall of information in younger and older adults. J. Health Commun **21**, 387–396 (2016)
7. ISI Web of Knowledge: Journal citation reports: journals from subject categories communication (2015). http://admin-apps.webofknowledge.com/JCR/JCR
8. Boerman, S.C., Van Reijmersdal, E.A., Neijens, P.C.: Using eye tracking to understand the effects of brand placement disclosure types in television programs. J. Advert. **44**, 196–207 (2015). 10.1080/00913367.2014.967423

9. Dix, S., Bellman, S., Haddad, H., Varan, D.: Using interactive program-loyalty banners to reduce TV ad avoidance. J. Advert. Res. **50**, 154–160 (2010). doi:10.2501/S00218499 10091312

10. Hartmann, P., Apaolaza, V., Alija, P.: Nature imagery in advertising: attention restoration and memory effects. Int. J. Advert. **32**, 183–210 (2013). doi:10.2501/IJA-32-2-183-210

11. Heath, R.G.: Emotional engagement: how television builds big brands at low attention. J. Advert. Res. **49**, 62–73 (2009). doi:10.2501/S0021849909090060

12. Heath, R.G., Nairn, A.C., Bottomley, P.A.: How effective is creativity? emotive content in TV advertising does not increase attention. J. Advert. Res. **49**, 450–463 (2009). doi:10.2501/S0021849909091077

13. Janssens, W., De Pelsmacker, P., Geuens, M.: Online advertising and congruency effects: it depends on how you look at it. Int. J. Advert. **31**, 579–604 (2012). doi:10.2501/IJA-31-3-579-604

14. Smit, E., Boerman, S., Van Meurs, L.: The power of direct context as revealed by eye tracking: a model tracks relative attention to competing editorial and promotional content. J. Advert. Res. **55**, 216–227 (2015). doi:10.2501/JAR-55-2-216-227

15. Steele, A., Jacobs, D., Siefert, C., Rule, R., Levine, B.: Leveraging synergy and emotion in a multi-platform world: a neuroscience-informed model of engagement. J. Advert. Res. **53**, 417–430 (2013). doi:10.2501/JAR-53-4-417-430

16. Treutler, T., Levine, B., Marci, C.D.: Biometrics and multi-platform messaging: the medium matters. J. Advert. Res. **50**, 243–249 (2010). doi:10.2501/S0021849910091415

17. Bassett-Gunter, R.L., Latimer-Cheung, A.E.: Martin Ginis, K.A., Castelhano, M.: I spy with my little eye: cognitive processing of framed physical activity messages. J. Health Commun. **19**, 676–691 (2014). doi:10.1080/10810730.2013.837553

18. Mackert, M., Champlin, S.E., Pasch, K.E., Weiss, B.D.: Understanding health literacy measurement through eye tracking. J. Health. Commun. **18**, 185–196 (2013). doi:10.1080/10810730.2013.825666

19. Turner, M.M., Skubisz, C., Pandya, S.P., Silverman, M., Austin, L.L.: Predicting visual attention to nutrition information on food products: the influence of motivation and ability. J. Health Commun. **19**, 1017–1029 (2014). doi:10.1080/10810730.2013.864726

20. Beattie, G., Webster, K., Ross, J.: The fixation and processing of the iconic gestures that accompany talk. J. Lang. Soc. Psychol. **29**, 194–213 (2010). doi:10.1177/0261927X0935 9589

21. Galesic, M., Tourangeau, R., Couper, M.P., Conrad, F.G.: Eye-tracking data: new insights on response order effects and other cognitive shortcuts in survey responding. Public. Opin. Q. **72**, 892–913 (2008). doi:10.1093/poq/nfn059

22. Bente, G., Rüggenberg, S., Krämer, N.C., Eschenburg, F.: Avatar-mediated networking: increasing social presence and interpersonal trust in net-based collaborations. Hum. Commun. Res. **34**, 287–318 (2008). doi:10.1111/j.1468-2958.2008.00322.x

23. Pan, B., Hembrooke, H., Joachims, T., Lorigo, L., Gay, G., Granka, L.: In Google we trust: users' decisions on rank, position, and relevance. J. Comput. Mediat. Commun. **12**, 801–823 (2007). doi:10.1111/j.1083-6101.2007.00351.x

24. Perego, E., Del Missier, F., Porta, M., Mosconi, M.: The cognitive effectiveness of subtitle processing. Media. Psychol. **13**, 243–272 (2010). doi:10.1080/15213269.2010.502873

25. Neale, L., Bellman, S., Treleaven-Hassard, S., Robinson, J., Varan, D.: Unlocking the 'reminder' potential when viewers pause programs: results from a laboratory test of a new online medium. J. Advert. Res. **53**, 444–454 (2013). doi:10.2501/JAR-53-4-444-454

26. Siefert, C., Gallent, J., Jacobs, D., Levine, B., Stipp, H., Marci, C.: Biometric and eye-tracking insights into the efficiency of information processing of television advertising during fast-forward viewing. Int. J. Advert. **27**, 425–446 (2008). doi:10.2501/S0265048708080050

27. Olmsted-Hawala, E.L., Holland, T., Quach, V.: Usability testing. In: Romano Bergstrom, J., Schall, A.J. (eds.) Eye Tracking in User Experience Design, pp. 49–80. Elsevier, Amsterdam (2014)

28. He, J., Siu, C., Chaparro, B., Strohl, J.: Mobile. In: Romano Bergstrom, J., Schall, A.J. (eds.) Eye Tracking in User Experience Design, pp. 255–290. Elsevier, Amsterdam (2014)

29. Loos, E.F., Romano Bergstrom, J.: Older adults. In: Romano Bergstrom, J., Schall, A.J. (eds.) Eye Tracking in User Experience Design, pp. 313–329. Elsevier, Amsterdam (2014)

An Eye Tracking Based Examination of Visual Attention During Pairwise Comparisons of a Digital Product's Package

Rafał Michalski[(✉)] and Jerzy Grobelny

Faculty of Computer Science and Management,
Wrocław University of Technology, Wrocław, Poland
{rafal.michalski, jerzy.grobelny}@pwr.edu.pl
http://RafalMichalski.com, http://JerzyGrobelny.com

Abstract. The paper presents results of the experimental investigation based on the eye tracking data regarding the pairwise comparisons of box package designs. Persons taking part in the study were asked to visually analyze and express their perceived purchase intentions towards various types of product packages. During the whole process subjects' visual activities were registered by an eye tracking system. The research explores two factors, where each is examined on two levels, namely: a box package with and without curved edges, and a package variant with and without a product image. The gathered oculographic data based on fixations were analyzed in defined areas of interests (AOIs). Finally, the obtained subjective subjects' preferences were compared and discussed with the objective eye tracking data.

Keywords: Eye tracking · Digital product presentation · Package design · Digital signage · AHP

1 Introduction

Research regarding human visual activity in a marketing context has a long history. Wedel and Pieters (2008) in their article reviewing eye tracking applications in this field refer to experiments conducted as early as in 1924. The development of more and more usable devices in the 90s of the 20th century resulted in a significant increase in the number of this type of studies. Furthermore, there are some methodological reasons that make the eye tracking studies attractive for scientists. In comparison with traditional methods, for instance, it allows for direct registration of quick attentional processes that are very often unconscious to a subject. Additionally, the researchers have a tool to verify existing results and models in a far more objective way than previously.

The research effort of the eye tracking based investigations in marketing has been directed, among other things, to examination of attentional dynamics concerned with printed advertisements, television commercials or web sites. In recent years oculographic studies also concern product packages. Among package design components that influence human being visual attention one usually includes (Piqueras-Fiszman et al. 2013): the package shape and texture, the location of informative items, labels etc.

© Springer International Publishing Switzerland 2016
M. Antona and C. Stephanidis (Eds.): UAHCI 2016, Part I, LNCS 9737, pp. 430–441, 2016.
DOI: 10.1007/978-3-319-40250-5_41

A number of latest studies in this regard deal with nutrition product packages. Graham et al. (2012) in their work presented a review of eye tracking analyses regarding identification and usage of nutrition information. The experiments allowed for creating detailed principles of the nutrition labels design. Some of the recommendations such as the clutter reduction of the label surrounding or the font size optimization were not possible to formulate earlier so precisely.

The application of scan paths tracking enabled the identification of relations between selected package attributes and customers' willingness to pay. Van Loo et al. (2015), for instance, showed that sustainability labels placed on the roasted ground coffee packaging lead to the increase of the acceptable price among people devoting more attention – measured by the dwell time and number of fixations – to these labels. In turn, Piqueras-Fiszman et al. (2013) documented an interesting phenomenon of the influence of ridged surface on extending the observer's penetration area towards edges and a flavor label of the examined jar of jam – and thereby increase willingness to try.

Chowdburry et al. (2012) examined scanpath patterns in mutated brands identification tasks. The exemplary illustrations of fixations and saccades registered during visual inspection of such products placed in shop shelves suggest that people apply the pairwise comparisons strategy in this type of visual search tasks. This mechanism was initially suggested by Van Raaji (1977) who directly observed of subjects' eye movements by means of a one-way mirror and recording camera. The findings of these papers constituted inspiration for the current study. The main goal of the present experiment is to try to identify the impact of specific package features on overt attention (Findlay and Gilchrist 2003) characteristics during performing pairwise comparisons of various package designs.

2   Method

2.1   Participants

A total of 23 student volunteers took part in the experiment. The age ranged from 19 to 47 years with the average of 22.2 and a standard deviation equaled 5.6. There were six males and 17 females participating in the study.

2.2   Apparatus

Custom made software was employed to present current study experimental stimuli. The same application was used for eliciting subjective weights according to the AHP methodology (Saaty 1977, 1980) based on pairwise comparisons. The gathered data were next exported to a statistical package for analyses. The examination was conducted in similar lighting conditions on a personal computer working under XP Microsoft Operating system and a 19 inches screen with a classic color scheme.

A SMI infrared eye-tracker system was used to track and collect oculographic data while making the comparisons. The system was composed of eye glasses and a laptop computer with a SMI iView ETG 2.2 recording application. The device allowed for recording eye ball movements at 60 Hz sample rate. Gaze analysis software (SMI BeGaze 3.5), was used for exporting raw data that were then analyzed in a statistical application.

2.3 Stimuli, Experimental Design and Dependent Variables

The study investigates a subjects' perceived willingness to buy a smartphone based on a digitally presented package. W prepared simple, three dimensional prototypes differed by two independent factors. Each factor was specified on two levels. The shape effect included a box package with or without curved edges, while the second one involved a package variant with or without a product image. A combination of these factors and their levels produced four different experimental conditions which are illustrated in Fig. 1.

(1)   (2)   (3)   (4)

Fig. 1. All four experimental conditions examined in the present study

A within subjects design was employed, thus each subject compared the set of all package variants. The subjective weights were computed based on these pairwise comparisons, by means of the AHP technique (Saaty 1977, 1980). Detailed calculation techniques may also be found e.g. in Michalski (2014).

Basic analysis of eye tracking data is usually based on saccades and fixations (Goldberg and Kotval 1999) which are the basic properties of a human visual behavior. A fixation refers to a situation when a person spends more time in a given location while a saccade is just a rapid jump of an eye ball between two fixations. In the presented analyses the fixation was defined according to a dispersion based algorithm with a minimum duration threshold (Salvucci and Goldberg 2000) when detected gazepoints lasted longer than 80 ms and their dispersion was smaller than 100 pixels (BeGaze Manual 2015).

Along with subjective preferences, the following objective data regarding participants' visual activity were used as dependent variables: dwell time, fixation durations, fixations count, fixated time, and pupil diameter.

2.4   Experimental Procedure

At first, participants were informed about the general objective of the study. After providing some basic data about themselves they put on the eye tracking glasses. Directly before the proper examination, the fast, one point calibration procedure was applied. The subjects' task was to assess which of the two presented smartphone packages would better persuaded them to buy the product. The image pairs were presented at random order by the experimental software. An example of such a comparison with a superimposed area of interests used for eye tracking data analysis is demonstrated in Fig. 2. During the whole process, subjects' visual activities were registered by the eye tracking system.

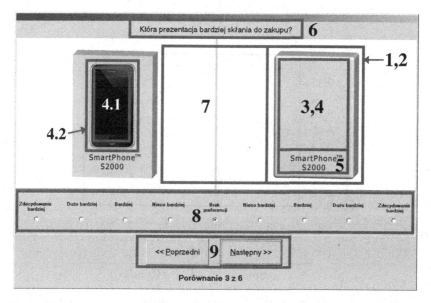

Fig. 2. An exemplary comparison presented by the experimental software. The superimposed Areas of Interests (numbers are explained in Table 3) were not visible during the examination.

3   Results

3.1   Perceived Purchase Willingness

Basic Statistics. The applied AHP framework allowed for controlling the subjects coherence of responses by computing the so called consistency ratio (CR) for each individual. The obtained values of CRs ranged from 0 to .042 with mean .016 and standard deviation of .0105. The observed values were far lower than the recommended .1 so all subjects' results were included in further analyses. The final hierarchy of examined conditions is presented in Table 1. Bigger mean weights denote higher preferences.

The results exhibit clear pattern showing that the inclusion of smartphone picture raises the average purchase intentions. Similarly, application of rounded box packages were more liked than the same variants with sharp edges. The observed pattern can be easily recognized in Fig. 3.

Table 1. Final hierarchy of investigated conditions based on mean weights of the purchase intentions. Standard deviations in brackets.

Hierarchy	Condition	Mean weight (SD)
1.	3. Rounded picture	.3162 (.0508)
2.	1. Sharp picture	.2724 (.0456)
3.	4. Rounded no picture	.2199 (.0391)
4.	2. Sharp no picture	.1915 (.0375)

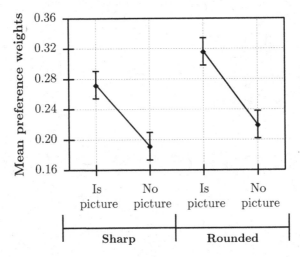

Fig. 3. Mean preference weights for all experimental conditions. Vertical bars denote 0.95 confidence intervals.

A series of LSD Fischer's pairwise comparisons between all experimental conditions revealed that differences between all of them were statistically significant at .05.

Table 2. Two-way (Shape × Picture presence) analysis of variance results

Effect	SS	df	MS	F	p	η^2
Package shape	.030	1	.030	16	.00015[*]	.15
Picture presence	.18	1	.18	95	<.0001[*]	.52
Package shape × Picture presence	.0014	1	.0014	.71	.40	.0080
Error	.17	88	.0019			

[*]$p < .001$; df–degrees of freedom; SS–sum of squares; MS–mean sum of squares; η^2–partial eta-squared

Analysis of Variance. A classic two way analysis of variance *Package shape* × *Picture presence* was used for formal verification whether the investigated factors and their interaction had a significant impact on mean willingness to buy a product. The computed data are put together in Table 2. The results revealed that both examined effects, differentiate average scores meaningfully: $F_{Shape}(1, 88) = 16$, p = .00015 and $F_{Picture\ presence}(1, 88) = 95$, p < .0001. The interaction between these factors was irrelevant.

Average values of subjective purchase intentions for the significant factors are graphically illustrated in Figs. 4 and 5 and clearly confirm the observation taken in the previous section. Rounded versions of the packages were better perceived than their sharp counter parts and box variants with pictures were better liked than options without them. The partial eta-squared values from Table 2 indicate that the Picture presence effect was decidedly more important than the Package shape factor in forming subjects' opinions.

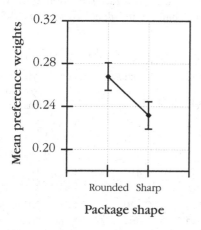 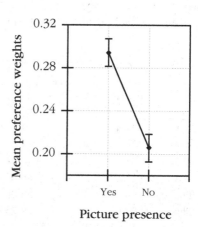

Fig. 4. Mean subjective purchase intentions for the *Package shape* factor. F(1, 88) = 16, p = .00015. Vertical bars denote .95 confidence intervals.

Fig. 5. Mean subjective purchase intentions for the factor. F(1, 88) = 95, p < .0001. Vertical bars denote .95 confidence intervals.

3.2 Eye Tracking Data Analysis

The obtained oculographic data were analyzed in particular parts of the presented stimuli by specifying the so called Area of Interests (AOI). By means of the SMI BeGaze 3.5 software two groups of AOIs were created. The first one concerned sections demonstrating the product package and included the following items: (1) Box rounded edges (EdgRnd), (2) Box sharp edges (EdgShr), (3) Box content without a picture (ConNoPic), (4) Box content with a picture (ConIsPic), and (5) Box captions (Caps). Additionally, the fourth AOI was divided into two subsections: 4.1. Phone edges (PhoEdg) and 4.2. Phone center (PhoCen). The second group comprised of regions related with the process of making comparisons, that is: (6) Task order (TskOrd), (7) Center area (Center), (8) Rating scale (Scale), (9) Buttons (Btns), and the remaining area where none particular objects were visible (10) White space (WhiSpa). The prepared AOI are schematically demonstrated in Fig. 2.

Basic Statistics. Table 3 presents major parameters regarding defined AOIs. The data provide a general overview of subjects' visual activity in specified regions. It may be observed that people spent most of the time both fixated and not looking at the region where the scale was located (AOI 8). The number of fixations and even the average fixation was also the biggest for this AOI. Among the least interesting locations were the place with the task order and the area between the two package images (AOI 6 and 7 respectively). One can also notice that number of fixation was decidedly bigger for conditions with a smartphone picture that without it: 410 versus 217, however the difference in mean fixations for these conditions seems to be negligible: 193 versus 190. A considerable difference between basic temporal parameters was obtained for the areas presenting the center of the smartphone and its edges. Although, both dwell and fixated times were longer for the smartphone's edges, the mean fixation time was longer for the center of the smartphone's picture than for its edges: 203 versus 185.

Table 3. Basic statistics of the main eye tracking data for all of the defined AOIs

AOI	Size (pixels)	Coverage (%)	Dwell time (ms)	Normalized dwell time (ms/coverage)	Fixation count	Fixation time (ms)	Average fixation (ms)
1. EdgRnd	29 469	4.15	39 102	9 422	191	36 588	192
2. EdgShr	29 469	4.15	39 615	9 546	210	36 770	175
3. ConNoPic	38 628	5.4	44 983	8 330	217	41 921	193
4. ConIsPic	38 628	5.4	85 843	15 897	410	77 927	190
4.1 PhoEdg	16 547	2.3	56 087	24 386	290	53 573	185
4.2 PhoCen	22 079	3.1	29 755	9 598	120	24 354	203
5. Caps	10 034	1.4	76 975	54 982	364	72 666	200
6. TskOrd	46 483	6.5	10 450	1 608	57	9 000	158
7. Center	47 972	6.8	12 795	1 882	70	11 681	167
8. Scale	97 679	14	238 175	17 013	911	203 467	223
9. Btns	51 512	7.2	53 988	7 498	244	49 182	202
10. WhiSpa	310 842	44	125 692	2 857	560	109 907	196

Analyses of Variance. A formal statistical verification of the influence of various types of AOIs (box captions, box content, box edges), package shapes (rounded, sharp), and the smartphone picture presence (with and without a picture) on essential temporal variables was conducted by means of a series of three-way Anovas. The obtained results for four dependent variables are given in Table 4. These data reveal statistically significant ($\alpha = .05$) impact of the *AOI type* and *Picture presence* effects on *Dwell* and *Fixated time* as well as on the *Fixation count*. The mean *Fixation duration* was meaningfully ($\alpha = .1$) differentiated by the *AOI type* $\times$ *Package shape* interaction. In all other cases the differences were statistically irrelevant. The statistically important relationships are graphically illustrated in Figs. 6, 7, 8, 9 and 10, where vertical bars denote .95 confidence intervals.

Table 4. A series of three-way (*AOI type* × *Picture presence* × *Package shape*) Anova results.

Effect	Fixation duration		Dwell time		Fixation count		Fixated time	
	F	p	F	p	F	p	F	p
AOI (A)	1.7	.18	3.4	.034[**]	3.9	.020[**]	3.1	.048[**]
PicPres (P)	.02	.89	4.7	.031[**]	6.0	.015[**]	4.6	.033[**]
PackShape (S)	.00	1.0	.48	.49	.61	.43	.77	.38
A × P	.51	.60	1.3	.26	1.5	.22	1.1	.34
A × S	2.8	.061[*]	1.1	.34	1.3	.29	1.0	.36
P × S	.44	.51	.76	.38	.24	.63	.86	.35
A × P × S	1.2	.29	1.6	.21	1.2	.29	1.7	.18

[*]p < .1; [**]p < .05; A - AOI Type, P - Picture presence, S - Picture shape,

A series of LSD Fischer pairwise comparisons for the significant interaction of *AOI type* × *Package shape* on mean fixation durations (Fig. 6) showed that for rounded package versions there was only one significant difference between *Captions* and *Content* (p = .095); for sharp conditions the difference between *Captions-Edges* as well as *Content-Edges* was significant (p = .045 and p = .0021 respectively); meaningful discrepancy between sharp and rounded conditions were noticed only for the *Content* (p = .012).

The LSD Fischer post-hoc analysis of the *AOI type* effect (Fig. 7) revealed significant differences between mean dwell times for *Captions-Content* (p = .044) and *Content-Edges* (p = .0077). Similar pattern was observed for mean fixated times with p = .073 and p = .011 respectively.

An analogical analysis was conducted for the AOI type effect on mean fixation time (Fig. 9). In this case, the LSD tests showed significant differences between Captions-Content (p = .0103) and Content-Edges (p = .0069). The difference between Captions-Edges was statistically irrelevant.

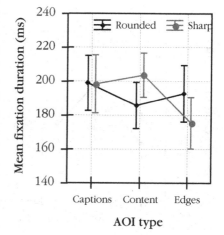

Fig. 6. Mean fixation durations for the *AOI type* × *Package shape* effect. $F_{(2, 1266)} = 2.8$, p = .061

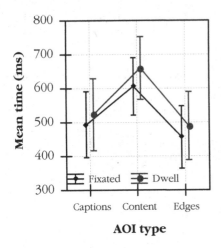

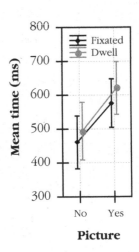

Fig. 7. Mean dwell and fixated times for the *AOI type* factor. $F_{Fixated}(2, 491) = 3.1$, $p_{Fixated} = .048$, $F_{Dwell}(2, 491) = 3.4$, $p_{Dwell} = .034$.

Fig. 8. Mean dwell and fixated times for the *Picture presence* factor. $F_{Fixated}(1, 491) = 4.6$, $p_{Fixated} < .033$, $F_{Dwell}(1, 491) = 4.7$, $p_{Dwell} < .031$.

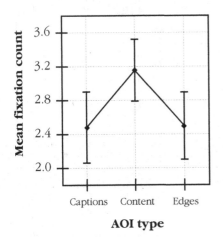

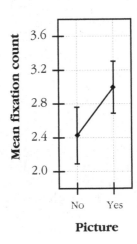

Fig. 9. Mean fixation counts for the *AOI type* factor. $F(2, 491) = 3.9$, $p = .020$.

Fig. 10. Mean fixation counts for the *Picture presence* factor. $F(1, 491) = 6.0$, $p < .015$.

An additional Anova was applied to check if there was any impact of *AOI type*, *Picture presence*, and *Package shape* on the pupil diameter. The biggest differences in mean values were observed for the *Picture presence* effect: for conditions with smartphone pictures the mean pupil diameter equaled 6.7 mm (Standard Mean

Error = .66) versus 5.2 mm (SME = .78) for cases without that image. Though the analyses generally showed no statistical significance for any of the examined factors, the probability for the *Picture presence* effect was on the verge and amounted to .136.

4 Discussion and Conclusions

The presented in this paper experiments were focused on examining the influence of package simple attributes on the perceived willingness to buy and, on the other hand shaping the visual attention process in pairwise comparisons. The study revealed the importance of graphical product presentation the on the package box as well as the package shape in determining the purchase behavior of a potential customer identified by means of AHP based pairwise comparisons.

Both the product image presence and rounded edges of the package cuboid decidedly raise purchase intentions. These outcomes correspond with previous research regarding the role of graphical information in cognitive processing (e.g. Underwood et al. 2001, Underwood and Klein 2002; Deliza et al. 2003) and with the bigger preference of mild and soft shapes over the edgy ones which is documented for instance in the works of Bar and Neta (2006, 2007), or Suzianti et al. (2015). The application of the eye tracking technique allowed for precise identification of the basic visual analysis parameters' nature and assessment of their influence on attentional processes during packages' comparisons.

The observation of the central area of the presented stimuli prevails in comparisons' strategies used by potential customers. The number of fixations and the fixated time observed in the *Content* AOI are markedly bigger than in other examined areas (Figs. 7 and 9). Interestingly, the role of the box captions and edges seems to be similar. Both factors have a significant impact on the package comparison process.

The major indicators that differentiate the consumers' visual activity, that is, the fixation count, dwell and fixated time in individual AOIs are bigger for conditions with a smartphone picture in comparison with cases where the image was not present (Figs. 7, 8, 9 and 10). Moreover, consumers' mean fixation duration in rounded packages is longer for *Edges* and shorter for the *Content* as compared with sharp edges package variants (Fig. 6). This finding is consistent with the results obtained by Piqueras-Fiszman et al. (2013) that suggest that the visual penetration field extends when the package box edge is atypical.

Another interesting result obtained in the present study is concerned with the increase of the eye pupil diameter (at the edge of statistical significance) for conditions including the product picture. Since this parameter is considered to be an indicator of emotions, is seems to be interesting to investigate in future studies the influence of graphical proposals having various features on the customer emotional level, for instance, by means of systems capable of identifying emotions directly from the face picture or video.

Acknowledgments. The work was partly financially supported by the Polish National Science Center grants no. 2011/03/B/HS4/03925. The experiment was conducted by means of the eye tracking glasses system made available by the Laboratory of Information Systems Quality of Use which is a part of a BIBLIOTECH project cofounded by the European Union through the European Regional Development Fund under the Operational Programme Innovative Economy 2007–2013.

References

Bar, M., Neta, M.: Humans prefer curved visual objects. Psychol. Sci. **17**(8), 645–648 (2006). doi:10.1111/j.1467-9280.2006.01759.x

Bar, M., Neta, M.: Visual elements of subjective preference modulate amygdala activation. Neuropsychologia **45**(10), 2191–2200 (2007). doi:10.1016/j.neuropsychologia.2007.03.008

BeGaze Manual: Version 3.5, SMI SensoMotoric Instruments, document number: 091222-P-1400-001-000-A March 2015

Chowdhury, A., Karmakar, S., Reddy, S.M., Sanjog, J., Ghosh, S., Chakrabarti, D.: Visual attention analysis on mutated brand name using eye-tracking: a case study. World Acad. Sci. Eng. Technol. Int. J. Soc. Behav. Educ. Econ. Bus. Ind. Eng. **6**(8), 1132–1135 (2012)

Deliza, R., Macfie, H., Hedderley, D.: Use of computer-generated images and conjoint analysis to investigate sensory expectations. J. Sens. Stud. **18**(6), 465–486 (2003). doi:10.1111/j.1745-459X.2003.tb00401.x

Findlay, J.M., Gilchrist, I.D.: Active vision. In: The Psychology of Looking and Seeing. Oxford University Press, New York (2003)

Goldberg, J.H., Kotval, X.P.: Computer interface evaluation using eye movements: methods and constructs. Int. J. Ind. Ergon. **24**(6), 631–645 (1999). doi:10.1016/S0169-8141(98)00068-7

Graham, D.J., Orquin, J.L., Visschers, V.H.M.: Eye tracking and nutrition label use: a review of the literature and recommendations for label enhancement. Food Policy **37**(4), 378–382 (2012). doi:10.1016/j.foodpol.2012.03.004

Michalski, R.: The influence of color grouping on users' visual search behavior and preferences. Displays **35**(4), 176–195 (2014). doi:10.1016/j.displa.2014.05.007

Piqueras-Fiszman, B., Velasco, C., Salgado-Montejo, A., Spence, C.: Using combined eye tracking and word association in order to assess novel packaging solutions: a case study involving jam jars. Food Qual. Prefer. **28**(1), 328–338 (2013). doi:10.1016/j.foodqual.2012.10.006

Saaty, T.L.: A scaling method for priorities in hierarchical structures. J. Math. Psychol. **15**(3), 234–281 (1977). doi:10.1016/0022-2496(77)90033-5

Saaty, T.L.: The analytic hierarchy process. McGraw–Hill, New York (1980)

Salvucci, D.D., Goldberg, J.H.: Identifying fixations and saccades in eye-tracking protocols. In: Proceedings of the 2000 Symposium on Eye Tracking Research and Applications, pp. 71–78. ACM, New York, NY, USA (2000). doi:10.1145/355017.355028

Suzianti, A., Rengkung, S., Nurtjahyo, B., Al Rasyid, H.: An analysis of cognitive-based design of yogurt product packaging. Int. J. Technol. **6**(4), 659 (2015). doi:10.14716/ijtech.v6i4.1105

Underwood, R.L., Klein, N.M., Burke, R.R.: Packaging communication: attentional effects of product imagery. J. Prod. Brand Manag. **10**(7), 403–422 (2001). doi:10.1108/10610420110410531

Underwood, R.L., Klein, N.M.: Packaging as brand communication: effects of product pictures on consumer responses to the package and brand. J. Mark. Theory Pract. **10**(4), 58–68 (2002). doi:10.1080/10696679.2002.11501926

Van Loo, E.J., Caputo, V., Nayga Jr., R.M., Seo, H.-S., Zhang, B., Verbeke, W.: Sustainability labels on coffee: consumer preferences, willingness-to-pay and visual attention to attributes. Ecol. Econ. **118**, 215–225 (2015). doi:10.1016/j.ecolecon.2015.07.011

Van Raaij, F.W.: Consumer information processing for different information structures and formats. In: Perreault Jr., W.D. (ed.) Advances in Consumer Research, vol. 4, pp. 176–184. Association for Consumer Research, Atlanta (1977)

Wedel, M., Pieters, R.: A review of eye-tracking research in marketing. In: Review of Marketing Research, vol. 4, pp. 123–147. Emerald Group Publishing Limited (2008). doi:10.1108/S1548-6435(2008)0000004009

A Pilot Investigation of the Association Between Eye-Tracking Patterns and Self-reported Reading Behavior

Erica Olmsted-Hawala[✉], Lin Wang, Diane K. Willimack,
Emily Stack, and Sabin Lakhe

U.S. Census Bureau, Washington, DC, USA
{erica.l.olmsted.hawala, lin.wang, diane.k.willimack,
emily.a.burke, sabin.lakhe}@census.gov

Abstract. Eye-tracking data combined with post-task debriefing was used in an exploratory usability study of two different stimuli: cover letters for a Web survey and the login page of the survey. Eye-tracking metrics in the form of fixation duration and number of fixations per character were combined with a post-task debriefing to analyze participants' information acquisition while reading the stimuli. Results show that participants read the letter and recalled salient portions of it. However, in the letter condition, while the eye-tracking data did not highlight any usability issues, the post-task debriefing identified areas of the letter that caused participants confusion. In the online Web survey condition, participants did not look at much beyond the center of the screen where the username and password fields were located. The post-task debriefing corroborated the eye-tracking data as the participants mentioned primarily focusing on the login information of the Web site.

Keywords: Eye tracking · Usability testing · Debriefing data · Reading behavior

1 Introduction

Eye tracking has been on the rise in user experience research, particularly in usability testing [1, 2]. Eye-tracking data can provide additional insight into the user experience. For instance, fixation duration captures how long a participant looks at something, while a gaze plot shows where the participant looked on a page over a period of time in a sequential pattern [3]. Eye tracking can help us understand what part of a user interface draws participants' attention. However, the use of eye tracking in usability research is still a relatively new and growing field. It is not always easy to interpret eye-tracking data. For example, a long eye-fixation duration could reflect either confusion about or engagement in the material [3–5]. In a typical usability study, a

---

This report is released to inform interested parties of research and to encourage discussion. The views expressed are those of the authors and not necessarily those of the U.S. Census Bureau.

M. Antona and C. Stephanidis (Eds.): UAHCI 2016, Part I, LNCS 9737, pp. 442–453, 2016.
DOI: 10.1007/978-3-319-40250-5_42

moderator conducts a debriefing interview after the participant completes tasks. During the debriefing, the researcher probes the participant with questions that arise from the observation of the participant's task performance. Analyzing eye-tracking data in conjunction with debriefing data in the context of the study may facilitate interpretation of the eye-tracking data and can lead to a more comprehensive picture of the participant's behavior.

With the prevalence of the Internet, the U.S. Census Bureau is moving more and more towards self–administered surveys, from paper to a Web-based online mode. To conduct a Web survey, the Census Bureau typically informs a respondent via a letter that he or she has been selected to participate in the survey. In addition to information about the purpose of the survey, the letter contains information such as whether the survey is mandatory or voluntary, the estimated amount of time it will take to complete the survey, when responses to the survey are due, the URL of the online survey, along with user name and login information. Some of this information is also shown on the login page of the Web survey or can be found by clicking on keyword links located at the top or the bottom of the survey screen. In other words, some of the same information is presented in both the letter and the login page. The Census Bureau is interested in knowing which pieces of information respondents attend to and how they behave with the different mediums. This knowledge can have an important impact on the design of a Web survey and letter. This paper presents the results of a usability study on participant behavior of reading two different stimuli: a letter and a login page of a Web survey (hereafter referred to as Web site). We examined participants' reading attention using eye-tracking technology and a follow up post-task debriefing question. We particularly investigated what parts of the letter or the Web site the participants saw, and what they would remember about what they had looked at and/or read.

2   Methodology

2.1   Study Design

We used a between-subjects design to investigate participants' behavior of reading a letter or a Web site. One group of participants was exposed to only the letter, while the other group was exposed only to the Web site. The same post-task performance assessment was conducted with both groups. In a typical survey production setting, the respondent will first receive a letter inviting them to participate in a Web survey. However, for this study we did not want the participants to have been exposed to any information about the survey prior to the test, as we could not be certain if they were exposed to both, where the information was learned. So, each participant was assigned to either the letter or the Web site condition. That is, the first participant was assigned to the letter condition, the next participant was assigned to the Web condition, then the letter condition, and so forth until all sessions were complete. It should be noted that the letter was displayed on the computer screen, rather than on paper, to enable evaluation via eye tracking.

2.2 Participants

Sixteen participants (8 interacted with the simulated production version of a letter and the other 8 interacted with the Web site) were recruited from Census Bureau's Business Register, the universe listing for Census Bureau establishment surveys. All were local to the Washington, DC area. (One of the Web participants refused to be audio or video recorded so we were unable to collect any eye-tracking data during his session. In addition, one of the letter participants' eyes were unable to be tracked with the TOBII software). All were fluent in reading and speaking English, had completed at least two years of college education and were within the age range of 34–68 years old. Participants took part in the research study at their place of work in a voluntary capacity; as such, they were not given any monetary incentive by the Census Bureau. See Table 1 for participant characteristics.

Table 1. Mean (and range) demographics by study condition

	Study condition	
	Letter	Web site
N	8	8
Gender	6 M/2 F	4 M/4 F
Age	50 (34–68)	54 (49–60)
Education	1 High school graduate	
	2 Some college	3 Some college
	3 BA/BS	3 BA/BS
	2 Graduate degree	1 Graduate degree
		1 Unknown
Race	5 White	6 White
	3 Black or African American	1 Asian
		1 Asian and White

2.3 Tasks

The task for the letter condition asked that participants read the letter on the laptop computer provided by the test administrator. Since the letter was displayed on the computer screen, the participants were informed that it was two pages long and that they would need to scroll to see all of the information. Participants were instructed to "Please read the letter the way you would if you had actually received it at your workplace, and then let me know once you are finished." Once the participant said they were finished, the test administrator stopped the eye tracking. A sample letter is depicted in Fig. 1.

The task for the Web site condition asked that the participant imagine that their business had been selected to complete a Census Bureau establishment survey on the

MRTS-L1
(06-11-2015)

UNITED STATES DEPARTMENT OF COMMERCE
Economics and Statistics Administration
U.S. Census Bureau
Washington, DC 20233-0001
OFFICE OF THE DIRECTOR

A message from the Director, U.S. Census Bureau

Your firm has been selected to participate in the Monthly Retail Trade Survey. The responses obtained from this survey will provide policy makers and business leaders with an up to date picture of the United States economic condition and are a key element in estimating the Gross Domestic Product (GDP) of the United States. The Census Bureau conducts the survey and requests your voluntary assistance under the authority of Title 13 U.S.C., Sections 131 and 182.

We have selected your firm for the monthly survey and have enclosed the materials you need to participate. We estimate this survey to take 7 minutes to complete. **Please read the instructions, complete the form, and return it by the due date printed on the form. You can complete your form online by following the instructions provided.**

Title 13 U.S.C., Section 9 also requires that we keep your answers strictly confidential. The information you provide may be seen only by persons sworn to uphold the confidentiality of Census Bureau information and may be used only for statistical purposes. Under the same law, your information will be used only to develop total U.S. estimates that do not disclose the individual activities of your firm. This information will be strictly safeguarded and cannot be used for taxation, regulation, or investigation purposes. Further, copies retained in your files are immune from legal process.

Please utilize your business expertise and judgment in completing the survey. If actual data are not available, carefully prepared estimates are acceptable. Use the 'Remarks' section to provide any needed explanations.

Thank you in advance for your cooperation. If you have additional questions, please call my staff on 1-800-772-7852 or visit our help site at https://econhelp.census.gov/mrts.

Sincerely,

John H. Thompson
Director

Enclosures

Census.gov

OMB Number and Expiration

You are not required to respond to this collection of information if it does not display a valid approval number from the Office of Management and Budget (OMB). The eight-digit OMB number is 0607-0717 and appears in the upper right corner of the report form/login screen.

Authority and Confidentiality

Title 13 U.S.C., Sections 131 and 182 authorizes the Census Bureau to conduct this collection and to request your voluntary assistance. By Section 9 of the same law, your report is confidential. It may be seen only by persons sworn to uphold the confidentiality of Census Bureau information, and may be used only for statistical purposes. The law also provides that copies of your report retained in your files are immune from legal process.

Burden Estimate Statement

Public reporting burden for this collection of information is estimated to average 7 minutes per response, including the time for reviewing instructions, searching existing data sources, gathering and maintaining the data needed, and completing and reviewing the collection of information. Send comments regarding this burden estimate or any other aspect of this collection of information, including suggestions for reducing this burden, to: ECON Survey Comments 0607-0717, U.S. Census Bureau, 4600 Silver Hill Road, Room EMD-8K122, Washington, DC 20233. You may e-mail comments to ECON.Survey.Comments@census.gov. Be sure to use ECON Survey Comments 0607-0717 as the subject.

Fig. 1. Sample letter

Web and that they had received these materials (an envelope with a paper that contained login information) in the mail[1]. The participants were then instructed to "Please open the envelope to find information on how to log in to the survey. I'm going to bring up the survey. Please read over the Web site and login to start the survey." Once the participant clicked on the login button, the task was finished and the eye tracking was stopped. The sample Web site is depicted in Fig. 2.

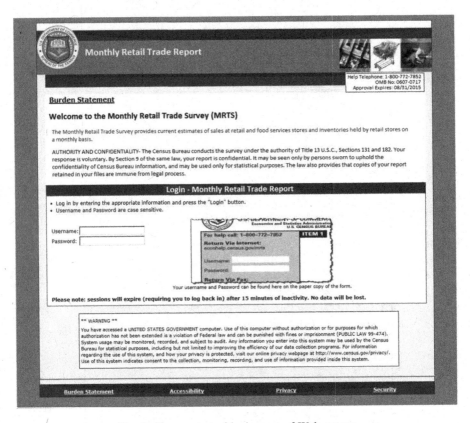

Fig. 2. Screen shot of login page of Web survey

Participants in each condition then engaged in a number of post-task debriefing questions and follow-up activities. The focus of this paper is the association between the eye-movement data and the first post-task debriefing question, a free recall question. The question was to elicit with verbal probing everything the participant had learned from what he/she had just seen. In the letter condition, the question was "Can you tell me about everything you learned from the letter? Anything else? Anything else? Anything else?" For the Web condition, the probe was the same except "Web site" was used in place of "letter."

---

[1] If it had contained all the mailing materials, the letter would have also been included, however as mentioned previously, we intentionally removed the letter from the mailings for the Web condition.

2.4   Procedure

During each one-on-one usability session, the participant was informed that the data were being collected for research purposes only. The test administrator asked the participant to read and sign a consent form stating that he/she understood his/her rights and was voluntarily taking part in the study. The test administrator began the recording after the participant signed the consent form. The participant completed a demographic questionnaire and was positioned in front of the laptop so that a brief eye calibration could be administered. After the participant performed the primary task, the test administrator began the debriefing portion of the study. The sessions lasted no longer than 30 min.

2.5   Equipment

The sessions were conducted at the participants' business establishments on a laptop (Dell Latitude E6540) that had a Tobii X2-60 eye-tracking device attached to the front of the laptop. For the Web version of the study, the participants used Internet browser IE Version 11. For the letter condition, a PDF was loaded into the eye-tracking software and when the test started, the letter appeared on the laptop screen. Analysis of the eye-tracking data was conducted with the Tobii Studio software [6].

2.6   Eye-Tracking Metrics

We assessed participants' attention to the letter or Web site with eye tracking. For the letter condition, we looked at total fixation duration, which is the total length of time spent fixating within the identified Areas of Interest (AOIs) in seconds to assess how long participants spent reading each part of the letter. We created the AOIs in the letter condition as simply one AOI for each of the paragraphs in the letter. We also looked at the fixation count so that we could get a measure of the number of fixations per character as the paragraph lengths varied and this measure normalizes the paragraph lengths so that we could compare the amount of time spent on each paragraph, relative to the length of the paragraph [7]. For the Web site, we created the AOIs on different chunks of information on the site, including:

- Top banner that has the Census logo and the name of the survey
- Burden statement link
- One paragraph below the burden statement link that describes what the survey does
- The next paragraph that mentions the authority and confidentiality statement
- Instructions located just above the login information
- Login area
- Example of where to locate the login information in the paper materials
- Warning message that is required on all Census survey Web sites
- Footer links

We looked at fixation duration in each AOI to determine where and for how long participants looked at certain areas of the Web site prior to login. See Appendix A and B for the visual of the pre-identified AOIs. For both conditions, we watched each participant's animated and static gaze plots. We also examined the relationship between what the eye-tracking data showed and what the participants' answers were to the free recall question. That is, we reviewed what participants mentioned during the free recall and whether there was evidence in the eye-tracking data of their attention to the area in the letter/Web site that contained that information.

3   Results

First, we present the eye-tracking results for the letter condition. Looking at the total fixation duration of participants on different parts of the letter, we found that five out of seven participants did not read the opening greeting of the letter, and four participants did not read the closing salutation from the Director. Four participants read the first paragraph that mentions the authority of the Census Bureau to collect the survey data. The paragraph that contained the survey's burden estimate had the longest fixation duration, with an average of 8.96 s. This was followed closely by an average of 8.69 s for the third paragraph, which explains that answers will be kept confidential and used only for statistical purposes. We examined the total number of fixations per character, including only the paragraphs where there was a count of at least six participants' eye movements, and we found that when we account for the paragraph length, the number of fixations per character is between 0.04 to 0.06. However the "Thank you" paragraph at 0.02 fixations per character is lower than the other paragraphs.

The data on the number of fixations per character indicates that participants were spending about the same amount of time on each paragraph of the letter. Therefore we conclude that there appears to be nothing in the burden estimate paragraph or the confidential paragraph that was unduly difficult to read or drew the eyes for a longer than normal amount of time. As mentioned earlier, the one paragraph that participants spent noticeably less time on was the "Thank you" paragraph. However, this is perhaps not so unusual as the paragraph included a telephone number and a URL, which was not readable as distinct words. It is possible that this content may only be read closely if participants were in a situation where they needed to call for assistance or access help.

Finally we reviewed participants' free recall verbalizations about what they remembered from the letter. Comments included content that indicated they had read and synthesized the salient pieces of information from the letter, including that it was a monthly survey, it would take 7 min to complete, and the answers would be kept confidential. Two participants commented on what they perceived to be contradictory pieces of information in the letter, and these points are indicators of what areas of the letter could be improved (e.g., usability findings on areas of improvement).

To summarize, eye movements, including gaze plots taken from the letter task, indicate that participants were reading the letter. Most participants read over key parts of the letter including the part of the letter that was bolded. Participants appeared to miss or skim over the letterhead and the signature block. As the number of fixations per character data highlight, the "Thank you" paragraph is also skimmed over. See examples of letter condition gaze plots from four different participants in Fig. 3.

Next we present eye-tracking results from the Web site condition. Analysis of fixation duration within the AOIs highlight that areas of the Web site that were not

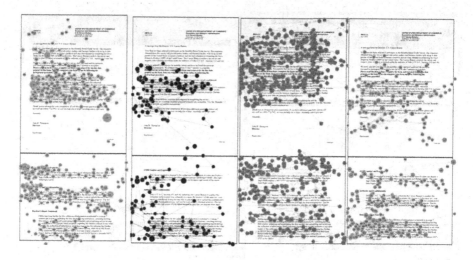

Fig. 3. Gaze plots of 4 different participants in letter condition

attended to include the links at the bottom of the screen (none of the participants looked in that area), along with the warning message (only one participant looked at that area of the screen) and the burden statement link (only one participant looked at that area of the screen). What did draw the attention of the participants' eyes was the username and password fields (participants spent an average of 1.83 s on this field) and to the right of that field, which displayed an example of where the participant would locate their username and password on the mailing materials (2.18 s on average). In addition, a few participants noticed the instruction just above the username and password field (spent on average 0.99 s). Three participants noticed the section of the Web site that begins "Authority and confidentiality," which explains that the response is voluntary and that the information that is collected will be kept confidential. They spent on average 30 s reviewing this area of the Web site.

The participants' free recall verbalizations about what they remember about the Web site mostly matched participant behavior of the eye-tracking data. Comments included that participants did not read the text, that they did not pay attention to the Web site as a whole, and that they did not remember much beyond the username and password area of the site. Four participants explicitly said they remembered the username and password areas on the screen. One participant mentioned that she thought the survey was mandatory (it was voluntary), and another participant mentioned that it was about retail stores and remembered reading about Census Bureau's authority (this information was contained on the Web site).

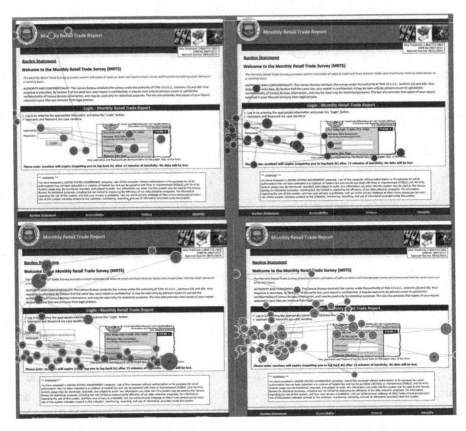

Fig. 4. Gaze plots of 4 different participants in the Web site condition

Looking at the eye movements and the free recall feedback together, we notice that participants did not spend time looking over the entire Web site but rather focused quickly on the username and login portion of the Web site. Gaze plots from participant behavior of the task give a visual perspective on how participants' were attending primarily to the username and login fields or the middle section of the Web site. See Fig. 4.

Comparing the results of the letter condition to the Web condition, we learned that participants in the letter condition appeared to read over the entire letter while participants in the Web site condition did not read over the entire Web site but instead focused on the area of the Web site where they had to make an action (e.g., begin the survey by logging in). The free recall verbalizations in the Web condition were quite a bit shorter in length and in content than the verbalizations from the letter condition; however for both conditions, the verbalizations mostly matched the eye-tracking data.

4   Limitations

The letter that participants interacted with was not on paper as it would be in real life but rather, in the test setting, the print letter had been saved as an electronic PDF so that it could be loaded onto the computer to make it possible to conduct eye tracking. Consequently, participant behavior may be different if they had received a paper letter at their place of business. The Web portion of the study did not have the letter included and as such is not true to what a participant would experience in real life. While this was intentional (as we didn't want participant performance to be influenced by materials they may or may not have read or seen in a prior task), it is not typical to the real-life situation, and participant behavior may be different outside of the laboratory setting. However, we feel the task itself is a typical task in that respondents are asked to go online, login, and begin the survey. In addition, limitations include the spatial accuracy of eye tracking. Gaze position calibration was a challenge, and head movement could compromise the recording of eye movements.

5   Conclusion

In general, we found that participants in the letter condition exhibited indications of reading the letter. Their eyes moved over key points of the letter. During the free recall component of the study we have indications that participants remembered some key points of the letter. On the other hand, other parts of the letter, while read, confused some participants. The participants' confusion was manifested in debriefing but not in the eye-tracking analysis, which indicates that eye-tracking alone is not always sufficient to understand participant interactions with letter materials.

For the Web site, we found that the task of reading over the Web site was ignored for the act of getting started with the survey. The eye-tracking behavior matches what participants said they recalled about the site: that they were focusing on logging into the survey.

Finally, this pilot study demonstrates that there is some association between the eye-tracking data and the debriefing feedback. Integration of eye-tracking data with other behavioral data appears a promising approach to usability evaluation. Further methodological development is warranted.

Appendix A. Screen Shot of Letter with AOIs

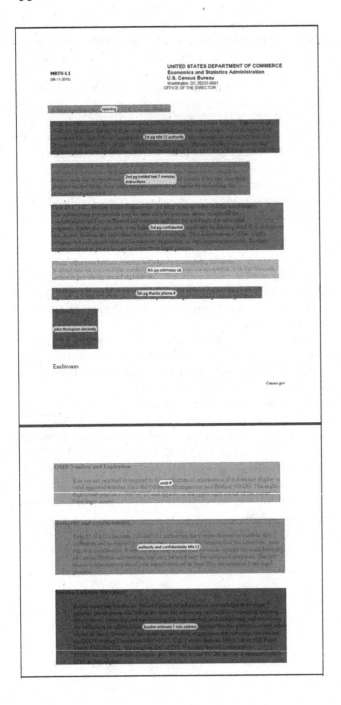

Appendix B. Screen Shot of Login Page of Web Survey with AOIs

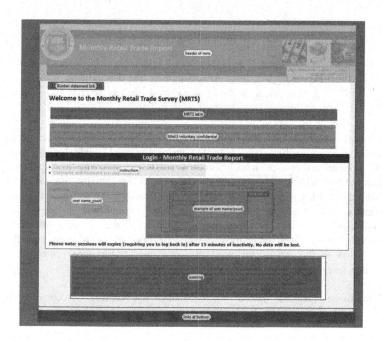

References

1. Bojko, A.: Eye Tracking the User Experience: A Practical Guide to Research. Rosenfeld Media, New York (2013)
2. Bergstrom, J.R., Schall, A. (eds.): Eye Tracking in User Experience Design. Morgan Kaufmann, Massachusetts (2014)
3. Ehmke, C., Wilson, S.: Identifying web usability problems from eye-tracking data. In: Proceedings of HCI 2007 People and Computers XXI – HCI, but not as we know it (2007)
4. Jacob, R.J., Karn, K.S.: Eye tracking in human computer interaction and usability research: ready to deliver the promises. In: Hyona, J., Radach, R., Deubel, H. (eds.) The Mind's Eye: Cognitive and Applied Aspects of Eye Movements, pp. 573–605. Elsevier, London (2003)
5. Poole, A., Ball, L.J.: Eye tracking in human-computer interaction and usability research: current status and future prospects. In: Ghaoui, C. (ed.) Encyclopedia of Human Computer Interaction, pp. 211–219. Idea Group, Pennsylvania (2005)
6. Tobii Studio version 3.1.3.6615-RC (2012). http://www.tobii.com/en/eye-tracking-research/global/
7. Olmsted-Hawala, E., Nichols, E.: Using eye tracking to evaluate email notifications of surveys and online surveys collecting address information. In: Presentation at American Association of Public Opinion Research (AAPOR) Annual Conference in Los Angeles, CA, 15 May 2014

Designing and Evaluating a Wearable Device for Accessing Gaze Signals from the Sighted

Shi Qiu[(✉)], Matthias Rauterberg, and Jun Hu

Eindhoven University of Technology,
Den Dolech 2, 5612 AZ Eindhoven, The Netherlands
{SQIU, G.W.M.Rauterberg, J.Hu}@tue.nl

Abstract. Gaze signals, frequently used by the sighted in social interactions as visual cues, are hardly accessible for low-vision and blind people. In this paper, we proposed a prototype, namely Tactile Band, to aim at testing the hypothesis that tactile feedback can enable the blind person to feel attention (gaze signals) from the sighted, enhancing the level of engagement in face-to-face communication. We tested our hypothesis with 30 participants with a face-to-face conversation scenario, in which the blindfolded and the sighted participants talked about a given daily topic. Comments from the participants and the reflection on the experiment provided useful insights for improvements and further research.

Keywords: Wearable device · Gaze signals · Eye-tracking · Accessibility · Engagement · Tactile feedback

1 Introduction

Gaze and mutual gaze are important in the development of trust and deeper relationships [1]. A common face-to-face conversation can contain a wealth of gazes and mutual gazes, which the sighed people take for granted in their daily routines. For example, a sighted speaker consciously or unconsciously uses gaze or eye contact to communicate with the conversation partner. Through the conversation partner's eyes, she can sense interest, engagement, happiness etc. Gaze signals are frequently used by the sighted in social interactions as visual cues. However, these signals and cues are inaccessible for the blind and hardly accessible for low-vision people. White et al. [2] interviewed 8 visually impaired expert users and a social communicative problem was indicated. The problem was that it was often difficult for them to meet people because they could not see and make eye contacts with the sighted people. McNeill also emphasizes that nonverbal cues such as gazes are integral to a conversation and that ignoring them means ignoring part of the conversation [3]. This becomes more serious when one of them is disabled (e.g. people with visual disability) and the others are not trained to interact with the specific disabled population [4].

In this paper, Tactile Band, a wearable device, was developed to help the blind person feel attention (gaze signals) from the sighted conversation partner in face-to-face communication. Tactile Band tries to map gazes to tactile signals, and let the blind

M. Antona and C. Stephanidis (Eds.): UAHCI 2016, Part I, LNCS 9737, pp. 454–464, 2016.
DOI: 10.1007/978-3-319-40250-5_43

person perceive them in real-time. 30 volunteers (15 blindfolded participants) were invited to evaluate the prototype in the preliminary experiment.

2 Related Work

One related research area is about gaze behaviors. A number of studies have investigated the importance of gaze behaviors of sighted people in social occasions. Argyle studied that in dyadic (two-person) conversations, about 75 % of the time people are listening coincides with gazing at the speaker [5]. Kendon suggested that seeking or avoiding looking at the face of the conversation partner has important functions in dyadic conversations, to regulate the flow of conversation and to communicate emotions and relationships [6]. Vertegaal et al. used an eye tracker to measure gazes at the faces of conversational partners during four-person conversations. The result indicated that gaze was an excellent predictor of attention in conversations [7].

The other relevant area is to make visual cues accessible to the blind people in face-to-face communication. Krishna et al. developed a wearable Social Interaction Assistant to help the blind and visually impaired people to know who was approaching and allowed them to choose whether to initiate a conversation [8]. ur Rehman et al. developed a haptic chair for providing facial expression information to the blind people. Nine vibrators were located in the back of the chair which indicated some specific facial features [9]. Krishna et al. also provided an assistive technology for accessing facial expressions of interaction partners. His research prototype was a vibrotactile glove worn by the blind person and it could convey the conversation partner's seven facial expressions such as happy, sad and surprise with different vibration patterns [10]. Finocchietti et al. proposed ABBI, an audio bracelet for the blind person's social interaction, aiming to rehabilitate spatial cognition on where and how the body was moving [11]. These examples were all about the assistive devices for accessing nonverbal signals such as facial expressions and body gestures. However, none of them was about providing blind people with access to gaze signals that are important in nonverbal communication.

In previous user study, we proposed a concept to help the blind people access and react to gaze signals in face-to-face communication. 20 blind and low-vision participants were interviewed to evaluate the features of this concept for their usefulness, efficiency and interest. We reported the evaluation in a conference paper [12]. Based on the evaluation, the concept is further developed into a prototype, namely Tactile Band, to aim at testing the hypothesis that tactile feedback can enable the blind person to feel attention (gaze signals) from the sighted, enhancing the level of engagement in face-to-face communication.

3 Experiment

3.1 Tactile Band Design

The Tactile Band was designed to exam the hypothesis that by enabling the blind person to feel attention (gaze signals) from the sighted, the tactile feedback can enhance the level of engagement in face-to-face communication. In our concept, SMI eye tracker[1], worn by the sighted, can detect her gazes on the blind person. Gaze signals are mapped to vibration signals of an actuator embedded in the Tactile Band, worn by the blind person on her forehead. The blind person perceives a slight vibration from the Tactile Band as a signal of the sighted looking at her face. Two vibration patterns are used to map basic gaze behaviors: the glance and the fixation. In the glance pattern, the sighted has a quick glance at the blind person's face to instantly trigger a slight vibration of the Tactile Band. If the sighted shortly looks away, the vibration stops in real-time. In the fixation pattern, the sighted gazes at the blind person's face for a while and looks away. In this process, the first fixation to the blind person's face triggers a slight vibration of the Tactile Band and lets her know the sighted is looking at her. If the sighted is still gazing at the blind person's face, she can feel a slight vibration with an interval in a loop until the sighted looked away. The reason of using intervals is to avoid continuous vibrations, which possibly becomes annoying.

A within-subject design was conducted and it included one independent variable with three levels (no Tactile Band, Tactile Band without vibrations and Tactile Band with vibrations) and one dependent variable (engagement in a conversation). In our preliminary experiment, blindfolded but sighted (hereafter blindfolded) participants were invited to the experiment as an alternative for the target blind users [13]. The level of engagement in a conversation was measured using questionnaires with two subjective measures: relationship quality and partner closeness. Besides the questionnaires, gaze information was collected through SMI eye tracker to help measure the sighted participants' engagement in conversations. A qualitative analysis on the results from a post-experimental questionnaire (five open questions) was performed to investigate participants' subjective attitudes towards the Tactile Band and to collect suggestions for further improvements.

3.2 Wizard-of-Oz Setup

The Tactile Band system used Wizard-of-Oz (WOZ) (Fig. 1) to simulate the final system's behavior as closely as possible: a human "Wizard" simulated the system's response in real-time, interacting with the users just like the envisioned system [14]. In the Wizard-of-Oz set up, two participants (A1: the blindfolded; A2: the sighted) had a conversation in Room 1, while a wizard situated in Room 2. A2 wore the SMI glasses – a wearable eye tracker C1. A1 wore the Tactile Band on her forehead. The wizard observed the real-time eye tracking video from C1 and controlled vibration actuator of the Tactile Band accordingly. The video with gaze information (recorded by the eye tracker C1) was used for the attention analysis after the experiment. Camera C2 captured the entire scene.

In the Tactile Band system, Eye Tracking Glasses (ETG) connected to an ETG-Laptop and detected gaze signals of the sighted participant in real-time. Wizard observed the real-time gaze video from iView ETG 2.0 (the controller and eye tracking

---

[1] http://www.smivision.com/.

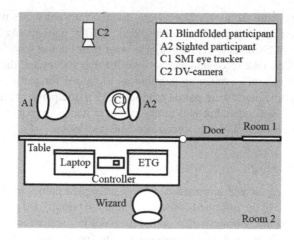

Fig. 1. Wizard-of-Oz environment

software) installed on an ETG-Laptop. If the gaze hit the facial region of the blind-folded participant, a slight vibration was triggered by the wizard. If the gaze was still in the facial region, slight vibrations with equal intervals were triggered by the wizard. The vibration stopped when gaze was out of the facial region. The moment of each vibration signal was recorded in the wizard computer (accurate to millisecond). Figure 2 shows an overview of the Tactile Band system.

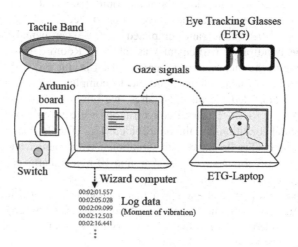

Fig. 2. Overview of the Tactile Band system

3.3 Participants

The participants were thirty student volunteers from Eindhoven University of Technology (11 females, M_{age} = 29.73, SD = 5.69; 19 males, M_{age} = 28.16, SD = 2.17) with ages ranging from 21 to 42. They were divided into pairs to have dyadic conversations and one of each pair was blindfolded. All the participants had normal or corrected-to-normal vision and were allowed to wear their contact lens, but not allowed to wear glasses due to the inconvenience to wear the eye tracker and the blindfold. We tried to recruit strangers as much as possible as a control for participants' previous familiarity. The participants were paired randomly: 17 participants never met before; 9 participants knew each other but had rarely or never had conversations; only 4 participants knew each other and had sometimes conversations.

3.4   Procedure

Two paired participants read informed consents and signed names in the office before being led to the lab. In the informed consent, we told the blindfolded participants: "You are wearing a band that vibrates when your conversation partner looks at your face in the experiment." After completing informed consents, one participant was blindfolded and we took both participants from the office to the nearby lab. In the lab, the blindfolded participant was taken to sit in the chair in Room 1, where we played some light music for relaxing. In Room 2, we helped the sighted participant wear the eye tracker and did the three-point calibration to accurately catch her eye movements. After calibration, the sighted participant went to sit in the other chair in Room 1, facing the blindfolded participant. After ensuring the blindfolded participant' comfort to the blindness, we turned off the music. Then we randomly picked one topic in fourteen daily topics from IELTS oral exams [15]. These topics were all about daily lives and easier for the participants to start such as the item "Describe a job you have done". Both participants were asked to share ideas about the topic. After that, the door was closed between Room 1 and Room 2 and the conversation started. After the average 10-min conversation, the sighted participant completed a post-experimental questionnaire in Room 1 and the blindfolded participant was taken to Room 2 to finish it with the blindfold off. Due to the pictorial measurements used in this process, the blindfolded participant was asked to take off the blindfold to complete the questionnaire. When both participants completed the questionnaires, we blindfolded the participant again and took her back to Room 1. Three conversations were taken place under the following experimental conditions for the blindfolded (I. no Tactile Band; J. Tactile Band without vibrations; K. Tactile Band with vibrations) with counter balancing to avoid carry-over effects. Each conversation lasted around 10 min and after each conversation, participants were asked to answer a post-experimental questionnaire. After three conversations and post-experimental questionnaires, we did a short interview to collect the blindfolded participant's comments and suggestions towards the Tactile Band. Each conversation was video-taped and the short interview was audio-tapped. The overall experiment lasted approximately 90–120 min.

3.5   Measurements

We measured the level of engagement in the face-to-face conversation with two subjective measures: relationship quality (IMI: Intrinsic Motivation Inventory questionnaire) [16] and partner closeness (IOS: The Inclusion of Other in the Self Scale) [17].

IMI included 45 items, assigned to 7 subscales. We were particularly interested in participants' mutual relationship in conversations. Therefore, relatedness subscale of IMI was used. It has 8 items, such as "It is likely that this person and I could become friends if we interacted a lot". IOS Scale was used to measure the closeness. It included seven increasingly overlapping circle pairs, which could indicate the distance of the relationship between themselves and their conversation partners. We also collected qualitative feedbacks from an open questionnaire and the interview. After three tests, we left the blindfolded participant alone to complete the open questionnaire with five questions included the item: "Do you have some suggestions for improving the Tactile Band?" After finishing these questions, we did a short interview (average around five minutes) to confirm the answers.

Gaze tracking data from the sighted participants in the tests were recorded and analyzed using the software BeGaze version 3.5, installed in the ETG-Laptop. Results were calculated over 45 conversations and last five minutes of each conversation video were analyzed. The facial region of the blindfolded participant was chosen as the area of interest (AOI) for measuring the fixation duration. This eye metric was selected based on the relevant literature on the attention analysis with eye movements [7, 18]. The AOI can synchronously match the dynamic facial region by setting key frames. When the sighted participant's gaze hit the dynamic AOI, gaze was registered for the attention analysis. Due to the frequent and strong head movements in tests, the dynamic AOI was not able to accurately catch facial regions of some blindfolded participants in videos. So ten sighed participants' eye-movement videos were used in the attention analysis and five were excluded. The corresponding eye metrics inside the AOI area were calculated using BeGaze and exported for analysis.

4 Results

4.1 Self-reports

Below we report both quantitative and qualitative results from the experiment.

Quantitative Results. We used SPSS for the data analysis. Blindfolded participants in 3 pairs out of 15 could not consciously sense vibration signals during the experiment, but they were possibly influenced by vibration signals unconsciously. Therefore, data from these blindfolded participants were not removed from the datasheet. The conversation quality was analyzed using RM-ANOVA with relationship quality and partner closeness as within-subject factors and the role (the blindfolded and the sighted) as a between-subject factor. Table 1 presents mean and standard deviation of relatedness and partner closeness across three conditions. Before running RM-ANOVA, we checked the data for violations of parametric analysis: the sphericity assumption was tested using Mauchly's test. There were no significant effects of relatedness $F(2, 56) = 0.64$, $p = 0.53$, and partner closeness $F(2, 56) = 0.20$, $p = 0.82$ in three conditions.

Since the blindfolded participants wore the Tactile Band, we analyzed them in three conditions separately. The datasheet was split into two groups: the blindfolded and the sighted. There were no significant effects for blindfolded participants in relatedness

F (2, 28) = 0.13, p = 0.88, and partner closeness F (2, 28) = 0.04, p = 0.96 in all conditions. There were also no significant results for sighted participants of relatedness and partner closeness in three conditions ($p > 0.05$).

Table 1. Mean and standard deviation of relatedness and partner closeness across three experimental conditions: (I) no Tactile Band; (J) Tactile Band with no vibration; (K) Tactile Band with vibration.

	I (N = 30)		J (N = 30)		K (N = 30)	
	M	SD	M	SD	M	SD
Relatedness	5.58	0.86	5.71	0.71	5.59	0.87
Partner closeness	3.07	1.14	3.17	1.15	3.17	0.87

Qualitative Results. We adopted conventional content analysis method that coding categories are derived directly from transcripts [19] to analyze comments from blindfolded participants answering five open questions. In total 70 quotes of user comments were collected and they were merged into three categories: the vibration feedback (20 quotes), the prototype (31 quotes) and suggestions (19 quotes).

We gathered positive and negative comments (Table 2) of the vibration feedback from the result of the question "What do you think about the vibration feedback, when your conversation partner looks at your face?" Two participants (P3, P11) mentioned they could not immediately map the vibration to the gaze signal in conversations. The other participant (P10) explained in the beginning the vibration feedback helped her concentrate on the conversation partner, but after while it became just a subtle clue that she often neglected.

Table 2. Positive and negative comments towards vibration feedback of the Tactile Band

Positive (frequency)	Good (2); help to concentrate (1); take conversation seriously (1); accurate (1); not obtrusive (1)
Negative (frequency)	Hard to map (3); neglect (3); unexpected (2); nothing special (2); strange (1); irritating (1); inconsistent (1); not necessary (1)

We asked participants the question: "Which aspects make you like/dislike the Tactile Band?" (Table 3) Six participants liked the Tactile Band. The example comments were: "The Tactile Band did not feel interfering too much. It was easy to wear and it had subtle cues." "It used soft material, which was comfortable to the skin."(P10, P14) Some participants also explained why they disliked the Tactile Band. The primary reason was they disliked having the Tactile Band on the head. The example comment was that "The head feels like a scary location for such direct vibrations. It might also be obtrusive for the conversation partner" (P14).

We received suggestions for improving the Tactile Band in two aspects: try other modalities to map gaze signals and improve the wearability of the Tactile Band

Table 3. Like and dislike the Tactile Band

Like (frequency)	Comfortable (5); subtle (3); not interfering (3); easy (1); relax (1); interesting (1); private (1); know being looked at (1); soft material (1)
Dislike (frequency)	Uncomfortable (4); strange (2); unexpected (1); dislike (1); weak (1); not attractive (1); scary (1); obtrusive (1); not good (1); awkward (1)

(Table 4). As for other modalities, two participants stated temperature changes could map to gaze signals. For example: the soft warmth on eyes indicated a kind of close feeling (P15). Other participants mentioned cue tone, soft touch and different intensity of the vibration. For the wearability of the Tactile Band, participants gave many suggestions and the top three were: at hand, around the arm and using the mobile device, where were more invisible during the conversation.

Table 4. Suggestions about the modality and the position of wearing the Tactile Band

Modality (frequency)	Temperature (2); cue tone (2); soft touch (2); vibration with different intensity (1)
Position (frequency)	At hand (4); in the arm (2); mobile (2); body (1); the shoulder (1); waist (1); around ear (1)

4.2 Gaze Signals

Fixation duration area was the facial region of the blindfolded participant. Mean and standard deviation of fixation duration were calculated for three experimental conditions (I, J & K) (Table 5). RM-ANOVA analysis revealed that, the main effect of fixation duration was not significant in all conditions, $F (1.41, 39.40) = 2.15, p = 0.14$.

Table 5. Mean and standard deviation of fixation duration (in milliseconds) across three conditions: (I) no Tactile Band; (J) Tactile Band with no vibration; (K) Tactile Band with vibration.

	Facial region	
	M	SD
I (N = 10)	280.88	28.14
J (N = 10)	268.35	32.37
K (N = 10)	256.92	26.32

5 Discussion

The quantitative results were not able to demonstrate the effect of tactile feedback on the engagement between the blindfolded and the sighted in face-to-face communication, but we gained valuable insights while running the studies. We realized our experiment has certain limitations and we also get some useful implications for further improvements in both the design and the experiment.

From observations, we found that: (1) the vibration signals were too subtle for three participants to sense them; (2) other participants could sense vibration signals, but with the engagement in the verbal communication, they started ignoring them. Simply increasing the intensity of the vibration may not be a good solution since it may become annoying in the conversation. We hope to improve our design and experiment as follows: improve the prototype such as the wearability, redesign the scenario in the experiment and give more time to the participants to get used to mapping between gaze signals and tactile signals.

According to the observations and user comments, we need to improve the wearability of the Tactile Band. For example, it could be worn on the wrist, which is less visible than on the forehead. The intensity of the tactile feedback could be fine-tuned. Other types of tactile feedback can also be explored besides vibration, such as a sense of pressure by changing the shape of the material. Since the auditory and tactile signals were two primary nonverbal signals for the blind people to sense in face-to-face communication [20], we also consider using auditory signals to map gaze signals. The scenario of dyadic conversation is mainly verbal communication, which is easier to cause conflicts with other auditory signals. Mapping gaze with auditory signals is far from a perfect solution in our case, but it may be possible under a certain condition. For example, one participant proposed to wear the ear phone in the conversation, mapping gaze signals with different cue tones from the ear phone. It can avoid extra auditory interfering to the conversation partner.

Besides the improvements of the prototype, redesigning the scenario in our experiment is also needed. In interviews, some blindfolded participants expressed several alternative contexts in which they would find them to be more useful. For example, a slight vibration (gaze) signal from the conversation partner predicts the start of the conversation to help them be more concentrated. We also consider in turn-taking, eye gaze plays an important role as it indicates where the speaker's focus of attention is directed [21]. An alternative scenario can be that, one sighted speaker discusses with two blindfolded participants in triadic (three-person) conversations. The sighted stops talking and gives her turn to one of two blindfolded listeners by the gaze signal.

Spending more time in learning the mapping between gaze signals and tactile signals may be helpful. The blindfolded participants knew the importance of the gazes and they had the direct and clear understanding of gaze behaviors. However, gaze is a visual cue in their perception. It will take some time, even a long-term training for them to map gaze signals to tactile signals, which is unnatural for them. As for the blind people, we found they tend to have the indirect and fuzzy understanding of eyes and gazes [20]. They knew the importance of gazes from descriptions in novels or by others. Mapping gazes with tactile signals is a new experience for them, which is likely to require more time for practicing to get used to.

6   Conclusion

In this paper, we focus on presenting an experiment with Tactile Band, a wearable device, which enables the blind person to feel attention (gaze signals) from the sighted and aims to enhance their mutual engagement in face-to-face communication. We set up a Wizard-of-Oz environment to conduct the user experiment with thirty participants in pairs. The results of the user experiment did not significantly demonstrate the effect of tactile feedback on the engagement between the blindfolded and the sighted in face-to-face communication, but we get many useful insights and design implications: (1) the prototype needs to be improved with the wearability with fine-tuned intensity for the tactile feedback. Other feedback can also be explored such as the cue tone or the sense of pressure by the shape changing of material; (2) an alternative scenario could be used in the experiment, which emphasize turn-taking in communication; (3) longer time in learning is necessary for better understanding of the mapping between tactile feedback and gaze signals. In our future work, we will improve the prototype and involve some target blind users in the evaluation.

Acknowledgments. We thank our participants from Hong Kong Blind Union, Yangzhou Special Education School in China. This research is supported by the China Scholarship Council and facilitated by Eindhoven University of Technology.

References

1. Argyle, M., Cook, M.: Gaze and Mutual Gaze. Cambridge University Press, Cambridge (1976)
2. White, G.R., Fitzpatrick, G., McAllister, G.: Toward accessible 3D virtual environments for the blind and visually impaired. In: 3rd International Conference on Digital Interactive Media in Entertainment and Arts, pp. 134–141 (2008)
3. McNeill, D.: Hand and Mind: What Gestures Reveal About Thought. University of Chicago Press, Chicago (1992)
4. Krishna, S., Balasubramanian, V., Panchanathan, S.: Enriching social situational awareness in remote interactions: insights and inspirations from disability focused research. In: International Conference on Multimedia, pp. 1275–1284 (2010)
5. Argyle, M.: The Psychology of Interpersonal Behaviour. Penguin UK, London (1994)
6. Kendon, A.: Some functions of gaze-direction in social interaction. Acta Psychol. **26**, 22–63 (1967)
7. Vertegaal, R., Slagter, R., Van der Veer, G., Nijholt, A.: Eye gaze patterns in conversations: there is more to conversational agents than meets the eyes. In: SIGCHI Conference on Human Factors in Computing Systems, pp. 301–308 (2001)
8. Krishna, S., Colbry, D., Black, J., Balasubramanian, V., Panchanathan, S., et al.: A systematic requirements analysis and development of an assistive device to enhance the social interaction of people who are blind or visually impaired. In: Workshop on Computer Vision Applications for the Visually Impaired (2008)
9. ur Rahman, S., Liu, L.: Vibrotactile rendering of human emotions on the manifold of facial expressions. J. Multimedia **3**(3), 18–25 (2008)
10. Krishna, S., Bala, S., McDaniel, T., McGuire, S., Panchanathan, S.: VibroGlove: an assistive technology aid for conveying facial expressions. In: Extended Abstracts on Human Factors in Computing Systems, pp. 3637–3642 (2010)
11. Finocchietti, S., Cappagli, G., Baud-Bovy, G., Magnusson, C., Caltenco, H., Wilson, G., Brewster, S., Rogge, A., Röder, B., Cocchi, E., Capris, E., Campana, P., Gilio, C., Gori, M.: ABBI, a New technology for sensory-motor rehabilitation of visual impaired people. In: International Conference on Enabling Access for Persons with Visual Impairment, pp. 80–84 (2015)

12. Qiu, S., Osawa, H., Rauterberg, M., Hu, J.: E-gaze: create gaze communication for persons with visual disability. In: 3rd International Conference on Human-Agent Interaction, pp. 199–202 (2015)
13. Sears, A., Hanson, V.L.: Representing users in accessibility research. ACM Trans. Accessible Comput. 4(2), 7 (2012)
14. Strauß, P.M., Hoffmann, H., Minker, W., Neumann, H., Palm, G., Scherer, S., Weidenbacher, U.: Wizard-of-oz data collection for perception and interaction in multi-user environments. In: International Conference on Language Resources and Evaluation, pp. 2014–2017 (2006)
15. IELTS Speaking Module - Part 2 - Sample Topics (2012). http://www.goodluckielts.com/IELTS-speaking-topics-2.html
16. McAuley, E., Duncan, T., Tammen, V.V.: Psychometric properties of the intrinsic motivation inventory in a competitive sport setting: a confirmatory factor analysis. Res. Q. Exerc. Sport 60(1), 48–58 (1989)
17. Aron, A., Aron, E.N., Smollan, D.: Inclusion of other in the self scale and the structure of interpersonal closeness. J. Pers. Soc. Psychol. 63(4), 596 (1992)
18. Mojzisch, A., Schilbach, L., Helmert, J.R., Pannasch, S., Velichkovsky, B.M., Vogeley, K.: The effects of self-involvement on attention, arousal, and facial expression during social interaction with virtual others: a psychophysiological study. Soc. Neurosci. 1(3–4), 184–195 (2006)
19. Hsieh, H.-F., Shannon, S.E.: Three approaches to qualitative content analysis. Qual. Health Res. 15(9), 1277–1288 (2005)
20. Qiu, S., Hu, J., Rauterberg, M.: Nonverbal signals for face-to-face communication between the blind and the sighted. In: International Conference on Enabling Access for Persons with Visual Impairment, pp. 157–165 (2015)
21. Jokinen, K., Furukawa, H., Nishida, M., Yamamoto, S.: Gaze and turn-taking behavior in casual conversational interactions. ACM Trans. Interact. Intell. Syst. 3(2), 12 (2013)

Density of Gaze Points Within a Fixation and Information Processing Behavior

Mina Shojaeizadeh$^{(\boxtimes)}$, Soussan Djamasbi, and Andrew C. Trapp

User Experience and Decision Making Research Laboratory, Worcester
Polytechnic Institute, 100 Institute Road, Worcester, MA 01609, USA
{minashojaei,djamasbi,atrapp}@wpi.edu

Abstract. The use of eye movements to study cognitive effort is becoming increasingly important in HCI research. Eye movements are natural and frequently occurring human behavior. In particular fixations represent attention; people look at something when they want to acquire information from it. Users also tend to cluster their attention on informative regions of a visual stimulus. Thus, fixation duration is often used to measure attention and cognitive processing. Additionally, parameters such as pupil dilation and fixation durations have also been shown to be representative of information processing. In this study we argue that fixation density, defined as the number of gaze points divided by the total area of a fixation event, can serve as a proxy for information processing. As such, fixation density has a significant relationship with pupil data and fixation duration, which have been shown to be representative of cognitive effort and information processing.

Keywords: Eye tracking · Cognitive effort · Information processing · Pupil dilation · Pupil dilation variation · Fixation density

1 Introduction

Eye movements can provide valuable data about a user's viewing behavior, and as such, the analysis of eye-movement data is becoming increasingly popular in human computer interaction (HCI) research [1, 2]. For example, fixations can provide invaluable data about a person's attention, awareness, and information processing behavior [1, 3]. Fixations refer to relatively stationary gazes during which we take "foveal snapshots" of interesting stimuli. These foveal snapshots are then sent to our brain for processing [1]. Thus, fixations form a fundamental unit of analysis in examinations of eye-movement data [3]. In this study, we examine one particular property of this important eye-tracking metric, namely its dispersion, or the density of the individual gaze points that form a fixation event. Because fixations are reliable indicators of cognitive processing [4], the distribution of gaze points within a fixation unit is likely to carry information about the intensity of cognitive processing. Fixation density represents both the number of gaze points, as well as their dispersion, during a certain fixation event. In this study, fixation density is computed as the number of gaze points within a fixation unit (event) divided by the area of the minimal bounding rectangle. A dense fixation unit is likely to represent more intense cognitive processing.

© Springer International Publishing Switzerland 2016
M. Antona and C. Stephanidis (Eds.): UAHCI 2016, Part I, LNCS 9737, pp. 465–471, 2016.
DOI: 10.1007/978-3-319-40250-5_44

Given this point of view, we expect to observe that gaze point density in a fixation is related to a number of known eye-movement metrics that represent cognitive processing, namely fixation duration, pupil dilation [5], and pupil dilation variation [6, 7].

2 Theoretical Background

Recent developments in eye-tracking technology have made it possible to capture a user's experience of a system through the analysis of eye movement data. Researchers in the field of Information Systems, Psychology, and Human Computer Interaction have been using eye-movement data to investigate users' attention, awareness, search behavior and preferences in a variety of ways [8, 9].

Eye-tracking data have also been used to discover user's cognitive states [10–12]. Understanding the relations between eye movements and human cognition has been useful in many domains such as studies of visual working memory [13]. Poole and Ball [3] identified different categories of eye-movement metrics, each reflecting the action of specific cognitive processes in the brain. These metrics include fixations, saccades, and pupil dilation. Fixations are defined as relatively stable gazes between saccades, and their interpretations differ depending on the context. Saccades are rapid movements of the eye when moving from one fixation to another [14]. There is evidence that cognitive load is likely to impact the length of fixation. A previous study using fixation data to find the correlation between a user's gaze and difficulty of the task shows a positive correlation between fixation duration and cognitive load [15]. Building on Just and Carpenter's [17] work, analyses based on the eye-mind assumption suggest that eye fixations can be used as a window into instances of effortful cognitive processing.

Fixations and saccades reflect very different types of eye movements. Fixations are related to information processing, whereas during saccades, visual information is not processed. Grounded in this distinction, a recent study discriminates between pupil data during fixations and saccades [7]. Because visual information is not processed during a saccadic event, in this paper, we focus on pupillary information during fixations only. Table 1 summarizes the eye-movement types and their respective metrics that were considered in this study.

2.1 Hypotheses

As shown in Table 1, longer fixations have been associated with a greater degree of attention, and thus more intense processing. Therefore, we expect to see that denser fixations have a significant relationship with fixation duration:

(H1)   Denser fixations are significantly correlated with fixation duration.

Pupillary data are known to serve as reliable proxies of cognitive processing [5], thus it is reasonable to argue that a fixations' gaze density and its corresponding pupillary data have a strong correlation. Thus, we assert:

(H2)   Denser fixations have a significant relationship with pupil dilation during fixations.

Table 1. Definition and application of different eye-tracking metrics used in this study as a representative of cognitive processing.

Fixation *Steady gazes with a minimum duration on a specific area of a stimulus*	Fixation duration: high fixation duration indicates high cognitive workload _ENREF_45 [15], and higher cognitive effort [1, 3, 18] Fixation density: total number of gaze points divided by the total minimal area to encapsulate all the gaze points [16]
Pupil dilation *Changes in pupil size*	Changes in the pupil diameter represents cognitive and mental workload [19–21]
Pupil dilation variation *Variation of changes in pupil size*	Standard deviation of pupil diameter [6]: related to both cognitive processing [7] and the characterization of differences between neutral and arousal elicitation [22, 23]

(H3) Denser fixations have a significant relationship with pupil dilation variation during fixations.

3 Methodology

The following sections provide a brief review of the laboratory experiments that were conducted to test our hypotheses.

3.1 Participants and Design

A total of 24 graduate students from various technical disciplines (e.g., computer science, electrical and computer engineering) in a northeastern university of the US were recruited for this study. Participants were assigned to complete a problem-solving cognitive task without any time limit. Because students are accustomed to taking timed tests, this setting was relevant and appropriate for manipulating cognitive load in our study.

We used the Tobii X300, a remote eye tracker with a sampling rate of 300 Hz and Tobii software version 3.2.3 to collect participant's eye-movements data. The I-VT filter was used with 30°/s saccadic velocity threshold. To track eye movements, each participant completed a brief eye-calibration process. While seated, participants were asked to observe a moving dot on the eye-tracking monitor. This calibration process, which required participants to follow the moving dot on the screen, took less than one minute.

3.2 Task

The problem-solving task used in this study required participants to provide correct answers to a set of mathematical questions. A set of 10 math questions were manually selected from a pool of problem-solving practice tests for the GRE cite available at www.majortests.com. The questions were then used to develop an online multiple choice math test.

3.3 Data Processing

The eye-movement data of 24 participants acquired from the Tobii eye-tracking software were further analyzed using MATLAB 2014b to calculate the average and standard deviation of the metrics mentioned in Table 1 and to compute the area encapsulating each fixation event for each participant. In addition, normalized values of fixation duration as well as fixation density for each participant were computed. Normalized fixation duration was calculated by dividing the total fixation duration by the total completion time of the task. The average values were then used in regression analyses, which are reported in the next section.

4 Results

The basic mean and standard deviation statistics of the variables under study, namely fixation density, pupil dilation during fixation, pupil dilation variation during fixation, and normalized fixation are reported in Table 2.

Table 2. Mean and Standard deviation of variables under study

	Mean – [unit]	STD
Fixation density	0.470 [mm^{-2}]	0.166
Pupil dilation during fixation	3.048 [mm]	0.385
Pupil dilation variation during fixation	0.014 [mm]	0.009
Normalized fixation duration	0.399	0.160

To investigate the relationship between fixation density (FD) and pupil dilation (PD), pupil dilation variation (PDV) and normalized fixation duration (NFD), we used three different regression models as outlined below.

$$FD = \beta_0 + \beta_1 \times PD \tag{1}$$

$$FD = \beta'_0 + \beta'_1 \times PDV \tag{2}$$

$$FD = \beta''_0 + \beta''_1 \times NFD \tag{3}$$

Unsurprisingly, the results of the regression analyses showed that fixation density is strongly (p-value = 0.004) and positively ($\beta_1 = 0.481$) correlated with normalized fixation duration. Twenty-three percent of the variation in model (3) was explained by normalized fixation duration, as displayed in Table 3. Our model (2) results showed that average pupil dilation *variation* was strongly (p-value = 0.001) correlated with fixation density. The relationship, however, was negative ($\beta_1' = -0.674$), meaning that higher fixation density was correlated with larger pupil dilation variations during fixations. Contrary to our expectation, the results were not significant in model (1): that is, the results did not show a significant relationship between average pupil dilation during fixation and fixation density (p-value = 0.953). These results together, which are displayed in Table 3, suggest that fixation density can be predicted by normalized fixation duration and average pupil dilation variation during fixation, but not average pupil dilation during fixation.

Table 3. Results of regression analysis for Fixation Density (FD) in terms of NFD, FD in terms of PD, and FD in terms of PDV.

	R^2	P-value	β
Normalized fixation duration	0.231	0.004	0.481
Average pupil dilation during fixation	0.009	0.953	−0.013
Average pupil dilation variation during fixation	0.454	0.001	−0.674

5 Discussion and Conclusion

Because fixations are a collection of gaze points that are close to each other in time and proximity, denser fixations represent a user's more focused attention, and thus a higher level of cognitive processing when viewing visual stimuli. Therefore, it is likely that fixation density is related to other eye movement metrics that are representative of a user's information processing behavior. In this paper, we investigated whether fixation density was correlated with three different eye metrics that are typically used to assess cognitive processing. Our results showed that fixation density was strongly correlated with pupil dilation variation and normalized fixation duration but not with pupil dilation. These results are consistent with prior research that indicates pupil dilation variation may be a more sensitive measure of information processing in HCI research [7]. Overall, the results provide evidence that fixation density, along with pupillary data, may also serve as an appropriate measure of information processing. These results have important implications because they provide a theoretical direction for incorporating fixation density in future HCI studies.

6 Limitations and Future Research

As with any experiment, our study had limitations, which we intend to address in follow-up studies. Our sample size was small, and the task was limited to a problem-solving cognitive task. Another limitation in our study was that the area for fixation was governed by a rectangle rather than a convex hull. Future studies are needed to replicate our analysis with larger sample sizes, different tasks, and convex hull as the area for fixation to increase confidence in the generalizability of our results.

7 Contribution

While there is evidence that fixations concentrated in a small area (fixation spatial density) is illustrative of focused and efficient searching [16], little work has been done to examine the relationship between fixation density and other eye movement measures that represent information processing. Our results show a strong positive relationship between fixation density and fixation duration and a strong negative relationship between fixation density and pupil dilation variation. These results contribute not only to HCI research but also to research in cognitive effort and information processing.

References

1. Djamasbi, S.: Eye tracking and web experience. AIS Trans. Hum.-Comput. Interact. **6**(2), 37–54 (2014)
2. Bergstrom, J.C.R., Olmsted-Hawala, E.L., Bergstrom, H.C.: Older adults fail to see the periphery in a web site task. Univ. Access Inf. Soc. **1**, 1–10 (2014)
3. Poole, A., Ball, L.J.: Eye tracking in HCI and usability research. Encycl. Hum. Comput. Interact. **1**, 211–219 (2006)
4. Pan, B., Hembrooke, H., Gay, G., Granka, L., Feusner, M., Newman, J.: The determinants of web page viewing behavior: an eye tracking study. In: Proceedings of the 2004 Symposium on Eye Tracking Research and Applications, pp. 147 – 154 (2004)
5. Klingner, J., Tversky, B., Hanrahan, P.: Effects of visual and verbal presentation on cognitive load in vigilance, memory, and arithmetic tasks. Psychophysiology **48**(3), 323–332 (2011)
6. Buettner, R., Sauer, S., Maier, C., Eckhardt, A.: Towards Ex ante prediction of user performance: a novel NeuroIS methodology based on real-time measurement of mental effort. In: 48th Hawaii International Conference on System Sciences (HICSS), pp. 533–542 (2015)
7. Shojaeizadeh, M., Djamasbi, S, Trapp, A.C.: Does pupillary data differ during fixations and saccades? Does it carry information about task demand? In: Proceedings of the Thirteenth Annual Workshop on HCI Research in MIS, Fort Worth, Texas, USA, 13 December 2015
8. Cyr, D., et al.: Exploring human images in website design: a multi-method approach. MIS Q. **33**(3), 539–566 (2009)
9. Tullis, T., Siegel, M.: Does ad blindness on the web vary by age and gender? In: CHI 2013 Extended Abstracts on Human Factors in Computing Systems, Paris, France, pp. 1833–1838. ACM (2013)
10. Eivazi, S., Bednarik, R.: Inferring problem solving strategies using eye-tracking: system description and evaluation. In: Proceedings of the 10th Koli Calling International Conference on Computing Education Research, Koli, Finland. ACM (2010)
11. Bixler, R., D'Mello, S.: Toward fully automated person-independent detection of mind wandering. In: Dimitrova, V., Kuflik, T., Chin, D., Ricci, F., Dolog, P., Houben, G.-J. (eds.) UMAP 2014. LNCS, vol. 8538, pp. 37–48. Springer, Heidelberg (2014)
12. Simola, J., et al.: Using 'hidden Markov model to uncover processing states from eye movements in information search tasks. Cogn. Syst. Res. **9**(4), 237–251 (2008)
13. Kaller, C.P., et al.: Eye movements and visuospatial problem solving: identifying separable phases of complex cognition. Psychophysiology **46**(4), 818–830 (2009)
14. Kahneman, D., Beatty, J.: Pupil diameter and load on memory. Science **154**(3756), 1583–1585 (1966)

15. Rayner, K.: Eye movements in reading and information processing: 20 years of research. Psychol. Bull. **124**(3), 372–422 (1998)
16. Cowen, L., Ball, L.J., Delin, J.: An eye-movement analysis of web-page usability. In: Faulkner, X., Finlay, J., Détienne, F. (eds.) People and Computers XVI—Memorable yet Invisible: Proceedings of HCI 2002, pp. 317–335. Springer, London (2002)
17. Just, M.A., Carpenter, P.A.: A capacity theory of comprehension: individual differences in working memory. Psychol. Rev. **99**(1), 122–149 (1992)
18. Djamasbi, S., Siegel, M., Tullis, T.: Visual hierarchy and viewing behavior: an eye tracking study. In: Jacko, J.A. (ed.) Human-Computer Interaction, Part I, HCII 2011. LNCS, vol. 6761, pp. 331–340. Springer, Heidelberg (2011)
19. Beatty, J.: Task-evoked pupillary responses, processing load, and the structure of processing resources. Psychol. Bull. **91**(2), 276–292 (1982)
20. Palinko, O., Kun, A.: Exploring the effects of visual cognitive load and illumination on pupil diameter in driving simulators. In: Proceedings of the Symposium on Eye Tracking Research and Applications, Santa Barbara, California. ACM (2012)
21. Iqbal, S., Adamczyk, P.D., Zheng, X., Baily, B.P.: Towards an index of opportunity: understanding changes in mental workload during task execution. In: CHI 2005: Proceedings of the SIGCHI Conference on Human Factors in Computing Systems, Portland, Oregon, USA. ACM (2005)
22. Lanata, A., Armato, A., Valenza, G., Scilingo, E.P.: Eye tracking and pupil size variation as response to affective stimuli: a preliminary study. In: 2011 5th International Conference on Pervasive Computing Technologies for Healthcare (PervasiveHealth), pp. 78–84, 23–26 May 2011
23. Bailey, B., Iqbal, S.: Understanding changes in mental workload during execution of goal-directed tasks and its application for interruption management. ACM Trans. Comput.-Hum. Interact. **14**(4), 1–28 (2008)

Exploring the Relationship Between Eye Movements and Pupillary Response from Formative User Experience Research

Jonathan Strohl[(✉)], Joseph Luchman, James Khun, Edward Pierce, and Kyle Andrews

Fors Marsh Group, Arlington, VA, USA
{jstrohl, jluchman, jkhun, epierce, kandrews}@forsmarshgroup.com

Abstract. Measurement of eye physiology is an increasingly utilized tool in studying the usability of digital products. Measures include fixation counts and fixation duration, both indicators of attention, as well as pupillometry, a measure known to correlate with workload and arousal. Although most eye-tracking systems collect pupillometry data, its utility has yet to be fully realized in usability testing. In particular, it is still unclear whether the measure provides additional insight into the user experience over and above that provided by traditional eye-movement measures. The present study seeks to examine the relationship between pupillary response and fixation in the context of a usability task. Specifically, we use data from a formative user experience research study to explore whether, and under which conditions, fixation measures and pupillary response measures correlate. A better understanding of the relationship will aid practitioners in the interpretation of pupillometry data.

Keywords: Eye movements · Pupillometry · User experience research · Usability testing

1 Introduction

The user's experience with digital products is often multi-faceted and complex. To better understand these complex interactions, researchers tend to advocate for the inclusion of multiple categories of metrics in order to produce a more complete understanding of the user experience [1]. While self-report (e.g., verbal comments, satisfaction questionnaire ratings) and performance are the two most commonly used types of metrics, physiological metrics (e.g., eye movements, pupillary response, galvanic skin response), which require specialized technology for observation, provide additional insight into the user experience. One such type of physiological data is eye movements, which can inform researchers about the allocation of visual attention on the design elements and language on a digital product. Eye movements can be used to provide an additional level of insight—over and above self-report and performance metrics—into the optimal design and language.

© Springer International Publishing Switzerland 2016
M. Antona and C. Stephanidis (Eds.): UAHCI 2016, Part I, LNCS 9737, pp. 472–480, 2016.
DOI: 10.1007/978-3-319-40250-5_45

As eye-tracking software and hardware continues to evolve and improve, pupillometry (the measurement of pupil diameter) is becoming more accurate and is being captured at a higher sampling rate. Improvements in eye-tracking hardware and software now allow analyses to be conducted that were once impractical for user experience research practitioners. Pupil diameter is a continuous variable that is measured and recorded at every observation captured by the eye tracker. Slight but measurable changes in pupil diameter have been attributed to differing levels of mental workload [2–4], cognitive processing [5], attentional effort [6], perception [7], memory [8, 9], decision making [10], and physiological arousal [11].

By measuring and analyzing pupil diameter during a person's interaction with a digital product, researchers can assess interactions with the product that require higher levels of mental workload to process. Researchers can then assess whether the increased levels of mental workload lead to comprehension problems or task failure. Combining pupillometry with traditional eye-movement data may lead to better informed design decisions and recommendations for digital product improvement.

Formative user experience research often consists of usability testing with eight to 10 participants to uncover errors and provide general feedback on design elements and language. While small, this sample size is typically sufficient to discover a relatively high proportion of possible errors given the homogeneity of responses. Pupillometry data is more typically included with cognitive research investigating executive functions. Not well understood is whether pupillometry data aids in the understanding of the user experience at these small sample sizes during commonplace internet interactions typical for this type of research.

Our current exploratory research investigates the relationship between eye-movement fixations and pupillary response. We approached this investigation with two broad research questions: (1) What is the relationship between pupillary response and fixation duration, and (2) What is the relationship between pupillary response and frequency of fixations?

2 Method

2.1 Data Source

Nine people participated in the study at the Fors Marsh Group User Experience Lab in Arlington, VA. One participant was removed due to a low eye-tracking capture rate, leaving eight participants (five female, three male), with a median age of 59 (range: 45–61) in the final data set. Participants were instructed to interact with an online calculator tool until they considered their experience complete. After completing the task, participants completed the System Usability Scale [12]. The moderator then conducted a debriefing interview with each participant about their experience using the site.

Data included in the analysis consisted of fixations and pupil diameters from participants while they used the calculator tool uninterrupted by the moderator. Data was collected using a Tobii X2-60(Hz) eye tracker from a system running Tobii Pro Studio version 3.2.3. The Velocity-Threshold Identification (I-VT) fixation classification algorithm [13] was applied to these raw data as preparation for analysis.

2.2   Within-Subjects Analysis

Our research question focuses on a general effect of (1) fixation duration and (2) number of fixations total on pupil diameter. To answer our research question, we first examined the correlation between participants' left and right pupils for each observation. Most observations had valid entries for both left and right eyes (80,627). The correlation was extremely strong ($r = 0.90$), so left and right pupils were averaged for ease of analysis. For single left (6,817) or right (6,512) entries, the single valid value was used as that observation's value.[1] The observation values were then aggregated by computing both the (1) average and (2) standard deviation across all observations within a single fixation. There were 8,843 total fixations across all eight participants in our data.

We used linear regression to estimate the effect that fixation duration and number of fixations had on the average pupil diameter. We chose the linear regression model as average pupil diameter was approximately and normally distributed and a good fit to the linear regression model.

We also included several control variables in the linear regression. All variables in the regression are discussed below.

1. Fixation duration:

   • Assesses the effect of length of a fixation on pupil diameter and should reflect mental workload independent of the below controls.

2. Number of fixations:

   • Assesses the effect of number of fixations on pupil diameter and should reflect mental workload independent of the below controls.

3. A set of dummy-coded indicator variables for each participant:

   • Removes each participant's natural level of pupil diameter. Some participants simply have larger pupils than others.

4. Each fixation's serial order:

   • Removes longer-term trends in pupil diameter across participants.

5. Standard deviation of pupil diameter:

   • Concurrent as well as one- and two-fixation lags to remove possible pupillary fatigue (i.e., from movement) effects on pupil diameter, which could change diameter toward resting levels.

6. Lagged pupil diameter:

   • One- and two-fixation lags remove any sedentary or inertia-like effects of diameter across fixations. To the extent diameter is similar across fixations, these effects will remove them.

---

[1] For single left or right eye measurement entries, there was not much variation in the average pupil diameters between the left (2.77 mm) and the right (2.72 mm) eyes.

Table 1. Within-subjects descriptive statistics

	Mean	Standard deviation	Minimum	Maximum
Average diameter	2.767	0.425	1.310	4.515
Diameter standard deviation	0.049	0.045	0.000	1.021
Fixation order	735.475	599.666	1.000	2542.000
Fixation duration	183.460	164.799	66.000	4250.000
Number of fixations	1469.710	734.573	362.000	2542.000

The descriptive statistics for several of the within-subjects variables are reported in Table 1. Nine fixations had no valid values on pupil diameter, which left the total number of usable fixations at 8,834.

2.3 Between-Subjects Analysis

Our research question did not require a strict focus on within-subjects data; we were also interested in obtaining relationships between the focal predictors of pupil diameter as aggregated between subjects.

Table 2. Between-subjects descriptive statistics

	Mean	Standard deviation	Minimum	Maximum
Average diameter	2.738	0.387	1.960	3.209
Diameter standard deviation	0.237	0.095	0.113	0.431
Fixation duration	177.170	28.360	138.983	225.633
Number of fixations	1105.375	678.358	362.000	2542.000

To do so, we obtained each person's average and standard deviation for pupil diameter at the fixation level, as well as each person's average fixation duration. We assessed the relationship between average diameter and standard deviation of diameter with number of fixations total as well as each person's average fixation duration using partial correlations controlling for each other variable. The between-subjects descriptive statistics for all eight participants are reported in Table 2.

3 Results

3.1 Within-Subjects Results

The results of the within-subjects regressions are reported in Table 3. Note that participant 8's dummy code was omitted due to overlap with other predictors.

The coefficient associated with fixation duration decreases pupil diameter, controlling for within-subjects effects and the previous two fixation periods. On average, a one second increase in gaze duration decreases pupil diameter by 0.0395 mm. The longer a person fixates, the smaller the pupil diameter is for that fixation. Conceptually, we expected fixation duration to decrease pupil diameter since it might reflect reduced mental and physiological workload.

The coefficient associated with total number of fixations increases pupil diameter, controlling for within-subject effects and the previous two fixation periods. Substantively, an increase of 100 fixations during the entire task would increase average pupil diameter by 0.00514 mm. More fixations, then, means larger pupil diameters. As we expected, the number of total fixations appears to be associated with increased pupil diameter and may be a useful indicator for level of workload in the context of a usability task.

Table 3 also shows that average pupil diameter from up to two previous fixations (i.e., lag 1 and lag 2 average pupil diameter variables) is serially correlated with the current period, suggesting that pupil diameters tend not to change greatly across fixations. The serial correlation between the fixations can also be observed below in Fig. 1. Figure 1 depicts the local polynomial-smoothed average diameter over the course of the entire task from fixation to fixation. The pupil diameters tend to be similar over time, move within a fairly narrow range, and tend not to change wildly over time. The stability in the trends in Fig. 1 is the reason for the effects obtained for the lagged pupil diameter variables.

Similarly, variance in pupil diameter from the previous fixation period (e.g., lag 1 standard deviation) predicts a smaller pupil diameter by approximately 0.191 mm for the current period, for every one standard deviation increase. The effect of the lag

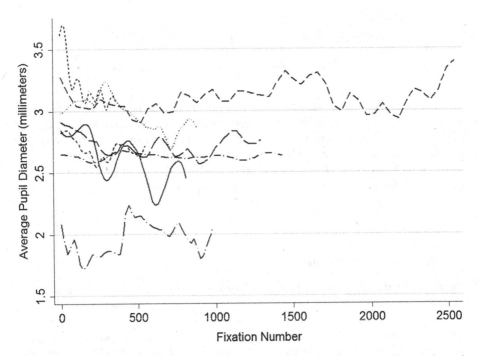

Fig. 1. Local polynomial-smoothed average pupil diameter over the course of the entire task from fixation to fixation.

Table 3. Within-subjects regression estimating average pupil diameter

Average pupil diameter (millimeters)	
Lag 1	**0.524***
	(0.010)
Lag 2	**0.235***
	(0.010)
Diameter standard deviation	
Concurrent	−0.071
	(0.045)
Lag 1	**−0.191***
	(0.045)
Lag 2	−0.050
	(0.045)
Fixation order	−0.000
	(0.000)
Participants	
1	.
	.
2	−0.015
	(0.009)
3	**0.140***
	(0.013)
4	**−0.194***
	(0.010)
5	**−0.030***
	(0.007)
6	**−0.061***
	(0.006)
7	**0.060***
	(0.008)
8	.
	.
Fixation duration	**<−0.001***
	(<0.001)
Total fixations	**<0.001***
	(<0.000)
Constant	0.638*
	(0.024)
N	8,800
Adjusted R^2	0.842

Standard errors in parentheses;
* $p < 0.05$

standard deviation from the previous fixation suggests—as opposed to the lag average finding—that lots of movement in the last fixation might fatigue the iris sphincter muscles and result in a movement toward a smaller resting diameter. Lots of contractions and expansions in diameter are likely to tire the iris sphincter muscle and are likely to move the diameter toward a person's average value (as can be seen in Fig. 1, in the separation between the lines, each person has different average diameters), which is usually smaller than the current size of the pupil—suggesting the pupil likely is expanding mainly during a fixation to result in a higher standard deviation.

Finally, a concern we had with these data was that the average and standard deviation would be strongly correlated as pupils are finite in terms of their dilation capability and we would expect large diameters to be associated with small standard deviations. The correlation between average pupil diameter and its standard deviation was, however −0.043. Thus, although the direction of the effect is as expected, the strength of the relationship was smaller than we were expecting. Additionally, the model does not suffer from unnecessary predictor multicollinearity with the inclusion of standard deviation controls. In other words, the standard deviation and average pupil diameter provide non-overlapping information and are effective control variables for estimating the effect of fixation duration.

3.2   Between-Subjects Partial Correlations

Results for the between-subjects partial correlations are reported in Table 4. The results for each variable correlated with average pupil diameter are in Column 1, and the results for each variable correlated with standard deviation of average pupil diameter are in Column 2. Because the correlations are partial, they control for the other variables. The only significant partial correlation was with the standard deviation of the pupil diameter with average fixation duration. On average, as average fixation durations increase, the variance of individuals' pupil diameters increase for each fixation (see Column 2).

Table 4. Partial correlation coefficients

	(1) Average pupil diameter (millimeters)	(2) Standard deviation of average pupil diameter
Average pupil diameter (millimeters)	.	−0.0186
Standard deviation of average pupil diameter	−0.0186	.
Average fixation duration	0.147	0.850*
Total number of fixations	0.0046	−0.702
N	8	8

4   Discussion

We explored the relationship between pupillary response and eye-movement fixations in data from formative usability testing. Three interrelated findings emerged:

1. Within subjects, longer fixation durations were associated with a decrease in pupil size.
2. Within subjects, an increase in total fixations was associated with an increase in average pupil size.
3. Between subjects, participants who fixated for longer durations had less consistency in their pupil size than those who fixated for shorter durations.

The first finding suggests that as a fixation becomes longer, the pupil becomes smaller, possibly as a result of fewer resources being expended. In other words, the pupil becomes smaller, potentially because looking in the same location requires fewer mental and physiological resources over time. This decrement in pupil size becomes more evident the longer the fixation becomes. The second finding, a positive relationship between number of fixations and pupil size, follows from the first. More frequent fixations during a task means less time the eye is resting and more time processing new information, therefore potentially increasing the average pupil size by requiring more resources.

Finally, the third finding—that those who fixate longer have less consistency in their pupil diameters than those who fixate for shorter durations—follows necessarily from the first two. If pupil size decreases over time within a given fixation as a result of reduced mental and physiological workload, then those with longer average fixations will have greater variance in pupil diameter.

This work, while exploratory, provides insight into the relationships between pupillary response and eye-movement fixations, and the former's potential utility in usability testing. Pupillary response has been found to be a useful measure of mental workload for the evaluation of interfaces with high cognitive demands; [14] however, not as much is known about the usefulness of the measure for less complex usability tasks. These findings demonstrate that in a usability task where participants are evaluating a website and not engaging in complex tasks, there is still significant variation in pupil diameter (and, by implication, workload), and that these variations in pupil diameter demonstrate consistent and interpretable relationships with fixation count and length.

Further research is needed to understand more fully how to interpret and apply pupillometry data in usability contexts, and whether the present results replicate in other commonplace online tasks. Future research is also needed to understand better the relationship between pupil diameter and different types of mental workload. Finally, it would be beneficial to research the relationship between pupil diameter and eye fixation, not just in the context of online task completion, but specifically their relationship to test outcome measures such as task success and satisfaction questionnaire ratings. It is possible that pupil diameter can provide additional insight into participants' subjective perceptions of task completion or satisfaction, not just task difficulty.

References

1. Tullis, T., Albert, B.: Measuring the User Experience: Collecting, Analyzing, and Presenting Usability Metrics. Morgan Kaufmann, Burlington, MA (2008)
2. Van Orden, K.F., Limbert, W., Makeig, S., Jung, T.P.: Eye activity correlates of workload during a visuospatial memory task. Hum. Factors **43**, 111 (2001)
3. May, J.G., Kennedy, R.S., Williams, M.C., Dunlap, W.P., Brannan, J.R.: Eye movement indices of mental workload. Acta Psychol. **75**, 75–89 (1990)
4. Ahlstrom, U., Friedman-Berg, F.J.: Using eye movement activity as a correlate of cognitive workload. Int. J. Ind. Ergononomics **36**, 623–636 (2006)
5. Allard, E.S., Wadlinger, H.A., Isaacowitz, D.M.: Positive gaze preferences in older adults: assessing the role of cognitive effort with pupil dilation. Aging Neuropsychol. Cogn. **17**(3), 296–311 (2010)
6. Alnaes, D., Sneve, M.H., Espeseth, T., Endestad, T., van de Pavert, S.H.P., Laeng, B.: Pupil size signals mental effort deployed during multiple object tracking and predicts brain activity in the dorsal attention network and the locus coeruleus. J. Vis. **14**, 1 (2014)
7. Duque, A., Sanchez, A., Vazquez, C.: Gaze-fixation and pupil dilation in the processing of emotional faces: the role of rumination. Cogn. Emot. **28**(8), 1347–1366 (2014)
8. Attar, N., Schneps, M., Pomplun, M.: Pupil size as a measure of working memory load during a complex visual search task. J. Vis. **13**, 160 (2013)
9. van Gerven, P.W.M., Paas, F., van Merrienboer, J.J.G., Schmidt, H.G.: Memory load and the cognitive pupillary response in aging. Psychophysiology **41**, 167–174 (2004)
10. Satterthwaite, T.D., Green, L., Myerson, J., Parker, J., Ramaratnam, M., Buckner, R.L.: Dissociable but inter-related systems of cognitive control and reward during decision making: evidence from pupillometry and event-related fMRI. Neuroimage **37**(3), 1017–1031 (2007)
11. Bradley, M.M., Miccoli, L., Escrig, M.A., Lang, P.J.: The pupil as a measure of emotional arousal and autonomic activation. Psychophysiology **45**(4), 602–607 (2008)
12. Brooke, J.: Usability evaluation in industry: SUS - a quick and dirty usability scale. In: Jordan, P.W., Thomas, B., Weerdmeester, B.A., McClelland, A.L. (eds.). Taylor and Francis, London (1996)
13. Olsen, A.: The Tobii I-VT Fixation Filter. http://www.acuity-ets.com/downloads/Tobii%20I-VT%20Fixation%20Filter.pdf
14. Bojko, A.: Eye Tracking the User Experience: A Practical Guide to Research. Rosenfeld Media, Brooklyn, NY (2013)

Unique Object Characteristics Differentially Affect Visual Attention During Viewing of Dynamic Stimuli: The Influence of Location and Luminosity

Brooke E. Wooley[1(✉)] and David S. March[2]

[1] MediaScience, Chicago, IL, USA
b.wooley@mediasciencelabs.com
[2] University of Tennessee, Knoxville, TN, USA
dmarch@vols.utk.edu

Abstract. Understanding which characteristics of dynamic stimuli affect visual attention is crucial to usability research. We explored how *object location* and *object luminosity* differentially affect visual attention. Thirty-seven American participants viewed 34 Australian commercials, which were broken down by scene (N = 606) to identify all pertinent Areas of Interest (N_{AOIs} = 2,695). Each AOI was subsequently coded for location and median luminosity. Luminosity was positively associated with attention capture ($\beta = .12$, p < .001), but negatively associated with sustaining attention ($\beta = -.06$, p < .000). Higher ($\beta = .04$, p < .000) or lower contrast with the immediate background ($\beta = .03$, p < .000) led to longer fixations, and central location drew visual attention ($\beta = .49$, p < .001) and sustained it ($\beta = .19$, p < .001) more than other locations. Our results show that object location and luminosity affect visual attention during dynamic stimuli, and likely influence subsequent cognitive or behavioral interaction with those objects.

Keywords: Design for all best practice · Evaluation of accessibility, usability and user experience · Visual attention · Eye tracking

1 Introduction

Eye-movement research has informed a number of technological and practical applications and has helped guide visual design improvements, which serve to enhance the usability of certain platforms and influence the behavior of the user. Due to advancements in eye-tracking technology, gaze tracking has become a very useful tool in the study of human computer interaction [1], human factors research [2], media and marketing research [3, 4], human development research [5, 24], and reading behavior [6]. For example, recent research has shown that the number and duration of fixations can explain 45 % of variance in the actual in-market sales performance of television commercials [7], and that fixations become more dispersed prior to viewers pressing the skip button to avoid online video commercials [8].

Like other automatic processes (e.g., heartbeat), it is very difficult to consciously suppress eye-movements [5, 9, 10]. Thus, the ability to track these movements can yield meaningful insights into unconscious cognitive activity and behavioral motivations.

© Springer International Publishing Switzerland 2016
M. Antona and C. Stephanidis (Eds.): UAHCI 2016, Part I, LNCS 9737, pp. 481–492, 2016.
DOI: 10.1007/978-3-319-40250-5_46

Because eye movements have a systematic means of expression, those movements can be measured consistently and reliably [11, 12] making eye tracking a very useful tool to usability researchers.

However, much of this research has been limited to the study of static images and static situations [13], in large part due to the difficulty in analyzing eye movement data in dynamic stimuli. The main difficulty preventing the expansion of eye-tracking research from the static to the dynamic domain has been that Areas of Interest (AOIs) in dynamic stimuli move around the frame 24 or 25 frames a second. Researchers have used laborious hand coding methods to identify when a viewer's gaze point enters and leaves a dynamically moving AOI. But now, eye-tracking software offers intelligent bounding boxes for AOIs that move with a scene, and if necessary, grow or shrink in size.

Given that many situations people come into contact with are dynamic in nature, it is necessary that usability researchers understand how people visually process dynamic stimuli. Thus, this study further explores which elements of dynamic images garner visual attention. Specifically, we identify how the location, luminosity, and contrast of an object with its background affect the visual attention it received and discuss how that visual behavior can inform dynamic stimuli design.

1.1 Influence of Object Location and Object Luminosity

Basic characteristics of static stimuli such as size, color, and luminosity can affect visual attention, as well as viewer goals and motivations [14].

Previous research on website usability has shown that viewers tend to allocate eye movements to the top and upper right corners of websites to facilitate in navigation and directed tasks (i.e., web search tasks) [15]. Eye movements during newspaper and magazine viewing also exhibit learned visual patterns in that readers tend to fixate on headlines and pictures first and then flow to the body text [16]. However, a central bias has been documented in natural static scene viewing, suggesting that the most important areas of visual media content should be centered in the frame [17]. Tatler [17] found that regardless of the features contained within images (e.g., chairs, buildings), viewers tend to fixate the center of the image more often than other areas, even during search tasks.

Brasel and Gips found similar patterns using dynamic stimuli, showing that viewers have a general tendency to fixate on the center of the screen during television programming [18]. It has been proposed that central bias during dynamic stimuli viewing may reflect viewers attending to multiple moving objects at once [19]. Thus, viewers would tend to fixate the center of the screen more often and for longer in order to allow the tracking of multiple moving objects within the visual field.

Similar to object location, object luminosity represents a highly salient visual characteristic to which the human eye is drawn. Eye-tracking studies have taken advantage of the fact that our eyes are well adept at identifying areas of contrast to explore the influence of luminosity on attention to visual objects [11]. Within the realm of media, researchers have shown that visual characteristics such as the brightness of products or text influence visual attention [3]. Advertisements from the yellow pages that exhibit bright colors or that contrast more with advertisements around them garner more visual attention [3]. Thus, it may not be simply that luminosity drives attention, but that contrast (i.e., luminosity of object minus background luminosity) is actually what draws viewer attention. This remains an empirical question that we will address herein.

Certainly, visual attention to areas and objects of interest is influenced by both location and the luminosity/contrast and the static or dynamic nature of the stimuli. There remains a need to investigate the conditions under which that visual attention varies in order to better inform the design of stimuli in media and other applications. Ultimately, identifying situations in which luminosity or contrast affect visual attention can inform design efforts to enhance interactions with visual stimuli.

1.2   The Current Study

The present study expands on previous eye-movement research by exploring how object location and object luminosity of visual elements affect visual attention toward those objects presented as dynamic stimuli. We collected eye-movement data from participants as they viewed dynamic visual content, specifically, television commercials. Televised advertisements served as a proxy for other dynamic stimuli humans encounter in that they present a variety of visual elements (e.g., animals, graphics, text, humans, objects) and visual situations, and they generally convey an entire idea within a relatively short period of time.

In order to evaluate the impact of object location and luminosity on visual attention, relevant areas of interest had to be first identified in every commercial. Each commercial was broken down into scenes and those scenes were content analyzed for their elements of interest. A scene began when either the camera cut to a new set of elements of interest or a new area of interest was introduced into the existing scene. The Area of Interest (AOI) identification process was informed by previous research in which content analysis was used to identify important factors in visual stimuli and advertisements [20]. Once scenes and relevant AOIs were identified, the location and luminance of each AOI was coded.

We hypothesized that areas of interest that were centrally located would receive more visual attention due to previous research concerning central tendency bias [17, 18]. We further expected that objects of high versus low luminosity and objects contrasting more with their background would draw visual attention, as previous research suggests these bottom-up factors attract visual attention.

Eye-movement data reveal cognitive processes on an implicit and continuous basis [11]. Using eye-tracking technology to identify which visual characteristics grab visual attention and sustain it in a scene can offer valuable insights into the fundamental design of a stimulus and how it could affect subsequent behavior. Designing visual content around what actually captures visual attention can allow for more streamlined and informative interactions.

2   Commercial Selection and Coding

2.1   Commercial Selection

The average amount of advertisements viewed during a 1-h long television program is roughly equivalent to 18-min on U.S. network television. Thus, thirty-five 30-s randomly selected Australian produced commercials were chosen from the top three Australian free-to-air commercial television networks. These commercials were embedded during pre-recorded Australian programming. This ensured a high level of attention to all the commercials and ensured that any effects revealed by the analysis could be attributed to the commercials' visual execution factors and not to individual differences in ad exposure and familiarity.

2.2   Commercial Coding

Scene Identification. As a first step, we completed content analysis of each commercial to catalogue important non-visual elements. This first step ensured that the correct visual elements could then be selected for further coding. The components coded during content analysis of the non-visual components of each advertisement were primarily derived from Stewart and Furse (e.g., information content, commercial tone, commercial setting) [20]. All of the non-visual execution factors were coded by watching and reviewing transcriptions of each commercial multiple times to identify the presence or absence of each variable.

We then coded visual execution factors, which were based on previous research investigating visual attention to different elements in a stimulus (e.g., size in pixels, type, movement, location, luminosity). The strategic-level coding revealed insights such as the number of scenes, main characters, product presence, graphical or animated components and more. Each of these categories had its own sub-variables for which each commercial was coded. Once these visual and non-visual execution factors were completely coded for any one commercial, scenes were then identified.

Each of the 35 commercials was broken down by scene. A scene was deemed to begin when either (1) the camera cut to a new set of AOIs, or (2) a new AOI was introduced into an existing scene. If a scene lasted less than 200 ms, they could not be well explored by the eye since the eyes take about 100–200 ms to re-orient after a scene change [21]; thus, the shot was deemed to be too short to warrant coding. All scenes had an area of 589,824 pixels (1024 × 576 pixels). Once a scene was created, it was then further broken down into AOIs.

Area of Interest Identification. Given that people are generally able to store around seven or fewer items at a time in working memory [22], it was decided that each shot would be broken down into no more than seven areas of interest (AOIs). This number also includes the "background" (i.e., all non-AOI pixels) of a snapshot as one of the seven AOIs. AOIs in a scene ranged from seven to a minimum of two (including the background).

AOIs were determined using several rules. Factors that have been shown to attract visual attention [6, 11] and thus, increased a visual element's likelihood of being chosen for AOI coding were: motion (if the AOI was moving), size (if the AOI took up a substantial part of the shot), location (if the AOI appeared near the center of the shot), and luminosity (if the AOI was especially bright).

Semantic factors that render an AOI important regardless of its size, location, or motion also affected whether an AOI was coded. For instance, objects such as human faces or eyes were almost always coded if they appeared in a scene. The AOIs relation to the product being advertised also increased an AOI's importance (i.e., if it was the product or product packaging).

The progression of the commercial was one the most important factors in determining AOIs for coding. Although the snapshots are static in nature, they represent dynamic moments in time possibly lasting from 500 ms to a few seconds in length. Thus, the coding scheme relied heavily on the objective of the commercial as a whole, as well as on auditory cues and the progression of visual elements throughout the commercial. For instance, a snapshot might include multiple faces, but unless the face was that of a main character or a speaking character, it may not have been coded as one of the seven AOIs. This was especially true for commercials with 'background casts.'

Once important AOIs were defined, each AOI was broken down further depending on the length of the scene. Scene length was coded and used to account for how visual attention allocation might differ in a scene that is 800 ms long versus a scene that is 3.5 s long. Scenes that lasted longer required a more detailed breakdown of important AOIs. However, the breakdown of AOIs was ultimately constrained by the maximum number of AOIs that could be defined within a snapshot (≤ 7).

AOI Location Coding. As it was hypothesized that the location of a visual object might have an influence on visual attention to it, we developed a way in which the location of an AOI could be systematically coded. We wanted to provide more than general location (i.e., "left" or "right"), since visual element location is often chosen very intentionally. By dividing the 1024×576-pixel snapshot into thirds, both horizontally and vertically, a grid was created so that each AOI could be coded as having occupied a specific location or set of locations. The location of an AOI was determined using the grid in Fig. 1 overlaid onto each snapshot. If an AOI existed in the middle of a snapshot, it would be coded as having a location of five (Location 5 = 1, all other Locations = 0). If an AOI existed in more than one rectangle, then all the rectangles occupied by the AOI were coded as its location.

1	2	3
4	5	6
7	8	9

576 pixels

1024 pixels

Fig. 1. Location grid with numbering scheme used during coding. This grid was overlaid onto each snapshot in order to code the location of each AOI appearing in the snapshot.

AOI Luminosity Coding. Luminosity was coded using the luminosity histogram in the Photoshop Elements program. Luminosity values disregard color information and represent the tonal intensity of an object on a scale from 0 (black) to 255 (white). Median luminosity value for each AOI was used as a measure of central tendency for luminosity, as it was robust to outliers, such as the presence of a few dark pixels. We also thought it important to explore how the brightness (or darkness) of an AOI against its background might affect visual attention to the AOI. Two foreground/background contrast variables were created from the luminosity (median) scores ("light on dark" and "dark on light" contrasts) by comparing the luminosity value of an AOI in a scene to the background AOI's luminosity value.

Coding Reliability. To check the reliability of the coding scheme, a subset of the commercials (15 %) was coded independently by a different coder. Intercoder reliability was tested using Krippendorf's alpha, confirming that both the location and luminosity codes were reliable (>0.67; range = 0. 70 to 1.00).

3   Methodology

3.1   Sample

Our original sample consisted of 49 participants (35 females). Data from 12 participants in the sample were excluded due to eye-tracking calibrations below the required accuracy threshold of "good" or "excellent" as reported by the Attention Tool 5.1 software plus hitting ten out of 12 targets in the validation stage. The final sample used in analysis was made up of 26 females (M_{age} = 39.4 years, SD = 8.64) and 11 males (M_{age} = 36.9 years, SD = 6.52).

Participants were recruited from the MediaScience® participant panel in Austin, Texas, USA and were screened for normal or corrected-to-normal vision. Over 20,000 panel members make up the MediaScience® panel in Austin embodying a wide range of demographics that closely represent that of the general U.S. population. Participants received a $30 American Express gift card for participating.

3.2   Apparatus

Participants' eye movements were recorded using Attention Tool 5.1 (iMotions Global) and tracked via a Tobii T60 eye tracker (60 Hz sampling rate, tracking accuracy of 0.5°) integrated just below a 573 × 579 mm stimulus presentation monitor. Participants were seated 60–70 cm eyes-to-monitor. Stimuli were presented via the Attention Tool program as well, which allowed for the rotation of stimuli, custom settings to present that stimuli, and screen recordings of what the participant sees.

3.3   Stimuli

The 35 commercials were presented during program content to simulate a normal TV viewing experience. We integrated the commercials into an episode of the Australian comedy documentary series, Caravan of Courage. The program was of Australian production to match the country-of-origin of the commercials. Because the episode was a one-hour program, five commercial breaks could be embedded in the program, each containing seven 30-s ads (i.e., a total of 35 ads). These five commercial breaks were labeled A through E and ad positions within those commercial pods were labeled one through seven.

Seven different presentation orders for the 35 commercials were created. These rotations were created by randomizing the entire list of 35 commercials into ad positions A1 (first ad in the first ad break) through E7 (last ad in the last ad break) such that (1) no one commercial could appear in the A1 (very first) or E7 (very last) position more than once, and (2) no ad could appear in any ad position more than once across rotations.

3.4 Procedure

A research assistant escorted a single participant to one of two identical viewing laboratories (each simulating a typical home living room) where the participant was seated at a desk equipped with a Tobii T60 monitor and computer speakers. Participants were told what they would be watching an episode of the comedy show, Hamish & Andy's Caravan of Courage and that their program would last approximately 1 h. The research assistant then adjusted the tracker to capture the participant's eyes and proceeded with a 9-point calibration. Once participants reached a successful calibration, they watched a video clip presenting a second set of 12 visual targets that served as a calibration validation. Once the participant was calibrated with the eye-gaze equipment and instructions were provided, the program content began and the research assistant left the room.

3.5 Analysis Strategy

Once data were collected, the dynamic AOI drawing tool in Attention Tool 5.1 was used to break down scenes into their respective dynamic AOIs. Once AOIs were coded, fixation metrics (fixation = eye-gaze duration > 100 ms), including if an AOI was fixated and for how long it was fixated, were automatically calculated for each AOI.

Mixed model methods were used in all analyses as this approach accommodates the non-independence of observations inherent in eye-movement data. Thus, Participant and Commercial were entered into the model as random intercept effects, and the visual execution factors served as the other independent variables. Two dependent variables were used: fixation, which was a binary (1/0) variable, and fixation duration, which was a continuous variable. The same predictor variables were used in each regression model.

A separate regression model was estimated for each of the two dependent variables: (1) the binary (1/0) dependent variable fixation, and (2) the continuous dependent variable percentage of total fixation time (fixation duration). In both models, the intercept term can be interpreted as the expected value of the dependent variable when the nine screen location variables and luminosity median are zero.

4   Results

4.1   Fixation Model Results[1]

Effect of Object Location on Attention Capture. AOI Location revealed significant predictors associated with a likelihood of acquiring fixation and a likelihood of not acquiring fixation. Screen locations in the center, center-top, and center-left (Locations 2, 4, and 5) were positively associated with fixation, while screen locations in the corners of the screen, or bottom-center (Locations 1, 3, 7, 8, and 9) were negatively associated with fixation (see Fig. 2). Thus, AOIs appearing into locations 2, 4, and 5 were significantly more likely to receive a fixation, and AOIs appearing in Locations 1, 3, 7, 8, or 9 were significantly less likely to acquire fixation.

Location 1 -.24***	Location 2 .13***	Location 3 -.07***
Location 4 .04*	Location 5 .49***	Location 6
Location 7 -.21***	Location 8 -.09***	Location 9 -.22***

Fig. 2. GLM results for the predictor variable Location displayed within the location grid. Standardized estimates are reported in each location. Red shading represents those locations associated with a lesser likelihood of predicting fixation; green shading represents those locations associated with a higher likelihood of predicting fixation. Location 6 was not a significant predictor. *p < 0.05, **p < 0.01, ***p < .001. (Color figure online)

Effect of Object Luminance and Contrast on Attention Capture. The overall *Luminosity* of an AOI was also positively associated with predicting fixation, such that the higher AOI luminosity values predicted fixation ($\beta = .12$, $p < .001$). Furthermore, the contrast variable, *Dark AOI on Light Background*, was significantly negatively associated with predicting fixation ($\beta = -.02$, $p < .001$), meaning that those AOIs having a lower luminosity value than the background on which they appeared were less likely to receive fixation. *Light AOIs on Dark Backgrounds* did not significantly affect attention capture.

4.2   Fixation Duration Model Results

Sustained attention was measured by the continuous dependent variable fixation duration. One of the main differences between this second regression model and the previous GLMM analysis is the dependent variable here did not include zeros. Any AOI that was

---

[1] Because predictors in the current model are measured on different scales, the regression coefficients have been standardized. These standardized beta estimates can be interpreted in terms of standard deviation units, and as such can be compared in terms of effect sizes, small = .1, medium = .2, and large = .5 (Cohen 1988).

not fixated on had fixation duration = 0 and therefore was not included in this analysis; if an AOI was not fixated on, it could not predict sustained attention.

Fixation durations on the AOIs in each commercial were collected in units of milliseconds. Fixation duration was converted into a standardized percentage by dividing the fixation duration of an AOI by the length in milliseconds of its associated scene. The transformed dependent variable represented the percentage of time an AOI was fixated on out of the time it was on screen.

Effect of Object Location on Sustained Visual Attention. Similar to fixation, the center and center-top of the screen (Locations 5 and 2) were significant predictors of longer fixation duration (see Fig. 3). The top-right corner of the screen (Location 3) was also associated with longer fixation duration. The other corners of the screen, the center-left, center-right, and the bottom-center (Locations 1, 4, 6, 7, 8, and 9) were all either significant predictors of shorter fixation durations (Locations 1, 4, 8, and 9), or non-significant predictors of fixation duration (Locations 6 and 7). Thus, AOIs appearing in Locations 2, 3, and 5 received longer fixation durations, while those in Locations 1, 4, 8, and 9 received shorter fixation durations.

Location 1 -.10***	Location 2 .07***	Location 3 .04*
Location 4 -.06***	Location 5 .19***	Location 6
Location 7	Location 8 -.07***	Location 9 -.11***

Fig. 3. LMM results for the predictor variable Location displayed within the location grid. Standardized beta estimates are reported. Red shading represents those locations associated with a lesser likelihood of predicting fixation duration; green shading represents those locations associated with a higher likelihood of predicting fixation duration. Locations 6 and 7 were not significant predictors. *p < 0.05, **p < 0.01,***p < .001. (Color figure online)

Effect of Object Luminance and Contrast on Sustained Visual Attention. The overall Luminosity of an AOI was positively associated with fixation but negatively associated with fixation duration ($\beta = -.06$, $p < .000$), such that AOIs with greater luminosity than the median were less likely to capture longer fixation durations. Furthermore, the contrast variables *Dark AOI on Light Background* ($\beta = .03$, $p < .000$) and *Light AOI on Dark Background* ($\beta = .04$, $p < .000$) were significantly positively associated with predicting with fixation duration. Thus, contrast between the foreground and background increased fixation duration, regardless of which AOI was lighter or darker.

5   Discussion

We found that AOI location was an important variable in visual attention to dynamic AOIs. Figure 4 displays the location grids from both regression models in order to facilitate comparison.

Attention Capture

Location 1	Location 2	Location 3
Location 4	Location 5	Location 6
Location 7	Location 8	Location 9

Attention Sustaining

Location 1	Location 2	Location 3
Location 4	Location 5	Location 6
Location 7	Location 8	Location 9

Fig. 4. The figure on the left indicates locations that were related to fixation capture while the figure on the right indicates locations that were related to fixation duration. Red shading represents those locations associated with a lesser likelihood of predicting fixation or fixation duration; green shading represents those locations associated with a higher likelihood of prediction fixation or fixation duration, gray indicates areas that were not significantly related to either. (Color figure online)

In both models, AOIs appearing in Locations 2 and 5 were significantly more likely to receive fixations and receive longer fixation durations. This result corresponds with previous research identifying viewers' central tendency bias, where most visual attention during dynamic content is focused towards the middle of the screen [18].

Location 4 was more likely to receive fixation but was less likely to receive longer fixation durations. This effect might be influenced by our participants' left to right reading behavior that biases visual attention towards items appearing at the left of a stimulus. Viewers from a culture that read right to left might reveal the inverse effect. This might also be why Location 6 was not a significant predictor of attention capture or sustaining attention, as many AOIs would make their exit from the scene through this location.

The bottom third of the location grid was mostly negatively associated with both fixation and fixation duration. This result indicates the presence of either an innate central tendency bias or possibly that the most important or relevant objects are centered in the frame during the creation of the stimuli, leaving less relevant things (e.g., small print or negative space) to appear in the lower locations. It is likely the interaction of the two; viewers tend to direct visual attention toward the center of the screen, even in the absence of accompanying audio [23], and realizing this tendency, creative decisions are made to place the most important objects in centralized locations, further reinforcing the central tendency bias.

The overall Luminosity of an AOI positively predicted fixation (attention capture) but negatively predicted fixation duration (sustaining attention). Dark AOIs on a Light Background captured fixation and both the Dark AOI on Light Background and Light AOI on Dark Background variables significantly predicted longer fixation durations. These results indicate that the salience of a bright (luminous) AOI contributed to capturing fixation, however, it seemed that the contrast of an AOI with its background was more important in sustaining visual attention. AOIs having a higher or lower luminosity than the background on which they appeared tended to receive longer fixations, suggesting that the degree to which an AOI contrasts with its background is more influential in visual attention than luminosity alone. Taken together, these results suggest that visual objects of high importance should be centrally located and contrast with the background on which they appear in order to garner more visual attention.

Because real commercials were used as stimuli in this study, the ecological validity of our results is greater, but there is also an unavoidable lack of control in the variables of interest. It may be the case that certain features in a scene (e.g., faces) would garner more attention regardless of their location. We cannot say for certain that it was an innate central tendency driving our results, but that perhaps advertisers put the most informationally salient features of an ad in the center of the screen. In future studies, dynamic stimuli created to manipulate the presence or absence and location of each variable would further clarify their impact on visual attention.

Previous research has shown that studying eye movements provides valuable insights into the ways users visually and behaviorally interact with stimuli. It is necessary to first understand how the user engages with and is influenced by the basic visual components of the display. These understandings can guide the people that design and create dynamic interfaces and content to best serve the user interacting with them. Using insights from studies such as this on visual attention, designers can create strategies to increase visual attention to items of interest, or perhaps to encourage *when* visual attention is lent to important objects, further enhancing, streamlining, and improving interactions with the content.

References

1. Jacob, R.J.K., Karn, K.S.: Eye tracking in human-computer interaction and usability research: ready to deliver the promises. In: Hyona, J., Radach, R., Duebel, H. (eds.) The Mind's Eye: Cognitive and Applied Aspects of Eye Movement Research, pp. 573–605. Elsevier Science, Amsterdam (2003)
2. Egeth, H.E., Yantis, S.: Visual attention: control, representation, and time course. Annu. Rev. Psychol. **48**(1), 269–297 (1997)
3. Lohse, G.L.: Consumer eye movement patterns on Yellow Pages advertising. J. Advert. **26**(1), 61–73 (1997)
4. Schiessl, M., Duda, S., Tholke, A., Fischer, R.: Eye tracking and its application in usability and media research. MMI-Interaktiv **6**, 41–50 (2003)
5. Gregory, R.L.: Eye and Brain: The Psychology of Seeing, 5th edn. Princeton University Press, Princeton (1997)
6. Rayner, K.: Eye movements in reading and information processing: 20 years of research. Psychol. Bull. **124**(3), 372–422 (1998)
7. Venkatraman, V., Dimoka, A., Pavlou, P.A., Vo, K., Hampton, W., Bollinger, B., Hershfield, H.E., Ishihara, M., Winer, R.S.: Predicting advertising success beyond traditional measures: new insights from neurophysiological methods and market response modeling. J. Mark. Res. **52**(4), 436–452 (2015)
8. Teixeira, T.S., Wedel, M., Pieters, R.: Moment-to-moment optimal branding in TV commercials: preventing avoidance by pulsing. Mark. Sci. **29**(5), 783–804 (2010)
9. Hillstrom, A.P., Yantis, S.: Visual motion and attentional capture. Percept. Psychophys. **55**(4), 399–411 (1994)
10. Loftus, G.R., Mackworth, N.H.: Cognitive determinants of fixation location during picture viewing. J. Exp. Psychol. Hum. Percept. Perform. **4**(4), 565–572 (1978)

11. Duchowski, A.T.: Eye Tracking Methodology: Theory and Practice, 2nd edn. Springer, London (2007)
12. Hammoud, R.I. (ed.): Passive Eye Monitoring: Algorithms, Applications and Experiments. Springer, Germany (2008)
13. Anderson, D.R., Burns, J.: Paying attention to television. In: Bryant, J., Zillmann, D. (eds.) Responding to the Screen: Reception and Reaction Processes, pp. 3–25. Routledge, New York (1991)
14. Rayner, K., Castelhano, M.S.: Eye movements during reading, scene perception, visual search, and while looking at print advertisements. In: Wedel, M., Pieters, R. (eds.) Visual Marketing: From Attention to Action, pp. 9–42. Taylor & Francis Group, New York (2008)
15. Roth, S.P., Tuch, A.N., Mekler, E.D., Bargas-Avila, J.A., Opwis, K.: Location matters, especially for non-salient features–an eye-tracking study on the effects of web object placement on different types of websites. Int. J. Hum.-Comput. Stud. **71**(3), 228–235 (2013)
16. Holmqvist, K., Wartenberg, C.: The role of local design factors for newspaper reading behaviour - an eye-tracking perspective. Lund Univ. Cogn. Stud. **127**, 1–21 (2005)
17. Tatler, B.W.: The central fixation bias in scene viewing: selecting an optimal viewing position independently of motor biases and image feature distributions. J. Vis. **7**(14), 1–17 (2007)
18. Brasel, A.S., Gips, J.: Points of view: where do we look when we watch TV? Perception **37**, 1890–1894 (2008)
19. Fehd, H.M., Seiffert, A.E.: Eye movements during multiple object tracking: where do participants look? Cognition **108**(1), 201–209 (2008)
20. Stewart, D.W., Furse, D.H.: Effective Television Advertising: A Study of 1000 Commercials. Lexington Books, Lexington (1986)
21. Le Meur, O., Le Callet, P., Barba, D.: Predicting visual fixations on video based on low-level visual features. Vis. Res. **47**, 2483–2498 (2007)
22. Miller, G.: The magical number seven, plus or minus two: some limits on our capacity for processing information. Psychol. Rev. **101**(2), 343–352 (1955)
23. Wooley, B.E., March, D.S.: Exploring the influence of audio in directing visual attention during dynamic content. In: Proceedings of Symposium on Eye Tracking Research and Applications, pp. 187–190. ACM Press, New York (2014)
24. Bergstrom, J.C.R., Olmsted-Hawala, E.L., Bergstrom, H.C.: Older adults fail to see the periphery in a web site task. In: Universal Access in the Information Society, pp. 1–10. Springer, Heidelberg (2014)

Author Index